National Intelligencer Newspaper Abstracts 1845

Joan M. Dixon

HERITAGE BOOKS
2006

HERITAGE BOOKS
AN IMPRINT OF HERITAGE BOOKS, INC.

Books, CDs, and more – Worldwide

For our listing of thousands of titles see our website
at
www.HeritageBooks.com

Published 2006 by
HERITAGE BOOKS, INC.
Publishing Division
65 East Main Street
Westminster, Maryland 21157-5026

Copyright © 2006 Joan M. Dixon

Other Heritage Books by the Author:

National Intelligencer Newspaper Abstracts, Special Edition: The Civil War Years, 1861-1863
National Intelligencer Newspaper Abstracts, 1846
National Intelligencer Newspaper Abstracts, 1845
National Intelligencer Newspaper Abstracts, 1844
National Intelligencer Newspaper Abstracts, 1843
National Intelligencer Newspaper Abstracts, 1842
National Intelligencer Newspaper Abstracts, 1841
National Intelligencer Newspaper Abstracts, 1840
National Intelligencer Newspaper Abstracts, 1838-1839
National Intelligencer Newspaper Abstracts, 1836-1837
National Intelligencer Newspaper Abstracts, 1834-1835
National Intelligencer Newspaper Abstracts, 1832-1833
National Intelligencer Newspaper Abstracts, 1830-1831
National Intelligencer Newspaper Abstracts, 1827-1829
National Intelligencer Newspaper Abstracts, 1824-1826
National Intelligencer Newspaper Abstracts, 1821-1823
National Intelligencer Newspaper Abstracts, 1818-1820
National Intelligencer Newspaper Abstracts, 1814-1817
National Intelligencer Newspaper Abstracts, 1811-1813
National Intelligencer Newspaper Abstracts, 1806-1810
National Intelligencer Newspaper Abstracts, 1800-1805

All rights reserved. No part of this book may be reproduced or transmitted in any form or by any means, electronic or mechanical, including photocopying, recording or by any information storage and retrieval system without written permission from the author, except for the inclusion of brief quotations in a review.

International Standard Book Number: 0-7884-4073-X

NATIONAL INTELLIGENCER NEWSPAPER
WASHINGTON, D C
1845

TABLE OF CONTENTS

Daily National Intelligencer
 Washington, D C, 1845--1

Appointments by the Govn'r of Md--42
Army appointments and promotions--127-129; 179; 271-273; 445-446

Casualties of the steamboat Swallow--141
Collection of late Jos Bonaparte--388
Conflagration in N Y--290-293

Commencements: Balt Academy of Visitation--297-298
                Columbian College--395-396
                Gtwn, D C--296-297; 300
                Mrs David H Burr's Seminary exams--60-61
                St Mary's Female Instit, Chas Co, Md--349
                Washington College, Wash, Pa—401

Constitution of the U S--258
Defenders of Balt, Md--358; 379

Disaster-steamer Marquette--274; 281
Geo Washington Parke Custis in N Y--324-325

Grocers-Wash, D C--236
New bldgs-Wash City--462-463; 474-475

Licenses-Ordinaries and Taverns--416-417
Maryland Line, 1781--171-176

Members of Cincinnati of Md--441-444
Naval Board of Engineers--302

Naval Court Martial of Capt Philip F Voorhees--199; 220; 247
Naval Midshipmen--258; 260

Ofcrs of the: Alabama--312
Brandywine--28 & 376
Columbus--147 & 450
Congress--100 & 424
Dolphin--451
Erie--120 & 275
Mississippi--311
Perry--375
Preble--385
Truxton--465
Union--39
Vandalia--152
Vincennes—147

Ofcrs of the Revolutionary Army, 1781--143-144
Pittsburgh in ruins--141

Reminiscences of Wash City--468
State of Indiana--222; 264

Tax sale-Wash City--372-375

Index---511

PREFACE

Daily National Intelligencer Newspaper Abstracts
1845
Joan M Dixon

The National Intelligencer & Washington Advertiser is hereafter the Daily National Intelligencer. It was the first newspaper printed in Washington, D C; Samuel H Smith, the originator. The same was transferred to Jos Gales, jr on Aug 31, 1810; on Nov 1, 1812, the paper was under the firm of Jos Gales, sr, & Wm W Seaton. The Library of Congress has microfilm of the paper from the first issue of Oct 31, 1800 thru Jan 8, 1870, the final paper. The Evening Star Newspaper of Jan 10, 1870 reports: The Intelligencer is discontinued: the proprietor, Mr Delmar, says that having lost several thousand dollars, & being in poor health, he has resolved to discontinue its publication.

Included in the abstracts are advertisements; appointments by the President; Hse o/Rep petitions; passed Acts; legal notices; marriages; deaths; mscl notices; social events; tax lists; military promotions; court cases; deaths by accident; prisoners; & maritime information-crews. Items or events which might be a clue as to the location, age or relationship of an individual are copied.

No attempt has been made to correct the spelling. Due to the length of some articles, it was necessary to present only the highlights of same. Chancery and Equity records are copied as written.

The index contains all surnames and *tracts of lands/places*. **Maritime vessels** are found under barge, boat, brig, frig, schn'r, ship, sloop, steamboat, tugboat, yacht or vessel.

ABBREVIATIONS:
AA CO	ANNE ARUNDEL COUNTY
CMDER	COMMANDER
CMDOR	COMMANDOR
D C	DISTRICT OF COLUMBIA
DWLG	DWELLING
ELIZ	ELIZABETH
ELIZA	ELIZA
MONTG CO	MONTGOMERY COUNTY
PG CO	PRINCE GEORGES CO
WASH	WASHINGTON
WASH, D C	WASHINGTON, DISTRICT OF COLUMBIA

BOOKS IN THE NATIONAL INTELLIGENCER NEWSPAPER SERIES-:
1800-1805/1806-1810/1811-1813/1814-1817/1818-1820/1821-1823/1824-1826/1827-1829/1830-1831/1832-1833/1834-1835/1836-1837/1838-1839/1840/1841/1842/1843/1844/1845
SPECIAL: CIVIL WAR 2 VOLS, 1861-1865

Dedicated to the memory of Andrew J S Dixon, Sr: b. Mar 1867-Gtwn, D C; d. 1935-Gtwn, D C m. Mar 19, 1889 Estelle Campbell: b. Nov, 1867, Balt, Md; d. Apr, 1950-Silver Spring, Md. [Grandparents of Roland C Dixon, my husband.]

DAILY NATIONAL INTELLIGENCER NEWSPAPER
WASHINGTON, D C
1845

WED JAN 1, 1845
Hse/o Reps: 1-Ptn of Gen Henry Sewall & 52 others, praying that Texas may not be annexed to the Union as slaveholding territory. 2-Memorial of Asahel Brainard, praying an increase of pension. 3-Ptn of Louis Chapperton, of Mich, for damages sustained during the late war. 4-Ptn of the heirs of John Mountjoy, dec'd, late of Ky. 5-Ptn of E W Gardner & 24 others, of Nantucket, against the annexation of Texas as a slave Territory. 6-Ptn of Job Bailey & others, for the abolition of slavery in D C. 7-Ptn of Jonathan Shofer, asking payment for a lost final-settlement certificate issued to Christian Orendorff. 8-Ptn of Mrs Hannah Everett, of Mass, praying that an appropriation may be made for the payment of her pension, agreeably to the terms of her certificate. 9-Cmte of Claims reported several bills: relief of Philip Swatzhawber; relief of Danl Homans; & relief of Wm Rich. 10-Cmte on Foreign Affairs: reported verbally favorably on the case of Henry Ledyard, late Charge d'Affiares to France. 11-Cmte on Invalid Pensions: reported unfavorable on the cases of Chas Larrabee, Wm Norman, & Chester Parish. 12-Same cmte: bill for the relief of Wm Gump; relief of John Frecklin; adverse report on the case of John Stone. 13-Cmte on Invalid Pensions: reported a bill for the relief of Arthur Frogge. 14-Cmte on Invalid Pension: reported a bill for the relief of Arsenith Orvis.

Robt E Klady, pilot of the steamboat **Buckeye**, at the time of the collison of that boat with the steamboat **De Soto**, by which a number of lives were lost, was tried at New Orleans recently for manslaughter. The jury was not able to agree, & were discharged.

On Dec 21, the dwlg house of Capt Wm Creel, about 11 miles east of Nashville, accidentally took fire & was entirely consumed. Capt Creel, in attempting to save some property, perished in the flames. He was near 70 years of age. A few nights previous, the house of Mr Jos Moore, about 2 miles eastwardly of the same place, was destroyed by fire, & a little dght of Mr Moore, 5 or 6 years of age, was burnt to death.

Benedict I Saunders, one of the most worthy citizens of Balt, died suddenly, while standing in the door of his store, in South Fred'k st, on Mon. The cause is supposed to have been an affection of the heart, his health having been bad for some years.

Senate: 1-Ptn of Pierre Choteau & others, asking the confirmation of titles to certain lands. 2-Ptn from the widow of the late Col Heman Allen, asking a pension. 3-Ptn of Sarah Bass, of Raleigh, N C. 4-Cmte of Claims: bill for the relief of Geo Whitten. 5-Cmte on Public Lands, reported back without amendment the bill for the relief of Wm Elliott. 6-Bills passed: bill for the relief of Wm Russell; relief of Wm Ritch; relief of David Shaw, & others.

Mr John J Salzwedel, an old & respectable citizen of Balt, died very suddenly of apoplexy on Sun, while out at the Reservoir house, near the Susquehanna Railroad depot.

A new & beautiful map of the U S, compiled by J Calvin Smith, Geographer, was published recently by Sherman & Smith, N Y.

Local News-Wash. Following were summoned to serve on the Grand Inquest:

John W Maury, Foreman	Thos Corcoran	John P Ingle
John Mason, jr	Chas A Burnett	Wm J Stone
R C Weightman	Thos Parker	Hamilton Lufborough
Philip T Berry	Lewis Carbery	G C Grammer
Darius Clagett	Geo W Philips	Thos Thornley
Henry Haw	Eleazar Lindsley	Benj K Morsell
David English	John Boyle	Wm H Campbell
Abner C Pearce	Henry McPherson	
	Wm W Corcoran	

Reward for the return of runaway negro girl from 14 to 15 years of age, calling herself Milly Allen. –Gen John H Eaton, at his residence in the District.

The copartnership existing under the firm of H C Spalding & Co, is this day dissolved by mutual consent, H C Spalding having bought out the entire interest of Isaac Clarke in the business. –Isaac Clarke, H C Spalding

Dissolution of the copartnership existing between the undersigned, under the name of Lewis & Hunt, is this day dissolved by mutual consent. The business in the future will be carried on by W B Lewis, at the old stand. –W B Lewis, Chas Hunt

THU JAN 2, 1845
Orphan's Court of Wash Co, D C. Letters testamentary on the personal estate of Jas T Davis, late of said county, dec'd. –Catharine S Davis, excx

J A Weisse, author of Key to the Franch Language, continues his Family Boarding School at the Highlands, Roxbury, near Boston, Mass.

Columbia Trunpike Road Co: notive given that an election for a President & 4 Dirs will be held on Jan 6. -Wm Gunton, Pres

New Year's Bouquets: Wm Buist, Florist, H st between 11th & 12th sts, Wash.

FRI JAN 3, 1845
Hse/o Reps: 1-Application of Jas Green for a pension: laid on the table. 2-Bill for the relief of Wm Rich: referred to the Cmte of Claims. 3-Bill for the relief of Wm Russell & others: referred to the Cmte on Commerce. 4-Joint resolution in favor of David Shaw & Solomon T Corser: referred to the Cmte on the Post Ofc & Post Roads. 5-Joint resolution of the House to change the name of the brig **Daniel Webster** to **Adela**, & that of the schnr **Mary Frances** to **Isabella**, was sent to the Senate for concurrence. 6-Ptn of Saml Forthingham, of Middletown, Middlesex Co, Conn, praying for an increase of pension.

Providence Journal of Tue. Sudden death. The Hon Jos L Tillinghast was found dead in his bed yesterday. He was a few years past 50.

A copy of the original edition [1667] of Milton's Paradise Lost was sold a few days since in Boston for $24.

Mrd: on Dec 31, by Rev Mr Knox, Mr Thos Tonge to Miss Eliz Dorrett, all of Wash City.

Mrd: on Dec 17, at Brandywine Mills, Summit Co, Ohio, by Rev Mr Cox, of Hudson, Lt Wm F Raynolds, U S Topographical Engineers, to Miss Mary Hanchett, y/d/o Hiram Hanchett, late of Buffalo, N Y.

Died: on Jan 2, Benjamin F, eldest s/o John W & Eleanor Hodgson, aged 2 years & 11 months. His funeral is this day at 2 o'clock.

Meder Pomroy, of Lenox, was run over by the Western railroad train in Pittsfield on Sat last. He was lying on the track in a state of intoxication.

For rent: 2 story brick back bldg, on 12th st, between C & D sts, containing 4 large rooms, all in good order.
-Mary B Alexander, Pa ave, between 12th & 13th sts

Senate: 1-Ptn of John Dillard, asking compensation for losses sustained in furnishing provisions for the Indians. 2-Ptn of the widow of Lt O'Brien, who lost his life in the service of Florida, asking a pension. 3-Ptn of John Carlow, asking a pension. 4-Cmte of Military Affairs: bill for the relief of Joshua Shaw. Also, a bill for the relief of Wm C Eastman. 5-Cmte on Commerce: bill for the relief of Thos Smith. 6-Bill reported for the relief of Mary Zantzinger.

I offer for sale a 2 story house & lot, on I st, between 4th & 5th sts. Call on Wm H Ward, 8th st, between I & K sts, or Albert Burch, Mass ave & 4th st. –Wm H Ward

Mrs S Crocker, late principal of the Young Ladies Seminary in Catskill, N Y, informs she has established a Writing Academy. She has taken a room in Todd's bldg, next door to his Fur Store, Wash. Miss Fagan, from N Y, will give lessons in elementary Drawing & Mezzotint Painting.

Criminal Court: the Court room was pretty much crowded yesterday during the trial of Mary Lackey Barry, alias Coyle, who was indicted for keeping a house of ill-fame in Wash City. The jury returned a verdict of guilty. [Jan 6th newspaper: Mary Lackey Barry was found not guilty.]

Wash Corp: 1-Ptn of Michl Hoover & others, praying a modification of the late law increasing the rent of Butchers' stalls: referred to the Cmte on Police. 2-Cmte of Claims: bill for the relief of Wm M Maddox, without amendment. 3-Cmte of Claims: asking to be discharged from the further consideration of the ptn of Mary M Ellis, was taken up, & the Board refused to discharge the cmte. Same cmte, adverse to the ptn of Wm Dalton: laid on the table.

SAT JAN 4, 1844
The nomination of Robt Walsh as Consul at Paris has been confirmed by the Senate.

The U S frig **Columbia**, Capt D Geisinger, arrived on Wed, after a passage of 42 days from Gibraltar, & 56 days from Mahon.

On Tue week Harvey R Morris, member of the N Y Assembly from Sullivan Co, was crossing Shawangunk mountain from Bloomingburg to Wurtsborough, in a one-horse wagon, with his wife. The horse slipped upon the ice & made a leap which upset the wagon, throwing both out. Mrs Morris was instantly killed, & Mr Morris was badly injured.

Mrd: on Dec 27, in Phil, by Rev Thos H Stockton, Col Wm Doughty, of Wash City, to Mrs Eliza Wilde, of Bloomfield, N J.

Mrd: on New Year's Day, by Rev French S Evans, Mr Chas Baker to Miss Charlotte M Calvert, both of Wash City.

Mrd: on Thu, in the Fourth Presbyterian Church, by Rev John C Smith, Cyrus W Hart to Miss Matilda Whitelock, both of Ohio.

Died: on Fri, after a painful illness, in his 75th year, Wm Alvey, of Montgomey Co, Md. He was much esteemed by those who knew him for his honesty & industry through life. His funeral will take place this evening at 3 o'clock, from Samuels' tavern, on 7th st.

Hse/o Reps: 1-Ptn of E H Holmes, for extension of a patent. 2-Ptn of Roswell Hale, of Adrian, Mich, for an increase of pension. 3-Claim of Capt John Martin, of Detroit, for payment for property destroyed during the war. 4-Claims of the Messrs Eldreds, of Detroit, for damages, on account of the seizure of the "Copper-Rock." 5-Ptn of Talmon G Keeler & others, of Chautauque Co, N Y, praying for a reduction of the rates of postage. 6-Ptn of Cmdor Jos Smith, commanding the American squadron in the Mediterranean, & 240 ofcrs & men of the U S frig **Cumberland**, praying that the spirit portion of the navy ration may be abolished.

The Hon Roger M Sherman died on Dec 30, at Fairfield, Conn, in his 72nd year. He was an assistant under the old Constitution, & a member of the famous Hartford Convention.

Circuit Court of Wash Co, D C: in Equity. E Hunt & others vs W R Hunt & others. Ordered that the sale made by J B H Smith, trustee for the sale of part of the real estate of the late Wm Hunt, to wit, the part of lot 1 in square 458, be ratified: amount of sale to be $638. –W Brent, clk

The old Pioneer [Catholic] Total Abstinence Society will meet in front of the Medical College, 10th st, tomorrow, at 3 p m, & form a procession & march to St Patrick's Church & renew the pledge for the present year. –John B Boon, Sec

Medical Society of D C: meeting on Jan 6 at 2 p m, at the City Hospital, on E st, between 4½ & 5th sts. –Jos Borrows, M D, Recording Sec

MON JAN 6, 1844
Wine Store: John H Buthmann, Pa ave, between 4½ & 6th sts, Wash.

Jos Eve, Charge d'Affaires to Texas, died at my residence in Jun, 1843, shortly after his recall. Gen Murphy, his successor, in his published correspondence with the State Dept, states that the records & correspondence of the Legation were in great confusion, & required the aid of a clerk to arrange them. I knew this accusation was unjust, if intended to apply to Mr Eve. I assisted Mr Eve, on his death bed, in arranging the correspondence, & recorded that which had accumulated during his illness, which had been long & painful. I delivered all to Mr Green, the U S Consul, in complete order, & took his receipt. I called on Gen Murphy, in company with Gen Memucan Hunt, formerly our Minister to the U S, & spoke of the injustice done to Mr Eve. He said the expression had been inadvertently made, & was not intended to case censure on Mr Eve. Rain & flooded streams during their transit, had greatly injured them. –Jas Love

Trial of Bishop Benj T Onderdonk, of the Easter diocese of N Y, closed on Thu in a judgment of guilty. The church mourns when one of its heads is convicted of offences against morality.

Hse/o Reps: 1-Ptn of Clara H Pike, wid/o the late Gen Zebulon Montgomery Pike, praying to be placed on the pension roll of the U S. 2-Ptn of Stephen Weston & 37 others, of Bloomfield, Maine, all legal voters, against the annexation of Texas. Also, of Geo F Cook & others, of Augusta, Maine, against admitting Texas as a slaveholding territory. 3-Ptn of Anna Greenman, praying for a pension. 4-Ptn of the heirs of Capt John Winans, for commutation of half pay as an ofcr in the army of the Revolution. 5-Ptn of Mary Guthridge, for a pension.

Mrd: on Dec 31, at St Andrew's Church, Balt, by Rev H S Keppler, Wm W Littell, of Va, to Harriet Matilda, eldest d/o Thos Robinson, of Balt.

Died: on Jan 1, at Gtwn, D C, Benj Fowler, aged 75 years. His remains were taken to Annapolis for interment; & the occasion was marked by the unanimous passage in the House of Delegates of Md, then in session, of the following resolution, moved by Mr Gallagher: Whereas this House have heard with deep regret intelligence of the death of Lt Col Benj Fowler, one of the gallant defenders of Balt, who so nobly distinguished himself as cmder of the 39th Regt of Infty at the battle of North Point: Therefore ordered, that, as a testimony of respect for the memory of the dec'd, his excellency the Govn'r be requested to cause the national flag to be displayed at half mast from the State House steeple during this day; & that the House now take a recess to attend the funeral of the dec'd.

Naval: the U S sloop of war **Yorktown** sailed Nov 30 for the coast of Africa. The U S sloop of war **Preble**, Lt Commandant Jas W Miller, left same day on a cruise for recruiting, having had some slight sickness on board.

Stray colt came to the subscriber's Farm, near Bladensburg, about 3 weeks ago, a black colt, which the owner can have by proving property & paying charges. –Tho Fenwick

Stop the thief! On Jan 1, the stable door was broken open, & his riding horse, was stolen. Liberal reward for return of the horse. –G M Dove, near Good Hope, Wash Co, D C.

Meeting of the Navy Yard [Anacostia] Fire Co, held on Jan 3, election for ofcrs as follows:

Jas B Ellis, Pres	John Davis, of Abel,
Wm Steward, V Pres	Treas
Chas Gordon, Sec	Jas Dickerson, Steward

Genteel furniture at auction: on Jan 6, at the late residence of Jas S Ringgold, dec'd, on Gay st, Gtwn, the entire stock of well-kept furniture. –Clement Cox, adm -Edw S Wright, auct

TUE JAN 7, 1845
Senate: 1-Ptn from the owners of the steamboat **George Washington**, for damages incurred by collision with the U S cutter **Colonel Harney**. 2-Ptn of Edw R Tyler, of New Haven, a mail-carrier, praying a reduction of postage. 3-Memorial from the heirs of the late Wm Woodworth, asking a patent. 4-Memorial of Thos Beveridge & others against the annexation of Texas. 5-Cmte on Private Lands Claims, reported a bill to confirm the title to a tract of land in the Territory of Iowa to the heirs of Julien Dubuque, dec'd. 6-Bill for the relief of Jos Ramsay: referred. 7-Bill for the relief of Hugh Wallace Wormley: referred. 8-Cmte on Naval affairs be instructed to inquire into the expediency of continuing the pension heretofore granted to the child of Fred'k A Bacon, late a passed midshipman in the U S Navy, who was lost in the U S schnr **Sea Gull**, in a gale off Cape Horn, in 1839. 9-Engrossed bills: relief of Mark Simpson; & relief of Geo Whitten.

Hse/o Reps: 1-Bill introduced for the relief of Zachariah Simmons & Jos Craig Miles: referred to the Cmte on Invalid Pensions. 2-Ptn of Wm G Sanders, for compensation for bldgs burned. 3-Ptn of John R Bold, of Medina Co, Ohio, praying for an increase of his pension. 4-Ptn of the heirs of Lt Ebenezer Jackson, dec'd, for commutation pay. 5-Ptn of Maria L Nourse, to be paid a sum of money ascertained to be due Jos Nourse. 6-Ptn of Levi Durand & others, for the passage of a law in relation to the Smithsonian bequest. 7-Ptn of Pethnel Foster, of Missouri, praying Congress to allow him a pension from Jul 1816, at which time he received a wound whilst in the service of his country during the late war with Great Britain. 8-Ptn of Jesse H Healy, heir at law of Hugh Healy, John Healy, & Patrick Healy, praying a grant of land as compensation for services rendered by his ancestors in the Revolutionary war. 9-Remonstrance of Ezra Batchellar & others, of North Brookfield, Mass, against the annexation of Texas. 10-Ptn of Nathan Rowley & 45 others, citizens of Ilinois, Indiana, & Missouri, praying Congress for a grant of unsold lands in the Vincennes district to complete the Wabash & Erie Canal.

Force's picture of Washington & Its Vicinity for 1845, with 41 embellishments, on steel & lithograph; to which is added the Wash Guide, containing a Congressional Directory, residences of public ofcrs, & other useful information. Will be published on Jan 9, & may be had at Mr Riordan's & at Mr Anderson's bookstores, at Mr Bayly's stationery store, at Mr Fischer's stationers' hall, & at the ofc of the publisher, corner of 10th & D sts.

By way of correcting some erroneous opinions as to who Wm Dove of recent notoriety is, the subscriber feels it is his duty to inform the public that his name is Wm T, & was once a grocer next door to the Nat'l Theatre, but in now engaged in the Lime business, near Gtwn. –Wm T Dove

It is reported that Mr T W Robeson, American Consul at Santa Martha, on the Spanish Main, died on Dec 4 last.

Mrd: on Jan 2, in Phil, by Rev T M Clark, Rector of St Andrew's Church, Capt W G Freeman, of the Adj Gen'l Dept U S Army, to Mgt C, d/o the late Thos B Coleman, of Lebanon Co, Pa.

Died: on Jan 6, in Wash City, Sarah Ann, w/o Prof Lehmanowski. Her funeral will take place today at 11 a m from the residence of her brother. [Jan 13th newspaper: obit of Mrs Prof Lemanowski, the authoress of Resignation; Poem on Africa; Work on Education, & various valuable essays, when she was Miss Sarah Ann Evans. She was a d/o John Evans, whose portrait stands in the Nat'l Institute, & a distant relation of Sir Wm Pepperell, the hero of Louisburg. Note different spellings of Lehmanowski/Lemanowski.]

Died: on Dec 31, 1844, at the residence of her father, in Fauquier Co, Va, Sarah Eliz, only child of Jno W & Maria F Patterson, aged about 5 years.

Auction on Thu on the Market space, by order of the Orphan's Court of Wash Co, D C, the good belonging to the estate of J J Mitchel, to wit: 1 trunk, a Lepine Silver Watch & Keys; black close coat, 1 pair of black pantaloons, 1 drab sack coat, 1 summer coat, 1 blue cloth coat, 2 pair summer pantaloons, 3 pairs summer cassimere pantaloons, 1 black velvet vest, 4 old vests, 1 black scarf, 5 handkerchiefs, 6 shirt collars, 2 purses, & 1 pair shoes. –W B Lewis, Auct

WED JAN 8, 1845
In Chancery. Robt Ramsay vs Ann McCormick & others. All those having claims against the estate of Jas McCormick, dec'd, are to present the same, with their vouchers, to the undersigned, on or before Jan 22; otherwise they may be excluded in the settlement of the estate. –Jos Forrest, Auditor

Senate: 1-Memorial of John Stryker & others, praying for compensation for losses by the Fire Ins Co of Charleston, S C. 2-Ptn of Jos Dudley & other citizens of N H, for an amendment in the pension laws. 3-Memorial of Edw S Osgood, praying to be released from a judgment obtained against him by the U S. 4-Ptn of Francis Sumter, adm of Gen Sumter, dec'd, praying remuneration for moneys advanced the U S during the Revolutionary war. 5-Bill introduced: bill for the relief of Jos Simmons, allowing him a pension. 6-Bills passed: bill for the relief of Mark Simpson; relief of Geo Whitten.

Death of a Veteran. Boston Transcript. Maj Benj Russell, age 83 years, died on Jan 4. Venerable by age, yet strong & lusty in his looks & feelings universally known, & every where respected.

A Music Teacher, competent to give instruction to young professors on the piano forte, & to teach the first class in the French language, desires a situation in a Young Ladies Seminary in any part of the U S. A letter address to John Thos Dunger, Mobile, Ala, will meet with prompt attention.

On Sun night last, the steamboat **Capitol**, bound from Pittsburg to this port, whilst at St Mary's landing, about 70 miles below this port, was destroyed by fire. A Mr Dalrymple, his wife, a son, [Master Jos D,] & dght, a young lady, were passengers on board. It is most probable that Mr Dalrymple & his son perished in their state-room. Mrs Dalrymple is also believed to have perished. The dght barely had time to save her life. Mr Dalrymple was from Lynn, Mass, & was moving to a farm in the vicinity of Carlinville, Ill. He had on board a large amount of valuable property, all of which was lost. A Mr McLane & his lady escaped in the clothes they were sleeping in. Mr McLane had upwards of $5,500 in gold in his trunk, which was lost.

Died: on Jan 5, Julia Barclay, aged 4 years & 5 months, d/o Maj Nicholson. Her funeral is today at 12 o'clock, from the residence of her father, near the headquarters of the marine corps.

Died: on Christmas eve, at the residence of his brother, Columbus, Ga, Thos Everett, aged 38 years, formerly of Balt, where many friends will mourn his death.

Died: on Jan 7, at her residence in Wash Co, Mrs Eleanor Gates Queen, consort of Mr Nicholas L Queen, in her 69th year. Her funeral will be at her late residence, on Jan 9, at 12 o'clock. [Jan 10th newspaper: obit of Mrs Eleanor Gates Queen: during the late holydays this good lady, as was her annual custom, invited her friends & numerous relatives to visit her, & expressed great gratification at seeing so many of them around her. She was a truly pious member of the Protestant Episcopal Church; but ever reminded her children of the religious duty to their own [the Roman Catholic] Church, which they had chosen for themselves. –S]

Died: on Jan 7, Fred'k Reitz, a native of Germany, aged 78 years, an old resident of Wash. His funeral will take place from Mrs Fowler's boarding house on E st, on Thu, at 2 o'clock.

For sale: the house & lot situated on B st, near the Railroad, at present occupied as a refectory by B H Shad. Apply to Jos Follansbee.

Godfrey Eckloff, Cheap & Fashionable Tailor, has removed his establishment from his former stand on 13th st to La ave, between 6th & 7th sts, where he is prepared to make to order every description of Fashionable Clothing.

THU JAN 9, 1845

Senate: 1-Ptn of Alex'r King, exec of Henry King, for arrears of pay for Revolutionary services. 2-Ptn of Frances Pottinger, widow of the late Lt Pottinger, of the Navy, for a pension. 3-Ptn of Susannah Knight, asking for a pension. 4-Ptn of Olives Niles, for an amendment of the pension laws. 5-Cmte on Military Affairs, made an unfavorable report in the case of Capt John Stockton. 6-Bill for the relief of the legal reps of Wm D Cheever, dec'd.

The Hon Ashbel Smith, for several years past Minister of Texas to France, arrived in Wash City on Tue last, on his return to Texas.

Galveston [Texas] News of the 24th give accounts of further Indian disturbances on the Guadaloupe river, below Victoria. Mr J R Kemper had been killed, & his house burned, his wife & children escaping by concealment in the woods. The Indians were afterwards pursued & 2 of the party killed.

The Hon Thos G Pratt was on Mon last duly installed in the ofc of Govn'r of the State of Md.

Mrd: on Jan 8, by Rev Septimus Tuston, A W Kirkwood to Miss Mgt E Young, d/o Mr Ezekiel Young, all of Wash City.

Mrd: on Dec 26, in PG Co, Md, by Rev Mr Dailey, Mr Z T Mattingley to Miss Charlotte A Jones, all of the above place.

Mrd: on Jan 7, by Rev Norval Wilson, Capt John McClelland to Miss Catharine E Hodson, both of Wash City.

Mrd: on Jan 8, by Rev W T Sprole, A F Kimmell to Miss Mary Ann S Lambell, all of Wash City.

Election will be held at the school-house on *Greenleaf's Point*, on Jan 18, to elect a member to the Board of Common Council to supply the vacancy occasioned by the resignation of John E Neale. Com'rs of election: Simon Frazer, Jas Johnson, & Geo W Thompson.

FRI JAN 10, 1845

Mr Ezra Coleman, of Phil, a brother of the inventor of the Aeolian attachment to the Piano Forte, has constructed an improvement on the locomotive engine, by which loaded trains may be carried up inclined planes without any stationary power. Machinery is placed on a frame, so that it requires little trouble to attach it to an engine. It propels a screw, which acts on rollers placed between the rails. The engine is at the perfect control of the director & there is no danger of a backward movement. –Phil Gaz

Senate: 1-Ptn of the heirs of the late Col T G Peachy. 2-Memorial of Silas Meacham, praying Congress to patronize his new invention of light for light-houses. 3-Memorial of Thos H Perkins & a large number of the citizens of Boston, remonstrating against the annexation of Texas in any form. 4-Ptn of C M Page, an examiner in the Patent Ofc, asking permission to take out a patent. 5-Memorial of the reps of Maj Gen Alexander, commonly known as Lord Stirling. 6-Bill introduced for the relief of John S Russworm.

Died: on Dec 19, in Wash City, at the residence of her son-in-law, Mrs Margaret Russell, in her 60th year, formerly of Balt, Md.

Hse/o Reps: 1-Ptn of Francis Summeraner, praying for a pension. 2-Ptn of Jas Morris, of Bates Co, Mo, praying Congress for the passage of an act placing him on the invalid pension list. 3-Ptn of Thos Marlin & others, asking the establishment of a post-route from Tuscumbia to Springfield, Mo. 4-Remonstrance of A H Brevard & 237 others, against the removal of the land ofc from Jackson to Fredericktown, Mo. 5-Ptn of Jas S McComas, of Harford Co, Md, to be allowed an amount due him for work done at the light-house, Piney Point, on the Potomac river. 6-Ptn of Sarah Teas, of Nelson, Va. Also, the ptn of Saml Hichock, of same county. 7-Memorial of Wm A Duer, adm, for a balance upon a contract for supplies to Sinclair's army. 8-Ptn of Jacob Lebengood, for a pension. 9-Ptn of Moses Noble, owner of the schnr **Ruth**, for a fishing bounty. 10-Ptnnof Wm Easby, surviving partner of Easby & Hanley, asking payment for 306 barrels of lime shipped to Old Point for the new ***Fortress Monroe***. 11-Ptn of Jas Farris, of Casey Co, Ky, asking for a pension. 12-Ptn of Sarah Hickney, of N H, asking an amendment of the pension laws.

Criminal Court-Wash: trial yesterday, of Wm S Moore, who discharged a loaded pistol in the lobby of the Hse/o Reps on Apr 23 last, by which John L Wirt, a police ofcr at the Capitol, was severely wounded. First indictment: assault with intent to kill the Hon Wm C McCauslen; 2nd, for an assault upon John L Wirt, with intent to kill Wm C McCauslen. Jury returned with a verdict of guilty of an assault upon Mr McCauslen, & not guilty of intent to kill, as charged in the 1st indictment; & not guilty as charged in the 2nd indictment. Jos H Bradley conducted the defence.

Wash Corp: 1-Ptn of Bernard Kelly: referred to the Cmte of Claims. 2-Cmte of Claims: reported a bill for the relief of Fred'k Hall: passed. 3-Act for the relief of R C Washington & others: passed. 4-Ptn & papers of Jemima Adams & others, excs of Geo Adams: referred to the Cmte of Claims. 5-Cmte of Claims: reported a bill for the relief of Mary M Ellis: which was read. 6-Bill for the relief of Wm M Maddox, was passed with an amendment. 7-Communication received from John E Neale, resigning his seat as a member of this Board. 8-Cmte of Claims: adverse to the ptn of Wm Dalton, & was recommitted to the Cmte of Claims.

Boston Courier: Eastham. In 1695, the town agreed that the order which was passed in 1675 for the destruction of crows & blackbirds should be continued, & that in addition every unmarried man in the township should kill 6 blackbirds or 3 crows while he remained single; as a penalty for not doing it, should not be married till he obeyed this order.

Medical Society of D C-Jan 6: following physicians were elected ofcrs for the year.

Dr F May, Pres	Dr Miller, Corr Sec	Dr Hall, Treas
Dr McWilliams, V P	Dr Jos Borrows, Rec Sec	Dr Howard, Librarian
Dr Sewall, V P		
Board of Examiners:		
Dr Lindsly	Dr Thomas	Dr W P Johnston
Dr Young	Dr J F May	

SAT JAN 11, 1845

To the Voters of PG Co. The vacancy in your delegation occasioned by the appointment of Col Wooton to the ofc of Sec of State of the State of Md, I desire to fill. I therefore take leave to offer myself as a candidate, & assure you that, if elected, my best services shall be devoted to the public interests. –Robt W Bowie, Mattapond, PG Co

Wanted, a boy about 12 or 15 years old, to attend store. Apply to Arnold & Crerar, Pa ave, between 9th & 10th sts.

Hussey's Reaping Machine of full size can now be examined in the basement of the Patent Ofc. I refer those who are interested to know what it will do, to the Hon Wm Lucas, member of Congress from Va, who has had 2 of them on his estate for 3 years. –Obed Hussey

Wanted, by a man & wife, having no children, a situation on a farm-the man as laborer or manager, his wife as housekeeper, or any other employment that would suit. Both are well acquainted with farming. By meeting with a good home & constant employment, they will hire on moderate terms by the month or year, & can come well recommended for honesty, sobriety, & industry. Apply to Mr Martin Murphy, near the corner of Pa ave & 4½ st, personally or by letter, post paid. The persons who advertise live in the country, & will be in the city on Jan 14.

The remainder of the Confectionary & Fancy Articles belonging to Mr J Murphy will be sold on Mon at 10 o'clock, in my store. –W Marshall, auct

Died: on Jan 9, in Wash City, Geo Washington Wilson, aged 43 years, for several years past a Clerk in the Genr'l Land Ofc of the U S. His funeral is today at 1 o'clock, from his late residence on Pa ave.

Died: on Jan 4, in Phil, Mrs Susan R, w/o Jos Bispham, of that city, & d/o the Hon E Tucker, of N J.

MON JAN 13, 1845
Hse/o Reps: 1-Cmte of Ways & Means are discharged from the consideration of the memorial of Wm Norris & Co, & that it be laid on the table. 2-Bill for the relief of March Farrington, made the order of the day for tomorrow. 3-Bill for the relief of Henry N Halsted: made the order of the day for tomorrow. 4-Cmte on Invalid Pensions: reported a bill for the relief of Justice Jacobs: referred to the Cmte of the Whole House. Same cmte, was discharged from the further consideration of the ptn of Aaron Rollins. 5-Cmte of Indian Affairs: adverse report on the memorial of Econchattimico, an Indian chief, & the cmte was discharged from the further consideration thereof. 6-Cmte on Invalid Pensions: bill placing the name of Benj Allen on the roll of invalid pensioners: referred to the Cmte of the Whole House. Same cmte was discharged from the further consideration of the ptn of the heirs of Chas Rumsey. 7-Cmte of Claims: to which was referred Senate bill for the relief of Wm Rich, reported the same with a recommendation that the bill do not pass: referred to the Cmte of the Whole House, & ordered to be printed. 8-Cmte of Claims: adverse reports on the ptn of Richd G Door & Martha Foot: laid on the table. Same cmte made adverse reports on the ptns of S Calvert Ford & of the widow of Southey Parker, dec'd: reports were laid on the table. 9-Cmte of Claims: bill for the relief of Harrison Wilson: committed to the Cmte of the Whole House. 10-Ordered, that the Cmte on the Post Ofc & Post Roads be discharged from the consideration of the memorial of John H Pennington, for an appropriation for experiments testing his invention for navigating the air. Also, that the memorialist have leave to withdraw the same from the files of the House. 11-Cmte on the Judiciary, asked to discharged from the further consideration of the ptn & papers of Henry Richards; which motion was agreed to, & it was laid on the table. Same cmte, reported a bill for the relief of the sureties of Wm Estes, late paymaster of the 4th Regt of Virginia troops, stationed at Norfolk during the late war: referred to the Cmte of the Whole. 12-Cmte on Military Affairs: favorable report on the case of John H McIntosh, with a bill for his relief: referred to the Cmte of the Whole House. 13-Cmte on Invalid Pensions: reported a bill for the relief of the widow Hannah Duboise; & was the same bill, verbatim, had been reported the last session, & was passed this House unanimously: bill to be engrossed.

Senate: 1-Act granting a pension to Geo Whitton: referred to the Cmte on Invalid Pensions. 2-Act for the relief of Mary Reeside, excx of the last will & testament of Jas Reeside. 3-Ptn of Ephraim Hatch & 85 others, of Chelsea, Vt, praying for a reduction of postage. 4-Ptn of Mary Briggs, of Rochester, Mass, widow of Arnold Briggs, a Revolutionary soldier, for a pension. 5-Papers in support of the application of Thos Bronaugh, of Hendricks Co, Indiana, for a pension. 6-Ptn of John P Whitman, respecting a military machine invented by him. 7-Ptn of Henry Tuckerman & others, of Ashburnham, Mass, against annexation of Texas. 8-Ptn & documents of Thos Thompson: referred. 9-Ptn & documents of Jos Taylor: referred.

Mrs Hamilton, the widow of Alex'r Hamilton, is now at Washington, with a view of procuring in some way the publication of her husband's papers under the auspices of Congress. The papers relate to the early political history of the country, & we understand, there are many letters from Gen Washington & other eminent public men of the time. –N Y Evening Post

Evan Parker, of Hamilton Co, Tenn, was killed a few days since by Lemuel Harvey, of the same county. An old quarrel about their lands renewed, Parker making the attack with a bowie knife, which Harvey wrested from his hand, & in turn inflicted the deadly wound.

Mrd: on Jan 9, by Rev Chas A Davis, Thos C Farquhar to Miss Harriet V Scrivener, both of Wash City.

Mrd: on Jan 9, by Rev Jas B Donelan, Mr Jas J Fowler to Miss Susannah Magill, both of Wash City.

Mrd: on Dec 31, by Rev Ulysses Ward, Mr Adam Talbert to Miss Eliz Crandell, both of Montg Co, Md.

Mrd: on Wed last, by Rev John B Ferguson, Mr Wm Mackee, [usually called Luckett] to Miss Rebecca Roberson.

Died: on Jan 10, of scarlet fever, Sarah Virginia Scheel, infant d/o John E & Sarah A Scheel, aged 1 year, 4 months & 10 days.

Died: Jan 5, at *Valentine's Grove*, his residence, in St Mary's Co, Md, Zachariah Spalding, in his 68th year.

The subscriber begs leave to say to his friends & the public generally, that he has repaired his old Establishment, which was consumed by fire on Dec 25, & is now prepared to serve them as usual with Cake, Nuts, Candies, & all varieties usually kept in a well regulated Confectionary. –Geo Norbeck, between 9th & 10th sts, Pa ave, Wash.

Appointments by the Pres, by & with the advice & consent of the Senate.
J B Lacey, of Va, to be Consul of the U S for the port of Nuevitas, Cuba, vice Wm Hogan, recalled.
Isaac L Todd, to be Assayer of the British Mint of the U S at Dahlonega, in the State of Georgia.
Jas B Longacre, of Phil, to be Engraver of the U S Mint at Phil, vice C F Gobrecht, dec'd.

For rent: the bldg on 12th st, which has been for some years occupied by Mr C B King as a studio & picture gallery, with domestic apartments in the basement story thereof. Apply to the proprietor on the premises.

TUE JAN 14, 1845
Hse/o Reps: 1-Ptn of Jas Williams, praying for compensation for services & expenses in arresting a deserter from the U S Army in 1814. 2-Ptn of Wm Culver, praying for remuneration for extra services in constructing the custom-house at New London, Conn. 3-Ptn of Jas Robinson & Eliz Robinson, for interest on the amount granted by act of Congress, approved Jun 13, 1836, for the half-pay of Lt Wilde, dec'd. 4-Ptn of Silas Waterman, for a pension. 5-Ptn from Jos Eaton & 49 others, of Plymouth, Vt, against the annexation of Texas. Same for H Safford & 33 other citizens of Muskingum Co, Ohio. 6-Ptn of Wm Jaynes, with additional testimony praying for a pension. 7-Ptn of Henry Nealy, for a pension. 8-Ptn of A Horback, of Pa, asking for the passage of a law authorizing the Post Ofc Dept to pay him the amount of a draft accepted by said Dept. 9-Ptn of Wm Pitman, of Alleghany Co, Pa, asking for a pension. 10-Ptn of John Ferguson, of Alleghany Co, Pa, asking for a pension as a soldier of the late war. 11-Memorial of John C Ivory & 1,371 others; of A B Carpenter & 54 others; of G B Walker & 76 others; of Jos Sneeder & 41 others, of W A Lacey & 104 others; of John F Kelso & 219 others; of T G Mason & 40 others; all praying a grant of land to the State of Indiana to aid in completing the Wabash & Erie Canal. 12-Ptn of Lucretia Foote, for a pension.

For rent: 2 story brick house on La ave for several years occupied by the subscriber. Apply to Saml Stettinius, or Thos W Pairo.

For rent: 2 story brick house with 10 rooms & kitchen, on 12th st, between F & G sts. –J M Krofft, corner of F & 12th sts.

Intelligence from Madrid to Nov 26 confirms the accounts of the execution of Benito Zurbano, s/o the revolted Gen, & also of his uncle Juan Martinez, both of whom were shot at Logrono, together with their 2 servants. Of Zurbano no authentic tidings had as yet reached Madrid. Some said that he had died, others that he was concealed on the banks of the Ebro, or he had found his way to Portugal. A report was prevalent in Madrid that Gen Prim had been rescued by a party of cavalry on his way to Cadiz, to be transported for imprisonment in Cuba.

At the late meeting of the Md Historical Society, Mr G B Coale presented an autograph letter: to Francis Hopkinson from Gen George Washington, dated Mount Vernon, May 16, 1785. Subject: on sitting for painters whilst they are delineating the lines of my face. [Regards to Mrs Hopkinson & yourself.] -Go Washington

For sale or to let: 2 story frame house, with brick basement, on East Capitol St, Capitol Hill. Apply to Isaac Bassett, on the premises. –Isaac Bassett

At Livingston, Dec 26, 1844, Mr Orra Mace, aged about 47 years, was killed instantly when thrown from his wagon, when the horses became unmanageable & descended a hill at a rapid rate. –Schoharie Republican

Died: on Jan 6, suddenly, at White Hall, his late residence, in King George Co, Va, Gustavus B Wallace, in his 68th year.

Died: on Jan 11, in his 46th year, Francis Cross, s/o the late Ely Cross.

Died: on Jan 11, near Washington, Mary, w/o Geo Oyster, in her 53rd year, for some years a resident of Gtwn, & a native of Emmittsburg, Fred'k Co, Md.

A hostile meeting between Mr Thos Butler King & Mr Chas Spalding, on Jan 6, at Amelia Island. Weapons-pistols, distance-10 paces. Two shots were passed without effect, when, on the intervention of friends, the affair was adjusted. Circumstances connected with the recent canvass of the 2 men while candidates for Congress was the difficulty. –Savannah Republican

The stables of Gen Harvie, near Richmond, Va, were consumed by fire on Wed, & with them 16 horses & mules. No doubt is entertained, that the stables were set on fire. –Whig

Senate: 1-Memorial of Danl Weed & 44 others, of Ipswich, Mass, for the abolition of slavery in D C. 2-Ptn from the heirs of Jas Delano, dec'd, for indemnity for French spoliations. 3-Ptn of Cadwallader Wallace, praying compensation for certain lands of which he was deprived by the treaty of Granville. 4-Ptn of Comfort Drew, the widow of a dec'd Revolutionary soldier, asking a pension. 5-Ptn of Jas Arnold, a soldier in the last war, praying a pension. 6-Cmte on Pensions: unfavorable report on the ptn of Jacob Fowler; & on the ptn of Catherine Leavitt; & on the ptn of Mary Carleton.

Obit-died: on Jan 2, at his residence, near Port Tobacco, Chas Co, Md, John J Jenkins, in his 58th year. A fatal paralysis suddenly deprived him of speech. He held the ofc of Judge of the Orphans' Court; & served as an independent legislator in the councils of the State. On a memorable occasion, he traveled on a litter, with 2 physicians in attendance, to Annapolis to give a casting vote for a measure which he believed to be for the good of his country. To his relative, friends, & neighbors, his loss is irreparable. -H

WED JAN 15, 1845
Hse/o Reps: 1-Ptn of Jeremiah Sims, praying for a pension. 2-Presented the ptn of Moses Wright; the ptn of Benj Hansford; ptn of Fielding Pratt; & the ptn of Isaiah Haden's heirs. 3-Ptn of Pliny Cutler & 40 others, of Boston, praying the abolition of the spirit ration in the navy. 4-Ptn of Gen Isaac Belknap, of Orange Co, N Y, for a pension.

Senate: 1-Ptn of Nathl Goddard & others, owners of the ship **Ariadne**, captured during the last war by a U S vessel & confiscated. 2-Ptn of the heirs of Nathl Ashby, an ofcr of the Revolution, praying for the commutation pay to which he was entitled. 3-Ptn of John Russell for a modification of the laws allowing bounty lands to the soldiers of the Revolution. 4-Cmte on the Judiciary: unfavorable report on the case of Jos Ramsey. The cmte, on motion, were discharged, & the papers referred to the Cmte of Claims. 5-Cmte on Military Affairs: an adverse report on the case of Capt John Stockton, which was afterwards recommitted, on motion of Mr Woodbridge, in the same cmte. 6-Resolved, That the Senate procure 1,200 additional copies of the report of J N Nicolet, which was ordered to be printed on Feb 16, 1841; & that he cause to be printed, from the copper-plate belonging to the Senate, the same number of copies of the map of the hydrographical basin of the Upper Mississippi river, with the said report. 7-Bill for the relief of John Woolley. 8-Bill for the relief of David Gurley. 9-Bill for the relief of Miles King.

Agency for the sale of Dale's Patent Scales: W M Randolph, opposite Brown's Hotel.

Mrd: on Jan 9, at Alexandria, by Rev Elias Harrison, Jas Eveleth, of Wash City, to Harriet, d/o the late Capt Jas Mackenzie.

Mrd: on Jan 9, by Rev Mr Tarring, Mr Wm Bird, of Wash, to Miss Virginia W Morrow, of Va.

Died: on Jan 10, at Goodwood, PG Co, Md, after a long illness, Rosalie Eugenia Carter, w/o Chas H Carter, & d/o the late Geo Calvert, of Riverdale.

Edw Sherry, convicted in the Kensington riots, at Phil, sentenced to 3 years in the Eastern Pen. Robt McQuillan, convicted of riot, sentenced to an imprisonment of 1 year.

Splendid lot of mutton for sale: in the Old Centre Market, raised & fed by Mr Jackland Smith, of Clarke Co, Va. –Philip Otterback, Chas Miller.

Yesterday Mr Jas Rhodes sold at his stall in our Centre Market some very superior lamb, fed by Chas Hill, in PG Co, Md.

THU JAN 16, 1845
An Owl was yesterday presented to the Museum of the Nat'l Institute by Mr G W Clark. We took to be a specimen of the great Cinereous Owl of Audubon, a species rarely found in the Atlantic regions. It was caught the night before last in a steel trap, on the farm of Mr Thos Jenkins, near the Navy Yard bridge, & measured between the tips of its wings 4 feet & 6 inches.

Senate: 1-Ptn of John B Randolph, passed midshipman in the navy, asking additional pay for extra services performed. 2-Ptn of Lorenzo N Clark, praying for indemnity for losses sustained as a contractor with the Gov't. 3-Bills engrossed: relief of Ava Andrews; of the heirs of Wm Fischer; & of Wm Elliott. 4-Cmte on Naval Affairs: unfavorable reports in the cases of Frances Pottinger & E M Cloud. 5-Cmte on Finance: favorable report in the case of Jas G King & others, for the redemption of Treas notes. 6-Cmte on Military Affairs were discharged from the further consideration of the case of W D Clagett.

For rent: 2 two-story basement brick houses on N J ave, in Phoenix Row, first houses below the Coast Survey Ofc, within a few yards of the Capitol. These house are finished with folding doors to the parlors, neat & convenient chambers, back & front porches, good yards, & in every respect comfortable residences. They will be rented for $100 per year. Apply to R Patten, Pa ave, between 10th & 11th sts.

Balt, Jan 15, A young man, Paul Roux, by papers in his possession, to be a hardware merchant of Mason, Ga, arrived in this city from Phil on Sat, & put up at the house of Thos Noland, keeper of a small tavern in South Chas st. On Mon he was found dead in his bed with his throat cut from ear to ear, & his skull broken with an axe. The murderer is supposed to be a young man named Henry McCurry, who roomed with the dec'd on Sun night, & left for Phil on Mon. Ofcrs have gone in pursuit of him. The dec'd was a member of the Old Fellows' Society, & his remains have been taken charge of by that society of this city, by whom they will be interred. -American

Pomonkey for sale: Valuable Potomac Fishery. The subscriber, finding the above estate too distant to receive the necessary attention, is desirous of disposing of it a private sale. *Pomonkey*, the residence of the late Col Fenwick, but more recently possessed by Mr R J Brent, from whom I purchased it, is on the Md side, 20 miles below Wash, & contains about 650 acs. The dwlg is commodious & in good order, & there is every out-house on the estate needed. Address the subscriber, near Chaptico, St Mary's Co, Md.
-Edmund J Plowden

Boarding: Mrs A Doniphan, near the corner of E & 13th sts. Her price is moderate, to suit the times.

On Dec 28, Dr Wm R Ball, of Alabama, was killed at Raymond, Miss, by Jeremiah B Granberry. Dr Ball had been sent by the Govn'r of Ala, with a requisition for the delivery of Granberry, who was under indictment in Barbour Co, Ala. On Sat Granberry was delivered over to Dr Ball by the Sheriff. After the surrender, Granberry proposed that they should walk out, as he wished to find whether a horse had been sent for him to ride. De Ball walked arm & arm with him down stairs. When they passed out of the court house, Granberry drew a pistol & fired it into the breast of Dr Ball. Dr Ball died in about a minute & a half after receiving the wound. Granberry was re-arrested, & placed in close confinement.

We see in the New Orleans papers that Francis Combs, s/o Gen Leslie Combs, of Ky, & one of the prisoners confined so long at Santa Fe, was shot near his plantation in the parish of Point Coupee, on Dec 31, by one of his neighbors, Geo O'Blemis, with whom he had had some difficulty. The murderer was arrested.

Died: yesterday, after an illness of some weeks, Patrick A Orme, in his 32nd of his age. His funeral is this day, at 2 o'clock, from his late residence on 7th st, near the Patent Ofc.

FRI JAN 16, 1845
Wash Corp: 1-Cmte of Claims: asked to be discharged from the further consideration of the ptns of Bernard Kelly & of John F Grimes. 2-Bill for the relief of Wm M Maddox was agreed to. 3-The Board resumed the consideration of the letter of J P McKean, Lt Commanding the Wash Light Infty. 4-Cmte of Claims: bill for the relief of Alvin Cole: passed. 5-Ptn of Wm Dowling, praying remission of a fine: referred to the Cmte of Claims. 6-Ptn of Wm Morrow, praying remission of a fine: referred to the Cmte of Claims. 7-Ptn of Wm Woodward & others, for improvement of Mass ave, from 5th to 7th sts: referred to the Cmte on Improvements. 8-Bills for the relief of Alvin Cole, for the relief of Fred'k Hall, & for the relief of R C Washington & others: referred to the Cmte of Claims. 9-Bill for the relief of Mary M Ellis: passed with an amendment proposed by Mr Davis.

Hse/o Reps: 1-Ptn of D Wendell Newhall & 489 other citizens of Lynn, Mass, for the adoption of a cheap & uniform system of postage. Memorial of D Wendell Newhall & 440 others, solemnly protesting against the annexation of Texas. 2-Ptn of Isaac Hulse & others, surgeons & assistant surgeons in the Navy, that the rank of medical ofcrs in the navy may be assimilated to that of the medical ofcrs in the army. 3-Ptn of Anna Graffan, of the city of Portland, Maine, praying for a pension. 4-Ptn of Peter Caville, of Buffalo, N Y, for an invalid pension. 5-Ptn & documents of Robt Dinsmore for a pension. 6-Ptn of B F Haskell & 330 others, for abolition of slavery in D C & the annexation of Texas. 7-Ptn of Mrs Ann Mix, wid/o the late Cmder Marvin P Mix, for compensation for the use of the manger stopper, invented by her husband.

Senate: 1-Ptn of Saml Norris & others, sureties of Laban C Howell, late Receiver of Public Moneys in Arkansas. 2-Communication from G W Patuck, in relation to the establishment of a mail route in Arkansas. 3-Bills passed: relief of the heirs of Wm Fischer; of Asa Andrews; & of Wm Elliott.

Fatal accidents on Tue upon the Balt & Ohio Railroad. 1-Mr John Slack, a carpenter, engaged at work on the Monocacy bridge, was run over by a locomotive & he died in a few minutes. 2-Mr Jacob Barnhardt, in the employ of the Company, managing a sawing machine, had been sawing timber near Sykesville, & tried to jump on one of the cars, but falling between the cars passed over his head & killed him instantly.

Wm Thornton, aged 10 or 11, s/o Col Wm M Thornton, of Cumberland, Va, was killed at or near Cartersville, Va, on Jan 8, by his friend, Wm Carrington, s/o Mr Jos Carrington, of Cartersville, of about the same age. Young Thornton threw up a stone for the latter to fire at as it fell, when, by his foot slipping, or by some cause, the contents of the piece were discharged in the face of his friend, who fell dead. -Whig

SAT JAN 18, 1845
Annual meeting of the Stockholders in the Wash & Norfolk Steampacket Co will be held at the Steamboat Hotel, opposite the Centre Market, on Jan 23, at 7 p m.
–Saml Bacon, Pres

The undersigned has taken a room on 4½ st, 3rd door south of Pa ave, for the purpose of taking Miniatures, where he may always be found between the hours of 8 a m & 5 p m.
–C Newmayer

Henry McCurry, the murderer of Paul Roux, of Ga, in Nolan's Hotel, on Mon, in Balt, was arrested on Thu & committed to prison to await the requisition of the Govn'r of Md.

Mrd: on Jan 8, by Rev John Montgomery, Morgan Vance, of Tenn, to Susan P Thompson, d/o Col Geo C Thompson, of Shawnee Springs, Mercer Co, Ky.

MON JAN 20, 1845
Hse/o Reps:; 1-Ptn of Jane Simpers & others, of Cecil Co, Md, praying Congress to grant them a pension for services rendered by their late father during the Revolutionary war. 2-Ptn of Jos Johnson for a pension. 3-Ptn of Cyrus Mendenhall, on behalf of the ship owners, mariners, & merchants on Lake Superior, praying the erection of light-houses. 4-Memorial of Dr Lawson, Surgeon Genr'l of the Army. 5-Resolved, That the Pres of the U S be directed to cause criminal prosecutions to be commenced against Caleb J McNulty, late Clerk of this House, for an embezzlement of the public money, & all persons advising or knowingly & willingly participating in such embezzlement, according to the provisions of the act of Congress, approved Aug 13, 1841. 6-Ptn of John Hutchins, of Adrian, Mich, for conveyance of land equitably belonging to him. 7-Ptn of John H Lincoln, for invalid pension. 8-Ptn of Sherman Pierce, for invalid pension. 9-Ptn of Alden Partridge for a loan of 150 stand of muskets to the American Literary, Scientific & Military Univ at Norwich, Vt.

Senate: 1-Bill for the relief of Gen Jos M Hernandez came up. 2-Bill for the relief of Matilda Drury & other reps of Capt Wm Smallwood Tillard, of the State of Md. 3-Report of the Cmte of Accounts disclosing a defalcation of Caleb J McNulty, Clerk of the House.

Mr Wm F Harnden, of the firm of Harnden & Co, died at his residence in Boston on Tue, of consumption.

A Noble Rebel: The memorialists call to the recollection of Congress that Lord Stirling was one of the earliest patriots of the Revolution. In 1775 he was appointed to the command of the first Continental regt that was raised in N J. In the winter of 1775-6, while the Asia man-of-war was in the bay of N Y, Col Lord Stirling embarked with a detachment of his own regt & some volunteers from Elizabethtown in 3 small craft, ran outside of Sandy Hook to sea, boarded, &, with musketry, carried a transport ship of 300 tons, armed with 6 guns, & freighted with stores for the enemy, & bore her triumphantly into Perth Amboy. In the battles of Long Island, Brandywine, Germantown, & Monmouth, he sustained a conspicuous & efficient part. Lord Stirling died in 1773. [The memorialists, one of whom is Judge Duer, of N Y-are the grandchildren & legal reps of Lord Stirling, by the intermarriage of his dght with the late Col Wm Duer, of N Y, who himself, like his father-in-law, was active in the Revolution, as a member of the Cmte of Public Safety in his State, & one of the delegates to the Continental Congress.]

Norwich [Conn] Courier: Richd Fanning was killed on Mon, when he is supposed to have jumped from the train while it was under full headway. He was carried to the city for medical aid, bur died in a few hours.

Baton Rouge [La] Gaz: a few days ago a worthy & industrious planter of West Baton Rouge, Jean Dominique Lanoux, residing about 12 miles below the Court-house, committed suicide by blowing his brains out. Severe family misfortunes, seem to be the cause. He was respected by all who knew him.

Died: on Jan 12, at Phil, Mrs Ellen Delaney, formerly of Wash City, after an illness of 10 weeks, which she bore with Christian fortitude.

Inauguration Ball: on Mar 4 next: meeting at Brown's Hotel on Wed next, at 8 p m. –Chas S Frailey, Sec

Washington City Orphan Asylum: following Ladies chosen Managers for the ensuing year.

Mrs Hawley, 1st Directress	Mrs Laurie, 2nd Directress	Miss Smith, Treas Miss Van Ness, Sec
Mrs Brown	Mrs Richd Smith	Mrs Gilliss
Mrs Lear	Mrs Stone	Miss Bingham
Mrs Henderson	Mrs Washington	Miss Ellen Key
Mrs R S Coxe	Mrs Tucker	
Mrs Luce	Mrs McLaughlin	

Poughkeepsie Ale just received & for sale. –Jourdan W Maury

Househole furniture, hackney carriage, & sleigh at auction on Feb 10, by deed of trust from Patrick Gowins, for certain purposes, at his residence at the corner of F & 22nd st. -Robt W Dyer & Co, aucts

TUE JAN 21, 1845
Senate: 1-Ptn of the widow of the late Gen Pike. 2-Ptn of Calvin Emmons, praying a renewal of his patent. 3-Ptn of Thos B Winston, praying to be relieved of a judgment. 4-Ptn of Lt J M Gillis, asking compensation for extra services performed whilst in the Exploying Expedition. 5-Cmte on Revolutionary Claims: reported without amendment the bill for the relief of John S Russworm. Adverse reports in the cases of Albert A Muller, & the reps of Jas Bell, dec'd. 6-Cmte on Commerce: bill for the relief of Noah Miller. 7-Engrossed bills: relief of Thos Smith; of Wm C Easton; of Mary E Zantzinger.

Wade Van Buren Barker, s/o Jas N Barker, who resides on Capitol Hill, who is about 16 or 17 years of age, was alone in an upper room of his father's house, when the report of a pistol was heard. The only person in the house at the time was a female servant, who gave the alarm, & Dr Hall & Dr J F May were sent for, but the young man died almost immediately. The pistol is supposed to have gone off accidentally; it was one of the rifle barrel pistols, manufactured by Kendall & Windsor, Vt-a very dangerous weapon, without any guard over the trigger, & very apt to go off with a slight touch. The pistol had Smith's improved patent stud-lock attached to it, & would carry a rifle ball a very great distance. The ball had entered the left temple, passed through the brain, & came out on the opposite side of the head. The ball was found on the floor, having struck the opposite wall.

Died: on Jan 19, Robt W Fenwick, in his 41st year, leaving a wife & 4 children to mourn his loss. His funeral will take place this morning at 9 o'clock, from his late residence on 7th st.

Died: on Jan 20, Mrs Eliz Williams, aged 70 years. Her funeral is this day at 3 o'clock, from the house of Dr Doniphan, near the corner of 13th & E sts, west.

WED JAN 22, 1845
Senate: 1-Ptn of Maria Taylor, of Ascension, La, for the confirmation of a land title. 2-Ptn of Pearson Cogswell, late marshal of the district of N H. 3-Ptn of Jas H Gayle, an ensign in the army, during the last war, asking a pension. 4-Memorial from the reps of Jas Roddy, dec'd, for compensation for losses sustained by certain contracts with the Gov't. 5-Ptn of P Prescott, the interpreter for the Indian agency at St Louis, for an increase of pay. 6-Cmte on Indian Affairs: bill for the relief of Reuben Gentry & others. Also, a bill for the relief of Geo Duvall.

The Nashville Whig of Jan 14: On Sun in our city, Thos H Fletcher, died. He had been for several days under high mental excitement in conducting the defence of W W Merchant, charged with murder. The trial closed, & the verdict was acquittal. Mr Fletcher evidently died of apoplexy.

The large barn belonging to Mr Thos Crown, in Anne Arundel Co, Md, was on Wed last, entirely consumed by fire. Believed to be the work of an incendiary.
–Annapolis Republican

Wash Corp: 1-Ptn of Philip Ennis: referred to the Cmte of Claims. 2-Presented: the credentials of John Van Reswick, member elect to supply a vacancy, appeared, was duly qualified, & took his seat. 3-Ptn from Francis A Tucker, commanding the Nat'l Blues, asking for the use of a room in the City Hall for the purpose of depositing their arms & equipments: referred to the Cmte on Police. 4-Cmte of Claims: bill report for the relief of Wm Dalton: passed.

Hse/o Reps: 1-Cmte on Revolutionary Pensions: bill for the relief of Geo Wentling: committed. 2-Ptn of R W Boyd, clerk in the ofc of the Surveyor Genr'l of La, praying compensation for extra services. 3-Ptn of Wm Neff, of Cincinnati, Ohio, & 400 other citizens of that city & vicinity, praying the passage of an act granting to Indiana public lands in the Vincennes land district, sufficient to complete the Wabash & Erie Canal to the Ohio River. 4-Ptn of C Benns, for remuneration for wrongful seizure of goods. 5-Ptn of Harvey Reynolds, for increase of pension. 6-Ptn of H Lowry, for services as pension agent. 7-Ptn of Danl Morse, for a pension.

From China: Mr T S Waldron, U S Consul & Navy Agent at Hong Kong, died on Sep 8.

Valuable 3 story brick house & lot for sale; by deed of trust from Miss Mary J Nourse to me, dated Nov 1, 1843, recorded in Liber W B, No 105, folios 27 thru 31, a land record for Wash Co, D C: sale on Jan 30, at the auction rooms of Robt W Dyer & Co, aucts, that valuable house & lot in sq 118, formerly owned by the Hon J K Paulding, & by him conveyed to said Mary J Nourse. This house is one of the Seven Bldgs, & fronts of course on Pa ave. The house & lot were sold at auction on Oct 23, 1843, & said Mary J Nourse became the purchases, & will be re-sold to obtain payment of so much of the purchase money as remains unpaid by said Mary J Nourse.
–H H Dent, Trustee -Robt W Dyer & Co, aucts

$4 reward for strayed horned cow. Above reward on delivery to the owner, living on Mass ave, east of 6th st, next door to Mr Thos Jarboe. –Sophia H Perrie [To hire, a likely servant boy, 14 years of age.]

Died: on Jan 20, from the effects of a wound received by the accidental explosion of a pistol he was handling, Wade, the s/o J N Barker, in his 18th year. His funeral is this day, at 1 o'clock, from his father's residence, South B st, Capitol Hill. [See Jan 21, 1845.]

Died: on Jan 15, at Cumberland, Md, after an illness of one week, Mr Saml Charles, Editor of the Cumberland Civilian, in his 45th year, leaving a wife & 5 children, most of whom are too young to be conscious of their loss. He through life set a bright example to those who survive him.

Appointments by the Pres, by & with the advice & consent of the Senate.
Andrew J Donelson, to be Charge d'Affaires of the U S to the Republic of Texas.
Consul of the U S:
Chas Graebe, of N Y, for the Kingdom of Hanover & Grand Dutchy of Hesse Darmstadt.
Alex'd Tod, for the port of Alexandria, in Egypt.
Robt L McIntosh, for the port of Touchoufou, in China.
Isaac Stone, for the port of San Juan de los Remedios, Cuba.
Gabriel G Fleurot, of N Y, for the island of Martinique.
Eneas McFaul, jr, for the port of Laguna de Terminos, Mexico.
Jas W Wright, for the port of St Jago de Cuba.
Alex'r G Abell, of Michigan, for the Island of Hawaii, one of the Sandwich Islands.
Register of the Land Ofc:
Jas W Barrett, at Springfield, Ill, vice Garret Elkin, removed.
John Gardner, at Winaman, Indiana
Receiver of Public Moneys:
Geo W Womack, at Greensburg, La, vice G P Womack, dec'd.
Parker Dudley, at Palmyra, Missouri
Bela M Hughes, at Plattsburg, Missouri
Sylvester W Higgins, at Detroit, Michigan
Seton W Norris, at Indianapolis, Indiana
Nimrod E Benson, at Montgomery, Alabama
Saml Wise, at Vincennes, Ind, vice Thos Scott, whose commission has expired.
Surveyor & Inspector of the Revenue:
A H Wilder for the port of Ipswich, Mass
Jas W Roach, for St Mary's river, Md.
Geo Hudson, for the port of Snow Hill, Md
Wm Walston, for the port of Accomack C H, Va
Wm Maxwell, for the port of Sunbury, Georgia
Benj Stiles, for the port of Hardwick, Georgia
Martin Russell, for the port of Troy, N Y
Chas A Judson, for New Haven, Conn, vice John T Collis, resigned.
Andrew Agnew, for New Brunswick, N J-re-appointment.
S H Page, for the port of Pontchartrain, La-re-appointment

Marshal of the U S:
Levi S Humphrey, for the District of Michigan, vice Joshua Howard, removed.
Moreau Forrest, for the District of Md, vice Thos B Pottinger, removed.
Henderson Willingham, for the District of Georgia, vice Edw Harden, appointed Collector of the Customs at Savannah.
Benning Mann, for the District of Connecticut, in the place of John B Eldredge, removed.
Robt C Ewing, for the District of Missouri, vice Wm C Anderson, declined, who was appointed in the place of Weston F Birch, rejected by the Senate.
Virgil D Parris, for the District of Maine, vice John D Kinsman, removed
John Lane, for the District of Ky, vice Wm B Blackburn, removed
Saml McClury, for the District of N J, vice J A Simson, removed.
Isaac O Barnes, for the District of Massachusetts, vice Solomon Lincoln, removed
Thos D Condy, for the District of S C
Saml Hays, for the Western District of Pa

Justice of the Peace:
Horatio Ball, for the county of Alexandria, D C

Atty of the U S:
Thos D Mosely, for the Middle District of Tenn, vice J M Lea, resigned.
Danl Mace, for the District of Indiana, vice Courtland Cushing, resigned.
Chas S Sibley, for the Middle District of Florida.
Nathl Denby, of Va, to be temporary Navy Agent at Marseilles, France, vice A G Benson, resigned.
Adam D Steuart, to be a Paymaster in the Army

Postmaster:
Edmund B Glasscock, at Augusta, Georgia
Wm D Marrast, at Tuscalousa, Alabama
Israel Hoge, at Zanesville, Ohio-re-appointment
Howell Hobbs, at Jackson, Miss

Midshipman Albert G Enos, having deserted from the U S ship **Portsmouth**, at Portsmouth, N H, has been dismissed from the naval service of the U S; the dismissal to take effect from Dec 10, 1844. –Navy Dept, Jan 14, 1845.

Law Notice: Basil Champer, formerly of Spencer Co, Indiana, & Theodore J Barnett, formerly of Indianapolis, have associated themselves in the practice of the law in New Albany, Indiana. Business requiring attention in any part of the State will be received.

THU JAN 23, 1845
French Hats: received 2 cases of French Moleskin Hats: from $1.50 to $5. Gentlemen wishing a neat & cheap Hat will do well to call & examine my stock. –E G Handy, between Coleman's & Brown's Hotels.

Life of Andrew Jackson, private, military, & civil, by Amos Kendall, to be completed in 15 numbers, with illustrations, at 25 cents each. –F Taylor, Wash

Sale this day of Trunks & Valises, at auction. –W B Lewis, auctioneer, Pa ave, near 11th st.

Clothing, books, instruments, by order of the Orphan's Court of Wash Co, D C: sale on Sat next, the personal effects of the late Jacob Nollner. -Robt W Dyer & Co, aucts

Household furniture at auction: on Jan 28, at the boarding-house of Mrs Dashiell, Pa ave, near 3rd st. -A Green, auctioneer [The house is for rent. Inquire on the premises, or of A Green, Concert Hall.]

Caution: Whereas, in the Circuit Court of the U S, a verdict has been recently rendered in my favor of $3,575, with costs, against Peter Hogg & Cornelius Delamater, Engine Bldrs in N Y, for an infringement of my patent right, in the use & manufacture of the Spiral Paddle Wheels, commonly called Ericsson Propellers, whereby the validity of my letters patent & their infringement as after said have been tested & established-All persons are hereby cautioned against using, manufacturing, or vending such Wheels without my consent, & are notified that arrangements can be made with the subscriber at 559 Pearl st, or his Attys, Clark & Campbell, 64 John st, N Y. –John B Emerson

<u>Annapolis, Md: the Senate of Md has rejected the following nominations made by the late Govn'r:</u>
Wm B Stone, to be Judge in the 1st judicial district, vice Stevens, dec'd.
Saml M Semmes, to be Judge in the 5th judicial district, vice Buchanan, dec'd.
John A Carter, to be clerk of Montg Co Court.
Wm H Gilpin, to be Register of Wills of Cecil Co.
<u>The following nominations of the late Govn'r have been confirmed:</u>
Stephenson Archer, to be Chief Judge of the Court of Appeals, vice Buchanan, dec'd.
Augustus R Sollers, to be Clerk of Calvert Co Court.

From Europe: the marriage of Queen Isabella II with Count Trapani, is said to be finally determined on.

Newark Daily Adv: the trial of Peter Parke, indicted for murder, terminated at Belvidere on Fri in a verdict of guilty. Two of the murderers, Jos Carter jr, & Peter Parke, his cousin, are identified & stand convicted. Abner Parke, either the father or uncle of Peter, it is believed his participataion in the dreadful tragedy will yet be fully established. He will be tried at the Feb term. The murders referred to were committed on May 1, 1843, when a family of 4 persons were murdered in their beds during the night, with the object of securing a large sum of money that was known to be in the house.

FRI JAN 24, 1845
Mr Jas Lewis, aged about 40 years, lost his life on Thu last, at the residence of his brother in Hamden, near Colchester line: he went to the well to draw water and being missed some 10 or 15 minutes after, the family found him in the well. He was got out immediately, but was found to be quite dead. There was considerable ice around the well, & it is supposed that he slipped & lost his balance. Mr Lewis was married but the day before the accident. –Delaware [N Y] Express

Harvard Univ: the 2nd term of the Law School will open on Feb 28, 1845. –Simon Greenleaf, Royal Prof of Law, Cambridge, Mass.

Fort Hill Square for sale: nearly 6 acs, on the Eastern Branch, near the Navy Yard. –A Green, Auct & Com Merchandise, Concert Hall.

Hse/o Reps: 1-Ptn of Mrs Hetty Fassett for a pension. 2-Ptn of C Gordon, for arrears of pension. 3-Ptn of Lydia Bean, praying for a pension. 4-Ptn of Mary M Hatch, wid/o Capt Robt Hatch, dec'd, for a renewal of her pension.

Patent Ofc, Apr 16, 1844. To the Hon H L Ellsworth, Com'r of Patents. The use of the hoop on which to attach the paddles, if covered by Mr Emerson's patent, would enable him to prevent the use of Ericsson's Propeller; but as there is not the least allusion to this feature in Mr Emerson's specification, I am satisfied that he will not be sustained by any Court; there is no mention of this feature in the specification, the drawing now in this ofc were filed here long subsequent to the practical application of the propeller by Capt Ericsson. –C M Keller, Examiner of Patents

Senate: 1-Ptn of the heirs of Harman Blannerhasset, asking compensation for the destruction of their father's property by a body of U S militia in 1806. 2-Memorial of J R Bryan, adm of Purser Garretson, dec'd, praying an additional allowance in the settlement of his accounts. 3-Ptn of Ebenezer Storer, an ofcr in the Revolution, asking a pension. 4-Memorial of Alden Partridge, principal of the Military School of Norwich, praying for the use of a certain portion of military equipments belonging to the U S. 5-Cmte on Private Land Claims: bill to confirm the title of certain lands claimed by Benj Ballard. 6-Cmte on Military Affairs: bill for the relief of Jas Smalley. Also, an unfavorable report on the ptn of Albert Day & others, of a company of Ohio volunteers.

By virtue of 2 writs of fieri facias, issued by Thos C Donn, Justice of the Peace in & for Wash Co, D C, at the suits of Wm Dant, surviving partner of John Dix, dec'd, use of Richd G Briscoe & Jos S Clark, trading under the firm of Clark & Briscoe, against the goods, chattels, lands, tenements, rights & credits of Chas Kiernan: the n w part of lot 6 in sq 536, & improvements thereon, in Wash City, on Feb 25: I will offer for sale the said property so seized & taken in execution, by public auction. –H R Maryman, Cnstbl

List of Ofcrs of the U S frig **Brandywine**: Bocca Tigris, Canton, River, Sep 21, 1844.
Cmdor-Foxall A Parker
Lts-Timothy A Hunt, J B Marchand, Wm T Muse, A L Case, R B Pegram, C Ap R Jones, W E Boudinot

Master-R H Wyman
Purser-D McF Thornton
Fleet Surgeon-Geo Blacknall
Assist Surgeons-A F Lawyer, R W Jeffrey
Lt of Marines-Archibald H Gillespie

Chaplain-Geo Jones
Sec-A R Bogardus
Cmdor's Clerk-Le Roy Parker
Purser's Clerk-Pollard Webb

Midshipmen-
Augustus McLaughlin
D C Hugunin
Wm H De Koven
Wm L Powell
Jas H Somerville
*Johh Laurens
John P Jones

Wm H Weaver
Jas Heron
Allan McLane
Chas M Mitchel
Wm H Murdaugh
Thos Young

Warrant Ofcrs-Thos G Bell, Boatswain; J W Pennington, Gunner; Wm Lee, Carpenter; Geo Parker, Sailmaker; Chas B Oliver, Master's Mate; John S Davis, Acting Master's Mate-all well. [*Copied as written.]

For sale or rent: large 3 story brick house, near **Greenleaf's Point**; at present occupied by Mason Piggott. Apply to Francis A Dickens

By virtue of a writ of fieri facias issued by Thos C Donn, Justice of the Peace in & for Wash Co, D C, at the suit of Enoch Ridgway, against the goods, chattels, lands, tenements, rights & credits of John Hollohon & Jas Hollohon: the equity of the above in & to lot G in sq 731, with a 2 story brick house thereon, situated on Capitol st, Wash City, D C: sale on Feb 25, 1845. –H R Maryman, Constable

By virtue of a writ of fieri facias issued by John D Clark, Justice of the Peace in & for Wash Co, D C, at the suit of Richd G Briscoe & Jos S Clarke, trading under the firm of Briscoe & Clarke, against the goods, chattels, lands, tenements, rights & credits of Wm B Dyer, in & to a lot of flushing, a lot of tweed, a looking-glass, 4 pairs of pantaloons, 1 vest, 2 pieces of cassimere, 2 pieces of cassinets, 9 vest patterns, 3 pieces of serge, 1 second-hand coat, 1 piece of plaid, 1 piece of canvas, 2 summer coats, a lot of buttons, & a wine case: sale in front of the Centre Market-house, Wash City, on Jan 30, 1845. –H R Maryman, Cnstbl

Senate: 1-Cmte of Claims: bill for the relief of J Throckmorton. Also, an unfavorable report on the ptn of T B Winston. 2-Cmte on Revolutionary Claims: unfavorable report on the claim of the widow of the late Col Heman Allen.

By virtue of a writ of fieri facias issued by Thos C Donn, Justice of the Peace in & for Wash Co, D C, at the suit of Jos S Clarke & Wm C Orme, late trading under the firm of Clarke & Orme, against the goods, chattels, lands, tenements, rights & credits of John Hollohon: in & to lot G in square 731, with a 2 story brick house thereon, on Capitol Hill, Wash City, D C: sale on Feb 25, 1845. –H R Maryman, Cnstbl

Mrd: on Jan 9, by Rev Wm Pinkney, Mr Warren Waugh to Miss Susan Brown, both of PG Co, Md.

Mrd: on Jan 19, at St Vincent's Church, Balt, by Rev Mr Gildea, Mr John McNerhany, of Wash, to Miss Rachel Maguire, of the former place.

Mrd: on Jan 21, by Rev Louis F Wilson, Wm T Snodgrass, of Berkeley Co, Va, to Miss Arabella E Tabb, of the same county.

Died: on Wed last, in Gtwn, Mrs Mary Baily, after a protracted illness, in her 77th year. Her funeral, from her late residence on High st, today, at 3 o'clock.

Died: on Jan 1, at Jacksonville, East Florida, of consumption, Lt S H Campbell, U S Engineers, aged 29 years.

Died: on Jan 18, in Wash City, Mr John Walker, formerly of Bermuda.

SAT JAN 25, 1845
Stolen, from the door of Sally Williams, a free colored woman, living on Capitol Hill, a buffalo Cow. Liberal reward on leaving her at Mrs Whitwell's, Duff Green's Row, Capitol Hill.

Property Agency: residence on 14th st, between F & G sts. As a citizen of Wash, I need no references. -Balaam Birch

Orphan's Court of Wash Co, D C. Letters testamentary on the personal estate of Geo Bell, late of said county, dec'd. –Basil Simms, Francis *Dutcher, adms [Feb 27th newspaper: Francis *Datcher, adms]

Died: on Jan 23, Rev Wm Hawley, Rector of St John's Church, in Wash City. His funeral will take place on Sun next at St John's Church, at 3½ p m. [Jan 27th newspaper: Obit-died: Rev Wm Hawley: for near 30 years maintained an unblemished reputation as a servant & minister of God; for many years manager of the American Colonization Society. Those deprived of his presence in their home, now sad & desolate, have out deepest sympathy. He shall rise again.]

The Rev Geo Fenwick, of Gtwn College, will preach in St Patrick's Church tomorrow, at 11 o'clock. A collection will be made for the poor.

Died: on Jan 21, of apoplexy, at Chambersburg, Pa, Danl Spangler, Cashier of the Bank of Chambersburg, aged about 50 years, leaving a disconsolate wife & 2 children. He was a most worthy member of society & an excellent bank ofcr, & his death is greatly regretted.

Died: on Jan 4, at **Fort Atkinson**, Mrs Sarah Louisa Dilworth, aged 17 years, w/o Lt Rankin Dilworth, of the 1st Infty.

Hse/o Reps: 1-Cmte on Military Affairs: joint resolution for the relief of John Stockton: committed to the Cmte of the Whole.

MON JAN 27, 1845
Hse/o Reps: 1-Ptn of Michl Johnson, of Glen's Falls, Warren Co, N Y, praying for relief. 2-Ptn of John Hollister & others, asking an appropriation for the payment of certain claims against the Ottowa Indians. 3-Ptn of Wm Wright: referred to the Judiciary Cmte. 4-Ptn of S Nicholson, for arrears of pay due: referred to the Cmte of Revolutionary Claims. 5-Ptn of Amasa Dunbar, for a pension: referred to the Cmte of Revolutionary Pensions. 6-Ptn of Juliana Birchmore, for a pension: referred to the Cmte on Invalid Pensions. 7-Ptn of Perry Burdeck, for a pension: referred to the Cmte on Revolutionary Pensions. 8-Ptn of the heirs of Marshal De Rochambeau, for compensation for father's services: referred to the Cmte on Revolutionary Claims. 9-Ptn of the heirs of Count De Grasse, praying for relief: referred to the Cmte on Revolutionary Claims. 10-Ptn of Susan Rogers, for a pension: referred to the Cmte on Revolutionary Pensions. 11-Ptn of Jas H Schnell, plant to light Capitol: referred to the Cmte on Public Bldgs. 12-Ptn of Huldah Saxton, for a pension: referred to the Cmte on Revolutionary Pensions. 13-Ptn of Mrs Anne Royall, for a pension: referred to the Cmte on Revolutionary Pensions. 14-Ptn of Theophilus Somerby, for a pension: referred to the Cmte on Invalid Pensions. 15-Ptn of Thos H Brown, for bounty land: referred to the Cmte on Public Lands. 16-Ptn of Susan Aldrich, for a pension: referred to the Cmte on Revolutionary Pensions. 17-Ptn of Kesiah Hobart, wid/o Danl Hobart, for a pension: referred to the Cmte on Revolutionary Pensions. 18-Ptn of Lucien Fainam, & others, of Ill, for the relief of W Jones. 19-Ptn of S P Buel, & others, of N Y, to procure release of persons at Van Diemans Land: referred to the Cmte on Foreign Affairs.

Accident on Troy road on Jan 20: Mr McKelsey, residing in Bethlehem, with his dght, the wife of T G Oliver, of Albany, were in a collision with another sleigh, & the shafts of the cutter pierced the temple of Mrs Oliver & killed here instantly. Mr & Mrs Kelsey were dangerously hurt. Mrs Oliver was 25 years of age, & the mother of several children. The jury returned a verdict against Robt Black & ___ Mackay, the two who collided with the McKelsey sleigh, as their furious driving caused the lady's death.

Another veteran Jerseyman has taken his final leave: Mr Thos Cobb, who died at Jersey City on Jan 17, was aged 85 years. He was born at Parsippany, Morris Co, Jan 16, 1760, & at age 16 volunteered his services in defence of his country. He was in the battles of Monmouth, Germantown, Yorktown, White Plains, & Springfield. He was one of the detachment sent against the Indians at Wyoming, & was with Washington at Valley Forge. He was also near the great commander at West point when Andre was captured, & attended his execution. Two years before the close of the war he was promoted to a captaincy on account of his faithful services. –Newark Daily Adv

The Albany Atlas contains an account of the defalcation of A H Lovett, the teller of the Commercial Bank of Albany, to the amount of $34,524.02. He confessed the defalcation; was arrested & is in custody. His sureties in the sum of $10,000 are his brother, J E Lovett & Joel R Wing, of Albany.

Bangor [Maine] Gaz: on Thu a fire broke out in the dwlg house occupied by Chester Wells, near Hampden, & a boy about 9 years old & a girl 15 years old, were, with the bldg, completely consumed-the remainder of the family barely escaping with their lives.

On Jan 10, Miss Clara Webster, a celebrated English dancer, of Drury Lane Theatre, aged 21, fell victim to fire, which caught her light dancing garments while performing in the ballet of the Revolt of the Haren, & caused her death within 3 days afterwards. [Foreign news.]

Mrd: on Jan 16, by Rev Mr Tarring, Levin H Manders to Miss Mary Ann Akars, all of Wash City.

Died: on Fri, in Wash City, after a long & painful illness, Frances Caroline Walker, 2nd d/o the late Saml P Walker, a young lady endeared to a large circle of relatives & friends. Her funeral will be from the residence of her mother, this day, at 1 o'clock.

Died: on Thu last, at Richmond, Va, Col Wm Campbell, Senator in the State Legislature from the district composed of Bedford & Franklin Counties.

Household & Kitchen furniture at auction: at the residence of Mr Wm W Acken, on I st, near 9th st: on Jan 29th. –A Green, Auct

Orphan's Court of Wash Co, D C. Ordered, on application, that letters of adm on the personal estate of Jane Bell, of said county, dec'd, be granted to Ulysses Ward. –Ed N Roach, Reg/o wills

City Ordnance-Wash: 1-Act for the relief of Wm M Maddox: fine imposed on him for a violation of the law in relation to gravel foot walks, is remitted.

Obituary: on Dec 28, at Liverpool, aged 83, W Fawcett, the celebrated engineer. We have to record the death of Mr S Heine, the celebrated banker, of Hamburg, aged 77. On Dec 21, at Greenwich Hospital, aged 56, Capt Thos Huskisson, brother to the late Right Hon W Huskisson. Lady Ann Culling Smith, sister of the Duke of Wellington, expired at Hampton Court Place on Dec 16. The celebrated hero of our India armies, Gen Sir Wm Nott, G C B, expired at Carmarthen on Jan 1. He was in his 65th year. Mr Corbould, the artist, who was about to be united to Lady Chantrey, was riding, on Dec 26, in the neighborhood of Silver Hill, near Robertsbridge, when he was struck with apoplexy & immediately expired.

Elegant private mansion in New Haven, Conn, for sale: Residence of the late Saml St John, on the corner of Elm & Church sts: house was erected a few years since, of the best materials, without regard to costs. The furniture will be sold with the property if desired. –Isaac H Townsend, S D Pardee, Excs & Trustees

TUE JAN 28, 1845
Geo W Humphreys, Surgeon Dentist, has removed near 10th st, on Pa ave, over Mrs Bihler's, & next door to Parker's fancy store, where he may be found at all hours. He had many years of practice in the South.

Mr L W Treat, formerly from Hartford, Conn, about 25 years old, an esteemed master mason, was accidentally shot on Jan 11 near Milwaukee, by a friend with whom he was hunting, & died the next day.

Senate: 1-Cmte on Revolutionary Claims: unfavorable report on the ptn of Frances Edwards. Unfavorable report on the ptn of Sally Bass. Unfavorable report on the ptn of the heirs of the late Nathl Ashley. 2-Cmte on Pensions: reported without amendment, the bill for the relief of David Cursier. Also, an unfavorable report on the ptn of Jas Arnold.

WED JAN 29, 1845
Senate: 1-Memoril from Asa Whitney, praying a grant of lands to aid him in the construction of a railroad from Lake Michigan to the Pacific Ocean. 2-Ptn of the Rev John Hough & Saml L Hough, for a pension. 3-Ptn of John Cocke, late Cherokee Com'r, praying to be released from a judgment obtained against him by the U S. 4-Cmte on Private Land Claims: reported a bill for the re-location of certain lands granted to Gen Lafayette.

Mr Jacob Myers, residing near the Shannondale Springs, Va, came to an untimely end last week by the running away of his team, which he was driving. He had been to Harper's Ferry & was returning, & the horses became frightened, at Beeler's Hill, & he was thrown from his saddle & dragged some distance. When found he was sensible, but expired a soon afterwards, leaving a wife & children to mourn their loss.

Hse/o Reps: 1-Cmte of Claims: reported a bill for the relief of Chas R Allen; & a bill for the relief of Jacob L Vance: both committed to the Cmte of the Whole. Same cmte: unfavorable reports on the cases of Chas Townsend, Andrew Waggoner, & Derrin Farrer: laid on the table. 2-Cmte of Claims: to be discharged from the case of F W Heinsman, adm of Capt John Jackson, dec'd: referred to the 4th Auditor of the Treasury. 3-Cmte on Commerce: recommended the passage of the bill from the Senate for the relief of Wm Russell. 4-Committed to the Cmte of the Whole House: relief of Wm Ellery & others; relief of D Grant & others; relief of Barnabas Baker, jr & others; relief of the owner & crew of the schnr **Two Brothers**; relief of the owner & crew of the schnr **Florilla**. 5-Cmte on Commerce: bill for the relief of Jos Holmes & others, owners & crew of the schnr **Industry**, reported the same with amendments. 6-Cmte on Military Affairs: bill to pay Capt John B Crozier's company of mounted volunteers of Tennessee militia: committed. 7-Cmte on Naval Affairs: adverse report on the memorial of Cmder J D McKnight: laid on the table. Same cmte: bill for the relief of Peter Von Schmidt: committed. Same cmte: bill to authorize an allowance to Purser D M F Thornton in the settlement of his accounts: committed. 8-Cmte on Invalid Pensions: bill for the relief of Capt Asahel Brainard, reported the same without amendment, & asked for immediate action on it. Mr Brinkerhoff made a feeling & eloquent appeal in behalf of the the old soldier, after which the bill was passed by acclamation, & now needs the approbation of the Pres to become law. 9-Cmte on Invalid Pensions: bill granting a pension to Geo Whitten: committed. Same cmte: bill for the relief of Jos Craig Miles: committed. Same cmte: bill for the relief of John A Wright; bill for the relief of Danl H Warren: committed. Also, an adverse report on the case of John Martin: laid on the table. Same cmte: bill for the relief of Thos Gronough: referred to the Cmte of the Whole. Same cmte, bill for the relief of Francis Summeraner: committed. 10-Cmte of the District of Columbia: bill for the relief of Jas Dixon: committed. 11-Cmte on Public Lands: bill for the relief of Abner E Van Ness: committed. 12-Cmte on Public Bldgs & Grounds: adverse report on the ptns of Thos C Wells & Wm Leach. 13-Cmte on the Judiciary: bill for the relief of Jos Ramsey: committed. 14-Cmte on Revolutionary Claims: papers to be delivered there, connected with the application of Robt Wilmot, an ofcr of the Revolution, for commutation pay. 15-Cmte on Private Land Claims: bill for the relief of the heirs of John Hart, dec'd: ordred to be engrossed. 16-Cmte on Indian Affairs: bill for the relief of Geo B Russell: committed. 17-Cmte on Invalid Pensions: to inquire into placing Amos Doughty, of Gardiner, Maine, on the pension list. 18-Cmte on Invalid Pensions: to inquire into increasing the pension allowed to Thos P Franklin, for disabilities occasioned in the discharge of his duty during the siege of Yorktown. 19-Resolved: that Fred'k Christmon, Francis Davidson, & Andrew McLaughlin have leave to withdraw their papers, which have been referred to the Cmte on Revolutionary Pensions.

Mrd: in Williamsburg, Va, at the residence of Prof Tucker, of Wm & Mary College, Edmund Berkeley, of Loudoun Co, Va, to Miss Mary Lawson Williams, y/d/o the Hon Thos L Williams, of Knoxville, Tenn. [No date-current item.]

Died: on Jan 12, in Leetown, Va, Mr Adam Wever, in his 93rd year, & for more than half a century a citizen of Jefferson Co, Va.

Died: in Mecklenburg Co, N C, in his 92nd year, Maj Thos Alexander: a soldier of the Revolution; was by blood allied to the Polks & Alexanders, two most distinguished families of that period. –Raleigh Reg [No date-current item.]

Died: on Sep 8, 1844, in China, Mr Thos Westbrook Waldron, aged 30, formerly of Portsmouth, N H. Cmdor Parker, of the frig **Brandywine**, writes to a friend in Boston: Mr Waldron was attacked with cholera on Sat & died on Sun. A monument will be erected over his grave by the Ofcrs of the Navy on this station & the American residents here.

On Jan 14, the 12 year old s/o Dr Lee Twyman, of St Chas, Missouri, accidentally hung himself, while engaged at playing.

A Liverpool paper says that Wm Towns, a soldier in the 21st Fusileers, now in India, confessed that he murdered a gamekeeper in Essex, about 9 years ago, & that a man named Chalker, who was executed for the murder, was innocent.

Orphan's Court of Wash Co, D C. Letters of adm on the personal estate of John Boda, late of the U S Navy, dec'd. –S A Paigh, adm

Orphan's Court of Wash Co, D C. Letters of adm on the personal estate of Patrick A Orme, late of said county, dec'd. –Fras Dodge, jr, adm

Orphan's Court of Wash Co, D C. Letters of adm on the personal estate of Basil Loveless, late of said county, dec'd. –Charlotte Loveless, Benoni Loveless, adms

THU JAN 30, 1845
Senate: 1-Ptn from Alex'r Tait, one of the mechanics employed in the bldg of the Patent Ofc, for arrearages of pay. 2-Ptn from C Evans, praying that his invention to prevent the explosion of the steam-boilers may be applied to all steam vessels in the service of the U S. 3-Bills referred: joint resolution for the benefit of Francis Slocum. Bill for the relief of the heirs of J Hart, dec'd. 4-Bills introduced: bill for the relief of Wm P Allen & Martin Thomas. 5-Cmte on Judiciary: reported a bill to authorize the settlement of the accounts of the late Jos Nourse. Same cmte: adverse report on the ptn from Wm & Mary College. 6-Cmte on Military Affairs: adverse report on the ptn of Alden Partridge. 7-Cmte on Finance: were discharged from the further consideration of the papers of Harvey & Hogg: ordered to lie on the table.

Hse/o Reps: 1-Resolved, That the Sec of War be directed to communicate to this House a copy of the report, journal, & map of Capt J Allen, of the 1st Regt of Dragoons, of his expedition during the past summer to the heads of the rivers Des Moines & Blue Earth, in the Northwest. 2-Bill for the relief of Jeremiah Moors: referred to the Cmte of Claims. 3-Bill for the relief of F M Irish: referred to the Cmte of Claims.

The Phil Grand Jury have recorded their opinion that the conduct of ex-Govn'r Porter, in throwing open the prison doors, almost without restriction, for the egress of murderers, incendiaries, robbers, & rogues of all descriptions, was a great deal too bad. Judge Jones, of the Quarter Sessions, said his conduct had been of the most outrageous character-all efforts of the Court to uphold the laws & preserve the public morals & protect society had been rendered void by this trifling with & glaring mockery of justice.

Female Teacher Wanted: address the subscriber, *Flint Hill*, Rappahannock Co, Va. –Jas Jett

Rockville Academy: classical dept has been for more than 12 months under the c/o Mr Oris C Wright, A B, as Principal. Wm McClenahan has charge of the English Dept. –John Mines-Pres; Richd I Brown-Sec

Trustee's sale: by deed of trust from Edw W Beatty dated Aug 26, 1840, recorded in Liber W B 83 Folios 27 to 33 of the Land Records of Wash Co, D C: sale on Feb 20 next at the auction room of Edw S Wright, of Gtwn, of said county, all that valuable Mill Property, with appurtenances now or lately in the occupancy of said Beatty, on the C & O Canal: the property includes 1 ac 3 roods & 34 perches of land, subject to a right of way over the same in favor of the owner of an adjoining mill-site. Improvements are a 3 story stone Mill, with modern machinery in good repair. –Clement Cox, Trustee
-Edw S Wright, Auct

FRI JAN 31, 1845
Hse/o Reps: 1-Ptn of Steven York, of Clarence, N Y, for compensation for property lost during the late war with Great Britain. 2-Ptn of Saml D Sizer, of Springfield, Mass, asking compensation for an invention for packing & boxing muskets & for services in relation thereto. 3-Ptn of Drummond Farnsworth & 4 others in behalf of the Liberty party of the State of Maine, in State convention, that Rev Joshua Leavitt may have a seat assigned him as a reporter in the House. 4-Ptn of Jacob Ames & others, of Chesterville, Maine, against annexation of Texas. 5-Ptn of John Chaney, for arrears of pension. 6- Memorial of Thos Jarrett, praying indemnity for loss of a vessel in the last war whilst in the use of the Gov't. 7-Ptn of Moses Stewart & 87 others, ofcrs & students of the Theological Seminary & of Phillips Academy at Andover, Mass, respectfully & earnestly requesting that a law may be passed which shall materially diminish the present rates of postage. 8-Ptn of Cadwalader Evans in reference to his invention of a safety valve. 9-Ptn

of Richd Buchanan, of Spottsylvania Co, Va, to be restored to the pension roll. 10-Ptn of Jas Howland & others, for placing buoys in Buzzard's Bay.

Senate: 1-Bill for the relief of Seth M Leavenworth. 2-Cmte on Naval Affairs: adverse report on the claim of Hugh Wallace Wormley. 3-Engrossed: bill for the relief of the legal reps of Jas Bell, dec'd.

Servant Wanted: who understands opening oysters & waiting on table. Liberal wages will be given, on application to Thos Baker, Franklin Inn, 8th & D sts, Wash.

Died: on Jan 10, at Oxford, N H, Mrs Eliz M Bissell, aged 37 years, w/o E M Bissell.

Obit-died: on Sat last, at Germantown, Pa, Alex'r Provest, aged 71. He was known not only in his native place & the county of Phil, but throughout the State, as connected with our internal improvements from their birth. His death, as his life had been, was that of the Christian. –Germantown paper

Annual meeting of the stockholders of the Steamboat Phoenix will be held on Feb 3 at 11 a m. –Stephen Shinn, Treas: Alexandria, Jan 31, 1845

Coal Wharf, foot of 17th st, near Gen Van Ness' residence: superior coal for sale. –Calhoun M Deringer

Wash Corp: 1-Bill for the relief of P Hilton & Wm H Clamfit was passed. 2-Cmte of Claims: asked to be discharged from further consideration of the ptn of Philip Ennis: ordered to lie on the table. 3-Cmte of Claims: bill for the relief of Geo Savage: recommended its rejection: laid on the table. 4-Bill for the relief of Patrick Moran: passed.

On Wed a fire was discovered in a small frame bldg belonging to Mr Henry Walker, north of Pa ave. It was tenanted by a colored man, was, with the poor occupant's furniture, destroyed by the flames. The fire is considered to have been the act of an incendiary.

SAT FEB 1, 1845
Hse/o Reps: 1-Cmte on the Militia: referred the memorial of Saml Colt, on the subject of his water-proof cartridges, reported a joint resolution directing that $50,000 of the annual appropriation for arming the equipping the U S militia be expended in the same.

Died: on the 22nd ult, at Zanesville, Ohio, in her 38th year, Mrs Mary Bernard Smallwood, w/o Rev W A Smallwood, of that place, & d/o the late Col Brearley, of N J.

Rev Walter Colton, Chaplain in the U S Navy, will preach tomorrow at 3½ p m, in the F st Presbyterian Church, [Dr Laurie] on the Characteristics, Condition & Claims of Seamen.

Mr G W Wilson, editor of the Upper Marlboro Gaz, chaged by a post ofc agent with being concerned in a recent robbery there, has been found not only innocent, but entirely clear of the least ground of accusation or suspicion. –Balt Clipper

Mr J Bayly, of Franklin, N H, a man of great respectability, aged about 50, committed suicide on Sat week, by shooting himself through the head in his own house. Pecuniary embarrassment is believed to have been the cause of the act.

Orphan's Court of Wash Co, D C. Letters of adm on the personal estate of Fred'k Reitz, late of said county, dec'd. –John Reitz, adm

MON FEB 3, 1845

City Ordnance: 1-Act for the relief of John P Hilton & W H Clampit: fine imposed upon them for an alleged obstruction of the street be & the same is hereby remitted; provided they pay the costs of prosecution. Approved, Feb 1, 1845.

Wm Miller, convicted of the murder of Geo West, at Sandlake, May 17, 1844, was executed at Troy N Y on Tue. The execution was private, a gallows being erected in the hall of the jail.

E H Roper offers for sale his house on K st, between 11th & 12th sts, near the Franklin Row: contains 9 rooms, & has a pump of excellent water in the yard. Apply to E H Roper.

For rent: house on Massachusetts ave, containing 8 rooms & a cellar. I have, as usual, household furniture, which will be sold for cash. –T M Milburn, Pa ave, between 9th & 10th sts.

Hse/o Reps: 1-Cmte on Military Affairs: adverse report on the ptn of Capt Alden Partridge, for a loan of muskets for the use of his military school at Norwich, Vt. 2-Memorial of Chas Reeder, Engineer, asking appropriation for the purpose of testing the utility of his invention for preventing explosions of steam boilers. 3-Ptn of D M Dobson & 108 other citizens of Indiana, asking a mail route from Spencer, by Mill Grove, to Putnamville. 4-Ptn of Ephraim Goulding & others, of Middlebury, Mass, in favor of a reduction of postage.

Mrd: on Jan 14, by Rev Van Horseigh, Jas Smithson & Pauline Rosemond Lehman, all of Wash City.

Mrd: on Jan 30, by Rev Mr Owen, Mr David Jas Efflin to Miss Susan Ann Birch, all of Wash City.

Mrd: on Jan 2, by Rev Mr Weeks, of Gtwn, Mr John Webb to Mrs Mary E Tilley, both of Wash City.

Died: on Feb 2, Mr John Emmerich, a native of Hesse Darmstadt, Germany, in his 57th year. Hid funeral is on Tue next, at 2 o'clock.

Died: in Anne Arundel Co, Md, after a painful illness, Mrs Henrietta Hammond, widow of the late Rev Henry Hammond, in her 68th year. [No date-current item.]

Died: on Feb 1, in Wash City, Eliz, d/o Rev Geo W & Eliz Janeson, aged 7 months & 6 days. Her funeral will be from the residence of her father on 9th & H sts, this morning, at 10 a m.

Wm J Neal, living in Newark, attempted to take the life of his wife on Mon, by discharging at her a gun loaded with buck-shot. He was an intemperate man, & had threatened her life & that of her son before. The woman fell at the flash, & was but slightly grazed by the shot. The brute was secured in jail

House for rent: 2 story brick house on D & 6th sts. Apply to Mrs Hunt, La ave & 6th st.

For rent-new 3 story brick house on H, between 7th & 8th sts, being the east house of the block recently created by Isaac Clarke. Inquire of H King.

Headquarters, Nat'l Blues: meeting this evening at 7 p m. By order, D Westerfield, jr, Sec.

Sale by order of the Orphan's Court of Wash Co, D C: on Feb 4, at the store of P A Orme, dec'd, on 7th st. –Francis Dodge, jr, adm -A Green, auct

TUE FEB 4, 1845
Senate: 1-Ptn of Eliakim Morse, of Mass, praying for indemnity for French spoliations prior to 1800. 2-Ptn of John Wood & others for certain mail routes. 3-Ptn of Ebenezer Ballard, asking a pension. 4-Ptn of Jas Irwin, for compensation for losses sustained by certain contracts with the Gov't for the removal of the Indians west of the Mississippii. 5-Ptn of John Baldwin, praying for the just allowance of his awards under the Mexican treaty. 6-Cmte on the Judiciary: beill for the relief of John P Skinner & the legal reps of Isaac Green. 7-Cmte on Pensions: bill for the relief of John Woodley.

Horse just arrived from Greenbriar Co, Va, for sale. Can be seen at the Franklin Stable, 8th & D sts. -Jacob Rowles

Miss Margaret G Meade has enlarged the school rooms & secured the aid of 2 teachers, who reside with her, & she is now enabled to increase her Day School, & that she has yet room for more boarders. Miss Mead's residence is on G st, between 21st & 22nd sts, north side, Wash.

The undersigned, Com'rs, appointed by Worcester County Court to value & divide the estate of Eliz Coltman, dec'd ,late of said County, do give notice that we shall meet at the house of Wm S B Coltman on the premises on Apr 9, at 10 o'clock, to proceed in the business for which we are appointed.

Cord Hazzard	Peter Dickerson	Saml D Harpff
John E Hayward	Moses C Smith	

Teacher wanted: in the fourth Election District. Genteel board can be obtained convenient to the school. -Henry H Hawkins, Bryantown, Chas Co, Md.

Died: on Jan 29, at **Keswick**, the residence of her father, Jane W Page, d/o Dr M Page, of Albemarle Co, Va, aged 16 years & 3 months. Farewell, lovely saint! May we, in your own precious words, meet in Heaven.

Died: on Feb 1, in Wash City, Eliz, aged 7 months, d/o Rev G W & Eliz Samson.

WED FEB 5, 1845
Ofcrs attached to the U S steamer **Union**:

Wm McBlair, Lt Commanding	J V Guthrie, Acting Master
Roger Perry, Lt	Chas Deas, Passed Midshipman
Jones W Plummer, Surgeon	J D Marshall, Capt's Clerk
Chas Murray, Purser	Levi Griffin, 1st Assist Engineer
Wm P Williamson, Chief Engineer	A S Palmer, 2nd do
A D Harrell, Acting Master	M M Thompson, 3rd do

Gov Edwards, of Missouri, pardoned the abolitionist Work, who was sentenced to the penitentiary about 3 years since for assisting in the escape of negroes from Marion Co. His punishment was fixed at 9 years.

Hse/o Reps: 1-Cmte of Claims: asking to be discharged from the further consideration of the ptns of Allen Matthews & of Geo Hunter: agreed to. 2-Cmte of Claims: asking to be discharged from the further consideration of the ptn of Geo Hereus: agreed to. 3-Cmte of the Police: asked to be discharged from further consideration of the ptn of Wm McCarty: agreed to. 4-Cmte on Foreign Affairs, reported a bill for the relief of Com Thos Ap Catesby Jones: committed to the Cmte of the Whole House. 5-Cmte on Invalid Pensions: bill for the relief of Jos Watson: committed to the Cmte of the Whole House. 6-Ptn of Geo W Johnson & 10 others, against the annexation of Texas. 7-Ptn of John Boden

Fitch, praying for a grant of land or money to himself & the other heirs of John Fitch, in consideration of the great benefit conferred by the said John Fitch as the first inventor of steam navigation in this country. 8-Ptn of Jos Morrison, of Kalamazoo Co, Mich, against the annexation of Texas. 9-Bill for the relief of Jos Simmons: referred to the Cmte on Invalid Pensions. 10-Bill for the relief of the legal reps of Jas Bell, dec'd: referred to the Cmte on Revolutionary Claims. 11-Ptn of J Homan, of Wash City, praying compensation for iron furnished in 1819 for building a jail. 12-Cmte on the Post Ofc: bill for the relief of Fuller & Saltmarsh. Also, made an adverse report on the claim of W P Allen & Martin Thomas.

Mrd: on Feb 2, by Rev H Myers, Mr Theodore Gaubert to Miss Mary A Hunt, both of this place.

Mrd: on Feb 4, at St Peter's Church, in Wash City, by Rev Mr Van Horseigh, Mr Francis Barry, jr, to Miss Mary Jane Lowe, all of Washington.

Destructive fire at the candle manufactory of Messrs Hancock & Mann, at Canton, Balt, on Mon. The factory employed altogether about 200 hands, who were dependant upon labor afforded them there for subsistence for themselves & families.

Wash Corp: 1-Ptn of E Simons & others: referred to the Cmte on the Canal. 2-Cmte of Claims: referred the ptn of the excs of Geo Adams, dec'd, reported a resolution instructing the Mayor & Register to settle on principles of equity, the claims of Mr Adams: read & amended. 3-Bill for the relief of Eliz Purrell: referred to the Cmte of Claims. 4-Bill for the relief of Robt Cohen: referred to the Cmte of Claims. 5-Bill for the relief of Alvin Cole: passed. 6-Cmte on Claims: asking to be asked to be discharged from further consideration of the ptn of Wm Dowling: agreed to. 7-Cmte on Claims: asked to be discharged from further consideration of the ptn of Wm Greer: Board refused to discharge the Cmte.

THU FEB 6, 1845
Notice: by virtue of a distrain, we shall sell on the premises, on Feb 6, sundry mscl property, seized & taken to satisfy rent due & in arrears to Robt Keyworth by Mary Lipscomb, widow of Conway Lipscomb, dec'd. -J A Ratcliff, T Donaldson, Constables. [Articles included window curtain, tub & basket, hone, scissors & strops, maps, spittoons, trunk, chairs, brushes & combs, axe, shovel, bucket, towel roller, & oil can.]

Was committed to the jail of Balt City & County, by Wm A Schaeffer, a justice of the peace, on Dec 15, 1844, Benj Roberts, charged with being a runaway slave, but says he was free born, & raised near Little Hutford, Cummins Co, N C. Said negro is about 23 years old. The owner, if any, of the above, is to come forward, prove property, pay charges, & take him away, otherwise he will be discharged according to the law.
–Danl Steever, Warden.

Howard Hotel, N Y, Thomas & Roe, Proprietors: at the corner of Broadway & Maiden Lane, in N Y C, is now open. –M J Thomas, Stephen R Roe, late cmder of the Hudson river steamboat **Empire**.

Was committed to the jail of Balt City & County, by Jacob Beckley, a justice of the peace, on Jan 18, 1845, Alex'r Dorsey, charged with being a runaway slave, but says he was free born, & raised near Leonardstown, St Mary's Co, Md. Said negro is about 40 years old. The owner, if any, of the above, is to come forward, prove property, pay charges, & take him away, otherwise he will be discharged according to the law. –Danl Steever, Warden.

Was committed to the jail of Balt City & County, by Wm A Schaeffer, a justice of the peace, on Dec 15, 1844, Geo Colwell, charged with being a runaway slave, but says he belongs to Archibald Flemming, of Wash City, D C. Said negro is about 23 years old. The owner, if any, of the above, is to come forward, prove property, pay charges, & take him away, otherwise he will be discharged according to the law. –Danl Steever, Warden.

Mrd: on Tue, by Rev Mr Pyne, Lewis Warrington, jr, U S Navy, to Miss Mary C, d/o Wm B Scott, all of Wash City.

Mrd: on Feb 4, in Wash City, by Rev Dr Laurie, Mr Vincent W Moore to Miss Mary G Moore, both of Jefferson Co, Va.

Mrd: on Feb 3, at St John's Church, in Gtwn, D C, by Rev Mr Shiraz, Alex'r G Abell, U S Consul to the Sandwich Islands, to Miss Sarah J, d/o the late R C Austin, of Gtwn.

Died: on Jan 27, in Anne Arundel Co, Md, Mr Edmund Clagett. The dec'd was one of those happy few, who, while living, had no enemy.

Died: on Feb 4, in Alexandria, suddenly, Mrs Julia Martin, widow of Jas Martin, late of Wash Navy Yard, in her 82nd year. Her funeral will take place this day at half-past 1 o'clock from the house of Mr Aaron W Miller, on L st south, between 4th & 5th sts. Her friends are invited to attend.

FRI FEB 7, 1845
Senate: 1-Cmte of Claims: bill for the relief of Jos Ramsay. 2-Ptn of Jas Giddings & others, of Chautauque Co, N Y, praying for the reduction of the postage rates & the abolition of the franking privileges. 3-Ptn of Mr Wm Pumphrey, of Louisiana, for the confirmation of a tract of land. 4-Papers of Jacob Baker, of New Orleans, in relation to certain claims against the U S Gov't. 5-Ptn of Sarah Grosvenor & others, of Southbridge, Mass, against the annexation of Texas. 6-Ptn of Chas Coppel, of Marksville, La, praying for a confirmation to a tract of land. 7-Ptn of Mathias Gish & 228 other citizens of Montgomery Co, Ohio, praying for an appropriation to complete the Cumberland Road.

Appointments last week made by the Govn'r of Maryland, with the advice & consent of the Senate of the State of Md.
Anne Arundel Co: Clerk of the County Court: Jos H Nicholson
Reg of Wills: Benj E Gantt
Fred'k Co: Clerk of the County Court: Wm B Tyler
Reg of Wills: Thos Sappintgon
Talbot Co: Clerk of the County Court: Jas Parrott
Reg of Wills: John H Harris
Caroline Co: Clerk of the County Court: John H Fountain
Reg of Wills: W A Ford
Worcester Co: Clerk of the County Court: Gordon M Handy
Surveyor: Powell Patty
Harford Co:
Clerk of the County Court: H D Gough
Reg of Wills: C W Billingslea
Kent Co: Clerk of the County Court: J N Gordon
Reg of Wills: J F Brown
Queen Anne's Co: Clerk of the County Court: John Tilghman
St Mary's Co: Reg of wills: Geo Coombs
PG Co: Reg of Wills: Jas Harper
For Lottery Com'rs: Jas Harwood, Thos K Carroll
Insolvent Com'r of Balt City & County: Hugh d Evans, Neilson Poe, John Philpot

John Powers, recently pardoned by Pres Tyler from the Ky penitentiary, in which he had been incarcerated for robbing the mail, has been arrested at New Orleans charged with abducting a slave & committing forgery.

Mrd: Jan 30, by Rev Mr Wilmer, Col J W Ware to Miss Edmonia J, d/o Edw J Smith, all of Clarke Co, Va.

Died: on Jan 30, at Charleston, S C, Mr Job Palmer, one of the patriarchs of that city & a worthy of the Revolution, at the extreme old age of 97 years & 5 months. He was born at Falmouth, Mass, on Aug 26, 1747, & ere he had reached maturity, or shortly after, migrated to Charleston, where he continued to reside until the day of his decease. Himself the s/o a clergyman, who ministered in the priest's ofc at Falmouth about 40 years, he was the ancestor of numerous descendants of 3 generations, & has given 2 sons & 2 grandsons to the Christian ministry. A carpenter by trade, his intelligence, skill, & worth place him high in the rank of our most respectable mechanics; & by honest industry, he earned a competency which enabled him to rear & educate a large family. With numerous other patriots in the civil line, he went through the perils, & bore his part in the trials, privations, & sufferings incident to the war of the Revolution. -Courier

Died: yesterday, Roberta Carter, aged 8 months & 12 days. Her funeral will take place from her mother's residence on Mass ave, between 4th & 5th sts, at 12 o'clock tomorrow. Relatives & friends of the mother are respectfully invited to attend.

Died: on Jan 27, at *Cloverfields*, the old family residence, in Albemarle Co, Va, Wm D Merriwether, sen, in his 84th year.

Died: on Feb 4, at Norfolk, Louisa Pleasance, d/o Lt Wm McBlair, U S Navy, aged 7 months.

The w/o Mr Enos Simpkins, of Bridgeton, West Jersey, was choked to death on Fri by getting a piece of ham fast in her throat. She had gone to the closet to cut ham for supper, & put a small piece in her mouth which she had attempted to swallow. Her death was so instantaneous that no person had time to do anything to afford her relief.

N Y Post: Francis McCully, an American by birth, & from his infancy a resident in the town of Paterson, N J, where he has been engaged in the construction of machinery, has recently made an important simplification in the process of spinning cotton. A small model, containing about 132 spindles, is now in operation at the factory of Gen Godwin, in Paterson. Mr McCully, the inventor, has already secured patents in England, France, Belgium, Mexico, & this country.

SAT FEB 8, 1845
Tribute to a dec'd Naval Ofcr: letter from the Sec of the Navy, dated Navy Dept, Feb 1, 1845, in testimony of their respect for the late Wm D Newman, a Cmder of the U S Navy: While his death may justly be regarded as a great loss to the service, our sympathies are yet more strongly excited by the melancholy & painful circumstances under which a life so honorable & useful was terminated. –J Y Mason to Lt C H McBlair, U S Navy, Balt, Md.

Lt E G Tilton, late Acting Cmder of the U S ship **St Louis**, who returned home a few days ago in the ship **Paul Jones**, at N Y, received a letter from the American merchants resident there, tendering him their warmest thanks for the promptness with which, on his own responsibility, proceeded with the **St Louis** to Whampoa, on Jun 17 last, & from thence with sufficient force to Canton, for the protection of the lives & property of all foreigners, at a time when they were in imminent danger. They intend to forward to him, as soon as it could be made ready, a service of plate as a token of their esteem.

Mr Lewis C Levin, indicted upon charges growing out of the riots in Phil some months ago, is now entirely acquitted of the charge of treason.

Lt J E Blake, of the U S Topographical Engineer Corps & party, have completed a survey of a route for a railroad across the peninsula of Florida. They were at St Augustine on the 25th ult.

Capt H L Thistle, U S Timber Agent, has recently seized a large quantity of red cedar & other timber, at the mouth of the Suwannee river, cut upon the public lands by certain individuals.

Mr Lowe, the popular clerk of the boat **Belle of Nashville**, was killed on Fri last, by falling down the after hatchhole of the boat, during her trip from Cincinnati to this place. He was a gentleman of much worth, & has left a wife & several children.
–Louisville Courier

Senate: 1-Ptn of Nancy Calimes, praying Congress to pass an act to enable her to bring back certain slaves from Texas. 2-Cmte on the Post Ofc & Post Roads: a resolution from the Senate, in favor of David Shaw & Solomon T Corson, with an amendment. 3-Cmte on the Judiciary: bill from the Senate for the relief of Asa Andrews, & for the relief of Miles King, without amendment: with an unfavorable report on the bill for the relief of Asa Andrews, recommending that it do not pass. The bills were then committed to the Cmte of the Whole. 4-Cmte on the Judiciary: asking to be discharged from the memorials of Benj Fry, John H Overstreet, & Geo B Didlake, & that they lie on the table: agreed to. 5-Cmte on Revolutionary Claims: bill for the relief of the heirs of Philip R Rice: committed to the Cmte of the Whole House. 6-Cmte on Indian Affairs: bill for the relief of John Hollister: committed to the Cmte of the Whole House. Same cmte: adverse report on the case of Wm J Pine; also, adverse report on the ptn of Fleming Wood. 7-Cmte on Military Affairs: asking to be discharged from the case of Eliz Campbell, & that it be referred to the Cmte of Claims: agreed to. 8-Cmte on Naval Affairs: asking to be discharged from the ptn of Francis Holton, & that it lie on the table: agreed to. Also, an adverse report on the ptn of Jane Baker: laid on the table. 9-Cmte on Naval Affairs: asking that the cmte be discharged from the ptn of Saml Colt: agreed. 10-Cmte on Revolutionary Pension, a bill for the relief of Geo Rouse & a bill for the relief of Lucy Davis: which bills were committed to the Cmte of the Whole. Same for the bill for the relief of Wm Couch. 11-Cmte on the Public Lands: bill for the relief of John G McCloud. 12-The calendar of private bills was called over today, & no objection was made to the bills & joint resolutions of the following titles-Bill for the relief of:
*Elliot Smith & Nathan Farnsworth
*John Adams & John Adams, jr
*Elisha Morrell, adm of Jos Icard, dec'd
*Arthur R Frogge, of Fentress Co, Tenn
*Chas R Allen, of Richmond, Va
Gideon Batchelder & others
*Legal reps of Alex'r Mitchell
*Wm Gove & Asenath Orvis

*Jacob L Vance, of Ohio
*Walker, Kinkle, & Caruthers
*Sellers & Pennock
*Jos & Lindsay Ward
*Isabella Baldrige, wid/o Capt John Baldrige, dec'd
*Jas Curwen, surviving partner of Curwen & Willins

*John H McIntosh	*Benj S Roberts	Mark Simpson
*Jos Ramsey	**Jas S Campbell	*John E Wright
*Geo B Russell	*Susannah Scott	*Danl H Warren
*March Farrington	*Richd Elliott	*Thos Bronough
*Henry N Halsted	*Eliz Fitch	*Francis Summeraner
*John P Converse	*Isaac Allen	*Jos Watson
*John Boyd	*Elijah Blodget	*Harvey & Slagg
*Justin Jacobs	*Philip Schwartztrawber	*Jacob Boston
*Harrison Whitson	*Danl Homans	*Saml Neely
J McFarlane	*Wm Rich	*Bennet M Dell
*Wm Gump	Jas Ritchie	*Ira Baldwin
*John Ficklin	*Lot Davis	*Stanley White
*Jos M Rhea	*Adino Goodenough	*Dunning R McNair
*Edw A Lambert	*Peter Von Schmidt	*Geo Wentling

Bill supplemental to an act for the relief of *John Hollinsworth, of Blount Co, Ala, approved Jun 28, 1838.
*Capt John B Crozier's company of mounted volunteers, Tenn militia.
Resolution authorizing an allowance to Purser D W Thornton, in the settlement of his accounts.
Bill for the benefit of *Jos Craigmiles, of Tennessee
Bill placing the name of *Benj Allen upon the invalid pension roll.
12-Cmte of the Whole: bill for the relief of Jas C Watson, of Georgia: asked to be discharged from its further consideration, & that the bill be brought into the House & laid on the Speaker's table: passed in the affirmative. 13-Ptn of John Washington, of Fayette Co, Pa. [No other information.] [*Feb 10th newspaper: Read the 3rd time & passed, & sent to the Senate for concurrence.] [**This bill provides for the payment of property [on then frontiers] destroyed by Indians in the Revolutionary war.]

Hse/o Reps: 1-Cmte of Ways & Means: asking to be discharged from the memorial of Wm Depew, & that it be laid on the table: agreed to. 2-Cmte of Claims: adverse report on the ptns of John Stein & Thos Thompson: laid on the table. Also, adverse report on the ptn of Jas Paxton; also, an adverse report on the ptn of Saml A Morse: both were laid on the table. 3-Cmte of Claims: bill for the relief of John W Hockett: committed. Aslo, same cmte, an adverse report on the ptn of the heirs of Mary Ker: laid on the table. 4-Cmte of Claims: bill for the relief of John R Williams: was committed to the Cmte of the Whole. 5-Cmte on Commerce: asking to be discharged from the ptn of B B Swasey, & that leave be given him to withdraw his ptn.

The following gentlemen, all Democrats, were on Mon last elected to the ofcs mentioned, by the 2 branches of the N Y legislature.

Nathl S Benton, of Herkimer, Sec of State

Azariah C Flagg, of Albany, Comptroller

Benj Enos, of Madison, Treasurer

John Van Buren, of Albany, Atty Genr'l

Hugh Halsey, of Suffolk, Surveyor Genr'l

Henry Storms, of N Y, Commissary Genr'l

Martin Van Buren & Wm C Bouck, Regents of the University, vice Jos Russell, resigned, & Wm Campbell, dec'd.

Died: on Feb 4, at Alexandria, suddenly, Mrs Julielimus Martin, widow of the late Jas Martin, [for many years master blockmaker of the Wash Navy Yard,] in her 75th year.

Died: on Jan 24, at Phil, Mrs Mary P Tompkins, aged 43 years, w/o Maj Danl D Tompkins, U S Army.

Died: on Feb 2, in Dumfries, Va, Mr Wm Duffey, aged 62 years. He was a native of Ireland, but for many years a resident of Alexandria.

Rev Levi R Reese, of Balt, will preach in the Methodist Protestant Church on 9th & E sts, on Sabbath next at 11 o'clock; & Rev Thos F Stockton, of Phil, will preach there on the same evening at 7 o'clock. Seats free.

N J Appointments: from the Trenton State Gaz:
Oliver S Halsted, Chancellor
Jos F Randolph & Thos P Carpenter, Associate Judges of the Supreme Court
Abraham Browning, Atty Genr'l
Elias P Seely, John C Ten Eyck, Wm C Morris, & Isaac W Scudder, Prosecutors of the Pleas

Letter in the St Louis Republican, dated at Jefferson City on Jan 24, says that Lewis Rogers, s/o the old chief of the Cherokee Nation, was recently waylaid & murdered. That portion of the Cherokees known as the Old Settlers, or the Rogers party, were in council near **Fort Gibson**, Ark, when Lewis Rogers, receiving information of the illness of his family, started immediately home. He had not proceeded far when he was attacked by 6 or 7 men, who fell upon him with bowie knives & killed him. He lived long enough to give the names of the blood-thirsty beings, to some of his friends. For a long time an old feud existed between the Ross & Rogers parties.

MON FEB 10, 1845
Hse/o Reps: 1-Be it enacted by the Senate & Hse/o Reps of the U S A in Congress assembled, that the sum of $18,100, with interest, at the rate of 6%,per annum from May 15, 1838, until paid, be, & the same is hereby appropriated to & for the use & benefit of the heirs & legal reps of Jas C Watson, late of Georgia, dec'd; & that the same be paid to the heirs or legal reps of said Jas C Watson, dec'd, by the Sec of the Treas. 2-Ptn of Saml Fisher, praying that a special law may be passed enabling him to procure a patent for his invention for retarding wagons & carriages.

The undersigned, passengers on board the new ice steamer **Powhatan**, bear testimony to the ability of Capt Rogers & the boat under his command, when the loss of a rudder, by an accident, occurred upon leaving Wash City. [Letter dated Washington, Feb 8, 1844.]

A C Spain, Columbia, S C	T C Denham, Balt
Edw L Fant, Balt, Md	C Brackenbridge, Va
B B Butterfield, Boston, Mass	A C Caldwell, N C
Nelson Head, Rockville, Md	S M Tinsley, Va
Dean Walker, Mass	Robt B Bagby, Va
Wm R Hunter, Darlington, S C	Richd Gardner
A A Denman, N Y	A Faiter
Wm M Baggeld, Va	E V Lightfoot, Va
R W Latham, Balt	

Caution: We, the undersigned, forewarn all persons from buying of John Evans the property & increase left by Thos Jenkins to his dght, Susannah Evans, during her natural life. –Thos Jenkins, adm on the property. Ann Smoot, Chloe Barr, Jas T Boiseau, heirs of the property.

Mrd: on Feb 3, by Rev Mr Coskery, Jas P Fugitt to Caroline Louisa, d/o the Lt John A Cooke, U S Navy, all of Wash City.

Senate: 1-Ptn of Cmdor Jesse D Elliott, praying reimbursement for expenses incurred by him for entertaining foreign Ministers & their suites while commanding the naval forces in the Mediterranean. 2-Cmte on Revolutionary Claims were discharged from the consideration of the case of the heirs of John Hart, dec'd, & referred to the Cmte on Private Land Claims.

By virtue of a writ of fieri facias, issued by T C Donn, a J P of Wash Co, D C, at the suit of W P Shed, use of John Hughes, against the goods & chattels of Wm B Guy, I have seized & taken in execution all the right, title, claim, & interst, at law & in equity, of the said Wm B Guy in & to one bay horse & wagon, & one body; & I hereby give notice, that on Feb 13, on the green opposite the center Market-house, I will offer for sale the said property so seized. –J a Ratcliff, Constable

Danl S Dickinson was on Tue elected Senator of the U S by the Legislature of N Y for 6 years from Mar 4 next. The Whigs voted for John C Clark, & the Natives for Robt Taylor.

Appointments made by the Govn'r of Md, with the advice & consent of the Senate of Md: 1-R W Gill, to be Clerk of the Court of Appeals. 2-A C Magruder, to be Chief Judge of the First Judicial District.

City Ordnances: Wash. Act for the relief of Alvin Cole: that the 2nd fine imposed upon Cole, by judgment of J D Clark, for an alleged violation of the act in relation to running an omnibus without a license, be & the same is hereby remitted; provided the said Cole pay the costs of prosecution.

Criminal Court-Wash. 1-U S vs Mary Ann Hall: no verdict rendered. 2-Susan Goodyear, indicted for receiving 3 silver spoons belonging to the Pres' House, knowing them to be stolen, was acquitted. Geo Avery, also indicted for the same offence, was acquitted. 3-F S Merritt, indicted for gambling: acquitted. 4-*Owen McGee, indicted for robbing his uncle, Patrick McGee: verdict-guilty. Recommend that his honor Judge Dunlop will give him the least punishment the law awards. 4-Chas Lucas & Danl Linkens were indicted for rescuing Emory Hamilton, while in custody of Thos Orme. The District Attorney entered a nolle prosequi in this case. [*Feb 14 newspaper: Owen McGee was sentenced to 1 year imprisonment in the penitentiary, to take effect from Feb 19.] [Feb 17th newspaper: Owen McGee was granted a pardon by the Pres of the U S, on Sat last.]

TUE FEB 11, 1845
British Navy List for 1845. British Army List for 1845. New annual Army List, by Capt Hart, 40th Regt, being the 6th annual volume, giving the dates of commissions & war services & wounds of every ofcr in the army, ordnance, & marines, corrected up to Dec 27, 1844, 1 vol octavo. Capt Marryatt's Code of Signals, 1 vol, London, 1844. Watson's Telegraphic Vocabulary. The Duties of Judge Advocates, by Capt Hughes, 12th Ret, Deputy Judge Advocate Genr'l, 1 vol, London, 1845. Campbell's Lives of British Admirals, 8 volumes. Grotius on War & Peace. –F Taylor, bookstore

Mrs R M Poulton informs that she has just received her London & Paris Prints for this month. Her residence is on 10th st, between Pa ave & C st.

For rent: the 1st floor & cellar of the Warehouse occupied by Messrs Wm Noyes & Sons. Possession may be had immediately. –J T Ryon & Bro, La ave, near the Bank of wash.

Jas W Berry & Co: Commission Merchants & Brokers, Pa ave, opposite Coleman's Hotel, offer for sale-leaf lard, bacon, java, gunpowder, black teas, wrapping paper, apple vinegar, & New Orleans molasses.

Senate: Ptn of Wm Miller, a soldier in the last war, asking a pension. 2-Memorial from the Cherokee Indians for indemnification. 3-Cmte on Pensions: reported a bill for the relief of Jos Morrison. Same cmte: discharged from the further consideration of the ptn of Obadiah Blanding; & the papers were referred to the Cmte on Revolutionary Pensions. 4-Cmte on Patents: reported a bill to extend a patent heretofore granted to Wm Woodworth. 5-Bill for the relief of Seth M Leavenworth was read & passed.

John H Saunders, Atty at Law: ofc north side of E st, between 6th & 7th sts. [Ad]

Negro man for sale, about 25 years of age, a good house servant or coachman. Inquire of Mr Thos Williams, corner of 7th & Md ave.

The schnr **Salada**, from Marblehead for N Y, went ashore about a mile form the lighthouse on race Point, [Cape Cod,] on Fri night. The vessel & cargo are a total loss, & the following persons perished: B T Ames, master; Thos Payton, of Fredericksburg, Va; & John Williams, colored, of Balt. Peter Peterson, the mate, was saved.

The schnr **Reeside**, from Boston for N Y, went ashore on Long Island, & broke in pieces. It is apprehended that all on board have perished. She was a Boston & N Y packet, commanded by Capt Langley.

WED FEB 12, 1845
Gen John Carr, of Clark Co, Indiana, died at his residence on Jan 20, after an illness of 10 weeks. For many years he filled a seat in the U S Congress. On the field, during the late war, he distinguished himself as a soldier & a patriot.

Hse/o Reps: 1-Ptn of Ransom White, praying compensation for a pilot boat which was pressed into public service during the war of the Revolution. 2-Memorial of Birkhead & Pearce, of Balt, asking for a remission of duties paid on guano, & that the article may be hereafter admitted free of duty. 3-Ptn of Caleb Belcher & others, asking a pension for Phoebe Grave, the widow of a Revolutionary soldier. 4-Ptn of Elisha Doane & others, seamen, asking that they be paid for services on board vessels of the U S Navy. 5-Ptn of John Turner, of Wayne Co, Ky, asking for a pension. 6-Ptn of Jas Marsh & Son, praying Congress to purchase their floating dry dock in the city of Charleston, for the use of the U S at that harbor. 7-Ptn of Geo G Smith, Francis Alexander, & others, artists of Boston, praying that Congress would purchase the portraits of the 5 first Presidents now on exhibition in the Library. 8-Ptn of Richd Atwill & others, of Boston, for a reduction of postage.

Mrd: on Feb 4, by Rev Wm Matthews, John W Skidmore, of Alexandria, to Mary A, y/d/o the late Saml Wimsatt, of Wash.

The marriage of Congrave Warner & Eliz Crocket was made null & void by the Senate of Missouri. The parties were at a wedding, & upon a banter given, they rode to a justice's, where the ceremony was performed. Upon their return, the lady insisted that it was all a joke & refused to consider it otherwise.

Died: on Feb 9, after a lingering illness, Wm Hudson Stewart, in his 52nd year. He was a native of Mount Holly, N J, & emigrated to Wash City in his boyhood. He has left a wife & 2 children, together with a large number of friends & relatives, to deplore his loss. His funeral will be on Wed at 1 o'clock.

Died: on Feb 4, in PG Co, Md, Thos Kraig, aged 3 years, y/c/o Dr Chas & Sarah Maria Bowie.

Died: Jan 9, Saml Columbus, only s/o Richd & Sarah Wimsatt, of Washington, aged 2 years & 4 months.

Waterton, N Y, Feb 4. Mournful tragedy. On Thu last Geo Brown, s/o Mr Brown, [residing in the village of Tylerville] had, with 2 or 3 other young men, been out hunting when on an eminence opposite the dwlg of Mr Simeon Oaks, & about 25 rods distant, he saw his dght Jane M, enter a small rear bldg, when one of the company said "now shoot & frighten her," upon which young Brown instantly fired at the bldg, & unfortunately with fatal effect, the ball entering her shoulder & passing through the heart. In the evening she died. The families of Messrs Oaks & Brown, who have for many years lived on terms of the strictest friendship, is now one of deep anguish. –Black River Journal [Jul 2nd newspaper: Court of Oyer & Terminer of Jefferson Co-Jun 18: verdict of guilty of manslaughter in the 3rd degree. Prisoner sentenced to the State prison in Clinton Co for 4 years.]

Senate: 1-Ptn of Jane Hawkins, widow of a dec'd seaman, for a pension. 2-Memorial of Hugh W Dobbin, praying for arrears of pension. 3-Ptn of True Putney & Hugh Riddle, praying compensation for work done on the public warehouse in Balt.

Appointments by the Pres, by & with the consent of the Senate.
Jos Graham, of Ohio, to be Consul at Buenos Ayres.
Oscar F Bledsoe, to the U S Atty for the District of Mississippi.
Saml H Hempstead, to be U S Atty for the District of Arkansas.
John McClung, to be U S Marshal for the District of Delaware.
Perry Douglass, to be Surveyor & Inspector of the Revunue for the port of New London, Conn.
Thos Lloyd, to be Surveyor of the Revenue for the District of Balt, Md.
Robt B Risley, to be Collector of the Customs for the District of Great Egg Harbor, & Inspector of the Revenue for the port of Bargaintown, N J.
Geo C Shaw, to be Naval Ofcr for the District of Newport, Rhode Island.

The Texas Nat'l Register announces the following recent deaths in that country: 1-On Jan 12, John W Smith, Senator from Bexar Co, for more than 20 years a resident. 2-On Jan 5, in Gonzales Co, Allen Walker, a native of N Y, long a resident of Mississippi before emigrating to Texas. 3-At Washington, Wm B Goodman, formerly of Tennessee, a resident in Texas from 1841. [No date.]

THU FEB 13, 1845
The Pres of the Senate announced the result to the joint meeting, in compliance with the law of Mar 1, 1792, & the resolution of the 2 Houses, made the following declaration: I do declare that Jas K Polk, of the State of Tenn, having a majority of the whole number of votes of the Electors of Pres & V P of the U S, is duly elected Pres of the U S for 4 years, commencing with Mar 4, 1845. And I do further declare that Geo M Dallas, of Pa, having the majority of the whole number of votes of the Electors of Pres & V P of the U S for V P, is duly elected V P of the U S for 4 years, commencing with Mar 4, 1845.

Hse/o Reps: 1-Cmte on Foreign Affairs: Bill for the Benj E Green, be allowing him $1069.45, for services as Charge d'Affaires in Mexico. Also, a bill for the relief of Armond T Donnet, by allowing him $3,069.86, for services as Charge d'Affaires in Portugal.

Coal, hickory, oak & pine wood for sale. Potomac Bridge & corner of E & 10th sts. –J S Harvey & Co

Valuable river land for sale: the undersigned, having determined to remove to the South, will dispose of his farm in Northumberland Co, Va: spacious dwlg house & all necessary out-houses, containing 350 acs. He will also dispose of 135 acres in the same county, with a large 2 story frame dwlg, with laundry, kitchen, granary, & barn, all in good repair. The farms are within a few miles of Cone landing. Information can be given by inquiring of the undersigned at Heathsville, in Eastern Va. –S M Conway

Orphan's Court of Wash Co, D C. In the case of Richd Dement, adm of John J Dement, dec'd: Mar 4 next has been appointed for the final settlement of said estate.
–Ed N Roach, Reg o/wills

N Y C Geo W Newcombe, a distinguished miniature painter of N Y C, died very suddenly yesterday of apoplexy. He was an Englishman by birth, & much esteemed for many excellent qualities.

Died: yesterday, at the dwlg of Jno G Law, after an illness of a few hours, Miss Martha Dudley, in her 17th year. Her funeral is today at 3 o'clock from St Matthew's church. Members of the Ladies Sodality, as well as the teachers & children of the Sunday School, are also invited to attend the funeral.

Died: at Petersburg, Va, Wm Pilling, formerly of Wash City. His funeral is today at 2 o'clock, from the residence of his brother, Jos Pilling.

Died: on Feb 3, in Nashville, Tenn, after a severe illness, Hester, d/o the late Jos Jefferson, comedian, of Phil, & w/o Alex'r Mackenzie, formerly manager of the theatres in Balt, Wash, Ill, & now of Nashville.

FRI FEB 14, 1845

Historical Society of Pennsylvania: letter from Job R Tyson, one of the V Presidents, to Granville Penn, a grandson of Wm Penn: dated Phil, Aug 1, 1844: addressed to Stoke Park, near London. Bringing tidings of the death of its Pres, Peter S Duponceau, who died in May last, in his 84th year. Though bent almost to deformity, & suffering much from obtuseness of hearing, & the almost total privation of sight, he prosecuted his studies with unabated diligence to the last. His death, aided by a bequest in his will, has induced us to removed to a bldg better suited for the commodious arrangement of the library & archives. A society was formed in this city some years ago for the purpose of commemorating the anniversary of Penn's landing, on Oct 24, 1682. His birthday occurred the next day: his birth occurring on Oct 14-old style. [Peter S Duponceau was a munificent benefactor of the Society.]

New Books: Sparks' Library of American Biography, vol xii. New series, vol ii. Containing lives of Jas Otis, by Francis Bowen, & of Gen Jas Oglethorpe, by W O Peabody. Boston, Little & Brown. 405 p

After Santa Anna's capture he was confined for a few days in the Castle of Perote, but at the latest date was said to be on his way to the city of Mexico, under a strong escort. It is stated that the Gov't had ordered all his property to be seized] confiscated, & the general belief was that he would himself be condemned & executed.

Capt Simmons, of the brig **Faith**, who arrived in Balt last week, discovered an island in the Pacific which is not laid down in any chart. He was on his way from Otaheite to Valparaiso, & fell in with this island in lat 21 10 & long 138 54: about 6 miles in circumference, surrounded by a reef of black coral rocks, covered with cocoa trees. He called it the Isle of Faith.

The Cecil [Md] Democrat states that Alex'r Shaw, residing about 8 miles from Elkton, near the Big Elk Creek, had been horribly murdered. He was found in his sleeping room, covered with a sheet. He was so disfigured that no one would suppose a human being could have committed so dreadful an outrage.

A letter of Jan 28 from Bellevue, Wash Co, Missouri, states that Thos Bird, of that place had met his death from a gun-shot wound at the hands of Jas Minor, with whom he had a lawsuit. The assassin fled, & a reward of $200 is offered for him.

Senate: 1-Ptn of Wm Carman, a drafted soldier in the Revolutionary war, for a pension. 2-Memorial of Enos Stevenson, informing Congress that he has discovered a machine for taking the yeas & nays in a very expeditious manner, & praying its adoption by their honorable bodies. 3-Ptn of Mary McNelly, praying for a pension. 4-Ptn of W H Ivey & others, mechanics & laborers in the Washington Navy Yard, praying compensation for loss of time in the suspension of their labors. 5-Cmte on the Post Ofc & Post Roads: reported a bill for the relief of Thos Rhodes. 6-Cmte of Claims: bill without amendment for the relief of John Adams & John Adams, jr; the bill for the relief of Edmund A Lambert; & the bill for the relief of Bennet M Dell. 7-Cmte on Naval Affairs: reported without amendment the bill for the relief of Peter Von Schmidt. 8-Cmte of Claims: reported a bill for the relief of Gen John Cocke.

Hse/o Reps: 1-Memorial of Jeremiah Dunham, of White Co, Indiana, praying compensation for services as blacksmith for the Miami & Pottawatamie Indians. 2-Ptn of Hugh Matthews, of Sumter district, S C, praing for a pension. 3-Ptn of Chas H Sanborn, a citizen of N H, praying Congress to prohibit the importation of wine, rum, brandy, & other spirituous liquors.

Died: on Wed, after a illness of a few hours, Miss Martha Dudley, in her 17th year. Last evening the obsequies for the dec'd took place at St Matthew's Church: Rev Mr Myers delivered the sermon: the multitude moved off in solemn procession, the corpse being borne on a bier supported on either side by 6 ladies & an equal number of gentlemen, until they reached St Patrick's church, in the vault of which the body was deposited. May she rest in peace. -M

Obit: died-Wm H Stewart: the writer of this communication had an acquaintance of near five years with him; he was a true patriot, as he proved himself in the last war, in the defence of Balt, at North Point. His patriotism was sincere as his friendship was lasting. -D

Died: on Jan 28, at Meredith, Hon Saml A Law, in his 74th year. He was born in Nov, 1771, at Cheshire, Conn, & in 1788 entered Yale College, at which institution he graduated in 1792. After the Law School at Litchfield, Conn, he was admitted to the Bar in 1795, & rec'd honorary degrees from the Colleges of Columbia & Harvard. In 1798 he came into this county as agent for the owners of the Franklin Patent, & commenced the settlement at the place of his late residence. Later he was appointed Judge of Common Pleas, which ofc he performed for several years. –Delaware [N Y] Gaz

Congressional Burial Ground: the broken shaft erected over the gallant Gen Brown, in that cemetery, was placed there by Congress, who appropriated $5,000 for the support of his family. A monument should be ordered to be erected without delay over the body of Gen Macomb, like that which covers the remains of Gen Brown. –W

Wash Corp: 1-Mayor nominates John Dewdney as the additional police ofcr of the 1st Ward: confirmed. 2-Memorial of S Hyatt & 88 others, property holders, praying a reduction of the present rate of taxes: referred. 3-Bill for the relief of Geo Savage: passed. 4-Cmte of Claims: bill for the relief of Geo Hervus.

Frisby Maurice Nowland, a native of Cecil Co, Md, who resided in 1826 thru 1828, in Chilicothe, Ohio, subsequently for a short time in Cincinnati, Ohio, & in Louisville, Ky, but about 1830 to 1832 at or about New Philadelphia, Ohio, & has not since been heard from by his friends in Md. Information is now desired where he resides, if living; therefore, should this notice reach him, he will report himself to me immediately; & if any member of Congress, or any other persons from the Western States, have any knowledge of Mr Nowland, he or they will confer a favor by giving me such information, as they may possess as to his residence, if living, or as to his death. –Alfred C Nowland, Elkton, Cecil Co, Md

SAT FEB 15. 1845
N Y Fancy Store: Falconer Smyles & Co, 377 Broadway, N Y. [Ad]

Caution: the public are cautioned against trading for a note drawn by B Milburn for $50, in favor of Jas R Ferguson, sometime between Dec 23 & 30th last, at 6 months after date, as said note was given under a wrong impression, which the subscriber believes he will be able to prove in a court of chancery. The money is not due to said Ferguson, & if a transfer shall have been offered, the holder will please communicate that fact to the undersigned. –Benedict Milburn. [The subscriber has 4 frame houses, [3 of them entirely new] which he would dispose of on accommodating terms. 3 of them on south F, between 4½ & 6th sts, & the other on north R, between 10th & 11th sts. Also, several lots on easy terms.

For rent: 3 story brick house on F st, between 13th & 14th sts, lately occupied by Mr Ferguson. –Jos Abbott

Senate: 1-Cmte of Claims: bills without amendment: act for the relief of Wm Rich; relief of Harrison Whitson; relief of Philip Schwartstraber. 2-Cmte on the Judiciary: bill for the relief of Benj S Roberts, without amendment. 3-Bill for the relief of John Russworm: ordered to be engrossed.

Last Chance. The ready made clothing at the store of Jas B Holmead, 4½ & Pa ave, will be closed this afternoon, at 6 o'clock.

Mons Gabriel De Korponay has arrived for the purpose of giving instruction in the principal fashionable dances prevailing in the highest circles of European & American society. Among them the well known dances La Polka, the new quadrilles, the waltz de deus pas, the Mazourka, German cotillion, new gallope, & all American dances. Madame Korponay will assist. Instruction will be given in French, German, Italian, & English. 6 lessons for $6.

Died: on Thu last, at the residence of his father, in Wash City, Beale Bordley Crawford, counsellor at law, of Chambersburg, Pa, & s/o Hon T Hartley Crawford, Com'r of Indian affairs. His funeral will be on Sun next at 2 o'clock.

Died: yesterday, after an illness of 48 hours, Therese Cornelia Maria, d/o J H & Eliz Henry, in her 2nd year. Her funeral is to take place Sun at 3 o'clock, from the corner of 25th & F sts.

Boarding: Mrs C Lipscomb on D st, opposite the Intelligencer Ofc. [Ad]

MON FEB 17, 1845

Carriages manufactured to order at the shortest notice, at his old stand, 3rd & Pa ave. Old carriages repaired or taken in exchange for new ones. Carriages sold on commission. -Michl McDermott

Hse/o Reps: 1-Cmte of Claims: bills committed: relief of Saml D Enochs; relief of John Carr, John Batty, & Saml Stevenson; relief of Geo D Spencer. 2-Cmte of Claims: adverse reports on the cases of Jeremiah Smith, jr, Thos T Wright, John Francis, Chas Duvall, & Teakle Savage, adm of Bolitha Laws: laid on the table. 3-Cmte of Claims: reported a bill for the relief of Peter Schaffer & a bill for the relief of Jas McAvoy: committed. 4-Cmte on the Public Lands: bill for the relief of Mary Anne Brunner, reported back with amendment: then committed. 5-Cmte on the Post Ofc & Post Roads: bill for the relief of Seth M Leavenworth, reported the same without amendment: then committed. 6-Cmte on Revolutionary Claims: bill for the relief of the legal reps of Christian Orendorff: committed. Same cmte: reported that John T Wilmot have leave to withdraw his ptn: agreed to. 7-Cmte on Public Expenditures: made a report on the memorial of Lt John T McLaughlin, of the U S Navy. 8-Cmte on Private Land Claims: bill for the relief of A B McMillen: committed. Same cmte: adverse report on the case of Chas Chappell: laid on the table. Also, same cmte: bill for the relief of the heirs of Wm Fisher, made a report in writing against the passage of the bill: then committed. 9-Cmte on Military Affairs: bill from the Senate for the relief of Wm C Easton, reported the same without amendment. 10-Cmte on Military Affairs: bill for the relief of Joshua Shaw, reported the same without amendment: committed. Also, same cmte, an adverse report on the ptn of Dijah Brown: laid on the table. 11-Cmte on Naval Affairs: asked to be discharged from the further consideration of the ptn of Ebenezer Atwell, & moved that it lie on the table: agreed to. Same cmte: bill for the relief of the legal reps of Jas H Clarke, late purser in the navy: committed. Also, same cmte: asked to be discharged from the memorial of Chas F Guillon, & that it be laid on the table: agreed to. 12-Cmte on Revolutionary Pensions: adverse reports on the ptns of Richd Wells & Benj Guthrie: laid on the table. Same cmte: asked to be discharged from the ptns of: [following ptns to lie on the table: agreed to.]

Carter B Chandler	Saml Saint John	Johnanna French
Lydia Baker	Wm Stanwood	John B Finley
Susan Aldrich	Michl Spatz	Gabriel Green
Alithea Allen	Geo Singley	Christian Gelvert
Danl & Betsey Clapp	Reuben Taylor	Fred Pearl
Ann Dunyea	Henry Lotz	Roswell Woodworth
Jos Davidson	Edmund Leavenworth	
Susan Rogers	John Everly	

13-Cmte on Revolutionary pensions: reported a bills for the relief of Patrick Masterton; relief of Lemuel Moody; bill for the relief of Peter Wilson: bills were read & committed. 14-Cmte on Public Bldgs & Grounds: proposition of John Skirving to ventilate the Hall of the Hse/o Reps: made a report declining the proposition: laid on the table. 14-Cmte on Invalid Pensions: bill granting a pension to Jas Davis: committed. 15-Cmte on the Post Ofc & Post Roads: joint resolution for the relief of Wm B Stokes, surviving partner of J N C Stockton & Co: committed. 16-Cmte on Private Land Claims: bill for the relief of the legal reps of Wm Dickson: committed. 17-Ptn of Francis Fitch, of Cecil Co, Md, praying Congress to permit Guano to be imported without paying any duty. 18-Ptn of Jas Harper & other editors & authors, praying that the postage of magazines & other periodicals may be put on the same footing as that of newspapers. 19-Ptn of N Groton & 319 others, praying for a reduction of postage.

Supreme Court of the U S: Feb 14, 1845. Henry M Phillips, of Pa, admitted an atty & counsellor of this Court. #59: Catharine Scholfield, appellant, vs Andrew Scholfield's exc. Argument of this cause was continued by Mr Davis for the appellant, & Messrs Neale & Coxe for the appellee.

Miss Sally Preston, d/o the Hon Wm C Preston, of S C, died at her father's residence in Columbia on Feb 8.

Senate: 1-Memorial of Wm Buchanan, of Md, praying a pension. 2-Memorial of Wm Duff, praying an examination of his invention to prevent explosions in steam boilers. 3-Ptn of Stephen Snow, a soldier in the last war with Great Britian, asking a pension. 4-Presented: Ptn of John F Wilmott, exc of the estate of Robt Wilmott. 5-Cmte on Naval Affairs: without amendment, the House bill for the relief of Jacob Boston. 6-Cmte on Revolutionary Claims: adverse report on the ptn of Obadiah Blanding. 7-Cmte on Foreign Relations: adverse report on the ptn of A P Brittingham.

New Orleans, Feb 5. Francis Boyce was arrested on Feb 4 charged with stabbing with intent to kill, Henry Ross, at the Franklin Restaurat, in Gravier st. Both were employed as cooks there. Another! Cola Herbisso, employed as a cook at the Restaurat of Mrs Verdie, corner of Gallatin & Ursuline sts, was arrested Feb 4 charged with inflicting a wound on the face of Mrs Verdi, severing entirely across the upper lip. Benito Dephant, exployed as a cook, in attempting to save Mrs Verdie, received a blow with the knife, which traversed the entire nose, nearly severing it in twain. Herbisso will be examinded this morning before Recorder Genois. Still another! H H Shroeder was arrested Feb 4, for assaulting a person whose name we did not learn, with a knife with intent to kill. And still another! An affray took place Feb 4 in the hat depository of the St Louis ballroom, between Mr H F Hatch & Mr Jackson, a nephew of Judge Jackson, because of some insult in the ball room, which resulted in Mr Jackson receiving 3 dangerous dirk wounds in the side, after having slapped the face of Mr Hatch. Mr Jackson has since died. Another yet! On Feb 4 Auguste Herrison & Jos Bonnedeau quarreled and blows passed between them, when Mr Herrison gave Bonnedeau 4 stabs in the chest & abdomen, which almost immediately resulted in death. -Bee

John W Van Cleve, of Dayton, of which place he is a native, is engaged on a scientific work relating to Natural History. It is to be a description of the organic remains found in western rocks, with their general & specific character, illustrated with engravings. Van Cleve has a mind very well adapted to treat the subject properly -Cin Chron

A young man named Hildebrand was shockingly mangled at Wheeling last Mon by the premature discharge of a cannon, which he was ramming at the time. He was engaged with others in firing a salute in honor of the arrival of Mr Polk.

On Fri last in Swanzey, N H, Capt David Reed, one of the most respectable citizens of Swanzey, went into the woods with his oxen for the purpose of drawing logs. He did not return and the next morning he was found with a large log lying across his leg, & frozen to death. He has left a wife & 7 children.

Baton Rouge Gaz of Sat: affray took place in St Francisville a few days ago, in the coffee house kept by Mr Fetters, between himself & his barkeeper, during which Mrs Fetters stepped between them to take a gun which her husband held in his hand, when the gun went off & killed her on the spot. –N O Bee, Feb 4 [No name given for the barkeeper.]

Trustee's sale of lot & bldg: deed of trust, dated Jan 13, 1843, by Jas Raley, recorded in Liber W B 99, folios 192 thru 195, a land record of Wash Co, D C. Sale of part of lot 5 in sq 525 at corner of 4th st & N Y ave, with one frame bldg nearly new. –Asa Gladman, Trustee -A Green, Auct

Mrd: Feb 4, by Rev J P Donelan, Mr Wm Welsh, of Columbia, Pa, to Miss Jane E Spalding, of Gtwn, D C.

Mrd: on Feb 3, at Trinity Church, Gtwn, D C, by Rev P O'Flanagan, Mr John Taylor Crow, of Gtwn Advocate, to Miss Chloe Ann A Boncher, of Gtwn, D C.

Died: on Feb 8, at the residence of Alex S Grigsby, Centreville, Va, Mrs Mildred Grigsby, relict of the late Aaron Grigsby, aged 78 years. The dec'd was 40 years a professor of the Christian religion, & in her last hours afforded her friends strong indications of unshaken confidence in the Redeemer.

Died: on Feb 9, in St Mary's Co, Md, Chas Neale, in his 85th year, the eldest s/o the late Jas Neale, Commissary General during the Revolution.

Died: on Feb 11, at Wilmington, Delaware, suddenly, Dr Allen McLane, a gentleman eminent in his profession, & a citizen of great worth.

Died: on Wed, at Balt, after a long illness, Thos Wilson, for many years a partner in the old & respectable house of Wm Wilson & Sons, & extensively known as an intelligent, sagacious, & upright merchant.

Obit-died: a brave & upright & honest patriot has fallen. Departed this life on Feb 1, Col Klimkiewicz, a native of Poland, who distinguished himself in the defence of liberty, sacrificed all his pecuniary interests, & spared not his blood in vindicating the rights of man. He was confined for 6 years in a dungeon at Kamienice Podolski as a prisoner of State. When the police master, Maj Alex'r Michael entered his dungeon in the hope of bribing him with a promise on the part of the Emperor of Russia with a pardon, & the restoration of his confiscated property, adding he would be looked upon & treated as a faithful subject of his Majesty, he indignantly replied: "Retire, miscreant! Thou who grovellest at the feet of thy Ministers, how darest thou present thyself before an honest patriot. Forget not that in my viens flows the blood of the illustrious Thadeus Kosciusko. Sir, I am a free citizen of Volhynia, & know the laws of thine own country better than thou dost. It is understood that a biographical notice of this brave man is in a state of preparation for publication in aid of his family. -Virginia

Providence Journal says that a serious division has happened in Rhode Island among the religious sect, the Friends. The cause of dissension goes back to the visit of Jos John Gurney, whose doctrines are objected to be a portion of the society, who are styled Wilburites, from John Wilbur, a preacher in the southern part of the State. Each party claims to be the genuine followers of Geo Fox. At the Quarterly Meeting in Providence last week the Wilburites were excluded, & held a separate meeting in another house.

TUE FEB 18, 1845
Two calves taken up estray: owner can have them by proving property & paying charges. –Osborn Acton, Twenty Bldgs Hill, near ***Buzzard Point***.

Caution: a counterfeit Check was paid at the Union Bank of Md on Feb 13, for $1,755.57. In case it should be offered, if possible, notify the police & the subscriber. –R Mickle, Cashier of the Bank.

Senate: 1-Cmte on Foreign Affairs: unfavorable report on the claim of John Baldwin, for Mexican indemnification. 2-Cmte of Claims: act for the relief of the heirs of Alex'r Mitchell, without amendment. 3-Cmte on Revolutionary Claims: unfavorable report on the ptn of Francis Sumter. 4-Cmte on Pensions: adverse report on the act granting a pension to Susannah Scott, wid/o Wm Scott. 5-Bills ordered engrossed: relief of the reps of Henry King; relief of Peter Von Schmidt. Bill authorizing a re-location of land warrants granted to Gen Lafayette.

Loudoun land for sale: I will sell on Mar 26, the *Cottage farm*, the late residence of Mrs Francis Armistead. This tract contains 526 acs, more or less; is 2 miles from the flourishing little village Aldie; commodious dwlg-house, a good kitchen, & meat-house, all in good condition, save the barn, which can be repaired at a very trivial expense. The dwlg-house is constituted of brick & stone; 2 stories high, with a spacious passage, & 2 rooms 21 by 19 feet on the lower floor, & a passage & 4 comfortable rooms on the 2nd floor. Immediate possession can be had. –Barrow Frere, Loudoun Co, Va.

$100 reward for runaway negro boy, Henson Johnson, light copper color, his face a little pitted from being poisoned, age is 18 years. –Wm L Berry, living near Upper Marlborough, PG Co, Md.

Caution: the public are cautioned against taking or trading for 3 notes, drawn by me in favor of Asahel Bliss, dated Feb 6, 1845. The above notes will not be paid, having received no consideration for the same. -Wm Moore

WED FEB 19, 1845
Laws of the U S, passed at the 2nd Session of the 28th Congress. 1-Act for the relief of Gideon Batchelder & others: to pay for any stone delivered in 1838 & 1839, towards the erection of Sandy Bay breakwater, near Gloucester, Mass: the price not to exceed the previous price. 2-Resolution authorizing an allowance to Purser D M F Thornton, in the settlement of his accounts: he is to be credited with $858.23 in his accounts with the U S, that sum being in full for the value of his stores destroyed or injured on board the U S ship **Erie**, during a hurricane on Sep 3, 1827. 3-Act for the relief of Asahel Brainard: pay to him the arrears of a pension, at the same rate per month as now received by him, as a captain of a rifle company in the service of the U S during the late war with Great Britain; said arrears to be computed from Sep 17, 1814, to Feb 24, 1843, deducting therefrom any pension which may have been received by said Brainard between the said dates. 4-Act for the relief of Jas Ritchie: settle the accounts of Ritchie, as hospital surgeon at the port of New Orleans during 1842 & 1843, on the same principles as were applied to the

settlement of similar accounts before the order of Dec 12, 1840, was issued. 5-Act for the relief of Mark Simpson: his name is to be placed on the roll of invalid pensioners, & that he be paid a pension, at the rate of $6 per month, during his life, to commence on Jan 1, 1844. 6-Act granting a pension to Jas Duffy: his name to be placed on the roll of invalid naval pensioners, & to pay him a pension, at the rate of $2.50 per month, during his life, to commence on Dec 1, 1842. 7-Act granting a pension to Geo Whitten: late a private in the 21st Regt of Infty, to be paid a pension, at the rate of $5.33 per month, to commence on Jan 1, 1843, & to continue during his natural life, he having been wounded in battle at Williamsburg, in Upper Canda, Nov 11, 1813. 8-Act for the relief of J McFarlane: to settle his accounts-as hospital surgeon at the port of New Orleans during 1842, on the same principles as were applied to the settlement of similar accounts before the Treasury order of Dec 12, 1840, was issued.

Senate: 1-Communication from the Navy Dept, being the report of Lt Gillis from the dept of charts. 2-Additional evidence in the claim of W W Buchanan. 3-Cmte on Pensions: unfavorable report on the ptn of Ellison Williams. 4-Cmte on Indian Affairs: reported a bill for the relief of Wm Henson. Also, a bill for the relief of Catlin, Peoples & Co. Also, a bill for the relief of W H Thomas. 5-Cmte on Naval Affairs: reported a bill for the relief of Cmdor Jesse D Elliot. 6-Engrossed bills passed: relief of the legal reps of Geo Duvall; relief of J A Throckmorton.

The New Orleans Tropic states that Wm L Hodge, Wm Christy, & Randell Hunt, have been appointed Commissioners by the U S Senate to take testimony relative to the general bearing & operation of the Naturalization laws, & the frauds that may have been committed.

Natchez Courier: on Feb 8 the steamboat **Pathfinder**, from Yazoo, a few miles below Grand Gulf, Miss, took fire. Those known to be lost are Messrs S S Caldwell, Huggins, & Butler, of Grenada, Miss; Mr Carleton, of Tallahatchie; Mr Pinchback, of Ill; the steward of the boat, & one of the crew, names unknown.

Mrs David H Burr's French & English seminary for Young Ladies: semi-annual Examination on Feb 7, when the honors were awarded to:

Miss L Howison	Miss E Cross	Miss E Blackwell
Miss E Todd	Miss R Howle	Miss E Wheeler
Miss S Pyne	Miss J Stettinius	Miss E Smith
Miss H Stettinius	Miss E Tayloe	Miss J Howle
Miss S F Little	Miss H Buit	Miss V Aulick
Miss L Morrison	Miss F Washington	Miss M Hanly
Miss F Kendall	Miss M Thomas	Miss E Rigdon
Miss S French	Miss E Thomas	Miss E Redfern
Miss L Wadsworth	Miss M Jackson	Miss Adelaide Smith
Miss J E Luce	Miss M Hewitt	Miss M J Handy

Miss M Kearney   Miss F Burr   Miss F Burr
Miss E J Stephens   Miss E Goddard

The celebrated historical series of Portraits of our first Chief Magistrates, by the late Gilbert Stuart, which for the last 4 years have graced the walls of the Library of Congress, will, if not now purchased by the Gov't. in all probability, pass into a foreign kingdom, as the proprietor of these pictures is now in Wash City for the purpose of making a final arrangement concerning them. The Washington, Adams, & Jefferson, as declared by Stuart himself, as the best heads that he ever painted of those illustrious men. Benj West, an American, & Pres of the Royal Academy of Painting in England, pronounced Stuart to be the best painter of the human head since the days of Vandyck, & that about 2 years ago it was reported in the British papers, that the Emperor of Russia had given 1,200 pounds, about $6,000, for the Stuart's Washington once owned by the late Marquis of Lansdown.

Timothy Walker Fiske, of N H, a midshipman in the Navy, was found dead in his bed at Jones' Hotel, Phil, on Sun. From the evidence, it appeared he had returned from a cruise, arrived in Phil about Feb 3. He had been stationed at the Naval Asylum, but went to Jones' Hotel on Fri. A bowl was found which had contained coffee, & in it were discovered the dregs of laudanum. In the grate a bottle was found, but the fire had removed all traces of the laudanum. A letter was written by the dec'd, addressed to a brother midshipman named Lowe, bequeathing to him his effects. The dec'd had been laboring under despondency, caused by disappointments.

Hubbard Williams, s/o John Williams, of Harrison Co, Ky, was killed on Feb 7, when out hunting, &, after discharging his gun, was stooping over the wadding whilst it was burning, when the stopper of his powder horn dropped out, the contents ignited, & an explosion took place, terminating his existence in about 4 hours. He was about 14 or 15 years of age.

Hse/o Reps: 1-Ptn of Noah Ely & 68 others, citizens of Otaego & Chenango Cos, praying for the establishment of a mail route from Oneonta to New Berlin, by way of Butternuts. 2-Ptn of Alex'r Stephenson, of Kosciusko Co, Indian, for relief. 3-Ptn of Geo Swope & 42 others, citizens of Phil Co, Pa, praying for an alteration of the naturalization laws.

On Mon last W M Johnson, about 18, went to the Patriotic Bank in Wash City & presented for payment a check for $535; check appeared to be a forgery. He was arrested & held to bail for his appearance at the next Criminal Court.

Notice: the copartnership heretofore existing between Theodore A Dwight & Geo C Thomas, jr, under the firm of Dwight & Thomas, is this day dissolved by mutual consent. –Geo C Thomas, jr, Genr'l Agent

Mrd: on Feb 13, at Luton Farm, by Rev Mr Trott, Mr Jas L Cross to Miss Lucy B M Fitzhugh, all of Fairfax Co, Va.

Died: on Feb 13, in Wash City, in her 78th year, Lucretia Sears, wid/o Geo Sears, formerly an eminent merchant of Balt, & mother of Abby, w/o Jas W McCulloh, First Comptroller of the U S Treasury.

Died: on Feb 10, Mrs Dorothea Wailes, in her 78th year. The dec'd was a native of St Mary's Co, Md, but resided in Wash City for 30 years previous to her death.

Died: on Feb 11, in Annapolis, Md, Mr Gotleib I Grammer, sr, in his 78th year. He was a native of Wirtemburg, Germany, but for the last 40 years a resident of Annapolis.

Strawberry plants for sale: 50 plants for $2.50. –John H Bayne, near Alexandria

Orphan's Court of Wash Co, D C. Letters of adm on the personal estate of Jos Hay, late a surgeon in the Virginia State line, dec'd. –Francis A Dickins, adm

THU FEB 20, 1845
Senate: 1-Cmte of Claims: reported without amendment, the following House bills: relief of Jacob S Vance, of Ohio; relief of Chas R Allen; relief of John R Converse. 2-Act for the relief of Harvey & Slagg, with a report. 3-Cmte on Military Affairs: reported an act for the relief of John H McIntosh. Also, an act for the relief of Capt J B Crozier's company of mounted volunteers. 4-Cmte on Pension: unfavorable report on the claims of W W Buchanan, which was ordered to be printed.

Farm for sale: the undersigned is authorized to offer for sale a fine farm, adjoining the lands of Messrs Pierson, Gales, & Kendall, containing about 300 acs: also a handsome & neat new dwlg-house, barn & stable, & all the necessary appendages for a farm. This tract of land can be divided into 2 farms. –N Callan, jr F st, or to Thos or Edw Fenwick, on the premises.

Millinery & Fancy Head Dresses for parties. Mrs E Torrence, next door to Mr Denham's dye-house, between 9th & 10th sts, south side of Pa ave, Wash.

The subscriber has for sale at Mr Green's Furniture Ware-room 2 splendid Pianos, one of the richest mahogany, 6 octaves, the other 7 octaves, made in Gothic style, of the best rosewood. –Louis Hern

Notice. The public is notified that, in consequence of my ill health & inablility to attend to my affairs, I have appointed my son, B I Semmes, jr, as agent & atty to transact all my business, & he alone is authorized to contract debts on my account. –Raphael Semmes

FRI FEB 21, 1845
Col David Chambers, the Speaker of the Senate of Ohio, [& formerly a Rep in Congress,] was many years ago an editor of a daily newspaper in Ohio; & John M Gallagher, the Speaker of the House, is now the editor of the Springfield Republican.

John Ross, principal chief, Richd Taylor, John Looney, Wm S Coodey, Aaron Price, Moses Daniel, T Walker, & John Spears, have been appointed a Delegation by the Nat'l Council of the Cherokee Indians, & directed to proceed to Wash City without delay, with full powers to negotiate a treaty that will embrace & settle all matters which are open between their people & the U S Gov't.

The little Josephine Bramson, a child but 9 years of age, of whose surprising skill on the Piano forte the N Y press has teemed with praises, will give a Concert on Tue next, assisted by her yet younger sister, only 6 years of age, & her brother of 11, whose extraordinary performance on the violin has obtained for him the title of the "young Ole Bull". The Concert will take place at Carusi's Saloon, particulars to be announced.

Wash Corp: 1-Ptn of Wm Woodward & others, praying the curbstone to be set & footway paved on Mass ave & I st: referred to the cmte on Improvements. 2-Ptn of Jas Maher, praying a remission of a fine: referred to the Cmte of Claims. 3-Bill for the relief of Wm Morrow: referred to the Cmte of Claims.

Julius A Peters' Wine Store, Pa ave, near 10th st, Wash. [Ad]

Hse/o Reps: 1-Ptn of John Blackwell & others, asking that lands may be given to poor families who are not able to purchase. 2-Ptn of Jas Smith on behalf of Benj Kerlin, an insane soldier, praying a pension. 3-Ptn of S C Holden & others, citizens of Batavia, N Y, praying for a reduction in the rate of postage. 4-Ptn of J S Marcy & 28 others, for the annexation of Canada to the U S. 5-Cmte of Claims: act for the relief of Wm Wise: passed. 6-Act for the relief of Wm Morrow: passed.

Sandwich Islands: 1-The U S frig **Savannah**, Com Armstrong, was at Hilo, Sandwich islands, on Sep 21 last; also the British ship **Carysfort**, Lord Geo Paulet. 2-News had been received at the island of the arrival in Columbia river of a Belgian brig from Antwerp, having nuns & ecclesiastics for the Roman Catholic Mission. 3-Affray at Wallamet, which led to the death of G W Le Breton, who was wounded while attempting to arrest an Indian, who had threatened the lives of several persons.

Mrd: on Feb 19, by Rev Eells, Jas Williams to Miss Sarah B Moore, all of Wash City..

Mrd: on Feb 13, by Rev Norval Wilson, Mr Jas Wescott to Miss Harriet Ann Calvert, both of Wash City.

Died: on Feb 19, Mrs Harriet Ann Wescott, w/o Mr Jas Wescott, in her 20th year. Her funeral will take place this day, at 3 o'clock, from the residence of her father, Mr Chas Calvert, on 19th st, between I & K sts.

Died: on Feb 19, in Wash City, of consumption, Mr Geo Smith, formerly of Winchester, Va.

Pittsburg, Pa: on Feb 17 the iron vessel **Hunter** was launched at the iron ship yard of Mr Tomlinson. This vessel is about 130 tons burden, & built on Lt Hunter's plan of submerged propellers. She belongs to Lt McLaughlin, of the U S Navy, & is intended for commercial uses; or, as is reported, is to go to Russian, to give the Autocrat a specimen of American skill & of Lt Hunter's plan of propulsion. –Gaz

Cupping & Leeching: 10 years experience in the business. Ladies who may prefer a female cupper or leacher are informed that Mrs Devaughan, who has 8 years in the above business, will attend them. –John Devaughan: residence on 9th st, between D & E sts, where they can be seen day or night.

Senate: 1-Ptn of Wm A Wellman & others, praying the Sec of the Navy may be authorized to purchase, for distribution among the U S naval seaman, a publication called the Sheet Anchor. 2-Ptn from the widow of Dr Jas R Putnam, praying that an examination may be ordered to be made by the War Dept into a machine for dredging, & that a patent may be given her by the U S. 3-Cmte on Foreign Affairs: discharged from the further consideration of the ptn of John Strobecker, claiming indemnity for loss of insurance. 4-Cmte of Claims: act for the relief of Danl Homans, with amendments. Also, a bill authorizing the payment of a sum of money to Robt Purkis.

For rent: 2 frame houses on 4½ st, south of Md ave. Inquire of Mr W Wise, adjoining the premises, or of Chas Miller, at the Centre Market. –Chas Miller

For rent: the house of the subscriber, on 19th st near Pa ave is offered for rent, with or without board, either in whole or in part, to a family or others who desire a temporary residence in the metropolis, on reasonable terms. –A Favier

SAT FEB 22, 1845

Trustee's Sale: in execution of a decree of the Court of Chancery, the subscriber offers at public sale, on Mar 31 next, on the premises, all those lots of ground in the city of Annapolis, with the bldgs thereon, which are known as Swan & Iglehart's Hotel. Immediately after the sale, there will be offered, by another trustee, all the personal property attached to & used with the aforesaid establishment, including beds, bedding, & other articles, sufficient for the accommodation of 100 persons. –Thos S Alexander, trustee

Chancery sale: by virtue of a decree of the Court of D C, sitting in Chancery, for Wash Co, made in the matter of Geo Parker, cmplnt, against Catherine W Hand, [widow & excx of Chauncey M Hand,] Catherine C & other heirs at law of Jos W Hand, will offer for sale at public auction, on Apr 7, all that piece or parcel of ground in Wash City, being part of lot 11 in sq 690, on N J ave, northwardly to the s e corner of Jas Young's lot; with 3 story brick bldgs. –Richd Wallach, trustee -Robt W Dyer & Co, aucts [Apr 8th newspaper: above sale postponed until Apr 15. -Robt W Dyer & Co, aucts]

By virtue of 2 writs of fieri facias issued by B K Morsell, a J P for Wash Co, I shall expose to public sale, on Feb 27, opposite the Centre Market House, in Wash City, one gray mare & one cart & gear, seized & taken as the property of John Huddleston, & will be sold to satisfy 2 judgments in favor of Patrick Moran. –R T Mills, Constable

Orphan's Court of Wash Co, D C. Letters testamentary on the personal estate of Wm H Stewart, late of said county, dec'd. –Sarah G Stewart, excx

Died: Feb 12, at his residence in Montgomery Co, Md, Henry Chew Gaither, aged 67, one of the oldest & most respectable citizens of the county. He had repeatedly represented his native county in the State Legislature: & a large circle of friends unite with his afflicted widow & son [the present Senator from the county] in mourning the loss of a kind neighbor, a devoted husband, & a most affectionate father.

Died: at her late residence, **Mount Pleasant**, Chas Co, Md, Mrs Mary Sheirburn, wid/o the late Jos Sheirburn, in her 59th year.

Late from Europe: 1-The Lady of Sir Chas Bagot, late Govn'r of Canada, died on Feb 2. 2-The death of the Duchess of Nassau, d/o the Emperor of Russia, is announced by the Wiesbaden correspondent of the Frankfurter Journal under the date of Jan 29.

MON FEB 24, 1845
Senate: 1-Memorial of John S Allen praying that an improved method in the construction of firearms invented by him may be adopted by the U S for the use of the army. 2-Cmte on Commerce: reported a bill for the relief of Elliot Smith & Nathan Farnsworth. 3-Resolved, that the Sec of War transfer to the Senate the report of Gen Roger Jones, Col Mason, & P M Butler, who have recently prosecuted an examination into the causes & extent of the discontents & difficulties among the Cherokee Indians, with the instructions, correspondence, & evidence connected therewith; & also a copy of any correspondence held by said board with the heirs of reps of the Ridges & Boudinots, or any of them. 4-Memorial from John Hall, of Berks Co, Pa, now 83 years of age, one of the surviving crew under Capt John Paul Jones, asking a pension. 5-Cmte on the Library: asked to be discharged from the further consideration of the ptn of Thos N Bryan, & that he have leave to withdraw his papers.

Hse/o Reps: 1-Bill for the relief of J Thockmorton: referred to the Cmte of Claims. 2-Ptn of Jas Little, for remuneration as keeper of the **Congressional Burying Ground**. 3-Ptn of Rees C Jones, of Pa, for the extension of a patent-right. 4-Ptn of Geo W Jackson, of Western Va, praying compensation for extra material put on the Cumberland road. 5-Cmte of the Whole: amendment proposed allowing to Wm L Goggin, of Va, pay & mileage while contesting the election of Thos W Gilmer at the last session of the present Congress. 6-Amendment came up appropriating $9,456 for the payment of the salary & outfit of Henry Ledyard, late Charge d'Affaires in France: House was not divided on the question. 7-Ptn of Edw Howe, jr, & 75 others, in favor of the Senate bill for the reduction of postage. 8-Mr Atkinson moved the following: "For rent of rooms paid A Cowdrey, Clerk of the Easter District of Virginia, for the Federal Court, at Norfolk, $25." Amendment was rejected.

Alex'r Hamilton, from the "Custis Recollections & Private Memoirs of the Life & Character of Washington." Hamilton was the patriot, soldier, statesman, jurist, orator & philosopher, & he was great in all of them. Born in the island of Nevis, the first rudiments of his education were obtained in Santa Cruz, from which, at very early age, he came to America, & completed his studies at Columbia College, in N Y. The Revolution found him engaged in an extensive mercantile concern, where he laid aside his ledger & his pen, ere he drew his sword, for the natural rights of mankind. Capt Hamilton, with his full company of artillery, remained in N Y until the vessel **Asia**, Admiral Pandeput, fired upon the city. Retreat became necessary. At the passage of the Raritan, near Brunswick, Hamilton attracted the notice of the Cmder-in-Chief. Washington ordered Lt Col Fitzgerald, his aid-de-camp, to ascertain the young ofcr, Hamilton, & bid him repair to headquarters at the first halt of the enemy. Lt Col Hamilton was at the side of the Chief during the most eventful periods of the Revolutionary war. Close to Washington, his master, ready for instant service was the stout yet active Billy, the celebrated servant during the whole of the war. Shortly after the surrender of Yorktown, Col Hamilton retired from the army, preserving his rank, but declining all pay or emolument. He studied law & was elected to the N Y Legislature, & then to the old Congress. He was elected a member of the Convention of 1787. Robt Morris declined the appointment of Sec of the Treasury & recommended Alex'r Hamilton. Washington hestitated not a moment in making the appointment of Hamilton as Sec of the Treasury. In 1795 Hamilton resigned his seat in the Cabinet & retired to private life-saying a rising family hath its claims. We close our brief memoir.

The Hon Geo B Eckhard, Judge of the City Court of Charleston, S C, died last Tue, after a short illness, in his 51st year. His kindness of heart endeared him to a large circle of attached friends.

The ship **Coromando**, Capt Hedge, of & for Boston, from Liverpool, Dec 17, was fallen in with at sea on the 11th ult, & the crew of 21 were taken off by the British brig **Brothers**, & carried to Halifax the 8th inst.

On Sat near Norwalk, Conn, Alfred Hyatt, a drunkard, was frozen to death. He was sent home from the groggery to his family, but did not reach there.

Appointments by the Pres, by & with the advice & consent of the Senate:
Saml Nelson, to be Assoc Justice of the Supreme Court of the U S; vice Smith Thompson, dec'd.
Jos Eaches, Bernard Hooe, & Robt Brockett, to the Justices of the Peace in Alexandria Co, D C.
Thos W Herndon, of N C, to be U S Consul for the port of Galveston, Texas; vice Duff Green, resigned.
Washington Reed, of N C, to be U S Consul for the port of Sugua la Grande, in Cuba; vice P J Devine, rejected by the Senate.
Wm P Chandler, of Delaware, to be U S Consul at Puerto Cabello, Venezuela; vice F Litchfield, dec'd.
Receiver of Public Moneys:
Oliver B Hill, at New Orleans; vice Thos Barrett, appointed Collector there.
Elijah H Gordy, at St Stephens, Ala.
Edw F Comegets, at Tuscaloosa, Ala.
Lunsford R Noel, at Danville, Ill.
David E Moore, at Demopolis, Ala.
Matthew Gayle, at Cahaba, Ala.
Register of the Land Ofc:
Arthur Bridgeman, at Fairfield, Iowa; vice Wm Ross, dec'd.
John S Horner, at Green Bay, Wisc.
Robt A Forsyte, at Detroit, Mich.
Wm Dowsing, at Columbus, Miss.
Andrew J Edmunson, at Pontotoc, Miss.
Lewis B McCarty, at Demopolis, Ala.
Thos J Hudson, at Tallahassee, Florida; vice Robt S Hackley, dec'd.
Josiah A Noonan, to be Postmaster at Milwaukie, Wisc.
Robt W Carson, to be Postmaster at Galena, Ill.
Danl B Turner, to be Postmaster at Huntsville, Ala; vice Geo Cox, resigned.

Richmond Enquirer: obit of Mrs Joanna Bouldin, wid/o Maj Wood Bouldin, dec'd, who died on the 15th ult in Charlotte Co, Va, in her 93rd year. She was the sister of John Tyler, formerly Govn'r of Va, who was the father of Pres Tyler, whose aunt, therefore, she was. She was taught music by Bramme; delighted mostly in Scotch music & songs. In painting & drawing she was instructed by the celebrated Gilbert Stewart. She was beloved by all her friends; affectionate to her children, by whom she was almost adored; a kind, gentle, & indulgent mistress. In short, no one perhaps ever lived so long & passed so blameless a life.

Mrd: Feb 20, by Rev Alexander Shiras, Mr Chas Abbot to Miss Sarah A, d/o Dr John Austin, all of Gtwn.

Died: on Feb 19, Mary E, d/o Wm & Rebecca Nevitt, of Fairfax Co, Va, in her 26th year, after lingering in pain for 3 weeks, from a burn occasioned by her clothes catching fire.

Jas Juler, Dead or Alive. Jas Juler, by trade a watch & clockmaker, left England for the U S in the fall of 1815; the first account of him was at Richmond, Va, in the following year. If alive, & he will write to his brother, Mr Geo Juler, North Walsam, Norfolk, Eng, he will hear of something very much to his advantage; if dead, any person giving such particulars of his death as can be legally acted upon shall be most liberally rewarded through any banking house in N Y or elsewhere having connexion with those in England. In a former residence in America to 1815 he took the Christian name of George instead of his real one. Should he be living he is in his 69th year, about 5 feet one or two inches in height. His left leg affected by a scald, when a child, from the knee to the ankle.

A late graduate of Waterville College, Maine, is desirous of obtain a situation as Teacher in some one of the Southern States. A situation in some private family, with a liberal salary, would be preferred. Address N Milton, Wash.

City Ordnance-Washington: 1-That the penalty incurred by Geo Savage, as security for Jacob Penn, be & the same is hereby remitted. Approved, Feb 13, 1845. 2-Chas A Davis & John R Queen were appointed to the Cmte on the part of the Board of the Common Council. Saml Byington & Walter Lenox were appointed on the part of the Board of Aldermen.

TUE FEB 25, 1845

Trustee's sale: by deed of trust from Francis Hill, et al, to me, dated Jan 6, 1843, & recorded in Liber B, #3, page 502, of the records for Alexandria Co, D C: sale in Wash City-Mar 1, that valuable property in said county, adjoining the Little Falls Bridge across the Potomac, now in the occupancy of said Hill. It includes about 15 acs, improved by a large stone mill with ample water power, now used for the manufacture of paper, ample bldgs for the hands employed about the mill, & other useful bldgs. Also, will be included in the sale, machinery, now set up in the bldg. –Clement Cox, Trustee -Robt W Dyer & Co, aucts [Mar 29th newspaper: this same property is advertised again for sale. Richd A Hill, the purchaser, failed to comply with the terms of the sale. Sale is postponed until Sat next.]

Inauguration Ball meeting at Brown's Hotel on Feb 26, at 8 p m. –Chas S Frailey, Sec

Oysters for sale: the schnr **John Anderson**, direct from York river, has just arrived with Oysters of the first quality. Apply to Capt P G Williams, on board, at the steamboat wharf.

Senate: 1-Memorial of Alex'r Vattemare: referred to the Cmte on the Library. 2-Cmte on Pensions: reported an act for the relief of Saml Neely: passed. 3-Cmte on Pensions: unfavorable report in the case of the heirs of Martha Hough; of Moses White; of Stephen Snow, in the case of Jos M Rhea; of Lucy Ann Roberts; of Wm Cannan; & of John Hall. Same cmte: unfavorable reports on the House bills for the relief of Justin Jacobs; & on the House bill for the relief of Jos Craignilas, of Tenn. 4-Cmte on Patents: bill for the relief of Uri Emmons.

The Hon Henry W Dwight, of Berkshire, Mass, [which district he represented in Congress for 2 or 3 terms about 20 years ago,] died suddenly on Fri at the Franklin House, N Y C, on his return from a visit to Washington, from congestion of the brain & bowels.

For sale or rent: handsomely finished house on H st, between 9th & 10th sts, in the neighborhood of the Patent & Post Ofc bldgs. For particulars, apply to Mr Duncanson, Post Ofc bldg.

The U S ship **Princeton**, Capt Stockton, put ot sea from N Y on Fri last.

Mrd: on Feb 20, at Mount Independence, Fauquier Co, Va, by Rev Mr Dodge, Mr Saml T Ashby, of Wash, to Miss Martha T, d/o Capt Andrew Chunn.

Died: on Feb 8, at her father's residence in Columbia, S C, Miss Sally Campbell Preston, only child of the Hon Wm C Preston. [See Feb 17th newspaper.]

Fine farm for sale in Montg Co, Md: containing 372 acs, with commodious & comfortable dwlg, & all necessary out-bldgs. Apply to John F Callan, Wash.

WED FEB 26, 1845
A Centenarian-A Whig of '76. John Adams, of Harford township, in this county, has just completed his 100th year on the 2nd of this month, or, as he counts it, Jan 22 old style. He followed his sons into this State some years since, from Ashburnham, Worcester Co, Mass, which, if we mistake not, was his native place, being extensively connected with the Adamses of that part of New England, & we believe a distant relative of the 2 Ex-Presidents of that name. The true patriotic blood of the Revolution flows in his veins; he volunteered his services, on several occasions, even when the most imminent danger threatened, & even took the pains to send his hired man in his place when the health of his family required his presence at home. He never served long enough at any one time himself to answer the requirements of the existing pension laws, it is believed that a man of his remarkable age & early patriotism ought to be entitled to a liberal pension from his country by a special act of Congress, at least since he has attained the age of 100 years. He works at his trade, shoemaking, with persevering industry even to this very winter. –Susquehannah [Pa] Reg

On Fri last John Gordon was executed in the State prison year at Providence, R I, convicted of being a participator in the murder of Amasa Sprague.

A day or two ago "an oak tree was cut down at a short distance from Harrisburg, [& near an old Revolutionary relic known as ***Paxon's Church***,] which, upon counting the growths, proved to be near 400 years old, & perfectly embedded in it, at a height of nearly 30 feet from the ground, was found a well-shaped stone motar & pestle, & an instrument resembling our axe, though much smaller in size. They are very hard flinty stone, & in their finish exhibit much skill. –Phil Enquirer

Wash Corp: 1-Ptn of John Donovan, praying remission of a fine: referred to the Cmte of Claims.

Letter, translated from the German, contains some interesting particulars respecting a branch of the Washington family. The letter from Gen Washingto, to which the writer alludes, may be seen in Sparks' Washington, vol xi page 393; & other particulars in vol i page 554. Jas Washington is there mentioned as having been a merchant in Rotterdam: Munich, Feb 21, 1844. The family of Washington is descended from a good old English family, which, in early times, owned considerable possessions in the counties of York & Northampton, & other places. It became connected, by marriage, with the family of Shirley, Earl Ferrers. Sir Lawrence Washington married Eliz, a d/o the 2nd Earl Ferrers. It was also connected with that of Villiers, Duke of Buckingham. A branch of the family, from unknown causes, for they were wealthy, emigrated about 1650 to America; & the well known Gen & Pres Geo Washington was descended from it. My great grandfather, Jas Washington, was so deeply implicated in the unfortunate affair of the Duke of Monmouth, at the time of Chas II, 1683 & 1684, that he was obliged to fly from England, &, after losing by shipwreck on the coast of Portugal every thing of his personal property, that he had been able to carry away from England, he came to Holland. He became the founder of that branch, which then began to flourish in Holland, & is still in existence in the persons of 2 individuals, cousins, lts in the army & navy. I possess an autograph letter of Geo Washington, from ***Mount Vernon***, dated Jan 20, 1799, in which Washington states that his ancestors came to America nearly 150 years ago. I have 3 sons, the eldest, Ludwig, 16, is a page of his Majesty the King; the 2nd, Max, 14, is pupil in the Royal Corps of Cadets; & the 3rd, Karl, 10, frequents the public school. By my 2 marriages with dghts of families of the highest nobility in the land, my children are in agreeable circumstances, even when I shall be no more. I remain, your devoted, Baron Von Washington, Royal Bavarian Chamberlain, Lt Gen & Aid-de-Camp to his Majesty the King, Cmder of the Civil Merit of the Bavarian crown, of the Greek Order of the Saviour, of the British Military Order of the Bath, Knight of the Royal French Order of the Legion of Honor, & Lord of Notzing. To De J G Fluzel, Consul of the U S of N America in Leipzic.

Columbia [S C] Chronicle: Rev Ferdinand Jacobs, his wife, child, & nurse, all died on Jan 21 of pneumonia, at Yorkville, in that State. Mr Jacobs was Pastor of the Presbyterian Church & Principal of the Female Academy of that village. [Feb 28 newspaper: This is a mistake, as far as the Rev Mr Jacobs himself is concerned, it is believed. Letters from him have been received here since the date mentioned above. He mentions in those letters the death of his wife & child. Mr Jacobs is a native of this place, & a son of our old friend & fellow-citizen, Mr Presley Jacobs. His former schoolmates retain a lively recollection of him in by-gone days. –Alexandria Gaz]

Hartford [Conn] Times. The friends of Gen Saml L Pitkin, of East Hartford, became alarmed at his absence on Jan 18. He left his house to visit his powder mills, on the Hockanum river, in Scotland society, in that town. The result of a search was in finding his corpse in the Hockanum river. His throat was cut sufficiently to deprive him of life.

Gonsalvo Aldama, aged about 35 years, committed suicide at N Y on Mon, by throwing himself from the roof of a 3 story house in Barclay st, whilst in a state of unsound mind. He was a native of Spain.

Senate: 1-Bills passed: relief of Walker, Kinckle & Co. Also, relief of John Adams & John Adams, jr. 2-Bill for the relief of W D Cheever was ordered to be engrossed.

I hereby forewarn all persons against trading for or receiving a note drawn by me, some 5 months ago, for $50, in favor of Alex'r Johnson. The note was drawn conditionally, & the conditions not being complied with, & not having received value therefore, I protest against paying the same. –Nath Brady [I certify to the truth of the above facts as stated. –Zadock Williams.]

Gtwn Municipal election: election on Mon last for Mayor:
Henry Addison- 228
John Cox-155
John Kurtz-43
John Cox has held the ofc of Mayor for the long period of 24 years, & retires with the good wishes & respect of the citizens of Gtwn generally. Jos Libbey was elected Alderman last Mon to supply a vacancy. The following were elected members of the Board of common Council:

Levin Jones	Jeremiah Orme	O M Linthicum	E S Wright
Chas E Mix	Robt Ould	Wm R Ridgely	Wm H Edes
John Dickson	John H King	Robt White	

The Olympic Saloon, under the management of Mrs Timms, will re-open this evening, after a temporary suspension.

House & lot in Carroll's Row at auction: part of lot 12 in square 729, at A st south 1st st. –R C Weightman, Surviving Trustee -Robt W Dyer & Co, aucts [Sale Mar 19 next.]

Hse/o Reps: 1-Bill to extend the patent heretofore granted to Wm Woodworth: referred to the Cmte on Patents. 2-Bill for the relief of Noah Miller, of the State of Maine: referred to the Cmte on Commerce. 3-Ptn of Lewis Mann & others, citizens of Potter Co, Pa, praying the immediate adoption of a uniform & cheap system of postage. 4-Ptn of Thos Hambleton & 28 citizens of Pa, praying Congress to make the coastwise slave trade as penal as African slave trade. 5-Ptn of Caleb W Pain & 22 other citizens of Pa, against the annexation of Texas. Also, for the abolition of slavery in the District of Columbia.

Wash Corp: 1-Ptn from J D Marr & others: referred to the Cmte on Improvements. 2-Ptn from H Cruttenden & 537 others, for the establishment of a market at the open space formed by the junction of N Y & Mass aves with K st north: referred to the Cmte on Improvements. 3-Cmte on the Canal, asked to be discharged from the further consideration of the ptn of E Simms & others, asking that the privilege may be granted to Geo McDuell to erect scales at the corner of 14th & E sts for weighing coal, & hay, etc; & they were discharged accordingly. 4-Act for the relief of O J Prather: passed. 5-Cmte of Claims: Act for the relief of John H Eberbach: read twice. 6-Cmte of Claims: bill for the relief of R C Washington & others: reported the same without amendment.

The undersigned have this day formed a copartnership, under the style of Emack & Weinhagen, for transacting the English, French, German, & Fancy Importing business, in all its varieties, as heretofore conducted by Geo Weinhagen, at 330 Balt st, Balt, Md. –Wm Emack, Geo Weinhagen, Feb 19, 1845.

THU FEB 27, 1845
Copartnership notice: Wm Egan has this day associated with him his son, Henry Egan, & will continue the Dry Goods & Clothing business, at the old stand, under the name of Wm Egan & Son. Wash, Feb 25, '45.

Heidsieck Champagne: just arrived per schnr **Dodge**, & for sale. –Julius A Peters' Wine Store.

Senate: 1-Bill for the relief of W D Cheeves, which had been ordered to be engrossed, was passed. 2-Bill for the relief of Walker, Kinkle, Caruthers & Co, was taken up for consideration. 3-Cmte on the Library were discharged from the further consideration of the ptns of David Haas & Alex'r Vattemare. 4-Cmte on Naval Affairs to inquire into printing the Astronomical & Maguetie observations made by Lt Gillis under the instruction of the Navy Dept of Aug 13, 1838.

Merchants' Shot Tower Co of Balt: Eutaw st, Balt, Md, an assortment of Drop Shot of all sizes. -Thos J Clare, Sec

Merchants' Shot Tower Co of Balt: Eutaw st, Balt, Md, an assortment of Drop Shot of all sizes. -Thos J Clare, Sec

Hse/o Reps: 1-Mr Rathbun moved to reconsider the vote of yesterday directing the report of the Cmte on Public Expenditures on the case of Lt McLaughlin to be printed, & the motion to reconsider was laid over for the present.

Died: on Jan 17, at Norwich, Vt, Capt Alden Partridge, aged 71 years. He was for many years an ofcr of the army, & was for several years Superintendent of the Military Academy. After retiring from the army he founded an institution in which military & civil education were combined, which for some time was prosperous, & afterwards reopened a similar institution at Norwich, Vt, where he died. [Mar 1st newspaper: correction-Capt Alden Partridge is still living.]

Died: on Feb 18, at his residence, West River, Md, Mr Nathl Chew, aged 56, after a protracted illness, leaving a large circle of relatives & friends to regret his demise. He was a most estimable man.

Died: on Feb 20, at **Chestnut Hill**, the late residence of her father, John H Wood, Rappahannock Co, Va, Ann C Miller, w/o Middleton Miller, in her 18th year. The dec'd has left a disconsolate husband & a large number of relatives & friends to mourn over an irreparable loss. Blessed are the dead that die in the Lord.

Beef, Beef, Fine Beef! At his stalls in the Centre Market on Mar 1. -P Crowley

The Hon Kenneth Rayner positively declines being a candidate for re-election as a Rep in Congress from the State of N C.

Wilmington [Delaware] Journal announces the death of the Hon Arnold S Naudain, of that State; age was 67 years. It was but a few days ago that he was a visitor to this city, & was seen in the Senate chamber in apparently full & vigorous health. [Mar 1st newspaper: correction-Dr Arnold Naudain is still living.]

For rent: 2 story dwlg-house, on 6th st, between G & H sts. Inquire next door of M Faherty.

Orphan's Court of Wash Co, D C. Letters of administration, with the will annexed, on the personal estate of John Emmerick, late of said county, dec'd. -Saml Wroe, adm, with will annexed.

FRI FEB 28, 1845
Mrd: on Tue, by Rev John C Smith, Mr Wm A Waugh to Miss Juliana P Hoover, both of Gtwn.

Hse/o Reps: 1-Cmte of Ways & Means: reported a bill for the relief of Saml K George: committed. 2-Cmte on Private Land Claims: adverse report on the case of Robt Graham: laid on the table. Same cmte: adverse report on the case of Wm Pumphrey, of Louisiana: laid on the table. Same cmte: was referred the bill from the Senate, to authorize the relocation of certain land warrants granted to Gen Lafayette, reported the same without amendment: bill was passed. Same cmte: reported adversely on the memorial of Martha Porch: laid on the table. Same cmte: reported adversely on the memorial of John Davis Acerman: laid on the table. 3-Cmte on Indian Affairs: adverse report on the case of Israel Johnson: laid on the table. 4-Cmte on Military Affairs: bill from the Senate for the relief of Mary A E Zantzinger, wid/o Maj Richd A Zantzinger, dec'd, reported the same without amendment, & recommended that it do not pass: bill laid on the table. 5-Cmte on Naval Affairs: bill for the relief of Thos Brownell: committed. Same cmte: joint resolution for the relief of Rodman M Price, purser of the U S steam frig **Missouri**: read a 3rd time. Purser is characterized as one of great merit & hardship. 6-Cmte on Military Affairs: reported a joint resolution for the burial of the martyrs of the prison ships of the Revolutionary war, at the Wallabout, in N Y, which was read & committed. 7-Cmte on Naval Affairs: adverse reports on the cases of Isaac Bigelow, Jas Davis, & of citizens of Jefferson Co, N Y, for a bulkhead at Sackett's Harbor: laid on the table. 8-Cmte on Foreign Affairs: bill for the relief of John K Cook: committed. 9-Cmte on Revolutionary Pensions: a resolution granting leave to Jacob Addison to withdraw his pensions papers: which was agreed to. 10-Cmte on Foreign Affairs: reported that Peter Von Schmidt have leave to withdraw his memorial: which was agreed to. 11-Cmte of Claims: bill for the relief of the heirs of Jos Gerard: committed. Same cmte: bill for the relief of Saml Perry: committed. 12-Cmte on Invalid Pensions: bill for the relief of the heirs of Wm Evans: committed. Same cmte: adverse reports on the cases of Adams Payne, John Nappertandy, Andrew McDowell, Wm B Adams, Jonas D Platt, Chas Walworth, Benj Dwinell, Jas Wilson, & Aaron Wilson: laid on the table. 13-Cmte on Invalid Pensions: was discharged from the ptn of Elisha E Holmes: laid on the table. 14-Cmte on Patents: bill from the Senate to extend the patent heretofore granted to Wm Woodworth: reported the same without amendment. 15-Cmte on the Library: requested to be discharged from the ptns of Levi Durand & Edw Stiff, & from the resolution in relation to a proposed purchase of the Journals of the several State Legislatures. 16-Cmte on Revolutionary Claims: bill for the relief of the legal reps of Jas Bell, dec'd, reported the same without amendment: committed. Same cmte: bill for the relief of Benj J Porter: committed. Same cmte: bill for the relief of the legal reps of Christian Orendorff: committed. Same cmte: bill for the relief of the heirs & legal reps of Francis Sumter, dec'd: committed. Same cmte: adverse report on the case of Richd M Livingston: laid on the table. 17-Cmte on Public Expenditures: report on behalf of the minority of that cmte in the case of Lt John T McLaughlin, of the U S Navy: laid on the table. 18-Cmte on Engraving: resolved, that 5,000 copies of D D Owens' survey of the mineral lands in Iowa, Wisconsin, & Northern Ill, with illustrations, be published for the use of this House. 19-Ptn of Fred'k A Tupper, praying remuneration for services, not provided for by law, as U S weigher & gauger at Savannah, Ga.

The Hon Waddy Thompson, sen, departed this life at his residence, near Greenville, S C, on Feb 9, at an advanced age. He had been in feeble state of health for some weeks. –Mountaineer

At a late term of the Court in Chenango Co, N Y, Harriet Graves recovered $1,500 damages of a faithless swain, named Geo W Willis. He had paid his attentions to her for 4 years, when he departed. Multitudes of promises were proved. Both parties are said to be highly respectable.

Mrd: on Tue, by Rev John C Smith, Mr Wm A Waugh to Miss Juliana P Hoover, both of Gtwn.

Died: on Sep 4 last, at Tahiti, Society Islands, Saml R Blackler, U S Consul at those Islands, a native of Marblehead, Mass.

Died: on Feb 20, near **Mount Vernon**, Vt, old Saml Anderson, aged about 100 years, one of the former servants of Gen Washington, & liberated by that great man in his will. Old Samuel was a native African, had been tattooed in his youth, & bore the marks to the day of his death.

$200 reward: for the apprehension & delivery to me in person of my 3 negro men, Danl, from 40 to 45 years of age: formerly belonged to the estate of the late Robt Davis, near Charlotte Hall, St Mary's Co. He left in Sep, 1844. Edw, about 25. I purchased this fellow of the estate of the late Lyttleton T Adams. He left Feb 25. Sewall, about 32, left in Jan last. –John D Bowling, Aquasco, PG Co, Md

Brown's Portrait Gallery: W Fischer has just received a few copies of Brown's splendid Portrait Gallery of the following distinguished American citizens, with biographical sketches & fac similes of original letters.

Judge Marshall	Thos Cooper	Martin Van Buren
R Channing Moore	Wm White	Henry Clay
John Forsyth	N P Tallmadge	Thos H Benton
John C Calhoun	Dixon H Lewis	Levi Woodbury
Richd M Johnson	John Q Adams	Danl Webster
Gen Alex Macomb	Andrew Jackson	Silas Wright
Saml L Southard	Wm H Harrison	Felix Grundy
Henry A Wise	De Witt Clinton	John Randolph
John Tyler	Joel R Poinsett	

Texan lands for sale: 1,476 acs; 1,280 acs; 640 acs. All on the river Nueces, entered in the Land Ofc by the Hon A Jones. For further information apply to Saml Rose, Gtwn.

For rent: the store recently occupied by the subscriber, as a Boot & Shoe Store, on Pa ave, between 9th & 10th sts. Inquire of Malcolm Douglass, of the firm of Moore & Douglass, on the opposite side of the street, or of the subscriber, corner of 9th & H sts, fronting the Mall. –Wm Douglass

Senate: 1-Senate considered the bill for the relief of Wm Henson: passed. 2-Cmte on Naval Affairs: joint resolution for the relief of Lt J M Gilliss, of the U S Navy.

SAT MAR 1, 1845
Inauguration Dinner & Ball: on Mar 4, in his splendid Saloon at the Assembly Rooms. German band has been engaged. Tickets $1-to be had of Messrs Gilman, Patterson, & Fischer, Wash; at Mr Linthicum's, Gtwn; Mr Appich, in Alexandria; & at the door of the Saloon. –C Lapon

Subscriber offers at private sale, that beautiful & magnificent estate called **Rose Hill Farm**, located in Fred'k Co, Md, about 1 mile north of Frederick City. This farm contains 213½ acs. The Mansion-house, a fine Overseer's house, a large barn, stables, corn-house, spring-house, smoke-house, bath-house, ice-house, & all other conveniences desirable on such a farm. The Mansion-house is a 2 story brick bldg, 60 feet by 20 feet, with a 2 story portico in front & in the rear. This farm is bounded on the north by Mr Buck's farm. –Geo Slater, Lexington st, Balt.

An undivided moiety of **Cabin John Mill**, in Montg Co, Md, for sale. By deed of trust, executed by the late Andrew Way & others, on Aug 12, 1829: sale on Apr 2, of that tract of land, 33½ acres & the mill seat thereon, known as Cabin John Mills, with all the bldg & improvements thereon. –Rd Smith, Trustee

For rent or sale: 2 convenient houses on Mass ave, between 4th & 5th sts. –Chas Hibbs

Orphan's Court of Wash Co, D C. Letters of adm on the personal estate of Jane Bell, late of said county, dec'd. -U Ward, adm

Wm Keefe has taken the shop formerly occupied by Vernon & Bridget as a coachmaker's shop, on 18th st, between Pa ave & G st west.

Providence Journal: the Hon Asher Robbins died at Newport on Sun last, at the age of 88. He was a most distinguished citizen of Rhode Island: for 14 years the rep of his State in the Senate of the U S.

The Hon Patrick G Goode, one of the Reps from Ohio in the last & preceding Congresses, has been appointed President Judge of the 16th Judicial District of the State, by the Legislature of the State of Ohio on Feb 24.

Died: yesterday, Dr Phineas Bradley, in his 76th year, for many years eminently known throughout the country as Assist Postmaster Genr'l. His funeral will take place tomorrow, from the residence of the Rev L J Gilliss, on N Y ave, & his remains will be deposited at the burying-ground of **Rock Creek Church**.

Died: on the 25th ult, Wm Rosemond, only child of Jas R & Mary Glasgood, aged 18 months & 25 days.

The Martinsburg [Va] Gaz, conducted for the last 16 years by that Whig, Edmund P Hunter, has been transferred by him to Jas Erskine Stewart.

MON MAR 3, 1845
Senate: 1-Ptn of John Manning, for indemnity for French spoliations prior to 1800. 2-Cmte on Pensions: Bill for the relief of Geo Wentling. 3-Bill to enable the Chickasaw Nation to try the validity of their claims in the Courts of the U S being on its passage. There were between 2,000 & 3,000 claims of the Chickasaw Indians unsettled. Bill was passed: yeas-18, nays-15. 4-Amendment proposed providing for the payment of $1,450 to Arthur Middleton, jr, for diplomatic services in Spain: which was agreed to. 5-Cmte on Pensions: recommendation that they do not pass: relief of Richd Elliott; relief of Eliz Fitch; relief of Elijah Blodget. Also, favorably, without amendment, an act for the relief of Isaac Allen. 6-Cmte on Revolutionary Claims: were discharged from the further consideration of the bill for the relief of the exec of Robt Wilmot. 7-Cmte on Pensions: unfavorable reports on the ptn of Hezekiah Hamlet, Mary Ann O'Brien, Smith Crain, Mary Blakesle, & Benj Allen: ordered to be printed. 8-Sec of War to communicate to the Senate Brvt Capt Fremont's report of his late expedition to Oregon in 1843 & 1844, with the report of his expedition to the Rocky Mountains in 1842. 9-Sec of War to transmit to the Senate the report made by John Stockton, superintendent of the mineral lands on Lake Superior, with the map accompanying the same. 10-Resolved, That there be paid out to each of the messengers of the Senate, the same per diem as is now allowed to Robt P Anderson, commencing with the present session. 11-Bill for the relief of Wm Henson: referred to the Cmte on Indian Affairs. 12-Bill for the relief of Reuben Gentry, Wm Head, & others: referred to the Cmte on Indian Affairs. 13-Bill for the relief of the legal reps of Wm D Cheever, dec'd: referred to the Cmte of Claims. 14-Bill for the relief of John P Skinner, legal reps of Isaac Green: referred to the Cmte on the Judiciary. 15-Bill for the relief of Robt Purkis: referred to the Cmte of Claims. 16-Bill for the relief of John R Bryan, adm of Isaac Garretson, late purser: referred to the Cmte on Naval Affairs. 17-Joint resolution for the relief of Putney & Riddle was referred to the Cmte of the Whole House. 18-Joint resolution from the Senate for the relief of Mary W Thompson, wid/o Col Thompson, who was killed in Florida, was ordered to a 3rd reading. 19-Cmte of Ways & Means: moved an amendment to provide for the settlement of the accounts of Col H Whiting: agreed to.

Stop the Thief! Jas A Carter entered the Intelligencer Ofc, Petersburg, Va, on Feb 28, & took a black broadcloth dress coat, not much worn, 2 pair of cassimere pantaloons, a new black satin vest, & several articles, belong to us & others. He is very well grown for his age, 19, as he says, well made, & has a full head of red hair; is fond of liquor. $10 reward for his apprehension & recovery of the property. –P B Whitlock, Wm D Faucett

On Wed a pickpocket attempted to steal from Mr Sheldon Basset, of Penningham, Conn, his pocket-book while he was walking along Pearl st, N Y. Mr Basset felt the fellow's fingers at his coat, & finding his wallet gone, accused the man near him of the theft. Mr Basset's pocket-book dropped from the man's vest. He was taken to the police ofc, where he was recognised as Chas Davis, an accomplished member of the light-fingered fraternity.

Died: on Feb 28, at the residence of his father, in the city of Phil, John Biddle Chapman, aged 34 years, the eldest s/o Dr N Chapman.

Mr Chouteau returned last evening on the steamer **Omega**, with Mr Moses Russell, the man who, several days ago, under the name of John Taylor, swindled him out of about $2,500, by getting him to sell 80,000 lbs of lead on a forged certificate. Russell has been heretofore a respectable farmer, owning a farm near Jackson, Capt Girardeau Co, in this State, & has a wife & family. –St Louis Republican, Feb 16

Presidential Inauguration:
Aids to Chief Marshal.
Gen Wm F Sanderson, of Ohio
Col Jas C Zabriskie, of N J
Maj A T Hillyer, of N Y
Assist Marshals:
Hon Jas G Clinton, of N Y
Hon Richd Brodhead, of Pa
Gen Jas H Carson, of Va
Lund Washington, jr, of D C
–John M McCalla, Chief Marshal

Cmte of Arrangements of the Senate:
Levi Woodbury   Sidney Breese   Walter T Colquitt

Appointed Deputies of the Marshal of D C to act on the occasion of the Inauguration of the Pres:
Maj T P Andrews   Maj G W Cambloss   Maj Hiess
Maj A A Nicholson   Maj J N Barker   Jas Hoban
Chas S Wallach   Dr J B Blake   John Branch
P Barton Key   Turner Dixon   Henry B Tyler
H H Dent   Mr Torbut
John W Minor   Dr Lacey

One cent reward for runaway, an indented apprentice to the Cabinet-making business by the name of Gabriel Langley, about 20 years of age, small in stature. –Leonard O Cook

For rent: dwlg-house on Louisiana ave, nearly opposite the Unitarian church, & now occupied by the subscriber. Possession to be given on Apr 1 next. Apply on the premises-P R Fendall.

Copy of Certificate. Charleston, Feb 24, 1825. We, the undersigned, were this day present at a public trial by fire, of one of Scott's Patent Asbestos Chests in the Citadel square, & are convinced that his chests are fire-proof.

A Ottolengui	Saml P Matthews	Wm Libby
Chas P L Westendorff	Chas Clarke	G W Backus-Feb 25

[The patentee, John Scott, thankful for past favors. Address to Balt, instead of Phil, where he formerly resided. –John Scott, Calvert st, near Barnum's Hotel, Balt.]

Meeting of the Nat'l Blues this evening at half past 7 o'clock. M P Mohun, Sec

Nat'l Blues ordered to parade tomorrow, Mar 4, at 8 o'clock precisely. Full winter uniform, knapsacks, & pompoms. By order of the Capt. –Geo Emmerich, 1st Sgt

Wash Light Infty meeting this evening at 7½ o'clock. –Jos B Tate, Sec

On Fri last a marine named Palmer, & a boy named Evans, also belonging to the U S service, were drowned in the Eastern Branch, somewhere between the Anacostia & Beale's bridges. It appears that there were 4 persons in a skiff, which was upset. Palmer had gone to assist Evans, & both drowned.

TUE MAR 4, 1845

Laws of the U S, passed at the 2nd Session of the 28th Congress. 1-Act for the relief of Peter Von Schmidt: to be paid $300, for his translation of a pamphlet on the culture & preparation of hemp, published at Odessa, in Russia.

For sale: my entire stock of blooded Horses, about 20 in number. I also wish to dispose of Register as a stallion, who broke down in his last Fall training. –Francis Thompson, at Brown's Hotel

Fatal Duel. An affair of honor came off near the Hampton Course, at Augusta, Ga, on Feb 20, between Maj John Partlow, of Abbeville District, & John G Burton, of Newberry District, S C. Mr Burton fell fatally wounded at the first fire, & died 10 hours later at the Hubbard's Hotel, Hamburgh. Both of these gentlemen had married each other's sisters, & the difficulty is said to have originated in private affairs. A relative of Mr Burton, [Lt Goggins, of the U S Army,] fell in a similar rencontre years ago. -Carolinian

Gen Jas W Wilkin died at Goshen, N Y, Feb 23rd, in the 83rd year of his age. He was a Member of the Legislature in 1800, & voted for Jefferson Electors, & voted for Madison Electors in 1812. He was a sterling Whig, & the father of Saml J Wilkin, the late Whig candidate for Lt Govn'r.

Lt Robbins, of the Marine Corps, destroyed himself on Fri at the Naval Hospital, N Y. He was much distressed by the death of his father, the Hon Asher Robbins, & was quite ill at the City Hall; thence he was removed, evidently in a deranged state of mind, to the Naval Hospital.

Mrd: on Mar 2, by Rev Septimus Tuston, Mr Jos W Sandford to Miss Lucy Ann Thompson, both of Va.

Died: on Feb 15, in Williamsburg, Marian, the only child of Prof Chas Minnigerode, of Wm & Mary College, aged 11 months & 10 days.

Mrd: on Mar 2, in Balt, by Rev Josiah Verden, Mr John Varden Shields, of Wash, to Anna M Lee, of Talbot Co, Md, formerly of Balt.

Senate: 1-Cmte on the Public Lands: reported unfavorably for the passage of the following bills from the House: relief of John Hollingsworth; & relief of John Boyd. 2-Bill for the relief of Sandy Hill was passed.

Inauguration of the President Elect, on Mar 4, 1845.

WED MAR 5, 1845
Wm Riggin died Mon at his residence in Fayette st, Balt, at an advanced age. He long since retired from business, upon an ample fortune, & has always been highly esteemed for his sterling integrity. -Patriot

From the Madisonian of Monday. Floyd Waggaman will leave the city this afternoon to deliver to Maj Donelson, temporarily at Nashville, the Joint Resolution for the admission of Texas into the Union, which was signed by the Pres of the U S on Sat. Should it be found that our Charge has left Nashville, the bearer of dispatches has been directed to proceed immediately himself to Texas.

Savannah, Feb 28. A boat belonging to the British ship **St Martins**, in coming up to the city yesterday, when opposite Fig Island, struck a snag & immediately sunk. Capt Vaughan, of the **St Martins**, & Capt Duckett, of the British ship **Elizabeth**, were rescued. Two men drowned: Thos Dillon & another.

Inauguration at the Capitol, Mar 4, 1845. Jas K Polk, President of the U S: the Hon Geo M Dallas, Vice Pres of the U S, on taking the Oath of Ofc. Volunteer companies in front of the procession were:
Fairfax Cavalry, Capt Wilcockson
Potomac Dragoons, Lt Bomford
Independent Blues, of Balt, Capt Watson
Savage Factory Guards, Capt Williams
Wash Light Infty, Lt McKean
Nat'l Blues, Capt Tucker
Independent Grays, of Gtwn, Lt Pickrell
Union Guards, Capt Cathcart
Mechanical Riflemen, Capt McClelland
United Riflemen, of Gtwn, Capt Duvall
Columbia Riflemen, of Alexandria, Capt Coast
The military was under the command of Capt Mason, of the Potomac Dragoons. Procession was formed under the direction of Chief Marshal McCalla & his aids. The Pres elect left Coleman's Hotel, for the march to the Capitol, arriving about 12 noon. Various distinguished functionaries, judicial, civil, & military followed.
The marine band played national & appropriate music.
The Professors & Students of Gtwn College, closed the line of the procession.

Mr Robt Haley, of Wolfborough, N H, whilst passing in a sleigh across the railroad near Great Fall, was so badly injured by coming in contact with a train of cars that he survived only a few hours. He was a man not far from 70 years of age. A sister who was in the sleigh with him escaped uninjured.

Obit-died: on Feb 25, at Columbian College, D C, Mr Thos Joiner, late of Southampton Co, Va. Only one week previous to his death he came to the college to commence his studies. He complained of being unwell, from a cold taken on his way, & the next day took to his room, from which he never went out until he was carried to his grave. His disease was erysipelas. After suitable religious ceremonies, his body was borne in solemn procession by faculty, students & citizens, to the grave, in the college burying ground.

$5 reward for a small pocket-book wallet containing valuable papers. Leave or send to Mr D C Whitehill, 12th st, between E & F sts, for the above reward.

THU MAR 6, 1845
Julius A Fay's Boarding School for Boys will be opened on the first Mon of May next, at the beautiful country seat known by the name of *"**The Chateau**,"* about half a mile west of Elizabethtown, N J. Mr Fay graduated at Williams College in 1833.

Hse/o Reps: 1-Cmte on Public Expenditures: in the case of Lt John T McLaughlin while in command of the naval forces in the late Indian war in Florida. These expenditures were declared by the speakers to be extravagant beyond all precedent, & illegal. Ordered to lie on the table. 2-Mr E Joy Morris moved that the House resolve itself in Comte of the Whole, to consider the bill for the relief of the heirs of Robt Fulton, dec'd: 65 in favor & 63 against. This was the last heard of the Fulton claim. 3-Ptn of Jos Morril & 47 others, citizens of Dover, N H, that the "area of freedom" may be enlarged upon its Northern as well as Southern boundary by the annexation of the 2 Canadas to the Union. 4-Ptn of John T Williamson & Ellen P Bryan, for the passage of an act authorizing them to enter a quarter section of land in Arkansas.

Acts passed at the session of Congress that has just closed.
Acts for relief of:

Mark Simpson	Wm Rich
Jas Ritchie	Isaac Alden
J McFarlane	Harvey & Slagg
Jos Simmons	Legal reps of Alex'r Mitchell
Gideon Batchelder & others	John H McIntosh
Asabel Brainerd	Stanley White
Peter Von Schmidt	Saml Neely
March Farmington	Benj S Roberts
Thos Bronaugh	Dunning R McNair
Jos Ramsey	Philip Schwartztrawber, of Ohio
Danl Thomas	Walter, Kinkle, & Caruthers
Edw A Lambert	John Adams & John Adams, jr

Elisha Morrell, adm of Jos Icard, dec'd
Mrs Mary W Thompson, wid/o Lt Col A R Thompson
Pension to:

Jas Duffey	John E Wright
Geo Whitten	

Relocation of land warrants 3, 4, & 5, granted by Congress to Gen Lafayette.
Extend patent heretofore granted to Wm Woodworth.
Act authorizing an allowance to Purser D M F Thornton, in settlement of his accounts.
Resolution directing an examination of Putnam's ploughing & dredging machine.
Joint resolution for the benefit of Frances Slocum & others, of the Miami tribe of Indians.

The New Cabinet:

Sec of State, Jas Buchanan	Atty Gen, John Y Mason
Sec of the Treas: Robt J Walker	Postmaster Gen, Cave Johnson
Sec of War, Wm L Marcy	

Geo Bancroft was nominated by the Senate, in connexion with the above, to be Sec of the Navy, but that nomination was laid over by the Senate until today.

The Whig candidates for Congress in Connecticut, to be supported at the Apr election, are Jas Dixon, for Hartford & Toland district; Saml D Hubbard, for Middlesex & New Haven; John A Rockwell, for New London & Windham; & Trumen Smith, for Litchfield & Fairfield.

Destructive fire last night in Wash City: consumed the National Theatre, besides some 7 or 8 dwlg-houses on the s e corner of the same square, fronting on Pa ave & 13th st. It was lately purchased from the company who erected it by Mr Benj Ogle Tayloe, of Wash City. Our fellow citizens, Mr Chas J Nourse & Mr Louis Vivans were among the sufferers. [Mar 7th newspaper: it was Michl Nourse, not Chas J Nourse.]

Mrd: on Feb 19, in **Mount Vernon**, Ohio, John G Plimpton, firm of Tweedy, Jennings & Co, N Y, to Eliz S, d/o H B Curtis.

Died: on Mar 4, Wm Simmons, of Wash City. His funeral is this afternoon, at 3½ o'clock, from his late residence on I st, between 10th & 11th sts.

Leonard O Cook, Cabinet-maker & Undertaker, corner of 7th & B sts, near the Canal Bridge. [Ad]

FRI MAR 7, 1845

At New Orleans, on Feb 25, a quarrel took place at a Coffee-House, between Mr Trepagnier & Mr Bruneau, which resulted in the death of Mr Trepagnier.

Obit-died: on Feb 28, Dr *Phinehas Bradley; born in Litchfield, Conn, on Jul 17, 1769; commenced the practice of medicine at Painted Post, N Y; about 1800 he received an ofc in the Gen Post Ofc Dept, & subsequently was appointed 2nd Assist Postmaster Gen, which ofc he held until Sep, 1829. As husband, a father, a friend, a citizen, his name will be as ointment poured forth. The last few months of his life were blessed by the removal to the city of his only surviving dght, w/o the Rev L J Gilliss, who was recently called as Rector of the Church of the Ascension. The wife of his bosom & his children were there, bound in life by friendship, affection, & blood. [Mar 1st newspaper: *Phineas.]

Mrd: on Feb 20, at New Orleans, by Rev Dr Wheaton, Wm D Bugbee, formerly of Wash, to Miss Mary E, d/o Judge Dickinson, of Arkansas.

Died: yesterday, after a long & painful illness, of consumption, Mrs Mary Ann Smull, w/o Mr Jas T Smull, & only d/o Mr Benj Kinsley, aged 23 years. Her funeral will take place on Sun next, at 2 o'clock, at her father's residence at the Navy Yard.

Died: on Mar 2, at Phil, in her 81st year, Mrs Hannah McKean, relict of the late Hon Jos B McKean.

Died: on Mar 4, Martha Matilda, infant d/o Jas & Mgt Raley, aged 2 years.

To let: dwlg house, with basement & back bldgs, at G & 22nd sts, late in the occupancy of T R Wise, dec'd. Apply to M Adler or C E Eckel, Gtwn.

Principal sufferers of the fire that originated in the Nat'l Theatre: bldg cost $45,000, & lately purchased at public sale by Benj Ogle Tayloe, for himself & other gentlemen, for $13,500. Other sufferers were Gen Van Ness, Mr Richd Smith, Mr Harrison Smith, & Mr Larned. Wholly or partially destroyed: the brick bldg occupied by Mr Berry, marble-cutter; grocery store owned by Mr Alison Naylor, & occupied by Mr Hand; brick dwlg owned by Mrs O'Neal, & occupied by Mr Edmund Brown; brick dwlg owned by Mrs O'Neal, & occupied by Miss Stringer, dress-maker; dwlg on 13th st, owned by Mr Louis Vivans, & occupied by Dr Doniphan; brick dwlg, also on 13th st, owned & occupied by Michl Nourse. [Mar 8th newspaper: correction-Mr Richd Smith is not a proprietor of the *Nat'l Theatre*.]

Wash Corp: 1-Cmte of Claims: bill for the relief of Wm Morrow: passed. Same cmte: bill for the relief of Wm Wise: passed. Same cmte: bill for the relief of Wm Dalton: rejected. Same cmte: bill for the relief of Patrick Moran: ordered to lie on the table. Same cmte: ptn of Philip Ennis: passed. 2-Ptn of Mrs Maria Mason for reduction of the taxes on certain property: referred to the cmte of Ways & Means. 3-Cmte of Claims: bill for the relief of O J Prather: passed. Same cmte: referred the ptn of John W Vhrel, asked to be discharged from its further consideration: which was concurred in.

Jas Larned returns his grateful thanks to the firemen of Wash City, Gtwn, & Alexandria, for their kind efforts in extinguishing the fire of last evening, after it had destroyed his stables & much of the adjacent property, without any essential damage to his dwlg-house.

SAT MAR 8, 1845
For Boston: the brig **Brookline**, Capt Statz, can take some small packages for Boston, & will be ready for cargo on Mar 12. –S E Scott, Gtwn

For N Y: Regular Line. The packet schnr **Victory**, G Penfield master, will sail on Mar 11. For freight or passage, apply to the captain, on board, or to F & A H Dodge, Water st, Gtwn.

Jos Eaches [Whig] was on Wed last re-elected Mayor of the City of Alexandria by a majority of almost 4 to 1 over an opponent of opposite politics.

Vicksbrug Sentinel of Feb 18. The Choctaw Indians. The last remnants of this once powerful tribe are now crossing our ferry on their way to their new home in the Far West. They leave names to many of our rivers, towns, & counties; & so long as our State remains, the Choctaws, who once owned most of her soil, will be remembered.

Removal of the Seminoles. A number of wagons passed on to **Fort Gibson** last week, under contract to remove the Seminoles to the district of the creek country destined for their future homes. The removal will begin forthwith. According to the treaty they are to be subsited after arriving at their new homes 6 months-a length a time sufficient to enable them to open small fields & grow plenty of corn, beans, & potatoes for consumption the next year.

Oo-tah-cau-hur, convicted of the murder of his wife, was publicly hanged at this place on Mon last. He confessed to the perpetration of the crime, acknowledged the justness of his sentence, & professed a willingness to die. He met his awful doom firmly & without trepidation. –Cherokee Advocate

Mrd: Mar 5, by Rev Norval Wilson, Mr Mathew Galt to Laura C, only d/o Wm G Deale, all of this place.

Died: on Jan 10 last, at his residence, **Smithwood**, St Mary's Co, Md, Elwiley Smith, in his 81st year. He was a good man in every relation of life, kind & hospitable. He was taken with a chill before dinner, & asked to be led to his bed. He survived 5 days, retaining his mind to the last breath, answering questions put to him. In peace he went down to the grave, evincing no wish to live, or fear to die.

Local News. Jas Minor was arrested in this city on Mar 4, charged with suspicion of having committed the crime of murder in Wash Co, Missouri. A letter of the 26th ult from Bellevue, Wash Co, Mo, states that Thos Bird, of that place had met his death from a gun-shot wound at the hands of a man named Jas Minor, with whom he had a lawsuit. The assassin fled, & a reward of $200 is offered for him.

I beg leave to offer my thanks to my friends & fellow-citizens, who, at much personal hazard, assisted in the preservation of my property at the late destructive fire. When I arrived at the scene I found many on my bldgs deluging the roofs with water, which they had carried up by hand at great risk. –S Burche

The subscriber desires to express his thanks to his friends & fellow-citizens who exerted themselves & saved his furniture from the fire on Mar 5, & regrets to say that, although most of it was brought out of the house, a greater part of the furniture & clothing has been destroyed & lost. Those persons who have taken for safe-keeping, or by mistake, articles belonging to my family, or Mrs Stewart, who had a room in our house, will confer a favor by sending them to me at the Globe ofc, or informing me where they can be had. A large basket, containing most of the clothing of my wife & children, was taken out of the house by a woman soon after the fire commenced, & has not been returned. We are much in want of them. –Edmund F Brown

To those citizens who labored to save my house & furniture in the late fire, I return my unfeigned acknowledgments; to the fire companies-what? As many articles taken from the house are yet missing, any information respecting them will be thankfully received.
—Michl Nourse

Notice: By virtue of an order of distrain for rent due in arrears to Geo W McLean, by Robt Mills, I shall expose to public sale, on Mar 15, in front of the Centre Market House, the following goods & chattels, viz: 1 piano, 1 pair card tables, 2 centre tables, 3 sofas, 2 looking-glasses, 1 pair curtains, fender & andirons, 1 workstand, 16 chairs, 1 pair of ottomans, 3 astral lamps, lot of carpeting, piano stool & cover, 3 sideboards, 1 coffee urn, 1 pair mahg tables, fender, poker, tongs & stand, easy chair, candlestand, washstand, bow & pitcher, stove, wardrobe, feather bed, hair mattress, bedstead, 2 sheets, & 1 bolster.
-H R Maryman, Bailiff

MON MAR 10, 1845
Laws of the U S, passed at the 2nd Session of the 28th Congress. 1-Act for the relief of Saml Neely, of the State of Pa: to place his name on the pension roll, & to pay him at the rate of $6 per month, from & after Sep 4 last. 2-Resolution for the relief of Mrs Mary W Thompson: to audit & settle her accounts, for all services which shall appear to have been rendered by her husband, the late Lt Col W R Thompson, U S Army, for the Gov't, & to allow here the same rate of pay & emoluments as many have been allowed to any other ofcr of the line or staff of the army, or agent, who may have rendered services of the same grade: & the amount found due shall be paid money in the Treasury not otherwise appropriated, to the said Mrs Thompson. 3-Resolution directing an examination of Putnam's ploughing & dredging machine: patented to the late Dr Jas R Putnam, of New Orleans.

Trustee's sale: in execution of the trusts of a certain deed recorded in Liber W B #96, folios 136 thru 140, one of the land records for Wash Co, D C, on May 7 next, that piece or parcel of ground in Wash City, being all that part of lot 2 in square 293, heretofore conveyed by John P Van Ness & wife to Geo King, of Chas, & Hezekiah Langley, as tenants in common, by deed dated Sep 20, 1816, together with the bldgs & improvements thereon. —Chauncey Bestor, Trustee -Robt W Dyer & Co, aucts

Wholesale & Retail Temperance Grocery Store: Messrs Peddecord & Holland, at their old stand, Centre Market Space, next door to the Dry Goods Store of D Clagett & Co, have determined from this date to abandon the sale of Wines & Liquors.

Dryburgh Abbey, where the body of Sir Walter Scott is buried, is the property of the Earl of Buchan. Over the large gate, at the entrance to be abbey grounds, is a board on which is painted, in large letters, placed there in all seriousness by order of the Countess of Buchan: "Slaveholders from America not admitted." -Scotsman

Hse/o Reps: 1-Cmte on Military Affairs: made an adverse report on the ptn of Mary Colburn: laid on the table. 2-Cmte of Claims: adverse report on the case of the heirs of Dr John Gray: laid on the table. Also, a bill for the relief of Adam McCulloch: read & committed. 3-Cmte of Claims: bill from the Senate for the relief of Wm D Cheever, dec'd: reported without amendment. 4-Cmte on the Judiciary: in the case of Jos de la Francis: act to liquidate certain claims therein mentioned, passed Apr 18, 1814, [claims arising out of the taking possession of a portion of West Florida,] which bill was read & committed. 5-Cmte on the Judiciary: bill for the relief of Sarah B H Stith: read & committed. Same cmte: bill from the Senate for the relief of John P Skinner: committed. 6-Cmte on Indian Affairs: adverse reports in relation to Jas M Smith & L P Pease: laid on the table. Same cmte: bill from the Senate for the relief of Wm Henson: a recommendation that it do not pass: bill was then laid on the table. Same cmte: adverse report on the case of Bent St Vrain: laid on the talbe. 7-Cmte on Naval Affairs: adverse report on the ptn of Geo W Taylor: laid on the table. 8-Cmte on Roads & Canals: report adverse to the memorial of Asa Whitney for a grant of land for a railroad from Lake Michigan to the Rocky Mountains: laid on table. 9-Cmte on Accounts: adverse to the claim of J W Nye: laid on the table.

Died: on Mar 8, Mary, w/o Martin Murphy, aged 42 years. Her funeral is this day, at 3 p m, from her late residence, on Pa ave, near 4½ st.

Died: on Mar 7, after a protracted illness, Wm G Patterson, in his 35th year. He has left a wife, child, & aged father to mourn his irreparable loss.

Fire was discovered on Sat last in the upper part of a dwlg on Missouri ave, between 6th & 4½ sts. The house belongs to G Watterston & is occupied by Mrs Valentine. The fire was soon extinguished.

City Ordnances-Wash: 1-Act for the relief of Wm Wise: that the fine imposed for an alleged violation of the law relative to grocery licenses, be remitted: provided Wise pay the costs of prosecution. Same fine as above, remitted, for Wm Morrow: provided Morrow pay the costs of prosecution.

TUE MAR 11, 1845
$100 reward for runaway negro woman Sally, about 23 years of age. –Jas H Payne, Westmoreland Co, Va

Committed to the jail of Montg Co, Md, as a runaway, a negro man who calls himself Isaac Johnson: says he has been in Florida for the last 2 or 3 years, & belonged to John Patrick, who was killed while in the service of the U S; but it is thought he belongs in the neighborhood of the Johnson's Iron works. Owner is to come forward, prove property, pay charges, & take him away, or he will be discharged as the law directs.
-D H Candler, Sheriff

Orphan's Court of Wash Co, D C. Letters testamentary on the personal property of Henry Smith, late of said county, dec'd. –Lewis Johnson, A B Proctor, Excs

Mrs S Masi has several large rooms for those wishing board, at the conrer of 4½ st & Pa ave.

Household furniture at auction: on Mar 13, at the residence of the late Wm Simmons, on H st, between 10th & 11th sts. -Robt W Dyer & Co, aucts

$5 reward: strayed from the premises of the subscriber, 11th & L sts, a small dark bay Canadian Pony. Reward will be paid upon his safe delivery. –John Nourse

<u>List of Bills which passed the Hse/o Reps & upon which final action was not had in the Senate.</u>
Bill for the relief of:
Ira Baldwin
Jos Curwen
Jacob Boston
Bennet M Dell
Jos & Lindsay Ward
Wm Gove
Lot Davis
Isabella Baldridge
Wm Gump
John Ficklin
Jno R Frogge
Heirs of John Hard, dec'd
Pension to Benj Allen
heirs of Adino Goodenough

Asenath Orvis
Henry N Halsted
Harrison Whiston
Geo Wentling
Jacob L Vance
Chas R Allen
John P Converse
Geo B Russell
Danl H Warren
Francis Summerance
Jos Watson

To pay Capt John B Crozier's company of mounted volunteers, Tennessee militia.

Mr Tyler, the ex-Pres of the U S, has returned from Wash City to his residence in Chas City Co, Va.

<u>List of Bills & Joint Resolutions which passed the Senate, & upon which final action was not had in the Hse/o Reps:</u>
Bill for the relief of:
legal reps of Joshua Kennedy, dec'd.
heirs of Robt Fulton
Wm Elliott, jr
Asa Andrews
Wm Rich

heirs of Wm Fisher
W C Easton
Thos Smith
Wm Henson
Robt Purkis
J S Throckmorton
Mary A E Zantzinger
legal reps of Wm D Cheever
legal reps of Jas Bell, dec'd
Noah Miller, of Maine
Reuben E Gentry & others
legal reps of Geo Duvall
Joshua Shaw
Miles King & his assigns
John P Skinner & legal reps of Isaac Green
Wm Russell & others
Mary Reeside, exc of Jas Reeside, dec'd
Pierre Menard, Josiah T Betts, Jacob Feaman, & Edmund Roberts, sureties of Felix Saint Vrain.

Resolutions:
In favor of David Shaw & Solomon Corser
In favor of Bent, St Vrain & Co
Relief of Seth M Leavenworth
Relief of Putney & Riddle

List of Bills & Resolutions of the Hse/o Reps were postponed indefinitely by the Senate on the last day of the session, & have not appeared in our published reports.

Relief of

Jos M Rhea	Justin Jacobs
Elijah Blodget	Richd Elliot
Eliz Fitch	Elliot Smith & Nahan Farnsworth
Jos Craigmiles	Susannah Scott, wid/o Wm Scott

WED MAR 12, 1845

Detroit Adv of Fri week: Mr Worter Thompson, in passing a week ago yesterday over a small lake about a mile from Leoni, fell in. His wife hastened to his assistance, when she too fell in, & both perished. The neighbors rallied to the spot, but their help was in vain.

In firing the cannon in honor of the advent of the Democratic Administration, there was a premature discharge, by which David Keller, a resident of this village, was seriously injured. His arms were so mutilated as to require the amputation of both above the elbow. Mr Keller was alive at the time our paper went to press. He has a wife & family.
–Ontario Messenger, Mar 5

Tribute to a Patriot of other days: Mr Jefferson's elevation to the Presidency might have been defeated, after his election, but the firmness of such Federal patriots as Hamiton, Bayard, & Ogle. The sire of the late B Ogle, of **Bel Air**, [of the same name, Benj Ogle,] was Govn'r of Md at the time of the contest between Jefferson & Adams. Govn'r Ogle belonged to the old Federal, conservative, hold fast to that which is good school. The Democratic party, at the meeting of the Legislature, struck with admiration of his integrity, offered to re-elect him Chief Magistrate of the State; but, to avoid all implication, he refused the ofc, then one of no equivocal dignity. Govn'r Ogle was never insulted by the tender office from Mr Jefferson.

Mr Wm Simons died suddenly at Balt on Thu last. He had been to Wash to see the inauguration, & was on his return home. Cause of death is supposed to be apoplexy. He was the editor of the Providence [R I] Republican Herald, which paper he conducted about 30 years.

Money lost: on E st: the roll of money contained the name of Albert Barber. Finder will be liberally rewarded, if required, by leaving the same at Mr Callan's drug store, E & 7th sts. The loser is a very poor colored man. –Philip Noland

Two brothers of the name of Lenzler, from Saxonburg, Butler Co, Pa, were drowned near the Aqueduct at Pittsburg on Sat last. This is the 3rd pair of brothers that have drowned in the same place. -American

We learn by a letter from Chestertown, that the w/o the Hon Jas A Pearce died on Sat. She had been dangerously ill for some time, which had kept Mr Pearce from his seat in the U S Senate. –Balt Amer

The U S sloop of war **St Mary's**, Com'r Saunders, for the Mediterranean, dropped down under sail to the anchorage below Norfolk on Sat last.

Wash Corp: 1-Ptn from E H Metcalf & others for a pavement: referred to the Cmte on Improvements. 2-Bill for the relief of Patrick Moran: passed. 3-Ptn of Thos Miller, that means be taken to procure water at Pa ave & 14th st: referred to the Cmte on Improvements. 4-Ptn of Ann E Sleater & others, praying the curbstone to be set & footway paved on La ave & 10th sts: referred to the Cmte on Improvements. 5-Bill for the relief of Philip Ennis: referred to the Cmte of Claims. 6-Bill authorizing R S Patterson to extend his fence: referred to the Cmte on Improvements.

Mr O'Callaghan, the proprietor of the private express connected with the New Orleans Crescent City newspaper, was arrested there on Feb 27, & left there in custody of the U S Deputy Marshal for Savannah, to be tried on the complaint of an agent of the Post Ofc Dept, on a charge of violating the P O laws.

By letter we learn that at Middletown, Md, on Fri last, a s/o Danl S Biser, member of the House of Delegates, about 3 miles from that place, was assisting in cutting timber in the woods, &, on the fall of a large tree, a branch flew back & struck him on the head, fracturing his skull in the most shocking manner. He was conveyed to his home, where he lingered in the most agonizing manner until next morning, when he breathed his last. A messenger was sent to Annapolis to apprize his father. The boy was about 15. Several years ago, while Mr Biser was in the Legislature, he was called home because of the entire destruction of his house by fire, & the loss of nearly the whole of his household effects. -Sun

The iron revenue cutter **George M Bibb**, was launched at Pittsburg on Sat. Some 15 minutes before the time set apart for launching, the boat started from its fastenings & rushed on its ways into the river, which it nearly crossed. Mr Buckhart was dangerously injured, & Mr McKee had his arm broken. Several others were thrown into the river, but they were rescued.

Supreme Court of N J decision pronounced on Fri, in the case of Peter W Parke, by Chief Justice Hornblower, & in the case of Jos Carter by Justice Nevius. The Court refused to grant the motion for new trials in both cases. The prisoners will probably be sentenced to be executed, for being concerned in the murder of the Castner family. [May 26 newspaper: Jos Carter & Peter W Parke were sentenced to death on Thu last by Chief Justice Hornblower. They are to be executed on Aug 22. Parke manifested but little contrition on the occasion, but Carter was deeply affected, & wept loudly. They both said they were innocent. –Trenton Emporium] [Jul 7th newspaper: The trial of Abner Parke, in Warren Co Circuit, on the second indictment for being concerned in the murder of the Castner family, terminated on Sat in a verdict of acquittal. There are, we believe, 2 more indictments against the prisoner for the murder of other members of the family. –Newark Daily Adv] [Aug 25th newspaper: Jos Carter, jr, & Peter W Parke underwent the penalty of the law at Belvidere, N J, on Fri last, for the murder of the Castner family in May, 1843. They protested to the last their innocence of the crime for which they suffered.]

Mrd: on Feb 27, by Rev Mr Edmonds, Mr Wm Herbert to Mrs Emily Osburn, both of Wash City.

Mrd: on Mar 11, by the Rev N Wilson, Rev Wm H Laney to Miss Columbia, d/o Thos Wilson, of Montg Co, Md.

Died: on Feb 22, in Gtwn, Anne Catharine, 2nd d/o Dr Grafton & Mary M Tyler, in her 6th year.

Sons of Temperance meeting on Mar 12, at 4 o'clock. –J W Dexter, Recording Scribe

Lost, between the City Hall & the subscriber's residence, on 7th st, south of Md ave, a bundle of papers in relation to the estate of W Ratcliffe, dec'd. The finder will confer a favor by returning them to W Lenox or myself. –Matilda Ratcliffe

Household furniture at auction: on Mar 13, at the residence of the late Wm Simmons, on H st, between 10th & 11th sts. -Robt W Dyer & Co, aucts

Ball to be given at Carusi's Saloon, on Mar 12, for the benefit of those who suffered by the late fire at the Nat'l Theatre. Appointed managers:

Hon Jas Buchanan	P Barton Key	Thos H Blake
W W Seaton	J P Wolf	John Tyler, jr
Com L Kearney, U S N	John B Randolph, U S N	Andrew Porter
Dr Thos Miller	Lt Henry Prince, U S A	Lt Overton Carr, U S N
Gen Hernandez	A L McCrea	F L Waddell, of N Y
Capt J H Aulick, U S N	Alex Mahon	Henry May
Capt J C Casey, U S A	Hon Wm Wilkins	Robt Lawrence
Dr J M Thomas	Gen Geo Gibson, U S A	L Purdy
Lt W A Maddox-USMC	T L Smith	J W Butler
Dr R A Lacey	Capt F Forrest, U S N	John Y Mason, jr
Lt John Pope, U S A	Col Wm H Polk	M K Warrington, U S N

J Whitehorn, Portrait Painter, from N Y, will remain a short time in Wash. Professional services at the American Colonization Ofc, between 3rd & 4½ sts, Pa ave, where specimens may be seen.

THU MAR 13, 1845
Obit-died: on Mar 8, in Chestertown, Kent Co, Md, Mrs Martha Jane Pearce, w/o the Hon Jas A Pearce, of the U S Senate, from a chronic pulmonary disease. She was a d/o the late Rev Jas Laird, formerly Rector of Great Chaptank, Cambridge, on the eastern Shore of Md. Since her marriage she has resided chiefly in Chestertown. For many years she was a member of the Protestant Episcopal Church. Her funeral ceremonies were performed by Rev Dr C F Jones, Rector of Chester Parish, on Mar 10, & her remains were interred at Ellerslie, the country seat of her husband, on the same day.

Balt, Mar 12. Hon Leander Starr, of N Y, met with a serious accident on Sun last. He was accompanying a lady to her residence, when he fell into a newly dug cellar, which had been left unprotected, & severely fractured his collar bone. He is confined at Barnum's Hotel, where he will recover, though perhaps may be permanently injured for life. –Sun

Robt N Martin has been appointed by the Govn'r & Senate of Md to be Chief Judge of the Judicial District composed of Allegany, Wash, & Fred'k Counties, Md.

Laws of the U S, passed at the 2nd Session of the 28th Congress. 1-Compensation to Benj E Green, while officiating as charge d'affaires in Mexico, $1,069.40 2-Compensation to J Pemberton Hutchison, in full for diplomatic services at Lisbon during the interval between the suspensionof the mission of T L L Brent, & the recoginition of his successor at the court of Portugal, $2,900. 3-Salary as charge d'affaires & outfit to Henry Ledyard, while so employed in France, $9456. 4-Compensation to Arthur Middleton, in full for diplomatic services in Spain during several periods in 1836, 1837, & 1840, $1,454. 5-For adjustment of claims arising under the act of Mar 5, 1815, for the relief of Lt Col Wm Lawrence & others, being a re-appropriation of an amount heretofore carried to the surplus fund, $347.60.

Levi S Chatfield, of Otsego, formerly Speaker of the N Y House of Assembly, died suddenly, of an affection of the heart, a few days since. [Mar 15th newspaper: It turns out that Mr Chatfield is both alive & well. –Albany Evening Journal]

Paton Ross, for many years Recorder of Lancaster, [Pa] was found dead in his ofc on Mon, a few moments after having entered it in his usual health.

The present wealth of Mr Astor is computed at $28,920,000. Last year the city tax upon his real estate alone, [including near 1,600 bldg lots, nearly all coveted with houses] was over $34,000. –N Y True Sun

Mrd: on Mar 6, by Rev C B Dana, Andrew Wylie, jr, of Pittsburg, Pa, to Miss Mary Caroline, 2nd d/o Danl Bryan, of Alexandria, D C.

Died: on Feb 27, at **Greenwood**, PG Co, Md, Thos T Somerville, in his 57th year.

Free lecture by J B Gough, the celebrated temperance lecturer, will lecture on intemperance, its causes & cure, at Rev Mr Samson's Baptist Church, E st, on Thu, at 7:30 p m. A collection will be taken up to defray expenses. By order, Cmte of Arrangements.

Patapsco Female Institute, at Ellicott's Mills, near Balt, Md, Mrs Lincoln Phelps, Principal, will open for the summer session from May 7 next.

For sale: new brick house, on corner of 4th st & Mass ave, where for particulars, inquire of J A Burch.

FRI MAR 14, 1845
The trial of Henry McCurry, for the murder of Mr Paul Roux, late of Georgia, commenced at Balt on Mon last, & ended on Wed by a verdict of guilty of murder in the first degree. Punishment is death.

Ptns presented to the Hse/o Reps: of the U S by John Quincy Adams, with the disposal of them by order of the House. 1-Jas Wallace & 168 males, Mgt Miller & 107 females, living in Randolph, Washington, Perry & St Clair counties, Ill, to propose amendments to the Constitution: referred to the Cmte on the Judiciary. 2-Henry & Hannah Woodard & 857 citizens of Cortlandville, Cortland Co, N Y, abolition of slavery & slave trade in D C: referred to the Cmte on D C. 3-Wm Webb & 41 citizens of the State of Delaware, abolish slavery: referred to the Cmte on the Judiciary, Dec 16, 1844. 4-Seth Field & Eliza Field, N E, & 400 citizens of West Brookfield, Mass: abolish slavery & slave trade in D C & Territories, & other slave related matters: referred. 5-Joshua A Spencer & 27 others, on board steamboat **Columbia**, from Albany & N Y, Dec 6, 1844, remonstrance against annexation of Texas: referred to the Cmte of the Whole, Dec 19, 1844. 6-A DeHall Tarr & 55 citizens of Pa, amend the naturalization laws, 21 years' residence: referred Dec 19, 1844: to Cmte on the Judiciary. 7-Joanna French, wid/o Nathl French, of Canton, Norfolk Co, Mass: referred to Cmte on Revolutionary Pensions. 8-Anne Royall, wid/o Capt Wm Royall: referred to Cmte on Revolutionary Pensions. 9-Jas Thatcher & 6 inhabitants of Vassalborough, Maine, to abolish the U S Army: referred to the Cmte on Military Affairs. 10-Joshua Mitchell & 15 citizens of Phil, admit no slave State & reject Texas: referred to the Cmte of the Whole. 11-Jos Lindsey & 21 citizens of Phil, immediate aboliton of slavery in D C & the Territory of Florida: referred to the Cmte on D C & a select cmte. 12-Geo McCarty & 13 inhabitants of Mentz, Cayuga Co, N Y, in the case of the annexation of Texas declare the Union dissolved: referred to the Cmte of the Whole. 13-Butler Wilmarth & 11 men & 11 women, Phil, residing at Hopedale, Milford, Mass, to reject the annexation of Texas. 14-L Bissell & 22 citizens of Ashtabula Co, Ohio, reject annexation of Texas: referred to the Cmte of the Whole. 15-B B Hunter & 45 inhabitants of Ashtabula Co, Ohio, amendment of the Constitution, free basis of representation: Cmte on the Judiciary. 16-Abigail Church, wid/o John Church, pension claim: referred to the Cmte on Revolutionary Pensions. 17-Jas Morgan, of Brooklyn, N Y, pension for Revolutionary service: referred to the Cmte on Revolutionary Pensions. 18-John N Barour, of Cambridge, abolition of slavery: referred to the Cmte on the Judiciary. 19-Frances Pottenger, of Hagerstown, Md, for a pension: referred to the Cmte on Naval Affairs. 20-Saml Raub, jr, on explosions & collapsing of flues on steam-boilers, & extinguishing of fires: referred to the Cmte on Naval Affairs. 21-Peter Schiefflin & 12 citizens of N Y & vicinity, to define the rank & rights of persons in the navy: referred to the Cmte on Naval Affairs. 22-Elisha Numbers & 76 inhabitants of Edinburg, Ohio, expulsion of duelists: referred to the Cmte on the Judiciary. 23-Sherburn C Blodget, Gtwn, Mass, alteration of patent laws: referred to the Cmte on Patents. 24-O H Haven & 58 citizens of Will Co, Ill, education for colored children in D C & Florida: referred to the Cmte on the Judiciary. 25-J W Allen & 12 ministers of the gospel, Middlesex, Mass, two cents postage & abolish franking: referred to the Cmte of the Whole. 26-Richd Holden, a method of producing relative motion: referred to the Cmte on Naval Affairs.

27-Ptns on the annexation of Canada: referred to the Cmte of the Whole:
John A Millis & Edwin Sleeper & 56 citizens of Pa
S J M Hammond & 25 inhabitants of St Joseph Co, Mich
M Bickford & 28 citizens of a State bordering on a British province
Alex'r Salisbury & 46 citizens of States bordering on British possessions
Sherman Osborn & 50 inhabitants of Canton, Hartford Co, Conn
Wm Hoyt & 17 citizens of the U S, Kingston, Pa
T M Wilson & 45 citizens of Oswego, N Y
Nelson Danforth & 29 borderers on British possessions

28-Against annexation of Texas: Referred to the Cmte of the Whole:
Jas M Robbins & 31 inhabitants of Milton, Mass
Mary Ann Anderson & 125 ladies of Albany, N Y
Jabez Parkhurst & 38 inhabitants of Franklin Co, N Y
Solomon Cowles & 59 citizens of Norfolk, Conn
C P Perkins & 23 citizens of Harrisville, N H
Mary F Perkins & 43 ladies of Harrisville, N H
Chalker Buell & 49 electors of Oakfield, Genesee Co, N Y
Ephraim Lyman & 29 electors of Litchfield Co, Conn
Lydia White & 55 ladies of Vermont
Exra D Kinney & 7 inhabitants of Darien, Conn
Chas Forster & 99 inhabitants of Charlestown, Mass
Andrew S Rogers & 13 citizens of Penn Yan
J D Zimmerman & 39 citizens of Branch & Calhoun Counties, Mich
R G Lincoln & 78 legal voters of Hallowell, Maine
Joshua Judson & 35 inhabitants of Arlington, Vt
Jeremiah Knight & 64 inhabitants of Oneida Co, N Y
Wm Finch & 30 inhabitants of Rensselaer Co, N Y
Nathl Thomas & 23 men, & Eliz B Estey, & 13 women, inhabitants of Milton, Mass
Seth Hayes & 147 voters of Hartford, Trumbull Co, Ohio
A Richmond & 22 voters in Alleghany Co, N Y
John D Safford & 65 others of Pembroke, Genesee Co, N Y
Hugh Glem & 20 citizens of De Witt Co, Ill
Harvey North & 54 citizens of Knox Co, Ohio
Cornelius Bassett & 67 inhabitants of Lee, Mass
Geo G Lay & 18 citizens of Calhoun Co, Mich
Issac E Heaton & 43 inhabitants of Rock Co, Wisc
Benj Jones & 14 inhabitants of Washington, Lincoln Co, Maine
S A Bualison & 43 voters of Brookfield, Madison Co, N Y
Jos Pollard, of Mount Holly, Rutland Co, Vt
Benj Bloom & 27 citizens of Chanango Co, N Y
Robt Wilson & 46 citizens of Salem, Wash Co, N Y

29: Against annexation of Texas as a slaveholding Territory: referred to Cmte of the Whole:
Jas Averill & 77 inhabitants of Shrewsbury, Mass
John Davis & 154 electors of Ashford, Conn
N C Robinson & 19 inhabitants of Monroe Co, Maine
Edwin Barnard & 77 inhabitants of Seneca Ontario Co, N Y
Isaac N Davenport & 38 inhabitants of W Boylston, Mass
Danl Spalding & 70 inhabitants of Kalamazoo Co, Mich
Danl F Millikin & 32 citizens of Whitesides Co, Ill
Saml H Lloyd & 78 inhabitants of Attleborough, Mass
Otis Cary & 50 legal voters of Foxborough, Mass
Seba Carpenter & 78 inhabitants of Attleborough, Mass
Wm C Stinson & 21 inhabitants of Pittsfield, Maine
Guy C Hawkins & 35 inhabitants of Somerville, Mass
Jas D Farnsworth & 20 citizens of Middlesex, Mass
Solomon Cox & 282 inhabitants of Henry Co, Indiana
Chas P White & 101 inhabitants of Mansfield, Mass
Jos Hewett & 132 voters of Marshfield, Mass
Jas Kennedy & 47 inhabitants of Sterling, Lake Co, Ill
Jas G Dunlavy & 31 citizens of Putnam Co, Ill
Sylvester Talcott & 62 inhabitants of Winnebago Co, Ill
Wm R Howe & 32 citizens of Illinois
Abolition of slavery in the District of Columbia: referred to Cmte for D C:
Andrew Pettigrew & 74 inhabitants of Ludlow, Windsor Co, Vt
David Riggs & 25 electors of Middlesex, Conn
Ephraim Lyman & 28 electors of Litchfield, Conn
Ezra Kinney & 8 inhabitants of Darien, Conn
Gilbert Titus & 26 inhabitants of Rensselaerville & vicinity, Albany Co, N Y
Henry Hill & 46 inhabitants of Charlestown, Mass
Jessie McConnell & 120 citizens of Columbiana Co, Ohio
E G Cary & 95 inhabitants of Grant Co, Indiana
Jesse Thomson & 42 inhabitants of Oneida Co, N Y
Jefferson Mayell & 25 citizens of Albany, N Y
Wm C Stinson & 24 inhabitants of Pittsfield, Maine
Thos H Palmer & 25 freemen of Pittsford, Vt
B V Marsh & 68 inhabitants of Brandon & vicinity, Vt
Seth Hayes & 147 voters of Hartford, Trumbull Co, Ohio
Jonathan Soule & 88 citizens of Schenectady Co, N Y
Jonathan Howe & 26 inhabitants of Charlestown, Mass
Thos T Butler & 241 citizens of Indiana
John D Safford & 70 inhabitants of Pembroke, Genesee Co, N Y
Allan Pinkerton & 27 citizens of Kent Co, Ill
A Richmond & 43 inhabitants of Alleghany Co, N Y

Sarah H Wicks & 83 females residents of Oneida Co, N Y
Jas Thompson & 51 inhabitants of Chautauque Co, N Y
Buel Pickett & 14 electors of Fairfield & Litchfield Counties, Conn
30: Danl T Miller & 39 electors of Norfolk, Conn, case of Jonathan Walker: referred to the Cmte on the Judiciary. 31-A S Kendall & 58 voters of Groton, Mass, abolish spirit ration in the navy: referred to the Cmte on Naval Affairs. 32-Jonathan Hodges & 3 voters of Taunton, Mass, re-annexation of Algiers to the U S: referred to the Cmte on the Judiciary. 33-Wm Grace & 54 memorialists, a canal round the falls of St Mary's at the mouth of Lake Superior: referred to the Cmte on Roads & Canals.
34-Abolish the franking privilege/reduction of postage: referred to the Cmte of the Whole:
Wm D Hoyt & 40 inhabitants of Vermont
Timothy Bishop & 13 inhabitants of Casa Co, Mich
Ezra D Kinney & 13 inhabitants of Darien, Conn
Jesse Thompson & 43 inhabitants of Paris Hill & vicinity, Oneida Co, N Y
35-Danl F Millikin & 32 citizens of Whitesides Co, Ill, to repeal the Florida laws in support of slavery, & of the punishment of Capt Jonathan Walker: referred to the Cmte on the Judiciary. 36-Adam Huntsman & 17 others, a negotiation for exchange of territory: referred to the Cmte on the Judiciary. 37-John Coffin Nazro Israel, of Jerusalem Prospect, Maine, sundry alterations of the laws: referred to the Cmte on the Judiciary. 38-R Coulter & 357 citizens of Canonsburg, Pa, & vicinity, investigation of the duel: referred to the Cmte on the Judiciary. 39-W T Bascom & 101 citizens of Morgan Co, Ohio, to withhold appropriation for a Minister to Mexico: referred to the Cmte on the Judiciary. 40-Lewis Bradford & 102 inhabitants of Plympton, Mass, to amend the naturalization laws: referred to the Cmte of the Whole. 41-H G Parker & 177 inhabitants of Keen, Cheshire Co, N H, to establish schools in D C for all: referred to the Cmte on the District of Columbia. 42-H C Morehand & 55 citizens of Greensburg, Westmoreland Co, Pa, inquiry of the duel: referred to the Cmte on the Judiciary. 43-Geo E Buehler & 25 inhabitants of Gettysburg, Pa, annexation of Africa: referred to the Cmte on the Judiciary. 44-Levinus Sperry & 62 citizens of Fulton Co, Ill, slave laws of Florida; oppression of Jonathan Walker. 45-F R Bennett & 8 legal voters of Illinois, to exchange South Carolina for Texas: referred to the Cmte on the Judiciary. 46-Jacob Lybrand & 70 inhabitants of Wisconsin Territory, to liberate the slaves in Wisconsin: referred to the Cmte on the Territories. 47-Simeon Brown, jr, & 11 inhabitants of Xenia, Ohio, annexation of Cuba & Ethiopia: referred to the Cmte on the Judiciary. 48-Armor McFarland & 108 inhabitants of Utica, Licking Co, Ohio, to recognize the law of God: referred to the Cmte on the Judiciary. 49-Jonathan Hodges & 3 voters of Taunton, Mass, re-annexation of Algiers to the U S: referred to the Cmte on the Judiciary. 50-Jas Riley, railroad from the Atlantic to the Pacific: laid on the table. 51-Resolution for the benefit of Frances Slocum & her children & grand-children, of the Miami tribe of Indians: that the portion of shares of the annuities or other moneys which are now, or may become payable to the Miami tribe of Indians, due to the following named persons, members of said tribe of Indians, shall be hereafter & forever payable to them & their descendants at

Fort Wayne or Peru, or such other place, in Indiana, as the Sec of War shall direct, viz: To Frances Slocum, Ke-ke-no-kush-wa, Ke-po-ke-na-mo-qua, Wa-pa-noc-shi-no-qua, Ke-no-sack qua, Ching-shing-gwaw, Pe-tu-loc-a-to-que, We-saw-she-no-qua, Te-quoc-yaw, Spo-quang gwaw, Waw-pop-e-tah, So-eel-en-je-sah, No-ac-co-mo-qua, Coch-e-no-qus, Po-con-da-maw, Tah-he-qua, Ki-ko-o-qua, Te-quoc-yaw, junior, Loc-o-chu-qua, Peem-y-o-ty-maw, So-eel-en-je-saw, junior, & Pun-ge-she-no-qua. That if the aforesaid Indians, their descendants, or any part thereof, shall hereafter remove to the country west of the Mississippi river assigned to the Miami tribe of Indians, then & in such case the portions or shares of annuities, or other moneys payable to said tribe, shall be paid to such persons so removing at the place of payment of annuities to said tribe of Indians.
52-Act providing payment for certain military services in Florida:
Col Robt Brown's command, Apr 6 to Jul 22, 1838, except the company of Capt North, which shall be paid to Jul 12, 1838.
Maj Isaac Garrison's command, from Mar 19 to Jul 5, 1838.
Capt Arthur Roerts' company, from Sep 13, 1838, to Jan 13, 1839.
Capt J L Thigpen's company, from Mar 1 to Aug 31, 1838.
Capt Wm Williams' company, from Aug 16, 1838 to Feb 16, 1839.
Capt Wm Cone & John Bryan's companies, from Aug 18 to Sep 15, 1840.
Capt J L Stewart's company, from Aug 19 to Sep 13, 1840.
Capt Stephen Daniel's company, from oct 13 to Nov 26, 1840.
53-Act making appropriations for the support of the army for the year ending Jun 13, 1846: To settle the accounts of Lt Col H Whiting, being a re-appropriation of part of former appropriations for a road from ***Fort Howard*** to ***Fort Crawford***, & for barracks at ***Fort Brady***, which has been carried to the surplus fund, $845.72.

Notice: I wish to engage a Governess to my children, a Lady who can teach music on the piano, French & the usual branches of a good English education. To one who cam come well recommended, I will give $200 per annum, board, etc. My residence is healthy, & about 3 miles north of the town of Port Tobacco, Chas Co, Md. –Walter Mitchell, Port Tobacco, Md

Cabinet Furniture: Edwin Green, at his establishment on Pa ave, corner of 11th st, Wash.

Obit-died: on the 13th ult, in Wash City, in her 78th year, Lucretia Sears, wid/o Geo Sears, formerly an eminent merchant of Balt, & mother of Abby, w/o Jas W McCulloh, First comptroller of the U S Treasury.

The Arkansas Intelligencer learns through Mr J W Taylor, a respectable merchant of the Creek Nation, that the Pawnee Mahas attacked, about 10 days since, the Creeks who live upon Little river. The Creeks were attacked by the Pawnees, but repulsed them, after killing 6 of their warriors, & without any loss on their side. The Pawnees have returned to their homes upon the wild prairies for a reinforcement.

Mrd: on Mar 12, by Rev H Stringfellow, Dr Gwo W Humphreys to Susan Decatur, d/o the late Saml Robertson, Purser of the U S Navy, all of Va.

Mrd: in Portsmouth, Mass, by Rev Mr Clarke, Mr Jas M Stewart, of Alexandria, D C, to Miss Susan Ann Swett, of Newburyport. [No date-appears recent.]

Died: on Mar 7, at Alexandria, in his 69th year, Capt Elisha Washington Jackson, a native of Lancaster Co, Pa, but for many years a resident of Alexandria.

Lexington Inquirer of Fri last: death of our fellow townsman, Clifton R *Thompson, who was shot dead in the court-house, in Mount Sterling, on Wed, during the sitting of court, by *Henry Daniel, his brother-in-law. Daniel was immediately taken into custody by the civil authority. Thus has fallen, by the hand of violence, one of Fayette's most gifted, noble, generous & honorable sons. [Mar 21st newspaper: the w/o *Harry Daniel, on hearing of her husband's horrible murder of her brother, Clifton R *Thomson, became a maniac & has continued such ever since.]

Criminal Court-Wash: 1-John Weston alias John W Weston [an old offender] convicted of larceny. 2-Wm Dove, charged with rape, & under recognizance was brought to the Court by his bail; he was then continued on bail for his appearance from day to day in the sum of $1,000. 3-W Black, alias J Brown, alias Curry, was convicted of obtaining $10 from the Hon J Brown, of the U S Hse/o Reps, under false pretences. 4-Henry Cole, free negro, was convicted of stealing $35, the property of Harriet Johnson. 5-Edw Williams, free negro, was convicted of stealing a silver watch valued at $8, the property of H C W Voss.

For sale: 2 excellent brick houses, on the square west of the Catholic Church, one on 10th st, & the other on 11th st, adjoining the Catholic Male Orphan Asylum formerly the Central Academy. –John McLeod, at the Columbian Academy.

SAT MAR 15, 1845
Circuit Court of Wash Co, D C-in Chancery. Amos Binney, adm, vs the heirs of Jas Thomas, dec'd. By virtue of a decree passed in the above cause, dated Dec 12, 1844, will be sold at public auction, on Apr 10 next, lots 9, 10, & 11 in square 490, Wash City, with a large frame stable & other improvements thereon. This property is at the intersection of C & 6th sts. –D A Hall, Trustee -A Green, Auctioneer

Died: on Mar 8, at *Oatland*, the residence of Miss Mgt D Bowie, in Montg Co, Md, Mr Jas Bowie, in his 67th year. Kind & conciliating in his disposition, intelligent, with accomplishments of a scholar, he had attracted a large number of friends, who will sympathize cordially with his bereaved son & dght.

The U S frig **Congress**, arrived here today from a 3 years' cruise, 48 days from Rio de Janeiro to the mouth of the Chesapeake: ofcrs & crew all well. List of her ofcrs: Capt P F Voorhees; Lts R L Browning, John P Gillis, T A Jenkins, Richd Bache, D D Porter, Wm Ronckendorff, Surgeon Thos L Smith, Purser B J Cahoone. Marine Ofcrs: Lts B E Brooke & John C Grayson, Chaplain W G Jackson, Acting Master Jas L Blair. Professor Jno Pierce, jr, Assist Surgeon Oscar F Baxter, Capt's Clerk F H Fleming, Midshipmen C W Aby, J W Bennett, Edw Simpson, W N Jeffers, Peter Kemble, Thos C Eaton, Wm Reily, D P McCorkle, L P Ashmead, T S Fillebrown, W R Mercer, Chas C Bayard, S B Luce, Jno D Langhorne. Acting Midshipmen [from frig **Raritan**] R W Simms, W P Humphreys, John M Mechan, Wm B Hays, Chas Daurcited. Boatswain Wm Black, Gunner Saml G City, Carpenter Jas Magill, Sailmaker G D Blackford. Passengers: Mrs B J Cahoone; John Sergeant, jr, of Phil, bearer of dispatches from our Minister at Rio; Lts Acosta & Alvin, of the Brazilian navy, to pursue their profession in our naval service, having been on board several months, at the request of the Emperor, for that purpose, & now on a visit to our dock-yards; & 4 Brazilian boys, to be apprenticed to ship-bldg in our navy-yards. Also, the master & crew of the brig **Montevideo**, arrested by G W Gordon, the American consul at Rio, charged with aiding & abetting the slave trade on the African coast. Lt Porter proceeded forthwith to Washington, bearer of dispatches from the American Consul at Rio to the Sec of State. By the cruise of the **Congress** she has displayed our flag in France, Italy, Austria, Greece, Turkey, Syria, Egypt, Tripoli, Morocco, Sicily, Malta, Minorca, Gibralter, Madeira, Teneriffe, Brazil, & the Republic of Rio de la Plata.

Thos Chapman, of Camden, N J, widely known as a member of the Bar of N J, died while in conversation. He fell from his chair & immediately expired. He was about 50 years of age. He was a member of the Episcopal Church: & a number of years Prosecutor of the Pleas for Gloucester Co. -Phil Ledger

Sale of valuable property near St Louis: deed dated Dec 6, 1837, recorded in ofc book D #2, page 366, of the land records of St Louis, Mo, which deed was made by Wm A Williams & wife & Granville S Farquhar & wife to the subscribers, in trust for certain purposes therein mentioned: sale on May 19 next, a tract of land in said county of St Louis, Mo, estimated to contain 640 acs. It is in the neighborhood of Bellefontaine, on the Missouri river, 12 to 15 miles from the town of St Louis. –H T Weightman, P R Fendall, Trustees -Robt W Dyer & Co, aucts

MON MAR 17, 1845
Laws of the U S, passed at the 2nd Session of the 28th Congress: 1-Payment to Wm Armstrong, to make good the loss sustained by him in consequence of the explosion of the boilers of the steamer **Cherokee**, while transporting Gov't funds from New Orleans to the Indian country west of Arkansas, in 1840: $145.
2-Payment of the claim of Thos Dole, for good & provisions furnished the N Y Indians in 1839 & 1840, allowed by the accounting ofcrs of the Treasury: $964.81

City Ordinance-Wash. 1-Act for the relief of Fred'k Hall: fine improsed for a violation of the law in relation to licenses for hacks, is remitted: provided he pay the costs of prosecution. 2-Act for the relief of Wm Dalton: several fines imposed on him for violations of an ordinance relative to hackney-carriages is remitted, provided he pay the costs of prosecution. 3-Act for the relief of Patrick Moran: for a violation of an act relative to hackney-carriages is remitted, provided he pay the costs of prosecution.

The Hon Isaac C Bates, one of the Senator from Massachusetts, died last evening, at his lodging in Wash City, after an illness of 2 weeks. [Mar 18th newspaper: The funeral services will be today in the Senate Chamber at 12 o'clock; thence the funeral will move to the Railroad depot, where the body will be delivered to the friends & relatives of the dec'd, at their particular request, to be transported for interment to the place of his residence in Massachusetts.]

Appointments by the Pres, with the advice & consent of the Senate:
Jas Buchanan, of Pa, to be Sec of State
Robt J Walker, of Miss, to be Sec of the Treas
W L Marcy, of N Y, to be Sec of War
Geo Bancroft, of Mass, to be Sec of the Navy
Cave Johnson, of Tenn, to be Postmaster Genr'l
John Y Mason, of Va, to be Atty Genr'l
Alex'r H Everett, of Mass, to be Com'r to China
Benj G Shields, of Ala, to be Charge to Venezuela
Wm H Polk, of Tenn, to be Charge to Naples
Albert G Jewett, of Maine, to be Charge to Peru
Benj F Butler, of N Y, to be D A for the Southern District of N Y
Elijah F Purdy, of N Y, to be Surveyor of the Port of N Y
John Davis, of Pa, to be Surveyor of the Port of Phil
Wm Parmenter, of Mass, to be Naval Ofcr of Boston
Prosper M Wetmore, of N Y, to be Navy Agent at N Y
____ McLaughlin, of Tenn, to be Recorder of the Genr'l Land Ofc
Robt Armstrong, of Tenn, to be Consul at Liverpool
J V Bradford, of Tenn, to be a Purser in the Navy
J H Prentiss, to be Marshal for the Northern District f N Y
Naval Appointments:
Chas H Haswell, Engineer in Chief; & as Chief Engineers, John Faron, jr, Andrew Hebard, Jas Thompson, Wm P Williamson, Chas B Moss, Wm Sewell, jr & Wm W W Wood.

Died: on Mar 16, Mrs Sarah McPherson, in her 69th year. Her funeral will be from her late residence, on B st, between 10th & 11th sts, on Tue at 3 o'clock.

Died: on Sun, after an illness of a few hours only, Felix, aged 6 years, s/o C M Keller. His funeral will be from the residence of his father on 10th st, between F & G sts, this day at 4 o'clock p m.

TUE MAR 18, 1845
House for rent in the immediate neighborhood of the Capitol square. Also, a convenient 2 story brick house on Missouri st, between 4½ & 6th sts. –Geo Watterston

Patent Ofc, Mar 13, 1845. 1-Ptn of Ross Winans, of Balt, praying for the extension of a patent granted to him for an improvement in axles of railway & other wheeled carriages, for 7 years from the expiration of said patent, which takes place on Jul 20, 1845. 2-Ptn of Chas Evans, of Phil, for extension of a patent granted to him for an improvement in the Press, for 7 years from the expiration of said patent, which takes place on Jun 13, 1845. –Henry L Ellsworth, Com'r of Patents

Trustee's sale: deed of trust executed Feb 23, 1843, recorded in Liber W B #100, folios 1 thru 4, a land record of Wash Co, D C: sale on Apr 19, of part of square 878, in Wash City: with a large well-built ice-house: situated near the Navy Yard market-house, immediately in the rear of the residence of Dr Alex'r McWilliams.
–Henry May, Trustee -Robt W Dyer & Co, aucts

Boots, Shoes & Palm Leaf hats: will be sold for cash or good paper.
–W Noyes & Son, La ave, Wash

For sale: 2 story brick house on D st, at 13½ st. –Nicholas Callan, jr

Naval: the Boston papers announce the death of Col Wm H Freeman, of the U S Marine Corps, at Westboro', on Tue.

Mr David Yearsley, merchant, Nauvoosa, Ill, was robbed in Phil on Mon of $4,280. He was a passenger in the western train of cars, & had his wallet in his pocket a short time before the arrival of the train.

WED MAR 19, 1845
Act to establish certain post routes: [Those that identify as a "person" are listed below.]
N Y: from Almond, via Ebenezer Allen's house, & Cartwright & Waldroff's store, to Phillipsville
From Ithaca, by Rumsey's Settlement, Cayutaville, & Catharine center, to Havana
Pa: from Pittsburg, by Logan's Ferry, to Shearersburg
Va: from Tazewell court-house, via Clear fork of Sandy river, to it mouth; thence down said river to the house of Philip Lambert; thence to Eli Lusk's, on Little Huff's creek
N C: from Rutherfordton, via Poorsfield, Edwin Thorn's, Buck creek, & R H Hicks', to Shelby court-house

From Kinston, Lenoir Co, via R D Nunn's, Lewis Jones', & Stephen M Graddys', to Hallsville, Duplin Co

S C: from Newbury court-house, Shop Spring, John Williams', Wells store, Island Ford, & Saluda Homestead, thence to Woodville, in Abbeville district

Ky: from Somerset, Pulaski Co, Ky, to London, in Laurel Co, via John Rabbitts

From the Poplar Plains, Fleming Co, via the dwlg house of Wm Philips, in same county, & the dwlg house of Joshua Knap, Carter Co, to Grayson, the seat of justice in Carter Co

From Mount Sterling, in Montg Co, via the store of Thos T Dobbins, & North Middleton, to Paris

From Morefield, Nicholas Co, via the dwlg house of Thos Hawkins, on Licking river, Bath Co, & the dwlg house of Thos A Matthews, to Sharpsburg, in Bath Co

From West Liberty, Morgan Co, via the dwlg house of Danl Horton, to the dwlg house of Wm Brown, on Point creek, intersection the mail route from West Liberty, in Morgan Co, to Louisa, Lawrence Co

From Princeton, Caldwell Co, via the house of John W Jenkins, to Providence, Hopkins Co

Tenn: from Rodgersville, via Thos I Lee's, to Ruselville

From Lynchburg, Tenn, via Wm A Tucker's, Arnold's store, Shelton creek, & Jacob Hamilton's, to New Market, Madison Co, Ala

From Lynchburg, Tenn, via Jacob Awalt's, to Winchester Springs

From Fayetteville, via Stone Cracker & McCarty's Mills, Kinderhook, & Arnold's store, to Salem, in Franklin Co

From Jackson, via Brownsville, Wesley Haywood, to Memphis

From Somerville, Fayette Co, to J K Hervey's, thence 10 miles to Whiteville, Hardiman Co, thence to Meden, Madison Co, thence to Jackson

Ohio: From Finely, Hancock Co, via Cannonsburg, Wm Morrison's, in Orange township, & Armorsville, to round Head, Hardin Co

From Cincinnati, by Mears' Farm, Withamville, Amelia, Bantam, & Bethel, to Felicity

From Toledo, via Lyman Parker's Farm, Chatfield's Mill, Bridgewater, Angola, Jackson, Prairie Lima, & White Pigeon, to St Joseph, in Michigan

Indiana: From Rochester, in Fulton Co, via Troy, Gilead, Nicoma, & Jos Beckner's, to Wabashtown, in Wabash Co

From Lafayette, via Rensselaer, John Jones', in Porter Co, Valparaiso, to City West

From Mooresville, via Waidsville, Millgrove, Upper Falls, Eel river, & Saml Kaufmans' to Poland post ofc, in Clay Co

La: from *Fort Jesup* to G B Beers', on the Sabine river

From Nachitoches to Mount Lebanon, via St Maurice, Cedar creek, Saline Mills, Mr Prother's, Mobley's Mills, & Robinson's Mills, weekly

Arkansas: A post route from Perryville, via Wm Haton's, Green Smith's, Jas Briggs', Wm J Park's, to Park's post ofc, in Arkansas

Post route beginning at Little Rock: to Walter Canthron's, 10 miles; thence to Dallas, Arkansas

Post route from Columbia, Chicot Co, via Clarke's plantation, on the Bartholomew Fountain prairie, Longview, Burk's Landing, to Eldorado, the seat of justice of Union Co

Post route from Izard court-house, Arkansas, to Springfield, in Missouri, via John T Talbot's, Thos Stone's, on Little North Fork of White river

Post route from Little Rock, via the residence of Jas Lewson, jr, & North Fork settlement, the nearest route to Hot Springs

From Jos Tomlinson's, on the route from Washington, Hempstead Co, via Black Jack & Vache Grass, to *Fort Smith*

Missouri: from High Creek post ofc, Holt Co, to Danl Huntsacker's on the Nishenabotns

From Savannah, by Back & Moore's Mills, to the Three Forks of Nodaway river, to Andrew Brown,'s Mill

The dwlg of Geo P Fisher, of Dover, Dela, was destroyed by fire on Mar 10, whilst he was absent from home. Two of his children, a boy of 4 years & a girl of 2 years, were rescued from the burning bldg by an aunt, Mr Celia Richards; but they were badly burnt & are in critical condition.

Making a fence. Married, at barn-stable, by Rev John Gates, Mr John Post to Miss Sophia Rails. If this match don't make a fence of the first quality, we should like to know what stuff will.

The last Natchez Courier says: the town of Woodville has lost 2 estimable citizens: a rencontre occurred between Mr B F Herbert & Mr Fenner, both said to be mild, & honorable men, which resulted in the death of Mr Herbert. A few days later, a rencontre took place between Mr Fenner & a brother of the dec'd Herbert, which has resulted in the death of Mr Fenner.

The residence of Mrs Pike, wid/o Gen Pike, was recently destroyed by fire, with everything therein-the family barely escaping. It was a splendid residence, just completed, standing on the banks of the Ohio, about 3 miles above Cincinnati, on the Kentucky shore.

A large 4 story wooden bldg in Dedham, Mass, owned & occupied in part by the New England Silk Co, was consumed by fire on Tue, together with its contents. A portion of the bldg was occupied by Mr Lucius P Nutting, silkdyer, Messrs S & F Mann, manufacturers of marble paper, & the basement story by Mr Saml Bickner, machinist. Loss is estimated at $10,000 or $12,000. Bldg was insured about $3,000, & the same amount on the materials in the silk factory. About 75 operatives are deprived of employment.

$50 reward for runaway negro girl Kitty, sometimes called Catharine Traverse: about 17 years of age. -Henry J Ball, living near Centreville, PG Co, Md

$1,900 reward offered by the Govn'r & citizens of Ohio for the arrest of Henry Thomas, alias Thos Dean, charged with the wilful murder of Fred'k Edwards, of Bourneville, Ross Co.

A man named Cowdrey was killed at Malden, Mass, on Tue of last week by the bursting of a gun used in firing a salute in honor of the inauguration.

Criminal Court-Wash: 1-John Thomas, free negro, an old offender, convicted of stealing boots & shoes of the value of about $20, the property of Christian Klopfer. 2-Thos Tanner, jr, found guilty of burglariously entering the shoe store of Benj Thompson, on Feb 16, stealing shoes of the value of $80. 3-John B Frizzell was put on trial for receiving part of the stolen shoes, knowing them to have been stolen. He left them in the hen-house attached to Frizzell's dwlg, near the Chain bridge. 4-The U S vs Robt Johnson, free negro, charged with stealing a gold watch & chain, the property of Mary Heislip. He was entitled to be discharged because the owner of the property had not been produced to prove her property. [Mar 24th newspaper. Sentences: 1-John Thomas-18 months in the penitentiary. He attempted to cut his throat, but was overpowered & conveyed to the penitentiary with the other convicts. 2-Thos Tanner: 3 years in the penitentiary. 3-Frizzell: 2 years in the penitentiary.]

Mrd: on Mar 17, by Rev Mr Furgerson, Mr Lewis A Tarlton, of Wash City, to Mrs Julia A West, formerly of Balt.

Died: on Mar 13, suddenly, in Gtwn, D C, Mr Zachariah Gatton, aged 73 years, a native & resident of Montgomery Co, Md. He was a member & elder of the Presbyterian Church, an affectionate husband, kind father, indulgent master, & obliging neighbor. He has passed away leaving to his children & the community an unblemished reputation.

Died: on Mar 9, in her 30th year, at *Willow Brook*, her residence, Mrs Catharine Duckett, d/o the late Wm Bowie, of Walter, & consort of Thos Duckett, of PG Co, Md.

Died: on Mar 13, Maria Christina Smith, the beloved d/o John C & Matilda E Smith, of Wash City, at the age of 7 years.

Communicated: we are called to mourn the death of Mrs Mary S Magruder, consort of C C Magruder, of Upper Marlborough, Md, who died on Mar 5. She leaves a disconsolate husband & young ones whose wants a mother's love only can supply.

THU MAR 20, 1845
Exchange Hotel, Exchange Place, Balt, Md. The subscriber had purchased Mr Erastus Coleman's interest, & become sole lessee of the above establishment. –John West

$50 reward for notes lost yesterday, $295, between 7th st & the Treasury Dept. Reward if returned to the owner, at Patrick Moran's Railroad Hotel. –Stephen W Day

Valuable Mississippi land for sale: 1,560 acres in Hinds Co; 1,129 acres in same county, on Baker's creek; 1,040 acres in same county, 5 miles of Edward's Depot; 600 acres on the road to Vicksburg-with dwlg house; 240 acres in same county, with common dwlg & out-houses; 560 acres in Tallahatchie creek, Rankin Co; 160 acres of "wild land" in yazoo Co; 296 acres of "wild land" in Wash Co; 641 acres unimproved land in Hinds Co. The undersigned is desirous to dispose of the above lands. For further information address Amos R Johnston, Raymond, Miss, or the undersigned. Thos Hundley, Raymond, Miss

Valuable tract of land at auction: by virtue of 2 deed of trust, the one from Augustine Newton, dec'd, to Lawrence B Taylor, dated Mar 2, 1843, the other from the said Augustine Newton to Danl Dayton, dated Jan 16, 1844: sale on Apr 15, in front of the Marshall House, Alexandria, a tract of 248 acres, 8 miles from the town of Alexandria, now occupied by Mr Chas A Newton. There is a small comfortable dwlg-house on the premises, together with all requisite outbldgs. –Lawrence B Taylor, Trustee under 1st deed -Danl Dayton, Trustee under 2nd deed

FRI MAR 21, 1845
Laws of the U S, passed at the 2nd Session of the 28th Congress. 1-Act for the relief of Thos Bronough, of Ky: Sec of War to place him on the roll of invalid pensioners, at $4 per month, from Apr 12, 1844, & to continue during his natural life. 2-Act for the relief of Wm Rich: to be paid $252.22, being in full payment of any equitable claim he may have upon the U S for having relinquished his interest, as a custom-house ofcr in Vt, in the result of a suit at law, [in a case of smuggling, upon which he had expended a considerable sum of money,] to enable him to become a witness for the Gov't. 3-Act for the relief of March Farrington: Sec of War to direct his name be put on the roll of invalid panesioners, & be paid $8 per month, to commence on Dec 23, 1843, & to continue during life. 4-Act for the relief of Danl Homans: to be paid $3,257.36, being the amount due him for damages sustained by lightning, money retained, & extra work done on the marine hospital built by him for the U S in 1831, 1832, & 1833. 5-Act for the relief of John H McIntosh: to be paid $9,950, being the value of certain of his property destroyed by a military ofcr of the U S, under due authority. Sec of War shall cause to be ascertained the quantity & value of the cotton destroyed on the same occasion by order of the commanding ofcr; that the Sec of Treas shall pay the sum certified by the Sec of War for the same, not exceeding the sum of $4,331.25. 6-Act for the relief of Jos Simmons, of North Brookfield, Mass: name to be placed upon the roll as an invalid pensioner, to receive $8 per month, from & after Mar 4 last. 7-Act for the relief of Dunning R McNair, former mail contractor on route 1,115, from Bedford to Wash, Pa, to cause to be audited & paid, to McNair, at the rate of $11,550, from the time it shall be found the great western mail from Phil to Wheeling, Va, was put upon said route, until the same was

restored to the original route via Balt & nat'l road to Wheeling, under contract made with Stockton & Stokes, on Jun 3, 1837, deducting therefrom the amount heretofore paid the said McNair, under his conditional & privileged bid of carrying passengers. 8-Act for the relief of Elisha Morrell, adm of Jos Icard, dec'd: Sec of Treas to settle with & pay Morrell, one third of whatever sum may have been retained in the U S Treasuty on account of an award made by the com'rs under the convention with France on Jul 4, 1841, in behalf of Julien S Raulet, on account of the loss of the cargo on board of the vessel **Cadoz**, after deducting any commissions or charges which may have been allowed for attending to said claim. 9-Act for the relief of Harvey & Slagg, of N Y C: to pay the drawback of duties upon 10 cases of merchandise, duly entered for exportation at the N Y custom-house on Nov 4, 1839, examined by the proper ofcr, found correct, & sent alongside of the ship **Patrick Henry**, in charge of the proper ofcr of the customs, & which were actually exported on board said vessel, & landed in Liverpool; the payment of which drawbacks of duties was withheld by reason of informality in lading the said merchandise on board said ship: Provided, the Sec of Treas shall be satisfied that every other requirement of law shall have been fully complied with. 10-Act to extend a patent heretofore granted to Wm Woodworth: patents granted on Dec 27, 1828, for his improvement in the method of planing, etc, extended to the term of 7 years, from & after Dec 28, 1849. 11-Act granting a pension to John E Wright: to be placed on the roll of invalid pensioners at $6 per month, to commence from May 10, 1844, & to continue during his natural life. 12-Act to authorize a relocation of land warrants numbers 3, 4, & 5, granted by Congress to Gen Lafayette: that the legal holder or assignees of these land warrants, granted on Mar 27, 1804, to Gen Lafayette, & located at Point Coupee, La, of 1,000 acres each, & which locations are shown to have been made in material conflict with several older & better grants, shall, upon evidence of right to the warrants, be permitted to enter & locate a like quantity of land in any of the unappropriated public lands in the State of Louisiana: Provided, that, before any such register & receiver shall issue to such holders or assignees any certificate of relocation, they shall deposite a copy of their deraignment of title from Gen Lafayette, & a release of title to the lands located at Point Coupee. 12-Act for the relief of Jos Ramsey, of Wythe Co, Va: be & he is hereby, discharged from all further liability upon a judgment had & now outstanding against him, John H Price, & Saml McCamant, in favor of the U S, in the District Court of the U S, for the Western District of Va, at Sep term, 1839, of said court: Provided, that nothing herein contained shall operate to discharge the said John H Price & the said Saml McCamant in any way from their liability on said judgment. 13-Act for the relief of Stanely White: White purchased of the U S at the **Fort Wayne** land ofc, Ind, the west half of section 30, in township 30 north, of range 10 east, containing 330 acs, by paying John Spencer, the receiver of public moneys at said land ofc, the sum of $414.50, & receiving his duplicate receipt for the said sum, describing said land, dated Jul 18, 1836; & prior to said entry by White, on Jul 12, 1836, one Chas H Lewis entered at said ofc the s w qrtr of said section 30, township 30 north, of range 10 east, being the south half of said half section, containing 167 acs, for which he paid $209.20. & for which said last qrtr section a patent has been issued to the said Chas H Lewis: whereas, also, the said ofcrs of said land ofc made no return of said purchase by said Stanley White, except for the n w qrtr of said section, containing 164 acs, whereby the Com'r of the Gen Land Ofc is unable to order the refunding the said sum of $209.20 to the said Stanley White; & the said John Spencer is represented & believed to be totally insolvent. The Sec of the Treas is to pay to Stanley White, his assigns or legal reps, the sum of $209,20. 14-Act for the relief of Walker, Kinkle, & Caruthers: Auditor of the treasury for the Post Ofc Dept state the account of the above, for their service in transporting the mails from Feb 1, 1835, to Aug 6, 1836, allowing them at the rate of $2/3^{rd}$ the excess paid M A Price & Co, who became the contractors, & who on the said Aug 6 took possession of the routes, over & above the amount allowed to Walker, Kinkle, & Caruthers, under their contract for the same routes: Auditor to deduct any sum which may have been paid to them, & pay to them, the balance, if any. 15-Act for the relief of John Adams & John Adams, jr, of Mass, to be repaid the sum of $500, the amount paid by them in satisfaction of a fine imposed by Mr Charles, the revenue ofcr of Elizabeth City, N C, for an alleged violation of the revenue laws of the U S. 16-Act for the relief of Edw A Lambert: if satisfied that a mistake was made in his bid, or his contract, for the supply of stationery to the N Y custom-house to his injury, the Sec of the Treas shall pay the same out of any moneys in the Treasury not otherwise appropriated: Provided, the amount to said Lambert shall not exceed $127.41. 16-Act for the relief of Isaac Allen: name to be placed on the invalid pension-roll & pay him at the rate of $4 per month, commenced on Jan 1, 1840, & continue during his natural life. 17-Act for the relief of the legal reps of Alex'r Mitchell, dec'd: they are released from 4 judgments, & all liens & emcumbrances of said judgments, in favor of the U S, obtained in the U S district court for the western district of Va, against the said Alex'r Mitchell, in his lifetime, as security for Peter Yarnall & Saml Mitchell: Provided, that nothing herein contained shall operate to release the said Peter Yarnall or Saml Mitchell from their liability on said judgments. 18-Act for the relief of Benj S Roberts: to release & discharge him from all liability to the U S for or on oaccount of any judgment or judgments, decree or decrees, bonds or obligations in favor of the U S against him, he, the said Roberts, releasing & conveying to the U S all his right, title, & interest in & to all the lands mentioned in a certain mortgage-deed, made, executed, & delivered to the U S, on Apr 13, 1839, by the said Benj S Roberts: The Sec of the treas is directed to adjust the account for services, pay, & rations of Roberts, prior to his resignation of the ofc of lt in the line of the army of the U S. 19-Act for the relief of Philip Schwartztrawber, of Ohio: Sec of the Treasury to pay him for his services in taking care of the booms left on Red river by Capts Tyson & Shreve, the sum of $240.

The following are the appointments made by the Methodist Protestant Conference for this District: in Wash-first Church, J J Murray; 9th st Church, H D Moore; Gtwn, Josiah Varden; Alexandria, Dr J S Reese.

The **Boonsboro'** Odd Fellow states that about 160 families intend leaving Washington Co for Illinois this spring & summer. From the neighborhood of Boonsboro's a considerable number are going.

Household & kitchen furniture at auction on Mar 24, at the boarding-house occupied by Miss Lane, on Pa ave, between 3rd & 4½ sts. -Robt W Dyer & Co, aucts

For rent, the wharf & warehouse, adjoining the establishement of Thos Blagden, on the Eastern Branch, near the Navy Yard. For sale, square 900, near Pa ave, east of the Capitol. This square has been in cultivation for several years, & would suit well for a market garden or bldg. Inquire of Mr Jas Crandle, near the Marine Garrison.

Positive sale of 2 entire squares of ground in the 1st Ward: squares 138 & 139, between 18th & 19th sts west, Wash, the property of the late John Gadsby. Title indisputable. -Robt W Dyer & Co, aucts

One month from England. Obit-died: the Earl of Effingham died at Brighton at age 78. Sir Thos Fowell Burton died on Feb 19 at his seat in Norfolk, aged 59. His name is known throughout the world as the great friend of the negro race, & the advocate for their emancipation. He was also the projector of the Niger expedition. The Earl of Mornington, better known as Lord Maryborough, or as Wm Wellesley Pole, died in London, Feb 22, in his 82nd year. He was a brother of the Duke of Wellington, & of the late Marquess Wellesley. The Marquis of Westminister died at his country seat, Eaton Hall, near Chester, on Feb 16. He was in his 79th year. The Rev Sydney Smith, canon of St Paul's, died on Feb 23, after an illness of several months, in his 72nd year. Mr Laman Blanchard, the well known contributor to the London magazines, committed suicide on Feb 15. The death of Mr Blanchard, which occurred some short time ago, is supposed to have been the cause of the fit of despondency under which he labored at the time of his death.

Lands for sale in Gtwn at public auction: by deed of trust executed by the late Jos Nourse on Oct 7, 1835: sale on Mar 27, all that tract of land in said deed beginning at the stone marked on the north side N, & on the south side T, in the line dividing the tract called **Weston** from the lands of the said Jos Nourse, purchased by him of a certain Richd Harrison, at a point on the line, being the 13th line of the survey of **Weston**, as made by Francis Fenwick, according to the plat of said survey: containing 30 acs, more or less. -Rd Smith, Trustee -E S Wright, Auctioneer

10,000 prime inoculated Peach Trees for sale. –David Roe, Haddenfield, N J

Wash City lot #8 in square 104, on 21st st, for sale: an eligible position for a residence. –J Mason, jr

Fashionable & Cheap Clothing: at Roby's Cheap Lane Store, Pa ave, between 9th & 10th sts. –H N Roby

Criminal Court-Washington. 1-On Tue the case of Capt T Sangster, against assault on the ex-Pres J Q Adams, was submitted to the Court. Adams received a letter from Sangster that he did not commit the assault with any malicious intention, & he freely forgave him. The Court, however, sentenced Sangster to 30 days confinement in the county jail, & to pay a fine of $100. The judgment was temporarily suspended in order to enable a ptn to be sent to the Pres for a pardon. 2-Ellen Lindsley, free negress, was tried for stealing bed linen & apparel valued at $8, the property of Eliza Penn: found guilty. She was tried last term for setting fire to a stable & acquitted through a defect in the evidence. 3-Silas Kelly, free negro, found guilty of stealng a diamond breastpin of the value of $75, the property of the Hon W H Stiles. 4-Joanna Edwards, who is a professed fortune-teller, was found guilty of grand larceny, in robbing one of her female patrons & visiters of a reticule containing a small amount of money, a veil, a purse, gloves, gold bracelet, & other articles of the value of more than $7. 5-Asbury Tyler, alias Bush Brooks, was convicted of stealing a pistol, the property of Patrick Murphy. 6-Paul Jones, free negro, found guilty on 2 indictments of assault & battery on Geo Harris & on Mary Ann Harris. [Mar 24th newspaper. Sentences: Silas Kelly: 2 years in the penitentiary. Paul Jones: 1 month in the county jail & fined $5. Asbury Tyler: 2 months in the county jail & fined $5. Ellen Lindsley: 18 months in the penitentiary.] [Mar 25th newspaper: Capt Sangster was on Sat last pardoned by the President.]

Mrd: on Thu, by Rev John C Smith, Mr Amon Woodward to Miss Barbara Lowe, all of Wash City.

Mrd: on Mar 10, at New Orleans, by Rev Mr Scott, Major Washington Sewall, U S Army, to Mrs Mary Zantzinger, d/o the late B Bullitt, of Natchitoches, La.

Mrd: on Mar 11, in Portsmouth, N H, by Rev Chas Burroughs, Chas F Stansbury, of Wash City, to Lucy M Berry, of Portsmouth, d/o the late Lt Wm Berry, of the U S Navy.

Died: on Mar 19, John McFarland, aged 59 years, a native of Londonderry, Ireland, & for the last 25 years a resident of Wash City.

SAT MAR 22, 1845
Information wanted of Mrs Eliz Brooks Handy, writing from Buenos Ayres, South America, under date of Nov 24 last, desires imformation of her brethren. She writes as follows: "I am the only dght among 8 children. My father, Jonathan Brooks, was a wealthy farmer of Ashby, Mass, & married my mother in Ashburnham; her maiden name was Mary Heyward. My mother died when I was about 18 years of age, & in about a year afterwards my father also. Subsequent to this I came for my health to So America with a Mrs Austin. I was married here to Mr Calvin Handy. We soon returned home, & have continued traveling about until I have lost track of all my brethren. There are 7; the last I heard of one was that he superintended the salt works at Salina, N Y; another in some part of Canada; another at the South.

By order of distrain for rent, in arrears due Jas Moore by Wm Murry, or his subtenant, Jas C Young, I shall expose to public sale for cash on Mar 25, 1845, in Wash City, in front of the Centre Market-house, 5 horses, 3 carts, 13 cows, one carryall, 3 sets of harness, & a lot of manure. –H R Maryman, Bailiff

We the undersigned give notice to the public that we have revoked the powers of Mr Wileman Thomas as our agent for making sales of our lands in the western parts of Va. Richmond, Mar 19, 1845. –Wm Gray, Chas F Osborne

The subscriber wishes to engage the servies of a Governess, qualified to teach the higher branches of an English education, French, Music, & Drawing. –Robt Ghiselin, near Nottingham, PG Co, Md.

Lime for sale: just received from the kiln near Wmsport, Md. –Walter Warder, 12th st

Thos B Bigger appointed by the Pres of the U S to be Postmaster at Richmond, Va, to succeed B Peyton, whose term of appointment has expired. Richmond Enquirer: Peyton discharged the duties of the ofc with skill & fidelity, & to the satisfaction of the community.

Nashville Banner: connexion of Donald McLeod with that paper at its Editor is to end on Mar 24, & Gen Washington Barrow is to succeed him; a worthy successor to an accomplished Editor. McLeod resumes his professional career ar a popular lecturer & private instructor in Elocution, Composition, & the cognate branches of Rhetorical Education.

Presentment against Ex-Govn'r Thomas. The Grand Jury now in session in this city have found 2 presentments against F Thomas, of Md, for libel, arising out of his late publications here & elsewhere respecting his domestic grievances.

Died: on Mar 9, at **Oak Ridge**, his residence, in Nelson Co, Va, Robt Rives, [father of the Hon Wm C Rives,] in his 81st year. He was just old enough to take part as a volunteer on the plains of Yorktown. Retiring from the active scenes of commercial adventure while yet in full vigor, he devoted the last 30 years of his life mainly to the care & improvement of a large landed estate. -Enquirer

Died: on Mar 6, at her residence, **Bristol Manor**, Anne Arundel Co, Md, Mrs Ann Drury, w/o Mr Saml Duryr, sen, in her 86th year. She was one of the oldest inhabitants of Md, her native State, having resided there during her life.

Died: on Mar 19, Miss Mary Eliz Everett, aged 20 years.

It certify that Overton Talbert, of PG Co, brought before me a stray black horse, trespassing upon his enclosures. –Benj O Lowndes, J P [Owners to prove property, pay charges, & take him away. –O Talbert]

Atlantic House, corner of Pelham & South Touro sts, Newport, R I: will be opened Jun 10th next for reception of company. The house is entirely new. –Ab'm A Potter, Proprietor

MON MAR 24, 1845
Murder committed on Mon in Hanover, Mass. Three Irishmen, 2 brothers named Stapleton, & one named Dowlan, with others, workmen on the Old Colony Railroad, who had taken St Patrick's day for a holyday, were turned out from a grogshop kept by Seth Perry, & Perry then came to the door with 3 loaded guns, which he discharged at the crowd, killing the 2 Stapletons instantly, & wounding Dowlan so that he died a few hours afterwards. Perry & Enos Bates, supposed accomplice, have been committed to Plymouth jail.

Capt Saml H Marshall, of the American ship **Powhatan**, from Liverpool, was drowned in Mobile bay on Mar 11. His wife & children were on board his vessel, to which he was proceeding in a schnr. Going to look for the ship he stepped off the gangway. He was a native of Portsmouth, N H, & a worthy gentleman.

On Mar 10, as the steam towboat **Pilot** was going alongside the brig **Pioneer**, in the Mississippi, bound to New Orleans, all 4 of her boilers exploded, & she sunk immediately. Persons killed or wounded: H B Webster, Branch Pilot of the brig, badly wounded; Capt Brown, of the towboat, slightly injured; W B Fagan, 1st engineer, killed; Lathrop G Bean, 2nd engineer, badly injured; Wm Reilly, pilot, badly injured; Wm Davis, steersman, missing; Matthew Berry, deck hand, missing; Jos Lauson, fireman, slightly injured; Wm Coltdoff, deck hand, slightly injured; Isaac, deck hand, slightly injured; Wm Buckman, fireman, uninjured; Chas, Jerry, & Bill, negroes, belonging to Capt Gow, uninjured.

Murder in Miller township, Dearborn Co, Indiana, Sat last. Mr Merritt Scoggin, a respectable citizen, was shot through the head while sitting by his own fireside, & was instantly killed. Perpetrator is not known.

It is said that the only person who shares the captivity of Santa Anna, in the cold & gloomy prison of Perote, is his young & beautiful wife, who, by a thousand little acts of kindness & affection, soothes his sorrows, & renders less irksome the horrors of his prison-house. –Cincinnati Atlas

Farm for sale: on which the subscriber resides, in Montg Co, Md, containing 372 acs; commodious dwlg-house & all necessary other out-bldgs. –Jonathan Prout

Boston Evening Gaz, Mar 15. The death of a much esteemed ofcr of the Marine Corps, Lt Col Freeman, died from a kick received from a colt at his farm in Westboro about a week previous to his death. The remains of Col Freeman were brought to this city & deposited in the family tomb in the Boylston burying ground on Thu, followed by a large procession. The reason he was not buried with military honors was not given. He received a commission in Aug, 1812, & was attached to the frig **Constitution**, under Cmdor Bainbridge, as a 2nd Lt of Marines. He participated in the engagement of the **Constitution** with the frig **Java** in Dec, 1812, which resulted in the capture of that well-equipped & full-armed English frig. He was in the action under Cmdor Stewart, with the English vessels of war **Levant** & **Cyane**, in which he acted as a 1st Lt of Marines. He was in the attack on piratical vessels in the Island of Cuba with the lamented Wm H Allen, of the Navy, who was killed at his side. In Jul, 1831, he was brevetted a Lt Col. He leaves his wife & children. His fame belongs to the public, & should be cherished. [See Mar 18th newspaper.]

Orphan's Court of Wash Co, D C. Letters of adm on the personal estate of Geo Smith, late of Winchester, Va, dec'd. –Johnson Furr, adm

Hon John Quincy has resigned the Presidency of Harvard College. He says in his letter that when he attained his 70th year, he resolved, if life & health continued, to hold the ofc 3 years longer. That period having now expired, he withdraws.

Appointments by the President, by & with the advice & consent of the Senate:
David L Gregg, to be U S Atty for the district of Ill, in place of Mark Skinner-commission expired.
Andrew A Kincannon, to be U S Marshal for the northern district of Mississippi, in place of Alex'r K McClung, resigned.
John S Rockwell, to be U S Marshal for the district of Wisconsin, in place of Chas M Prevost-commission expired.
Henry Naylor, Thos Turner, John L Smith, Benedict Milburn, Joshua Pierce, Chas J Nourse, Saml Smoot & Henry Howison, to be Justices of the Peace in Wash Co, D C, & Chas Scott & Wm N Mills to be Justices of the Peace in Alexandria, D C; their commissions either having expired, or being about to expire.
Henry Addison, Mayor elect of Gtwn, to be a Justice of the Peace in Wash Co, D C.
Naval Appointments:
Geo W Latham, to be a Chaplain, vice John P Lathrop, dec'd.
Nath'l Frost, to be a Chaplain, vice Chapman Swan, dec'd.
Nathan C Fletcher, to be a Chaplain, to fill a vacancy.
Passed Midshipman Gough W Grant, to be a lt, vice Lt B S B Darlington, dec'd.
John O Bradford, to be a Purser, to fill vacancy.
Prosper M Wetmore, to be Navy Agent at N Y for 4 years, vice Jas H Suydam, rejected by the Senate.

Saml D Patterson, to be Navy Agent at Phil for 4 years, vice Thos Hayes, whose commission expired on Mar 15.
Geo Lotall, to be Navy Agent at Norfolk for 4 years from Mar 15, re-appointed.
Jos S Watkins, to be Navy Agent at Memphis for 4 years.
Marine Corps:
2nd Lt Robt C Caldwell, to be 1st Lt, vice Lt Geo W Robbins, dec'd.
John C Cash, to be 2nd Lt, vice Lt R C Caldwell, promoted.
Capt Thos A Linton to be a Major to fill vacancy created by the death of Brvt Lt Col Wm H Freeman.
Lt Henry B Tyler to be Capt, vice Capt Thos A Linton, promoted.
2nd Lt Wm L Young to be 1st Lt, vice Lt Henry B Tyler, promoted.
Geo Adams, of Mississippi, to be a 2nd Lt, to fill the vacancy occasioned by the promotion of Lt Wm L Young.

Mrd: on Jan 29 last, at Erie, Green Co, Ala, by Rev D P Bester, Herndon B Robinson to Virginia, y/d/o Wm Sawkins, of Wash City.

Died: on Mar 23, David French, aged 18 years. His funeral will be from his mother's residence, on Capitol Hill, this day, at 4 o'clock.

Henry Diffenbach, Painter & Decorator in Fresco & Oil: many years of successful practice in the decoration of the principal Royal Palaces in Europe. Having been but a short time a resident of Wash City, he can, at present, only refer to his work executed in Mrs Polk's residence, on Pa ave. Orders to be left at Mr J H Eberbach's, 8th & E sts, will be promptly attended to.

For sale: very valuable land for farming or sites for country seats on the heights above Gtwn: 120 acs, south of his residence, running back to the lands of Joshua Peirce. Also, a tract of about 15 acs, north of the residence of the subscriber, fronting the turnpike. Also, a tract of about 30 acres in the rear of & adjoining the farm of Mrs Lyles. Apply to Chas J Nourse, who offers for rent the beautiful country seat on the Heights of Gtwn, formerly occupied by the late Jos Nourse, & more recently by his widow, possession of which may be had on Apr 1 next.

Deed or writings copied: written in French or English. –Thos Bladon, n e corner of Pa ave & 2nd st

Bargains in fancy dry goods: -Geo Stettinius [Local ad.]

$10 reward for strayed or stolen bay horse, which was fastened at 1st & Market sts, Gtwn, on Mar 15. Reward if returned to my farm, **Dallecarlia**, opposite the Little Falls of the Potomac. –W B Thompson

TUE MAR 25, 1845
The subscriber, after Apr 1 next, will place in the hands of a collector all accounts rendered up to Jan last, with orders to close them at once. –S Parker

On Mar 9, at *Fort Stoddard*, as the steamboat **Red Rover**, from Wetumpka, laden with cotton, was descending the river, she came in contact with the vessel **Ruby**, striking her a little forward of the wheelhouse. The **Ruby** sunk in 50 feet of water. Mr John Carter Knight & a negro man drowned.

For rent: store #11 on Pa ave, next to A Lee's Lottery ofc. Also, the store & dwlg #14, at present occupied by Jas Riordan, as a book & stationery store. Possession given on Apr 1. Inquire of J P Pepper

Head's Mansion House, south 3rd st, Phil: refitted & well prepared to receive the traveling community. Mr Head, the former proprietor, will continue to assist in the general supervision. –W P Hunt

Public sale of valuable lots on 4½ st, in square 491. By virtue of a deed of trust from Wm Gadsby, dated Aug 5, 1842, recorded in the land records of Wash Co, D C, in book W B #95, folios 46 to 49: sale on the premises, near Mrs Peyton's, on May 1, 1845. Also, the southern part of lot 22 in the same square. Also, all the north part of lot 24 in the same square. –A Green, Auctioneer

Beautiful & most healthy residence for sale: I offer my farm known as *The Retreat*, in Wash Co, D C, 2½ miles from Wash, on the turnpike road leading from Gtwn to Rockville: contains 64 acs: improvements are on an extensive scale, & the mansion could be well adapted for the residence of a large family or a boarding school. Every thing about the premises is in complete order. –Richd P Pile

Obit-died: on Mar 4, of consumption, in her 25th year, Miss Mary Crowly. She was the pride of all who knew her.

Obit-died: on Mar 15, at the family residence, near Port Tobacco, Chas Co, Md, after a long & painful illness, Mrs Margaret Greenfield, w/o Henry H Hawkins. She was one of the best wives, a most affectionate mother, a kind & indulgent mistress, & a true benefactress to the poor of her neighborhood. Kept almost entirely from the sacred temples of her parish for the last 2 years by the destroying hand of a pulmonary disease, yet she suffered not that time to pass unprofitably with her God, making the Bible her chief study.

Died: on Mar 14, at Balt, in his 20th year, Pedro Mom, of Buenos Ayres, for the last 2 years a student of Mount St Mary's College, Emmittsburg, Md.

Mrd: on Mar 22, by Rev Septimus Tuston, Mr Fairfax F Vernon to Miss Ann Phillips, all of Wash City.

Died: yesterday, in Wash City, after a long illness, Mr Eleazer Peddecord, aged 23 years. His funeral will take place on Wed, at 3 o'clock, from his late residence, on Pa ave, near 4½ st.

WED MAR 26, 1845
Copartnership which has existed between E D Weatherbee & S A Peugh is this day mutually dissolved. Mar 22, 1845. –E D Weatherbee, S A Peugh

Mr Fuller, the driver of the Taunton & Duxbury stage, after the delivery of his passengers at Taunton last evening, & having taken care of his horses, hung himself in his own coach by a silk handkerchief attached to the strap of the middle seat. He has left a young wife. –Boston Transcript of Fri.

Genteel furniture at auction: on Mar 31, at the residence of Mrs Wall, 9th st, between D & E sts. -W Marshall, Auctioneer

Private residence for sale: commodious & pleasant dwlg house on 17th st, a few doors south of the late residence of Gen Macomb: with stabling, carriage & smoke-house, double lot, & fruit trees. Apply to S P Franklin.

Francis Davis, of New London, Conn, was run over by the railway train, within 2 miles of New Haven, on Thu, & killed instantly.

From the Balt papers: Mr Thos Lloyd has been removed from the ofc of Surveyor of the port of Balt, & Mr Wm H Cole, jr, appointed in his place.

Lt P O Hebert, of the U S Corps of Engineers, has been appointed State Engineer of the State of Louisiana.

Wash Corp: 1-Ptn of John Bohlayer: referred to the Cme of Claims. 2-Cmte on the ptn of the executors of Geo Adams, dec'd, reported a resolution referring the same to the Mayor for information. 3-Cmte of Claims: asked to be discharged from further consideration of the ptn of Jas Maher: under consideration. 4-Cmte of Claims: act for the relief of John Howell: passed. Same cmte: act for the relief of J M Peeree: passed.

Geo Morell, Chief Justice of the State of Mich, died at Detroit on Mar 8, at the age of 59. He was a native of Berkshire, Mass, &, in 1831, appointed a Judge of the U S Court for the Territory of Mich.

Trustee's sale of valuable lots: by virtue of an act of Congress, passed Jul 20, 1840, & of the decree of the Circuit Court of Wash Co, D C, made in the cause of Lewis Grant Davidson's heirs: I shall offer on Apr 17 next, the following lots, situated in Wash City:
Lots 1 thru 8 in square 161
Lots 1 to 21 in square 163
Lots 3 to 9 in square 163
Lots 13 to 19 in square 126
Llots 3 to 11 in square 15
Lot 18 in square 127
Lots 4, 6, 7, 8, 11, 13, 15, 16, & 17 in square 168
Lots 2, 3, 4, & 19 in square 169
Lots 1 thru 5 in square 170
Lots 1 to 20 in square 163
Lots 1 to 25 in square 183
Lots 1 to 6 & 8 thru 16, & 18, in square 184.
These lots are opposite the President's square. Plats of the lots can be seen at the ofc of Mr Redin, Gtwn. –Saml G Davidson, Trustee -Robt W Dyer & Co, aucts

THU MAR 27, 1845
The schnr **Mary**, of Deer Isle, Capt Rufus York, was at anchor in that harbor on the night of Mar 12. A large fire was kept in the stove. They awoke enveloped in flames. Capt York, although a good swimmer, sunk before he reached the shore, probably having been burnt. The others landed on a high bluff, half a mile from any house. When they reached there with blood marking their path. Young York, aged 18 years, died on Mar 14. Cole was supposed to be on the recovery on Mar 18. The body of Capt York had not been found. He leaves a sickly wife & a large number of children. The vessel, of which he was the owner, was nearly destroyed, & was not insured. –Boston Adv

Dealer in Paint, Oil, & Glass, C st, Todd's Bldg, Wash. –O Whittlesey

Salisbury [N C] Watchman, Mar 22. On Thu last was reported the deaths of Mrs Mary West, relict of the late Wm West, aged about 80 years, & her grandson, Henry Swink, aged about 12 years, living 4 miles north of this place, whose half consumed bodies were drawn from the flames of the burning & destroyed dwlg of the dec'd. A jury of inquest found that the dec'd had come to their deaths by the violence of some unknown person or persons on Thu, & that the bldg was then fired. Mrs West was known to be in possession of several hundred dollars in silver & paper money.

$450 reward for runaway servant woman Ann Fenwick. I am inclined to think she is in Gtwn, as I have been informed she has relations there. –Jas R Brent, his farm is in Port Tobacco, Md.

N Y Courier of Tue: accident yesterday at the black & whitesmith shop of Edw Duvall, #102 Charlton st. Duvall, about 33 years old, found a cannon ball in the sand & brought it to his shop. In opening it, the shell exploded killing Mr Duvall & 2 others instantly, & severely wounding several others. Mr Aaron O Price, bldr, aged about 39 years, was in the area. When the explosion took place, he received a blow on the back of his head from a piece of the shell, breaking the intire back of his skull & causing instant death. Richd Broderick, a lad 17 years of age, was passing at the time with a young associate by the name of Bennett, was killed by a piece of the shell, which struck him on the right side of the neck, severing the jugular vein, which killed him instantly. Robt Benentt, step-son of Abraham Moses, 280 Hudson st, was thrown into the air & has since died.

Died: on Mar 25, after a short illness, Mary Jane, w/o John McDermott. Her funeral will take place this afternoon, at 3 o'clock, from the residence of Michl McDermott, corner of 3rd & Pa ave.

Died: on Mar 20, at the residence of his father, after a severe & protracted illness, Andrew, 3rd s/o the Hon Richd Thomas, of St Mary's Co, Md, aged 7 years & 10 days.

Died: on Mar 18, suddenly, at **Fort Johnson**, N C, Grace Ann, w/o Dr Alex F Suter, U S Army, & d/o the late Chas F Dejen, of Leghorn, Italy.

FRI MAR 28, 1845
$100 reward for runaway, my boy Patrick, about 18 years old, of a light copper-color. He left without the least provocation. I purchased him of the estate of the late Thos Magruder, near Good Luck, in this county, with whose widow his mother now resides. He is also in the habit of visiting frequently Mr Fred'k Skinner's, near Centreville.
–Thos W Clagett

Removals & appointments by the Executive: N M Miller [transferred from 2nd Assist Postmaster Gen] to be 3rd Assist Postmaster Gen, vice John S Skinner, removed.
Wm Medill, of Ohio, to be 2nd Assist Postmaster Gen, vice N M Miller, transferred as above.
C K Gardner, to the Postmaster of Wash City, vice Wm Jones, removed.
Seth Barton, of La, to be Solicitor of the Treasury, vice C B Penrose, removed.
Robt Rantoul, to the U S Atty for the District of Massachusetts, vice Franklin Dexter, removed.
Marcus Morton, to be Collector for the port of Boston, vice Lemuel Williams, removed.
Isaac H Wright, to be Naval Ofcr for the same port, vice J Vincent Brown, removed.
Gen McNeil, to be Surveyor of the same port, vice ____ Grafton, removed.

The Cincinnati Atlas states that Mr J Crutchell, of that city, has invented a mode of generating gas by which a very superior light is produced at a cheap rate. The apparatus has been placed in several houses in Cincinnati, & also on board the steamboat **Pike**.

Providence Journal: Thos W Dorr is not seriously affected by his now voluntary confinement in the State Prison. His health has improved since he entered the prison.

Any body wishing to purchase a nice Saddle Horse, easy in his gaits, & perfectly gentle for lady or gentleman, has only to call at Mrs Dixon's Stable, on F st, between 11th & 12th sts. He is well worth $100, but, under the circumstances will be sold for $75. The advertiser has neither time nor inclination for chaffering.

The stage from Richmond to Lexington, Ky, was upset on Thu last, falling on Mr A C Franklin, of Fayette Co, & killing him instantly.

Albany, Mar 21. Railroad accident yesterday: Mr Clark Wilcox, who was formerly in the employ of the company, was hit by the train as he walked on the track. He was deaf. He leaves a wife & 4 children.

Benj A Lowndes offers for sale part of the farm on which he resides, near Bladensburg. He wishes to dispose of 100 to 120 acs.

SAT MAR 29, 1845

Obit-died: on Mar 9, in her 30th year, at *Willow Brooke*, her residence, Mrs Catharine Duckett, d/o the late Wm Bowie of Walter, & consort of Thos Duckett, of PG Co, Md. She has left a husband bowed down with grief, & 5 children, among them an infant 5 days & a child 2 years old.

Boots & Shoes for sale: A Coyle & Son. [Local ad.]

Mathew St Clair Clarke was removed from the ofc of Auditor of the Post Ofc Dept, & appointment was made of Peter G Washington, Chief Clerk in the ofc, to be his successor.

It is proposed to build a monument over the remains of 150 Revolutioanry soldiers, at *Ephrata*, Lancaster Co, Pa. During the Revolution, the church of the Seventh-day Baptists was used as a hospital, & thither the wounded from the battle of Brandywine were conveyed, & there the greater portion of them died.

Savannah, Ga, has been thrown into a most painful state of distress by the suicide of a young clergyman of the Episcopal Chuch of that place, the Rev Jas Jackson, late of the diocese of Massachusetts. He drowned himself & his body was found on Thu, in the river, opposite Bonaventure. –Savannah Republican

The copartnership existing between John Lynch & A Brown, under the firm of John Lynch & Co, is by mutual consent this day dissolved. –John Lynch, A Brown [John Lynch will continue the business.]

Chancery sale of real estate in Mississippi. Apply to J Roach, Com'r

Chas A Fletcher, a member of the late House of Delegates of the State of Md from Wash Co, died at his residence on Mon last, in his 39th year.

The remains of the late Hon Senator Isaac C Bates arrived at Northampton, Mass, on Thu. The funeral took place on Sat, at the First Church in Northampton: services performed by Rev Heman Humphrey, D D, late Pres of Amherst College, & Rev Dr Osgood, of Springfield. –Boston Transcript

Mrd: on Mar 25, by Rev Wm Walsh, Jas L White, of Wash City, to Miss Rachael E Gibson, of Kent Island, Eastern Shore of Md.

MON MAR 31, 1845

New English, Classical, & Mathematical Academy will be opened by the subscriber on Apr 15, in the school-house on H st, between 8th & 9th sts, recently occupied by J E Norris. –W S Graff

Embroidered Canton Crape Shawls received & for sale. –Thos McConnell, 49 Balt st, between Gay & Fred'k sts, Balt, Md.

For rent: the house now occupied by C B Penrose, late Solicitor of the Treasury, who will dispose of the unexpired time of his lease, when the occupant can retain it on the same terms for any period. The house is on G st. Apply to C B Penrose, on the premises, or to Jno H Houston.

The copartnership existing under the name of Peddecord & Holland has been dissolved by the death of E Peddecord. The surviving partner, J S Holland will continue the wholesale & retail Grocery business.

The U S ship **Erie** arrived at N Y on Fri from Port Praya, after a passage of 24½ days. List of her ofcrs & passengers:

C C Turner, Lt Commanding
Edw Donaldson, Actg Master & Executive Ofcr
A A Henderson, Assist Surgeon
D Loyd Winder, Passed Midshipman

N B Harrison, Passed Midshipman
Chas W Hays, Passed Midshipman
John H Poor, Capt's Clerk
John P Gregson, Master's Mate

Passengers: Lts Jas F Miller, Wm Taylor Smith, Wm Decatur Hurst, C S McDonough, Acting Master, F W Colby, Passed Midshipman

List of deaths of ofcrs & men belonging to the squadron, which occurred during the month of Dec, from diseases contracted on the coast of Africa:
U S ship **Saratoga**: John Smith, seaman
U S ship **Preble**: Wm A Henry, Passed Midshipman, attached as Acting Master

Emanuel Francisco, boy	Wm King, ordinary seaman
Thos Maher, seaman	Smith Owens, seaman
John Flanagan, seaman	Timothy West, seaman
Simon Talbot, seaman	Savory Allen, apprentice
Jas G Huston, yeoman	Jas H Shaw, sailmaker's mate
Wm Thompson, seaman	Robt Cleave, seaman
Jas Bryant, capt of the forecastle	John Bannister, boy

Jesse M Smith, midshipman, s/o Lt J Smith, who was lost in the ship **Hornet**

Extensive iron foundry of J R Dorr & Co, Detroit, was wholly destroyed by fire Dec 15.

At New Orleans, on Dec 19, Dr Saml Kennedy was found guilty of the murder of Benj Wood Wait on Dec 29 last.

Very handsome & superior furniture at auction: on Apr 7 next, at the residence of C B Penrose, on G st, between 19th & 20th sts. -Robt W Dyer & Co, aucts

Col Andrew Beirne, of Monroe Co, Va, is dead. He breathed his last in Gainesville, Ala. He served efficiently many years in the Legislature of Va, & was the predecessor of Gen Chapman in the U S Congress. [No date-current item.]

The removal of John S Skinner from the ofc of Assist Postmaster Genr'l is a national disgrace. He has done more than any man living for the true interests of the country, the improvement of Agriculture. Nor was the manner of his removal at all courteous or gentlemanly. The only notice or warning allowed him was a summons immediately to give up his place last evening-& this morning his successor took possession of his chair. –Corres of N Y Courier

<u>Appointments by the Pres, by & with the advice & consent of the Senate:</u>
Custom House Ofcrs. Collectors:
Richd Jordan, Saco, Main, vice Tristam Storer, whose commission expired.
Jas Osborne, Kennebunk, Maine, vice Danl Remick, whose commission expired
Wm M Jackson, Plymouth, Mass, vice Ebenezer Bacon, whose commission expired
Thos F Carpenter, Providence, R I, vice Wm R Watson, whose commission expired.
Norris Wilcox, New Haven, Conn, vice R R Hinman, whose temporary commission expired.
Abel Huntington, Sag Harbor, N Y, vice John H Payton, rejected.
Thos J Pastaer, Ocracoke, N C, vice Sylvester Brown, whose commission expired.

Naval Ofcr: Wm Parmenter, Boston, Mass, vice Geo Roberts, whose temporary commission expired.
Surveyors:
D F Seamans, Providence, R I, vice Wm P Greene, whose commission expired.
Winthrop Pickering, Portsmouth, N H, vice Jos L Locke, rejected by the Senate.
Asa Gray, Tiverton, R I, vice Geo Howland, whose commission expired.
Geo Brown, Pawtucket, R I, vice Silas Sisson, who did not qualify.
E F Purdy, N Y, N Y, vice Henry C Atwood, whose temporary commission expired.
John Davis, Phil, Pa, vice Thos A Cooper, whose temporary commission expired.
Robt Butler, Smithfield, Va, re-appointed.
Gordon Forbes, Yeocomico, Va, re-appointed.
Armand Lefils, Darien, Georgia, vice Edw Hopkins, resigned.
Land Ofcrs: Register:
Jacob Judy, Edwardsville, Ill, vice A W Jones, dec'd.
Wm M Jackson, Chicago, Ill, vice E B Williams, whose temporary commission expired.
Geo Mixter, Dixon, Ill, vice Benj Clifford, whose temporary commission expired.
Thos B Ives, Grenada, Mississippi, vice Wm Hunley, whose temporary commission expired.
Hiram Smith, Champagnole, Arkansas, new ofc.
Receiver:
Wm Wilson, Palestine, Ill, vice David McGahey, resigned.
Saml Leach, Quincy, Ill, vice E A Thompson, whose temporary commission expired.
Chas C Hascall, Genesee, Mich, vice R J S Page, whose temporary commission expired.
Edw Dobyns, St Louis, Missouri, vice Saml Merry, whose commission expired.
G S Gollady, Grenada, Mississippi, vice J H McRea, resigned.
A G Rust, Champagnole, Arkansas, new ofc.

City Hospital-Summer Arrangements. Patients will continue to be received as heretofore on paying to the Steward his compensation of $3 per week. For medicines, medical & surgical attendance, including the performance of operations, no charge will be made. The hospital patients will be visited daily at 12 o'clock, at which time the poor who desire advice & medicines must be in attendance. Part of the bldg has been appropriated to lying-in patients, to whom every attention will be given. Surgeons for the Spring & Summer: Professors Miller & Johnston. Physicians: Professors Lindsly & Riley.

Circuit Court of Wash Co, D C: admitted as attys & counselors of the Court:

A Thomas Smith	Richd H Hagner	Worthington G Snethen
A H Lawrence	Thos J Semmes	Chas E Stuart

Mrd: on Mar 5, at the house of Col Benton, in Wash City, by Rev Mr Spregle, Hon John B Weller, of Ohio, to Miss Susan Preston McDowal Taylor, d/o the Hon Wm Taylor, of Va, & a niece of the gentleman first named.

Died: on Feb 30, Chas M Heseltine, in his 36th year. His funeral will be from his late residence on D st, between 6th & 7th sts, tomorrow at 2 o'clock.

Died: on Feb 30, Edward, s/o John E & Susannah Holland, in his 8th year. His funeral is this day at 3 o'clock from the residence of his father on H st, between 6th & 7th sts.

Died: on Mar 30, in her 63rd year, Mrs Ann Husler, for many years a respected resident of Wash City. She endured a long & painful illness with a truly Christian fortitude. Her friends & the members of the Church to which she belonged are invited to attend her funeral this evening, at 4 o'clock, from her late residence, near the lower bridge.

Advertisement of Messrs Townsend & Clark, manufacturing Dentists, Balt, who insert artificial teeth with gums, that are said to be highly useful & to appear so natural as not to be noticed. Testimonials from Dr T P Jones, Dr Dunbar, & Benj Hallowell.

TUE APR 1, 1845
Sheriffs' sales for delinquency in non-payment of Taxes, are every 5 years, & this is the year of sale. -Jas E Heath, Auditor of Public Accounts, Richmond, Va.

Welsh slate for sale: call on S G Wilbur, slater, Balt, or on the subscriber on E st.
–Enoch Ridgway, slater

Fatal affray in Woodville, Ala, on Mon week, between Jos B Tutt & S S Horton, in which the former was killed by a pistol shot. Mr Horton has been held to bail in the sum of $2,000.

Thos Hale's extensive Dyeing & Printing Works at Rahway, N J, have been entirely consumed by fire, with all their contents. The insurance amounts to $15,000.

Washington College-Pa: winter session has just closed; students in attendance during the session was 160. The price of Boarding in the College bldg, under the superintendence of a steward, is $1.50 per week. The next session will commence on May 1.
–Alex W Acheson, Sec of the Board.

Excellent household & kitchen furniture at auction on Apr 4, at the residence of Chas M Keller, on 10th st, between F & G sts. -Robt W Dyer & Co, aucts

Died: on Mar 27, at his late residence in PG Co, Md, Zachariah Berry, sen, in his 97th year, an ofcr of the Revolution.

Died: on the 28th ult, at Park Gate, near Brentsville, Va, Mrs Euphan Brent, aged 80 years.

Died: on Thu last, at Balt, in his 85th year, Col Jas Mosher, soldier of the Revolution, formerly Pres of the Mechanics' Bank, & for many years Surveyor of the port.

Died: on Mar 13, at Salem, Mass, Miss Mary Peters, & on Mar 16, her twin sister, Miss Betsey Peters, aged 73 years & 4 months. That of the first was very sudden, while in the act of rising from her bed. There was no one in the house except her twin sister, who was in bed with her. The first to give the alarm was an aged sister, nearly 80 years of age, who happened to be passing the house about an hour after, & hearing the growns of her surviving sister, went in & found her sitting in a chair & uttering the most piteous moans, & saying "Mary is dead! Mary is dead! She continued for a few hours, when she became unconscious of every thing around her, & gradually sunk away without any apparent disease until Sunday, & died without a struggle. They were both interred in one grave.

Died: on Mar 18, at Springfield, Ill, at the residence of N H Ridgely, Cassandra B Niles, d/o Wm Ogden Niles, [late editor of Niles' Register,] in her 19th year. [Apr 2nd newspaper: obit of Cassandra B Niles: her death was sudden, so unexpected, & fell like a thunder-bolt on the community. If death had made his dreaded visit while at home, if those parents could have watched by her dying bed, ministered to her wants, consoled her parting spirit, it would have been a source of consolation to them, while it would gradually have prepared them for the awful visitation; but to be told in the same breath of her illness & death, will be to them a blow of deep agony. Her remains were on Wed last conveyed to the tomb.]

Died: on Sun last, Rosanna Howard, aged 11 years & 6 months, d/o Mr Henry Howard, of Wash City.

Detroit papers, on Mar 8, announce the death of Geo Morell, late Chief Justice of the State of Michigan, aged 59. He was a native of Lenox, Berkshire Co, Mass, & a graduate of William's College: in 1808 he studied at law at the ofc of John Russell, of Troy, where, among his fellow students, were the Hon Reuben M Walworth, the present Chancellor of the State of N Y, & the Hon Wm L Marcy, the present Sec of War. In 1811 he entered the practice of his profession in Cooperstown, Otsego Co; subsequently abandoned the practice of his profession for the Bench; in 1831 he was appointed one of the Judges of the U S Court for the then Territory of Michigan; on the admission of Michigan into the Union as a State, he was retained on the bench of the Supreme Court for 7 years, & near the close of his term, appointed the Chief Justice of the State. Judge Morell was the brother-in-law, & the guardian of the proprietor of this paper in early life. -N Y Courier & Enquirer

WED APR 2, 1845

Railroad accident: John McAin, a merchant from N C, was accidentally run over by a car at the Balt depot, in Market st, Phil, on Sat, & had his right foot crushed; his cloak caught on the rail & tripped him up. He was taken to the Pennsylvania Hospital. He had just arrived from N Y, & was about starting South.

The old Swedish custom of announcing each hour with a trumpet from the church steeple, & singing a song, to assure the people that no conflagration is to be observed, is still kept up at *Upsala*, & in all the ancient towns of Sweden. –James' Tour

Senor Haro y Tamariz, Santa Anna's late Minister of Finance, has arrived at New Orleans from Havana. He was the individual who took Santa Anna's propositions to the new Congress.

Edgefield [S C] Adv of Thu: On Mon last near Dunton's Post Ofc, a fatal affray took place between Mr Chas Price & Mr Benj F Jones, in which Jones was instantly killed by the discharge of a shot-gun in the hands of Mr Price. We also learn that a similar occurrence took place near Aiken between Mr Buckhalter & Mr Taylor, in which Taylor was dangerously wounded, & not expected to recover.

Jonas L Parker, tax collector of the town of Manchester, N H, was murdered on Mar 26. A wallet, containing $1,635 was found on the body; but a pocket-book, filled with a large lot of bills, which he had been seen to have during the day, is missing.

Mrd: on Mar 31, by Rev Septimus Tuston, Mr Elijah Peacock to Miss Ann Rose, both of Loudoun Co, Va.

Died: yesterday, Mrs Micha Ann Rhodes, consort of Mr Jas Rhodes, in her 46th year, after a short but painful illness. Her funeral is tomorrow at 10 o'clock, from the residence of her husband, near the Navy Yard gate.

Died: yesterday, of consumption, Mr Geo W Thorn, in his 22nd year. His funeral is today at 2 o'clock, from the residence of Mr Alexander, on N Y ave, between 12th & 13th sts.

Gen Chas R Floyd died at his residence in Camden Co, Ga, on Mar 22. He was a gallant soldier & chivalrous citizen, & rendered essential service to his native State, & has left many friends to bewail his decease in the prime of manhood. –Savannah Georgian

Judge Gilbert Leonard, of Plaquemines, La, was wounded in a duel with Philip Toca, about 10 days since. The Judge had a rib or two broken & a ball lodged in his shoulder.

The extensive flouring mill of Robt Halsey, on Owego st, Ithaca, was destroyed by fire a few days' since.

Appointments by the President:
Custom-house Ofcrs. Collectors:
Augustus Jenkins, Portsmouth, N H, vice Lory Odell, removed.
Marcus Morton, Boston, Mass, vice Lemuel Williams, removed.
Chas F Lester, New London, Conn, vice Gerard Carpenter, resigned.
Jos P Junkins, York, Maine, vice Jeremiah Brooks, removed.
Parker McCobb, jr, Waldoboro, Maine, vice Goe Allen, removed
Jas Taylor, Wiscassett, Maine, vice Moses Shaw, removed.
Naval Ofcr: Danl Vaughan, Portsmouth, N H, vice John McClinton, removed.
Surveyors: John McNeil, Boston, Mass, vice Jos Grafton, removed.
Wm H Cole, jr, Balt, Md, vice Thos Lloyd, removed.
Land Ofcr: John Dement, Dixon, Ill, vice Jas Swan, removed.

For rent: the house & lot now occupied by Lt Sands, of the Navy, corner of 8th & E sts: the house is a 2 story brick, with 6 excellent bed chambers: good brick smokehouse, stable, & carriage house. Possession on Jun 1, or before if desired. Apply to Edw Dyer.

Wash Library Co meeting on Apr 7, at the Library Rooms, on 11th st. Judges of Election: Messrs Wm Anderson, Z W Denham, & John Sessford, jr. –Jas F Haliday, Sec

To let: large 2 story brick house, D & 12th sts; carriage-house & stable attached to the dwlg-house. Possession immediately. Rent reasonable. –John P Van Ness

THU APR 3, 1845
Valuable land near Wash City at auction: on Apr 3 next, about 62 acs, distant a quarter of a mile from the city boundary, lying n e of the Capitol, near the ***Tiber Mill***, & bordering on the new county road leading from Bladensburg: will be offered in lots or in a body. Plot of the land may be seen at our auction store.
-Robt W Dyer & Co, aucts

For rent: commodious house on C st, between 3rd & 4½ sts, at present occupied by Mrs Abercombie, & adjoining the residence of Mrs D Galvin. Possession given immediately.

A Board of Naval Surgeons will be convened at the Naval Asylum, Phil, on May 1 next, for the examination of Assist Surgeons in the Navy. The Board will consist of Surgeon John A Kearney, Pres; Surgeons Isaac Hulse, B F Bache, Thos Dillard, & S Barrington, Members.

Orphan's Court of Wash Co, D C. Letters testamentary on the personal estate of Phineas Bradley, late of said county, dec'd. –W S Bradley, Executor

$100 reward for runaway negro Andrew, 25 years old. –Mortimer Smith, Chaptico, St Mary's Co, Md

Orphan's Court of Wash Co, D C. Letters testamentary on the personal estate of Phineas Bradley, late of said county, dec'd. –W S Bradley, Executor

$100 reward for runaway negro Andrew, 25 years old. –Mortimer Smith, Chaptico, St Mary's Co, Md

The dwlg-house of Mr Merrill, near Alexandria Bay, Jefferson Co, N Y, was burnt to the ground on Mar 20, with its entire contents. Two of Mr Merrill's children, who were asleep in the house, were burnt to death. The family were not at home at the time of the disaster.

The Trustees of District school #7, in Chas Co, Md, wish to employ for the residue of the year a Teacher. His salary will be $250, board included. By the order of the Board of Trustees, F B F Burgess, Sec.

Obit-died: Mrs Micha Ann Rhodes: language fails in endeavoring to pay an adequate tribute to her memory. As a dght, none could be more cheerfully submissive to parental authority; as a wife, none could be more tender & affectionate; & as a Christian, none more truly pious & exemplary. Long will St Peter's congregation mourn her loss. I understand that her funeral obsequies will be performed in St Peter's Church, Capitol Hill, this morning at 10 o'clock.

Hall of the Franklin Fire Co, Wash, Apr 1, 1845. Meeting due to the death of Geo W Thorn, late a member of this company. In consideration of the services & worth of Mr Thorn as a fireman, this company will attend his funeral tomorrow at 2 o'clock. Messrs Robt E Doyle, Thos J Fisher, & John T Mitchell be a cmte to make all necessary arrangements. –Robt Coltman, Pres -L A Iardella, Sec

Switzerland: It is believed that the Genr'l of the Jesuits at Rome has resolved to suppress the Jesuits' College in Switzerland, in order to prevent the civil war which is menaced by the continuance of the Jesuits in that country.

Theophilius Fisk will deliver a Lecture before the Union Literary & Debating society, in the room of the 10th st Baptist Church, this evening. Subject: the women of the Revolution, or woman's worth, influence, duties & responsibilities. –C Drew, Sec

Country residence wanted, & Gtwn property for sale or exchange. The subscriber wishes to purchase or rent a small country place, from 3 or 4 to 10 or 15 acs, within 3 miles of Gtwn, & will exchange or sell for such property, a new, well-built, 2 story frame house, with a large garden & stable, on 2nd st, Gtwn, near the College gate. Apply to me on Capitol Hill, N J ave, near the residence of Dr F May. –Mary A B Cummin

FRI APR 4, 1845
Army of the U S. War Dept, Adj Gen Ofc, Wash, 31, 1845. Genr'l Orders, #9.
Promotions & Appointments in the U S Army, made by the Pres, by & with the advice & consent of the Senate, since Jan 1, 1845.
Promotions-Corps of Engineers:
2nd Lt Henry W Halleck to be 1st Lt, Jan 1, 1845, vice Campbell, dec'd.
Brvt 2d Lt Gustavus W Smith to be 2nd Lt, Jan 1, 1845, vice Halleck, promoted.
1st Regt of Dragoons:
2nd Lt Andrew J Smith to be 1st Lt, Mar 4, 1845, vice Schaumburg, whose appointment ceased on that day.
Brvt 2nd Lt Thos C Hammond to be 2nd Lt, Mar 3, 1845, vice Smith, promoted.
Brvt 2nd Lt Rufus Ingalls, of the 2nd Dragoons, to be 2nd Lt, Mar 31, 1845, vice Rust, resigned.
1st Regt of Artillery:
2nd Lt Henry D Grafton to be 1st Lt, Feb 24, 1845, vice Aisquith, cashiered.
Brvt 2nd Lt Abner Doubleday, of the 3rd Artl, to be 2nd Lt, Feb 24, 1845, vice Grafton, promoted.
3rd Regt of Artl:
Brvt 2nd Lt Hachalish Brown, of the 4th Artl, to be 2nd Lt, Mar 1, 1845, vice Hillhouse, resigned.
8th Regt of Infty:
1st Lt Jas V Bomford to be Capt, Mar 4, 1845, vice Birdsall, dec'd.
2nd Lt Arthur T Lee to be 1st Lt, Mar 4, 1845, vice Bomford, promoted.
Brvt 2nd Lt Jas Longstreet, of the 4th Infty, to be 2nd Lt, Mar 4, 1845, vice Lee, promoted.
Brevet
2nd Lt John C Fremont, of the Corps of Topographical Engineers, to be Capt by brevet, Jul 31, 1844, "for gallant & highly meritorious services in 2 expeditions commanded by himself; the first to the Rocky Mountains, which terminated Oct 17, 1842; & the second beyond those Mountains, which terminated Jul 31, 1844."
Appointment. Medical Dept:
Chas C Keeney, of Mich, [late Assist Surgeon,] to be Assist Surgeon, Mar 19, 1845.
Casualties.
Resignations:
2nd Lt John Hillhouse, 3rd Artl, Mar 1, 1845.
2nd Lt Paul O Hebert, Corps of Engineers, Mar 31, 1845.
2nd Lt T M Rust, 1st Dragoons, Mar 31, 1845.
Assist Surgeon Jacob B Motte, Mar 14, 1845.
Deaths:
Capt Egbert B Birdsall, 8th Infty, at St Augustine, Florida, Mar 4, 1845.
1st Lt Stephen H Campbell, Corps of Engineers, at Jacksonville, Florida, Jan 1, 1845.

Dropped:
1st Lt Jas W Schaumburg, 1st Dragoons, Mar 4, 1845. [Name erased from the Official Army Register by direction of the Pres of the U S, but without reproach to Mr Schaumburg.]
Cashiered: 1st Lt Wm E Aisquith, Feb 24, 1845.
The Ofcrs promoted & appointed will join their proper stations & companies without delay; those on detached service, or acting under special instructions, will report by letter to the commanding ofcrs of their respective regts. By order: R Jones, Adj Gen
Memoriandum: Re-appointment:
Adam D Steuart, re-appointed Paymaster-Army, from Jan 14, 1845, when his former commission expired.

The Magnetic Telegraph-official. Post Ofc Dept, Mar 29, 1845. The appropriation of $8,000 to meet the expenses of the Magnetic Telegraph between Wash & Balt being placed under the charge & direction of the Postmaster General; & it appearing that, under a previous appropriation embracing the same object, which was made for the purpose of testing the practicability & utility of said telegraph, the Sec of the Treas, under authority conferred by act of Congress, had appointed S F B Morse superintendent, at a salar y of $2,000 a year, & 2 assistants, Messrs Alfred Vail-$1,400 & Henry J Rogers-$1,000,& 2 keepers of laboratory & inspectors of wires, at $300 each.
–C Johnson, Postmaster General

Wash Corp: 1-Ptn of Simon Fraser & others: referred to the Cmte on Improvements. 2-Ptn of A Rothwell & others, praying curbstone & footway on front of square 516: referred to the Cmte on Improvements. 3-Ptn of A B Gladmon & others, praying improvement of L st, from 6th to 7th sts: referred to the Cmte on Improvements. 4-Ptn of Jas Mankin & others, regarding gutters on 9th st: referred to the Cmte on Improvements. 5-Application from Rev Mr Gurley to enclose the public spring on C st: referred to the Cmte on Improvements. 6-Cmte of Claims: askng to be discharged from the further consideration of the ptn of Jas Maher: to be laid on the table. 7-Cmte of Claims: made on Nov 18 last, asking to be discharged from the furher consideration of the ptn of Lewis & Elwood, was taken up & agreed to. 8-Act for the relief of O J Prather: passed.

Late English papers. 1-A statue in honor of Chritopher Columbus is about to be erected at Genoa, his birth place. 2-Prince Tufiakin, formerly Chamberlain to the emperor of Russia, long a resident of France, died lately in Paris.

Trustee's sale: by deed of trust, executed Nov 25, 1842, recorded in Liber W R #96, folios 351 thru 360, one of the land records of Wash Co, D C: sale on Apr 26, all the west 30 feet, from front to rear, of that lot of ground in Wash City, known as lot 17 in square 453, with bldgs, improvements, & other hereditaments thereto belong. –Richd Wallach, Michl Nourse, Trustees -A Green, Auctioneer

$5 reward for strayed or stolen from the subscriber, living on 7th st, near the Almshouse, Wash, a horse, missing since last Sun. –Henry C Davis

In pursuance of a decree of the Circuit Court of Wash Co, D C, on Mar 25, 1845, the undersigned Com'rs appointed by said court to sell the real estate of the late Ann Larkin, [formerly Mrs McGunnigle,] will offer at public auction, on May 1 next, two 3 story brick houses on 10th st west, opposite Col Force's, one of them having spacious back bldgs. –D Saunders, John Boyle, Peter Force, J A M Duncanson, Jas A Kennedy

There died at Springton Forge, in West Marlborough township, Chester Co, Pa, on Mar 24, Mrs Esther Townsley, at the remarkable age of 103 years & 11 months. She was born in 1741, & survived through several generations, & at the time of her death her dght's family, in which she resided, was composed of the old lady, her dght, her grand-dght, her great-grand-dght, & her great-great-grand-dght; a regular descent of 5 generations. These were the only persons constituting the house-hold-5 persons each representing a generation. The age of her dght is 70 years, of her great-great-grand-dght about 3 years. Mrs Townsley was born in Ireland; her memory of the events of her early life was unimpaired. –Village Record

Obit-died: the death of Mr Eleazer Peddecord, at the age of 23 years, was a young gentleman of congenial habits & tastes, joined in wedlock to the lady of his choice; to her who was destined by an inscrutable Providence to be the sharer of his few remaining days of sorrow, & at last to close his eyes in death. The painful illness of Mr Peddecord was borne, on his part, with patience & resignation to the Divine will, & his end was peace. Watch! For in such an hour as ye think not the Son of Man cometh.
–H J W [See death notice in Mar 25th newspaper.]

Mrd: on Apr 2, by Rev Dr Laurie, Mr Henry B Clagget, of Alexandria, to Miss Eliz D Fuller, d/o A Fuller.

Died: on Fri last, very suddenly, in Raleigh, N C, Jas Wyche, Pres of the Raleigh & Gaston Railroad Co. He has left a wife & 9 children, we learn, to deplore his loss.

Meeting of the United Brothers of Temperance at the German Church, 1st Ward, on Apr 5, at 4 o'clock. Mr J C Theaker, of Ohio, will address the meeting.
–Edw Owen, Pres

SAT APR 5, 1845
Capt White, of the schnr **Meridian**, from Portsmouth, N H, lying in the dock at Richmond, Va, fell overboard on Mon night & was drowned. He has left a wife & family at the North.

Died: on Mar 11, after an illness of a few days, Mr Wm Kehoe, in his 54th year, leaving an interesting & devoted family to mourn their loss.

St Louis Republican: on Mar 17, at *Fort Scott*, as Capt B A Terrett, 1st Regt Dragoons, was dismounting his horse, having a loaded pistol in his hand, his horse started, & the pistol was accidentally discharged. The ball passed through his right lung, & he survived only about 20 minutes. The army has lost in Capt Terrett, a gallant soldier & an accomplished gentleman.

By virtue of 3 writs of fieri facias, issued by Thos C Donn, a J P for & in Wash Co, D C, at the suit of Julius A Peters, use of Matthew Bouvett, against the goods & chattels of Momus A Gilbert, & to me directed, I have seized & taken in execution all the right, title, & interest of the said Momus A Gilbert, in & to 6 looking glasses, a mahg sofa, 8 chairs, a breakfast table, 2 blankets, 1 table cover, 6 lamps, 5 window curtains, 2 bracket Candlesticks, 2 iron bedsteads, 1 baize-covered table, 1 washstand, 1 basin & ewer, & 1 small center table: sale on Apr 12, at the Centre Market, Wash City.
–R I A Culverwell, Constable

Wm R Riley has just received from the North a large & well assorted stock of Spring Dry Goods.

For rent: house at present occupied by the subscriber, over the shoe store so long kept by himself, on Pa ave, between 6th & 7th sts; & the furniture will also be sold. Possession about May 1. Also, a comfortable dwlg on 13th st south, near the Mall. Possession immediately. For sale: a number of valuable lots, in square 264, on 13th st south. Inquire of the subscriber, Walter Clarke.

Circuit Court of the U S for the District of Middle Tennessee. John McKeon & others, of N Y, cmplnts, against, Godfrey M Fogg, Adm of the goods & chattels, rights & credits of Miles McKeon, formerly of Nashville, Tenn, dfndnt. It was among other things decreed that notice be given of the pendency of this suit in the public papers in Tenn, & other newspapers, as designated in said order, that the next of kin of the late Miles McKeon, late of Nashville, Tenn, dec'd, who died at Nashville on Jun 5, 1844, living at the time of his death, & then residing in the U S A, should make application to be made parties to this suit, which is for a distribution of his personal estate. Any person claiming to be the next of kin of said Miles McKeon, residents in the U S at the time of his death, & in case any of them have since died, the personal rep or reps of him, her, or them so dying, are, by themselves or their solicitors, to come in & be made parties to this suit, make out their claim, at the next Circuit Court of the U S for the Middle District of Tenn, on the first Mon in Sep next. –Jacob McGavock, Clerk of said court

MON APR 7, 1845
For rent: 3 story brick house, with back bldg, on H st, between 10th & 11th sts. The house is new, having been built in 1843. Apply to the subscriber next door east.
–Wm S Clary, Agent

House for sale or rent: on Gay st, Gtwn: contains 2 parlors, 4 chambers, besides other rooms, with good cellars. There is a smoke & milkhouse, with a pump of good water, stabling, & a large garden. Also for sale, a farm of about 175 acs, near Tenallytown, on the Brookville Road. Apply to the subscriber in Gtwn. -Jas McVean

Bran or shorts for sale: cargo of the schnr **Bartol**. At my wharf in Gtwn on Apr 7.
–J W Fearson, Gtwn

Orders for Wigs & Toupets, or Scalps, at my room at Brown's Hotel.
–Thos Quirk, 490 Braodway, N Y

Jas S Holland has associated Washington Lewis with him in the Wholesale & Retail Grocery Business, under the name of Lewis & Holland. –Lewis & Holland

David F Kaufman has been appointed Charge d'Affaires to the U S. He is represented to be an ardent friend of annexation.

Died: on Apr 5, at Petersburgh, Va, after a short illness, Mrs Mary Rosina Stettinius, w/o Mr Wm Stettinius, of that place, & d/o Mr G C Grammer, of Wash City, in her 31st year. Her funeral will take place from the residence of her father on C & 4½ sts, this afternoon at half past 3 o'clock.

Died: on Mar 22, at Madison Barracks, Sackett's Harbor, N Y, Mrs Pamela Brown Vinton, w/o Capt D H Vinton, U S Army, & d/o the late Maj Gen Jacob Brown, aged 34 years. She was imbued with all Christian graces; exemplary as a dght, wife & mother.

Meeting of the Board of Trustees of the Public Schools, at City Hall at 4 o'clock, this evening. –Wm J McCormick, Sec

Obit-died: the Springfield, Ill, papers announce the death of Cassandra B Niles, d/o Wm Ogden Niles, late editor of "Niles Register," & grand-dght of the late Nezekiah Niles, the originator of the same celebrated paper. At 18 years & a few months this lovely flower has been called away from the things of "time & sense for those of eternity." Deprived, far from home, of the cares which maternal solicitude alone can render in grief, in pain, in death-sickness, she yet found friends to cheer her in the hour of deepest trial. This tribute by one who loved her for herself. –E A H

The Patapsco Female Institute, at Ellicott's Mills, near Balt, Md, Mrs Lincoln Phelps, Principal, will be open for the summer session from May 7 next.

Wash City Ordnances: 1-Act for the relief of O J Prather: The $22.21 be paid to Prather for leveling the surplus earth from south F st, deposited in the 2nd Ward.

TUE APR 8, 1845
Falcon Boat Club meeting this evening, at 7½ o'clock. –W C Bestor, Sec

For rent: large 3 story brick house, on s w corner of 12th & F sts. The key may be found in the ofc next door, on F st. For particulars, apply to S P Franklin.

Desirable private residence for rent: the new bldg now occupied by Maj T L Smith, late Register of the Treas Dept; on G st, between 10th & 11th sts; 14 rooms in the house; possession on Apr 22. Application to C Woodward, between 10th & 11th sts, Pa ave.

Mrd: on Mar 20, at Fredericksburg, Va, Dr Wm Wirt, of Balt, [eldest s/o the late Wm Wirt,] to Miss Bettie S Payne, d/o the late Daniel Payne, of the former city.

Mrd: on Mar 27, by Rev Mr Woodley, Mr John Goodrich to Mrs Susan M Bean, all of St Mary's Co, Md.

Mrd: on Mar 27, in Chas Co, Md, at the residence of Col Hugh Cox, by Rev Mr Wilmer, Hillery S Williams, of the Eastern Shore of Md, to Eliz A Richardson, of Alexandria, D C.

Died: on Sunday last, after a short but severe illness, Mr Gustavus Hill, aged 35 years. He has left a wife & 2 small children to deplore their loss. He was an affectionate husband & kind parent, & beloved by all who knew him. His funeral will take place this evening, at 3 o'clock, from his late residence, on 5th st, between G & H sts.

Died: on Apr 7, the Hon Richd Cutts, aged 74 years. His funeral is on Apr 9, at 4 o'clock, from his late residence, on 14th st, between Pa ave & F st.

Died: on Apr 18, at Phil, J Humphrey Bissell, of Charlotte, Mecklenburg Co, N C. He was a native of Simmsburg, Conn. At an early age he was graduated with distinguished honors at Yale College; engaged in the practice of law in Charles, S C; & of late years a successful explorer of the geological resources of the mining districts of the Carolinas & Georgia.

Dissolution of partnership by mutual consent. The business will be contined by R Estep, at the old stand. -R Estep, John T Catlett

Obit-died: on Mar 28, at Park Gate, Prince Wm Co, Va, Mrs Euphan Wallace Brent, at the age of about 81 years. She was born of Jas Wallace & Eliz Westwood, at Evrol, on Back river, Eliz Co, Va; & at the age of 19 was married to Bailey Washington, of Stafford Co, brother to Col Wm Washington, of the Revolution. After the death of Mr Washington, she married the late Danl Carroll Brent, of Richland, in the same county, &, surviving him by many years, she closed her life at her late residence. As a wife, neighbor, friend & companion, her long & well spent life, has descended to the tomb with the universal regrets of all who knew her.

Obit-died: at her late residence in Bladensburg, Md, Mrs Juliana Stephen, wid/o the late Chief Judge of the First Judicial district. The dec'd assumed the vows of baptism in the very flower of her youth, & sustained to the close of a long life the reputation of a devoted & consistent Christian. I will not attempt to portray her solicitude & vigilance as a mother. As a sister, she was kind, confiding, generous, & considerate.

WED APR 9, 1845
Licenses issued for using Carts, Wagons, & Drays, in Wash City, expire on this day, & must be renewed at this Ofc within 10 days, according to law. –C H Wiltberger, Register, Apr 7, 1845.

Obit-died: on Mar 18, in Phil, Col John H Bissell. At an early age he completed his academic education at Yale College with the honors of the institution; at age 19 he was called to the professorship of the Greek language in a College then recently established at New Orleans under the charge of a society of Catholics, all of whom were distinguished for great learning. On its dissolution Mr Bissell commenced the study of law in the ofc of the late Chancellor Livingston. He removed to Charleston city & practiced his profession there. On the discovery of the gold mines of N C, he sought that new field & has devoted himself to the development of its resources. To the pursuit of mining his loss will be deeply felt. The introduction of the processes employed in the mines of Austria would have soon been effected by him, as his arrangements were completed for that purpose. In life he was affiable, & had warm attachments to his friends.

Wm A Richardson, Merchant Tailor: opposite the Seven Bldgs. [Local ad.]

The Madisonian newspaper of this city has passed into the hands of Messrs Theophilus Fisk & Jesse E Dow, who propose to issue a new daily, semi-weekly, & weekly Democratic paper, under the title of The Constellation.

At Cincinnati, last week, Professor Locke amused his auditors by exhibiting to them a Talking Telegraph, recently invented by him. It does not articulate words, but it articulates the elements of words, viz letters.

Jas Jervey, for some years Pres of the State Bank of S C, died at Charleston last week.

Charleston Courier: Wm Ogleby, for the last 15 years British Consul at that port, has solicited & obtained her Majesty's leave to retire, & was about to return to Europe.

Andrew J McLain, presented before the County Court of Williamsport, Md, for voting twice at the same election in Oct last, sentenced on Tue to pay a $20 fine & 10 days' imprisonment in the county jail.

A boy named Adams, accidentally shot his sister in the head & instantly killed her, in the town of Webster, Mass, on Tue last. She was 15 years old.

By writ of fieri facias, issued by B K Morsell, Justice of the Peace for Wash Co, D C, at the suit of Robt Hodgkins, against the goods & chattels, lands & tenements, rights & credits of Wm A Maloy, I have seized & taken one horse & wagon, property of said Maloy; same for sale on Apr 19, in front of the Centre Market-house, in Wash City. –H R Maryman, Constable

By writ of fieri facias, issued by J H Goddard, Justice of the Peace for Wash Co, D C, at the suit of Christopher Cammack, against the goods & chattels, lands & tenements, rights & credits of Carroll Brooks, I have seized & taken one mantel clock, 2 looking glasses, & 1 silver watch, property of said Brooks: same for sale on Apr 19, in front of the Centre Market-house, in Wash City. –H R Maryman, Constable

By writ of fieri facias, issued by Wm W Stewart, Justice of the Peace for Wash Co, D C, at the suit of Geo Collard, against the goods & chattels, lands & tenements, rights & credits of David Westerfield, jr, I have seized & taken one sideboard & one stove, property of said Westerfield: same for sale on Apr 19, in front of the Centre Market-house, in Wash City. –H R Maryman, Constable

By writ of fieri facias, issued by Thos C Donn, Justice of the Peace for Wash Co, D C, at the suit of Wm Uttermuhle, against the goods & chattels, lands & tenements, rights & credits of Edw Grindall, I have seized & taken 1 clock, 1 table, 6 chairs, 1 lounge frame, 1 waiter, a lot of pipe for house, & 1 looking glass, property of said Grindall: same for sale on Apr 19, in front of the Centre Market-house, in Wash City. –H R Maryman, Constable

Attempt at arson & murder: made last Fri upon the premises & person of Mr J Gilpin, a citizen who has lately established himself there in the coopering business. The Mayor of Gtwn has offered a $200 reward for the apprehension of the diabolical offender.

Mrd: on Apr 8, at the U S Hotel, in Wash City, by Rev Mr Samson, Mr R B Taylor, of Va, to Miss Pamela M Sterne, of Va.

Died: on Mon, at Alexandria, after a protracted illness, Col Geo Brent, Collector of that port.

Died: on Apr 2, in Wash City, Judge Blueford West, aged about 38 years, a citizen of the Cherokee nation. A few days after his arrival here he was attacked with bilious pneumonia, which baffled the skill of medical men of great eminence, &, after 2 weeks' illness, terminated in his demise. Judge West was one of the old settlers of the Cherokee nation, & was called at an early age to preside over the chief tribunal of the country. –Globe

Died: on Mar 20, at Little Rock, Arkansas, after a lingering illness, at the residence of her husband, the amiable consort of Hon A H Sevier, Senator of the U S. Mrs Sevier was a d/o Col James, brother to the Hon Richd M Johnson, late Vice Pres of the U S, & inherited all the nobleness of soul belonging to her gallant sire. The melancholy intelligence of her decease reached the fond husband on the Mississippi whilst returning from an arduous & protracted session of the Senate. -Madisonian

THU APR 10, 1845
Connecticut election of last Mon: Roger S Baldwin, elected Govn'r. The State will be represented in the next Congress by 4 Whigs: Truman Smith, from Fairfield & Litchfield Cos, in place of Saml Simons. Saml D Hubbard, from New Haven & Middlesex, in place of John Stewart. Jas Dixon, from Hartford & Tolland, in place of Thos H Seymour. John A Rockwell, from New London & Windham, in place of Geo H Carter.

A man named Loomis was killed by the explosion of the powder mill at Enfield, Conn, on Mar 31.

Mr Hatch, on trial at New Orleans for the murder of Mr Jackson in a ball room, has been acquitted.

The undersigned wishes to obtain a situation as Princiapl of an academy or private School, after Jul 4 next, at which time his present engagement as teacher of a select school at the Univ of Va will expire. He is a graduate of the Univ of Gottingen, & has been a resident of this country for more than 10 years. Address: Henry W Maertens, Univ of Va.

Household & kitchen furniture at auction: on Apr 14, at the large boarding-house of Mrs Gassaway, on Pa ave, a few doors east of Coleman's hotel. –A Green, Auctioneer

Handsome & extensive sale of furniture: on Apr 22, at the residence of Mrs Hewitt, on 3rd st, between C & Pa ave. –Wm Marshall, Auctioneer

Furnished house to rent: on I st, formerly the residence of Mrs Tudor, & lately occupied by the Hon John Y Mason. For terms apply to Richd Smith, of the Bank of the Metropolis, or on the premises to C J Stewart, exec of the late Mrs Tudor.

Sale of valuable furniture: on Apr 16, at the late residence of M Gilbert, on F st, corner of 13th west, opposite the large grocery store of E Simms. Seized & taken as the property of M Gilbert, & will be sold to satisfy rent due to B F Pleasnats. –J M Waters, Bailiff

By order of distrain, & to me directed, I shall expose to public sale, on the green opposite the Centre Market, on Apr 12, 1 book-case, large imported feather bed, with bolster & pillows, & a lot of bed-clothes, taken as the property of Wm R Rose, to satisfy room-rent due & in arrears to John C McKelden. Also, 2 writs of fieri facias, issued by Thos C Donn, Justice of the Peace for Wash Co, D C, I have levied on the above goods, subject to the above claim, to satisfy 2 executions, one in favor of Jas B Holmead & the other in favor of J P McKean, against the said Wm R Rose. –J A Ratcliffe & Co, Constables

Iin virtue of 2 writs of fieri facias, issued by R H Clements, a Justice of the Peace for Wash Co, D C, at the suit of John F May & Alex'r Shepherd, against the goods & chattels, lands & tenements, rights & credits of Wm A Maloy, to me directed, I have seized 1 horse & wagon, property of said Maloy. Same to be sold in front of Centre Market House, on Apr 17, 1845. –H R Maryman, Constable

$100 reward for runaway negro man Stephen Boarman, about 22 years of age.
–Alexius Lancaster, living near Newport, Chas Co, Md.

Mrd: on Tue, by Rev Norval Wilson, Mr Wm C Wright to Juliet R, eldest d/o the late Edw Lewis, of this place.

Died: yesterday, Jas Nash, s/o Michl & Catherine Nash, aged 6 years & 6 months. His funeral is today at 2 o'clock.

FRI APR 11, 1845
Removals & appointments: The Balt papers of Wed announce:
Jas M Buchanan, Postmaster, in place of Thos Finley, removed.
Jas Polk, of Somerset, Naval Ofcr, in place of J K Handy, removed.
Jos White, Navy Agent, in place of Saml McLellan, removed.
Michl McBlair, Appraiser in the Custom House, in place of John Lester, removed.
Wm L Marshall, District Atty, in place of Z C Lee, removed.

Hillary Langtry appointed by the Pres of the U S to be Collector of the Customs for the Port of Alexandria. He was formerly a resident of that place. He was a merchant, &, removing to the West, settled in Columbia, Tenn, where he now resides. Edw Green, the present Deputy Collector is to continue in his ofc.

Obit-died: on Thu, at his residence in Wash City, after an illness of 3 weeks' duration in his 59th year, Thos Sewall, M D. He was born on Apr 16, 1786, at Augusta, Maine. He was graduated in medicine at Boston, & after a few years in Essex Co, removed to Wash City in 1820. He was a member of the first Faculty of the Medical College in D C. In 1821 he was appointed Prof of Anatomy there. In the spring of 1843 Dr Sewall visited Great Britain, Ireland, & some parts of the Continent. For the last 20 years of his life he was fighting off the fatal consumption. In 1828 he joined the Methodist Episcopal Church. His funeral will take place this afternoon at half past 3 o'clock, from the Wesleyan Chapel, at 5th & F sts. Condolences to his family.

Mr Benj Bushe died at Greensborough, Vt, on Mar 21, at the extraordinary age of 115 years. He was a native of Old Swansey, Massachusetts.

Brazil: the infant Prince was to be christened on Mar 25, King Louis Philippe being the Godfather.

Mr John McArn, a merchant from Fayetteville, N C, who a few days ago fell & had his foot crushed while attempting to get into a car at the railroad depot in Phil, died on Mon last, from his injuries.

Govn'r Steele, of N H, offers $1,000 reward for the murderer of Mr Parker at Manchester, to be paid upon conviction; or $500 for such information as shall lead to detection.

Richd M Waring: Hardware Store-near the corner of 6th st & Pa ave, Wash. [Local ad.]

Died: on Apr 7, after a brief illness, Mrs Anna C Slade, w/o Mr Wm O Slade, of Fairfax Co, Va.

Died: yesterday, after a lingering illness, Mr Jos Stone, aged 55 years. He was a native of Dezect, county of Kilkenny, Ireland. His funeral is from his late residence on F st, between 10th & 11th, this evening at 4 o'clock.

Died: on Apr 8, at N Y, Rev Jas Milnor, D D, Rector of St George's Church in N Y C, universally respected & beloved as an estimable & exemplary Divine. He was a native of Pa, & practiced law at one time in the city of Phil. He was also a member of Congress, & took an active part in the discussions of 1812. He was chosen rector of St George's chapel in 1816, & held the post until his death.

Medical Society of D C: meeting this day at 2 o'clock. –Jos Borrows, Recording Sec

Wash Corp: 1-Ptn of Josiah Essex, praying to be indemnified for certain injury sustained in erecting the new Almshouse: referred to the Cmte of Claims. 2-Ptn of Jas Carrico, praying the setting of the curb & footway on 16th st: referred to the Cmte on Improvements. 3-Ptn of John Purdy & others, remonstrating against the late general assessment of property, & praying a reduction of taxes: referred to the Cmte of Ways & Means. 4-Ptn of C Gautier & E F Valentine, praying the remission of fines: referred to the Cmte of Claims. 5-Ptn from Asaph H Parish, in relation to the number of houses in the city: read & laid on the table. 6-Cmte of Claims: unfavorable report on the ptn of Jos Bohlayer, & asked to be discharged from its further consideration: agreed. Petitioner has leave to withdraw his papers. 7-Cmte of Claims: asked to be discharged from the further consideration of the ptns of Mary Quigley & of Wm Dipple: agreed. 8-Ptn of Jas W Barker & others: referred to the Cmte on Improvements. 9-Cmte of Claims: reported a bill for the relief of Jos Peck: passed. 10-Ptn of Thos Lawson & others, remonstrating against the erection of a livery stable at a certain point in the 1st Ward: referred to the Cmte on Police. 11-Bill for the relief of Philip Ennis, reported the same without amendment.

For rent: a 2 story house on D st, near 7th. Inquire of Mrs Williams, on the premises.

SAT APR 12, 1845
Late calamity on the Hudson: wreck of the steamboat **Swallow**, Capt Squire, which left Albany on Mon, having on board passengers estimated at from 250 to 350. She struck upon the points of a small rock island between Hudson & Athens with such force as to lift the bow entirely out of the water, breaking the boat in two, & rendering her a complete wreck. About 100 of the passengers were brought down by the steamer **Rochester**, & 50 by the steamer **Express**. Recovered: one body has been recognized as that of Mrs Coffin, of West Troy; another as Mrs Walker, of N Y; & a 3rd is supposed to be Mrs Conklin, of Albany. With Mrs Walker was found pocket-book containin a large sum of money. Her husband recognised her by a miniature of himself attached to a gold chain, which she wore around her neck. The Albany Atlas of Wed says that last evening the vessel **John Mason** returned to the city bringing the bodies of the 2 Misses Wood, sisters of Dr Wood, & Wm Davis, the s/o Nathl Davis, of this city. The bodies of Miss Briggs & Mrs Spencer, of Troy, were taken up. [Apr 18th newspaper: Miss Cornelia Pratt was rescued by the courage of Mr Jas A Hicks. They both held onto a settee, which was repeatedly grasped by persons struggling in the water around them, & whom they were forced to beat off. When in the water about half an hour, they were rescued by a boat that came to them.] [May 2nd newspaper: the body of the little s/o Judge Mather, who was lost at the stranding of the **Swallow**, has been found.] [May 22nd newspaper: letter dated at Athens, on Sat last says: they have the steamboat **Swallow** on the beach, decks out of water; no bodies could be found; every berth examined. Efforts are now to be made to pump her out, to bring her to N Y.]

By a writ of fieri facias, issued by B K Morrell, a Justice of the Peace for Wash Co, D C, at the suit of Francis Hanna, against the goods & chattels, lands & tenements, rights & credits, of Thos Maloy, I have seized a mantel clock, 6 chiars, 3 tables, 1 safe, 2 tubs, 1 looking glass, 2 candlesticks, pair andirons, 1 water bucket, 1 trunk, 1 shovel, 1 skillet, & 1 washstand: to be sold on Apr 19, in front of the Centre Market House, in Wash City. –H R Maryman, Constable

Splendid American & French paper hangings for sale: large assortment. Also received several patterns of Embossed Papers, a new style. –J Alexander, Pa ave, between 12th & 13th sts, Wash.

Chas J Cone, a journeyman hatter in Danbury, Conn, was lately found dead in his shop from taking opium.

Mrd: on Apr 10, at the Church of the Epiphany, in Wash City, by Rev J W French, J H C Coffin, of the U S Navy, to Louisa Harrison, niece of the late Richd Harrison, of the Treasury Dept.

The funeral sermon of the late Mrs Wm Stettinius will be preached tomorrow, at half-past 7, in the Fourth Presbyterian Church, [Rev Mr Smith's.]

Miss Jane E Biscoe will open fashionable Millinery on Apr 12, next door to D Clagett.

Wm Bell, Balt Dyeing & Coat Dressing Establishment, south side Pa ave, near 4½ st. [Local ad.]

The corner-stone of the old Washington Hotel, in Broadway, near the corner of Chambers st, was taken up on Tue, after having lain undisturbed ever since 1808. Stewart, the wealthy dry-goods dealer in Broadway, is bldg a splendid structure for a store on this site. He hopes to make the forsaken east side of Broadway fashionable. The front, extending nearly a whole square, is to be of white marble, ornamented with a row of columns of the Corinthian order. Pretty well for a retail shop.

$100 reward for runaway negro boy Jim, about 18 years of age. –Wm Clark, living near Queen Anne, PG Co, Md.

MON APR 14, 1845
Died: on Apr 2, after a long & painful illness, Miss Gracey Ann, d/o the late Maj Alex'r Dent, of Chas Co, Md, in her 22nd year.

Died: on Apr 11, in Wash City, Mrs Miranda Van Ness, consort of Mr Geo Van Ness, in her 23rd year.

Those who lost their lives by the late disaster of the steamboat **Swallow**:
Mrs Conklin, of Bennington, Vt
Mrs Eliz Coffin, West Troy
Mrs Louisa Coffin, West Troy
Mrs Walker, of N Y
Miss L Briggs, of Troy
Miss Mary Torrey, of Pa
Mrs Parker, of Utica
2 Misses Wood, of Albany
Mr Wm Davis, of Albany
Miss Spencer, of Troy
Mrs Ann Lamberson, of Jamaica, L I
Mrs Brewster, of Mohawk Valley

Pittsburg in Ruins! Pittsburg Gaz of Fri: fire is raging as I write; the Momongahela Bridge has taken fire & is entirely consumed; 20 squares are entirely destroyed; all of Pipetown & all the bldgs around Bakewell's Glassworks, also consumed. The Pittsburg Bank, supposed to be fire-proof, is in flames. The Mayor's Ofc is on fire, & the new Post Ofc is in danger. The fire spread so rapidly that it was impossible to save property. The Chronicle lost its presses. The Presbyterian Advocate & Protestant Unionist ofcs are both destroyed. Pittsburg Chronical of Sat: houses consumed-1,200 of which 700 were dwlgs, depriving at least 4,000 persons of house & home. Only one life is known to have been lost-a Mrs Brooks, who was burnt in her house on 3rd st. The vaults of the Bank of Pittsburg & the iron safes of Mr Kramer & Sibbet & Jones, Brokers, have been opened & their contents found almost entirely uninjured. [Apr 17th newspaper: Mr Saml Kingston has been missing since the fire. He was last seen going into his burning ofc. It is feared he is lost. The Gaz says: "that every book & paper in the safe of Messrs Sibbett & Jones were burnt up, & the gold & silver melted together."] [Apr 19th newspaper: A married woman, the mother of 2 children, named McGowly, perished on 3rd st, & a man named Johnson is supposed to have been lost in Wood st.]

Staunton Spectator of Thu: fire in Bath & Pendleton; the houses of Mr Jas Crawford & Mr Inch were destroyed. A fire broke out in the Blue Ridge, above Waynesborough, which did much damage.

Obit-died: on Apr 5, in Wash City, after a short illness, Mrs Mary Rosina Stettinius, consort of Mr Wm Stettinius, & d/o G C Grammer, of Wash, in her 31st year. A husband who well knew her worth, & 2 children, the oldest scarcely old enough to appreciate her loss, remain to deplore this sudden bereavement. Many friends from 2 years' residence in this town have gathered around her. –Petersburg Intelligencer

The Hon Danl Waldo, of Worcester, Mass, has paid $1,000 towards the purchase of territory in or near Liberia, & the Misses Waldo, of the same place, $1,000 more.

Balt City Court: the first cases of offence under the new law, passed by the Leg of Md during its last session, prohibiting minors from running with fire-engines, were tried in the above court on Sat last, & the offenders were rigorously dealt with. They were John Dever, Jos Joseph, Wm Myers, & Saml Morris, each fine $10 & costs.

The powder mills of J P Garesche, near Wilmington, Del, were blown up on Thu, killing one man & wounding 2 or 3 others. Nearly 8,000 pounds of powder were destroyed.

Zanesville Gaz says that by the fire in that town on Mon last, the dwlg-houses of Messrs Parke & Eastman, Mrs Printz, & the business rooms on Main st of Messrs Briton & Gibbons, Williams & Greeland, Clements & Warner were completely destroyed. Mr John Cooper, s/o Judge Cooper, was found dead in his room.

Fred'k E Bailey, lately appointed Prosecuting Atty for York Co, Pa, committed suicide on Mon, by hanging himself in the attic story of his dwlg. He had been in the court-house at York until 4 o'clock, & about half past 5 he was found a corpse.

Died, on Jan 28, on the Kempt Road, near Ristigouche, Donald McLaren, aged 36, the mail courier. He had been employed the preceding 18 months in carrying the mail between Metes & Ristigouche, 97¾ miles, twice a week, having thus to walk on snow shoes in the winter season 195½ miles every 6 days, carrying a mail bag on his back frequently weighing 35 to 40 pounds. On his arrival at Metes, on Jan 15, he was obliged to lay up for 6 days, receiving the kindest care from Mr Page, the postmaster. Somewhat recruited, he returned to Ristigouche & resumed his trips. He met Peter Glasgow who was trapping marten. Glasgow decided to make after him because a snow storm was increasing. He found him the poor courier & they struggled to the first house, from whence a person was sent to Mr Dixon's. He was then carried to Mr Dixon's, where he received the best attention. The present courier, David McGregor, was formerly engaged in the duty, with his brother Alex'r, when this last was unfortunately drowned, 3 years since, on Lake Matapediac, while carrying the mail.

Household & kitchen furniture at auction: on Apr 16, at the residence of a lady leaving the city, on Capitol Hill, N J ave, [Dr May's row.] –A Green, Auctioneer

Household & kitchen furniture at auction: on Apr 18, at the Boarding-house of Mrs Thorp, on Pa ave, enar 6th st, opposite Colemen's Hotel. –A Green, Auctioneer

Local News: the funeral of the late Dr Sewall took place last Fri evening in the presence of a very numerous assemblage of mourners. Dr Sewall's practice was in Wash City for the last 25 years & it was most extensive. His remains were removed from his late dwlg, C & 4½ sts, to Wesley Chapel at half past 3 o'clock. The service was performed by Rev Norval Wilson, pastor of the church. The corpse was conveyed to the grave-yard of the Methodist Episcopal Church, near the Columbian College. Ex-Pres Adams, Senator Benton, & the Mayor of the city, were among the many distinguished in attendance.

Wash Ordinance: Act for the relief of Jos Peck: the penalty incurred by Peck, as security in the case of the Corp against Geo W McCallion, same is hereby remitted: Provided, he pay the costs of prosecution.

Sale of valuable Wash City lots Thur: 5 lots advertised by Mr Green were sold by auction: the first, being the corner lot on 6th & C sts, to Johnson Hellen, at .70 per square foot; 2nd to Geo Parker, at .50 per square foot, the 3rd & 4th to Hon Judge Thruston, at .45 per square foot; 5th to Mr Holtzman, at .45 per square foot.

Dr Wm Jones will in future give his undivided attention to the practice of medicine. His ofc is at his residence on C st, between 3rd & 4½ sts.

Factories in Gtwn: a large cotton factory is in the course of construction in Gtwn. It will occupy the site of the large flouring mill of Mr Geo C Bomford, which was destroyed by fire in Sep last. The bldg is to be 4 stories high, with machinery upon 4 floors. The flouring mill of Mr Davis at this place is known to be one of the largest & best in the country. All the machinery is of the most superior character.

TUE APR 15, 1845
The following is a list of the Genr'l Ofcrs of the Revolutionary Army in 1781, agreeably to rank:
Geo Washington, Cmder-in-Chief
Major Generals:
Israel Putnam, Conn
*Chas Lee, Va
Horatio Gates, Va
Wm Heath, Mass
Nathl Green, R I
Wm Alexander, Jersey
Earl of Stirling, Jersey
Arthur St Clair, Pa
Benj Lincoln, Mass
Brig Generals:
Wm Thompson, Va
John Nixon, Mass
Jas Clinton, N Y
Wm Moultrie, S C
Loughlin McIntosh, N C
Wm Maxwell, Jersey
Enoch Poor, N H
John Glover, Mass
John Paterson, Conn

Marquis de la Fayetts, France
Baron de Kalb, France
Robt Howe, N C
Alex'r McDougall, N Y
Baron Steuben, Prussia
Wm Smallwood, Md
Saml Parsons, Conn
Henry Knox, Mass
Duportaile, of Engineers, France

Anthony Wayne, Pa
Wm Woodford, Va
Peter Muhlenburg, Va
Edw Hand, Pa
Jedediah Huntington, Conn
John Starke, N H
Mordecai Gist, Md
Wm Ervin, Pa

Promoted after that period:
Danl Morgan, Va
Mr Sumpter, S C
Mr Marion, S C
-Boston Journal

Jos Greaton, Mass
Rufus Putnam, Mass
Otho Williams, Md

*Chas Lee, suspended for one year by sentence of court martial, for charges exhibited against him by Gen Washington, at the battle of Monmouth, in Jun 29, 1778; but his pride would not suffer him to resume his command at the expiration of his sentence; notwithstanding, he was still retained on the list of genr'l ofcrs until his death, which happened in Phil in 1782. His funeral was attended by the Pres of Congress & members, French Minister, & a vast number of the most respectable gentlemen of that city.

Soldiers of the Revolutionary & late wars, & their heirs, are informed that I have a list of all those entitled to lands who have not received them; &, by sending me their names, regts, ofcrs, & other particulars, postage paid, they will be informed whether they are entitled to lands or otherwise. –Edmund F Brown, Gen Agent & Notary Public, Wash, Apr 14, 1845. Reference to the following named gentlemen:

Hon J W Williams, Lancaster, N H
Rev D Benedict, Pawtucket, R I
Rev Danl Sharp, D D, Boston, Mass
Rev Baron, Stow, Boston, Mass
Rev Ch G Sommers, N Y C
Rev Ira M Allen, N Y C
Wm M Brown, N Y C
Saml H Congar, Newark, N J
Chas McKaraher, Phil, Pa
Rev A D Gillette, Phil, Pa
Thos C Clarke, Phil, Pa
Edmund Morris, Phil, Pa
Mr W Crane & Co, Balt, Md
Mr J C Crane, Richmond, Va
Rev H W Dodge, Upperville, Va
Hon R M Johnson, Great Crossing, Ky
Dr L D Boone, Chicago, Ill

Wm Stuart, P M, Chicago, Ill
L C P Freer, Chicago, Ill
Hon John Reynolds, Belleville, Ill
C W Coote, St Louis, Mo
Col John H Wheeler, Raleigh, N C
S J Wheeler, P M, Murfreesborough, N C
Rev J F Brown, Gainesville, Ala
Rev I T Hinton, New Orleans, La
Wm McDaniel, Cannonsburg, Pa
J E Black, Cannonsburg, Pa
Hon A H Sevier, U S Senator-Arkansas
Hon John Wentworth, H of R from Ill
Rev Dr Chapin, Wash
Rev Dr Muller, Wash
Rev O B Brown, Wash
Rev G W Samson, Wash

Valuable real estate for sale: the subscriber will sell 2 plantations lying in PG Co, Md, 3 miles north of Upper Marlborough. The mill tract, 387 9-10 acs, adjoins the lands of Chas Hill, Thos W Clagett, & Wm M Bowie: with a new dwlg-house, 4 large barns, a new saw-mill, & all necessary out-houses new & in complete order. The other plantation, 269 1-5 acs, adjoins the land of Otho B Beall & Washington J Beall: improvements are a dwlg-house, 2 large tobacco barns, stabling, & all other necessary out-houses. –Roderick McGregor

For sale: the subscriber, having removed to Md, will sell at public auction, on the premises, on Apr 21, lot 12 in square 252, on 14th st, containing 5,95¼ square feet, with a 2 story dwlg-house, & room enough in front to build another house with a front of 28 or 29 feet. –Lloyd M Lowe -Robt W Dyer & Co, aucts

For sale: house & lot nearly opposite the Navy Yard Market-house, at present in the occupancy of Mr Bright. This lot is part of lot 6 in square 881, & has a front of 36 feet on Market alley, & the house is suitable for a store & dwlg. Also, the house & lot on 11th st east, near the Eastern Branch bridge, recently occupied by Mr Carrico. The title to the above is indisputable, having been in undisturbed possession of the family upwards of 30 years. Apply to Cornelius Cox, at the City Post Ofc.

Orphan's Court of Wash Co, D C. Letters testamentary on the personal estate of John McFarland, late of said county, dec'd. –Ellen McFarland, Excx

Household & kitchen furniture for sale: Apr 17, at the residence of Mr Daniel, Capitol Hill. –A Green, auct

By virtue of an order of distress, & to me directed, I shall expose to public sale, for cash, on Apr 19, in Wash City, to wit: 1 dressing bureau & glass, 13 pictures & frames, 2 lamps, 2 pieces carpet, 1 small lot of crockery, knives & forks, 2 water buckets, 1 pair brass candlesticks, mantel ornaments, 1 mattress, 2 gilt frames, & a number of small articles, seized & taken for house rent due W G W White by Julia Fleet.
-R T Mills, Bailiff

Illusion that I would not have been removed if Gen Jackson had not ordered or assented to it. Recent letters, which will enable the public to judge how far there has been any abatement on his part of those feeling of warm & cordial friendship which have united us for more than a third of a century. **Hermitage**, Feb 11, 1845. Letter to Maj Wm B Lewis, 2nd Auditor U S Treasury. My Dear Major: I have been as well as I am able, [for I am very feeble,] looking over your various letters, enclosing to me copies of Mr Monroe's letters & mine to him, & I am over whelmed with gratitude to you for the solicitude, labor, & care taken to defend my character & fame from falsehoods & calumnies. I thank my God, in my old age & great afflictions, when I have become unable to defend myself, that I have such friends. –Andrew Jackson **Hermitage**, Mar 22, 1845. Letter to Maj Wm B Lewis. We all sincerely regret your indisposition-our hopes & united prayers are, that ere this a kind Providence has restored you to perfect health, & has in store for you a long life of health, prosperity, & usefulness, & a happy immortality. May God bless you with health & prosperity for many years, are the wishes & prayers of all inhabiting the **Hermitage**. Adieu. Andrew Jackson

Died: on Apr 1, of scarlet fever, aged 3 years & 10 days, Lelia Hay, d/o Rev W G H & Frances C Jones, of Clarke Co, Va.

Meeting of the ofcrs stationed at *Fort Scott*, Mo, Mar 19, 1845, Maj W M Graham, 4th Infty, called to the chair, & Lt E B Holloway, 4th Infty, appointed Sec. Subject: the loss of friend & fellow-soldier, Capt B A Terrett, of the 1st Regt of U S Dragoons, by a sudden & unexpected death. Copy of this be furnished his afflicted widow & family.

WED APR 16, 1845
In Chancery: Dillon vs Garretson et al. Decree of the Circuit Court of Wash Co, D C, dated Dec 19, 1844: will be sold at public auction, on Apr 30, 1845, on the premises, to wit: lot 1 in square 324, with brick bldg thereon; & lots 40 & 54 in sq 387, on south side of the Mall. The first named lot lies at the intersection of Canal & 11th sts.
–D A Hall, Trustee -A Green, Auctioneer

Valuable house & lots for sale at Public Auction: by decree of the Circuit Court of Wash Co, D C, as Court of Chancery, in the case of Jas Robertson et al vs Mrs Clara F Forsyth et al, passed on Jan 22, 1844, sale on May 8 next, all the following lots in square 27, in Wash City: lots 5, 8, 10, & east part of lot 9, with the improvements thereon, consisting of a large 2 story brick house & other bldgs. Mrs Clary F Forsyth, wid/o the late John Forsyth, right of dower shall be reserved, unless she agree before the sale to receive in commutation thereof such allowance out of the purchase money as the Court shall make.
–Richd Smith, Trustee -Robt W Dyer & Co, aucts

Trustee's sale of a very valuable farm near Wash City: by 2 deeds of trust executed by Perez Packard to me, one dated Jul 7, 1838, recorded in Liber W B 67, folios 237 & 238, & the other dated Oct 13, 1843, recorded in Liber W B 96, folios 12, 13, etc, among the land records of Wash Co: sale on the premises, on Jun 18 next: 200 acs, more or less, being the same land Jasper M Jackson purchased from a certain Jasper Mauduit, & which was conveyed to him by the last will & testament of said Jasper Mauduit, a part of which was taken up by the said Jasper Mauduit, & being all claimed by the said Jasper Mauduit in his lifetime, & lying between the lands known as Nicholas L Queen's lands on one side & the heirs of John Laird, dec'd, on the other, & being also all the land which was conveyed, or meant or intended so to be, to the said Perez Packard by Deborah Jenners, by her deed of indenture bearing date of Apr 3, 1836, which will more fully & particularly appear by reference to the said deed or the record thereof, reference being thereto hereby had for greater certainty; together with all & singular the bldgs, houses, improvements, rights, privileges, & apputenances to the same belonging, or in anywise appertaining, with all the right, title, interest, & estate of him, the said Perez Packard & Eliz, his wife, of, in, & to the same & every part & parcel thereof. At this time the lands are improved by a large barn & stable, & a comfortable farm house, with other necessary bldgs, all of which have been built within a few years apart. –E G Emack, Trustee
-Robt W Dyer & Co, aucts

Wash Corp: 1-Ptn from Fred'k Ford: referred to the Cmte of Claims. 2-Ptn of M P Mohum: referred to the Cmte of Claims. 3-Cmte of Claims: reported a bill for the relief of Chas Gautier: referred to the Cmte of Claims. 4-Cmte on Improvements: ptn of Wm B Berryman & others, for improvement of 12th st: read.

We understand that the Pres has this day dismissed Lt Wm Decatur Hurst from the Navy. It has been ascertained that Lt Hurst, while employed as 1st lt of the U S brig **Truxton** on the coast of Africa, & exercising the duties of chief executive ofcr of that vessel, engaged in a duel with a midshipman under his command. It is said, & not denied, that Lt Hurst, on an intimation of an intention by Passed Midshipman Creighton to appeal, for some alleged wrong received from Lt Hurst, to highter authority, told that ofcr that such appeal was unnecessary, as he, Lt Hurst, would give him personal satisfaction. The Pres has seized the earliest opportunity to express, by the strongest action, his disapprobation of the course pursued by an ofcr who should have set an example of discipline & subordination. -Globe

The U S ship **Columbus** & sloop of war **Vincennes** are to be fitted out immediately for sea, destined for the East Indians. Ofcrs, so far as ordered:
Columbus: Capt T W Wyman
Lts: Stephen Johnson, Percival Drayton, Oliver Tod, J W Walsh, Chas F McIntosh, & Jas H Strong
Surgeon B Ticknor
Passed Assist Surgeon C F Guillou
Assist Surgeons: D L Bryan & R E Wall
Purser John De Bree
Passed Midshipmen: Madison Rush, [Acting Master,] J C Wait, J M Wainwright, D McN Fairfax, A J Drake, W H Jamesson
Midshipmen: H A Colborn, W W Low, W C West, W D Whiting, B W Stevenson, T L Walker, J T Barrand, C K Graham, E A Selden, J Young, G M Dibble, J B Stuart
Prof of Mathematics: M Yarnall
Boatswain: V R Hall
Gunner: Thos Robinson
Sailmaker: R C Rodman
Carpenter: Jonas Dibble
For the sloop of war **Vincennes**:
Capt Hiram Paulding
Lts: H Ingersoll, Z Holland, J A Winslow, C M Armstrong
Surgeon: J B McKnight
Passed Assist Surgeon: A J Bowie
Purser: Chas Murray
Passed Midshipman Danl Ammen, Acting Master
The U S sloop of war **Saratoga**, Cmder J Shubrick, & the sloop of war **St Mary's**, Cmder John L Saunders, dropped down to Hampton Roads on Apr 12. –Constit'n

Household & kitchen furniture for sale, at Auction: on Apr 21, at the residence of Mrs A T McCormick, on Capitol Hill, Gen Duff Green's Row. –A Green, Auctioneer

Household & kitchen furniture for sale, at Auction: on Apr 23, at the residence of Walter Clarke, on Pa ave, between 6th & 7th sts. –Robt W Dyer & Co, aucts

Sporting Goods, Cheap, in Gtwn. –Smoot & Brother, Bridge st, near High st.

Let it be known from the Navy Yard to Gtwn Heights, that J T & C King are now selling the richest, newest, & cheapest Laces, Ribands, Nets, Edgings, Capes, & Caps. The Cheap Lace Store, between 10th & 11th sts. –J T & C King

The trial of Polly Bodine was terminated at N Y on Sat, the jury returning a verdict of guilty of murder, with a recommendation to mercy. She was removed in the custody of the sheriff, to her quarters in the Eldridge street prison. [Jan 4th, 1844 newspaper: The person who lately murdered Mrs Houseman & her child, on Staten Island, N Y, & afterwards fired her dwlg house to conceal the crime, is supposed to have been a sister of the murdered woman's husband, named Polly Bodine, who has borne a very bad character & previously lived in the family. A druggist of N Y named Waite is also suspected of having been concerned in the tragedy. Both have been arrested.]

THU APR 17, 1845
Teacher wanted: a person well qualified to teach young ladies is wanted to take charge of a female seminary in Chestertown, Md. –Jas B Ricaud, Chestertown, Md

Mr Jas H Carlin, a respectable citizen of Alexandria Co, on Sat, was accidentally killed by falling from his wagon while he was driving it from town to his residence in the country. The wagon was heavily laden, & as he fell to the ground the forewheel must have passed against his neck & strangled him. He was about 45 years of age, & has left a large family. –Alex Gaz

Wonderful bargains at my store: variety of fancy & ornamental Goods.
–Jas Clephane, Pa ave & 12th st

Second arrival of Spring Goods: W Egan & Son, south side Pa ave, between 6th & 7th sts.

A young man named Alex'r Reed, said to be a cadet from West Point, residing in Rivington st, rose from his bed on Sunday night, while in a state of somnambulism, & jumped from the 4th story of the house. He was taken to the City Hospital, where he died this morning. -N Y Correspondence

Valuable farm for sale in Loudoun Co, Va: under the provisions of a deed from John Thompson Mason to Robt I Taylor, Chas Fenton Mercer, & others, as trustees, of record in the county court of Loudoun, & of a decree of said court by which I have been appointed trustee in the place of the said Robt I Taylor, etc, I offer for sale the tract of land in Loudoun Co known as *Locust Hill*, containing 405 acs. This land lies about 3 miles north of Leesburg, near the road leading from Leesburg to the Point of Rocks, adjoining the lands of Thos Swann, Henry Cassaway, & others. Improvements are all good, consisting of a neat & substantial 2 story brick dwlg house, with the usual out-houses; a very good barn, erected within the last 3 or 4 years, upon the Swiss plan; also, another small dwlg house. Communications to be addressed to me at Martinsburg, Berkeley Co, Va. –Philip Pendleton, Trustee

Orphan's Court of Wash Co, D C. Letters testamentary on the personal estate of Thos Sewall, late of said county, dec'd. –Thos Sewall, Exec [And I hereby appoint Warren C Choate my agent, authorized to collect accounts due to the estate.]

The brother-in-law of Ex-Pres Tyler, Mr Gardiner, has received from Judge Nelson the appointment of Clerk of the U S Circuit Court in N Y C. -N Y Correspondence

Appointments by the Pres: Lewis Sanders, to be Navy Agent for the State of Ky, vice Jas Hamilton, removed. Danl Pierce, to be Naval Storekeeper at Portsmouth, N H, vice Chas W Cutter, removed. J F H Clairborne, to be Live Oak Agent for Louisiana, vice A G Southall, removed. –Constitution

A letter written on board the U S sloop of war **Vandalia**, on Mar 22, states that Mr John Overman, carpenter of the ship, died at Port au Prince of yellow fever on the 19th, & was buried the same day. He had been sick 4 days. Mr Overman was 29 years of age, & has left a wife & 4 children in Portsmouth, Va, where he belonged. Others have become sick, but there are no deaths to report.

The soap factory of Jas Buchan, in Elizabeth st, N Y, was destroyed by fire, with its contents, on Sun.

The post ofc at Webster, Maine, was destroyed by fire on Tue, with all the blanks & mail bags. Jacob Hill, the postmaster, lost all his private papers & library.

Naval: the U S sloop of war **St Mary's**, Cmder John L Saunders, dropped down to Hampton Roads on Sun. The handsome little iron steamer **Water Witch** has arrived from Washington, & is intended to be used for towing the public vessels & as a water tank. She has been placed under the command of Mr Edmund F Olmsted, master's mate of the ship **Pennsylvania**, who had previously had charge of the steamer **Engineer**, employed in the same service. The **Water Witch** is fitted with Hunter's propeller. -Herald

Fatal railroad accident on Sun as the train was proceeding towards Fred'k, & near Buzzard Rock, an old gentleman named Abel Chapman, who resided in that vicinity, was sitting upon the track. The engineer discovered him when the train was within 20 yards of him, but it was too late to check the speed of the train, & the engine passed over him killing him instantly.

Correspondent of the Boston Daily Advertiser, writing at Rome, Feb 15, gives the following interesting account of an interview with the Pope, a hale old man of nearly 80 years. Pope Gregory XVI maintains in the splendor of the Pontifical Court all the personal simplicity of taste & manners which were appropriate to his early life. The same bed which he used in the Benedictine monastery passed with him to his Cardinal palace, & he now sleeps on it in his regal chamber in the *Vatican*. He continued standing during an audience of half an hour, conversed affiably, & referred to the destruction of the Ursuline convent in 1834. He wore a velvet slipper, having a cross upon it embroidered in gold. The Catholics, on being presented, kneel & press their lips upon this cross. It is called in derision kissing the Pope's toe. This was not demanded of me. He is considered the head of the true church by more than one-half the Christian world.

Trustee's sale: by deed of trust to me, the subscriber, from Jos D Lafontaine, dated Apr 11, 1845, I shall sell at public auction, on May 2 next, on the premises now occupied by the said Jos E Lafontaine, on 15th st, nearly opposite the front of the Treasury bldg, in Wash City, all the furniture & household goods specified in the schedule annexed to the said deed of trust, to which, the same is recorded among the Land Records of Wash Co, D C, reference is made: all the goods now in & about the said premises. I shall also sell a lot of ground in Wash City, conveyed in said deed as lot F, subdivision of square 692, fronting on Md ave. Terms of sale, cash. –N Callan, jr, Trustee -Robt W Dyer & Co, aucts

Whilst the steamboat **Josephine** was on her passage up the Ohio river, on Apr 8, near Madison, Indiana, one of her boilers exploded. Mr Jas Ellis, a gentleman of Alleghany Co, Pa, was severely scalded & died soon after reaching Madison. No one else was injured.

Natchez Courier: on Fri last, at the Globe Hotel in this city, a rencontre took place between a man named Gadberry & another named Farmer. Farmer died on Sat last, it is supposed from the effects of the shot. Gadberry was committed for trial.

Land for sale: a farm in PG Co, Md: lies within 2 miles of Bladensburg, on the Annapolis road, & contains 312 acs; improvements are a comfortable dwlg-house & kitchen, 2 barns, & one quarter. This farm adjoins the farm of Mr Wm Cooper. Apply to Thos S Ferrall, Bladensburg, PG Co, Md.

FRI APR 18, 1845
The Freemen's Vigilant Total Abstinence Society meeting lately at the Club House, when the following were elected ofcrs of the Society:

Geo Savage, Pres
Jos Whipple, 1st V P
Edw Owen, 2nd V P
J E W Thompson, Treasurer
Z K Offutt, Rec Sec
Geo Cochrane, Financial Sec
J D Clark, Corr Sec

The copartnership heretofore existing under the name of John Tabler & Co, is this day dissolved by mutual consent. –John Tabler The undersigned have taken the above establishment. –Jacob Taylor, J A Clark

Valuable Grist & Saw Mill for sale: I wish to dispose of this mill property known as Seneca Mills, on Seneca creek. If not sold before, it will be offered at auction at Mr Edw S Wright's auction rooms, in Gtwn, on Apr 21. –Clement Smith, Gtwn

Celebrated Root Beer: Henry Keppler's well-known & popular Root Beer. Orders left at the subscriber's residence, 11th & C sts, will be promptly attended to. –Henry Keppler

R F Fichet, supposed to belong to Boston or its vicinity, jumped overboard from the steamboat **Narragasset** on her passage from N Y to Stonington on Sat, & was drowned. He was insane.

On Apr 1 the body of Mr Saml L Lewis, printer, & recently editor of the Yazoo Democrat, was found near Baton Rouge, drowned. He had for some time past shown symptoms of insanity. He fell from the steamboat **Rainbow**. A rope was thrown to him, but he declined to take hold of it. He has left a distressed wife & small family.

The U S ship **Vandalia** has arrived at Norfolk from Port au Prince, with a large portion of her crew dreadfully afflicted with fever. In addition to Carpenter Overman, who died before the ship sailed from Port au Prince, it is said that Lt Lockhart, Lt Geo Mason Hooe, Surgeon Channing, Purser Moore, Sailmaker Crow, & 16 of the crew have died on passage.

The New Orleans papers announce the death of Judge Gilbert Leonard. He died on Tue week from the effects of the wound received in the late duel with Mr Toca. The duel had its origin in the Plaquemine frauds at the late Presidential Election.

Capt John Power, who was some time since convicted in Ky of robbing the U S mail, & pardoned therefore by Pres Tyler, has since been convicted at New Orleans of inveigling a female slave, & has been sentenced to the penitentiary for 5 years.

Mrd: on Apr 16, by Rev Mr Pyne, Mr Chas Abert to Miss Henrietta Constantia Bache.

Mrd: on Apr 17, by Rev H Myers, Mr Richd Barnes to Miss Eliza Wilson, both of Montg Co, Md.

Mrd: on Apr 15, by Rev Mr Burnap, at Balt, Mr John Cranch, s/o Judge Cranch, of Wash, to Miss Charlotte D Appleton, d/o the late Chas H Appleton, of Balt, Md.

Died: on Apr 15, at his residence, in PG Co, Md, Wm Clark, in his 77th year.

Tyson & Brothers have opened a Grocery Store on Pa ave, 4 doors east of Colemen's Nat'l Hotel.

By virtue of 6 writs of fieri facias, 2 issued by C T Coote, & 4 issued by Wm Thompson, justices of the peace for Wash Co, D C, I shall expose to public sale for cash, the goods & chattels, property of Chas Lafon, to satisfy a judgment in favor of Edw Simms, a judgment in favor of Geo Collard, use of Edw Simms, a judgment in faovr of Wm H Harrover, & 3 judgments in favor of the Corp of Wash. –R R Burr, Constable –A Green, Auctioneer

SAT APR 19, 1845
European Hotel at Wash. Gentlemen from France, Spain, & South America will find themselves' at home. –Louis Galabrun, near the Treasury Bldg, Pa ave

Naval Agent's Ofc, Wash, Apr 17, 1845. Proposals will be received at this ofc on May 17 next, for furnishing all fresh beef & vegetables that may be required at this naval station during the fiscal year commencing on Jul 1 next & ending on Jun 30th following. –Wm B Scott, Navy Agent

Information wanted of John McNerhany, who left the city of Washington about a year ago for Chatham, New Brunswick, where his parents reside. Not having reached the place of his distination up to Apr 1, it is probable that he may have taken passage from N Y [where he was last seen] for New Orleans, in which latter place he has a married sister, named McDermott. Any information relative to his whereabouts, address to Francis McNerhany, Wash, D C, will be thankfully received. [New Orleans Picayune copy.]

Arrival of the U S ship **Vandalia** in Hampton Roads on Wed; since her sailing from Port au Prince on Apr 1, many of the crew are on the sick list & 19 have died. Among the deaths are the following ofcrs:

Geo Mason Hooe, 1st Lt	Saml Crow, Sailmaker
Lt Jas M Lockert	John Overman, Carpenter-before
Surgeon D S Green	reported
Purser Robt S Moore	

There are now 40 or 50 sick, & most of them are out of danger. –Norfolk Herald

Orphan's Court of Wash Co, D C. Letters of administration, with the will annexed, on the personal estate of Richd Cutts, late of said county, dec'd.
–J M Cutts, Richd D Cutts, Adms

The undersigned has learned with deep regret the current report among her friends, that she received a portion of the proceeds of a subscription for the aid of widows who suffered by the burning of the Nat'l Theatre. As there were but 2 widows who suffered on this occasion, myself being one, it was perfectly natural to suppose that such was the case; but as I do not wish my friends to retain the false impression, I take this method of contradicting it. Such a subscription was made, & one of the widows received something, but for myself, I have never received any portion of it. –S R Stinger

Mrd: on Apr 18, by Rev Jas Knox, Mr David Bassett to Miss Catherine Matilda, eldest d/o J A M Duncanson, all of Wash City.

Died: on Apr 17, of scarlet fever, Mary Clarissa Sweeny, aged 2½ years, d/o Mr Hugh Bernard Sweeny.

MON APR 21, 1845

All persons are cautioned against receiving or negotiating a promissory note drawn by the undersigned in favor of David Stuart, Balt, dated Wash City, Mar 18, 1845, for $1,236.90, 4 months after date, payable at the counting room of E J Sanders & Co, Balt. Said note was mailed at the post ofc in Wash City on Mar 24 last, & has never been received by the said David Stuart. –Semmes, Murray, & Semmes

Appropriations made during the 2nd session of the 28th Congress. 1-For compensation to Benj E Green while officiating as charge des affaires in Mexico: $1,069.40 2-For compensation to J Pemberton Hutchinson, in full for diplomatic services at Lisbon: $2,900,000. 3-For compensation to Arthur Middleton, in full for diplomatic services in Spain: $1,454,000. 4-To settle the accounts of Lt Col H Whiting: $843.72.

The Hon John Norvell appointed U S District Arry for the District of Michigan. He was one of the U S Senators from the State. –N Y Courier

The Hon Jas Shields, of Ill, appointed Com'r of the General Land Ofc, & commenced his duties on Fri.

At Louisville, a few days since, Mons Mallet, a teacher of dancing, came in collision with a wagon & was thrown with force to the ground. He walked afterwards & did not appear hurt, but he died the next day of his injuries.

Mrs Ann H Clark has just returned from the North, & is now opening a splendid assortment of Millinery. All repairing done in the neatest manner. Bridge st, Gtwn, D C.

For rent: that large 3 story brick bldg & 3 story back bldgs the property of the late Anthony Preston, on Pa ave, at present occupied by Mrs Preuss as a boarding house. Inquire of Mr B M Beall, on the premises, or to J Gideon, 9th st.

Wheatland in Market: fine estate 35 miles from Wash, D C, in Prince Wm, Va, in view of Brentsville: sale on May 20 next, the same being the first day of the Superior Court for Pr Wm Co, if not sooner disposed of. Mr F Brawner, the present tenent, will show the farm. It consists of more than 500 acs. –John Gibson, Agent & Atty for F Vincent.

By virtue of a writ of fieri facias, issued by Jas Marshall, a Justice of the Peace for Wash Co, D C, at the suit of Robt M Combs, against the goods & chattels, lands & tenements, rights & credits of Levi Beach & Wm F Austin, I have seized the interest of Levi Beach in a 2 story frame house on square 536, in Wash City, on Va ave: sale on May 21 next, on the premises. –Ignatius Howe, Constable

The residence of Wm Rust, near Upperville, Va, was burnt down on yesterday week, & all the furniture destroyed, except a bookcase with Mr Rust's papers.

The author of the Curtain Lectures, of which we have published one or two, is dead. His name was Laman Blanchard, & his contributions to the London Punch were among the best articles in that paper. He wrote this whilst his wife was lying at the point of death. In a fit of delirium he committed suicide by cutting his throat. –Balt Patriot

Notice: the removal to Albany of Hon John A Collier, who with his 2 sons, bid adieu to the village of Binghampton. Last winter Hon Mitchell Sanford has removed thither from Catskill, & Hon David Russell is soon to take his place also at the Bar of Albany. The prior removal to Albany within a few years past of Hon Danl Cady from Johnstown, argues an increase of legal business at the capital. –N Y Tribune

Died: on Apr 19, in Wash City, Rose Standish, infant d/o Horatio King, aged 17 months. Her funeral will take place at the house of her father, on 2nd st east, Capitol Hill, at 4 o'clock this afternoon.

Wm Davis, formerly one of the deputy keepers of the N Y C prison, has been convicted of aiding Alex'r Hong, a convict, to make his escape.

TUE APR 22, 1845
Agent for Claims at Washington: Chas De Selding, Genr'l Agent, 11 Todd's Bldgs, Pa ave, Wash.

Wash City Canal: proposals for renting of section wharves will be received until May 1, 1845. —Jacob S Bender, Com'r W C Canal

Atlantic House, Pelham & South Toure sts, Newport, R I: house is now completed & will be open on Jun 10 next for the reception of company. —Ab'm A Potter, Proprietor

English papers: Miss Mary Linwood died at her house in Belgrave Gate, Leicester, on Mar 9 last, in her 90th yer. She was a native of that town, & her specimens of needlework have been one of the great objects of attraction in the rooms in Leicester square, London, for nearly half a century. Her productions bore so close a resemblance to the most finished painting that a very close inspection was necessary to discover their peculiar mode of execution.

Benton [Miss] Banner: on Mar 31 John B Hixon was shot dead a few miles from that place by Lewis Lott. Hixon, it seems, had maltreated his wife, who has sought refuge in her father's house, which he had forbidden, in consequence of which he threatenened violence upon the persons of his wife, Mr Lott, & other members of his family. He finally came & demanded his child, with a double barreled gun in his hand, riding into the house on horseback, when Mr Lott fired & killed him, & was examined & acquitted.

Appropriations made during the 2nd session of the 28th Congress. 1-To R P Anderson, for printing & binding for the Navy Dept, by contract: $1,321. 2-To credit Rodman M Price, as purser of the U S steamship **Missouri**, with such amount of the slops, small stores, & money, with which he stands charged on the books of the 4th Auditor of the Treas, as the accounting ofcrs shall be satisfied was consumed or lost by the burning of said vessel, not, however, to exceed: $12,060. 3-To the Choctaws: for life annuity to chief, Bob Cole, stipulated in the 15th article of the treaty of Sep 27, 1830. 4-Relief of John H McIntosh: for property destroyed by order of the military ofcrs of the U S: $9,950. For cotton destroyed on the same occasion, by order of the commanding ofcr: $4,531.25. 5-Relief of Edw A Lambert: to correct a mistake made in his bid, or his contract, for the supply of stationery to the N Y custom-house: $127.41. 6-Relief of Dunning R McNair: for carrying the great Western mail from Bedford to Wash, Pa, at the rate of $11,550, from the time it shall be found that the great Western mail from Phil to Wheeling, Va, was put upon said route, until the same was restored to the original route, via Balt & the Nat'l road to Wheeling: indefinite. 7-Relief of Benj S Roberts: indefinite. 8-Relief of Elisha Morrell, adm of Jos Icard, dec'd: on account of an award made by the com'rs under the convention with France, of Jul 4, 1841, in behalf of Julien S Raulet, on account of the loss of the cargo on board the vessel **Cadoz**: indefinite. 9-Relief of Danl Homans: for damages sustained by lightning, money retained, & extra work done on the marine hospital built by him: $3,257.36. 10-Relief of Mrs Mary W Thompson: for services which shall appear to have been rendered by her husband, the late Lt Col A R Thompson, U S Army: indefinite. 11-Relief of Wm Rich: for relinquishing his interest as a custom-house ofcr in Vt, in the result of a suit at law, to enable him to become a witness:

$252.22. 12-Relief of Philip Schwartztrawber, of Ohio: for his services in taking care of the booms left on Red river by Capts Tyson & Shreve: $240.00. 13-Payment to Wm Armstrong, to make good the loss sustained by him in consequence of the explosion of the boiler of the steamer **Cherokee**, while transporting Gov't funds from New Orleans to the Indian country west of Arkansas, in 1840: $141.00. 14-Payment of the claim of Thos Dole, for goods & provisions furnished the N Y Indians, in 1839 & 1840, allowed by the accounting ofcrs of the Treas: $964.81. 15-Relief of Harvey & Slagg: for the drawback of duties upon 10 cases of merchandise: indefinite. 16-Relief of John Adams & John Adams, jr: for a fine imposed by Mr Charles, the revenue ofcr at Eliz city, N C: $500.00 17-Relief of Stanley White: for land improperly patented to Chas H Lewis, by the U S: $209.20. 18-To R P Anderson, for printing & binding for the Navy Dept, by contract: $1,331.00 19-Act providing payment for certain military services in Florida: To Col Robt Brown's command, from Apr 6 to Jul 22, 1838, except the company of Capt North, which shall be paid to Jul 12, 1838: indefinite. Maj Isaac Garrison's command, from Mar 19 to Jul 5, 1838: indefinite. Capt Arthur Roberts' company, from Sep 13, 1838, to Jan 13, 1839: indefinite. Capt J T Thigpen's company, from Mar 1, to Aug 31, 1838: indefinite. 5-Capt Wm Williams' company, from Aug 16, 1838 to Feb 16, 1839: indefinite. Capt Wm Cone & John Bryan's companies, from Aug 18 to Sep 15, 1840: indefinite. Capt J T Stewart's company, from Aug 19 to Sep 13, 1840: indefinite. Capt Stephen Daniel's company, from Oct 13 to Nov 26, 1842: indefinite.

To the memory of the late Richd Cutts: born on Jun 22, 1771, at Cutts' Island, Saco, in the province or district of Maine, then constituting a part of the commonwealth of Mass, descended fom one of the earliest founders of New England: received his early education at Harvard Univ, where he graduated in 1790, in his 20th year. At age 29, in 1800, he was elected by the people of his district a member of the Hse/o Reps of the U S-through 6 successive Congresses. Mr Cutts was appointed by Pres Jas Monroe 2nd Comptroller of the Treas, which he held until 1829, since which he has resided in Wash City in the retirement of private life. In 1804 he was united in marriage with Miss Anna Payne, a sister of Mrs Madison. By her he had 4 sons & 2 dghts, 4 of whom, 3 sons & 1 dght survive, & followed his remains in filial anguish to the grave, near to those of their departed mother & sister, the former of whom had been withdrawn from their devoted affection in 1832, & the latter in 1838.

The Rev John Henshaw, of the Protestant Episcopal Church, was accidentally drowned near Brooklyn, in Noxubee Co, Miss, a few days since.

Died: on Apr 18, Chas Laskey, in his 33rd year, a native of Cornwall, England, but for the last 20 years a resident of Wash City.

Died: on Mar 7, at his residence in Wilmington, Dela, Elder John Purnell Peckworth, pastor of the first Baptist Church in that place, in his 75th year, formally pastor of the Baptist Church in Alexandria, D C.

Died: on Mar 24, at New Orleans, Georgeanna, w/o Wm M Lambeth, & y/d/o the late Geo Slacum, of Alexandria, D C, leaving 4 young children; the tenderest of whom, an infant son, aged 16 days, followed on Apr 7th its mother, as we trust to a better world.

Caution: I caution the public against trusting any person whatever for good or otherwise on my account, as I am determined to pay no bills contracted in my name or on my account by any one except myself in person. –Henry Harvey

Josiah Dixon, Merchant Tailor, Coleman's Nat'l Hotel, entrance on 6th st. [Local ad.]

For rent, a commodious 3 story house, on Pa ave, next to 3rd st. The key may be found at Dr Schwartz's apothecary store, next door.

WED APR 23, 1845
Wash Corp: 1-Bill for the relief of Isaac Beers: passed. 2-Cmte of Claims: act for the relief of John Barnes: read twice. 3-Cmte of Claims: asking to be discharged from the further consideration of the ptn of Edw Sweeney, was reconsidered, & the ptn was recommitted to the cmte.

Orphan's Court of Wash Co, D C, Apr 22, 1845. In the matter of the real estate of the late Lewis G Davidson. The trustee reported the following persons became purchasers of the respective lots, to wit:
Wm Bagmam, Lot 1 in square 163: $149.22½
Walter Butler, Lot 3 in square 163: $74.22
Cornelius Clarke, Lot 10 in square 163: $176.30
Geo Krafft, Lot 10 in square 163: $81.67½
John Sherbaus, lot 17 in square 163: $85.39
Columbus Alexander, lot 18 in square 163: $89.10
Richd Cruikshanks, lots 1 & 20 in square 165: $1.663.48
Aaron O Dayton, Lot 3 in square 165: $429.00
Richd Smith, lot 4 in square 165: $363.00
Geo J Abbott, lot 5 in square 165: $478.50
Chas A Schneider, lot 6 in square 165: $265.12½
Ordered that the sale be ratified. –Nathl Pope Causin. –Ed N Roach, Reg of Wills

Valuable household & kitchen furniture at auction: on Apr 28, at the residence of Douglas Howard, n w corner of F & 6th sts. –A Green, Auctioneer

Nicholas G Gordon, whose trial at Providence, R I, for the murder of Amasa Sprague, resulted in the disagreement of the jury, has been admitted to bail in the sum of $10,000, & is at large.

Capt P F Voorhees, of the U S ship **Congress**, just arrived at Norfolk, has addressed a note to the Sec of the Navy, with reference to statements published in the Gov't paper of Buenos Ayres, to the effect that the death of the late Com Newman, of the frig **Bainbridge**, was caused in some way by him. He says that it is utterly untrue, & that none but the most friendly relations ever existed between them. He says: Com Newman came to me in great agony of feeling, in consequence of having been fired into, unprovokedly, by one of the cruisers belonging to the squadron of Buenos Ayres, & I endeavored to soothe him to the uttermost. On the morning preceding the evening of his death, I also wrote him a soothing note, which I presume may now be in possession of his widow. The death of the late Cmder Newman was certainly brought about by his having been fired into by a cruiser of Buenos Ayres; & it is my humble opinion that he would now be on the land with the living but for that outrage.

Thos Pollard, of Boston, a very estimable gentleman, staying temporarily at Richmond, Va, for his health, suddenly ruptured a blood vessel, on Mon, while ascending the staircase at the Powhatan House, & immediately breathed his last from excessive hemorrhage. He was about 55 or 60 years of age; unmarried, living independently, & leaves few near relatives; but his correspondence proves he had many friends in New England, who, with us, will mourn his sudden departure. –Whig

$50 reward for runaway negro Edmond, about 21 years old. –Thos Ap C Jones, near Prospect Hill, Va.

Houses for rent: in the First Ward. For terms apply to Mrs Dorcas Walker, on 18th, between I & K sts.

John Burns was shot in Phil on Sat, & died on Sun. The gun was fired from a house, & 5 men were arrested immediately.

The Hon Jas Cooper, at present a Rep in the Legislature of Pa from Alden Co, & the Hon Chas B Penrose, of Carlisle, late Solicitor of the U S Treas, intend removing to Lancaster city in a few weeks. [Apr 26th newspaper: the Hon Jas Cooper has no intention of removing from his present residence in Gettysburg. –Harrisburg Telegraph]

Isabella Walker, age 19 years, was killed at Valley Falls, R I, on Apr 12, by being caught in the machinery of a factory where she was at work.

The new Methodist Episcopal Church lately erected in the Northern Liberties was on Sun last dedicated for public worship, Rev Wm Ryland preaching. Amongst those in the congregation was the Pres & lady, the Secs of State & War, the Atty Gen, Ex-Pres Adams, & the Mayor of Wash. Rev Henry Slicer made an address. The sum of $1,100.28 was collected.

On Wed last Ambrose Jones was tried at Grenville Courthouse for the murder of his stepmother in Feb last, & found guilty. The old lady was 65 years of age, & was the only white person living on the place, her husband having died a few years previous. She was found dead in the garden, with her skull & one arm broken. Jones is about 50 years of age, & has a wife & several children, most of the latter grown. –Columbia [S C] Chronicle [Apr 28th newspaper: sentenced to be hung on the first Fri of Jun. On Mon last, Jones committed suicide by hanging himself with his suspenders & a rope made by tearing & twisting his blanket. He left a note: Col D Hoke: Dear Sir: I have saved you the trouble. Ambrose H Jones. I am innocent of the charge. Jones made his will near the middle of that day. His wife took leave of him about half an hour before he was found dead, but he asked her to return in an hour, which she did. In company with the jailor, he was found dead.]

Died: on Apr 22, in Gtwn, in her 76th year, Mrs Betty H Blake, relict of the late Dr Jas H Blake, of Wash City. She was well known to most of the old inhabitants of the District, & enjoyed the respect & esteem of a large circle of friends & acquaintances. Her funeral will take place this afternoon, at 4 o'clock, from the residence of her son-in-law, Wm A Gordon, & 1st st.

Died: on Mon last, in her 63rd year, Mrs Ann Dyer, relict of the late Capt Wm B Dyer, formerly of Balt, but for many years a highly respectable inhabitant of Wash City. She was an exemplary member of the Methodist Episcopal Church; leaving as a legacy to her children an example worthy of imitation. The remains of the dec'd will be removed from the residence of her son-in-law, R W Bates, on Apr 23, to the Foundry Meeting-house, on 14th st, where the funeral services will be performed.

Died: on yesterday, Mathew Sexsmith, aged 76 years. His funeral will take place on today, at 3 o'clock, from his late residence, Pa ave, between 9th & 10th sts.

THU APR 24, 1845
Sale of valuable property at public auction: by deed of trust from Michl McCarty, dated Apr 20, 1844, recorded in the land records of Wash Co, D C, in book W B #109, folios 55 to 57, & for the purpose of satisfying the debt intended to have been secured by that conveyance, will be sold at public auction, on the premises, May 17, 1845, all the right, title, interest, & estate in & to the unexpired term & time of McCarty in: part of lot 29 in square B, in Wash City, on Pa ave; the said devised by Fred'k May to McCarty by deed dated Aug 17, 1836, as recorded in said land records, in book W B 59, folios 391 to 394, for 99 years, renewable forever, at an annual rent of $114.90, with the right to purchase out the fee for the sum of $1,915. There is upon the said premises a 2 story brick house, used as a store & dwlg, & other improvements. By order of the Trustees, Ed W Simms, R E Simms. -Robt W Dyer & Co, aucts

Household furniture at auction on Apr 25, at the residence of Lt Humphreys, on Pa ave, near the corner of 17th st west. -Robt W Dyer & Co, aucts

New Book: The Pictorial History of the U S of America, from the discovery by the Northmen, in the 10th century, to the present time. By John Frost, L L D, Professor of Belles-Letters, Central High School, Phil. Embellished with 350 engravings from original drawings, by W Croome: 4 volumes in 2; 8vo Phil. Simeon Collins, 1844.

Obit-died: Mr R W Watkins, of Md. As a husband & father his devotion to his family was incessant & untiring; as a master he was kind & humane. -W
[No date-current item.]

Died: on Apr 15, at Newport, Chas Co, Md, at the residence of his mother, Wm F Budd, aged 24 years & 17 days, after an illness of 10 days. But an hour before his death, the prayer was read by him according to the usages of the Roman Catholic Church, of which he was a member. He was the joy & comfort of an aged & widowed mother, whose hope in life seemed to have rested on his aid. He also leaves a sister & young brother.

FRI APR 25, 1845
Mrs Spalding, on 4½ st, a few doors above Pa ave, is prepared to accommodate with board gentlemen, with or without their families, by the month, week, or day. Terms moderate.

Copartnership. The subscribers have associated themselves together for the wholesale & retail Grocery Business, under the firm of Browning & Belt, & have taken the large storehouse formerly occupied by Edw S Wright, between the stores of Wm F Seymour & R H L Villard, Bridge st, Gtwn. -N Thos Browning, John M Belt

House & lots at auction on Capitol Hill, on May 3 next, lots 17 & 18 in square 725, with the 2 story frame house thereon, on the brow of the Hill, to the n e of the Capitol, overlooking the valley through which the railroad passes, being the same bldg which was formerly occupied by the late Jas Greenleaf. A neat cottage has been erected on the north. Title is unquestionable. -D A Hall, Trustee & Agent -A Green, Auctioneer

The subscriber still continues to recover claims, & to give his advice & assistance in all cases within his sphere as an agent & counsellor at law. -Estwick Evans, 7th & N Y ave, Wash

The Waterford Chronicle announces the death of Regina Maria Roche, the celebrated authoress of that old fashioned novel, The Children of the Abbey. She died at her residence in Ireland, at age 81 years.

The New Orleans papers announce the death of John Hill Stickney, aged 47 years, brother of S P Stickney, of the Nat'l Amphitheatre. Mr Stickney was for many years connected with the several equestrian & dramatic companies of distinction both in Europe & this country.

Mrd: on Apr 23, by the Rev H H Bean, H Allen Taylor, of Balt, to Ann E Van Ness, d/o Gen A Henderson.

Norfolk Herald: Geo Lewis was terribly crushed in the machinery used for raising vessels in Mr Calley's ship yard, that he expired almost instantly. He was the only s/o a poor widowed mother.

City Ordinance-Wash. Act for the relief of Isaac Beers: fine imposed for keeping 2 dogs without paying license, is hereby remitted: Provided, that the said Beers pay the costs of prosecution.

SAT APR 26, 1845
Household & kitchen furniture, silver & plated ware, & coppers, at auction: on Apr 29, being articles from the houses lately occupied by Momus Gilbert, taken under a bill of sale. -Robt W Dyer & Co, aucts

Jason Mahan, charged with counterfeiting coin, & G W Curtis & Jas Higgins, charged with uttering the same, were put on trial before the U S Circuit Court of Phil on Wed, when each of them plead guilty. -Clipper

The copartnership existing under the name of Shepherd & Harkness has been dissolved by mutual consent. –Alex Shepherd, John C Harkness The undersigned having this day entered into copartnership, for the purpose of conducting the Lumber, Lime, & Coal business at the well known stand formerly occupied by Shepher & Harkness, on 7th st, adjoining the Centre Market. –J C Harkness, John Purdy

Mrd: on Thu last, in Wash City, by Rev O B Brown, Mr Wm McCoy, of N Y, to Miss Mary Jane Dodd, of Wash City.

Died: yesterday, in his 5th year, Charles Constantine, s/o the late Thos T & Barbara Ann Parker. His funeral tomorrow at 3 o'clock.

Loudoun land for sale: the subscriber offers for sale 2,740 acres of valuable land, in Loudoun Co, Va, bounded on the west by Broad Run: land has been divided into several farms. Farms may be had at private sale by applying to Mr Judson H Chittenden, at Gunnell's [Dranesville P O] on the Wash & Leesburg turnpike, or to Mr Benj Bridges, residing in the immediate vicinity. –Wm B Chittenden, Richmond, Va

N Y correspondence: Gorham Parks, of Maine, has been appointed Consul of the U S at Rio Janeiro, vice Mr Gordon, to make a place for whom the former excellent Consul, Mr Slacum, was removed.

An uncle in Scotland has recently died & left Fanny Wright property worth L100,000. She is now in Jersey city, & will remain in this country for a few weeks to take legal steps preliminary to taking possession of this large legacy. –Albany Citizen

John Carr, of Anne Arundel Co, Md, was thrown from his horse on Apr 16, near Annapolis, & died a short time afterwards. He leaves a wife & 2 children to mourn his irreparable loss.

St Mary's School, Raleigh, N C. Rt Rev L S Ives, D D, Visiter; Rev Aldert Smedes, Rector. Next session will commence on Jun 10th, & continue 10 months.

Constable's sale: by virtue of a writ of fieri facias, issued by Henry Addison, a Justice of the Peace for Wash Co, D C: sale on May 3, on the premises, lot 7 in square 692, [subject to an annual gound-rent of $24.05, payable half-yearly,] with the improvements thereon, seized & taken as the property of Jos D Lafontaine, & the interest of the said Lafontaine will be sold to satisfy a judgment due Edw S Wright. -Wm H Barnaclo, Constable

On the petition of Oliver C Harris, of Waterville, N Y, praying for the extension of a patent granted to him for an improvement in the paint mill, for 7 years from the expiration of said patent, which takes place on Mar 15, 1846: said petition will be heard at the Patent Ofc on the first Mon in Aug next. –Henry L Ellsworth, Com'r of Patents

MON APR 28, 1845
Among the passengers by the barque **Hecla**, arrived at N Y from St Croix, is Thurlow Weed, editor of the Albany Evening Journal.

The Sicilian frig **Urania**, Com Lettiere, of 46 guns & 335 men, arrived at N Y on Sat, in 57 days from St Helena.

Roxbury, Mass. The extensive Ropewalk of Messrs John Webber & Son was consumed by fire with all the contents on Wed. Dwlgs of the workmen were destroyed. A woman, with an infant in her arms, jumped from a 3rd story window. The infant was killed & the woman was seriously injured. Two children are missing.

The storm of Fri was very violent at York, Pa. The ofc of Messrs A & E Denmead & Co, attached to their shed for framing bridges, was struck by lightning, killing Wm Wilson, s/o Mr Wilson, tavern keeper at Cockeysville, & stunning Matthew Placide.

Trustee's sale: by virtue of a deed of trust from John E Dement et al, to me, dated Feb 16, 1843, recorded in liber W B #106, folios 144 to 150, of the land records of Wash Co: sale in Wash City, on May 13, a tract of land, part of *Gisborough Manor*, now in the occupancy of said Dement, containing 90+ acs, in said county. Land is on the main road from Wash City to Piscataway, & adjoins the lands of Dr Chas B Hamilton & other land of said Dement. Tract has a new dwlg. –Jas C Barry, Trustee -Robt W Dyer & Co, aucts [Jul 14th newspaper: At the request of Mr John E Dement, & with the consent of the Trustee, the above sale is postponed till this Mon. -R W Dyer & Co, aucts}

The Rev Edw Dromgoole Sims died at his residence in Tuscaloosa on Apr 13$^{th.}$ While superintending some work in his garden the preceding Sat he suddenly fell, & was taken to his dwlg in a state of insensibility, from which he never recovered. He was born in Brunswick Co, Va, Mar 24, 1805; graduated in the Univ of N C in 1823, & became a tutor of that institution. He filled various other positions. In Dec, 1841, he was elected as Prof of English Literature in the Univ of Ala, & filled that chair until his lamented death.

Mrd: on Apr 10, in Boston, Mass, by Rev Dr Fiske, Mr P Dickinson, [of the firm of Cowan & Dickinson, Knoxville, Tenn] to Miss Susan Penniman, of New Braintree, Mass.

Circuit Court of Wash Co, D C-in Chancery. John Alves & Duncan Alves, vs Jos T Hall, Caroline D Alves, & others. Ratify sale by Com'rs of lot 2 in square 186 in Wash City: same sold to Wm W Corcoran for $593.12. –Wm Brent, clk

To let: the 2 houses near the corner of I st & 17th st, nearly opposite Mrs Macomb's, the east fronts thereof are painted a lead color. –Thos Munroe

For sale: a 2 story brick house on Capitol Hill. Apply to Jas D Waller, on the premises, or to Chas W Stewart, next door.

Circuit Court of Wash Co, D C. Trial of unusual interest. The plntfs, Saml Dinsman & others, marines, formerly in the service of the U S, during the celebrated Exploring Expedition, have brought an action against their former commander, Capt Chas Wilkes, for assault & battery & false imprisonment on board the ship **Vincennes**, while engaged in that service. The marines assume the position that they were not, at the time of the infliction of punishment, in the service of the U S. Capt Wilkes maintains that they were, hence his legal power to coerce them for any refusal on their part to attend to the duties of the marine service. [May 3rd newspaper: In the cases of Dinsman, Babb, & Roberts, vs Wilkes: a verdict was rendered yesterday for Dinsman & Babb. Damages, $500 in each case. In the case of Roberts vs Wilkes, the jury gave a verdict for the dfndnt.]

Col Cunningham, one of the Reps of Beaver Co, Pa, died on Apr 18, in a canal-boat, near Johnstown on the Conemaugh. He had been long in delicate health. He was attended in his last moments by his colleague, Mr Nicholason, & Mr Sankey, of Mercer Co, & was buried on Sat at Saltsburg. He discharged all his duties as father, citizen, & rep, sedulously & faithfully.

Charleston, S C papers announce the death of Dr Wm Reed, aged 91 years, at his plantation on Cooper river, on Apr 20. This venerable patriot was a member of Gen Washington's Staff during the Revolutionary war. He was buried at Charleston with the honors of war.

A fine lad, about 9 years of age, named Hill, while fishing at Lenox's wharf, on Sat, fell into the Potomac, & was drowned. Dr Morgan tried to resucitate the boy, but it proved ineffectual.

A sudden & tremendous gust visited Wash City on Fri: 2 lofty brick chimneys were blown down, from the rear of the large house occupied by Mrs Potter, on Pa ave. A house belonging to Mr Wm Morrow, now being erected near the railroad depot, was blown down. Lightning struck the chimney on the house of Mr Quigley at the Navy Yard. The son & dght of Mr Quigley were struck & severely stunned. The young lady did not recover until the following day. Young Quigley recovered from the shock in a few hours. A cow not far from the residence of Mr Quigley was instantly killed by the lightning. [Apr 30th newspaper: Mrs Lewis, the d/o Mr Quigley referred to, did not recover to her right senses until Mon. Dr McWilliams considers her entirely out of danger. Her face become totally changed & elongated, so much so as not to be recognised by her intimate acquaintances. She has of course entirely recovered.]

TUE APR 29, 1845
Cherokee Country: the delegation appointed by the Nat'l Council left Tahlequah for Washington on Apr 1. It consists of John Ross, Jos Vann, David Vann, & others. Col Washington & Col Armistead left Tahlequah for *Fort Gibson* on Mar 28.

For rent: 2 story brick house on Md ave. Possession immediately.
–Mrs R Cheshire, 4½ st.

A good chance for a nice house. To rent, & possession on Mar 15, the house in which Mr Skinner resides, in F st. The house is in complete order. Apply to Saml Brereton, F & 7th sts.

Estray cow came to the residence of the subscriber, on the gravel turnpike leading to Fairfax court-house, on Apr 23. Owner to prove property & pay the cost of this ad.
–Isaac H Robbins

We have been presented by a friend in New Bedford with an egg with this inscription: "Presented by Capt R R Crocker, of New Bedford, Mass, Apr 1845." This is the egg of a penquin, taken from the Island of Ichaboe in Dec, 1844, 58 feet below the surface of guano, & must be 6,408 years old. –Boston Atlas

Valuable real estate for sale: on Jun 11, near Luray, Page Co, Va: **Blackford Estate**. It contains **Isabella Furnace**, about 25 acs; **Speedwell Forges**, 1,000 acs; Land near the furnace & forges, containing about 245 acs; a tract of Land adjoining the last, containing 240 acs; a tract of Land adjoining the latter, containing 250 acs; & 3 tracts adjoining the former, containing each 114, 115, & 151 acs. –Chauncy Brooks, Pres Western Bank of Balt

I offer for sale the entire stock of Blooded Horses, the property of the late T R S Boyce, dec'd. [Pedigree information followed the names of the horses.] -Noah Gassaway, Exc of T R S Boyce's Estate

$50 reward for runaway, my servant George, about 40 years of age. Address, Millville, King Geo Co, Va. -R H Montgomery

Mr Valentine Gay, of Maine, about 50 years old, was killed on Fri on the Lowell railroad, upon which he was walking. He stepped from one track to avoid the baggage train, & was caught by the passenger train, & instantly killed.

WED APR 30, 1854
Mrs Wilkins, wid/o the late Wm Wilkins, & mother-in-law of J Glenn, met with an accident on Fri last. She was on her way home, when on the pavement of the Maypole Tavern, corner of Paca & German st, a horse belonging to Mr McPherson, of Fred'k Co, which a small colored boy was riding, took fright, ran upon the pavement, & fell with his whole weight upon the lady, causing severe contusion upon the head, crushing one of her ankles, & causing severe internal injuries. She was conveyed to her dwlg on Chas st. She is lying in a very precarious condition, not having spoken since the accident. -Clipper

Augustine Haines, of Portland, appointed District Atty of Maine, in place of Gorham Parks, appointed Consul at Rio Janeiro.

Barre [Mass] Patriot: Mr Wm White, of that town, at the recent term of the Supreme Court, in Worcester, recovered $816. 65 damages against the town of Phillipston, for an injury he received in consequence of the road not being sufficiently broken out. His left hand or wrist was maimed so badly as to partially deprive him of its use for life.

The sale of the pictures belonging to Cardinal Fesch's gallery, & left by him to Jos Bonaparte, commenced at Rome on Mar 17. A landscape by Hobbema brought 6,400 crowns, nearly $7,000.

The large clock factory of Chauncey Jerome, at Bristol, Conn, was destroyed by fire on Wed. The loss is not far from $25,000, on which is an insurance of $10,000 at the Aetna ofc, Hartford.

Saratoga Whig: the inventive genius of the late Obed M Coleman, the inventor of the Aeolian Attachment, was exhibited in his 16th year, when he perfected the Automaton Lady Minstrel & Singing Bird, the figure of a lady & bird, the former performing popular airs upon the accordion, while the bird perched on her shoulder, warbled wood-notes wild. He disposed of this for $800, & being thus somewhat relieved from extreme poverty he removed to Saratoga, & built his Aeolian Attachment, which took 2 years.

Died: on Apr 26, of consumption, at the residence of his father, in Alexandria, Henry Yeates, only s/o Wm Yeates, in his 29th year.

For rent: 3 story brick house on Capitol Hill. Inquire of Saml Burche, or of the subscriber, on N J ave, near the residence of Mr Blagden. –Rebecca Burche

For rent, & possession given on May 1, the neat cottage residence near 12th st & Md ave. Inquire of Edmond Brooke, near the premises.

To be sold at public auction on May 26, at the Centre Market, one gray Mare & one sorrel Horse, the property of Robt Little, for livery due to G W Young.
–Wm Kelly, Agent

THU MAY 1, 1845
N Y papers announce the death of Danl Oakey, one of the oldest & most respectable residents of that city.

Persons wishing to make good investments in real estate are requested to the sale of the property of the late Ann Larkin, [formerly Mrs McGunnigle,] on May 1, on 10th st west, the whole of lot 17 in square 348, with improvements. –A Green, auctioneer

Horse for sale at the stable of Messrs Walker & Kimmell, between 4½ & 6th sts, & C st & Pa ave.

Fine lot of Virginia horses just arrived, & for sale at Franklin stable, corner of 8th & D sts.
–J Rowles, Proprietor

Tavern for rent: the new 3 story brick bldg on the corner of 7th & I sts. –Jas H Shreve

For sale: household furniture, bar fixtures, & kitchen utensils of that well known establishment, the Washington Coffee House, near the Centre Market. Inquire on the premises of W Lenox, Atty at Law

Mr Moses Ward, one of the distributing clerks in the N Y Post Ofc, whilst engaged in his duties, on Sun, fell suddenly on the floor, & before medical aid could be procured, was a corpse. Apoplexy was the cause.

Deaths by lightning: on the 5th ult, in front of the residence of Green Fenn, of Westville, Miss, when it struck persons in the piazza near the base of a tree, 3 were instantly killed: Mrs W B Fenn, aged about 19 years, G G Fenn, aged about 11 years, the former a brother & the latter an only s/o G Fenn; & D B Halford, aged about 10 years, s/o Mrs Halford, who had stopped out of the rain, on his way home from school.

By an order of distress to me directed, I shall expose to public sale on May 3, at Green's warehouse, on 6th st near Pa ave, the goods & chattels seized & taken as the property of John Truscott, & will be sold to satisfy house-rent due to Danl S Harkness.
–John Wright, Bailiff -A Green, auct

Mrd: on Apr 29, by Rev H Myers, Capt John F Lee, U S Army, to Miss Ellen Ann Hill, of Wash City.

Mrd: on Apr 29, at *Avondale*, PG Co, Md, by Rev Thos Lilly, Chas C Hill to Miss Emily R Snowden, d/o Mrs E W Snowden, all of PG Co, Md.

FRI MAY 2, 1845
The Hon Caleb Cushing arrived at Newburyport, Mass, his place of residence, on Thu last, & was received with various demonstrations of regard. A salute was fired by the Artl company in his honor.

Brooklyn Evening Star: Mr Covert, on Sun, at Whitehall, about 1 mile from the village of Cold Spring, L I, was shot through his window & died almost instantly. Mrs Covert was standing near her husband.

Mrd: on Apr 30, by Rev Mr Tarring, Mr Wm F Gardiner to Miss Mary Jane Young, both of Wash City.

Mrd: on May 1, by Rev Jas B Donelan, Mr Robt P Wade, of Montg Co, Md, to Miss Eliza M Peckham, of Wash City.

Mrd: on Jan 3 last, by Rev Dr Brackenridge, R Caton Woodville to Mary T Buckler, d/o Dr John Buckler, of Balt.

Mrd: on Apr 15, in Ponola Co, Miss, by Rev Jesse Stratton, John E Morse, of Wash City, to Miss Eliz K, only d/o Col Andrew Stratton, of Ponola Co, Miss.

Died: on Apr 30, in his 19th year, Wm Henry Howard, s/o Henry & Rosa Howard; of a severe & painful illness of many weeks. His funeral is this evening at 4 o'clock.

Wash Seminary, N Y ave, between 17th & 18th sts. The subscriber having purchased this Institution of A H Evans, will conduct it in such a manner as to give satisfaction to those who attend. –Wm S Graff

Robt Seabrook, from S C, stopping at the Astor House, had his trunk opened on Thu, & about $480 in gold coin stolen thereform. A Mr Edwards has been arrested. –N Y Post

Justices of the Peace for Wash Co, D C, paid their respects to the Pres yesterday, at the Executive Mansion, according to previous arrangement among themselves. They were received with great courtesy.

Benj K Morsell	S Drury	Joshua Pierce
N B Van Zandt	R H Clements	C H Wiltberger
John D Clark	Josh Beck	N Callan
Wm Thompson	E W Smallwood	Thos Donoho
N Brady	B B French	A T Smith
Jas Marshall	H C Williams	J L Smith

New Commission Warehouse: east of Mr John T Ryon's Grocery Store, 7th & La ave. Will always keep on hand choice family Groceries, Provisions, & Chinaware. –H J Gould & Co

Dissolution of partnership existing under the firm of Thos Berry & Co: by mutual consent. Thos Berry will continue the business. –Thos Berry, Wm Dougherty

SAT MAY 3, 1845
Household & kitchen furniture at auction: on May 5, at the house formerly occupied by the Hon Mr Wickliffe, on 7th st, opposite the Gen Post Ofc. –A Green, auct

<u>Naval Intelligence</u>: Cmdor Jas Biddle, to command the U S East India Squadron.
<u>Promotions</u>: Passed Midshipmen C Van Alstine, A G Clary, & H L Chipman, to be Lts, vice Lts Saml Lockhart & Geo M Hooe, dec'd, & Wm D Hurst, dismissed.
<u>Appointments</u>: John Y Mason, jr, to be a Purser, vice R S Moore, dec'd. Washington Sherman, to be an Assist Surgeon, vice Wm Pitt Canning, dec'd.

Mr Benj True, the oldest printer in Boston, died there on Tue, aged 80 years.

Mr Thos Gaffield, of Boston, & Wm Edwards, of Haverhill, went out to ride on Mon from there, & were soon after found dead at the bottom of a steep hill, over which it was evident the horse had fallen, as he was found entangled with the broken chaise & much injured.

At Brownsville, Pa, on Sat last, a horse attached to a carriage, became frightened & ran off at top speed. Mrs West, an elderly lady, was thrown out & severely injured. She died that evening; Mrs Tilton, was bruised, & her child escaped injury.

New Boarding Establishment: Miss R S Lane has taken those 2 commodious dwlgs at F & 19th sts, formerly occupied by Mrs Lindenberger, & is prepared to receive 3 or 4 families or single persons.

By virtue of a decree of the Circuit Court of Wash Co, D C in Chancery, wherein Jas Carrico is cmplnt & the heirs-at-law of the late Danl T Patterson et al are dfndnts, the subscriber will offer at public vendue on Jun 3, on the premises, the east part of lot 12 in square 170 in Wash City, & improvements, subject to the life estate therein of Eliza J Hayne. –J B H Smith, Trustee -Robt W Dyer & Co, aucts

House for rent & carriage for sale. The house lately occupied by the Hon C B Penrose is for rent. Apply to J H Houston, or to the subscribers. Also for private sale a very handsome Family Carriage, which can be seen at McDermott's Coach Shop, or on application to us. -Robt W Dyer & Co, aucts

Valuable farm for sale. By virtue of a deed of trust from the late Tench Ringgold to me, & at the request of his heirs & the parties interested in such deed, I will sell, at public auction, on the premises, on Mar 23, a tract or parcel of land in Alexandria Co, on the Gtwn road, & within a few miles of Wash City & Gtwn, lately the residence of the said T Ringgold, containing 140 acres thereabouts, with a comfortable dwlg. Further information from me, or apply to Lt Ringgold, Arsenal, Wash. –W Redin, Trustee, Gtwn. The undersigned will offer at the same time & place 100 acres of land adjoining the above property. Terms at sale. –T L Ringgold

Sale of splendid furniture, large mirrors, at auction: on Apr 7, at the residence of Emlan Physie, on north B st, in the house formerly occupied by the Hon Richd M Johnson, all the furniture in the house. –Boteler, Donn & Co, auctioneers

Orphan's Court of Wash Co, D C. In the case of Peter O'Donoghue, adm, with the will annexed, of Jeremiah O'Sullivan, of Wash Co, dec'd. The adm aforesaid will settle the estate, & make payment & distribution, of the assets in the hands of the adm, so far as collected, on May 20 next. –Ed N Roach, Reg/o wills

Boys' Hats. Opening this morning at Todd's Fashionable Establishment, sign of the Golden Hat, west of Brown's hotel. Also, a beautiful assortment of Bohemian Gipsy Hats, for misses & children. –W B Todd, Fashionable Hatter

Mrd: on Apr 24, by Rev Mr Vanhorseigh, John Serro, Engineer U S Navy, to Miss Martha A Granger, of Wash.

Mrd: on May 1, in Wash City, by Rev Dr Muller, Mr Wm Linkins to Miss Mary Ann Woodward, d/o Wm Woodward.

Died: on May 2, in his 73rd year, Wm Hilbus, an old & respectable resident of Wash City. His funeral will take place Sat at 4 o'clock, from the residence of his son-in-law, Mr John Ousley, 15th & E sts.

MON MAY 5, 1845

Centre Market. We had an excellent market last Sat. Some remarkable fine lamb raised by Mr Dorsett, in PG Co, was sold by Mr Chas Miller. Messrs Otterback, Speisser, Rhodes, & other victuallers, sold excellent veal & lamb at fair prices. Messrs John Walker, Henry Walker, Crowley, John Little, Saml Little, & other victuallers, sold very fine beef.

Tobacco for the Navy: Bur of Provisions & Clothing, May 2, 1845. Proposals for tobacco will be received until Jun 3 next, for furnishing & delivering at the U S Navy yards at Boston, N Y, & Norfolk, where samples are deposited, such quantity of Tobacco [probably, in all, about 100,000 pounds, more or less] as may be required by the Chief of this Bureau, or the commandants of the said Navy Yards, during the fiscal year-Jul1 next & ending Jun 30, 1846.

Appointments by the Pres: 1-Robt H Morris, Deputy Postmaster in N Y C, in place of John Lorimer Graham, removed. 2-Ely Moore, Marshal of the Southern district of N Y, in place of Silas M Stilwell, removed. 3-Michl Hoffman, Naval Ofcr in N Y C, in place of Jeremiah Towle, removed.

Mrd: on Thu last, by Rev Mr French, Henry N Cox, of Wilson, Westmoreland Co, Va, to Miss Susan G, d/o the late Wm Worthington, of Wash City.

Died: on May 3, in Wash City, in her 68th year, Mrs Mary Cleary, relict of the late Michl Cleary, of Occoquan, Va. Her funeral will take place this Mon at 8 o'clock, from the residence of her dght, Mrs Mary Ann Spalding, on 4½ st, near Pa ave. Requiescat in pace. –W

The Misses Hawley, dghts of the late Rector of St John's Church of Wash City, will on May 5, open a school for young ladies. For further particulars call on them at their residence, F st, between 12th & 13th sts.

Trustee's sale: by deed of trust from Geo Hill, jr, dated Dec 4, 1841, & recorded in Liber W B #90, folios 405 thru 407, of the Land Records of Wash Co, D C, I shall offer on May 5, a negro woman named Louisa, aged about 34 years, to serve until Dec 4, 1851, & then to be free; & her female child Rosannah, now aged about 12 years, a slave for life. –Henry Haw, Trustee -E D Wright, auct

Sale of land. Order of Chas Co Court, the undersigned will sell on Jun 10, on the premises, that portion of the real estate of the late Lawrence Posey designated in the partition as Lot #2, containing by recent survey about 300 acs. Improvements are a dwlg-house & convenient out-houses. –W Penn, W D Merrick, Philip Marshall, Josias Hawkins, Geo Dent, Com'rs

Last Fri some wicked person set fire to a frame stable occupied by Thos Woodward, the Deputy Marshal. It could not be saved. Mayor Addison offers a reward of $200 for the detection & conviction of the incendiary.

TUE MAY 6, 1845
Miss Winter informs her customers that she has removed to rooms in the house of Mr Noell, blindmaker, Pa ave, near 10th, where she carries on the mantua making.

Balt Custom House. John R Diggs, Robt M Welch, Edw A Slicer, Hamlet Duvall, Saml Harker, Beale Randall, Wm Krebs, & Michl McDonald have been appointed Inspectors of the Customs at the port of Balt, in the place of Jonathan Creery, Geo C Veazy, Francis Reilly, N N Robinson, John Lowry, Thos Carroll, Chas Soran, & Thos E Tilden, removed. S C Roszell appointed Marker, vice Sebastian Sultzer, removed, & Robt M Welch appointed Boarding Ofcr.

The following interesting document, exhibiting the arrangement of the Maryland Line on Jun 1, 1781, authenticated by the signature of Gen Smallwood, was found among the military papers of the late Gen Gist, who commanded the 2nd Brigade of that gallant corps:

First Regt
When Commissioned
Otho H Williams, Col   Jan 1, 1777
John Stewart, Lt Col   Feb 10, 1781
John Eccleston, Major   Dec 10, 1777
Captains
Jonathan Sellman   Jan 10, 1777
Edw Teall   Jun 10, 1777

Wm Reily	Oct 13, 1777
John Sprigg Belt	Dec 15, 1777
Christian Orndorff	Apr 1, 1778
Richd Bird	Jun 12, 1780
Geo Armstrong	Feb 11, 1780
Lloyd Beall	Feb 10, 1781
Thos B Hugo	Jun 12, 1781

Lts

Wm Lamar	Nov 15, 1777
Jas Ewing	May 29, 1778
Jas John Skinner	Sep 18, 1778
Isaac Duvall	Apr 10, 1779
John Hamilton	Jun 1, 1779
Wm Woolford	Sep 11, 1779
Wm Raison	Jan 26, 1780
Joshua Burgess	Mar 11, 1780
Hezekiah Ford	Aug 16, 1780
John J Lowe	Jan 20, 1781
Edw M Smith	Feb 19, 1781
Saml Edmiston	Mar 14, 1781
John Trueman	Mar 16, 1781
Richd Pindell, Surgeon	[blank]
Ezekiel Hayne, Mate	[blank]

2nd Regt

John Gunby, Col	Apr 17, 1777
John Eager Howard, Lt Col	Mar 11, 1779
John Dean, Major	Mar 11, 1779

Capts

Alex'r Truemen	Jan 1, 1777
Jonathan Morris	Apr 14, 1777
Walker Muse	Jun 10, 1777
Wm Wilmot	Oct 15, 1777
John Jordan	Dec 26, 1777
Thos Mason	Jun 8, 1779
John Gassaway	Apr 2, 1780
Adam Hooper	Mar 16, 1781
Saml McPherson	Apr 25, 1781

Lts

Edw Dyer, Capt Lt	Sep 10, 1780
John A Hamilton	Feb 1, 1778
Christopher Richmond	May 27, 1778
Wm Adams	Jun 8, 1779
Nicholas Gassaway	[blank]

Arthur Harris	Oct 26, 1779
Thos Price	Feb 11, 1780
Wm Murdock	Apr 1, 1780
Zedekiah Moore	Sep 10, 1780
Mark McPherson	Jan 1, 1781
Wm Smoot	Mar 16, 1781
Jas Arthur	[blank]
Walter Warfield, Surgeon	[blank]

3rd Regt:

Peter Adams, Lt Col Commanding	Aug 1, 1779
Henry Hardman, Major	Mar 29, 1779
Thos Landsdale, Major	Feb 19, 1781

Capts:

Henry Dobson	Jan 10, 1777
Jos Marbury	Jan 1, 1777
Lilburn Williams	Apr 16, 1777
Robt Chesley	Jun 10, 1777
John Smith [6]	Nov 9, 1777
Jas Woodford Gray	Dec 25, 1777
Edw Spurrier	May 20, 1779
Benj Price	Jul 1, 1779
Richd Waters	Apr 7, 1779

Lts:

Francis Revelly	Apr 15, 1777
Jas Gould	Mar 11, 1778
Jas Winchester	May 27, 1778
Philip Reid	Oct 13, 1778
John Hartshorn	May 21, 1779
Rignal Hillary	Jul 15, 1779
Philip Hill	[blank]
Wm Pendergast	Oct 29, 1779
Henry Baldwin	Feb 11, 1780
David Lucket	Apr 7, 1780
Walter Dyer	Sep 5, 1780
Nathan Wright	Jan 1, 1781
John Boone	Apr 12, 1781
Levin Denwood, Surgeon	[blank]

4th Regt:

Thos Woolford, Lt Col Com'g	Oct 23, 1779
Levin Winder, Major	Apr 17, 1777
Alex Rosburgh, Major	Apr 7, 1780

Capts:

John Lynch	Jan 1, 1777

Jacob Brice	Jan 1, 1777
Henry Gaither	Apr 17, 1777
John Courts Jones	Sep 20, 1777
Richd Anderson	Nov 15, 1777
Geo Hamilton	Jan 25, 1778
David Lynn	May 22, 1779
John Mitchell	Jul 15, 1779
Jonthan Gibson	May 1, 1780

Lts

Nicholas Mangers	Apr 15, 1779
Jas Simmes	May 27, 1778
Peter Hardcastle	Sep 14, 1778
Benj Garnett	Oct 13, 1778
Wm Stoddert	May 21, 1779
Levascha d'Naubunne	[blank]
Nathan Smith	Sep 15, 1779
Edmund Compton	Feb 18, 1780
Joshua Rutledge	May 1, 1780
John Brevett	Sep 20, 1780
John McCoy	Jan 1, 1781
Robt Hatherston	Apr 25, 1781
Henry Gassaway	May 12, 1781
Wm Kelty, Surgeon	[blank]

5th Regt:

Benj Ford, Lt Com't	[blank]
John Davidson, Major	Jan 12, 1781
Benj Brooke, Major	Mar 16, 1781

Capts:

Wm Dent Beall	Jan 1, 1777
John Smith, [3d]	Jan 1, 1777
Edw Oldham	May 20, 1777
Horatio Clagett	Oct 10, 1777
John Galt	Dec 10, 1777
Perry Benson	Mar 11, 1778
Jas Somerville	Jun 1, 1779
Edw Edgerly	Sep 10, 1779

Lts:

Jas Bruff	Oct 7, 1777
Gassaway Watkins	Sep 14, 1778
Jacob Norris	Nov 26, 1778
John Lynn	Jun 1, 1779
Saml Hanson	Aug 1, 1779
Thos Rowse	[blank]

Robt Denny	Jan 3, 1780
Benj Tickle	Feb 19, 1780
Roger Nelson	Jul 15, 1780
Thos Boyd	Jan 1, 1781
John Sears	Jan 1, 1781
Henry Clements	Apr 25, 1781
Adam Jamieson	Jun 1, 1781

Supernumeraries in the 7 regts of the Md line:
Col Josias Carvill Hall, of the late 4th, supernumerary Jan 1, 1781.
Lt Col Nathl Ramsey, do 3d do.
Lt Col Edw Jillard, do 4th do.

Accurate list, up to the present time; part of the line being in Carolina & part in Md, the arrangement could be completed on Jan 1, pursuant to the resolution of Congress, but the rank has been adjusted, upon the principle of seniority, to that date, & the promotions regularly made since to such vacancies as have happened. The soldier of the late 7 Md Regts being incorporated, now form the 1st & 2nd Regts, those now levied, & about to be levied in the State, to be first marched to the southward, form the 3rd Regt; & it is proposed, as soon as the State completes her quota, or levies more, sufficient to form the 2 other Regts, to dissolve the incorporation of the 1st & 2nd, & assign the non-commisioned ofcrs & old soldiers of those Regts to the 1st, 2nd, 3rd, 4th, & 5th, to which they formerly belonged, in which the non-commissioned ofcrs & soldiers of the late 6th & 7th-the Md part of the Rifle & German Regts-the Md Companies raised in the State, in other Continental Corps, & the Md Artl, are to be equally divided, unless the Artl should be continued as a Corp, which the State has made application for to Congress. This disposition, as soon as circumstances may admit, seems most just & desirable to the ofcrs in general, & must tend to promote the service, by placing a proportion of the old troops in each of the present Regts. The Md part of the Rifle & German Regts not being incorporated, or considered as distinct Corps, nor included or arranged in the Md Line, have together with such companies as above said & the Md Artl, been considered a part of the State quota. I am therefore induced to show their pretensions to such provision as has been granted, or may hereafter be made by Congress for them. The dates of Commissions, & the promotions they might have been entitiled to at the time of dissolution, I have in few instances been able to ascertain, for want of proper returns of their respective state of rank & vacancies; nor from the cause could I ascertain or include the names or rank of any ofcrs commanding the companies coming under the above description, except in Col Nathl Gist's Regt.

Ofcrs in the Md Artl
Captains: Wm Brown, Richd Dorsey
Capt Lts: Ebenezer Finley, Jas Smith
1st Lts:

Robt Wilmot	Nicholas Rickets	Clement Skerrett
Jacques Bacques	Young Wilkinson	Jas McFadon

2nd Lts:

Isaac Rawlings	John Chevere	John Carson

Ofcrs in the Md part of the Rifle Corps
Capts:

Thos Hussey Lucket	Jas M Lingan	Lt Elijah Evans-but
Adamson Rannihill	Texin Davis	claims a captaincy

Ofcrs in the Md part of the German Corps:
Lt Col Lodowick Welmer, commissioned Aug 9, 1777
Capts:

Chas Baltzell, May 10, 1777	Christ'r Myers, Mar 12, 1778	Michl Boyer, May 25, 1778

Lts:

Martin Shugart, May 25, 1778	Ensign Jacob Reybold, Jul 24, 1778
Jacob Gromath, Jan 4, 1778	Surgeon Alex'r Smith, Aug, 1778
David Morgan, Apr 8, 1778	

Ofcrs in the Md part of Col Nathl Gist's Regt:
Maj Nathl Mitchell
Capts:

John Gist	Jos Smith	Jos Britain

There are many other ofcrs not included here who raised their companies in, & went from, the State of Md into the Continental line, who come under the same description with those above enumerated; therefore, upon application, the expediency of admitting their claims must necessarily come under consideration. -W Smallwood, M G

Gen Chas M Reed, of Erie, has sent a letter to the Mayor of Pittsburg, enclosing for himself & father, Rufus S Reed, the sum of $500.00, for the relief of the sufferers.

Knapp, Burrill, & Tompkins, 3 anti-renters of Delaware Co, N Y, were sentenced last week to the State prison for 2 years each. A fourth, Kelly, was fined $250.

During the storm of Sun week 2 persons of the name of Knox, residing not very far from Sykesville, Carroll Co, Md, met with their death from the effects of lightning.

Hamburg [S C] Republican: on May 7, an affray took place at Edgefield courthouse, between Mr Lovitt Gomillion & Mr W Murrell, during which Mr Murrell fired a pistol, the ball wounding Mr J Whatley severely in the thigh.

Whipping a Clergyman. The St Louis Republican of Sat says: a rencounter took place in the street today, in which F Kennett inflicted personal chastisement on the Rev Mr Linn, the pastor of the Centenary Church in this city.

Mrd: on May 3, at the E st Baptist church, by Rev G W Samson, Mr Jas W Lindsay to Miss Amanda T Graves, both of Madison Co, Va.

Mrd: on Apr 11, at Newbern, N C, by Rev Danl Stratton, Dr John Graham Tull to Miss Julia West Hollister, d/o the late Wm Hollister.

Died: on Sunday, of consumption, Mrs Ann Sessford, in her 26th year. Her funeral will take place this afternoon, at 3 o'clock, from the residence of her sister, on D st, between 9th & 10th sts.

Handsome residence for a gentleman: to let, & possession immediately, that spacious brick house & premises, the residence of the late Robt Sewall, consisting of 4 large lofty dry cellars, handsome entrance, 4 spacious dining, drawing, & sitting rooms, with 4 equally spacious rooms over the same, & 4 large garrets, with housekeeper's room, store room, kitchen, servants' room, & chambers over the same, a fine stable for 4 horses, large carriage house, standing single on the highest part of Capitol Hill, Wash, within 250 yards of the s e corner of the Capitol gardens. Inquire of S Scott, on the adjoining premises.

Cheap Auction Dry Good: just opened, direct from the Phil auctions: assortment of fabric, gloves, hoods, & bonnets. –Geo F Allen, Pa ave, between 11th & 12th sts.

WED MAY 7, 1845
A destructive storm passed over the plantation of the late Judge Rhea, on Thompson's Creek, East Felicison, on Apr 16. Every bldg in the course of the tornado was prostrated, & every tree topped as though an axe had been used. The overseer, Beverly Phelps, a meritorious young men, with the field hands, ran under the gin house. It fell beneath the crash, & crushed Mr Phelps & 7 of the negroes. Mr Phelps & 3 negroes were instantly killed. 4 others had broken limbs.

The Nashville papers announce the death of the Hon David W Dickinson, a member of the last Congress from Tenn. He died on Apr 27, near Franklin, Tenn.

Mr Danl McCullogh,of Gladden's Grove, Fairfield District, S C, has commenced erecting a bldg for a cotton factory.

Public Baths, C st, between 4½ & 6th sts. $10 for the season, & be estimated to one bath per day, Sun excepted, for themselves, or son, or dght, or the lady of the house. Single bath .25. -P Aiken

Patent Agency at Wash, D C. Z C Robbins, ofc on F st, opposite the Patent Ofc.

Preparatory Departmental of the Columbian College. The next term will commence on May 12. –T W Tobey

Pleasant residence to rent. Inquire of Mrs John Coyle, south B st, Capitol Hill.

Farm for sale: the subscriber will offer at public sale, on the premises, on May 26, the farm on which he resides, in Montg Co, Md, containing 372 acs; with comfortable & commodious dwlg & out-bldgs. -Jonathan Prout

Notice. I forewarn any person from buying any execution or debt on the property of Matthias Jeffers, on Capitol Hill, under the expectation of receiving any of the proceeds of the deferred payments, as the notes I hold on the property are not satisfied, & will overbalance what the property sold for. -John P Pepper

Mrd: on Apr 29, by Rev Lemuel Wilmer, S Wilmer Cannell, of Phil, to Sally Nivison, d/o Humberston Skipwith, of Va.

Died: on May 4, after a short illness, Mr John Brannan, sen, a native of Ireland, but for many years a respectable inhabitant of Wash City.

Masonic: meeting of Columbia Chapter, #15, on May 7, at their Hall, 12th & Pa ave. -Wm Greer, Sec

Henry Workman was killed at Louisville, on Apr 26, while in a fit of drunken anger when tried to beat his wife. His brother opposed him, & Workman attempted to stab him. His brother struck him on the head with a stone pitcher that proved fatal, & he died in a few hours.

In store, 30 drums fresh Figs, which will be sold at .10 per lb, if applied for soon. English walnuts, of prime quality, at .08 per lb. -H J Gould, 7th & La ave

Wash Corp: 1-Bill for the relief of Eliz Purrill was taken up & disagreed to. 2-Bill for the relief of R C Washington & others: passed. 3-Ptn from John T Lenman: referred to the Cmte of Claims. 4-Ptn from Wm Pettigrew: referred to the Cmte of Claims. 5-Ptn of John L Wilson, praying remission of a fine: referred to the Cmte of Claims. 6-Cmte on Improvements: ptns of Wm Gunton & others, for repair of La ave: passed. 7-Cmte of Improvements: ptn of A P Skinner & others, for the conveyance of water in the 2nd Ward: passed. 8-Cmte of Claims: bill for the relief of Chas Gautier: passed.

THU MAY 8, 1845
In the case of John Campbell, tried in Phil on Sat on a charge of murdering Lewis Greble during the riots in Kensington last year, the jury acquitted the prisoner, the Judge of the Supreme Court charging that although he fired a gun during the riots & was active in the fight, he was justifiable in defending his life & property.

Promotions in the Army made by the Pres of the U S since the promulgation of Genr'l Orders, #9, dated Mar 31, 1845.

1st Regt of Dragoons:
1st Lt Wm Eustis, to be Capt, Mar 17, 1845, vice Terrett, dec'd.
2nd Lt Jas H Carleton, to be 1st Lt, Mar 17, 1845, vice Eustis, promoted.
Brevet 2nd Lt Rufus Ingalls, of the 2nd Dragoons, to be 2nd Lt, Mar 17, 1845, vice Carleton, promoted.
Brevet 2nd Lt Cave J Couts, of the 2nd Dragoons, to be 2nd Lt, Mar 31, 1845, vice Rust, resigned.

7th Regt of Infty:
1st Lt Danl P Whiting, to be Capt, Apr 18, 1845, vice Davis, dismissed.
2nd Lt Henry Little, to be 1st Lt, Apr 18, 1845, vice Whiting, promoted.
Brevet 2nd Lt John M Jones, of the 5th Infty, to be 2nd Lt, Apr 18, 1845, vice Little, promoted.

The extensive foundry & machine shop at Louisville, Ky, owned by Mr John Curry, was entirely consumed by fire last week. The loss is variously estimated at from $20,000 to $60,000.

Mr John Faxon, of Quincy, Mass, was instantly killed on Fri last by being thrown from his wagon. He was 54 years of age, a good citizen, a kind father & husband, & much respected in his native town, where he had always resided. He leave a wife & 9 children to mourn his loss. -Transcript

The horses of the Camden, S C stage, on Apr 29, near Columbia, became frightened & upset the stage, severely injuring some of the passengers. Mr Danl McLean had the ankle bone of his left leg torn from its socket; Col Stevenson, of Mobile, was severely hurt; & Shelly, the driver, had his should blade put out of place. The other passengers, Messrs Hale & Dickerson, escaped unhurt.

Trustee's sale: by deed of trust from Jos Nourse to the subscriber, dated Apr 30, 1829, recorded in the land records of Wash Co, D C, in Liber W B #25, folios 479 thru 483: sale on May 31, on the premises, all that lot of ground in Wash City numbered 8 in square 168, with the bldgs & improvements thereon. –J I Stull, Trustee
-Robt W Dyer & Co, aucts

By virtue of 2 writs of fieri facias, issued by Clement T Coote, a J P for Wash Co, D C, at the suits of John R Murray & John H Semmes, trading under the firm of Murray & Semmes, against the goods & chattels, land & tenements, rights & credits of Jas I Martin, to me directed, I have seized & taken in execution furniture & accessories, & one gun, the property of said Martin. Sale of same, on May 15, in the house occupied by Martin, near the railroad depot, on Pa ave. –H R Maryman, Bailiff

By an order of distrain for rent in arrears due Saml Burche by Jas I Martin, I shall expose to public sale for cash, on May 15, in the house of Jas I Martin, near the railroad depot, on Pa ave, in Wash City, goods & chattels of said Martin. –H R Maryman, Bailiff

Appointments by the Pres:
Edmund Burke, Com'r of Patents, vice Henry L Ellsworth, resigned.
Otis N Cole, Collector, at Sackett's Harbor, N Y, vice John O Dickey, removed.
Phineas W Leland, Collector of Fall River, Mass, vice Chas J Holmes, removed.
Edwin Wilbur, Collector of Newport, R I, vice Wm Ennis, removed.
Thos M Pettit, of Phil, to be Atty of the U S for the eastern district of Pa, vice Henry M Watts, removed.
Henry Horn, Collector of Phil, vice Calvin Blythe, removed.
Henry Welsh, Naval Ofcr, Phil, vice Joel B Sutherland, removed.
Geo F Lehlman, Deputy Postmaster, Phil, vice Hoy, removed.
Jas A Nichols, Collector at Perth Amboy, N J, vice Solomon Andrews, removed.
Geo W Phillips, of Wash, Richd Jones, of Gtwn, & Wm Minor, of Alexandria, to be Inspectors of the Penitentiary in the District of Columbia.
Reappointments-to renew commissions which had expired. 1-Robt White, J P for Wash Co, D C.
J F Cox, Henry Naylor, Joshua Pierce, John Cox, Lewis Carbery, Robt White, members of the Levy Court of Wash Co, D C.

Harrisburg, May 6, 1845. On arrival of the packet-boat **Juniata**, Capt Hoffman, at our wharf on Sat, a passenger giving his name as Chas Howard, was arrested for stealing a cloak belonging to Susan Webb, of Greenwich, Mass, a passenger from Pittsburg. After he was committed to jail a search found in his boot several stolen checks & drafts.

Mrd: on May 1, at St Matthew's Church, by Rev J P Donelan, Mr J H Drury to Miss Mary C Donelan, all of Wash City.

Mrd: on Apr 29, at Annapolis, by Rev Mr Van Dusen, Wm H Thomas, of St Mary's Co, Md, to Miss Ellen Mackubin, d/o Geo Mackubin, of Annapolis.

Mrd: on Apr 30, in Balt, by Rev Jas Sewall, Mr David A Gardner, of Wash City, to Mrs Ursula Reeve, of Brooklyn, Long Island, N Y.

Mrd: on Apr 23, by Rev Mr Martin, Mr Zephaniah G Robey, of Chas Co, Md, to Miss Sarah M Hatton, of PG Co, Md.

Died: on Mar 8, in England, at Southwood, Highgate, Lt Gen Thos L'Estrange, in his 90th year. He served during the American Revolutionary war, in North & South Carolina, on Staten Island & Long Island, N Y, & in Rhode Island.

Died: on Mar 16, in Cumberland st, London, in his 86th year, Adm Jas Carpenter. He entered the Navy as a midshipman Apr 11, 1776, & served as a lt in the action between Adm Graves & the Count de Grasse, off the Capes of the Chesapeake, on Sep 5, 1781. Adm Carpenter was the senior admiral of the white, & had served in the British navy nearly 70 years.

Died: on Apr 27, at his residence in Cumberland Co, Va, in his 61st year, Thos T Swann. He was confined to his bed for several weeks, & suffered great pain, but not a murmur was heard to escape his lips; he trusted on Him in whom he believed, & neither feared nor dreaded death. As a husband & parent, he was affectionate & indulgent; as a master, kind & humane.

Obit-died: on Apr 8, in St Mary's Co, Md, Priscilla, w/o Wm Hebb. She was an affectionate wife, dutiful & exemplary mother, & devoted Christian.

Firemen's Convention: meeting this day at 8 o'clock. –Jos Borrows, Pres of the Convention

FRI MAY 9, 1845
Foreign obituary. The Earl of Egremont died on Apr 2. He leaves no issue, & his titles are extinct. The Marquis of Devonshire died very suddenly on Apr 12, while riding on his horse over his estates at ***Blessington***, near Dublin. He was in his 57th year, & died of apoplexy. Dowager Vicountess Chetwynd expired on Apr 27. Her ladyship was in her 73rd year. The Earl of Abergavenny died on Apr 5, at Eridge Castle, near Tunbridge Wells, of apoplexy, in his 57th year. Lt Col Clive died on Apr 14, aged 51. He served in the Peninsular war, in 1814, & was at the battles of Quatre Bras & Waterloo. On Apr 2, Adm Sir P C H Durham died at Naples, in his 83rd year. He was ofcr of the deck on board the ship of the line **Royal George**, when she foundered at Spithead in 1782, & was the only ofcr who survived that catastrophe.

$5 reward. Broke away from the subscriber on Mon, in Gtwn, a dark bay Mare, with saddle on. Anyone letting me know where she may be found, will receive the reward. –Simon Fraser, south F st, near the Mansion House.

400 kegs of Lewis' White Lead just received & will be sold cheap. –Chas Stott, 7th & Pa ave, Wash

Very Singular. Worcester Co, Mass, has the honor of being the birth-place of 3 members of the present Cabinet, viz: Messrs Bancroft, Walker, & Marcy-the 2 former were natives of Worcester, & the latter was born in Southbridge. –Balt Sun

Mrd: on May 7, at St Patrick's Church, by Rev Mr Matthews, John H P O'Neale to Miss Louisa Maria Vivan, all of Wash City.

Jos Bonaparte, the younger, a Roman prince, by the title of Prince Musigrand, eldest grandson of Jos Bonaparte, called Count of Survilliers, so long an inhabitant of this city & N J, arrived 3 days ago & took possession of the large mansion & domain called ***Point Breeze***, near Bordentown, devised to him by his grandfather. He was born in Phil & is the eldest s/o Chas Bonaparte, Roman prince, by the title of Prince of Canino, inherited from his father, Lucien Bonaparte. Chas, the Prince of Canino, married Jos' eldest dght, Terraide, some time resident at Phil, where their eldest son was born, who comes now, just 21 years of age, to take possession of the paternal American homestead. The numerous friends of his much-respected grandfather will wish that he may succeed by similar deportment to render himself as welcome where we believe he means to reside.
–U S Gaz

Drowned, on Apr 26, at the foot of Bade's Island, in the Ohio river, by falling overboard from the guards of the steamer **Bertrand**, Chas Fleming, aged 3 years, 1 month & 18 days, y/s/o John F & Emily Summers, of Jackson, Miss.

Miss Gordon, whilst crossing one of the principal streets of Boston, a few days since, was run down by a horseman galloping along at a furious rate. She was conveyed to the hospital, & died on Fri. The fellow was arrested, & we trust will be suitably punished.

Died: on Wed last, suddenly, at the U S Arsenal in Wash City, Dr Marcus C Buck, Military Storekeeper-a native of Va, & a gentleman universally esteemed for his strict honor & humane & generous disposition.

Died: on May 8, John McClelland, one of the oldest residents of Wash City. His funeral is on May 10, at 3½ o'clock, from the 2nd Presbyterian Church, on N Y ave, between 13th & 14th sts. [May 12th newspaper: obit of John McClelland: he was in his 72nd year.]

Died: on May 3, at his residence, at Mont Alto Furnace, Pa, Saml Hughes, in his 71st year. He was formerly a resident of Hagerstown, & was long a distinguished lawyer.

Supreme Court of the U S-Dec Term, 1844. #74. Thos Mancy & al, plntfs in error, vs Thos J Porter. The death of Thos J Porter, the dfndnt in error, having been suggested on a prior day of the present term of this Court, to wit, on Apr 28, by Mr Brinley, counsel for the plntfs in error, the said counsel now moves the Court for an order to make the reps of said Porter parties to this suit: on consideration whereof it is nowhere ordered by the Court that unless the proper reps of Thos J Porter, dec'd, shall become parties within the first 10 days of the ensuing term of this Court, the plntfs in error shall be entitled to open the record for the purpose of having it reversed: Provided, that a copy of this order be published according to the requirements of the 28th rule of Court. Feb 21, 1845.
–Wm Thos Carroll, C S C U S

SAT MAY 10, 1845
Wood Park for sale: beautiful residence, in Orange Co, Va: contains 722 acres & lies 3 miles from Orange court-house. Marcus Bull, jr, who resides on the farm will show it. Information can be had by addressing him at Orange Court House, or David Horner, postmaster, same place. –Marcus Bull

New Orleans, May 1. Capt Craglievich, of the Austrian ship **Elizawetta**, now in this port, was murdered on Tue. He was on his first trip to this port, having selected New Orleans as his trading point in the U S. The crew of the vessel, & others, who wanted the loading of her, got into an affray, when the captain interferred to suppress the disturbance. He was struck on the head with a hammer, inflicting a wound of which he died on Tue.

Boston Daily Adv: Mr Healy, the young American artist, is among the passengers who arrived in the steamer **Hibernia**, being commissioned by Louis Philippe to take for him the portraits of Gen Jackson, John Q Adams, Danl Webster, Henry Clay, & other distinguished Americans.

Mr Hendrich B Wright, who was President of the last Locofoco Nat'l Convention, has been appointed Treasurer of the U S Phil Mint, in place of Maj Roach, removed.

Raleigh Register: Wm W Cherry died after a brief illness. He is spoken of as having been a man of very brilliant talents. [No date-recent news.] [May 15th newspaper: Departed this life on Apr 1, at Jackson, in Northampton Co, N C, Col Wm W Cherry. He died in the county adjoining Bertie, in which he resided. Having made a speech during the day at Jackson, he was taken so suddenly ill at night as to prevent his being carried to his family. He was educated at the Univ of N C: later commenced the practice of law. He was a warm-hearted generous man. His family & friends mourn his death. –W]

Michigan city, storm of Apr 24. Luke Murray was killed. At or near Napierville, Ill, one lady named Vought was killed. A multitude of houses were blown down or unroofed.

By virtue of an order of distrain, for rent in arrears due H R Maryman by Jas T Adams, I shall expose to public sale, for cash, on May 17, in front of the Centre Market-house, in Wash City, goods & chattels of said Adams. –Henry S Wood, Bailiff

John Goldin, a native of Ireland, aged 30 years, was instantly killed on the Charlestown Railroad on Wed, in attempting to get on one of the cars as it was starting.

Mrd: on May 4, by Rev Jas B Donelan, Mr Wm H Havenner to Miss Ann Hazle.

Mrd: on May 8, by Rev G W Samson, Mr Stephen Stevens to Miss Ann White, both of Wash City.

Died: on Wed last, Mrs Eliza Causin, d/o the late Gov Stone, of Md, & w/o Dr N P Causin, of Wash City. Her funeral is Sun at 4 o'clock, from the residence of Dr Causin, on 11th st.

Died: yesterday, of pulmonary consumption, in her 20th year, Miss Mary C Lancaster, lately of Chas Co, Md. Her funeral will take place at St Peter's Church, Capitol Hill, today, at 4 o'clock. Friends of the family & the public in general are respectfully invited to attend.

MON MAY 12, 1845
The Hon Leverett Saltonstall died at his residence in Salem, Mass, on Wed, after a short illness. He had served frequently as a member of both branches of the Legislature of his State, & twice as a Rep in Congress. He was about 64 years of age, & died from an affection of the heart. [May 13th newspaper: Mr Saltonstall was the representative of a family that has been conspicuous in our history from the earliest settlement of New England. His ancestor, Sir Richd Saltonstall, was the first named associate of the 6 original patentees of the colony of Massachusetts Bay, & was appointed the first assistant. On board the ship **Arabella**, while lying at Yarmouth, in the Isle of Wright, he, with Govn'r Winthrop & others, signed the humble request of his Majesty's loyal subjects, the Govn'r & Company late gone for New England, to the rest of their brethren in & of the Church of England, in which they take a tender leave of their native land on their departure for their poor cottages in the wilderness. They arrived at Salem, in the **Arabella**, on Jun 12, 1630, & brought with them the charter of Chas I. Sir Richd Saltonstall has been styled "one of the Fathers of the Massachusetts Colony." He was a patron of Harvard College, & left it a legacy in his will made in 1658. Richd Saltstall, s/o Sir Richard, settled at Ipswich, & was chosen an assistant in 1637. He was one of the few persons who knew where the regicide Judges, Whalley & Goffe, were concealed, & in 1672 gave them L50. He was a relative & friend of John Hampden, grandson of the parliamentary leader. All his male descendants in Mass, except 2, have been graduated at Harvard. His son, Nathl Saltonstall, settled in Haverhill in 1659, & was chosen an assistant in 1679. He took an active part in deposing the tyrannical Royal Govn'r, Sir Edmund Andross, &, after his removal, became one of the Council of the Revolutionary gov't, & so continued till the charter of Wm & Mary, & was then appointed one of his Majesty's Council. He opposed the proceedings against the witches in 1692. He died in 1707. Gurdon Saltonstall, the eldest s/o Nathl, was the Govn'r of Connecticut. He was a benefactor of Harvard College. His widow bequeathed to it L1,000 for the use of 2 students designed for the ministry. Richd Saltonstall, grandson of Col N Saltonstall, was appointed a Judge of the Superior Court in 1736, & held the ofc till his death in 1756. His son, Col Richd Saltonstall, was sheriff of the county, & commanded a regt in the French war. The late Dr Nathl Saltonstall was 2nd s/o Judge Richd Saltonstall, & the father of our fellow citizen just deceased. His son, the Hon Leverett Saltonstall was the worthy descendant of the long line of ancestors. He was educated at Harvard College &

was graduated in 1802; maintined a high literary ran in a class unusually large & remarkable for genius & ability. He commenced the practice of law in 1805. He was a member of the American Academy of Arts & Sciences & of the Massachusetts Historical Society. To all his friends he has left a precious & invaluable legacy-the remembrance of his virtues, the recollection of his Christian life & of his Christian death.]

Isabella Hagan, a vagrant, who some weeks since stole an infant child from a house in Southwark, was tried on Thu, in the Criminal Court, & convicted. It was the first of the kind that has ever taken place in Criminal Sessions. –Phil American

New Bedford has been scourged with scarlet fever, especially among the children. There are no less than 25 bodies waiting for interment at the same time on one day of last week.

Among the passengers by the steamer **Hibernia**, is Joel W White, late U S Consul at Liverpool. He is the bearer of important dispatches from the U S Leg at Belgium to the Sec of State.

Rev Sydney Smith, a Clergyman of the Church of England, notwithstanding his losses by American stocks, died worth a very large sum of money. In his will his wife was appointed execx, & he left L30,000 to his son, L10,000 to his wife, & distributed the rest of his property, which amounts to some L80,000, among his former servants & others.

City Ordinance-Wash. 1-Act of the relief of Chas Gautier: fine imposed on him for selling on the Sabbath, be & the same is hereby remitted, provided he pay the costs of prosecution.

Anthony Sloat [about 26 years old] was committed, suspected of robbing Mr Wm Samuels of $123 in gold & silver. He will be examined this afternoon by the committing magistrates. [May 19th newspaper: When Sloat was examined before Justice Goddard & Thompson at the watch-house, the prisoner was recognised as the man who was convicted on Oct 27, 1841, in our Criminal Court, of robbing Mr John N Kendall, in Wash City, on Aug 11, of a pocket-book containing bank notes of the value of $100. He was sentenced to 2 years in the penitentiary, & was discharged about 18 months ago, & it appears he was living in N Y.]

Sale at auction on May 13, of household furniture, at the residence of the Hon H I Ellsworth, on C st, between 3rd & 4½ sts. –Boteler, Donn & Co, aucts

Mrd: on May 8, in Wash City, by Rev Dr Wyatt, of Balt, Dr Geo Clymer, U S Navy, to Mary, d/o Cmdor Shubrick.

Mrd: on May 8, by Rev H Tarring, Mr Geo O'Barron to Miss Harriet Williamson, eldest d/o Benj Williamson, all of Wash City.

Died: on May 9, Mr Thos McIntosh, a native of Scotland, but for the last 35 years a resident of Wash City, in his 60th year.

Improved refrigerator, manufactured by him, which for utility & economy surpasses all others. A small quantity of ice will keep a reservoir of water [attached] perfectly cool, the ice not mixing with the water. –Jos H Nevett, Pa ave, opposite Fuller & Co's hotel.

TUE MAY 13, 1845

The Hon Wm H Roane, formerly a Rep as well as a Senator in Congress from the State of Va, died at his residence in Richmond Co on Sunday last. [May 14th newspaper: The Hon Wm H Roane died at *Tree Hill*, Henrico Co, Va. His remains were taken for interment to the family burying ground of the late Judge Lyons, in Hanover Co.]

Appointment by the Pres. Geo W Johnson, of Wisconsin Territory, surveyor of public lands in Wisconsin & Iowa, vice Jas Wilson, removed.

The Richmond Enquirer, conducted so long by Thos Ritchie, has passed into the hands of Thos Ritchie, jr, & Wm F Ritchie, sons of the late editor.

Gardening: orders may be left with, or reference may be made to J F Callan, E & 7th sts, Joshua Pierce, of *Linnean Hill*, or Wm D Brackenridge, Green House, Patent Ofc.
–Jas Watt

Recent deaths: copied from an English newspaper. At Maynooth, Mrs Smith, aged 117, having lived to see her 6th generation. In the Isle of Wight, D P Blaine, aged 74 years, author of the Enclyclopedia of Fields Sports. At Newcastle, Mrs Nicholson, aged 103 years; she retained all her faculties to the last; her mother died at age 102 & a sister 103. At Doncaster, Mrs Ann Firth, 101 years.

Died: on Apr 27, at Warrenton, N C, in her 5th year, Sarah Pierrepoint, d/o the Rev Camoron F McRae, minister of the church in that place.

Household & kitchen furniture at auction: on May 15, at the store of J B Holmead, 4½ st & Pa ave. -A Green, auctioneer

Veal for sale at my stall, on this morning, that Show Calf raised & fatted by Chas Calvert, of PG Co, Md. -Henry Walker, Centre Market

Farm for sale: the subscriber offers his country residence, in Farifax Co, Va, 5 miles from Alexandria. The farm contains 150 acs: improvements are a well built frame dwlg house, containing 12 rooms. Immediate possession will be given if required. –Richd Davis

Frescati still for sale: being anxious to equalize the property of my children & to diseneumber myself from the weight of care & trouble consequent on such an estate, I again offer this desirable Farm for sale. No epidemic within the recollection of the undersigned for 40 years: society in its vicinity being equal perhaps to any in Va: estate has about 1,300 acres of land; is lies amidst the Southwest Mountains, within 5½ miles of the railroad depot near Gordonsville, Orange. The dwlg-house is of brick, large, commodious, & elegant: all bldgs erected within the last 22 years. An undisputed title can be conveyed. My post ofc is Gordonsville, Orange Co, Va. –Frances T Barbour

By order of the Orphan's Court of Wash Co, D C: sale on May 13, today, at our auction rooms, all the interest of A Vancoble, dec'd, in Woodworth's Patent Planing Machine. Terms cash. –C W Boteler, adm -Boteler, Donn & Co, aucts

Wed May 14, 1845

Public sale of valuable iron works, 7,000 acs, on which are erected a Furnace & Forge, Mansion House, 25 houses for workmen & other bldgs, called *Mount Holly* Iron Works, in Cumberland Co, Pa. For information address, post paid, W Patton, jr, Farmers' & Mechanics' Bank, Phil; Wm Grimshaw, Harrisburg, Pa, their atty & agent, or to M Thomas & Son, Auctioneers, 94 Walnut st, Phil.

Wash Corp: 1-Nomination by the Mayor for Guardians of the Poor: Alex'r McIntire, Flodoardo Howard, Leonard Harbaugh, Henry Stone, John B Ferguson, & Noble Young. For the Board of Health: Dr W M Magruder, J D Barclay, Dr Thos Miller, Jas Larned, Dr H Lindsley, G C Grammer, Dr J F May, John P Ingle, Dr Jas G Coombe, John B Ferguson, Dr Noble Young. 2-Ptn from R B Owens & others: referred to the Cmte on Improvements. 3-Ptn of John Shaw, of Gtwn, for remission of a fine: referred to the Cmte of Claims. 4-Cmte of Claims: ptn of Wm Green: read twice. 5-Cmte on Police: ptn of F A Tucker, asking the use of a room in the City Hall for the use of the Nat'l Blues: asked to be discharged from its further consideration. 6-Cmte on Police: asked to be discharged from further consideration of the ptn of Thos Lawson & others, remonstrating against the erection of a livery stable in the First Ward.

Valuable farm land for sale in Loudoun Co, Va. Under the provisions of a deed from John Thompson Mason to Robt I Taylor, Chas Fenton Mercer, & others, as trustees, of record in said county, by which I have been appointed trustee in place of said Robt I Taylor, etc, I offer the tract known as *Locust Hill*, containing 405 acs. Improvements consist of a substantial 2 story brick dwlg house, with usual out houses. Communications to be addressed to me at Martinsburg, Berkeley Co, Va. –Philip Pendleton, Trustee

$200 reward for runaways negro man Andrew Coger, about 38 years of age. Also, my negro man Nace Hawkins, about 33 years of age.
–John W Guy, Pomonkey, Chas Co, Md

Appointments by the Pres:
Harman Alexander, Register of the Land Ofc at Palestine, Ill, vice Jas M McLean, removed.
J Travis Rosser, Collector of the Customs at Petersburg, Va, vice Hugh Nelson, removed.
John Duncan, Appraiser of Merchandise at New Orleans, vice Robt M Wellman, removed.
Wm F Wagner, Marshal of District of La, vice Algernon S Robinson, removed.
Pierre T Landry, Surveyor Genr'l of La, vice Francis D Newcomb, removed.
John R Macmurdo, Treasurer Branch Mint at New Orleans, La, vice Horace C Cammack, removed.
Fred'k R Conway, Surveyor of Public Lands in Missouri & Illinois, vice Silas Reed, removed.
Wm A Sparks, of S C, Consul at Venice, vice Jos Binda, removed.

The U S storeship **Lexington**, Lt Ellson commanding, arrived at Charleston, S C, last Sat from Mahon, via Gibraltar, having on board the remains of Cmdor E R Shubrick, who died some time since whilst in command of the U S ship **Columbia** on the passage from Rio to Mahon.

Mrd: on May 8, by Rev Henry Tarring, Mr Wm T Jones to Miss Lieuzippy A Teachen, both of Wash City.

Died: on May 13, Danl H Durham, in his 23rd year, eldest s/o Jas H Durham, formerly of Albany, N Y. His funeral is this evening at 4 o'clock, from the residence of his father, 13th & I sts.

Died: suddenly, yesterday, Mary Amelia, d/o Jas H & Anna S Boss, aged 2 years & 8 months. Her funeral to take place this afternoon at 3 o'clock from the residence of her parents, Mass ave, near 4th st.

Bedford Mineral Springs, south of the borough of Bedford, Pa. Espy L Anderson, proprietor has fitted up & newly furnished the above celebrated watering place. It will be under the superintendence of Mr A S Barnum, proprietor of Barnum's Hotel, in Cumberland, Md. [Barnum's Hotel will of course continue.]

THU MAY 15, 1845
Prof Geo Tucker has resigned his chair as professor of Moral Philosophy in the Virginia University. The Visiters will fill the vacancy on Jul 1. [May 22nd newspaper: He has occupied his post 20 years-being one, & the last one, of the professors originally selected by Mr Jefferson at the commencement of the institution. We hear Mr Tucker's purpose is to make Phil his future residence, where he will devote the remnant of his days to the cultivation of literature, & the enjoyment of literary society. –Richmond Whig.]

New Orleans papers state that Solomon Downs, of Ouachita, has been appointed U S District Atty for the District of La, in place of Baylie Peyton.

John Appleton, of Maine, appointed chief clerk in the Navy Dept, in place of Dr Orris A Brown, resigned. –U S Journal

Thos Lloyd, of Port Tobacco, Chas Co, Md, appointed Keeper of the Light-boat at Upper Cedar Point, Potomac river, vice J A Neale, removed. Thos Shorter appointed Keeper of the Light-boat at Lower Cedar Point, Potomac river, vice Capt Smoot, removed.

Military Movements. The Union states that Col Kearney, with several troops of his regt of dragoons, & in pursuance of standing orders from the Genr'l-in-chief of 1842, will set out from **Fort Leavenworth** [on the Missouri] some time in this month, to make an extensive tour of the prairies beyond. If his horses should be able to maintain themselves on pasturage alone, he may go as far as **Fort Laramie**, a trader's work in the South Pass of the Rocky Mountains.

Mr Seth S Snow was killed instantly by a whale, off Race Point, Provincetown, last Tue. As soon as the whale was discovered, 2 boats, one with 5 & the other with 4 persons, made in pursuit, & each boat succeeded in fastening their irons, when the whale turned upon them, & coming upon one boat head foremost, utterly demolished it, killing Mr Snow, leaving the others afloat in the water. The other boat severed their line & rescued the drowning persons, when the whale made for them also, but by hand pulling they reached the shore in safety, the whale following as far as the depth of the water permitted. This is said to be the first instance in which a whale has attacked a boat in this manner upon our shore. –Boston Courier

Orphan's Court of Wash Co, D C. Letters testamentary on the personal estate of Andrew Ruppert, late of said county, dec'd. –E Ruppert, Excx

Orphan's Court of Wash Co, D C. Letters of administration on the personal estate of John Blackburn, late of the U S Marine, dec'd. –Wm J Burneston, adm

Rev Ninian Bannatyne, elected co-pastor of the F Street Presbyterian Church in Wash City, on May 13, to be associated with Rev Dr Laurie, who has for so many years ministered to that congregation.

Mrd: on May 8, in Phil, by Rev S C Taylor, Capt Richd C Brown, of Canada, to Miss Emily A, d/o the late Abraham Fowler, of Wash City.

Mrd: on May 13, in St Matthew's Church, by Rev H Myers, Mr John B McGill to Miss Isabella R Ratary, both of Wash City.

Mrd: on May 8, at Newport, R I, by Rev Mr Hall, Camillus Saunders, of Raleigh, N C, to Harriet Hamilton, d/o Capt Wm V Taylor, U S Navy, of the former place.

Died: on May 13, after a protracted & painful illness, Wm H Duncan, printer, in his 23rd year. His funeral is this evening, at 4½ o'clock, from the residence of Jas Moore, north Capitol st, above B st.

Albany Evening Journal: Judge Sutherland, whose health has been long declining, & who reached this city a few days since, on his return to Geneva, from a winter's residence at the South, now languishes in a state which forbids the hope of his recovery. P. S. We learn, just as our paper is going to press, that Judge Sutherland is no more! He was an eminently good man, & will be universally & deeply mourned.

$400 reward for runaway negro men: Lewis Grant, about 20; Warren, who is brother to Lewis, about 17; Joe, brother to the 2 former; Nace Easton, about 27.
–Thos McPherson, John Core, living near Pomonkey Post Ofc, Chas Co, Md.

For rent: the store on Pa ave, between Brown's & Coleman's Hotels, for many years occupied by E G Handy as a hat store. Apply to Jourdan W Maury, next door to Coleman's Hotel.

FRI MAY 16, 1845
Jas Matthews & Marcus Snow were consigned, last week, to the N Y state prison for 4 years, by the Onondaga Oyer & Terminer, for an attempt to do violence on a young girl named Forbes. This girl, being an orphan, went from Utica to Syracuse in the hope of obtaining a place as servant. –Commercial Adv

$300 reward for runaways, 2 slaves, Wm-28 & Peter-about 21 years of age.
–Arthur H H Bernard, residing 2 miles below Fredericksburg.

$700 reward for runaways negroes: John-25 years old; Baptist, about 21; Hillary Chandler, about 28; Judson, about 24; George, about 19; & Sandy, about 35 years old. Address to Pomonkey Post Ofc, Chas Co, Md, to either one of the subscribers.
–Wm Thompson, John H Diggs, Mrs Ann Ward, & Miss Emeline Ward

The widow of Alex'r Hamilton was invited to visit the N Y Legislature on Mon last. She was conducted up the middle aisle, when Mr Lee, stepping a few paces in advance of her, said, "Mr Speaker, I present to this House the wid/o Gen Alex'r Hamilton, the d/o Gen Philip Schuyler." The lady then took her seat, & after having listened some minutes to the proceedings, rose, bowed to the Speaker, & took her leave, the House honoring her departure by standing until the doors closed upon her retreating form.

We learn from Cumberland, Md, that at the town election on Mon, Capt Thos Shriver was re-elected Mayor, & the entire Whig Council ticket prevailed by a majority of nearly 100 votes.

Albany, May 13, 1845. In the sudden death of Jared L Rathbone, our city loses an old & highly esteemed merchant. He was the senior partner in the house of Rathbone & Chapin. He was a native of Salem, Conn, from which place he came to this city in 1812. –Evening Journal [No date-recent news.

The Miners' Journal: accident in the mines of Messrs Wm Milnes & Co on Thu of last week. 4 men & a boy were severely burnt. Patrick Bodkin is since dead. Thos Bodkin & Wm Powell were badly burnt, but are now doing well; Tiley, the boy, & Mr Buckley, were not so much injured.

Buffalo Commercial Adv of Tue. Account given this morning by Mr Pliny Allen, on board the ship **St Louis**, of a colony now on their way to Wisconsin. The entire colony is composed of the Allen family. There are 3 generations, numbering in all 112 souls, of whom 50 are now on their way, to be followed by the remainder. The patriarch of the family, Philip Allen, is with them, aged 88 years. He is the father of 5 sons & 3 dghts; he was a soldier of the Revolution & receives a pension from his country, & has resided in Rochester for the last 27 years. Though feeble he is cheerful. The Allen family is located at Walworth, Walworth Co, Wisconsin Territory, where they have purchased a large tract of land, in the centre of which they intend to build a village, which is to be called Allen City.

We learn from Mr Wm F Bayley, that his Stationery Warehouse, on Pa ave, was entered last Wed, & the money drawer emptied of its contents.

Mrd: on May 13, by Rev Mr Eggleston, Baruch Hall to Virginia B, d/o Wm H Gunnell, all of Wash City.

Obit-died: on may 7, Eliza Stone Causin, consort of the respected Dr N P Causin, & d/o the late Gov Stone, of Md. This friend, whom I highly esteemed, had been an invalid for many years. She was an excellent wife, devoted mother, & kind mistress.

Furnished house for rent: house occupied by Mrs Sarah T Hughes, on 13th st, between G & H sts. Inquire at the house.

In order to settle & divide the estate of the late Saml Wimsatt, the subscriber will sell at auction, on May 25, on the premises, 3 houses & lots, & 2 vacant lots, all near Bradley's Steamboat Wharves. One house fronts on 11 st in square 353, at present occupied as a grocery store & dwlg; the other 2 houses are good 2 story frame dwlgs, fronting on 11th st in square 354. –Richd Wimsatt, Exc -Robt W Dyer & Co, aucts

For rent: a neat 2 story frame house on 6th st, between E & F sts. Inquire at Noah Fletcher's.

For rent: 2 new brick houses on I st, between 4th & 5th sts. For further information please apply to Thos W Burch, 5th & H sts, Wash.

SAT MAY 17, 1845
Orphans Court of St Mary's Co, Md. Letters of administration on the personal estate of Edw P Stone, late of said county, dec'd. –Matthew A Stone, adm

The subscriber, finding it impossible to close his old business, for want of time & attention, has appointed Mr John Scrivner his collector. –D Clagett

Information is requested concerning Mr Robt Richardson, formerly of James City Co, Va, who removed thence to Tennessee some years since. If he be living, or any of his heirs or excs, by addressing a letter to D B A at the ofc of the Nat'l Intell, Wash, he or they will receive acceptable intelligence.

Died: on Thu, in Wash City, Mr Reuben M Whitney, in his 57th year.

Died: on May 12, in Wash City, of a short but severe illness, Miss Marietta Morley, aged 20 years, formerly of West Springfield, Mass.

Died: on May 15, Louise Favier, aged 6 years & 9 months, after an illness of 3 weeks, leaving a father & 3 sisters to mourn her loss. Her funeral is today at half past 9 o'clock.

On Tue a woman named Pennoyer was committed to prison in N Y on the charge of having murdered her brother, Mr Scudder, at Hoboken, by administering arsenic. She was locked up in her cell in the county jail, but was discovered this morning suspended over a stove pipe, quite dead. She used her shawl. She was a widow, exceedingly good looking, & not over 30 years of age, it is said. Scudder has left a son about 16 years old. –Evening Mirror

$100 reward for runaway, my servant Geo Edwin, who is usually called Ned Rustin, about 22 years of age. –Ann Harrison, Pomonkey, Chas Co, Md

Obit-died: on May 4, at her residence in Leonardtown, Md, Ellen, w/o Dr Wm J Edelen. Her sickness was 12 days, but was attended with much painful suffering. Mrs Edelen was not a captivating woman; her sincerity of character & her earnest feelings alike suppressed the wish & forbade the attempt to win admiration. As a wife & mother, she was an admirable & beautiful example. Her death is a heavy loss to her husband & her children. She was buried at Newtown on May 6.

Appointments by the Pres:
Loren Spencer, [Missouri] Recorder of Land Titles in Missouri, vice Fred'k R Conway, appointed Surveyor Genr'l of Illinois & Missouri.
Jas K Hutton, Collector, Wash, N C, vice Thos H Blount, resigned.
Appraisers:
Geo W Pomeroy, N Y C, vice Mathias B Edgar, removed.
Saml Jones Willis, N Y, vice Amos Palmer, removed.
Benj E Carpenter, Phil, vice Saml Spackman, removed.
Geo W Doty, Lt in the Navy, vice Wm A Jones, resigned.
Danl Dobbins, re-appointed-Capt of a cutter in the revenue service, vice Gilvert Knapp, dismissed.
John Norvell, Atty U S for District of Michigan, vice Geo C Bates, resigned; to take effect Jun 1, 1845.
Chas G Hammond, Collector at Detroit, Mich, vice Edw Brooks, resigned.
Saml C White, Surveyor at Accomac Court-house, Va, vice Wm Walston, removed.

Second Presbyterian Church: funeral sermon, occasioned by the death of Mr John McClelland, late an Elder of the Church, will be preached today at 4 o'clock.

MON MAY 19, 1845
The subscriber will take boarders during the summer, at his residence 3 miles north of the Capitol. –J Brooks

Rockville & Wash Turnpike Road Co: meeting of stockholders on May 26, 11 a m. –Geo Sweeny, Treas

Thos F Harkness has removed from Pa ave to a store on 7th st, next door to Mr L Harbaugh's grocery store, & invites his old friends & the public in general to give him a call & examine his stock of Cloths, Cassimeres, Vestings, Drillings, & other goods suitable for the season.

Lot on the Island for sale: lot 24 in square 388, fronting 25 feet on E st south, between 9th & 10th sts west, 125 feet deep, on which is a small frame tenement. For terms apply to Wm Douglas, south B st, fronting the Mall, or to –Jno D McPherson.

Steven Thomson Mason, of Va, appointed by the Sec of War Military Storekeeper at the Wash Arsenal, in place of Marcus C Buck, dec'd.

The ship **Columbus**, Cmdor Biddle, Capt J W Wyman commanding, is on the eve of departure for China. She takes out Hon Alex'r H Everett, the newly appointed Minister or Com'r of our Gov't to China. Mr Everett's lady accompanies him. They will probably reside at Macao. –N Y Mirror

Nashville Banner: an enterprise is on foot for establishing a colony of Dutch emigrants in Morgan Co, Tenn: about 200,000 acres have been purchased, & 200 to 300 emigrants are daily expected to arrive. They have recently purchased from Dr John Shelby his valuable flocks of Bakewells & Southdowns sheep.

Magnetic Telegraph Co: W W Corcoran & B B French, Trustees of the Company. [Meeting notice.]

The steamship **New York** arrived at New Orleans on May 10 from Galveston, whence she sailed on May 8. Among her passengers were Maj Donelson, the U S Charge, & Gov Yell, of Arkansas. Mr Wickliffe, the ex-Postmaster Genr'l, was at Galveston on May 7.

Mrd: on May 15, in St Patrick's Church, by Rev Wm Matthews, Benj C Ridgate to Miss Mgt E King, of Wash City.

Mrd: on May 15, by Rev H Myers, Mr Geo Laudner to Miss Eliz Helfrick, both of Wash City.

Died: on May 16, Joseph, s/o Michl & Catherine Nash, aged 9 months.

A few week since, Milton Fowler intruded into the Pres' House & frightened the female inmates. Geo E H Day, of Painesville, Ohio, learning that Fowler lived in the adjoining county, visited the confined man, & found that he had no criminal intention. He was released Thu afternoon. –U S Journal

TUE MAY 20, 1845
Convention for: Mutual abolition of the Droit d'Aubaine & of Taxes on Emigration, between the U S A & His Royal Highness the Grand Duke of Hesse, concluded Mar 26, 1844. Both equally desirous of removing the restrictions which exist in their territories upon the acquisition & transfer of property by their respective citizens & subjects, have agreed to enter into negotiation for this purpose. Full powers have been conferred on Henry Wheaton, the U S Envoy Extra & Minister Pleni at the Court of his Majesty the King of Prussia, & His Royal Highness the Grand Duke of Hesse upon Baron Schaeffer-Bernstein, his Chamberlain, Col, Aid-de-camp, & Minister Resident near His Majesty the King of Prussia, who, after having exchanged their said full powers, found in due & proper form, have agreed to the following articles. On the death of any person holding real property within the territories of one party, such would, by the laws of the land, descend on a subject or citizen of the other, were he not disqualified by alienage, such citizen or subject shall be allowed a term of 2 years to sell the same, which term may be reasonably prolonged according to circumstances, & to withdraw the proceed thereof, without molestation, & exempt from all duties of detraction on the part of the Gov't of the respective States. Citizens or subjects of each contracting parties shall have power to

dispose of their personal property with the States of the other, by testament, donation, or otherwise; & their heirs, being citizens or subjects of the other contracting party, shall succeed to their said personal property, whether by testament or ab intestato, & may take possession thereof, either by themselves or by others acting for them, & dispose of the same at their pleasure, paying such duties only as the inhabitants of the country where the said property lies shall be liable to pay in like cases. In the case of the absence of the heirs, the same care shall be taken of such real or personal property, as would be taken in a like case of property belonging to the natives of the country, until the lawful owner , or the person who has a right to sell the same, may take measures to receive or dispose of the inheritance. Disputes are decided according to the laws & by the judges of the country where the property is situated. Done in Berlin, on Mar 26, 1844. Done at Wash City, May 8, 1845. –Jas K Polk, Pres -Jas Buchanan, Sec of State

The Hon Nicholas Sickles, of Kingston, N Y, died on May 13. He was a native of Kinderhook, & several years ago was Rep in Congress.

Demise of a venerable citizen of Balt. On Mon, Richd Caton died after a short illness, at the advanced age of 83 years. He was a native of Lancashire, Eng, & has been a resident of Balt for the last 62 years. He married the eldest d/o the late Chas Carroll, of Carrollton, & is the father of the Marchioness of Wellesley. He has long had the management of large landed estates; an accomplished gentleman of the old school. -Balt Pat

Pittsburg American: fire occurred in Alleghany City on Sat: burned at various places along the canal bank, gives supposition that it was set on fire. Various transportation houses, & depot, were consumed, among which were those of Messrs H & P Graff, Wallingford & Taylor, Bingham & Co, & J McFaden & Co. The warehouse of Messrs D Leech & Co on the lower isde of Federal st, escaped untouched. Houses lost were those of John Kelly, teacher; Mr McGrew, turner shop; Saml Baird, dwlg; Mr Carothers, dwlg; Mr Shutter, dwlg; Francis Sellers, boat store; Wrightman's machine shop. No lives were lost.

Death recorded under the N Y obituary head is that of John Megarey, a young artist of considerable talent, s/o Henry I Megarey, once & for many years among the foremost booksellers in Broadway, now engaged in publishing large engraved views of the principal American cities.

Runaway slave, negro man Tom Wright, was committed in Alleghany Co jail, Md: age about 30 years. If said negro is not proven to be a slave by his owner or agent in 60 days he will be set at large. Law of 1802, chapter 96. –Norman Bruce, Sheriff of Alleghany Co, ofc-Cumberland, Md.

Slavery in N J. A rule has been granted in the Supreme Court of N J requiring John A Post, of Passaic Co, to show cause on Tue why an attachment should not issue against him for disobeying a writ of habeas corpus, served on him in vacation, requiring him to bring William, a colored man in his custody, before the Court. A writ of habeas corpus has been granted, directed to Edw Van Buren, of Bergen Co, requiring him to being up the body of Mary Foutoute, a colored women. The object of these cases is to establish the position that under the new Constitution there can be no slavery in New Jersey.

Died: suddenly, of congestive fever, in Barnesville, Montg Co, Md, Mr Isaac Bell, of the State of N Y, aged about 35 years. Delirium rendered him unable to tell the address of his relatives. He has said his mother's maiden name was Poole, & that he had not been at home for years. Unfinished letters to his parents & other friends can be obtained by addressing D Hershey, Barnesville, Mont Co, Md. –H Editors favorable to the cause of humanity are requested to copy this. [No date-recent news.]

New Shoe Store: Thos N Brashears informs that he has left the employment of A Hoover & Son, where he has been for the last 4 years, & has opened a store on his own hook in the house recently occupied by Mr Jack as a shoe store, opposite Brown's Hotel.

Union Tavern, Gtwn, D C. By virtue of sundry deeds of trust, & to accomplish the purposes contemplated by the parties to the said deeds, the subscribers will offer for sale, at public auction, on Aug 27 next, 11 of 12 undivided parts or shares of all those lots of ground numbered 169, 170, 176, & part of lot 177, in Beall's addition to Gtwn, in D C, with extensive bldgs, so long known as The *Union Tavern*. The title to the propery is believed to be good, & the portions offered for sale without incumbrance of any kind except the dower right of a widow lady in one undivided 12th part, subject to which the property will be sold. –Wm S Nicholls, John Kurtz, Ed M Linthicum, Trustees

Valuable land near Wash City for sale: on Jun 10 next, all that very desirable farm on which the subscriber lives: contains about 220 acs: there is a dwlg-house, & all necessary out-houses. It is contiguous to the beautiful places of Dr Causin, T Carbery, & others, on the turnpike road, & to Messrs Ray & Shepard, on the Rock creek Church road. –Henry Ould -A Green, auctioneer

Pittsburg, May 10, 1845. I do hereby certify that on Apr 10, 1845, when my ofc in this city was destroyed by the great fire, my books & papers, specie, etc, were preserved perfectly uninjured, although in the midst of the flames during the whole period of the awul conflagration, by an Asbestos Fire Proof Chest, manufactured by John Scott, 16 south Calvert St, Balt, Md. –Allen Kramer [Mr K is an Exchange Broker in a large business.]

House & lot for sale: on Md ave, & 4½ st. Apply to T L & A Tho Smith: ofc on F st, near the Treas Dept.

WED MAY 21, 1845
Mrs Freeland, w/o Mr Edw Freeland, of Pottsville, Pa, fell whilst attempting to run across the track of the Mount Carbon Railroad, on Thu last, & was horribly mutilated, a train of cars passing over her. No hopes of her recovery.

The copartnership existing between John R Ardasr & John Cospar, in the business of Carpenters, was dissolved May 1 by mutual consent. John Cospar will continue the business.

$100 reward for runaway negro man Henry Neale, about 24 years of age. –Jos W Coombes, *Pleasant Hill*, Chas Co, Md

The undersigned, late teacher in the Preparatory Dept of Dickinson College, Pa, has taken the School recently taught by Mr J J Sandford, near the Gen Post Ofce, & will open his school on May 26. –J J Potts

Washington [Texas] National Register of May 1: Rencontre on Fri on the premises of Cl Walton, about 7 miles east of this place, which resulted in the parties killed-John L Laguire & John Nix; the latter has left a wife & several small children. Mr Strickland, wounded, still survives, but his recovery is doubtful. On the next day, J L Nickleson, Asa Ufford, & Chas B Snow, with a slave, the property of Col Walton, were arrested by the Sheriff, & brought before Chief Justice Ewing & S R Roberts, & Nickleson was committed to this county jail to await his trial at the next term of the District Court for the murder of the above named.

Rich Dinner sets: Chas S Fowler, store on 7th st, opposite the Nat'l Intell ofc.

Wash Corp: 1-Cmte of Claims: relief of John H Eberbach: passed. 2-Ptn from Wilhelm Grupe: referred to Cmte of Claims. 3-Cmte of Claims: asked to be discharged from consideration of the ptn of Saml Lewis. 4-Cmte of Claims: bill for the relief of John F Lenman: passed. 5-Ptn of Wm Dowling, praying remission of a fine: referred to the Cmte of Claims. 6-Appointed Com'rs to hold elections in the several Wards:

Saml Drury	John C Harkness	John B Ferguson
R W Bates	G C Grammer	Thompson Van Reswick
Wm Degges	John C McKelden	Wm Ashdown
Willard Drake	John T Frost	Lewis A Newman
J S Harvey	Wm J McCormick	Robt Clarke
Nicholas Callan, jr	Benj B French	Jas Gordon

Nat'l Saloon: Ice cream, Soda Water, Strawberries & Cream: will open on Mon next, at much cost, on 6th st, adjoining the Nat'l Eating-house. Mrs Walker will superintend the Saloon. –W Walker

50 years ago: turning over the pages of the Gaz of the U S, published at Phil, for 1790, 1791, & 1792. May 16, 1792: On Fri last the Govn'r of this State laid the corner stone of the Pres' House in 9th st. Inscription on the stone:
This Corner Stone was laid
On the 10th day of May, 1792.
The State of Pennsylvania out of debt.
Thomas Mifflin, Governor."
May 15, 1792: the intended bridge over Rock Creek, opposite the Federal City, in Virginia, is now begun, under the immediate direction of Mr Harbaugh. There arrived at the port of New York, from Jan 1, 1791 to Jan 1, 1792, 120 ships & barques, 280 snows & brigs, 1 galliot, 1 polacre, 158 schooners, 158 sloops-total from foreign ports 718, & coasters 1,101; being 151 vessels from foreign prots & 407 coasters more than arrived at Phil during that period."
"Georgetown, Jul 2, 1791. On Mon last, being the appointed day, the Pres of the U S arrived in this town; & on Wed put the finishing hand to the location of the Federal City."
"Alexandria, Apr 21, 1791. On Fri, 15th inst, the Hon Danl Carroll & Dr David Stewart arrived in this town, to superintend the fixing of the first corner-stone of the Federal District." [The paper of the 30th of Apr gives a long account of the proceedings.]— copied as in the newspaper.
In the original plan of the City of Washington, as submitted to Congress by the Pres in Jan, 1790, we find mention of the subjoined "magnificent intentions." Which are unfortunately not yet entirely realized: "An equestrian figure of George Washington, a monument voted in 1783 by the late Continental Congress. "An historic column, also intended for a mile or itinerary column, from whose station [at a mile from the Federal House] all distances & places through the continent are to be calculated." A naval itinerary column, proposed to be erected to celebrate the first rise of a navy, & to stand a ready monument to perpetuate its progress & achievements."
"A church intended for national purposes, such as public prayer, thanksgivings, funeral oration, etc, & assigned to the special use of no particular sect or denomination, but equally open to all. It will likewise be a proper shelter for such monuments as were voted by the late Continental Congress for those heroes who fell in the cause of liberty, & for such others as may hereafter be decreed by the voice of a grateful nation.
"Five grand fountains, intended with a constant spout of water."
"A grand cascade formed of the water of the sources of the Tiber."
"A grand avenue, 400 feet in breadth, & about a mile in length, bordered with gardens, ending in a slope from the houses on each side. This avenue leads to the monument of Washington, & connects the Congress Garden with the Pres' Park. 15 squares were to be divided among the several States in the Union for each of them to improve: the centers of these squares designed for statues, columns, obelisks, etc, such as the different States may choose to erect."
"The water of <u>Tiber Creek</u> to be conveyed to the high ground where the Congress House stands, &, after watering that part of the city, its overplus will fall from under the base of

the edifice, &, in a cascade of 20 feet in height & 50 in breadth, into the reservoir below, thence to run in three falls through the gardens in the grand canal.
The plan of the city, from which the above particulars have been extracted, was drawn up by Peter Chas L'Infant.

From the far West. Van Buren [Ark] May 3.
1-The report of the murder of a party of Creeks, who went out on the prairies to trade, is confirmed. Among them were Jess Chisholm, Jno Spaniard, D G Watson, Nick Miller, Mr Colker, Jno Connor, Bill Connor, Jno Kitchum & several others.
2-The U S Com'r, Gen Mason, with his 2 dghts, & Col S C Stambaugh, left this city on Mon for Washington.
3-An affray occurred at Evansville, Wash Co, on Sat, between Thos Bridgewood & some person whose name we did not learn, in which Bridgewood shot the latter in the side; & it is thought that the wound will prove mortal.
4-Mr Clark Landers, long a resident of this county, was drowned, about 2 weeks since, while crossing the Red River. He had removed his family to Texas, & was on his return to this county when the accident happened. -Intelligencer

Henry H Sylvester, of N H, has been appointed Chief Clerk in the Patent Ofc, [Dept of State.]

A Naval Court Martial is to be commenced in this city on Jun 2, said to be principally for the trial of Capt Philip F Voorhees, on charges growing out of his proceedings while in command of the frig **Congress**, in the Platte river, during the months of Sept & Oct of last year. The Court is composed of the following ofcrs: Capt Chas Stewart, Pres; Capts Chas G Ridgely, John Downs, Stephen Cassin, Lawrence Kearney, David Geisinger, Chas S McCauley, John H Aulick, French Forrest, Benj F Hallett, of Boston, Judge Advocate. [Jun 13th newspaper: Midshipman Thos S Fillebrown was examined; Lt Brooke of the Marines was examined.] [Jun 14th newspaper: Lt Brooke stated that Silas E Burroughs was in the cabin at the time of the conversation between Capts Fitton & Voorhees. He said the firing at or into the frig **Bainbridge** was known on board the **Congress** some days before the capture of the Argentine squadron; but the particular circumstances of that capture were not communicated until Capt Newman came on board the **Congress** on the day of the capture. Rev Mr Jackson was re-examined. Lt Robt L Browning was examined.]

City Ordinances-Wash. 1-An Act for the relief of R C Washington, H C Spalding & Co, Henry Carter, & Hall & Brother. That the fines imposed on the above, for an alleged violation of the law in relation to licenses for sales of dry goods, be remitted: provided they pay the cost of prosecution.

Gtwn Adv: fire last night at the store of Mr Saml Kelly, High st. Not much damage. Fire was attempted on a frame back bldg on the premises of Mr Lindsley, Prospect st. The bldg was partially saved.

Mr Geo A Goddard, stock & exchange broker of Boston, was killed there on Thu. While on his way, in his chaise, to his residence in Milton, his horse took fright, & threw Mr Goddard down, his head & one of the wheels came violently in contact, & when taken up he was dead. He was a worthy man & has left a family. -Adv

Genteel furniture at auction: May 27th, at the residence of Mr Seibert, Pa ave & 1st st. —Wm Marshall, auct

Hanover Landing for sale: 163 acs, 1 mile from Hanover College. Address, post paid, A Hays, Madison, Ind.

Mrd: on May 15, by Rev Jas T Johnston, Chas Sinclair Taylor, of Glenwood, Jefferson Co, Va, to Harriet B, y/d/o Wm Fowle, of Alexandria.

Mrd: on May 12, at **Fruit Hill**, near Chilicothe, Ohio, by Rev Jas B Britton, the Hon Wm Allen, of the U S Senate, to Mrs Effie McArthur Coones, d/o the late Gov McArthur.

Died: in Wash City, after a severe illness of 2 days, Mrs Mary E Evans, aged 28 years. Her funeral is at 10 a m today from her late residence on La ave, between 4½ & 6th sts. [No date-current item.]

Obit-died: on Apr 21, 1845, in childbed, Mrs Eliz Eliza Goldin, consort of Richd R Goldin, in her 24th year, after a severe illness, until death released her from her sufferings. She has left a kind & affectionate husband.

THU MAY 22, 1845
Deaths in England: the venerable Earl of Stanford, Geo Harry Grey, expired at Enville Hall, Staffordshire, on Apr 26, in his 80th year. Lt Gen R N Hopkins, one of the oldest field ofcrs in the army, died on Apr 26, in London, at age 88 years. The Hon Lady Sinclair, d/o the first Lord Macdonald, died at Edinburgh on Apr 21, aged 76. Duncan, the promising artist, died in the same city at age 39. On Apr 20, the eminent artist Thos Phillips, died at his residence, Hanover Square, London, in his 75th year. Col Sir Geo Chas Haste, C B, died on Apr 21, at Woolwich, in his 59th year. Recently, in the county of Waterford, Mrs Sweeney, in her 129th year. She was born in the second year of the reign of Geo the First. On Apr 22, at Cork, Col John Townsend, of the 14th Light Dragoons, aide-de-camp to the Queen. He served in that regt 40 years, was engaged in numerous actions, concluding his chief war services in the attack on New Orleans on Jan 8, 1815.

$10 reward for large bay Horse. Strayed away from the subscriber's stable near the Navy Yard. –Josias Clements [Deliver at the Railroad depot.]

Butler [Pa] Democrat: announces the death of the Hon John Gilmore, at that place, on Sun last, aged 65 years.

For rent: 3 story brick house, being the centre bldg of the block known as Granite Row, near the West Market, in the 1st Ward. Apply to Alex McIntire, next door north of St John's Church.

Valuable property at auction on Jun 4 next: by order of the present owners, who have made a power of atty to the subscriber, fully authorizing him to dispose of the same, part of square 74, with the 2 story brick bldg now in the occupation of Lund Washington, jr, & Mrs Hannah Wells, fronting on Pa ave, & well known as the Six Bldgs.
–John C Vowell, Atty for Geo Beale Brown -Robt W Dyer & Co, aucts

Trustees sale of valuable property at auction: on Jun 23 next, on the premises, part of square 355, with a large 3 story brick house, known as the Steamboat Hotel, corner of 11th & G sts, fronts 70 feet 10½ inches on G st, & runs back 137 feet on 11th st. –Wm Douglass, Thos R Riley, Trustees -Robt W Dyer & Co, aucts [At the same time, we shall sell also, on the premises, part of square 355, fronting 29 feet on G st, & 137 feet deep, with a new 2 story frame house, containing 7 rooms. This property adjoins the property described above. -Robt W Dyer & Co, aucts]

Mrd: on March 27, by Rev David Kerr, Rector of St John's Church, Thibodaux, La, Wm Robt Jordan, formerly of Va, to Miss Mary Louisa Tanner, of the parish of Terrebonne, La.

Mrd: on Apr 17, by Rev David Kerr, Jos Nicholas Tanner, of the parish of Terrebonne, La, to Miss Marian Oceana Woodson, formerly of Va.

FRI MAY 23, 1845
Caution to the public. Absconded from the subscriber, on May 21, a manumitted servant, Maximilian Norris, better known by the sobriquet of Magic, given to him in infancy. He is in his 19th year, bound by the act of manumission to serve until 25 years old.
–T Watkins

For rent: the dwlg part of a 3 story brick house on Pa ave, next door to Massi's Jewelry store. –J P Pepper

White sand for sale: to bricklayers, plasters & others. Also on hand, sharp bay sand. –John T Killmon, Pa ave Also, Groceries, in addition to his stock, all of which will be sold on very best terms.

Household & kitchen furniture auction: on May 28, at the residence of Mrs S T Hughes, 13th st, between G & H sts, her entire household. –A Green, auct

Naval Medical Board of Examiners convened at Phil for the examination of Assist Surgeons for promotion, & adjourned on Fri last. The following found qualified for promotion:

Dr Chas J Bates, of the date of Mar, 1838.

Dr Jas McClelland, of the date of Mar, 1838.

Dr J O'Connor Barclay, of the date of Oct, 1839.

Dr Wm A Nelson, of the date of Oct, 1839.

On Mon last, while 2 young men, Thos Ruth & John Larmand were putting up a gutter to a house in Richmond, Va, occupied by Mr D C Randolph, the scaffolding gave way & Ruth fell to the pavement, & was so much injured that he died the same evening. Larmand save himself by seizing hold of the hooks driven in to secure the gutter, where he remained supended till rescued by means of a ladder.

Mrd: on May 15, by Rev Mr Dodge, at Green Garden, Loudoun Co, Va, Dr Z T Chunn, of Fauquier, to Miss Mary S, d/o Dr Bushrod Rust, of the former place.

Mrd: on May 15, by Rev Mr Tarring, Mr Wm D Crampsey to Mrs Eliza Leatherbeury, both of Washington.

Mrd: on May 18, by Rev Jas B Donelan, Mr John Wise to Miss Bridget M Gallagher, all of Wash City.

Died: on May 13, in the city of Wmsburg, Va, Mary Fairlie Tyler, d/o Robt & Priscilla Tyler, aged 4 years & 4 months.

Died: on Wed, of the croup, Rebecca Maria, infant d/o John L & Rebecca Maria Smith, aged 10 months.

Dry Goods store: Wm M Perry, 2nd door west of 7th st, opposite Centre Market. [Local ad.]

SAT MAY 24, 1845
$400 reward for runaways, 4 negroes: Wm is 18 or 20 years of age; Geo is 16 or 18 years of age; Levi-[age not given;] Henry is about 25 years of age. –Sarah Marshall, near Pomonkey Post Ofc, Chas Co, Md

Valuable farm for sale: on Jun 16, on the premises, the farm occupied by W E Stubb, in Montg Co, Md, 10 miles from Wash, containing 282½ acs, with 2 dwlg-houses & other necessary out-bldgs. –John Boyle

Valuable lot at auction: on Tue, in front of the premises, lot #1 in square 409, fronting 99+ feet on Va ave & 110 feet deep on 8th st, nearly opposite the residence of Capt Black. -Robt W Dyer & Co, aucts

The N Y papers of Wed announce the death of Robt C Cornell, Pres of the Farmers' Trust Co of that city; & also of Jas Smith, 2 of the most useful & estimable citizens of that city. [May 26 newspaper: Mr Cornell was a native of N Y C; was the Govn'r & active manager of the N Y Hospital; was Pres of the Public School Society; was Pres of the Manumission Society; & only 1 hour before his death was chosen Pres of the Deaf & Dumb Institution made vacant by the death of Dr Milnor. Within a very short time we have lost 3 of our most active citizens in the cause of benevolence, vis: John R Willis, Rev Dr Milnor, & Robt C Cornell. –N Y Express]

Appointments by the Pres:
Robt McKelly, Register of the Land Ofc at Upper Sandusky, Ohio, vice Abner Root, removed.
Christian Huber, Receiver of Public Moneys at Upper Sandusky, Ohio, vice Moses H Kirby, removed.
Ephraim D Dickson, Register of the Land Ofc at Fayetteville, Ark, vice Jas H Stirman, removed.

Flood in Germany. The last account from **Bremen** were of 41 houses swept away by a breach in one of the dikes. Six persons have been ascertained to have been lost. –Mirror

Mrd: on May 22, by Rev Wm T Sprole, at the F st Presbyterian Church, Jas M Smith to Miss Martha L Boutwell, all of Wash City.

Mrd: on May 21, at Beddington, Berkeley Co, Va, by Rev John Light, the Rev J T Ward, formerly of Wash City, & now Pastor of the M P Church at Cumberland, Md, to Miss Catherine Ann Light, of the former place.

Died: on May 18, at Warrenton, N C, in his 2nd year, Cameron Farquhar, child of the Rev Cameron F McRae, of that place.

Obit-died: on May 13, at Phil, in her 38th year, Eliza R Tuston, only d/o the late Wm Tuston, & sister of the Rev Septimus Tuston, of Wash. At an early age she was called to experience the bereavement by which the hopes of a family become suddenly extinguished. To her remaining parent she clung with instinctive fondness, like the ivy to the pillar. After a lingering illness, she peacefully sunk into the arms of death.

Obit-died: The mortal remains of the late Mrs Georgiana Slacum Lambeth, who died at her residence, in New Orleans, on March 24 last, & of her son, Geo Meredith Lambeth, who died on Apr 7 last, were, on May 13, consigned by her mourning relatives & friends to the family burial place, in **Christ Church Cemetery**, near Alexandria, D C.

Extensive sale of land & negroes: pursuant to the decree of the Circuit Superior Court of Law & Chancery of Fauquier Co, pronounced on May 11, 1845, in a cause depending in said court in the name of Fitzhugh vs Fitzhugh, on Jun 23 next, at the front door of the courthouse, will be offered for sale a large number of very valuable slaves. There are about 60, & consist of the slaves of the late Thos Fitzhugh, dec'd, that were allotted by Com'rs Beale, Combs, & Stovin, pursuant to the order in the said cause of Oct 16, 1844, to the heirs & reps of Wm Fitzhugh, of Nicholas Fitzhugh, of Geo Fitzhugh, & of Mary Fitzhugh. On Jun 24 will be offered for sale, 3 parcels of land, being those portions of the real estate of the said Thos Fitzhugh, dec'd, that were allotted by the said com'rs severally to the heirs of the said Wm Fitzhugh, of the said Geo Fitzhugh, & of Henry Fitzhugh, & are designated on the plot & survey of Wm McCoy which accompanied the report as lots 4, 6, & 9. Lot 4 was allotted to the heirs of Wm Fitzhugh, contains 463+ acs, & is the house part or north end of the *Owl Run Farm*. Lot 6 was allotted to the heirs of Geo Fitzhugh, contains 267+ acs, & is the house part of the *Ajax Farm*. Lot 9 was allotted to the heirs of Henry Fitzhugh, contains 333+ acs, being the south end of the *Page Land Farm*, & 87+ acs, the north end of the *Ajax Farm*. On Jun 30, on the premises, will be sold 2 other parcels of land, being those portions of the said real estate of the said Thos Fitzhugh, dec'd, that were allotted to the heirs of the said Mary Fitzhugh & the heirs of the said Nicholas Fitzhugh, designated on the said plot as lot 1 & lot 2. Lot 1 contains 322+ acs, & was allotted to the heirs of the said Mary Fitzhugh; lot 2 contains 369+ acs, & was allotted to the heirs of Nicholas Fitzhugh. These lots comprise the upper & middle parts of the *Mountain Run Farm*, Culpeper Co, & lie near the village of Stephensburg, in that county. The *Page Land*, *Ajax*, & the *Owl Run Farms*, of which lots 4, 6, & 9 are parts, lie in Fauquier Co, contiguous to each other, & about 8 or 10 miles from Warrenton. The boundaries of the several lots may be ascertained by the aforesaid plot, in the clerk's ofc. By order of the com'rs. –Jas A English, Auctioneer

MON MAY 26, 1845
Great bargain in real estate: the subscriber, having determined to quit farming, will sell his farm, lying within 1 mile of Colesville, Montg Co, Md, containing 192 acres of land, with good improvements. There is also on the premises a large Tannery establishment. The property is offered at $35 per ac. –John Poole

Babe, who was convicted in N Y a year or 2 ago, of murder & piracy on board the schnr **Sarah Lavinia**, of Alexandria, has received another respite from the Pres of the U S. This, we believe, is the 6th time. This one will not expire till Jun 5, 1846.

City Ordinances: 1-Act for the relief of John H Eberbach: fine imposed for the violation of the law in relation to tavern licenses, for selling without a license, the same is remitted: provided he pay the costs of prosecution. 2-Act for the relief of John Barnes: fine imposed for a violation of the act relative to enclosing footways, be remitted: provided he pay the costs of prosecution.

Mr Henry Brent, our esteemed fellow-townsman, left for Europe a year ago to study in the schools of France & Italy the paintings of the great masters, & of accomplishing himself in the art of painting. The following are copies he has made & returned with, to be placed for exhibition in the studio of Mr John Cranch, at the foot of Capitol Hill. 1-Le Retour des Bergers, by Claude. 2-Une Danse au Soleil couchant, by Claude. 3-Le Paturage, by K Dujardin. 4-Depart pour la chase, by Wignants. 5-Paysage, by Claude.

The storeship **Lexington**, Lt Commanding Ellison, arrived at Charleston from Gibraltar a few days ago, has gone round to N Y where she arrived on Fri. Wm P Griffen, lt; Isaac N Briceland, passed midshipman; Hiram Sandford, 1st assist engineer, came passengers in this vessel

Law case before the courts in New Orleans, in which a child is claimed by 2 sets of parents: John & Martha Paul on the one side, & Mrs Hughes on the other. One asserts that the child was born in New Orleans in 1835, the other that he was born in N Y in 1837. The Court decided that Mrs Paul was the mother of the child, in virtue of which decision she took him under her maternal protection.

A fire on the farm of Mr John Hodges, near Upper Marlborough, Md, on Thu, destroyed a granary & stable, with the contents of both. The loss is probably $1,000.

Col Wm Edgar, a most worthy citizen of N J, died on Fri at his residence in Rahway, aged 78 years. He leaves a large family to inherit his name & virtues. –Newark Adv

Mrd: on May 1, by Rev Mr Morgan, at the residence of Dr N G Friend, in Green Co, Ala, Dr R Gale, Surgeon of the Marine Hospital at Mobile, to Mrs Frances Jeffries, d/o Wm Robertson, of Petersburg, Va.

Died: on May 25, of scarlet fever, Samuel, y/s/o Samuel & Eliz Redfern, aged 9 years & 5 months. His funeral is today, at 3 o'clock, from the residence of his father, corner of 19th st & Pa ave.

TUE MAY 27, 1845

To builders: the undersigned propose to buil an edifice to be called Jackson Hall, on the north side of Pa ave, between 3rd & 4½ sts. This notice is to invite proposals for the erection of this bldg. The plans will be exhibited by J C Rives, at his house.
–Blair & Rives

Charleston Courier of Sat: the Hon John Campbell, for many years a Rep in Congress from the Peedee district of S C, died at his residence in Marlborough district on May 19, of hemorrhage of the lungs. Mr Campbell was in the prime of life. He graduated at the S C College in 1819.

Appointments by the Pres:
Patrick Collins, Surveyor of the Revenue at Cincinnati, Ohio, vice Isaiah Wing, removed.
Elias Rector, Marshal of Arkansas, vice Henry M Rector, removed.
Thos M Carr, of N Y, U S Consul for Morocco, vice John F Mullowney, recalled.
Simeon M Johnson, Consul for port of Matanzas, iin Cuba, vice Thos M Rodney, recalled.
Benj P Jell, Register Land Ofc, Washington, Ark, vice Saml C Wheat, removed.
Wm Adams, Receiver of Public Moneys, Johnson C H, Ark, vice Alfred Henderson, removed.
John Bruton, Register of Land Ofc, Johnson C H, Ark, vice Jas Woodson Bates, removed.

Vicksburg Sentinel: Judge Coalter has sentenced Horace Pagaud, convicted of forging Treas warrants of the State of Miss, to 30 years in the penitentiary. This is the lowest the law would allow.

Thornton A Freeman, a deputy postmaster in Carroll Co, Mo, who abstracted a large amount of money from the mail last year, was on Apr 8, sentenced to 13 years in the penitentiary in Missouri at hard labor.

For rent: the house formerly occupied by Mrs Ronckendorff, on Pa ave, between 4½ & 6th sts. Inquire of Mr Lee, next door to the premises.

Wanted, a first rate Cook; also, a good Washer & ironer. Apply at Miss Gurley's, C st, next to the Exchange Hotel.

Cow Estray: $3 reward. Strayed from the neighborhood of the Potomac Bridge on Thu: a small white milch cow. –Wm B Berryman, 12th & C st south

Mrs R S Meade will receive company to the number of 12 or 15 at **Lucky Hit**, Clarke Co, Va, on Jun 1 next. Terms: $4 for adults, & half that price for children & servants.

I certify that Jacob Rowles, of Wash Co, D C, brought before me, a sorrel Horse & a bay Mare, as estrays trespassing upon the enclosures of Washington Berry. –Thos C Donn, J P [The owner of the above creatures will come forward, prove property, & pay charges. –Jacob Rowles, Livery Stable, 9th st.]

For rent: 2 story brick dwlg near the corner of I & 7th sts, & adjoining the residence of A Rothwell. Apply to Messrs Robt W Dyer & Co, or the subscriber, John F Boone.

Died: on May 16, at Columbus, Ga, Dr Wiley B Ector, late Editor of the Columbus Enquirer, in his 53rd year, after a painful & protracted illness of more than 4 months.

Died: lately, at his residence in Bainbridge, Decatur Co, Ga, Bennett Crawford, [brother of the late Hon Wm H Crawford,] leaving a large & devoted family.

Died: on May 14, at the residence of her father, Col Geo A Bayard, Pittsburg, Pa, Margaretta Baden, w/o Jas B Briggs, of Cleveland, Ohio. She died in full faith of the religion of Christ.

WED MAY 28, 1845
Wash Corp: 1-Cmte of Claims: act for the relief of John Howell, & act for the relief of I M Peerce: laid on the table. 2-Cme of Claims: ptns of Jas Davis, of Geo Dunbar, of Elias Abrams, of M P Mohun, of Fred'k Ford, of Wm Pettigrew, of Wilhelm Grupe, of Jas Fitzgerald, of W Ward: laid on the table. 3-Confirmed as members of the Board of Health: Dr W B Magurder, John D Barclay, Dr Thos Miller, Jas Larned, Dr H Lindsly, G C Grammer, Dr J F May, John P Ingle, Dr J G Combe, John B Gerfuson, Dr Noble Young, & Marmaduke Dove. 4-Confirmed as Guardians of the Poor: Alex'r McIntire, Flodoardo Howard, Leonard Harbaugh, Henry Stone, John B Ferguson, & Noble Young. 5-Nominations from the Mayor for assesors, viz: Saml Drury, Wm Cooper, & Lewis A Newman. 6-Bill for the relief of John Donovan: laid on the table. 6-Resolved: thanks of this Board presented to Jas Adams, for the able & impartial manner in which he has discharged the duites of the presiding ofcr of the Board: adopted. 7-Bills for the relief of John T Leaman; relief of John Donovan: passed. 8-Cmte on Improvements: ptn of Jas Tucker & others; ptn of John Marron & others: passed.

Horrid murder committed near West Chester, Pa on Sun. An intemperate young man named Jabez Boyd went to the house of Mr Jas Patton, a respectable farmer, during the absence of Mr Patton & his wife at church, where he found a servant girl & 2 of Mr Patton's children, a boy about 14 years of age & an infant. Boyd beat the boy as to fracture his skull & causing his death. The servant girl escaped with the infant and went to the neighbors, who sounded the alarm. The murderer has been arrested.

On Tue last, at a military muster in Hughesville, Pa, David McCarty, who had been stationed to keep guard, while in the discharge of his duty had occasion to resist an attemped intrusion upon the parade ground of a man named Elijah Sanders, & in doing so presented his gun, which was seized by the other in a contemptuous manner, when by some means the charge went off, mangling the body of Sanders in a most horrid manner. The poor man expired a few hours afterwards, leaving a wife & several small children.

The beautiful Miss McTavish is about to be married to the Hon Henry Howard, s/o the Earl of Carlisle, & brother to the Duchess of Sutherland. Mr Howard is an attaché to the British embassy in Paris. –London Court Journal May 3.

Letter written at Abbeville on May 22, published in the Augusta Chronicle of Sat, says that the Hon Geo McDuffie was attacked suddenly on May 21 with paralysis. He had lost the use of one side & his speech.

History of Wyoming. The Hon Chas Miner will shortly put to press his history of the Wyoming valley.

A Board for the examination of Midshipmen is to convene at the naval asylum, Phil, on Jun 2 next, of which Cmdor Geo C Read is appointed Pres, Cmdors Thos Ap Catesby Jones & M C Perry, & Capts E A F Lavalette & Isaac Mayo, members.

The marble bust of Gen Harrison, executed by the lamented Clevenger while in Italy, & purchased from his widow by the citizens of Cincinnati, has arrived in safety in that city. It is pronounced by good judges a work of great truthfulness & merit.

In a breach of promise case recently tried in England, Mr Justice Coleridge said he believed the love letters of even the cleverest men never did much credit to their heads.

Tragic affair: from the Marengo [Ala] Patriot: a few days ago Mr B M Mayfield, with his wife & dght, were returning home from church, when Mr Mayfield was attacked from behind by Theophilus Fisher, who struck him several blows; Mayfield stabbed Fisher, whereupon Fisher drew a pistol, but the crowd stopped him. Fisher died next morning, & Mayfield surrendered himself. Verdict: necessary self-defence.

The Liberia Herald says that the U S sloop of war **Preble** has lost 17 by death & 70 on the sick list.

War Dept, May 6, 1845. Appointed inspectors of the U S Military Acad for the year: Maj Gen Scott, Brig Gen Brooke, Brig Gen Gibson, Brig Gen Towson, Col G Bomford, Surgeon Gen Lawson, & Maj Levi Whiting. –W L Marcy, Sec of War. By order: R Jones, Adj Gen

Mrd: on May 19, in Centreville, Md, by Rev Washington Roby, Rev John I Murray, pastor of the First Methodist Protestant church of this city, to Miss Elizbbeth E Emory, of Queen Anne's Co, Md. [Note: Elizbbeth as written.]

Mrd: on May 25, in Wash, by Rev John **I** Murray, Mr John H Wise to Miss Eliz Jane Charles, all of Wash City.

Mrd: on May 25, in Wash, by Rev John J Murray, Mr Colley W Bean to Miss Emeline Wilkison, both of Wash City.

Died: on My 22, in Wash City, John H Yetman, aged 65 years, formerly of Richmond Co, Va. He was long a consistent member of the Baptist Church in the county where he resided.

Died: a few days ago, at his plantation, near Mobile, Ala, Col John B Hogan. He was a gallant ofcr during the late war, & served the Gov't with much energy in the last Creek war in Alabama. He has represented his county repeatedly in the State Legislature, & was for a number of years Collector of the port of Mobile.

Died: on May 27, Andrew, s/o Jas & Margaret Fitzgerald, aged 6 months.

Carusi's Saloon for sale or lease, situated at the n e corner of 11th & C sts, fronting 110 feet on 11th st & 55 feet on C st. Professional engagements require his undivided attention. –Lewis Carusi

Penitentiary for the District of Columbia: proposals for repairs of wharf must be directed to the Warden. -John B Dade, Warden

Land for sale: on the premises, 187 acres in Alexandria Co, with a small house, partly frame & log, & a stable. –Robt Widdicombe

Valuable stand for rent, on Pa ave, 3 doors west of the Railroad ofc. Calculated for a confectioner or baker. Best in the city for a refectory. –S Burche

THU MAY 29, 1845
Mr Jas Wade, a very respectable citizen of Trenton, Tenn, while gunning with a neighbor, Mr Jos Harrison, on May 12, became separated from him, & was shot by Harrison, who mistook him for a wild turkey. He was seated among the bushes imitating the note of the wild turkey. He died almost instantly.

Orphan's Court of Wash Co, D C. Letters of administration on the personal estate of Thos McIntosh, late of said county, dec'd. –Jas T McIntosh, adm

Robt Bland, the keeper of a coffee house, was shot by his friend & brother Englishman, Mr Saml Pownil, who keeps a variety store on 3rd st, west of Western Row. Bland died of his wounds, & Pwonil was arraigned on a charge of fighting a duel. –Cincinnati Atlas

Mrd: on May 28, by Rev Geo W Samson, Mr Jos H Davenport to Miss Ann Davenport, both of Lytwalton, Lancaster Co, Va.

Died: on May 21, at West River, Md, after a prolonged illness, Mrs Sarah Winterson, consort of Gassaway Winterson. The dec'd was a most excellent woman, & has left an affectionate husband, 2 tender offsprings, & a large number of friends to regret her death.

Died: on May 27, Algernon Mortimer, infant s/o Geo W & Susan B Cambloss, aged 13 months.

Died: yesterday, Georgianna, aged 3 years, d/o Geo M & Georgianna Davis, adding one more to the little children of whom the Saviour of the world said, "Send them not away, but suffer them to come unto me, for of such is the kingdom of heaven." Her funeral will be from the residence of her grandfather, Lewis Johnson, G & 11th sts, at 4 o'clock today.

Died: on May 18, in N Y, Medora, infant d/o Hon Jos L & Milinda Williams, of Knoxville, Tenn, aged 1 month.

For rent: desirable front room, house on E st, adjoining the residence of David Saunders, which, with board, can be had on moderate terms. –Catharine Rice

FRI MAY 30, 1845
Rivers S Wilson, a member of the Bar of N Y, of highly respectable standing, committed suicide on Tue in the Park, rear of the City Hall, by blowing away the right side of the fore part of his head with a pistol. The cause of the deed appears to have been pecuniary embarrassment. He was about 30 years of age, of Scottish extraction, & came from Canada a few years since. He has left a wife & 2 children. –News

Valuable property at auction: by authority vested in me as exec of Andrew Scholfield, dec'd, I offer at public sale, on the premises, all of square 863, with commodious Cottage, calculated for 1 or 2 tenements. It is on Md ave & 6th st; rents readily & has not been without good tenants for the last 5 years. Also, lot 7 in square 576, with 2 frame tenaments, under rent to good tenants: on Md ave, west of the Capitol Grounds. Also, all of the east portion of lot 8 in square east of square 87, on N Y ave, near 21st st.
–Geo Scott, exc -A Green, auctioneer

The Camden [opposite Phil] Race on Wed. When Peytona & Fashion were brought out, & the race to begin, there was a sudden movement, & the stand wavered, tottered, & cracked. The whole center of the ponderous mass, containing 2 stories fell with tremendous crach. Some of the sufferers are: Mr P O Daniel, Mr E Ovenshine, Mr Stratton, W P Way, Mr McElroy, Mr Price, Jas Torbert, Garrick Sharpe, John Kisley, Reuben Haines, ___ Copeland, ___ Singleton, Jas McMan, ___ Riley, Wm Beebe, Patrick Quigly, Thos Reynolds, Thos J Hough, Saml McKinney, Wm Calhoun, & Wm Franks. Most of the sufferers were conveyed home, & while on the ground were attended by Dr McClelland & several other physicians.

Appointments by the Pres: 1-Danl B Richardson, Register of the Land Ofc at Ouschita, La, vice Henry O McEnery, removed. 2-Nicholas B Boyle, of D C, Consul of the U S for the Port of Mahon, in the island of Minorca, vice Obadiah Rich, resigned.

Died: on May 28, at the Washington Navy Yard, Julia M, infant d/o Lt Henry Pinkney, U S Navy.

Mrs Turpin, corner of 7th & Pa ave, has still 2 or 3 front rooms suitable for a family. Terms moderate.

$1000 reward for return of pocketbook lost on May 26, between the Southern Mail Boat Landing & the Railroad Depot, Wash: contains $8,000, in notes. –M Fridenberg, North 2nd st, #207, Phil.

In Chancery. John King against Mary A Webster, Eliz Webster, & others, heirs at law, & Jas Marshll, adm of Geo Webster, dec'd. The Trustee appointed for the sale of the property in the proceedings of this cause mentioned, having reported to the Court, that on Jun 6, 1844, he sold at public auction, all that piece of land lying on the east side of Anacostia river, beginning at the n w corner of Nathl Brady's lot, purchased out of the same tract, etc, as surveyed & plotted by Lewis Carbery, on Nov 28, 1828-to Philip Otterback, he being the highest bidder, for the sum of $100.75 an acre, amounting to $1,435.06. It is by the Court, this May 26, 1845, ordered that the sale be ratified. –W Brent, clk

SAT MAY 31, 1845
Small but desirable Farm for sale: situated a little below the junction of the Old Leesburg road & the Middle turnpike: the western part of this tract, for nearly a half mile, binds on the Leesburg road. About 25 acres are cleared on which there is an old dwlg house & out-houses, all in a dilapidated state. –Christopher Neale & Thos Grimes, Attys in fact for Mary P Allison, Matilda Allison, & Jas H Allison, heirs & devisees of Jno Allison & D F Allison, dec'd.

St Peter's Church, Capitol Hill, the Rev W Moriarty, from Ireland, will preach tomorrow, at 11 o'clock.

Store & house for rent: the store now occupied by Mr Wm Whitney, on Pa ave, between 6th & 7th sts, as a Shoe Store, & the House above occupied by Mrs Harrison as a Boarding House, will be rented separately or together. Possession given Aug 6. Inquire of Mrs Sarah T Hughes.

Household & kitchen furniture at auction: on Jun 3, at the residence of Mr Vass, on 6th st, between E & F sts. –A Green, auctioneer

Household & kitchen furniture at auction: on Jun 5, at the residence of Mrs Doctor Brereton, on C st, between 3rd & 4½ sts. –Robt W Dyer & Co, aucts

John Miller, Confectioner, informs he can be ready at the shortest notice. His store is at the old stand, corner of F & 9th sts, between St Patrick's Church & the Patent Ofc.

Old Point Hotel, celebrated Water Place, will be open for visiters Jun 10. In sight of the Capes, & in 3 or 4 hours sail of Yorktown & Jamestown. The tables will be supplied with Hogfish, Sheepshead, Hard & Soft Crabs, Oysters, Turtles, & Terrapins served up by Jack McRae, of Petersburg. Mr T H Ramsey, formerly of the Farmer's Hotel, Fredericksburg, & late of the Bollingbrook Hotel, Petersburg, will attend to the reception of visiters. –Jas S French

MON JUN 2, 1845
An iron house has been constructed in the short space of 6 weeks by Mr Wm Laycock, of Liverpool, for Mrs Brown, of Nova Scotia. The house is 38 feet by 34 feet.

On Fri at the Boston Iron Co in Roxbury, on the mill dam, Jas German, an Irishman, between 23 & 24 years old, was killed when his clothes caught in the machinery, & his body was drawn in between the wheels. He was unmarried.

A bean, which had lodged in the windpipe of a child of the Rev Hezekiah Crout, at Westminster, Md, was extracted by Dr Payne who operated on the boy, making an incision, taking the bean out with an instrument.

Painful affair took place on Apr 9 in Chickasaw Co, Miss. A dispute had existed between Dr Thos C Boon & his brother-in-law, Thos Murray. In the midst of high word, Murray fired upon Boon the contents of a heavily charged rifle, which killed Boon in a few minutes. Murray has escaped.

Public Notice. Notice is hereby given, that, from & after this date, I will not pay any debts that may be contracted by my wife, Catherine Douglass, she having, by her change of habits, forfeited any claims to my support or protection. –Henry Douglass

We learn from Tenn of the death of John A McKinney, of Rogersville. He died after a very short illness in Tazewell, Claiborne Co, on Apr 12, whither he had gone to attend court. He was a lawyer of considerable distinction, & formerly U S dist atty for East Tenn. -Banner

Indian name of Lake Superior. The original name of Lake Superior is Algoma. The Buffalo Commercial suggests that the new steamboat now bldg at Buffalo by Gen Chas M Reed, of Erie, be named **Algoma**. -Albany Argus

On Sat the lifeless body of Mr Geo Cameron, an inoffensive & ingenious mechanic, was found with the hands & head resting against the front door of his dwlg, on C st, near 12th. The dec'd is supposed to have died in a fit, or from mere exhaustion, he being very infirm & nearly 70 years of age. He lived alone in the tenement which he occupied, & no one was at hand to assist him when he fell.

Notice. The Vestry of Washington Parish have appointed Mr John H O'Neill to be keeper of the Washington Parish Burial Ground, commonly called the *Congressional Burying Ground*, in place of Jas Little. From Mr O'Neill's experience as a gardener, he is well qualified to renew the sodding on graves, & to ornament them by planting shrubbery about them. –John P Ingle, Register

Mr Hector Perkins, of Balt, who was wounded in the battle of Chippewa, 30 years ago, had to have his leg amputated on May 25. For nearly 31 years he has suffered occasional pain, but for several months past he has suffered most intensely, until at last he consented to lose his leg. He has been doing well.

City Ordinances-Wash. 1-Act for the relief of John T Lenman: the fine imposed, in relation to the violation of an act prohibiting the fastening of horses to trees or the boxes enclosing them, he, & the same is remitted: Provided: he pay the costs or prosecution.

Mrd: on May 29, by Rev F S Evans, Mr Wesley T King to Miss Matilda Piercey, d/o Geo W Venable, all of Wash City.

Mrd: on May 29, in St Matthew's Church, by Rev H Myers, Mr Francis M Strother to Miss Jane E Cusick, both of this place.

Died: on Jun 1, Alex'r Shepherd, late of Wash City, aged 42 years, leaving a wife & 7 children. His funeral is from his late residence near Rock Creek Church, today at 4 o'clock. [Jun 6th newspaper: Obit-died: Alex'r Shepherd: devoted husband, affectionate father, sincere friend, & kind master. Throughout his long & severe illness his hopes were built upon the Rock of Ages. –C]

Circuit Court: since last Mon the jury has been engaged in the trial regarding an issue from the Orphans' Court, to try the validity of a will made by the late Mrs Catharine Calder, of Gtwn, by which she emancipated a number of servants. Some depositions have been taken touching the condition of the mind & faculties of the testrix at the time & previous to her making the will. The learned counsel employed by the contending parties, who are Jacob G Smoot & Helen, his wife, vs Robt White & Wm Jewell. Messrs Bradley, Marbury, & Redin are counsel for the plntfs; & Messrs C Cox & Addison for the dfndnts.

TUE JUN 3, 1845

Household & kitchen furniture at auction: on Jun 4, on H st, between 18th & 19th sts, near Mr S Redfern's, [the flag will designate the house.] –Robt W Dyer & Co, aucts

Situation wanted as Teacher, at the South, either in a public school or in a private family, by a young gentleman who is a graduate of one of the New England Colleges. Address W S Paulding, Burlington, Vt.

Persons are cautioned against receiving a note drawn by me in favor of Saml Phillips, & endorsed by Thos G Turton, at 18 months, dated Jan 1, 1845, for $139.97. Also, a note drawn by J L Waring, & endorsed by me, for $85, at 18 months, the notes were obtained by Saml Phillips by fraud. –R W Turton, Nottingham

Wilson K Shinn, late a Senator in the Legislature of Va, died at his residence in Clarksburg, on May 26, in his 36th year.

Jos Osgood, who was sent to the House of Correction last week for having stolen 2 horses & chaises, one of them belonging to the City Marshal, committed suicide at that institution. He had taken a bottle of arsenic from another prisoner, who had it for medicinal purposes. –Boston Traveller

Another death by Quackery. A coroner's jury at Newburg, N Y, returned a verdict of death by lobelia, in the case of Jas Roe, who died there a few days since, under the treatment of a man named Caulkins.

On Fri last a s/o Doct Ring, of Pleasnat Valley, watching the cutting down of a tree in the town of Hyde Park, was struck in front of the ear by a limb, & he died in 2 hours. He was about 15 years of age.

Accident at the residence of Mr Kelley, of *Acre's Hollow*, Middleburgh, N Y, on May 21. While raising a barn, part of it fell, seriously injuring 15 persons. Elisha Guensey had both thighs broken & could not live. Jacob Bert had his thigh broken; Burton Nethaway was injured in the head, & deranged; Nicholas Becher had his breast bone broken in.

The New Haven Herald states that the venerable widow of the late Hon Elbridge Gerry, now a resident of that city, has become the legatee or inheritor of a handsome fortune, by the death of a brother in England. The amount is said to be $50,000.

The Oldest Minister in the World: is the Rev Mr Harvey, a Baptist clergyman, 109 years of age, & is still living at Frankfort, N Y, & is engaged every Sabbath in his profession.

The Massachusetts Colonization Society held its anniversary on Wed, Prof Greenleaf presiding. Report was read by Rev Jos Tracey. The Society was organized May 26, 1841. Hon Danl Waldo, of Worcester, & his sisters, have given $2,000 to the Society.

It having been recently discovered that the whole of the architrave of St Paul's Cathedral was composed of white marble, workmen, within the last few days, have been removing the thick coating of black paint which for years it had been covered, revealing, as they proceed, carvings of the most beautiful description.

I certify that Benj M Wall, of PG Co, brought before me as estrays, a bay Horse & a bay Filly. Owner is to prove property, pay charges, & take them away.
–Hanson Penn, J P for PG Co, Md

Appointment by the Pres: John F Bacon, of N Y, Consul of the U S for the port of Nassau, New Providence, vice Timothy Darling recalled.

Genr'l Orders, No. 23: War Dept, Adj Gen Ofc, Wash, May 31, 1845. The resignations of the following ofcrs have been accepted by the Pres, to take effect at the dates set opposite their names: 1-Capt C A Waite, 2nd Infty, as Adj Q M, May 8, 1845. 2-2nd Lt G D Hanson, 8th Infty, Jun 1, 1845. 3-2nd Lt A P Stewart, 3rd Artl, May 31, 1845. By order: R Jones, adj Gen

Wash City elections held yesterday:
1st Ward: For Alderman:
*John D Barclay-129
For Common Council:
*Chas A Davis-87   Wm Wilson-71
*Geo W Harkness-78   Richd M Harrison-26
*Saml Stott-73
2nd Ward: For Alderman:
*John Wilson-132   Chas L Coltman-52
For Common Council:
*Jas F Haliday-114   J E Dow-68
*Lewis Johnson-113   N B Vanzandt-65
*S D King-105   J L Smith-46
3rd Ward: For Alderman:
*John W Maury-269   Jos Bryan-67
For Common Council:
*John T Towers-247   John Y Bryant-103
*Saml Bacon-246   Jon T Walker-80
*Saml Burche-212   S H Hill-72
4th Ward: For Alderman:
*Jas Adams-78   Jas Young-54

For Common Council:
*B B French-79 *John Kedglie-66
*Peter Brady-67
5th Ward: For Alderman:
*J C Fitzpatrick-101 Nathl Brady [dec']–7
For Common Council:
*J L Maddox-70 J McCauley-42
*J W Jones-55 A M Miller-35
*J Van Reswick-49 S Beach-34
[Jun 4th newspaper. *-those elected. Also included were those of the 6th Ward: Alderman-Marmaduke Dove. Common Council: Alex'r Lawrence, Jas Cull, & Geo H Fulmer. –W W Seaton, Mayor] [Jun 6th newspaper: information on the 6th Ward: For Alderman: *M Dove-121; John R Queen-120. For Common Council: *Alex Lawrence-143; *Jas Cull-139; *G H Fulmer-124; Thos Kelly-105; Jas Gordon-87; W D Aiken-8.]

Mrd: on May 29, at Richmond, Va, by Rt Rev Bishop Johns, Wm F Turner, of Jefferson Co, to Miss Ellen Beirne, y/d/o the late Col Andrew Beirne, of Monroe Co, Va.

Mrd: on May 27, at **Mount Air**, in Chas Co, Md, by Rev Mr Stonestreet, Mr Richd M C Throckmorton, of Loudoun Co, Va, to Miss Mary Ophelia, d/o Robt Digges, of Chas Co.

Died: on Jun 2, at **Eastern Hill**, D C, Wm Ignatius, infant s/o Dr W A & R C Manning, aged 8 months & 11 days.

Died: on Jun 2, at the Navy Yard, Wash, James E Arvin, y/s/o Dennis & Mary Callaghan, aged 13 months & 27 days. His funeral is this evening, at 3 o'clock.

WED JUN 4, 1845
Fatal steamboat accident. One of the boilers of the steamer **Paul Jones**, Capt Moffett, which runs between Balt & Havre de Grace as a tow-boat, exploded yesterday near North Point, whilst going up the Pataspsco river, when the following were killed: Mr John Parsons-engineer & Mr Geo Gill-fireman.

A man named Carr was killed on the Columbia Railroad on Thu when his horse became frightened, & ran across the tracks. The locomotive came in contact with the cart, & the driver was thrown some distance, causing death immediately.

The 5 persons indicted for killing Joe & Hiram Smith appeared in court, at Hancock Co, on May 19. Their trial was fixed for the 21st. Few Mormons were in attendance, & no distubance took place of any kind.

The late European steamer brings news of the death of Thos Hood, the well-known author. He had been ill for many months, & suffered much. He was the son of a bookseller. [No date-current item.]

Nashua Telegraph says that a few days ago John Bartley, 14 years old, of Windham, Mass, killed a white-headed eagle, which measured 7 feet from tip to tip of his wings.

Foreign Items. 1-Queen Victoria has appointed Chas Duncan Wake, now British Vice Consul at Copenhagen, her Majesty's Consul at Charleston. 2-The Duke of Wellington completed his 76th year on May 1, & is yet in good health.

Orphans Court of Wash Co, D C. Letters testamentary on the personal estate of John McClelland, late of said county, dec'd. –Mary McClelland, excx; John McClelland, exc

Naval Court Martial: in the case of Capt Philip E Voorhees, on charges growing out of his proceedings in Sep & Oct last, while in command of the frig **Congress**, commenced yesterday at Coleman's Hotel. Court is composed of: Capt Chas Stewart, Pres; Capts Chas G Ridgely, John Downs, Stephen Cassin, Lawrence Kearney, David Geissenger, C S McCauley, John H Aulick, & French Forrest. Benj F Hallett, of Boston, Judge Advocate. Richd S Coxe, Counsel for Capt Voorhees. Only witness examined was Lt Jenkins. [Jun 5th newspaper: Sailingmaster Blair was introduced as a witness.]

For rent: 2 small & convenient houses, on 19th st, between I & K sts. Rent moderate. Apply to Ann Kedglie.

Honor to the late Col Wm S Foster, of the 4th Regt of U S Infty: the ofcrs of the 4th Regt, in 1842, presented to the dght [now residing in Cincinnati] of the late Col Foster, a beautiful silver vase, as a testimony of their respect for his services. The artist was Mr E Kirk, of Balt, & the execution does him great credit. It is an Etruscan vase or urn. On one face a shield, with the American arms, surrounded by 2 laurel branches, bears the inscription "***Fort Erie***, September 15, 1814," on which day he [then Capt Foster] distinguished himself by his gallant conduct, for which he received from Pres Madison the brevet rank of Major. On the face a shield, surrounded with Indian weapons, bears the inscription, "Okee-cho-bee, December 25, 1837;" on which day he distinguished himself as Lt Col in the command of the 4th Infty, on an occasion when the Seminoles gave battle with more force than on any other field in Florida. For his services on that day he received the brevet of colonel. The centre of the urn bears the following: "To Mary Jane, daughter of Brevet Colonel W S Foster, from the officers of the 4th regiment of Infantry, U S army, as a memento of their respect for his gallant services." The lid of the urn is surmounted with an elegant magnolia blossom, emblematical of Florida, that "land of flowers," where his more recent services were performed.

Fire last night in the brick stable in the rear of Mr Edw Simms' grocery & spirit warehouse. It is supposed that the fire was wilfully set.

Appointed as delegates to represent Division #3 in the Temperance Union of D C for 1 year from May 28 last, viz: Brothers Ulysses Ward, John Sexsmith, Flodoardo Howard, Wm Whitney, L A Gobright, Sylvanus Holmes, Jas B Ford, & R Flowers.
–J W Eckloff, Rec Scribe

Mrd: on May 27, by Rev Dr Muller, Mr Fred'k Lakemeyer to Miss Eliz, eldest d/o Mr John C Roemmele, all of Wash.

THU JUN 5, 1845
The ship **Erbus**, Capt Sir John Franklin, & the ship **Terror**, Capt Crozier, have sailed on another voyage of discovery. Each ship has been supplied with 200 tin cylinders for the purpose of holding papers, which are to be thrown overboard, with the statement of the longitude & other particulars worthy of record, written in 6 different languages, & the parties finding them are requested to forward the information to the British Admiralty.

Douglas Jerrold is now said to be the writer of Mrs Caudle's famed "Curtain Lectures" in the London Punch.

New Drug Store: corner of 9th & I sts, Wash. –E F Buckingham

Valuable real estate for sale: about 200 acres in PG Co, Md. Apply to Geo A Digges, residing near Bladensburg.

$25 reward for runaway negro woman, Henrietta, about 19 years of age. I purchased her from the estate of Francis Beall, dec'd, near Vansville, where her relatives now live. She has also a brother & sister in Gtwn. -A B Berry

A new magazine, entitled "The National," made its appearance yesterday. It is under the editorial supervision of Redwood Fisher. This issue contains a history of the Electro-Magnetic Telegraph, by F O J Smith. The remaining contents are appropriate & instructive.

Mrd: on May 19, at Bristol, Indiana, Sylvester Larned, Atty at Law, Detroit, Mich, to Helen P, d/o R R Lansing, of the former place.

FRI JUN 6, 1845
On Mon last, while laborers were digging away the banks in Lancaster st, Albany, a portion of the bank tumbled down, & Jas Highland was taken out dead; 3 others were badly injured.

In 1840 the bones of the great Missourium of Missouri was discovered. The same discoverer, Dr Albert C Koch, has brought to light the fossil remains of a monster in the animal creation that he gives the name of Zeulodon Silliman, in compliment to Prof Silliman, of Yale College. Its length is 104 feet, the solid portions of the vertebra are from 14 to 18 inches in length & from 8 to 12 inches in diameter, each averaging 75 pounds in weight. This discovery may be set down to the State of Alabama, & to a county adjoining Mobile, namely, Washington, being imbedded in a yellow lime-rock formation, near the old Washington court-house. Dr Koch is a German by birth & education.

Providence Journal announces the death, at Coventry, R I, on May 17, of Wm Anthony, f/o the editor of that paper. Mr Anthony was upwards of 70 years; he was the s/o Danl Anthony, an elder of the Society of Friends. Mr Anthony, the father, was one of the first in this country to engage in the cotton manufactures; in 1788 entered into it with Andrew Dexter, & had drawings from Bridgewater, & manufactured some rude machinery, even before the arrival of Slater, who first established factories upon the English model in this country. In 1805 Mr Wm Anthony entered into the manufacture of cotton & pursued it prosperously from that time.

Public sale of 150 or 160 acres of land, more or less, 1 mile from Bladensburg, on the Marlborough road. It adjoins Mr Jones' tract of land north, & Messrs Darnal & Magruder south & east. You may call on Mr Horatio Newman, residing on the premises, or inquire of the subscriber, near the Potomac bridge, Wash.
-Wm Lloyd, Atty for Horatio Newman

Ho! For Oregon. Oregon emigrants: the First Company consisted of 176 males & 117 females & 64 wagons; the Captain is Mr Everett. The 2nd company is commanded by D Luther & has 166 males & 117 females; & 58 wagons. The 3rd company was commanded by Capt Parker, & consists of 60 males & 100 women & children; & 43 wagons. The whole number of work cattle 1,148, of loose cattle 1,228, of horses & mules 211, & of firearms 334.

Mrd: on Jun 3, by Rev Mr Pyne, Mr Thos J Fisher to Miss Charlotte M Sioussa, both of Wash City.

Mrd: on May 29, by Rev John Claxton, Mr Albert Young to Miss Rachel Ann Briscoe, all of St Mary's Co, Md.

Beautiful country seat for rent: property formerly occupied by the late Jos Nourse, 1 mile above Gtwn, adjoining the country residence of Mr Causten. Apply to Chas J Nourse, Exchange Ofc, Pa ave.

Court Martial of Capt Philip F Voorhees: charge-Disobedience of orders. Specification 1st: on Mar 14, 1844, dispatched in the U S frig **Congress** to Montevideo: did on Sep 29, 1844, wrongfully capture & take forcible possession of an armed vessel **Sancala**, belonging to a Gov't at peace with the U S Gov't. Specification 2: on Sep 29, 1844; did disobey the order of Capt Danl Turner by wrongfully capturing & taking forcible possession of a squadron of armed vessels belonging to a Gov't at peace with the U S Gov't. 3-Specification: did on Sep 29, 1844, wrongfully release prisoners & property captured by, or in custody of, a squadron of vessels employed in blockading the port of Montevideo, the said squadron belonging to a Gov't at peace with the U S Gov't. Specifications 4 & 5 dealing with the same. [Jun 7th newspaper: Lt Porter was next sworn & examined.] [Jun 17th newspaper: Lt Browning was examined: communications of Mr Hamilton to Capt Voorhees were put in as evidence, but were objected to by the Judge Advocate.] [Jun 20th newspaper: Mr Jas L Blair, Lt Bache & Lt Gantt were examined. Mr Coxe, dfndnt's counsel, gave notice of his readiness to make his defence on Sat next.]

SAT JUN 7, 1845

The trials of the persons charged with the murder of the 2 leading Mormons, Hiram & Joe Smith, were commenced at Carthage, Ill, on May 21. The parties arraigned are J C Davis, late an Illinois Senator; T C Sharp, editor of the Warsaw Signal; Mark Aldrich, Wm N Grover, & Col Levi Williams. A correspondent of the St Louis Republican says that "almost every body attending court comes arned to the teeth, & frequently muskets & rifles will be seen taken out of wagons with as much deliveration as if they were attending a militia muster instead of attending a court of justice. This is a bad state of things, but extraordinary cases demand extraordinary remedies."

Paving Stones-wanted immediately, 30,000 square yards, to be delivered on 7th st wharf, or on 7th st west, between the Canal & H st. –Patrick Crowley, Contractor for paving & grading 7th st.

The undersigned wish to employ a Teacher to take charge of Primary School #4, in the village of Nottingham, PG Co, Md, on Jul 1. –Jno M S McCubbin, M D; Jno T Stamp; Henry M Chew, Trustees

Piano Fortes for sale: has on hand a beautiful new Boston Piano, & one of his own make. –J F Kahl, Piano Forte maker, Pa ave, south side, between 12th & 13th sts.

Our friend N P Willis sailed from here in the Britannia steamer for Liverpool on Sun last, to take his only child, a dght 3 years of age, to her relatives in England, in obedience to the dying request of the late Mrs Willis. He will remain abroad a few months, corresponding with the Mirror, & then return to his editorial chair. These particulars we have from himself. –Boston Post

The Editor of the Louisville Journal, with Ole Bull, & a few others, recently made a brief visit to this mightiest of wonders: beautiful, wild, majestic, & mysterious. Ole Bull took his violin into the cave & gave some of this nobliest performances at the points most remarkable to their wonderful echoes.

The will of Mr Philip John Miles, of Bristol, has just been proved. The personal property exceeds a million. Each of his sons, 8 in number, has L100,000. His dghts were provided for at their marriage.

The following are the "bids" made for painting of the Pres' house: Hurdle & Co, of Alexandria, $2,625; Williams, of Phil, $2,956; Bunker, of N Y, $2,996; Moore & Kellar, of Phil, $3,995; Seely, of Wash, $4,383; Purdy, of Wash, $4,000. Two-thirds of the house are to receive 2 coats of paint, & the other third a single coat. Hurdle & Co have received the contract. –Balt Sun

Capt Peter Flowery, of the schnr **Spitfire**, indicted at Boston for an alleged participation in a slave-trading expedition of that schnr, was brought up for trial on Wed in the U S Circuit Court, Judge Sprague presiding. The indictment charged him with sailing as master of the vessel, intending to employ her in the trade, & that he aided Don Juan Martinez, who was owner, in fitting her out. The indictment is framed upon a law of Congress passed in 1818, forfeiting the vessel, & fining in not over $5,000, & imprisoning between 3 & 7 years, the aider & abetter. [The **Spitfire** had been called the **Caballero**.] Examined were: R S Smith, one of the crew of the vessel **Manchester**; Saml Wilcox, midshipman on the vessel **Truxton**; Antonio del Majo, a Spaniard, & one of the crew, examined through an interpreter. N Y Enquirer

Mrd: on Jun 5, by Rev G W Samson, Mr Saml Pumphrey to Miss Eliz Ann Wake, both of Wash City.

Mrd: on Jun 5, by Rev John P Donelan, Mr Saml E Smith to Miss Eliz St Clair, all of Wash City.

Mrd: on Tue last, by Rev Mr Tarring, Mr David Jenkins, of Wash, to Miss Mary Ann Hall, of Greenburg, Green Co, Pa.

Died: yesterday, Mrs Catharine N, consort of Jos Carter, in her 38th year, leaving an afflicted husband & 4 children to mourn her irreparable loss. Her funeral is this afternoon, at 4 o'clock, from her late residence on 12th st.

Died: on Jun 6, Ida, y/d/o Robt & Mary Keyworth. Her funeral is this afternoon at 4 o'clock.

Mechanical Riflemen: to meet at the Company's Armory, for parade, in full summer uniform, with knapsacks & 1 days' provision, on Jun 9, at 6 o'clock. –J B Mazeen, O S

MON JUN 9, 1845
Wash Co, D C: I certify that Jos L Shoemaker, of said county, brought before me a stray trespassing on his enclosures a dark bay Mare. –Thos Holtzman, J P [Ownere is to prove property, pay charges, & take her away. –Jos L Shoemaker, Gtwn, about half a mile west of the end of 7th st.]

Pleasure Excursion: the Grand Division of the Order of the Sons of Temperance on Jun 24, down the Potomac, on the commodious steamer **Columbia**, Capt Guyther. The following Brothers compose the cmte for the reception of the Ladies:

Darius Clagett	Ulysses Ward	Wm Whitney
Lambert Tree	Selby Parker	Christopher Cammack
S Holmes	Dr Flodoardo Howard	J B Wingerd
John D Clark	J L Henshaw	Geo Savage
Cmte of Arrangements:		
Chas W Boteler, jr	John A Burns	Z K Offutt
Robt W Davis	L A Gobright	H S Davis

The State of Indiana as illustrated in a small volume entitled the "Indiana Annual Register & Pocket Annual for 1845. [Population in 1800 was 4,875, & by the census of 1840, 685,856.]
1672: The country visited by the missionaries Allouez & Dablon.
1683 to 1763: Claimed by France, & trading posts founded at Vincennes, **Fort Wayne**, etc.
1763: Claim of France relinquished to Great Britian.
1784: Ceded by Virginia to the U S.
1800: Northwestern Territory divided, & Indiana Territory erected.
1804: First newspaper printed at Vincennes, by Elihu Stout, Jul 4.
1807: Indiana University established.
1816: State of Indiana admitted into the Union.
1825: Seat of Gov't removed to Indianapolis.
1836: Law passed for a general system of internal improvements.
1842: Imprisonment for debt abolished.
1843: A tax levied for the establishment of a Deaf & Dumb Asylum in the State.
The Indiana Historical Society was established in 1831.

The Ancient & Honorable Artillery Co of Boston celebrated their 207th anniversary on Monday. A sermon was preached by the Rev Dr Vinton, of the Episcopal Church.

Fifth Ward lock-up house for sale: on the premises, on Jun 14.
–John Magar, Acting Com'r 5th Ward.

Circuit Court of Wash Co, D C, in Chancery. Alex'r Hanna & Louisa C his wife, cmplnts, & Eliz Bohrer, Eliza Grammer, Chas West & Mary his wife, Catherine, Anna, Eliza, William, & John A Grammer, Henry F Mayer, Henry Emmons & Henrietta his wife, & Ernestina M Mayer, dfndnts. The bill in substance: that Fred'k Grammer being seised of lot 5 in square 294, lot 13 in square 548, & lot 14 in square 378, in Wash City, departed this life; the cmplnts & dfndnts above named are now entitled to the same as his heirs at law, in undivided & unequal portions; that the said lots are not susceptible of divison; that some of said dfndnts are minors, to whose advantage as well as of said other heirs it will be to have the said lots sold; that all the said dfndnts are non-residents of this District; & the object of the bill is to have the said lots sold & the purchase money divided among said cmplnts & dfndnts according to their respective shares in said lots; it is ordered that the dfndnts are to be & appear in this court on the third Mon of Oct next to answer said bill, otherwise the same will be taken for confessed against said dfndnts. –W Brent, clerk -Redin for cmplnts.

Circuit Court: the case of Jacob G Smoot & Helen his wife, vs Robt White & Wm Jewell: the jury has been engaged for 8 days & confined 3 days & nights, not having reached a verdict. The Gtwn Will case will probably have to be re-tried. Many respectable witnesses, many of whom are ladies & acquaintances of Mrs Calder, the testatrix, gave testimony as to the state of her mind at the time of her making the will.

Alexandria will case before the Circuit Court: Walter S Alexander vs Geo Wise & others: already tried twice in Alexandria Co, & the jury discharged, not being able to agree. Disputing the validity of the will: was the testator incapable; was the writing purporting to be his will procured by means of an undue influence. Counsel in the above cause are- for plntfs, R J Brent, Henry May, & Messrs Swann & Swann; for dfndnt, Gen Jones & J H Bradley.

Jas Herbert, charged with stealing, on Mar 15, 1845, a horse, the property of Wm B Thompson, of Gtwn, was committed on Sat last to the Wash Co jail by Justice Thompson. He was arrested at Leesburg, & removed to Wash City under the authority & order of the Govn'r of Va.

Claiborne Wilson fell into the Eastern Branch last Fri , while fishing near the Brewery. Fortunately he was saved by a kind hearted bystander, who jumped into the water & saved the boy from a watery grave.

For sale: 2 story frame house on L & 15th sts, with a good stable. –Jos A Deeble, agent

To let: first-rate dwlg, containing 10 rooms, on 13th st west, between G & H sts north. Apply to Geo Parker, or to the subscriber. –Geo Cover

TUE JUN 10, 1845
House & lot at auction: part of lot 6 in square 881, with a 2 story brick & frame house, lately occupied by Mr Bright: fronts 36 feet on Market alley. –A Green, auctioneer

On Fri last the Athenaeum bldg, at Harvard College, put up for the reception of the Panoram of Athens, was destroyed by fire. Every exertion was made to save the painting without avail; it was taken down & rolled up, but no passageway sufficiently large to admit its removal could be made before the flames spread. It was a present from Hon Theo Lyman, & was painted by Messrs Barker & Burford, in London.

N Y, May 28, 1845. The "Old Fort" discovered by Dr Locke in Highland Co, Ohio, in 1838, denoted a period of 600 years from its abandonment; that is, 284 years before Christopher Columbus first sailed into the western ocean. The trees on Grave Creek mound denote the abandonment of trenches & stone look-outs in that vicinity to have been in 1338. [Trams Am Ethnological Society, Vol 1, N Y, 1845.]
-Henry R Schoolcraft

Fred'k White Sulphur Springs, 6 miles east of Winchester, Va, are open for the reception of company. Improvements have been increased for the last 5 years. –Branch Jordan, Proprietor

Fauquier White Sulphur Springs is open for the reception of visiters: 50 miles from Alexandria, 35 from Fredericksbrug, & 20 miles east of the Blue Ridge.
–Danl Ward, Agent

Potomac land for sale: by virtue of the last will & testament of Wm H Sydnor, dec'd, late of Northumberland Co, Va: sale on Aug 11 next, that valuable farm called *Cupid's*, on Cupid's creek, in said county, containing 731+ acs, with houses suitable for a genteel family, as for all the purposes of a farm. The subscriber reserves to himself the privilege of one bid. –Thos S Sydnor, Exc of Wm H Sydnor, dec'd

The schnr **Mary Jane** at auction: by virtue of a deed of mortgage, with power of sale, from Benj Harris: sale on Jun 20. It is now lying at Mr Griffithe Coombs' wharf, at the termination of 3rd st, on the Eastern Branch, near the old Sugar House. This vessel is only 3½ years old. –Wm T Rice R W Dyer & Co, aucts

Circuit Court of Wash Co, D C. In the matter of the division of the real estate of the late Ann Larkin, formerly McGunnigle, it is this 7th day of Jun, 1845, ordered by the Court, that the sale made on May 22, 1845, of the real estate of the above, to wit, of lot 17 in square 348, with 2 three story houses thereon, be ratified & confirmed. The property was sold for $4,025; the north house to J B H Smith, the south house to John Gregory.
–Wm Brent, clerk

Shannondale Springs, Jefferson Co, Va, opened in early June. Mr A P Fitch is in charge again this year.

Appointments by the Pres:
Wm D Pritchard, Collector of the Customs, Camden, N C, vice Geo W Charles, removed.
Benj Davis, Register of the Land ofc at Palmyra, Missouri, vice Cyril C Cady, removed.
Warner Lewis, Register, Dubuque, Iowa, vice Wm H H Scott, removed.
Stephen Langworthy, Receiver, Dubuque, Iowa, vice Thos McKnight, removed.
Chas Parker, Surveyor of Revenue at Snow Hill, Md, vice Geo Hudson, removed.
Jesse Williams, Sec in & for the Territory of Iowa, vice Saml J Burr, removed.
Edw Johnston, U S Atty for the Terriroty of Iowa, vice John G Deshler.
Ver Planck Van Antwerp, Receiver of Public Moneys at Fairfield, Iowa, vice Saml J Bayard, removed.
Bernhart Henn, Register of the Land Ofc at Fairfield, Iowa, vice Arthur Bridgman, removed.

Mrd: on Jun 29, at the residence of the Hon Chas H Carroll, in Livingston Co, N Y, by Rev H B Bartow, Thos T Gantt, of St Louis, Mo, to Miss Mary C Tabbs, d/o the late Moses Tabbs.

Died: on May 30, at Princeton, Gibson Co, Indiana, the Rev Nicholas Snethen, of the Methodist Protestant Church, aged 76 years.

Died: on May 30, at the St Charles Hotel, New Orleans, Jas Jenkinson Wright, late U S Consul at St Jago de Cuba, a native of Dublin, aged 64 years. He has been a leading merchant in St Jago de Cuba for the last 30 years, & was universally esteemed for his generous & intrinsic good qualities.

Died: on Mon, Florida Henning, d/o R W & Sarah Bates, aged 18 months. Her funeral is this evening at 4 o'clock, from the residence of Mr Bates, on Pa ave, near 18th st.

Died: on Monday, in Wash City, Wm Fulton, only child of John A & Agatha C Lynch, aged 2 years & 3 months. His funeral will take place this evening at 4 o'clock, from the residence of his parents on East Capitol st, Capitol Hill.

Died: on Jun 7, after a few hours' severe illness, Richmond Johnson, y/c/o Edmund & Eliz Ann Coolidge, aged 10 months & 22 days.

Died: on Jun 7, Agnes Lowrey, infant d/o Mrs Susan D & the late Alex'r Shepherd, aged 14 months. Her remains were deposited in the same grave with her father, who was buried on Jun 2.

Died: on Jun 2, of scarlet fever, Henry, 2nd s/o Dr Franklin Waters, of PG Co, Md.

WED JUN 11, 1845

The trial of Peter Flowery, late master of the schnr **Spitfire**, in the U S Distric Court of Boston, terminated on Sat, when the jury rendered a verdict of guilty, but recommended the prisoner to the mercy of the Court.

In Jefferson Co, Va, Nelson Hooper, from 27 to 30 years of age, has been tried for the murder of Wm Brooks, in Morgan Co, on Feb 17 last. The defence made was insanity. Jury returned a verdict of guilty of murder in the 2nd degree, & ascertain the term of his imprisonment in the public jail, or penitentiary house, in Richmond City, to be 18 years.

On Sun, Wm A Houston, aged 52 years, formerly in the U S army, on alightning from one of the Harlen cars at the depot in Centre st, N Y, was instantly killed by being crushed between the car he was leaving & one which was proceeding up town. The dec'd was nearly related to Gen Saml Houston, of Texan celebrity, & had served as a sergeant in the Black Hawk & Florida wars. Having been frostbitten in the service, he was a pensioner. About 2 weeks ago he went up to New Rochelle to exercise his calling as a painter & glazier. Yesterday he came down to the city to visit his wife. –True Sun

Accident in Phil on Sat: Danl Farrar died from foul air, when working with others on installing a new well.

Orphans Court of Wash Co, D C. In the case of Clement Cox, adm of John Kincaid, dec'd; 2nd Tue in Jul next appointed for the settlement of the estate.
–Ed N Roach, Reg of wills

Orphans Court of Wash Co, D C. Letters of administration on the personal estate of Henry Benter, late of Norfolk, Va, dec'd. –Eva Ruppert

Villains did not succeed in robbing the grocery store of Mr Sylvanus Holmes, on 7th st, a few nights ago. They were alarmed by a dog that was kept about the premises.

Mr Edw McCubbin was accidentally knocked down last Sat by a stage, while he was crossing from 7th st to the Centre Market. We are glad to learn he is not seriously hurt.

Dr Jas E Morgan, having now permanently located himself, offers his professional services. Ofc on Missouri ave, 2nd door east of 4½ st; & on the Island, near the Steamboat wharf.

THU JUN 12, 1845

Orphans Court of Wash Co, D C. House & lot at auction, on Jun 2: lot D in square 797, on I st, between 3rd & 4th sts, with the improvements, being part of the estate of the late Geo Bell. -R W Dyer & Co, aucts

Orphans Court of Wash Co, D C. Letters testamentary on the personal estate of Alex'r Shepherd, late of Wash Co, dec'd. –Susan D Shepherd, excx; Sylvanus Holmes, excr [I hereby authorize Rev John C Smith to sign all necessary papers in the settlement of the above estate for me, & in my name, as my atty. –Susan D Shepherd, Excx of A Shepherd]

The trial of the persons charged with the murder of Joe Smith, in Carthage, Ill, has resulted in a verdict of acquittal. The same persons stand charged with the murder of Hiram Smith, & gave bail in the sum of $5,000 for their appearance at the next term of the court, to answer the charge.

Mr Wm V Buskirk, late Sec of State of the State of Md, committed suicide at Cumberland on Mon, while sitting in the portico of the court-house in that town. He shot himself with a gun, which he discharged against his head by means of the ramrod. A note was found on his person addressed to Saml M Semmes. Mr Buskirk was about 50 years of age, & had of late been intemperate. -American

Miners' Journal of Sat: sudden death of Dr Berryman. While making a professional visit near Port Carbon, on Wed, his horse became frightened & ran. The Dr was thrown from the carriage & struck his head; a concussion of the brain was produced, of which he died on Thu.

Ran away from Ossian Hall, Fairfax Co, Va, on Jun 7, a negro girl named Jane Lee, aged 13 years. $25 reward if taken in Wash Co; $15 if taken in Alexandria Co; & $10 if in Fairfax Co. –Francis A Dickins

Died: yesterday, Richd Patrick, eldest s/o Chas & Susan V McNamee, aged 3 years. His funeral will take place this afternoon at 4 o'clock from the residence of Mr Tonge, 7th st.

Died: on Jun 10, Margaret, y/d/o Ferdinand & Mgt Jefferson, in her 4th year.

Desirable country residence for rent until Nov next: 2 story frame house & 50 acres of land: part of the summer retreat of Miss Carroll, known as the *Cottage*, in Montg Co, Md. –E B Davidson

Spring Garden for sale: wishing to remove from Charlotte Hall, I offer for sale my house & lot in said village. There is an academy of long standing within 200 yards of the house, at this time under the superintendence of the Rev John Claxton, assisted by Mr Jas Miltimore & Mr N Merriam. I am determined to sell on accommodating terms. –Margaret Estep

For rent: dwlg house on I st, near St Matthew's Church, recently occupied by Lt Farley, & next door to W W Corcoran. –Susan D Shepherd, excx; Sylvanus Holmes, excr

FRI JUN 13, 1845
$50 reward for runaway negro man Washington Johnson, about 20 years of age. –W F Berry, Upper Marlboro, PG Co, Md

Henry Schley, the late able & efficient Clerk of Fred'k Co Court, was elected Cashier of that institution.

Monroe, Mich, Jun 4: Louis A Hall, a teller in the Bank of River Raisin, was assassinated by Geo Wells, of Detroit, & in consequence of his wounds is now at the point of death. Wells is in custody. Wells is the s/o the Rev Mr Wells, formerly of the Presbyterian Church in this city, but now chaplain of the military post at Prairie du Chien. [Jun 26th newspaper: Lewis A Hall has so far recovered as to be able to ride out, & no further doubt is felt of his entire recovery.]

The new Gothic edifice recently erected at the corner of H & 11th sts, for the worship of the congregation under the pastoral charge of the Rev Dr Muller, will be opened for public worship on Jun 15.

Died: on Jun 12, in Wash City, after an illness of 2 days, Mrs Sarah Commerford, a native of King George Co, Va, but for the last 39 years a resident of Wash. Her funeral will take place from the residence of her son-in-law, Mr Michl Nash, this day, at 4 o'clock.

Died: yesterday, in Wash City, of cholera infantum, terminating with a disease upon the brain, Margaret McLellan, y/c/o Chas & Rowena C Whitman, aged 7 months & 15 days. Her funeral will be at the house of Mr Saml Hanson, N J ave, Capitol Hill, this morning, at 9 o'clock.

SAT JUN 14, 1845
The dwlg of Mr Printup, a farmer, near Fultonsville, on the Erie Canal, was burnt on Sat, & 2 of his children perished in the flames. Mr Printup was severely burnt, & hardly expected to live.

Miss Hannah Cornell, d/o Henry Cornell, of the town of Chemung, N Y, aged about 16 years, was drowned on Mon last while attempting to cross the Chemung river on horseback.

House for rent: 2 story brick house on the avenue, a few doors west of the War Dept, & next door west of Com Warrington's residence. A notice on the gate will indicate where the key may be had. –Louis Vivans

In Chancery: Wm B Stone & Walter Mitchell, Excs of Alex'r Greer, against Wm D Prout & others, heirs at law, Rachael Prout, widow, & Chas S Fowler, adms of Wm Prout, dec'd. Trustee reports he sold the following real estate in the decree made on Sep 17, 1843; & on Nov 27, 1844, to the persons & at & for the prices hereinafter mentioned, viz:
Lot 3 in square 4 to John C Harkness: $97.12
Part of lot 1 in square 494 to Geo B McKnight: $294.37
Lot 1 in square 494 to Geo B McKnight: $108.00
Lot 11 in square 873 to John Lee: $138.60
Lot 12 in square 873 to John Lee: $134.16
Lot 9 in square 877 to Chas Lyons: $112.76
Lot 33 in square 878 to Henry Naylor: $4.27
Lot 34 in square 878 to Geo B McKnight: $41.97
Lot 35 in square 878 to Geo B McKnight: $66.50
Lot 36 in square 878 to Geo B McKnight: $105.21
Lot 10 in square 897 to Geo B McKnight: $38.31
Lot 11 in square 897 to Geo B McKnight: $28.59
Lot 12 in square 897 to Geo B McKnight: $44.81
Part of lot 13 in square 897 to Little: $93.00
Lot 3 in square 899 to Geo B McKnight: $45.50
Lot 4 in square 899 to Geo B McKnight: $98.13
Lot 8 in square 925 to Geo B McKnight: $46.87
Lot 9 in square 925 to Wm Easby: $89.83
Lot 13 in square 926 to G B McKnight: $46.58
Lot 24 in square 926 to G B McKnight: $45.21
Lot 15 in square 926 to G B McKnight: $54.36
Lot 16 in square 926 to G B McKnight: $55.63
Part of lot 17 in square 926 to G B McKnight: $43.04
Lot 2 in square 926 to Henry Naylor: $88.91
Lot 9 in square 949 to G B McKnight: $72.20
Lot 10 in square 949 to G B McKnight: $49.16
Lot 11 in square 949 to G B McKnight: $51.90
Lot 11 in square 950 to Jas Marshall: $49.82
Lot 12 in square 950 to R W Dyer: $49.09
Lot 13 in square 950 to G B McKnight: $49.09
Lot 14 in square 950 to G B McKnight: $49.09
Lot 15 in square 950 to G B McKnight: $51.17
Part of lot 16 in square 950 to Jas Rhodes: $26.05
Lot 17 in square 950 to G B McKnight: $30.13
Lot 18 in square 950 to G B McKnight: $42.23
Lot 19 in square 950 to G B McKnight: $42.59
Lot 20 in square 950 to G B McKnight: $45.40
Lot 5 in square 975 to G B McKnight: $93.43

Lot 6 in square 975 to Chas Newton: $53.39
Lot 3 in square 1001 to G B McKnight: $18.44
Lot 6 in square 1001 to G B McKnight: $48.17
Lot 14 in square 1001 to H Naylor: $8.32
All the purchasers aforesaid, with the exception of Geo B McKnight, had complied with the terms of the sale, as require by said decree. Same is comfirmed on Jun 4, 1845.
-W Brent, clerk

Public sale of *Greenwood*: by decree of Balt Co Court, as a Court of Equity, the undersigned trustee will offer for sale at auction, on Jul 3 next, at the Exchange in Balt City, Greenwood, on Bel-Air road, the Mansion formerly belonging to Philip Rogers, & about 17½ acres of ground, adjoining the place formerly owned by Isaiah Mankin. The Mansion needs repairs, but with the materials in part worked out, & which will go to the purchaser, it is thought that from $1,500 to $2,000 will put it in good order. It is 62 feet front by 43 feet 8 inches deep. A plat of the whole of *Greenwood* will be exhibited at the sale, & may be seen before at the ofc of the Trustee, 22 north Charles st, or of the Surveyor, Mr Bouldin, in the basement of the Record ofc, back of the Court-house. After the above sale, will be offered, the rest of Greenwood grounds, about 45 acs, in lots, beginning with those on both sides of John st. –Edw Hinkley, Trustee

Circuit Court of Wash Co, D C-in Chancery. Amos Binney, adm of Amos Binney, dec'd, cmplnt, vs the heirs of Jas Thomas, dec'd, Byron Wilkinson, Paul Spofford & Thos Tileson, & Levi Pumphrey, dfndnts. Supplemental bill. In 1829 Jas Thomas, since dec'd, conveyed, by way of mortgage in fee, to Amos Binney, cmplnts intestate, lots 9, 10, & 11 in square 490 in Wash City, to secure a debt, now exceeding $5,000; that he subsequently mortgaged the same property, by different deed of conveyance, to the dfndnts, Wilkinson, Spofford & Tileson, & Pumphrey, in the order in which they are named to secure the aggregate amount of about $3,414, with interest with the respective dates of the morgages, that is, about the year 1841; that the said cmplnt, in 1843, filed his original bill in this case against the heirs of the said Jas Thomas, to procure a foreclosure of his said mortgage first named; &, having then no notice or knowledge of the other mortgages, he did not make the other dfndnts above named parties thereto, but proceeded to a decree of foreclosure & sale of the said premise thereon; that the sale was fairly conducted, & produced the sum of $6,441.69 or thereabouts. The object of this supplemental bill is to make the said Byron Wilkinson, Paul Spofford & Thos Tileson, who are not residents of D C, or within the jurisdiction of the Court, dfndnts in the said case, to the end that they may declare whether they will redeem the said premises from the mortages prior to theirs, & whethere they will pay the debt due to the cmplnt, or, in default thereof, be foreclosed of all claim upon said premises. Absent dfndnts to appear in this Court on or before the 3rd Mon of Oct next, & make answer to the said bill, or, in default thereof, that the same be taken for confessed against them.
-W Cranch -D A Hall, for cmplnt

Appointment by the Pres: Cornelius W Lawrence, Collector of the port of N Y, to take effect on Jul 1 next, in place of C P Van Ness, resigned.

Naval Ofcrs: Capts, Cmders & Lts, only, are to wear epaulets, & they shall wear one on each shoulder, over the shoulder strap; yet never without swords, when absent from the ship. The bullions of the epaulet shall be of silver gilt; those of capts & cmders to be in 2 rows, the outer row to be half an inch in diameter, & 3 inches long, & 20 in number; those of Lts 3/8ths of an inch in diameter, & 3 inches long, in 2 rows, with a proportionate number in the outer row. Straps of all epaulets shall be of navy gold lace, with a worked edge & crescent, according to the pattern.

Mr Francis Butler, of Farmington, Maine, committed suicide by cutting his throat on May 27. His age was 63. He was the richest man in that county, & has all his life been a prudent & money-making man. He committed suicide because laboring under derpression of spirits, consequent upon some unfortunate circumstances, by which it not improbable he should lose a few thousand dollars.

Mrd: on Jun 12, by Rev W T Sprole, Geo Wm Phillips, of Boston, to Miss Mary Anne, d/o the late Geo Blagden, of Wash City.

Died: on Jun 10, of paralytic, Miss Rachel Adams, of Chas Co, Md, in her 83rd year of her age.

Died: on Jun 2, Mrs Ellen E Ficklen, w/o J B Ficklen, & y/d/o Thos McGehee, of Person Co, N D, in her 22nd year.

Died: on Jun 12, Chas Pinkney, s/o Theodore & Emily E Kane, aged 17 months. His funeral is this morning, at 11 o'clock.

MON JUN 16, 1845
Capt Johnson, of the U S Army, & a resident of Greensburg, Westmoreland Co, Pa, died very suddenly in Pittsburg a few evenings since. He arrived in Cincinnati in a steamboat, was put into an omnibus, & died while on his way to the hotel for invalids in Alleghany City. He died of consumption. His remains were buried by the ofcrs & military of the garrison & the city volunteer companies.

The Montreal Courier announces the death of Sir Richd Downes Jackson, K C B Lt Genr'l, commanding her Britannic Majesty's forces in British North Ameirca. He died on Jun 9, having been suddenly seized by apoplexy. He entered the army as ensign in 1794.

We learn by a passenger, from Nashville, that Gen Jackson died on last Sun. [Jun 17th newspaper: the news of the death of Gen Andrew Jackson, Ex-President of the U S, is confirmed by the Western papers. He expired at the Hermitage on Jun 8.]

Deacon Ebenezer Silliman, of Wethersfield, Conn, was seriously injured, if not killed, on Fri, by being thrown from his wagon in the town of Durham. He was taking the remains of his wife to Guilford for interment; & when on the stone causeway or bridge, the horse took fright & jumped off, falling about 25 feet. Deacon Silliman was taken up lifeless, & the horse was killed outright.

Appointments by the Pres:
Isaac A Hedges, Surveyor & Inspector of the Revenue of St Louis, Missouri, vice Oliver Harris, removed.
Thos J Gantt, U S Atty for the district of Missouri, vice Wm H McPherson, removed.
Edw W Green, Deputy Postmaster at New Bedford, Mass, vice Simeon Baily, removed.
Wilson Knott, Deputy Postmaster at Newark, N J, vice Jno J Plume, removed.

The Albany Citizen says that among the letters & papers of Gen Philip Schuyler is one in which he speaks of the existence of a box or camp-chest, left in Albany, which contained much valuable correspondence & information relative to events connected with the American Revolution & the history of that period. On the occasion of the late visit of Mrs Alex'r Hamilton, the only surviving d/o Gen Schuyler, search was instituted for this long-missing box, & was luckily found among the lumber & rubbish of some quiet nook, where it had undisturbedly reposed for 50 years. It was removed from its resting place & sent to Mrs Hamilton.

Died: on Jun 13, in Wash City, Mr John McQuillan, aged 60 years.

Died: on Jun 13, in Wash City, Agnes, infant d/o Edw & Margaret S Smith, aged 2 months & 26 days.

Take notice: Any person found trespassing on my farm, near Rock Creek Church, with dog or gun, shall certainly be prosecuted after this notice. –Thos Murphy

For rent: commodious store & warehouse on 7th st, adjoining the china & glass store of Chas S Fowler. Apply at the ofc, 5th st & Louisiana ave. –Johnson Hellen

Presley Simpson has taken the Store heretofore occupied by Mr Wm Orme, Pa ave & 11th st, where he will keep a Family Grocery Store.

During the thunder storm of Tue last, the hotel of Saml Colp, at Barren Hill, on the Ridge Turnpike road, was struck by lightning, & his son, Wm Colp, a young married man, was killed while leaning against the wall in the bar-room. -Phil Ledger

The Columbian Horticultural Society met last Sat: Mr Clagett exhibited 2 fine specimens of Smith's White & the Royal George Gooseberries. Monsieur Vivans exhibited some fine Dahlias & Yellow Onions. Miss M C Call, a handsome bouquet of Dahlias & Roses.

TUE JUN 17, 1845
For sale or rent: commodious 2 story brick dwlg-house on La ave, between 6th & 4½ sts. Inquire of E Guttschlich, near the corner of 6th & La ave.

Episcopal High School of Va: Rev F A Dalrymple, Rector: located in Fairfax Co, 3 miles west of Alexandria, D C.

Columbia Academy is now offered at private sale: located on 9th st, between G & H sts. The lot is 59 feet 6 inches fronting 9th st, by 140 feet deep. A few yards to the south of it, on the same square, is the 4th Presbyterian Church of the Ascension, which will be finished in a short time, & on the adjoining square is St Patrick's Church. –John McLeod

From a Sault Ste Marie correspondent of the Detroit Free Press: Mr Chas T Miller, one of the U S Deputy Surveyors for the mineral region, died at the Saulte on Jun 3.

Eminent citizens connected with the Gov't who have died within the last 4 years:
Pres Harrison, Ex-Pres Jackson
Sec Upshur, Sec Gilmer, Atty Gen Legare
Judges Thompson & Baldwin, of the U S Supreme Court
Senator Southard, N J; Senator McRoberts, Ill; Senator Linn, Mo; Senator Porter, La; Senator Fulton, Ark; Senator Bates, Mass; Senator Betts, Conn.
Gen Macomb & Gen Eustis
Cmdor Hull, Cmdor Claxton, Cmdor Shubrick, Cmdor Porter, Cmdor Kennon
Judge Rowan, Ky; Judge Buchanan, Md; Judge Gaston, N C
Those who have played no unimportant part in the history of the country:

Bishop Griswold, Vt	John Holmes, ex-Senator, Maine
Rev Dr Channing, Mass	Judge Cowan
Rev Dr Breckenridge, La	Gen Morgan Lewis
John Forsyth, ex-Sec of State	Asher Robbins, R I
Gen Porter, ex-Sec of War	Virgil Maxcy
Nicholas Biddle	Ex-Govn'r Mason, Mich
Thos Morris, ex-Senator, Ohio	Govn'r Kavanagh, Maine
Jas Lanman, ex-Senator, Conn	

On Jun 5, in the coal mines of Geo M Hollenback, near Wilkebarre, Pa, 3 miners, Jos Walker, John Casery, & John O'Neil, were instantly killed, & Robt Johnson, seriously injured. The coal which had been left overhead & not intended to be mined, gave way while the men were at work under it, crushing them.

The whaling ship **Maria Theresa**, Capt Fisher, which sailed from New Bedford, May 1, for the Indian Ocean, returned again on Jun 9, having had her 1st ofcr, a boat-steerer & 3 of her men washed overboard on Jun 14. Capt Fisher & 4 of the crew were also washed overboard at the same time, but succeeded in regaining the ship.

A gold medal, of massive size, has recently been sent to Mr John Mears, jr, of this city, from the Emperor Nicholas, of Russia. A short time since, the medal & a letter were received from the Russian Minister at Wash: the Plough you intended to present to the Emperor has been received, & its usefulness acknowledged. His Imperial Majesty had ordered me to present to you in his name the great gold medal, with his effigy, & the motto, Praemia Digno. –Alex de Bodisco [Wash, May 20, 1845.]

Mrd: on Jun 10, by Rev Mr Pyne, John C Ten Eyck, of Mount Holly, N J, to Julie, d/o the late John Gadsby, of Wash City.

Died: on Jun 13, Mr Auguste Royer, a native of France, but for the last 10 years a resident of Wash City.

Died: on May 31, at St Thomas' Manor, Chas Co, Md, after a long & painful illness, Mrs Eleanor Neale, w/o Capt Jas H Neale, in her 36th year.

Died: on Jun 11, at West River, Md, Cornelia Maxcy, y/c/o Francis & Mary G Markoe, jr, of Wash, aged 1 year & 2 days.

The Arkansas Intelligencer of May 24 states that a Court Martial will sit at **Fort Smith** on Jul 2, to investigate certain charges preferred against Col Harney, of the Dragoons.

By a deed of trust, dated Jan 16, 1845, recorded in Liber W B #116, land record of Wash Co, D C, made by Jos Jewett & Patrick H King, for certain purposes expressed, I shall sell on Jun 27, on the premises now occupied by said Jewett & King, on Pa ave, commonly known as Congress Hall, a large variety of Household & Tavern furniture. –Walter Lenox, Trustee -A Green, Auctioneer

For rent: small house on H st, Captiol Hill, now occupied by Capt Crabb. Inquire of Capt Crabb, or B Thruston.

Hanover Landing for sale: 163 acs, a large white brick house; one of the healthiest places on the Ohio: 1 mile from Hanover College, 4 from Madison. Address, post paid, A Hays, Madison, Indiana.

Farm for sale: the farm of the late Alex'r Shepherd: in Wash Co, in sight of Rock Creek Church: 200 acs. For particulars apply to Mrs Shepherd, on the premises, or to S Holmes, at his store on 7th st. –Susan D Shepherd, excx; Sylvanus Holmes, excr

WED JUN 18, 1845
Albany, N Y: on Jun 13, on the Mohawk & Hudson railroad, the engineer of a wood train, Wm Groat, at full speed, collided with a passenger train. Mr Friend W Forbes, [glassblower, from Hay's & Coffin's works, in Camder Co, N J, where he has left a wife & 5 children,] was crushed and both legs mangled. Amputation of one of these limbs was performed and should he live, the other leg must be amputated also. Mr Forbes left his home to visit his father in Oneida Castle, in this State. He is about 35 years of age. -D of New Jersey

Nicholas Co, Ky: A few days since, Mr Jonathan Parish attempted to repair the lock of a loaded gun without removing the percussion cape from the nipple, & while thus engaged the gun went off, & the ball lodged in the side of his wife, who was sitting nearby, causing her death in a few hours.

Trustee's sale: deed of trust to me from Jos D Lafontaine, dated Apr 1, 1845, I shall sell, all the right, ritle, & interest of Jos D Lafontaine in lot 4 in subdivision of square 692, on Md ave, together with the improvements, bldgs, & appurtenances. –N Callan, jr, Trustee -R W Dyer & Co, aucts

Valuable household & kitchen furniture at auction: on Jun 25, at the residence of Dr Powell, on E st, between 9th & 10th sts. –A Green, Auctioneer

Appointments by the Pres: 1-Louis McLane, of Md, Minister Pleni & Envoy Extra to the United Kingdom of Great Britain & Ireland, vice Edw Everett, recalled. 2-Saml W Spencer, Collector of the Customs at Apalachicola, Fla, vice Hiram Nourse, resigned. 3-Ezra Chesebro, Collector of the Customs at Stonington, Conn, vice Giles R Hallam, resigned.

Criminal Court-Wash: to serve on the Grand Inquest during the present term:

John W Maury, Foreman	Benj K Morsell	John F Cox
	Geo Parker	Geo W Riggs
John Mason, jr	Jacob Gideon	Abner C Pierce
R C Weightman	Thos Fenwick	Henry C Mathews
Hamilton Lufborough	Henry McPherson	Saml Bacon
John Kurtz	Jos Forrest	Thos Thornly
John Boyle	Eleazer Lindsly	Geo W Phillips
Henry Haw	Lewis Carbery	
John Cox	John C Rives	

Boarding: the undersigned would be happy to accommodate a Mess of gentlemen at his house, recently occupied by Gen Scott. The house is pleasantly situated on Pa ave, between 17th & 18th sts. –A Julien, French Cook.

On Sun, a colored boy, Thos Selden, about 10 years old, was drowned while bathing in the Wash Canal. Dr J E Morgan was present to tender assistance, but to no avail.

We, the undersigned, Grocery Merchants in Wash City, agree that on Jun 19th, we will order our stores to be closed precisely at 8 o'clock. [This is to leave a couple of hours for out-door exercise & enjoyment for the comfort & health of their clerks & other employees.]

Geo & Thos Parker	John T Ryon & Brother	John T Killmon
Edw Hall	S J Ober	John A Donohoo
Saml Bacon & Co	Middleton & Beall	T C Duckworth
B L Jackson & Brother	S Holmes	H J Gould & Co
Randolph & Keller	Simms & Son	H Allen
Murray & Semmes	W H Upperman	Lewis & Holland
R W Beall	Tyson & Brothers	John Sexsmith
Leonard Harbaugh	W B Brashear	Presley Simpson

City lots for sale: lots 5, 6, & 10 in square 212, adjoining the residence of Chas Hill: title indisputable. Inquire of A Green, Auction & Commission Merchant, Concert Hall, Todd's bldg.

Trustee's sale of valuable lots: by deed of trust, dated May 39, 1844, recorded in Liber W B 109, folios 153 thru 156, in the Land records of Wash Co, D C: part of lot 22 in square 254 on F st, between 13th & 14th sts, with improvements. Lot 19 in square 221 on H st. –E Owen, trustee -A Green, auct

Orphans Court of Wash Co, D C. Letters of administration on the personal estate of John Brannan, late of said county, dec'd. –Eliza Brannan

THU JUN 19, 1845
A visit to Chas Thomson: on a summer morning in 1820, at his mansion in Chester Co, Pa. Mr Thomson was then about 97 years of age, seated on a sofa, reading a small Greek Testament, without glasses. He says he has been blessed. He points to the portrait of his first wife, of whom he was married to for more than 43 years. He turns to the portrait of his second wife: she, too, was a kind & good wife. He has a kind sister who had resided with him more than 70 years. -M

Mrd: on Jun 17, by Rev Mr Eby, Mr Pliny Wood to Miss Eliz Dove, all of the Navy Yard, Wash.

The funeral of Gen Andrew Jackson. On Jun 10th, every place of business was closed, & our citizens, for the most part, went up to the Hermitage to pay the last solemn rites to the distinguished dead. The Sermon was preached by Rev Dr Edgar. The body was placed by the side of her whom in life he had loved so well.

Annals of the Revolution. Annapolis, Oct 20, 1774. Teas, & the vessel bringing it, burnt by the owners: the brig **Peggy Stewart**, Capt Jackson, from London, having on board 2,320 pounds of that detestable weed tea, arrived here on Fri last. The teas was consigned to Thos Chas Williams & Co, merchants in the city. As published in the Md Gaz: "We, Jas Williams, Jos Williams, & Anthony Stewart, do severally acknowledge that we have committed a most daring insult & act of the most pernicious tendency to the liberties of America; we, the said Williams, in importing the tea, & the said Stewart in paying the duty thereon; incurred the displeasure of the people now convened." After which they went on board & set the tea & the vessel on fire, & in a few hours the whole, with the vessel, was consumed.
+
Annals of the Revolution. Jan 29, 1776: Resolved, that Messrs Saml Purviance, Isaac Grist, Benj Griffith, Wm Buchanan, & Thos Harrison, be a cmte to devise & point out to the Council of Safety the best modes for fortifying & defending Balt town, & to make out an estimate of the expense of each.

Died: on Jun 16, at Phil, Edw L Carey, s/o the late venerable Mathew Carey, aged 40 years. Mr Carey was a member of the firm of Carey & Hart, leading book publishers. He had recently been elected Pres of the Academy of Fine Arts, but declined the station in consequence of ill health.

Died: on Jun 18, John Edw Neale, s/o John E & Mary Neale, aged 8 years.

Dr A Myers, German Physician, will undertake to cure the consumption, [if taken in time.] He can be seen at Mr Eberbach's, corner of 8th & E sts. No charge made unless a cure be affected.

Very fine household & kitchen furniture at auction: on Jun 26, at the residence of Lt Ward, 17th & H sts. -A Green, auct

FRI JUN 20, 1845
For sale or rent: good 2 story brick house on square 293, fronting on C st, near 12th st west. For terms apply at the Patriotic Bank. –G C Grammer, Pres

Wanted, a vrssel to carry 1,500 barrels to Kingston, Jamaica. –Clement Smith, Gtwn

Among the passengers for Liverpool in the steamer **Cambria**, which sailed from Boston on Mon last, was the Hon R B Rhett, Rep in Congress from S C.

The people of Cincinnati are rejoicing over the completion of the Miami Canal, by which a regular & direct communication is established between Cincinnati & Toledo, [at the head of the Maumee Bay,] on Lake Erie. It extends from Cincinnati to Defiance, & is 178 miles in length.

It is understood that Rev W G Jackson, of the Episcopalian Church, has accepted the Chaplaincy of the Univ of Va. He will enter his duties the ensuing session, which commences in Oct next.

Appointments by the Pres: 1-John J Peavey, of Maine, as Consul of the U S for the port of Pictou, Nova Scotia, in place of Jas Primrose, recalled. 2-John M Wimer, Postermaster at St Louis, Mo, vice S B Churchill, removed.

Naval Intelligence. Cmder Wm J McCluney appointed to command the sloop-of-war **John Adams**. Lts Harry Ingersoll, Zachariah Holland, A A Holcomb, Francis Lowry; Surgeon Saml Barrington; Passed Assist Surgeon J Winthrop Taylor; Purser Geo F Sawyer; Chaplain Geo W Latham; Prof of Mathematics J P Espy; Midshipmen John Gale, Jas E Jouett, J D Langhorne, Alfred Baily, Arthur H Otis; Boatswain John Munro; Gunner Danl James; & Carpenter J M Webb have been ordered on the same ship. The U S ship **Jamestown**, bearing the broad pennant of Com Chas W Skinner, arrived at Port Praya May 11th, from Monrovia. Letter from an ofcr on board the **Jamestown**, dated May 17, says that John S Limetz, who had been sick for some time with a severe pain in the head, died.

Information received of the death of Geo P Fleschman, dentist, a citizen of the U S, who was drowned in the harbor at Nassau, N P, on Apr 13, while attempting to board a transport ship. The U S Consul at Nassau, has taken possession of his effects.

New Orleans Tropic: on Jun 10 in the public school of the Second Municipality, Jacob Polhemus, about 10 years old, died after having put his head through a hole in a door and becoming lodged there until life was extinct. He had been put in a room in the basement to chastise him for some misconduct. He was the s/o a widow lady on Nayades st, & her bereavement was most pitiful. The teacher is overwhelmed with grief.

SAT JUN 21, 1845
Wm Strickland, of Phil, the distinguished architect, is to superintend the erection of the State Capitol bldgs at Nashville.

The trial of O'Blenis, of Pointe Coupee, La, for the murder of young Frank Combs, has resulted in the discharge of the jury. The prisoner was remanded to jail for another trial.

On Wed last, Mr Horace Coval, Principal of an Academy in White Plains, Westchester Co, N Y, came to his death by falling head-foremost from the 3rd story of his dwlg, a height of about 20 feet.

The Great Indian Council met last month: Gov Butler & Col Logan, U S Agents for the Cherokees & Creeks, were in attendance, with Lt Flint, U S Army. The Muscogees shake hands; the Osages grasp as high as the elbow; the Caddoes embrace with an old fashioned country hug. The Caddo Chief is a man of remarkable beauty, his features evincing a high degree of intellect & an ardent spirit. Black Dog, the Osage Chief, is about 7 feet-powerful frame, with a voice attractive & commanding. Wild cat only got in the day of adjournment; he was very quiet, & has been for weeks very ill.

Mr Van Zandt, an aged gentleman, who was knocked down the other day by a horse which had taken fright at the explosion of a fire-cracker, died yesterday of the injury sustained. -N Y Commercial Adv [No date.]

Dry Goods & Bonnets. –John Allen, Pa ave, between 9th & 10th sts.

In Brooklyn, N Y, Brig Gen Gilbert Reed, a member of the Bar of that city, went to the house of his father-in-law, Andrew Demarest, in Poplar st, & woke up Mr Chas Demarest, saying he was very sick. Mr Demarest's wife procured a mustard plaster but this gave him no relief & he asked for laudanum, which he said was the only medicine that gave him relief in such attacks. He took 5 or 6 teaspoonsful, when the pain somewhat abated. His peculiar hard breathing alarmed them & Dr Van Pelt was brought in. Mr Reed died on Tue, from too free use of laudanum, while suffering a severe attack of bilious cholic. -News

Notice: was committed to the jail of Fred'k Co, on Jun 16, as a runaway, a black man, Jas Crawford, about 30 years of age; says he went from Ky to Ohio, & from thence he arrived here. The owner, if any, is to come & have him released, otherwise he will be discharged according to law. –Geo Rice, Sheriff of Fred'k Co, Md.

Am immense multitude, some 12,000 people, of both sexes, assembled at St Louis to witness the execution of T H Hocker for the murder of Delarue. Such painful spectacles are avoided in many of the States by the humane provisions for private executions. [Jun 23rd newspaper: the murder was committed in England, near London, & the execution took place in London, & not in St Louis. –N Y Commercial Adv

Notice: was committed to the jail of Fred'k Co, on Jun 16, as a runaway, a black man who calls himself Ben; about 22 years of age; says he belongs to Mr Rawlings of Montg Co, & made his escape from the jail of said county. The owner, if any, is to come & have him released, otherwise he will be discharged according to law. –Geo Rice, Sheriff of Fred'k Co, Md.

A little boy of 6 years old, s/o Mr Lewis Cobbett, of West Dedham, became very sick from tobacco given to him by Hank, a clerk, in Mr Jason Ellis, jr's store. He died on Jun 5. Mr Ellis discharged the clerk. –Dedham Democrat

The iron bolt to which Christopher Columbus was chained during his imprisonment in St Domingo has been received at Newbern, N C. It was procured by Robt S Moore, late purser in the U S Navy, recently deceased. It is indeed a courious & interesting relic.

On Thu last, Rev Jas Graham, of Wilkinsburg, was thrown from his horse, which took fright from his hoisting an umbrella, & was so badly injured that he has since died. –Pittsburg Chronicle

Appointments by the Pres:
Commercial Agent: David Naar, of N J, at the island of St Thomas, West Indies.
Custom-house Ofcrs:
Rysap Rawls, Collector at Edenton, N C, vice Thos J Charlton, whose commission will expire Jul 1, 1845.
Murray Whallon, Collector of the Customs at Presque Isle, Pa, vice Chas W Kelse, whose commission will expire Jul 10, 1845.
Alcee Labranche, Naval Ofcr at New Orleans, La, vice Martin Duralde, whose commission will expire Jul 1, 1845.
Land Ofcrs:
Aaron Snider, Receiver of Public Moneys at Jackson, Mo, vice Ralph Gould, whose commission will expire Jul 1, 1845.
Amzi L Wheeler, Receiver of Public Moneys at Winsmac, Ind, vice Jeremiah Grover, whose commission will expire Jul 8, 1845.
John F Read, Register of the Land Ofc at Jeffersonville, Ind, vice Jas Scott, whose commission will expire Jul 1, 1845.
Alex'r J Irwin, Receiver of Public Moneys at Green Bay, Wisc, vice Stoddard Judd, whose commission will expire Jul 1, 1845.
Philip E Engle, Receiver of Public Moneys at Crawfordsville, Ind, vice John Beard, whose commission will expire Jul 1, 1845.

Notice. All persons indebted to the subscriber on account of the business recently conducted by Mr Henry Carter, at the corner of 8th st & Market Space, are to call at the store & settle their accounts with Mr Kirkpatrick Mitchell, who is authorized to settle the same. New firm to be established at the old stand under the name of Gibson, Mitchell & Co. –W G W White

For rent: large 3 story fire-proof store now occupied by E P Scott, & formerly by King & Scott, near the Market Space, fronting on the Canal & Cherry st. Apply at my store on Water st. –Z M P King, Gtwn

Household & kitchen furniture at auction: on Jun 24, at the residence of Capt Titcomb, on H st, between 7th & 8th sts. –A Green, auctioneer

The public are cautioned against purchasing lot 16 in square 42 in Wash City; said lot, through inadvertency, conveyed to Wm T Wilson, by the subscriber, about Jul 10, 1844, instead of conveying only 20 front feet thereof; he, said Wilson, having a deed drawn up for the whole lot instead of a portion thereof, & brought to the subscriber for his signature, which was signed, believing it was correct. Wilson conveyed said property to Geo Krafft, althought he, said Krafft, was cognizant of the fact that said property, beyond the 20 feet, was so obtained & so dishonestly held & transferred. I also inform the public that the said Wilson has in his possession 2 notes given by Krafft of $100 each, dated this day, & believed to be payable in 6 to 12 months, in part payment thereof. –Wm H *Parke [Jun 25th newspaper: reply by Geo Krafft. I deem it due to my own character to say that I knew about the property, conveyed to me, is wholly untrue. I purchased the lot from Wm T Wilson, who had a deed for it from *Parker; I never heard of any dispute about Wilson's title until after the sale to me by Parker. I paid a full price for the lot to Wilson, who had a good deed & I mean to keep it. –Geo Krafft]
[Note: *Parke & Parker.]

$100 reward for runaway negro man Jim Ormes, about 24 or 25 years of age. He has a wife living at Mr Walter S Hilleary's, near Bladensburg. Jim left home on Jun 12. Thos E Berry, living near Queen Ann, PG Co, Md.

By an order of distrain, I shall expose to public sale, on Jun 26, 6 doors east of Coleman's Hotel, the following property, to wit: bonnets, artificial flowers, capes, ribands, stockings, scarfs, cherry table, centre table, astral lamp, books, trimmings, corsets, whalebone, looking-glass, cane chairs, jet pins, gloves, kettle, bedstead, bucket, pine table, knives, coffee port, snuffers, & sundry other articles, taking as the property of Mrs Loring, & sold to satisfy house rent due & in arrears to J P Pepper. –J A Ratcliff & Co, Bailiffs

Mrd: on Jun 19, by Rev Geo W Samson, Mr John T Killmon to Miss Mary J Sheriff, both of Wash City.

Mrd: on Jun 19, by Rev H Myers, Mr Wm B Brashear to Miss Adeline Mazine, all of Wash City.

Died: on Jun 20, Anne, w/o Jas Gill, in her 18th year. Her funeral will take place at 4 o'clock today, from the house of J Whipple, near the Navy Yard. The friends of the family, & the United Brothers of Temperance of D C, are respectfully invited.

Died: on Jun 20, Mrs Mary Peirce, in her 60th year. She was a consistant member of the Methodist Episcopal Church. Her funeral service will take place at Wesley Chapel today at 4 o'clock.

MON JUN 23, 1845
Special meeting of the Grand Lodge of Free & Accepted Masons of D C, at the Masonic Hall on Jun 25, at 7½ p m, for taking into consideration what appropriate honors shall be paid to the memory of our dec'd Brother, Gen Andrew Jackson, late M W Past Grand Master of the Grand Lodge of the State of Tenn.
–H C Williams, Grand Sec Grand Lodge, D C

Rooms for rent: house is on F st, next door to Corcoran & Riggs. –R Widdicombe

Meeting of the Franklin Fire Co on Jun 23, at 7½ o'clock. –L A Iardella, Sec

For rent: new 3 story brick house; also a pump in the yard. Also, 2 large well-furnished parlors & 2 chambers on G st, near the State Dept. –D A Gardner

Letter of King Charles V [Don Carlos] to his son, Charles Louis, the Prince of the Asturias, abdicating his claim to the throne of Spain. Having determined to retire from political affairs, I took the resolution of renouncing in your favor my rights to the crown, transmitting them to you. From this day I assume the title of Count de Molino, which it is my intention to bear hereafter. Charles [Bourges, May 18, 1845.] When Divine Providence called me to the throne of Spain at the death of my well-beloved brother & lord, King Ferdinand VII, I saw in my new position a sacred duty. [Bourges, May 18, 1845.] Reply of his Royal Highness the Prince of the Asturias. An obedient & submissive son, my duty is to conform to the sovereign will of your Majesty. I have in consequence the honor to lay at your feet the act of my acceptance. I assume from this day the title of Count Montemolin. –Charles Louis [Bourges, May 18, 1845.]

The 26th anniversary of Queen Victoria's birthday was celebrated, not on Sat week, when it occurred, but on Tue last, as being a more convenient day.

Foreign Obituary 1--The celebrated marine artist, Huggins, died in London a few days ago, much respected. 2-The eminent German author & critic, Schlegel, died a few days ago, aged 79. 3-Vice-Admiral Villaumez, distinguished ofcr of the empire, & senior Adm of the French Navy, died at Suresnes, near Paris, on May 17. 4-The death of Cardinal Luigi del Drago is announced by the Diario di Roma. He was born at Rome in 1776, & raised to the Cardinalat in 1832, by Pope Gregory XIV. 5-Mrs Kemble, wid/o the celebrated actor, John Philip Kemble, died on May 19, at age 90 years, having survived her husband more than 20 years. She had in her time been a celebrated actress, & commenced her career when Garrick was in the zenith of his fame. She had been visited by some of the first families of nobility & gentry, & was excellent company.

Appointments by the Pres:
Franklin Cannon, Register of the Land Ofc at Jackson, Mo, vice Greer W Davis, removed.
Abraham Morrell, of N Y, U S Consul for Turk's Island, West Indies, vice Jno Arthur, recalled.
John W Holding, of Md, U S Consul for the port of Santago de Cuba, in place of Jas J Wright, dec'd.
Chas N Lawson, Surveyor & Inspector of the Revenue at Carter's Creek, Va, in place of Robt Edmonds, whose commission will expire on Jul 8, 1845.
Wm Pelham, Surveyor Genr'l of Arkansas, is re-appointed to the same ofc from Jul 10, when his present commission will expire.
Appointments to take effect Jun 29, when the present commissions expire.
Stanly G Trott, Postmaster at New London, Conn, in place of J H Turner.
Geo M Horton, Postmaster at Geneva, N Y, in place of Jas Rees.
John K Wright, Postmaster at Reading, Pa, in place of Chas Troxell.
Richd H Stanton, Postmaster at Maysville, Ky, in place of Jas W Coburn.

Hon Killian K Van Rensselaer died at his residence in Albany on Wed last, aged 82. He was a member of Congress for 6 years from the Albany district, from 1805 to 1811.

Being in Havana in 1835, I went to see the spot which contains the mortal remains of Christopher Columbus. These remains are placed in the wall of the Cathedral Church of Havana, on the west side of the grand altar. Columbus died at Valladolid, 1506, aged 70 years. In 1513 his remains were removed to Seville; in 1536 they were transported to the city of St Domingo; & in Jan, 1796, they were taken by a Spanish squadron to Havana, & placed in the Cathedral. A white marble tablet has been set into the wall to designate the spot which contains the relic. On the tablet is a likeness of Columbus, in profile; with the following inscription:
"O! restos e y magen del grande Colon!
Mil siglos durad gu___edos en la Orna,
Y en la remembranza de nuestra Nacion.
Fcit Habana, 1832."
Translation given by an ofcr of the U S Navy, then in Havana:
"O rest the image of the great Columbus!
May it endure a thousand ages, guarded in this Urn,
And in the remembrance of our Nation."

I hereby notify the public that Mrs A C Loring, late Milliner, of this city, broke into my premises, lately occupied by her, [on Pa ave,] on Jun 21, before daylight, & took a quality of goods, which were in the possession of Jas A Ratcliffe & Thos Donaldson, bailiffs, taken for rent due in arrears to me. –J P Pepper

Pursuant to an order of the Lord Chancellor, any person claiming to be the heir at law & next of kin, or entitled under the statute of Distributions [in case he were now dead intestate] to share in the estate of John McDougle, formerly of Lloyd's Coffee House, in London, underwriter, but now of Dunston Lodge Asylum, near Newcastle upon Tyne, in Northumberland Co, [being of unsound mind,] are to come in] prove their kindred before the Comer's in Lunacy, at their ofc, 45 Lincoln's Inn Fields, in Middlesex Co, Eng, or in default thereof they will be excluded the benefit of the said order. Apr 25, 1845.
–Ed Winslow

Orphans Court of Wash Co, D C. Letters of administration on the personal estate of Janette Taylor, late of the State of N Y, dec'd. –Geo L Lowden, Charleston, S C

$100 reward for runaway mulatto woman Judy Burryl, 25 or 26 years old.
–Wm Major, jr, living near Culpeper Court-house, Va.

Mrd: on Jun 19, by Rev Mr Pyne, Mr John J Williams to Miss Eliza Maria Coburn, d/o John Coburn, all of Wash City.

Mrd: on Jun 18, at Charleston, S C, by Rev D Gilman, Col W Gates, U S Army, to Miss Harriet Louisa, d/o Mr Artemus Carter, of Portland, Maine.

Died: on Sat, at the residence of her father, Mrs Clementina Mary Davidson, w/o Lt Delozier Davidson, U S Army, & d/o the Hon T Hartley Crawford, aged 19 years. The death of this young wife will bring the deepest affliction to the bosom of a young & absent husband, as it has done to her family.

Died: on May 26, at Pittsfield, Mass, Hon Jonathan Allen, in his 76th year, leaving an interesting family & a large circle of warmly attached friends to lament their heavy bereavement. The subject of this notice was a s/o the late Rev Thos Allen, first Pastor of the Congregational Church in that town, & father of Maj Geo Allen, of the U S Army. Amongst the very first of those who imported into the U S Merino sheep from Spain, he lived not only to see the vast benefits but to witness his native mountains & valleys white with the descendants of the original flocks.

Died: on May 25, in Waterford, N Y, of an organic affection of the heart, Mrs Ann Eliza Ellis, w/o the Hon Chessenden Ellis, [late member of Congress from the Saratoga district,] in her 43rd year. Mrs Ellis had spent the past winter in Washington with her husband, where her health began to decline. The day after her return, she was prostrated by a debility from which she could not be raised.

The apothecary store of Mr John F Callan was robbed on Fri night.

Criminal Court-Wash: 1-Augustus Lucas found guilty of rescuing a prisoner at Gtwn: fined $50 & to be imprisoned 20 days, & to give security for his good behavior & to keep the peace for 2 years in the sum of $300. 2-Alex'r Dubant found guilty with a riot at the circus in 1842. He was then tried & convicted of an assault & battery on Julia Fleet, a free colored woman.

Patent for sale. Interest of the late Geo S Wharton, of Pa, in the Circular Bullet Mould patented by Danl Pettibone, & recorded anew Mar 2, 1849. -R W Dyer & Co, aucts

TUE JUN 24, 1845
Information wanted of Saml Sheckels, a pensioner of the U S for a wound received in the Florida war. If alive, he will please make known his present residence. If dead, any information concerning him will be thankfully received. A letter from him dated Somerville, Tenn, 1837, was the last that was heard of him. -Bradley & Thruston

House for rent: 2 story brick house, with finished basement, on E st, between 9th & 10th sts. –R S Patterson, corner 9th & Pa ave.

Store & house for rent: store now occupied by Mr Wm Whitney, on Pa ave, between 6th & 7th sts, as a Shoe Store, & the House above, occupied by Mrs Harrison as a Boarding House, will be rented separately or together. Possession given Aug 6. –A Green, Auct

For rent: commodious house on Capitol Hill, N J ave, now in the occupancy of Mrs Cummin. Possession will be given at any required time. For further particulars inquire of Mrs Cummin, or G Coombe.

Foreign Item: Mme de St Elme, authoress of the Memoires d'une Contemporaine, whose death was announced, was born at the Hague, of Protestant parents. After the death of her first husband, she married the Count de St Elme, one of Napoleon's ofcrs.

Old Point Hotel, at **Fortress Monroe**, Va, a celebrated Watering Place, was opened for visiters on Jun 10. Charges will be moderate. –Jas S French

Trustee's sale of valuable real estate: decree of the Circuit Court of Wash Co, D C: sale on Jul 15th next: lot 1 in subdivision 12, on High st, having a 10 feet allet on its north boundary, which separates it from Mr E M Mosher's dwlg. –Jno Marbury, Trustee -E S Wright, Auct

A Va farm, **Jaqueline Hall**, at Auction: on Jul 28, 1845, at Orange Court-house. The Farm is between the Court-house & Barboursville: consists of 364 acres with a handsome & very convenient 2 story mansion, all in good repair: with all necessary out-bldgs. The society is as good as any in Va. Address, Liberty Mills, Orange Co, Va, post paid. –John J Ambler

The post ofc at Rome, Geo, has been robbed lately & suspicion fell upon the postmaster at that place, Doct Patterson. The Coosa River Journal says, on Jun 1, the ofc of Col T C Hackett, which adjoins that of the postmaster, was entered & a small trunk containing $1,060 & valuable papers was taken out. The postmaster is in prison-he denies his guilt. His appointment is said to be among the first of the new Administration. –Balt Sun

Order of the Orphan's Court of Montg Co, Pa: notice is given to John Maguire, eldest son & heir at law of Archibald Maguire, late of the township of Whitemarsh, in said county, dec'd, & to all others whom it may concern, that an inquest will be held at the late dwlg-house of the dec'd, on Aug 5, for the purpose of making partition of the real estate of the dec'd to & among his children & legal reps, if the same can be done without prejudice to or spoiling of the whole. –Jas Wells, Sheriff: Norristown, Pa, Jun 22, 1845.

Criminal Court-Wash: 1-Yesterday John Davis, free negro, was found guilty of manslaughter in the murder of Chas Carroll, a colored boy, apprentice to Mr John Y Young, of Gtwn. A fight had taken place between Carroll & a colored man, Jerry Grandison, in the course of which Davis, taking sides with Grandison, struck Carroll a severe blow on the head with a stick, which caused his death in 3 days. [Jul 2nd newspaper: 1-Davis sentenced to 6 years of hard labor in the penitentiary.]

Mrd: on Jun 19, by Rev John Davis, Wm Berry to Rachel Rigsby, all of Wash.

Mrd: on May 29 last, at *Rose Valley*, by Rev Mr Callahan, Dr Jas Nelson, of Westmoreland Co, Va, to Miss Jane Cecelia, d/o the late Jas Kirk, of St Mary's Co, Md.

Mrd: on Jun 4, by Rev Geo Adie, Asher W Gray, of Leesburg, to Martha L, 2nd d/o Horace Luckett, Dresden, Loudoun Co, Va.

Died: on Jun 5, at his residence, in Prince Wm Co, Va, Jas M Tyler, in his 40th year.

Mammoth Drawings of the Drunkard's Stomach are being exhibited at the Club-house every Tue at 8 o'clock. The drinkers of intoxicating liquors are particularly invited to come & see what liquor does for them. –Geo Savage, Pres F V T S

WED JUN 25, 1845
On Wed last 2 ladies were driven to King's wharf, in Bath, Maine, & as the horse was turning, a rein caught in one of the shafts & the horse backed into the river. Miss Ryan escaped, but Mrs Nichols, w/o J H Nichols, sunk with the cab, & was drowned. The body was subsequently recovered.

John C Smith, Pres of the Ins Co of North America, & for many years a highly respected merchant of Phil, died suddenly on Sunday morning.

U S District Court, sitting at Balt, on Mon last, Judge Heath passed sentence upon Jason L Pendleton, captain, & Robt Baker, first mate, of the brig **Montevideo**, who were convicted of a misdemeanor, as ofcrs of said brig, in being concerned in the slave trade on the coast of Africa. In consideration of his already having been in jail for 6 months, the jury's recommendation to mercy, the Court would only adjudge Pendleton to be confined in the common jail for 12 months & to pay a fine of $1,000, & to remain imprisoned until the fine & costs be paid. The mate, Baker, was sentenced to 6 months in prison, & fined $500, & to remain in prison until the fine & costs be paid. -Clipper

Garrick Sharpe, the printer employed at the U S Gaz ofc, who had his leg fractured by an accident at the Camden race course, was on Sun forced to undergo amputation of the limb. He is now doing very well.

Nashville Whig of Tue: murder in Tippah Co, Miss, of Beverley Adcock & wife & 2 children as they were emigrating to Missouri, by a man named A J McCannon, who committed the murder for no other apparent object than plunder.

The new Court Martial, convened to try Capt Voorhees on another charge, assembled yesterday at Coleman's Hotel: following ofcrs constitute the present Court:

Cmdor John Downes, Pres	Capt David Geisinger
Capt Stephen Cassin	Capt Chas S McCauley
Capt Henry E Ballard	Capt Silas H Stringham
Capt Lawrence Kearney	Capt French Forrest
Capt Geo Washington Stover	B F Hallet, Judge Advocate

Circuit Court of Wash Co, D C: in Chancery. The Pres & Dirs of the Bank of Wash, vs Clifton Wharton, Washington Wharton, Franklin Wharton, Wm Lewis Wharton, Alfred Wharton, Clifton Wharton, & Henry Wharton, heirs-at-law of Franklin Wharton, late of Wash City, dec'd, & Saml Miller & Edw W Duvall, adms of said Franklin Wharton, dec'd. The intestate died indebted to the complnts in divers sums of money, & did not leave sufficient personal estate to pay his debts; that certain real estate, whereof the said intestate died seised, was by that Court decreed to be sold for the payment of said intestate's debts, on a bill filed in this Court by John H Ladd, Jos B Ladd, & John Wheelwright against said dfndnts; that a greater part of said real estate was sold under said decree, but did not produce a sum sufficient to pay said debts, & that the residue remaining unpaid is insufficient to supply the deficiency; that, beside the property so decreed to be sold, the intestate died seised of an estate in fee simple of part of lot 6 in square 802 in Wash City, with a valuable wharf & warehouses thereon. The object of the bill is to obtain a decree for the sale of said part of lot 6 in square 102 with appurtenances, for the payment of intestate's debts. The dfndnts reside out of the jurisdiction of this Court. Same are to answer this bill by the fourth Mon in Nov next. W Brent, Clerk -J Hellen, for cmplnts

Died: on Tue, after an illness of a few hours, Rose Alber, d/o Edw Simms, aged 2½ years. Her funeral will take place today at 4 o'clock.

For rent: new brick house on I st, between, 9th & 10th sts. Inquire on the premises or of Wm D Acken.

G L Gillchrest has opened a Family Grocery Store on 7th st, next door to McKelden's Bakery. His stock is fresh & mostly from N Y.

Wash Corp: 1-Nominations from the Mayor:
*C H Wiltberger, for ofc of Register — *Jos H Bradley, Atty
*Jos Radcliff, First Clerk — *Jacob Kleiber, Messenger
*Wm E Howard, 2nd Clerk — Richd Butt, Intendant of the Asylum
Wm P Elliot, Surveyor
City Com'rs:
Saml Drury — Thos J Barret-Acting
John Sessford — John Magar-Acting
Wm Cooper, jr — Ignatuis Howe-Acting
Police Constables:
Fielder B Poston — Jas M Wright
John Waters — Thos J Barret
John W Dexter — John Magar
Richd R Burr — Ignatius Howe
Com'rs of the Centre Market:
*J H Goddard — *Walter Clarke
*Wm Orme
Clerks of Market:
*Wm Serrin — *H B Robertson
*John Waters — *Peter Little
Inspectors & Measurers of Lumber:
*David A Gardiner — *Benj Bean
*Wm G Deale — *Wm Douglass
*John W Ferguson — *John G Robinson
Wood Corders & Coal Measuring:
*Jas Gaither — *Nathl Plant
*John P Hilton — *Richd Wimsatt
*Saml Kilman — *John B Ferguson
Gaugers & Inspectors:
*Nicholas Callan — *Florian Hitz
Measurers of Grain, etc:
*Jas Gaither — *John B Ferguson

Com'r of West Burial Ground:
*Saml Drury
*O S Wilson
Com'rs of East Burial Ground:
*Jas Marshall
*John P Ingle
Scavengers:
*G T McGlue
*Luke Richardson
*Jas Hollidge
*Wm Johnson
*Launcelot Wilson
*Confirmed

*J C Harkness
*Guy Graham, Sexton

*Thos J Barret, Sexton

*Jas Hollidge
*John Cox
*Osborn Turner
*John Cox, jr

2-Ptn from G C Grammer was referred. 3-Ptn from Jas Pillings & others: referred to the Cmte on Improvements. 4-Ptn from Alfred Prather: to lie on the table. 5-Ptn of John N Ashton, praying remission of a fine: referred to the Cmte of Claims. 6-Ptn of Wm A Scott, praying remission of a fine: not sworn in as required by the rules of the Board. [*Partial list of confirmed can be found in the Jul 9th newspaper.]

THU JUN 26, 1845

Rock Creek Church: a rural excursion, a shady retreat, & cool refreshements. The Ladies belong in the Church will prepare a supply of Ices. Lemonade, Tea, Coffee, Sandwiches & Cakes in the grove near the church, on Jul 3 & Jul 4. The proceeds to be appropriated to the wants of the Church.

Mr Wetton, stage agent at Lowell, Mass, lost his life on Sat in attempting to arrest the horses attached to a stage at the door which had got frightened by thunder. The horses threw him down, & the coach ran over & killed him instantly.

For rent: 2 large new frame houses on 23rd st, near I st west. Inquire of Saml Drury, with whom the keys are left, or to the propriety, Jos Libbey, Water st, Gtwn.

The Balt American states that a valuable present has recently been made to the Md Historical Society by R Gilmor, of that city, consisting of 3 large folio volumes, elegantly bound in Russia, containing a series of documents, relative to the history of Md, & the wars on the northern frontier conducted by Sir Wm Johnson. The papers were chiefly taken from those which fell into his possession among the documents presented by the late Horatio Ridout, son of the Sec of Govn'r Sharp.

McCurry, the murderer of Paul Roux, who is to be executed at Balt tomorrow, is said to have made a full confession of his crime. [Jun 28th newspaper: Henry McCurry was executed yesterday. There were probably not less than 15 or 20 thousand persons, men, women, & children, there to witness the event.]

The Rochester Democrat announces the death of Mr Levi P Dickinson, a highly respectable merchant of that city, who had passed the winter at the South in the hope of recovering his health, but who died soon after reaching home on Thu last. He was a young gentleman generally & greatly beloved.

The case of the U S vs Wm B Vaux, indicted for robbing the mail at Westfield a year ago last Dec, was tried before the U S Court at Canandaigua a few days ago. The prisoner, an old offender, was found guilty, & sentenced to Auburn State Prison for the term of 6 years.

Mrd: at London, England, in the District Church of St Paul's, Knightsbridge, the Hon Henry Geo Howard, y/s/o the Earl of Carlisle, to Miss Mary Wellesley McTavish, d/o Mr & Mrs John McTavish, of Balt, Md. [No date-current item.]

Died: on Jun 18, Festus Dickinson, Couseller at Law, of the Bowling Green, Caroline Co, Va. The severity of this private & public bereavement is seen in the inconsolable grief of his family, relatives, & friends.

Died: on Jun 22, at the residence of Dr Phillipps, in Bristol, Pa, John Tyler, s/o Robt Tyler & Priscilla E Tyler, aged 11 months & 15 days.

For rent: new 2½ story frame house on 9th st, near M. Inquire of J E Kendall, City Post Ofc, or Jas G Marr, Grocery Store, s w corner of 9th & M sts.

For rent: commodious Frame House, on 7th st, near Md ave. Inquire at the house, or at the Hardware store of R M Waring, corner of 6th & Pa ave.

Boarding: 4 excellent rooms, at his residence, 7th & D sts. –John Macleod

FRI JUN 27, 1845
The faithful Chief Clerk of the Second Auditor's ofc, Jas Eakin, has been dismissed from ofc. Those who are accustomed to settle their accounts during the last 40 years at this ofc, will be surprised to learn of this.

$20 reward: strayed or stolen from the commons adjoining the Gov't stables, a bright sorrel horse. $5 reward if delivered to me at the above stables; if stolen, $20 for the conviction of the thief. –John Lee

St Louis Republican: the Osage Indians have among them about 20 white children, whom they purchased from the Comanches, by whom they were stolen from their parents in Texas & New Mexico. The Osages will only sell them for horses or goods. Should not the U S ofcrs look to this, & is it not the duty of the Indian Agent in inquire into this?

Mrd: on Jun 12, at *Tuleyries*, the residence of Col Tuley, Clarke Co, Va, by Rev W G H Jones, Jos Tuley Thomas, of Phil, to Miss Belinda J Mitchell, of Va.

Died: on Jun 19, Wm Henry, s/o Wm & Ann Dodson, aged 3 years.

Criminal Court-Wash. 1- Henry Winters, negro boy, indicted for an attempt at arson: found guilty. 2-Jas Newell & Wm Hines: guilty for rioting. 3-Lewis Lee, free negro, guilty of stealing $5.25, the property of Catharine Hays. 4-Chas Roden, free negro, not guilty for stealing 2 earrings & a knife. 5-Chas Roden, free negro, found guilty for an assault & battery upon the d/o Mr H Trusmels, of Gtwn, by shooting her with a musket. [Jul 3rd newspaper: 1-Lee sentenced to 2 years in the penitentiary. 2-Roden sentenced to 2 months in jail & fined $20. 3-Winters sentenced to 4 months in jail & fined $10.]

R Estep, of the late firm of Estep & Co, informs his customers that their bills will be vendered them by Jul 1, at which time he will be pleased to receive their amounts.

SAT JUN 28, 1845

In New Orleans, on Jun 14, there was fatal affray in Philippa st, in which a young man, Robt Creswell, a clerk in a mercantile house, was stabbed so badly that he died in a short time. The deed is supposed to have been perpetrated by another clerk named Switzer, who fled. There has been an old grudge between them. On the preceding Mon an affray took place at Baton Rouge between Berry Lively & Ezekiel Furgason, which resulted in the death of Lively. Furgason made his escape.

L C Hornsby, indicted at New Orleans for the murder of D H Twogood, & convicted of manslaughter, is to be tried again.

At Berne, N Y, a few days ago, the 12 year old d/o John Banner, was hung to death by a school-house window falling on her neck. School-house windows, to prevent this recurrence, should move up & down with weights.

For rent: 3 story brick house in Smith's block, on 1st st, Gtwn. Apply to Chas Vinson. –N B Vinson

Powhatan House, Richdmond, Va. Board per day: $1.50. –Chs I Dibrell

For sale: valuable farm of Loudoun Land: I offer the whole of my landed estate, within 11 miles of Leesburg, consisting of 606 acs, divided into 2 parts; one containing 206 acs, the other contains 400 acs. The latter part has a 2 story dwlg-house, 75 feet in length, with a cellar 50 feet long. Apply to the undersigned, or in his absence to Theodore N Davisson. –T M McIlhany, Hillsborough, Loudoun Co, Va

Parlor & Chamber furniture at auction: on Jul 1, at the residence of Mrs Sweeney, on Capitol Hill, East Capitol st. –A Green, auctioneer

$100 reward for runaway negro man Jerre Hawkins, about 30 years of age. He was bought out of the late Govn'r Kent's estate, & has relations living at Mr Chas B Calvert's, near Bladensburg, & in Wash. –Jos K Roberts, near Bladensburg, PG Co, Md.

Appointments by the Pres:
Geo H Walker, Register of the Land Ofc at Milwaukie, Wisc, vice Paraclete Potter, whose commission will expire on Jul 1, 1845.
Nathan Bardin, Surveyor & Inspector of the Revenue at Bristol, R I, vice Elkanah French, whose commission will expire Jul 8, 1845.
Lycius Lyon, Surveyor Genr'l of Ohio, Indiana, & Michigan, from Jun 30, 1845, vice Wm Johnson, resigned.
Henry Hicks, Collector of the Customs for the District of Delaware, vice Arnold Naudain, whose commission will expire on Jul 1, 1845.
Robt H Merchant, Surveyor & Inspector of the revenue at Dumfries, Va, vice Geo H Cockrell, whose commission will expire Jul 8, 1845.
John B Guthrie, Surveyor & Inspector of the revenue at Pittsburg, Pa, vice Wm B Moury, removed.

Postmaster:
Wm N Friend, at Petersburg, Va, in place of John Minge, removed.
Jos M Doty, at Ogdensburg, N Y, from Jul 10 next, when the commission of the present incumbent will expire.
Whitacre O'Neal, at Steubenville, Ohio, from Jun 29, when the commission of the present incumbent will expire.
Benj F Rawls, at Columbia, S C, from Jun 29, when the commission of the present incumbent, A H Gladden, will expire.
Wm G Smith, at Macon, Ga, on Jul 1, in place of Kneeland Tyner, whose commission espires on Jun 29.
Geo Crawford, at Cincinnati Ohio, on Jul 1, in place of Wm H H Taylor, whose commission will expire on Jun 29.
J B B Hall, at Wheeling, Va, on Jul 1, in place of David Agner, whose commission expires on Jun 29.
Chambers McKibbin, at Pittsburg, Pa, on Jul 16, in place of R M Riddle, whose commission will expire on Jul 15.

Died: on Jun 27, aged 9 months, Wm Gaston, s/o Wm A & Eliz T Kennedy. His funeral will be at their residence on 6th st, between E & F sts, this morning at 9 o'clock.

Geo W Kline, of Lebanon, Pa, in a moment of mental aberration, a few days ago committed suicide by shooting himself. He was perfectly easy in his wordly affairs, & was much respected & beloved.

Totonto [U C] Examiner: Maj Chas Beale, of Woodstock, Brock District, committed suicide at the British Coffee-house in this city on Thu last. It appears that he had been taking prussic acid medicinally, & it is supposed took an extra portion, which caused his death. On a post mortem, 3 large tenpenny nails were found in his stomach.

MON JUN 30, 1845
The celebrated German author Schlegel, who died recently, left by his will his writing desk to the King of Prussia. Half his fortune goes to his wife, who lives with her father, the ecclesiastical Counselor Paulus at Heidelberg, & who quitted her husband a year after their marriage, which was celebrated in 1819.

Soda Water: F W Fuller, Druggist & Chemist, corner of Pa ave & 12th st, Wash.

$50 reward for runaway negro Roderick, 30 years of age. He has a wife in Upper Marlborough, the property of Mrs Sarah Duvall, & a free brother, Robt Dueany, living in the adjoining county, near the village of Queen Ann, with whom he is probably lurking. –Wm J Belt, living in the Forest of PG Co, Md.

We learn that a severe affliction has befallen the family of the late U S Senator N P Tallmadge, now of Wisc, in the death of a very promising son, recently a graduate of Union College, Schenectady. –Balt Amer [No other information.]

The Postmaster Genr'l has removed Mrs Karch, a widow lady, who has held the ofc of Postmistress at Lebanon, Dela, for some years past, & appointed in her place one Jos Hartman, editor of a Locofoco German newspaper. Mr Cave Johnson ought not to have done this; & as for Mr Jos Hartman, he ought to ride behind upon a pilion & "sew nether socks" all the rest of his days. –N Y Courier

A Russian, named Emerett, in 1835 visited Cincinnati a poor ragged cobbler. He went South & engaged in the manufacture of lucifer matches. He returned to Cincinnati a few days since worth $26,000.

TUE JUL 1, 1845
$100 reward for runaway negro man Hillary Beender, 40 years of age. –Edmund J Plowden, living near Chaptico, St Mary's Co, Md.

Trustee's sale of valuable property: deed of trust from Matthias Jeffers & others to me, dated Jul 25, 1842, Recorded in liber W B 96, folios 55 thru 60, of the land records of Wash Co, D C: all the west half part of lot 5 in square A in Wash City, with 2 story brick dwlg & other improvements. –John Kurtz, Trustee -R W Dyer & Co, aucts

House of Assembly of R I on Wed in relation to the ptns in favor of the liberation of Thos W Dorr. Thos W Dorr was released from prison on Fri; on which occasion, as we learn from the Providence Journal, some of his friends, who betrayed & deserted him in the hour of danger, took occasion to manifest their devotion to him by firing cannon. They formed a procession & escorted him to the house of Hezekiah Willard. This act of amnesty appears to have been the result of a compromise between the adverse parties.

Mrd: on Jun 24, at **Belair**, by Rev Mr Keech, M A Earl, of Phil, to Miss Caroline H McCormick, of Harford Co, Md.

Valuable hotel for rent: Loudoun Hotel, now occupied by Miss Janney: a large & substantial stone tavern in the town of Middleburg, Va: contains about 20 rooms. –H B Powell, Trustee under the will of the late Col Noble Beveridge.

Valuable real estate for sale: 65 acres in Wash Co, D C, 1½ miles from Wash City, formerly owned by Mr Jas Williams, adjoining the lands of Messrs Gales & Chapin, on the Bladensburg & Balt road. Improvements are a 1½ story house, well finished. Possession next fall. Apply to the subscriber, living thereon. –John A Bartruff

WED JUL 2, 1845
Among the venerables in the procession in N Y C on Tue, was the High Constable Jacob Hays, who, although in his 79th year, trudged on foot throughout the entire route. –Courier

Supreme Court of La: on Jun 21: the case of Sally Muller vs Louis Belmonti & John F Miller, called in warranty. Sally claimed to be born in Germany of German parents; of coming to this country when an infant with her parents, who died shortly after their arrival. John F Miller alleged that she was born a slave & was his property; as such he brought her up, & as such he sold her to Belmonti. The Court declared the plntf, who has been in bondage about 25 years, to be free.

Monrovia, Liberia, Africa, Apr 25, 1845. Letter from Galway Smith to John McDonogh. Opportunity by Capt Lewin of writing you: all your people are doing well: Elijah Gibson, the free colored man who came from New Orleans with his children about a year ago, begs me to give you his love, & wants to tell his friends, Mr Seymour, Mrs Eleanora Johnson & her husband, Mr John Baptist, Mr John Goff, Mr Saml Jones & his cousin Billy, to bring their friends & relations to this fine country, where they will be happy & soon be rich. P S-Tell Mr Augustin, Edward, Madam Blen, & all the colored people of New Orleans, to come to this fine country.

$50 reward for runaway negro Bill Cook, about 22 years of age. $100 reward for negro Gasaway Tailor, about 24 years of age. –Otho B Beall, near Upper Marlborough, PG Co, Md.

The remains of Gen Sentmanat, who was executed by the Mexicans for endeavoring to overthrow their dominion at Tabasco, were brought to New Orleans on Jun 20 by the schnr **Water Witch**. They were to be interred on Jun 22.

Ky Commonwealth: we understand that the Hon Henry Daniel was last week acquitted on the trial of the indictment against him in the Montgomery Circuit Court for the murder of his brother-in-law, Clifton R Thomson.

The Alabama Planter is the new weekly paper just started in Mobile by W W McGuire.

Mrd: on Sun last, in Balt City, by Rev Mr Backus, Gen John T Mason to Frances Romyn, d/o the late Wm B Magruder, of that city.

Geo Fred'k Archibald, s/o Thos Archibald, was instantly killed on Thu at the brickyard of his father, in Troy, N Y, by being caught between the frame-work of the machine for grinding clay & the sweep, to which a horse was attached.

John Wilbor, jr, of South Kingston, R I, was killed at his lumber yard at Fall river on Mon last, when 2 piles of boards suddenly fell over & crushed him to death. He was about 25 years of age, & has left a wife & family.

Criminal Court-Wash. 1-Saml Sumby, free Negro, convicted of stabbing, with intent to kill, his wife: to be imprisoned 3 years in the penitentiary. 2-Peter Dubant, convicted of a riot: fined $10. 3-Saml Adams, convicted of a riot: fined $30. 4-Jos Hilton, convicted of a riot: fined $30. 5-Hinds & Newell, convicted of a riot: fined $25 each. 6-John Sheahan, convicted of a riot on Pa ave, to be imprisoned 20 days in jail & fined $20. 7-John Barrett, convicted of same offence; same punishment. 8-Morris Holland, Wm Donovan, & Timothy Sullivan, convicted of a riot: to be imprisoned each 10 days in jail & each pay $20 fine. 9-Henry Lacy, convicted of an assault & battery: fined $20. 10-Frank Tolson, free negro, convicted of an assault & battery: fined $10. 11-Robt Tennesley, a youth, was tried on Mon on a charge of theft & found not guilty. The defence was conducted by Jas Hoban & E Swann. 12-The trial of Caleb J McNulty is fixed for Jul 7.

Wash Corp: 1-The ptn of Thos Donoho & others, asking that pipes be laid from the spring on square 377 to the centre of square 378 & the erection of a hydrant: referred to the Cmte on Improvements. 2-Ptn of E W Smallwood & 45 others, asking removing the Railroad Depot to the city boundary: referred to the Cmte on Police. 3-Ptn of Geo Humes & 132 others, asking removal of the same, to Delaware ave: referred to the Cmte on Police. 4-Ptn of R M Combs & others, for a reduction of taxes: referred to the Cmte of Ways & Means.

Wm Jackson was recently tried in Dearborn Co, Indiana, for the murder of Merritt Scroggins, & acquitted by the jury. –Balt Patriot

THU JUL 3, 1845
For rent: 2 story brick dwlg, with kitchen attached, on H, between 18th & 19th sts. Inquire of the subscriber adjoining. –David Hines, Agent To Let-new 3 story brick house on H st, between 7th & 8th sts, adjoining the residence of the Hon W J Brown.

City Court of Balt, on Mon last, the case of Martin [alias Michl] McDuffy, indicted for perjury testifying before the Insolvent Com'rs, in order to go security for a person whom he desired to petition out of jail. The penalty of the bond was $6,000, &, being sworn, he testified that he was worth some property in the city & elsewhere, which was found to be false. He was found guilty & sentenced to the penitentiary for 5 years.

Beallair at private sale: subscriber offers this desirable estate, 5 miles from Harper's Ferry, containing about 530 acs. Improvements consist of a comfortable stone dwlg house & all necessary out-bldgs. For information address the subscriber on the premises, near Halltown, Jefferson Co, Va. –Lewis W Washington

Pittsburg Post: two little girls, ages 4 & 5 years, children of Mr Albertson, of Alleghany, were drowned on Thu in crossing the Monongahela river in the ferry boat. They were sitting in a buggy, on the boat, when the horse scared at a steamboat which was passing, & backed the vehicle off into the river. Their parents were unable to rescue them. The scene on the boat was distressing in the extreme.

Appointments by the Pres: Michl Edwards, Surveyor & Inspector of the revenue at Wheeling, Va, vice Saml Atkinson, whose commission will expire Jul 22, 1845.
Postmaster:
Jacob Medary, at Columbus, Ohio, from Jul 29, in place of John G Miller, whose commission will expire on Jul 29.
Henry F Baker, at Winchester, Va, from Jul 29, in place of John Wall, whose commission will expire then.
Benj F Johnson, at Frankfort, Ky, on Jul 1, in place of Wm Hardin, resigned.
Freeman C Everts, at Toledo, Ohio, on Jul 1, in place of Andrew Palmer, resigned.
Pearson Mundy, at Watertown, N Y, on Jul 1, in place of John F Hutchinson, resigned.
Wm L'Hommedieu, at Norwich, Conn, in place of John H Townsend, removed.
Geo Sanderson, at Carlisle, Pa, in place of Wm M Porter, removed.

Alarming fire yesterday in the brick dwlg at the corner of F & 14th sts, occupied by Mrs Bihler. Mrs Bihler & a servant were awaked, & were in danger of being burnt in the fire. $4,500 were insured on Mrs Bihler's house & furniture; & $1,000 was insured on 2 adjoining burnt bldgs, owned by Mrs Webb & Mrs Balser.

Mrd: on Jul 1, by Rev Geo W Samson, Mr Benj Leddon, jr, to Miss Margaret Coates, both of Wash City.

Mrd: on Jul 7, by Rev J M Brown, Mr W Chauncey Brooks to Miss Lavinia V Brigham, d/o Mrs A Brigham, all of Kanawha Co, Va.

Mrd: on Jul 2, by Rev H Stringfellow, Jas R Smith, of Phil, to Mary Catherine White, of Wash City.

Mrd: on Tue, at *Wilson's Delight*, Montg Co, Md, by Rev Chas A Davis, Lewis Magruder, of PG Co, Md, to Susan, d/o Thos Wilson.

Died: on Jul 2, at his residence, in Wash City, of an affection of the brain, John P Latruitte, aged 60 years, leaving a wife & 4 children to mourn his loss. His funeral will be on Thu, at 10 o'clock, from his late residence, on First st, a few doors north of Pa ave.

Small but desirable farm for sale: the subscriber offers the farm upon which he resides, lying about 1¼ miles north of the Capitol, on the west side of Rock Creek Church road: tract contains about 30 acs. As this land is a part of the tract formerly belonging to Mr Jas Moore, sr, it is deemed unnecessary to describe it more particularly. –David Moore

The creditors of Wm Ogden Niles, whose claims originated prior to May 8, 1839, are to file their claims, on or before Sep 1 next; otherwise they will be excluded from any dividend on the same. –Thos G Hill, Trustee, 150 Lombard st, Balt, Md.

FRI JUL 4, 1845
Lexington [Ky] Observer of Jun 28. Mr Jacob F Todhunter, s/o Mr P E Todhunter, of Jessamine Co, was born deaf & dumb. He is now about 25 years of age, & has received a very fine education at the Deaf & Dumb Asylum at Danville. He was, these past few months, under the charge of Mr Robt T Anderson.

Valuable brick house & lot at auction: on Jul 21, lot 8 in square 533: being on D st south, near Md ave, immediately opposite the property of Lewis Machin. –A Green, auct

Awful accident at Rockport, Mass, on Thu. While blasting rocks a premature explosion took place, which caused the instant death of Mr Thos Peach. Two other persons were injured.

Rev Jas H Thornwell, Prof of the Evidences of Christianity in Columbia College, S C, was on Thu unanimously elected pastor of the Second Presbyterian church of the city of Balt, to succeed the Rev Dr Breckinridge.

Constitution of the U S: Done in Convention Sep 17, 1787. In witness whereof we have hereunto subscribed our names. Go Washington, Pres, & Deputy from Virginia.

<u>N H</u>
John Langdon
Nicholas Gilman
<u>Mass</u>
Nathl Gorham
Rufus King
<u>Conn</u>
Wm Saml Johnson
Roger Sherman
<u>N Y</u>
Alex'r Hamilton
<u>N J</u>
Wm Livingston
David Brearly
Wm Patterson
Jonathan Dayton
<u>Pa</u>
Benj Franklin
Thos Mifflin
Robt Morris
Geo Clymer
Thos Fitzsimons
Jared Ingersoll
Jas Wilson
Gouverneur Morris

<u>Dela</u>
Geo Reed
Gunning Bedford, jr
John Dickinson
Richd Bassett
Jacob Broom
<u>Md</u>
Jas McHenry
Danl of St Tho Jenifer
Danl Carroll
<u>Va</u>
John Blair
Jas Madison, jr
<u>N C</u>
Wm Blount
Richd Dobbs Spaight
Hugh Williamson
<u>S C</u>
John Rutledge
Chas C Pinckney
Chas Pinckney
Pierce Butler
<u>Ga</u>
Wm Few
Abraham Baldwin
Wm Jackson, Sec

Appointments by the Pres:
John Hoban, U S Atty for D C, from Jul 3, in place of Philip R Fendall, whose commission will expire then
Robt White, Collector of the Customs, Gtwn, D C, vice Henry Addison, whose commission will expire Jul 8, 1845
Chas Linsley, U S Atty for the district of Vt, from Jul 22, in place of Chas Davis, whose commission will expire on that day
Thos B Hahn, Postmaster at Canandaigua, N Y, in place of Jonas M Wheeler, who commission expired on Jun 29
Jas Fischer, Surveyor & Inspector of the Revenue at Pawtucket, R I, vice Peleg Aborn, whose commission will expire Jul 22, 1845

Vanilla Beans. 4 lbs fresh Vanilla Beans, just received & for sale by-Chas Stott.

Board of Naval Ofcrs convened at the Naval Asylum, in Phil, on Jun 2, for examination of the Midshipmen entitled to promotion, finished their labors on Jul 1. 46 presented themselves, & the following 37 passed. Their names are alphabetically arranged, but not according to rank.

Henry Ashton
Henry N T Arnold
W W Bassett
Chas H Baldwin
Jas D Bullock
Julius S Bohrer
E Ross Colhoun
Richd M Cuyler
Jos S Day
Alex J Dallas, jr
Reginald Fairfax
Aaron K Hughes
John R Hynson
Jas Higgins
Wm E Hopkins
Wm R Low
Jas M Ladd
Julian Mayers
Tenant McLanahan

Somerville Nicholson
Thos Pattison
Alex C Rhind
Wm W Roberts
Abner Read
Beverly Randolph
Geo M Ransom
R Clay Rodgers
Henry K Stevens
Robt W Shufeldt
John Stuart
Wm F Spicer
Paul Shirley
Chas C Simms
Maurice Simons
Edw C Stiles
Wm A Webb
Jas Wilcoxson

The corner-stone of the new Presbyterian Church intended for the Rev Septimus Tuston & his congregation was laid on Wed. The site is upon 8th st, between H & I sts; & the stone was laid by the Grand Lodge of Masons of D C, Dr W B Magruder, Grand Master, officiating. The opening prayer was made by Rev Mr Samson, & other ceremonies were performed by Rev H Smith, Rev Mr Eggleston, of Balt, & Rev Dr Muller, of Wash City. Rev Septimus Tuston delivered an impressive address.

Some villain or villains, on Wed, broke into Mr Munk's locksmith shop, on D st. They failed to get into the front shop, but a lighted lamp was left in the back shop, which set fire to a wooden box. The shop narrowly escaped destruction.

Mrd: on Jun 17, in Galveston, by Rev John Brands, the Hon Wm B Ochiltree, Sec of the Treas of the Republic of Texas, to Mrs Maria Louisa Reid, d/o Mr Nathan Smith, formerly a resident of Wash City.

Died: on Thu, in Wash City, Mrs Mehetabel M Samson, w/o Rev A Samson, aged 64 years & 8 months. Her funeral will be on Sat, at 10 o'clock, from the residence of her son, Rev G W Samson, on 9th st, between H & I sts.

Boarding: Mrs M Crim, 108 Walnut st, between 4th & 5th sts, Phil, having connected with her old establishment the commodious house adjoining. Warm & cold baths are attached to the house.

For rent: pleasant residence near the Episcopal Church, [the Rev Mr Bean's.] Also, a 3 story house on Capitol Hill, next door to Col Gardiner's. Inquire at Mr Jas Owner's, Va ave, or of Mr Nixon, Pa ave

MON JUL 7, 1845
Gen J B Dawson, Member of Congress from the Third District of Louisiana, expired at his residence near St Francisville on Jun 26. He was a man of generous impulses & chivalrous bearing, universally popular in Feliciana, & his loss is much regretted by all who knew him. –Picayune

Navy Dept, Jul 2, 1845. The Board, composed of Cmdors Geo C Read, Thos Ap C Jones, & M C Perry, & Capts E A F Lavalette & Isaac Mayo, recently convened at Phil for the examination of midshipmen, adjourned on Jul 1. The following if the list of midshipmen, in order of rank assigned them by the Board:

Edmund R Colhoun, of Pa
Jas D Bullock, of Georgia
Chas H Baldwin, of N Y
Robt W Shufeldt, of N Y
Beverley Randolph, of Va
Henry K Stevens, of S C
Abner Read, of Ohio
Alex'r C Rhind, of N Y
Richd M Cuyler, of Georgia
Alex'r J Dallas, of Pa
Geo M Ranson, of N Y
Wm F Spicer, of N Y
Edw C Stiles, of Pa
Wm W Roberts, of N C
Reginald Fairfax, of Va
Somerville Nicholson, of N Y
Wm W Webb, of Va
John Stuart, of Michigan
Jos S Day, of Vt
Maurice Simons, of S C
Jas Wilcoxson, of N Y
Wm E Hopkins, of Va
Paul Shirley, of Ky
Chas C Simms, of Va
Wm R Low, of N H
Robt C Rodgers, of Delaware
Henry N T Arnold, of N Y
Jas M Ladd, of Maine
John R Hynson, of Md
Tenant McLanahan, of Md
Thos Pattison, of N Y
Henry Ashton, of Md
Wesley B Bassett, of Conn
Julian Myers, of Georgia
Jas Higgins, of N Y
Julius S Bohrer, of D C

Midshipman A K Hughes, who was unable, from ill health, to appear for examination with his date in 1844, & been passed by the present Board, has been assigned rank at the foot of the passed midshipmen of May 20, 1844.

Jonathan F Woodside, late U S Charge d'Affaires at Copenhagen, died very suddenly at his residence in Chillicothe, Ohio, on the *2nd ult, aged 50 years. [*Print difficult to read- the 2nd appears correct.]

Alexandria Gaz: Philip R Fendall, the U S Atty for D C, removed on the expiration of his commission, on Jul 3. His talents were constantly employed for right purposes, & directed honorably & uprightly. His successor is Mr Hoban, a gentleman of the Washington bar, of talents & experience in his profession, who we wish every happiness in his new & honorable position.

The U S ship **Princeton**, Cmdor Stockton, arrived at Annapolis on Jul 3 from Galveston, Texas, after the short passage of 9 days.

Official: Dept of State, Jul 3, 1845. Information received from the U S Consulat Fayal of the death of Horace Barnes, of Plymouth, Litchfield Co, Conn, who died in the hospital of that island on Apr 12 last. A sealed bag, containing his effects, will be sent to the collector of Boston by the brig **Harbringer**.

Mrd: on Thu, in Wash City, by Rev Geo W Samson, Mr Jos B Pleasants, of Richmond, Va, to Miss Rosa A Smoot, of Wash City.

Mrd: on Jun 20, in Wilmington, Dela, by Rev P Riley, Wm Chase Barney, of Balt, Md, to Eliz, d/o Chief Justice Booth, of Delaware.

Died: on Jun 28, at the family residence on the Patapsco, near Ellicott's Mills, Mrs Eliza C Gray, w/o Edw Gray, in her 58th year.

Died: on Jun 27, at the residence of her son, Edw Stabler, Sandy Spring, Montg Co, Md, Deborah Stabler, in her 82nd year.

Died: on Jul 5, Jacob Walter Ker, s/o Saml W & Mgt W Handy, aged 9 years & 9 months.

Died: on Jul 5, Gertrude Newton, infant d/o Chas W & Gertrude Pettit, aged 9 months.

Warsaw [Illinois] Signal of Jun 25: letter from the editor, dated at Carthage, on Jun 24, from which it appears that Dr Marshall, of the latter place, has been killed by M D Deming, the Sheriff of the county, in a scuffle. The difficulty grew out of a purchase of a tract of land at a tax sale. Deming is in custody.

A Card. The subscriber will be absent nearly 2 months from home, & returns his most sincere thanks to the fire companies, & the good citizens of Wash, for their kind exertions in saving from destruction his store-house whilst his stabling was wrapped in flames.
–Edw Simms

Notice. The subscriber will be absent from the city about 3 weeks, & requests those who have business with him to call on N Callan, F st, near 15th. –Thos W Pairo

Solebury township, Bucks Co, Pa, on Fri last: Mr Amos Pearson, with his son & a colored man, were unloading hay in his barn when by some means the hay & straw in the other part of the barn were set on fire. They escaped, but the son was much burnt. 2 other sons of Mr Pearson escaped, but one of the brothers perished in the flames & the other is so much injured, his life is despaired of. The dwlg & out-bldgs burnt to the ground, leaving no bldg on the premises.

U S Circuit Court in Boston, before Judge Story, on Sat, Moses Guild was discharged under the bankrupt law. The objecting creditor alleged that he had fraudulently concealed property received by him since his failure in 1836 to the amount of more than $70,000. The jury, on the appeal, found for Mr Guild, & his discharge was accordingly ordered.

Providence Journal: on Sat, at Woonsocket Falls, in firing cannon in commemoration of the release of Thos W Dorr, by mismanagement in loading, a discharge took place before the ramrod was withdrawn, by which 2 men were seriously injured-one of them, a young man by the name of Briggs, died on Sat.

Jul 4th celebration: in the open space between the Pres' Mansion & the canal were 6,000 or 8,000 persons, congregated to witness a display of fireworks. Near the close of the display, as the pyrotechnist was about firing a stand of 12 rockets, it fell, so as to direct the missiles, not upwards, but ranging a few feet above the crowd on the flat, though precisely in the right direction to strike among those on the surrounding ground. Mr Jas Knowles, a worthy citizen of Wash, was transfixed through the heart by one, & was instantly killed. His poor wife hung on his arm at the time. Others were less injured. The wife of the unfortunate man was borne past us on the arms of 2 gentlemen, & her heartrending shrieks are yet ringing in our ears. Mr Wm Magee had his arm dreadfully lacerated, with 2 children in his arms, which were also injured. The colored woman, Georgianna Ferguson, was not injured & is likely to survive. Mr Magee, who is attended by Dr Dawes, is in a critical situation. Christian Manuyette, a member of the Morgan Riflemen, whose arm was shatterd by the premature discharge of a cannon at Gtwn, had his arm amputated about the elbow by Dr Lieberman. One of his eyes was nearly blown out. An appeal to the Humane: Poor Knowles, the young, amiable, & respectable mechanic, born in Gtwn, & raised as an apprentice in Wash, who was killed on Fri, has left a wife & child, who are suddenly reduced to the most distressing proverty by the death of their dearest friend. Who will step forward to their relief? Apply to Mr Gardner, with whom he served his apprenticeship, & has since worked for the last 2 years, 2 doors from Douglass' green-house, near the Treasury

For rent: 2 story brick house in a very pleasant part of the city. Rent low. Inquire at the auction store of Mr Wm Marshall, Pa ave, between 9th & 10th sts.

To let, from Aug 1 next: 4 story bldg, on Pa ave, between 3rd & 4th sts, now occupied by the Miss Polks. –Jno A Donohoo

For rent: store #11, Pa ave, next to A Lee's Lottery Ofc. Apply to J P Pepper.

For rent: valuable boarding-house in the village of Bladensburg, PG Co, Md, lately occupied by Mr Truman Belt. Apply to Harriet Ross, residing near the village.

By virtue of 4 writs of fieri facias, issued by Thos C Donn, J P for Wash Co, D C, at the suits of Ward & Burch, Jno France, S J Ober, & Darius Clagett, against the good & chattels, lands & tenements, rights & credits of Mathias Jeffries: sale of one piano forte & 1 bureau; in front of the Centre Market House, in Wash City.
–Richd I A Culverwell, Constable

TUE JUL 8, 1845.
By virtue of 3 writs of fieri facias issued by Thos C Donn, J P for Wash Co, D C, at the suits of Henry Lee & Jas Esprey, trading under the firm of Lee & Espey: against the goods & chattels, lands & tenements, of John H Smith: seized-1 sideboard, one lot of china & glass ware, mantal clock, 3 mahg tables, 6 cane seat chairs, one doz yellow chairs, andirons, tea-board, 2 small waiters, pine candle stand, ingrain carpet, rag carpeting, milk pans, plough, cupboard, old-fashioned bureau, washstand, basket carriage, 3 feather beds, child's chair, 4 cows & one calf, lot of tools, etc. Sale on Jul 12, on the premises of said John H Smith, on square 939, corner of 9th & C sts.
–Richd I A Culverwell, Constable

Farmers' & Mechanics' Bank: trustees have this day declared a dividend of 2½ % out of the profits for the last 6 months, which will be paid to Stockholders or their legal reps on demand. –Alex Suter, cashier

Wash, Jul 2. Dissolution of the copartnership heretofore existing between the subscribers, under the firm of Jno T Ryon & Brother, was dissolved, by mutual consent, on Jul 1. John T Ryon will continue the business for his own account.
–Jno T Ryon, Richd J Ryon

Mr Chas A Higgins, formerly a resident of Macon, Ga, & lately for a few weeks a broker in Wall st, N Y, was arrested on Wed, charged with having passed off his own notes, with the name of Mr Lambert Suydam forged on them as endorser, to the amount of about $10,000.

$10 reward for strayed or stolen Roan Horse, on Jul 4, from a farm bordering on the n e boundary of Wash City. -Edmund Brooke, jr

Election in Indiana takes place in Aug. The rival candidates for Congress throughout the State are:

Whigs	Locos
G P R Wilson	*Robt D Owen
Roger Martin	Thos J Henley
Jos C Eggleston	*Thos Smith
*Caleb B Smith	M H Hull-[Abolition]
Jas Foley, Wm Herrod	Wm W Wick
Eli P Farmer	*John W Davis
E W McGaughey	*Jos A Wright
Albert L Holmes	*John Pettit
*Saml C Sample	C W Cathcart
L G Thompson	*Andrew Kennedy

* Old members

Boston, Jun 27, 1845. To Nathan Lord, D D, President of Dartmouth College: For the purpose of giving further aid to the institution at this time, I send you enclosed my check on the Columbian Bank for $9,000. This sum, with the donation of $1,000 sent to you in Aug, 1843, making $10,000, I wish may be invested for the establishment of a Professorship of Natural Philosophy at Dartmouth College. -Saml Appleton

Circuit Court of Wash Co, D C: to divide the real estate in said county of which Julius Forrest died seized. Chas G Wilcox & Anna M S Wilcox his wife, vs Alex'r M Marbury & Sophia Marbury his wife, & David C Forrest. Com'rs appointed have divided the said real estate into 2 equal parts: Division #1, consisting of lots 13 & 14 & part of lot 15 in square 254, allot to Anna M S Wilcox, the cmplnt. Division #2, consisting of part of lot 9 in square 225, which was conveyed by Brent, Monroe, & Forrest to Wm Thornton, by deed dated Apr 3, 1807, & recorded in liber S, #18, at folio 96, & by the said Wm Thornton to Julius Forrest, by deed dated Dec 17, 1826, & recorded in liber A M, #37, at page 468; & also lot 10, in square 656, & lot 11 in square 661, all lying in Wash City, D C, which said division #2 they, pursuant to the said commission, allot to David C Forrest, the dfndnt. -W Brent, clk

To whom it may concern. The undersigned, having administered on the estate of Chas Byrnes, who died in Oct, 1842, in Clearspring, Wash Co, Md, would hereby inform the legal heirs of said estate, whose residences are unknown to him, that he has funds in his possession, being the proceeds of said estate, which will be paid to them on their appearing & substantiating their claims. -John G Stone, Adm-Clearwater

Mrd: on Jul 3, at *Ever-May*, Gtwn, D C, by Rev R T Berry, Dr A D Woodruff, of Haddonfield, N J, to Ann G, d/o the late Lewis Grant Davidson, of the former place.

Mrd: on Jun 19, by Rev Mr Wheat, Thos W Preston, of St Louis, Mo, to Mary, eldest d/o David Craighead, of Nashville, Tenn.

Died: on Jun 16 last, at *Afton*, the residence of her father, near Culpeper court-house, Va, Sally Peyton Maury, w/o Fayette Maury, & d/o Saml K Bradford, after an illness of 3 months. She was a communicant of the Protestant Episcopal church. She died in her 27th year, leaving her husband & 3 young children to lament their bereavement.

Died: on Jun 12, at the residence of his father, in Taycheedah, Wisconsin Territory, after a severe illness of 3 weeks, Mr Wm Davies, 2nd s/o Hon N P Tallmadge, aged 20 years.

Only 6½ cents for an Elegant Fan at the Cheap Lace Store, Pa ave, between 10th & 11th sts. –J T & C King's

House & lot for sale: on C st, in reservation #10, in Wash City, recently occupied by Rev Chas Rich. Apply to Mrs Brereton, on the premises.

Household & kitchen furniture at auction: on Jul 10, at the residence of Capt Crabb, on B st, near N J ave, on Capitol Hill, to satisfy rent due the Hon Judge Thruston. –W Green, auctioneer

WED JUL 9, 1845
Having inserted, at the request of Wm Chase Barney, an annunciation of his having been married to Miss Booth, of Delaware, we insert the following denial of that marriage, which reached our hands yesterday. Newcastle, Jul 4, 1845. The U S Gaz of this date has been shown to me, in which a notice is inserted that my dght, Eliz Booth, was married on Jun 20 last to a certain Wm Chase Barney. I, as the father of the young lady, beg you to contradict this matter, & also to request the editors of other papers in which the notice may be inserted also to contradict it. I am, very respectfully, your obedient servant, Jas Booth.

Extract of a letter of Goethe to Schiller, dated Stuttgart, Aug 30, 1797. I found Prof Mueller at the portrait of Graff, which Graff painted himself. He is also busy with the death of a general, & that an American, a young man, who fell at Bunker Hill. The picture is by an American, Trumbull, & has merits of the artist & faults of the amateur. The merits are very characteristic & admirably handled portrait faces; the faults disproportions between the different bodies & between their parts. The engraving makes a very good whole, & is in its parts excellently done.

Horses for sale: just received at the Farmers' Hotel, 8th & D sts, 26 head of superior Horses. Apply to Owen Connolly, Proprietor.

Appointments by the Pres:
Wm Nichols, Collector of the Customs at Newburyport, Mass, vice Henry W Kinsman, whose commission will expire Jul 10, 1845.
Gideon S Bailey, U S Marshal for the Territory of Iowa, in the place of Isaac Leffler, removed.
Benj B French, a Justice of the Peace in Wash Co, D C; his former commission having expired on Jul 2.
Enoch Fowler, Naval Ofcr for the district of Newburyport, Mass, vice Thos M Clark, whose commission will expire Jul 10, 1845.
Geo F Worth, Postmaster at Nantucket, Mass, vice S H Jenks, whose commission has expired.
John Forsyth, Postmaster at Columbus, Ga, from Jul 22, vice G W E Bedell, whose commission will expire on that day.
Thos Shepherd, Postmaster at Northampton, Mass, vice Amos H Bullen, removed.

The Hon Louis McLane, the newly appointed Minister to London, will leave the U S by the steam-packet on Jul 16.

Columbia House, Chestnut st, between 6th & 7th sts, Phil: taken over the house formerly known as the Marshall House. –Bagley, Mackenzie & Co. –Jas Bagley, late of Jones' Hotel; H C Mackenzie, formerly of the Washington House; & Peter L Ferguson.

Peter Martin, a young man, arrested on Sat, charged of feloniously entering the dwlg-house of Mr Jacob S Van Tyne, on Jul 4, & stealing wearing apparel & a box containing a small amount of money. We learn that the accused was yesterday admitted to bail.

Wash Corp: 1-Act for the relief of A C Kidwell: referred to Cmte on Improvements. 2-Act for relief of John Donovan: laid on the table. 3-Relief of Robt Cohen: same.

THU JUL 10, 1845
Note: copy of the Defence of Philip F Voorhees, a Capt in the U S Navy, prepared & delivered by his counsel, Richd S Coxe, on Jun 21, 1848, before a Grand Naval Court Martial, upon charges preferred against him by the Sec of the Navy, relative to the rencontre between the U S frig **Congress** & the Argentine squadron, etc, during the past year, in the river La Plate. [8½ columns] [Aug 15th newspaper: Navy Dept, Aug 12, 1845. On Jun 24 last, you were found guilty of every specification & guilty of the charge, & sentenced to be reprimanded in the general order by the Sec of the Navy & to be suspended for 3 years from that date. You are therefore suspended from command. This letter of reprimand will be published in a general order.
–Geo Bancroft: Sec of the Navy.]

$2 reward for lost, on Jul 5, 2 sheets of paper, rolled together, being designs for a 2 story cottage. Leave at the carpenters' shop of Messrs Edmondson & Henning, on the alley between 8th & 9th & H & I sts.

Chancery Notice. Whereas Eliz Hutchison, late of Fairfax Co, Va, departed this life about 1833, leaving to Jane Morgan, Conny Hogin, alias Hagan & Jas Ashford, her 2 full sisters & half brother, a legacy of $500, to be divided among them according to law, contingent upon the event of a certain Mary Ward's dying without 'marrying & having issue," the testatrix directing the interest of said legacy to be paid to the said Mary Ward during her natural life, & the principal also should she marry & have issue. Also, a legacy of $50 to the children of Joel Fagg, of $50 to Jos Fagg, & $100 to Sabert Ashford, & whereas the said legatees are supposed not to be residents of the State of Va, & it is not known, so far as it can be as yet ascertained, whether they or any of them are dead or living; & whereas, by an order of the Circuit Superior Court of Law & Chancery for Loudoun Co, Va, aforesaid, in the case of Athelia Hutchison against the excs of Chas Lewis dec'd, who was exc of said Eliz Hutchison, & others, made at the Apr term, 1845, I, the Com'r of said Court, are to notify the said legatees of said Eliz Hutchison, dec'd, their or either of their descendants, if any of them be now living, to present their claims, with the evidence thereof, before me, at my ofc in Leesburg, Loudoun Co, Va,; to furnish me with the best evidence they can, whether they or any of them, their or either of their descendants, were living or not at the period of the death of said testatrix, & whether they, be now living, together with their places of residence & years of majority.
–F W Luckett, Com'r

Wash Co, D C: Wm A Woodall, of said county, brought before me an estray bay mare. She had on a good saddle & halter, nearly new, maker's name Wm M Brown, of Alexandria, D C. –B K Morsell, J P

David Levy & J D Westcott, [Dem] were on Jul 1 elected by the Legislature of the State of Florida to be Senators of the U S from that State.

Richmond Whig: proprietorship of that paper is Mr Ro H Gallaher, under date of May 1, 1845, formerly owned by Alex'r Moseley. The editorial dept is still to be under the control of John Hampden Pleasants, aided from time to time by his fomer associate John S Gallaher.

Chas B Calvert, of PG Co, has been suggested in the Balt Patriot as a suitable person to represent the first Congressional District of Md.

The Hon Reverdy Johnson, [U S Senator of Md,] with Mrs Johnson, will sail for England in the New York packet of Jul 10, & will return early in the fall.

The gov't paper states that Gansevoort Melville received the appointment of Sec of Legation to London.

N P Willis-by a letter, dated Jun 14, from London, in the N Y Mirror, we regret to learn that this gentleman was quite ill with a brain fever. He was terribly sick on board the steamer during the whole of the passage.

Died: last evening, Lewis G Gassaway, a Clerk in the Genr'l Land Ofc, in his 35th year. His funeral will take place this evening, at 5 o'clock, from his late residence on the corner of 20th st & N Y ave.

Died: last evening, Mrs Mary E Berret, consort of the late Jos H Berret, of Md, in her 56th year. Her funeral solemnities will take place at the residence of her son, John J Berret, on 6th st, this evening, at 5:30 p m.

Died: on Jun 10, at Fairfield, Caroline Co, Va, Mrs Mildred W Thornton, relict of the late John Thornton, aged 68 years.

Last week, in Boston, Chas H Flint, about 8 years old, was playing in a room with his mother & a young man named Brewer; he took up a pistol & snapped it at them. Mr Brewer took it out of his hand & snapped it quickly, when it went off, hitting the boy in the temple. He died on Jun 27. -Ledger

FRI JUL 11, 1845
The w/o Mr F L Morris, of New Orleans, who had just returned from attending her husband, who died at the bay of St Louis, Mo, found that her house & all had been consumed by fire, & her 3 children & mother-in-law thrown pennyless upon the world. A Subscription was about to be made for her by the citizens.

Wm Wyman, formerly Pres of the Phoenix Bank at Charlestown, Mass, had been again arraigned before the Court at Concord, under a new indictment of the grand jury, & has given bonds in the sum of $50,000 for his appearance for trial at Lowell, in Oct. [Sep 15th newspaper: trial terminated at Concord, Mass, Sep 10: verdict of not guilty.]

An entire Mastondon Skeleton has just been constructed in Newark, N J, from the bones recently found in a small pond on the top of a mountain near Hackettstown, Warren, Co, N J. I measures 22 feet in length, about 11 feet hight, & 16 feet in girth.

Violent thunderstorn on Thu last at Portland, Maine. Lightning struck the house of Mr Warren Cox, killed his wife instantly, & prostrating the whole family, but doing them no serious injury. The houses of Judge Emery & Mr Nathan Woodbury were also struck, but no serious damage done.

Extraordinary Fecundity. The w/o Mr Elijah Marshall, of Silver Lake township, in this county, was delivered on Jun 22 of 4 living children at birth. They are all dghts, doing well at the last accounts. Although but 26 years of age, Mrs Marshall has already been the mother of 11 children. –Montorse [Pa] Democrat

From a correspondent at Ilchester Mills, near Ellicott's, in Howard District, that on Jul 4, some boys commenced throwing stones, which ended in a stone, thrown by a s/o Franklin Ijams, striking Thos Ellett on the head causing his death the next day. They were both about 20 years of age. -Sun

On returning from a race at the Beacon course, at N Y, Mr John Van Sicklen, on Mon, accidentally drove his wagon against a pile of bricks in the street, and was thrown from the wagon and broke his neck. He died yesterday. He was an estimable man in private life, attached to a large circle of friends. -News

The late Thos Hood-from the July Knickerbocker. Weighed down with disease himself, plying his laborious task as an author with incessant devotion, earning his bread, he found time, to give the world substantial proof that the pain & sorrow under which he struggles had chastened his spirit & enlarged his heart to a sympathy with the sufferings of others. Mr Hood's disease we infer to have been consumption. He died at age 47, & has left behind a widow with a small family, who, to the honor of Sir Robt Peel be it said, have been endowed with a liberal life-pension from the English Gov't.

From the New Haven Herald: Thos G Woodward has retired the editorship of that paper, which will be conducted by his former partner, J B Carrington. The Herald is a good Whig paper. –N Y Tribune

W H Polk, brother of the President, arrived at Liverpool on Jun 12, in the packet ship **Yorkshire**, Capt Bailey, from N Y, on his way to Naples.

Geo Harrison, a respectable citizen of Phil, died on Jul 6, at his residence in Chestnut st, at age 84 years. For 20 years he filled the ofc of Navy Agent of the port of Phil, having been appointed by Pres Madison.

The U S schnr **Flirt**, Lt Commanding Watson, went to sea on Thu with the following passengers to Carthagena: the Hon B A Bidlack, Charge d'Affaires to New Granada, Dr Edw Berandon, Sec of Legation, Nicholas Quifaro, Interpreter, & Mr Wallace Bidlack.

In the reigh of James I, Hugh Myddleton, an ingenious man, undertook to bring a river of pure water above 38 miles out of its natural course for the supply of London. At the present time the New River, which was the work of Myddleton, supplies 13 millions of gallons of water every day.

Dr Saml Ackerly died on his farm at Staten Island, on Sunday last. He was a native of N Y C, & inherited from his father ample pecuniary means, & received the best medical education, under the superintendence of his brother-in-law, the late Dr Saml L Mitchell. During the war between this country & Great Britain he was hospital surgeon.

Gen Garrigues D Flaugeac, a member of the Legislature of Louisiana for several years past, & a captain of artillery at the battle of New Orleans under Gen Jackson, died at his residence in Opelousas on Jun 26, aged 68 years.

Mr John H Crawford was attacked by a large alligator a short time since while hauling a seine in the Savannah, Ogechee & Altamaha canal, about 5 miles from this city. He was seized by the thigh, & broke his hold by forcing the alligator to relax his hold, by putting his fingers in the agressor's eyes. The wounds received although severe, are not considered dangerous. –Savannah Sentinel

Criminal Court-Wash: The U S vs Caleb J McNulty: indictments for embezzlement of Public Moneys while Clerk of the House of Reps; cases called today: 6 indictments, founded upon distinct transactions, alleging acts of embezzlement, contrary to the act of Congress, approved Aug 13, 1841. Each indictment contains 3 counts. The first, embezzlement of so much money, by converting it to his own use; 2nd, by investing it in property & merchandise; 3rd, by loaning it to certain individuals, to whom the prosecution undertakes to trace it. [Jul 12th newspaper: Chauncey Bestor, cashier of the Patriotic Bank was examined.]

Died: on Jul 3, after a short illness, at his residence, Orange Court-house, Mr Robt Taylor, sr, in his 82nd year. He was greatly distinguished for probity of character, & highly esteemed by a numerous circle of relatives & friends.

Died: on Jun 22, in Cincinnati, of consumption, Alden Spooner Merrifield, aged 33 years, a native of Windsor, Vt, late one of the editors of the New Orleans Tropic.

Died: on Jul 5, Geo Mark, s/o Geo W & Mary Phelps.

Masonic: meeting of Lebanon Lodge $7, at their Hall, Pa ave & 12th st, Fri. –D O Hare, Sec

SAT JUL 12, 1845
War Dept, Jun 25, 1845. The <u>Franking Privilege</u> of this Dept & all its Bureaus will cease after Jul 30th. All ofcrs of the Army, & others subject to the orders of this Dept, will be required to observe the same economy in their public correspondence, & to keep & certify their postage accounts in duplicate, as required in all other public disbursements, in relation to postage accounts. –G Bancroft, Acting Sec of War

Army General Order: War Dept, Adj Gen Ofc, Wash, Jul 7, 1845. Gen Orders #31. Promotions & appointments in the Army, made by the Pres of the U S since the promulgation of general orders #9, Mar 31, 1845.

1-Promotions

1st Regt of Dragoons:

1st Lt Wm Eustis to be Captain Mar 17, 1845, vice Terrett, dec'd.
2nd Lt Jas H Carleton, to be 1st Lt, Mar 17, 1845, vice Eustis, promoted.
Brevet 2nd Lt Rufus Ingallas, of the 2nd dragoons, to be 2nd Lt, Mar 17, 1845, vice Carleton, promoted, instead of Mar 31, vice Rust, resigned, as heretofore announced.
Brevet 2nd Lt Cave J Couts, of the 2nd dragoons, to be 2nd Lt, Mar 31, 1845, vice Rust, resigned.

3rd Regt of Artl:

Brevet 2nd Lt Lucien Looser, of the 2nd artillery, to be 2nd Lt, May 31, 1845, vice A P Stewart, resigned.

5th Regt of Infty:

1st Lt Wm Chapman, to be Captain, Jun 8, 1845, vice Johnston, dec'd.
2nd Lt John A Whitall, to be 1st Lt, Jun 8, 1845, vice Chapman, promoted.
Brevet 2nd Lt Martimer Rosecrants, to be 2nd Lt, Jun 8, 1845, vice Whitall, promoted.

7th Regt of Infty:

1st Lt Danl P Whiting, to be Captain, Apr 18, 1845, vice Davis, dismissed.
2nd Lt Henry Little, to be 1st Lt, Apr 18, 1845, vice Whiting, promoted.
Brevet 2nd Lt John M Jones, of the 5th Infty, to be 2nd Lt, Apr 18, 1845, vice Little, promoted.

8th Regt of Infty:

2nd Lt Calvin Hetzel, to be 1st Lt, May 30, 1845, vice Johnson, cashiered.
Brevet 2nd Lt Jas O Handy, of the 5th Infty, to be 2nd Lt, May 30, 1845, vice Hetzel, promoted.
Brevet 2nd Lt Jacob J Booker, of the 1st Infty, to be 2nd Lt, Jun 1, 1845, vice Hanson, resigned.

II-Appointments

Corps of Engineers:

1-Cadet Wm H C Whiting, to be 2nd Lt, Jul 1, 1845.

Ordnance Dept

Stevens T Mason, of Va, to be military storekeeper, May 15, 1845.

III-The following named Cadets, graduated of the Military Academy, are attached to the army as supernumerary ofcrs, with the brevet of 2nd Lt, in conformity with the 4th section of the act of Apr 29, 1811; to take rank from Jul 1, 1845:

Brevet 2nd Lts attached to the Corps of Engineers.

2-Cadet Edw B Hunt
3-Cadet Louis Hebert

Brevet 2nd Lts attached to the Corps of Topographical Engineers.

4-Cadet Wm F Smith
5-Cadet Thos J Wood

Brevet 2nd Lts attached to the Ordnance Dept.
6-Cadet Thos G Rhett
7-Cadet Chas P Stone
Brevet 2nd Lts attached to the Dragoon Arm.

Company	Regiment
22-Cadet B W Armstrong	G-1st dragoons
23-Cadet Wm T Allen	F-2nd dragoons
27-Cadet John W Davidson	K-1st dragoons
29-Cadet Jas M Hawes	G-2nd dragoons
30-Cadet Newton C Givens	D-1st dragoons
31-Cadet Richd C W Radford	H-1st dragoons
32-Cadet Deloss B Sackett	E-2nd dragoons
39-Cadet Jos McElvain	I-1st dragoons

Brevet 2nd Lts attached to the Artillery Arm.

8-Cadet Fitz-John Porter	D-4th Artl
9-Cadet Josiah H Carlisle	E-2nd Artl
10-Cadet Geo Edwards	G-2nd Artl
11-Cadet Henry Coppee	B-2nd Artl
12-Cadet Francis Collins	A-4th Artl
13-Cadet Jos F Farry	G-4th Artl
14-Cadet Louis D Welch	H-3rd Artl
15-Cadet Geo P Andrews	E-3rd Artl
16-Cadet Thos B J Weld	E-1st Artl

Brevet 2nd Lts attached to the Infantry Arm.

17-Cadet John P Hatch	A-3rd Infty
18-Cadet John A Richey	I-4th Infty
19-Cadet Henry Merrill	F-5th Infty
20-Cadet Patrick A Farrelly	H-4th Infty
21-Cadet Abram B Lincoln	A-1st Infty
24-Cadet Jas G S Snelling	I-8th Infty
25-Cadet Edmund K Smith	H-5th Infty
26-Cadet Thos J Montgomery	H-8th Infty
28-Cadet Jas N Ward	F-6th Infty
33-Cadet Barnard E Bee	B-3rd Infty
34-Cadet Wm Rhea	E-6th Infty
35-Cadet Gordon Granger	F-2nd Infty
36-Cadet Henry B Clitz	A-7th Infty
37-Cadet Wm H Wood	H-7th Infty
38-Cadet David A Russell	B-1st Infty
40-Cadet Thos G Pitcher	A-5th Infty
41-Cadet Wm L Crittenden	K-5th Infty

The foregoing assignments to regts & companies will be regarded as a temporary arrangement, necessary for the convenience of the service. Vacancies will be filled according to seniority in the particular arm, in conformity with the established rule.

IV-Casualties

Disbanded

Under the 4th section of the act of Congress entitled "An act respecting the organization of the army, & for other purposes," approved Aug 23, 1842, the ofc of one inspector genr'l being abolished, the Pres directs, pursuant thereto, that Col Sylvester Churchill, the junior inspector general, be honorably discharged from the army.

Resignations-3:

Capt Carlos A Waite, of the 2nd Infty, as assistant quartermaster, [only,] May 8, 1845.
2nd Lt Grafton D Hanson, 8th Infty, Jun 1, 1845.
2nd Lt Alex'r P Stewart, 3rd Artl, May 31, 1845.

Deaths-3:

Capt Burdett A Terrett, 1st Dragoons, at **Fort Scott**, Mo, Mar 17, 1845.
Capt Alex'r Johnston, 5th Infty, at Pittsburg, Pa, Jun 8, 1845.
Military Storekeeper Marcus C Buck, ordnance dept, at Wash Arsenal, D C, May 7, 1845.

Dismissed-1:

Capt John P Davis, 7th Infty, assist quartermaster, Apr 8, 1845.

Cashiered-1:

1st Lt Thos S J Johnson, 8th Infty, May 30, 1845.

V-The ofcrs promoted & appointed will join their proper stations & companies without delay; those on detached service, or acting under special instructions, will report, by letter, to the commanding ofcrs of their respective regts.

VI-The usual leave of absence, allowed by the regulations is hereby granted to the several graduates; at the expiration of which, [Sep 30,] they will join their proper station & companies.

VII-Acceptances, or non-acceptances of appointments, will be reported to the Adj Gen of the Army; &, in case of acceptance, the birth-place of the person appointed will be stated. By order: R Jones, Adj Gen

Memorandum-The name of Jos Smith, a brevet 2nd Lt in the 5th Regt of Infty, having been changed, by the Legislature of the State of N H to Jos Parker Smith, he will hereafter be known & recognized in the army accordingly.

Dr Lindsly has removed to the late residence of Dr Sewall, corner of 4½ & C sts.

War Dept, Jun 25, 1845. The Franking Privilege of this Dept & all its Bureaus will cease after Jul 30th. All ofcrs of the Army, & others subject to the orders of this Dept, will be required to observe the same economy in their public correspondence, & to keep & certify their postage accounts in duplicate, as required in all other public disbursements, in relation to postage accounts. –G Bancroft, Acting Sec of War

Notice: By virtue of an order of distrain from Nicholas L Queen, adm of Nelly G Queen, dec'd, against the goods & chattels of Jehiel Brooks, for rent due in arrears to the estate of said Nelly G Queen, dec'd, I have seized the following property, viz: negroes Isaac, about 46 years; Augustus, about 11 years; Jas, about 10 years; Wm Thomas, about 8 years; Jacob, about 6 years; Henry, about 6 years; Leonard, about 25 years; negresses Maria, aged about 36 years; Mary Jane, about 4 years; Eliza, about 6 months; Eveline, about 30 years; Sarah Ann, about 3 years; Mary Virginia, about 2 years, all slaves for life; & negro Basil, about 39 years, slave for about 5 years; 6 milch cows, 3 heifers, 2 yearlings, 3 bay horses, 2 sows, & 7 pigs. Public sale of said property on the premises of said Jehiel Brooks, in Wash Co, on Jul 19, 1845. Terms cash: Michl Reardon, Bailiff

Steamboat disaster: late fatal explosion of the boilers of the steamer **Marquette**: John Hazard, 2nd engineer, [who was killed,] was a joiner or a carpenter by trade, & could not obtain a certificate from the Board of Engineers in Mobile, as an engineer, although applied for. Saml Hays, the chief engineer, [who is under arrest,] did obtain a certificate from the Board as a 2nd class engineer on May 10 last, having been several times before rejected as an engineer in any capacity. The 3rd engineer [also killed] was a negro- perfectly irresponsible. List of the killed & wounded by the above explosion: Died in the Charity Hospital: Bernard, 14 years old, from, Indiana; John Hazard, 2nd engineer of Marquette, from Providence, R I; Wm Ramsey, carpenter, from Franklin Co, Ala; John Melton, from Indiana; 2 children, named Troy, one 5 years of age & the other 6 years of age; Hannibal, Capt Turpin's slave, [3rd engineer] & 2 white men, whose names are unknown; Wm B Daniels, carpenter, from Boston, Mass. Neal Harkins, steamboat hand, from Ireland; & John L Dearman, a farmer, from Tenn, are very severely wounded. Daniels is not expected to live. Andrew Troy, carpenter, from Ireland, & his wife Mary Ann,] the parents of the 2 children, who are dead,] & John W Lee, a flatboat man, from the State of N Y, are expected to recover; Francois La Glaise & Christopher Gueydan, both from France, were but slightly injured. At Dr Stone's Hospital there are 2 persons, Ostrander, 1st pilot of the **Marquette**, & _____ Hathaway, clerk of the steamer **Belle Poule**, who was a passenger: Theodore Ostrander is wounded mortally. Hathaway's arm is shattered & his face bruised a good deal-wounds not considered dangerous. The Coroner has, in addition to those above mentioned as dead, held inquests on Saml Hays, 1st engineer of the **Marquette**; Jas Coleman, a deck hand, & 3 white men, whose names are unknown. It is almost certain, that Wm Hartwell, a passenger, of Alabama, formerly clerk of the steamboat **Bourbon**; Griffith Armstrong, steward of the boat, & Mrs Decker & her child, are lost. [Jul 15th newspaper: Examination of Capt E A Turpin, the master, & of Saml Hayes, the 1st engineer of the steamboat **Marquette**; testimony of Theodore Ostrander, the pilot. The Court decided to send the case before the grand jury of the Criminal Court. Bail was reduced to $2,000] [Dec 22nd newspaper: Capt Turpin failed to appear in the U S District Court at New Orleans & answer the charge of manslaughter preferred against him. His bonds for $5,000 were therefore forfeited. The engineer of the boat appeared, but his trial was postponed.]

J A Ratcliff's Shaving & Hair Dressing Establishment, on D st, next door to Beker's Tavern, between 7th & 8th sts, Wash, D C.

For sale: a Hack, in excellent order, for sale cheap, for cash. Inquire at Julius A Peters' Wine store, Pa ave, near 10th st. Also, a brown Mare, used to hacking or carting, & warranted sound.

Died: on Jul 11, in Wash City, George W Phillips, s/o Geo Phillips, dec'd, aged 22 years. His funeral will take place on Sun next, from the residence of his mother, on East Capitol st, Capitol Hill.

The U S store-ship **Erie** sailed from N Y on Tue for the Pacific. List of her ofcrs:
Chas C Turner, Commanding　　　　　Chas Murray, Purser
Edw Higgins, Acting Master　　　　　　A A Henderson, Assist Surgeon
Passed Midshipmen:
N B Harrison　　　　　　　　　　　　Jas D Bulloch
Chas W Hays
John H Poor, jr, Captain's Clerk
Passengers:
J McClelland, Passed Assist Surgeon　　Dr W D Jamison, of Balt

The copartnership under the firm of Farquhar & Morgan is this day dissolved by mutual consent. -Thos C Farquhar, Thos P Morgan. The business will be conducted hereafter, at the old stand, by Thos P Morgan.

MON JUL 14, 1845
The Hon Wm Hughlette, formerly a Senator from Talbot Co, Md, has accepted the post of Collector for Talbot.

Mr Henry M Payne who was recently shot at by robbers in Wash City, was [he says] waylaid & attacked by 3 robbers on Wed, near Oxford, Mass, where he resides. He exchanged shots with them & they ran away. –N Y Courier

The Boston papers announce the death of the Hon Danl Waldo, a highly respectable citizen of Worcester, Mass. He had attended to his business as usual on Tue, & the next morning he was found dead in his bed.

A week since, Mr Knight Armstrong, of Burrillville, R I, drank some rum which had been poisioned. Suspicion rested on Mr Danl Cooper, his near neighbor & brother-in-law. On Wed, Mr Cooper went into his barn & hung himself. He left a paper protesting his innocence & made arrangements for his own funeral. -Prov Journal

A Monument is shortly to be erected near that of Kosciusko, at West Point, to the memory of the gallant Major Dade.

At Syracuse, on Jul 4, the d/o John Spencer, was killed almost instantly, by the discharge of a cannon. The accident occurred at a picnic party.

The late Geo Harrison, of Phil, lately died at his residence in Phil, in his 84th year. Born in the city of Phil, he always dwelt there. He was selected by the Navy Dept to fill a general agency at that port, which he continued for many years. In 1809, the ofc of permanent Navy Agent was created by law, & that post was at once offered to him by Pres Madison. He filled it for more than 20 years. –U S Gaz

Edw Comens, about 6 years of age, drowned in Genesee Valley Canal, Rochester, Tue.

Chas Roberts, who resided in Arch st, Phil, was found dead in his bed, evidently without a struggle, probably of an apoplectic attack. –U S Gaz

Mr Gilbert Coutant died this morning, having numbered his four score years. He has filled many offices, both in the religious denomination of which he has been a member for 56 years & in the civil depts of N Y C & State. –Com Adv

The Kennebec [Me] Journal says that on Jul 3, Miss Patty Crommett, respectable milliner of Augusta, was put into a mesmeric sleep by Dr Josiah Dean, of Bangor, when a tumer, weighing 2 pounds & 6 ounces, was taken out by Dr H H Hill. She was wholly insensible & knew nothing of what had been passing. In attandance were Dr Issachar Snell, Dr Cyrus Briggs, Dr Lott Myrick, & Mr Nichols, a student in medicine, of Augusta & Dr John Hubbard, of Hallowell. There were also present, as assistants & spectators, Rev Mr Burgess, Jas L Child, & Mrs Hannah Smith, of Augusta.

Cold blooded murder a few days ago, at Greenville, S C: Deter Wells shot a young man named Robt Headden, who survived only a few hours. Wells was arrested & committed to prison.

Valuable residence for sale: on Jul 24, in front of the premises-the large & convenient brick House, containing 6 lots, in square 764, being near the residence of Danl Carroll, of Duddington. But a short walk from the Capitol or Navy Yard. -R W Dyer & Co, aucts

Jas Stimpson, of Balt City, praying for the extension of a patent granted to him for "wrought iron railroad plates for streets," for 7 years from the expiration of said patent, which takes place on Aug 23, 1845; also, for an extension of the patent to the same for "turning short curves on railways," for 7 years from the expiration which takes place on Aug 30, 1845. –H H Sylvester, Acting Com'r of Patents

Petition of Wm Carlock, of N Y C, for extension of a patent granted to him for "an improvement in the manufacture of stocks for the neck," for 7 years from expiration of said patent, which takes place on Aug 9, 1845. –H H Sylvester, Acting Com'r of Patents

Boxes New Cheese received per schnrs **Frank & Victory**, & for sale: W H Tenney, s e corner of Bridge & High sts, Gtwn.

Valuable lot at auction: on Jul 15, lot #_, fronting 66 feet on Prospect st, belonging to the estate of the late Wm M Worthington. -Edw S Wright, auctioneer [Note: lot number was blank.]

$50 reward for runaway: my negro boy Williamson Dobson, about 18 years of age. He has a brother called Griffin, belonging to Cmdor Jones, where he said on the road he was going. –Cyrus C Marsteller, Haymarket, Prince Wm Co, Va

Outrageous attack near the Eastern Branch: Mr Albert B Berry, of PG Co, was returning in his buggy from this city to his home last Thu evening, & he was attacked by 2 men & wounded severely, leaving him in a dangerous condition. On Fri warrants were issued on the affidavit of the brother of Mr Berry, requiring the arrest of Saml & Thos Hays, on suspicion of committing this assault. They were held in custody to bail in the sum of $500 each; whereupon Levi Hays, a brother of the accused, sworn that he was worth $1,000 free of all debts, was accepted as security, & the prisoners were discharged from custody.

John Hines was attacked near the West Market last Thu, by 2 young men, one of whom fired a pistol at Mr Hines & lodged a ball in his arm, which was extracted by Dr J F May. [Jul 18th newspaper: correction: It was not Mr John Hines, but Mr Wm Hines who was wounded in the manner above described.]

A few days ago, Mr Geo W Phillips fell from the upper part of a bldg now being erected on East Capitol st. The injuries he sustained caused his death, we are sorry to learn, on Friday.

Obit-died: on Jul 2, in Wash City, aged 20 years, 11 months & 8 days, Danl Paradise. His surviving relatives & friends grieve at his loss.

John B Boone has opened a wood yard at the corner of 9th st & the canal. He respectfully solicits a share of public patronage.

For rent: commodious brick dwlg-house on Pa ave, near the Navy Hospital. For terms, apply to Wm Easby, or Thos Plumsill, agent. Also for rent: dwlg-house near the West Market, next door to Mr Richd Ricketts, & a few doors from Mr Bender's. Apply to Geo Fletcher, or to Thos Plumsill, agent.

Died: in Fairfax Co, Va, Julius, infant s/o Thos W Dickins. [No date-current item.]

Sale of very superior household furniture at auction: on Jul 28, at the large boarding house of Miss Polk, on Pa ave, between 3rd & 4½ sts. –Boteler, Donn & Co, Auctioneers

TUE JUL 15, 1845
Rev Danl B Woods' Seminary for Young Ladies, 225 Spruce st, below 8th, Phil, will re-open on Sep 1.

Watches & jewelry at auction: a large lot belonging to the estate of the late J P Latruitte, dec'd. –A Green, auctioneer

Public sale of the Eutaw House Hotel, corner of Balt & Eutaw sts, fronting 112 feet on Balt st & 186 feet on Eutaw st to an alley: house is 5 stories in height, covered with slate. This bldg was erected in 1835 expressly for a hotel. It is completely furnished.
–Jacob Albert, Robt A Taylor, Saml Jones, jr, Trustees

Wakefield for sale: about 1,320 acres on the Potomac river: with an overseer's house, granary, & all the outhouses necessary for the use of the farm. The estate is bounded on 3 sides by Bridge creek, the river, & Pope's creek. It is the birthplace of Washington. With the estate I wish to dispose of from 18 to 20 likely negroes, consisting of a fair proportion of men, women, boys, & children. Apply at the ofc of the Balt American.

Mrd: on the 8th Sunday after Trinity, at Rock Creek Rectory, by Rev W A Harris, Fred'k Anderson to Eliz Grimes.

Public sale: by virtue of a decree of the Circuit Superior Court of Loudoun Co, pronounced Apr 22, 1845, in the case of Lowe vs Miller, I shall sell at public auction, at the tavern of Elijah Peacock, on Leesburg & Gtwn Turnpike Rd, on Aug 2, a steam-engine of 10 horse power, with 2 large boilers, in good condition, in use but a few years. –R H Summers, Com'r

Farm for sale: desirous of removing to the South, I will sell the farm on which I reside, being part of a tract called *Clover Farms*, containing by plat 189 acs; farm is about 5 miles from Bladensburg, & about 1 mile from the Balt & Wash Railroad at Scaggs' Crossing. All persons wishing to view the land will call on Mr John B Beall or the subscriber. –John E Beall

Letters remaining in the Post Ofc, Wash City, Jul 15, 1845.
Argais, P A	Alexander, L Gibson	Arnold, Henry
Anderson, Wm J	Arvin, Geo H	Alerson, Miss Evel'e
Acosta, Col Joaquin	Anderson, Mrs L B	Alvey, Miss Eliza'h

Arnold, Mr
Armstead, Joh
Ball, Mrs F
Bonds, Levi
Brent, Wm L
Brandt, Henry
Brown, John E
Brown, John-2
Boyd, J Granville S
Brook, Gideon
Banks, J
Bayne, Mrs Matilda
Bull, Jas H
Ball, Mrs Mary Ann
Barry, Mrs Eliza
Berry, A B
Bolend, Miss Marcia
Burneston, Wm J
Butler, Wm
Brackenridge, Mrs E
Bleeker, Lt W W
Bradley, Gen Wm
Burnett, Miss C
Baker, Mrs Ellen
Barrett, Mrs Eliz'h
Breamen, W J
Bishop, John
Bartow, Dr E H
Butterworth, J F
Brannan, John
Bevan, J A-3
Bowen, Thos H
Butler, Capt P M
Baker, Miss C H
Braxton, Richd
Cherry, Geo W
Cox, Wm
Cook, Wm
Clark, Wm
Chase, Mrs Catherine
Crooks, Alex'r
Cree, Jas
Clark, Oswald B

Cummin, Mrs M A B
Corwin, Thos
Clampit, Wm
Conly, John
Colemen, Charlotte
Catlett, John Tabb
Chambers, John-2
Calvert, Geo
Corrigan, Michl
Cassedy, Mrs Mgt
Chapman, David
Conclean, John
Custis, Wm H
Clarvoe, John H
Chamblin, Henry
Campbell, Mrs M A
Cochran, S
Crockett, Col G S
Colemen, Robt P
Campbell, Alex'r
Currie, W C
Collins, Capt C C
Cornish, Wm
Copeland, Thos
Dix, Miss Phoebe
Dawes, Isaac
Dodge, J
Day, Mrs Louisa
Douglass, Malcolm
Duncan, PdMid J M
Dorrand, Rev G W
Donaldson, Robt B
Davis, A C, U S N
Dillingham, Paul
Dickinson, T D
Deneal, Kindlaw
Dixon, Mrs Mary
Duncan, Mrs S
Darragh, C
DuPontarie, H
Derringer, B M-2
Ford, Mrs Maria
Ford, J H

France, J H
Fulton, Thos H
Freeman, Mrs M
Fletcher, Miss E Z
Fleming, Archibald
Fenner, Wm
Fithian, Wm
Glenn, Jos B
Glenn, Mrs Eliz
Graeve, Ludwig
Green, Geo
Griffin, Ellen
Goldsborough, C
Goodrick, F S
Galoway, Francis A
Gorman, Peter
Gilbert, M
Griggsby, Miss E
Giddings, Sam S
Grammer, F A
Garrett, Alex'r
Goodlow, Dan R
Grayson, Lt J C
Gover, Miss Sally
Graham, Maj J D-3
Haines, Col E S
Hall, Miss Ann
Hughes, Thos
Hall, Levi A
Horn, Michl
Hill, Wm B
Hill, Mrs Ann
Hill, Chas-2
Hall, Maj Wm M
Hussey, Mr
Hungerford, O
Herrick, Joshua
Hanson, Mrs Elea'r
Hanson, Andrew
Howard, Miss Sarah
Hoffman, Otto
Hilton, Mrs Susan
Humphrey, H B

Hamill, Saml R	Lewis, Mid R F	McArann, Miss E E
Harrison, Almon	Lakin, Miss Winifred	Naile, Purser T B
Hanson, Miss R D	Lemon, Chas	O'Brien, Wm
Hanscom, Alfred H-2	Lester, C Edw	Orton, Ray S
Hernandez, Gen J M	Lewis, Miss Eliz	Palm, Wm
Handley, Miss M I	Lewis, Mrs Carter	Price, W F
Hutchins, S P-2	Loomis, S L	Pickett, Jas
Holmead, John	Mackey, Owen	Philips, H Robt
Henderson, Mrs A	Myers, Chas	Powell, Miss Louisa
Harris, Capt Arnold	Martin, Isabella	Palmer, Richd
Harris, Warner	Marks, Jos	Polkinghorn, Alfred
Houston, Gen Sam of Texas	Mountz, Geo W	Pierson, John
	Masa, jr, A	Parker, Henry
Hynson, J Ringgold-2	Mountz, Mrs Sarah	Perry, Com M C
Hanson, Lt C	Morse, John B	Parsons, Maj John-2
Iardella, John	Mott, Jordan L	Packard, Timothy
Isherwood, Robt	Moore, Mrs Cerusa	Parker, Wm
Island, Eliza	March, C C	Hamilton, Mrs
Jones, Dangerfield	Masterson, Wm W-2	Potter, Dr
James, Israel E	Mandlebaum, S E	Pickerell, Ignatius I
Israel, Miss Mary J	Massoletti, J R-2	Packard, Prof
Johnston, Andrew	Manning, Mrs C R	Quantrill, Maj Thos
Jamaison, Harriet	Maddox, Lt W A T	Quimby, Thos R
Johnson, G W	Mullin, Mrs Nancy	Rice, Geo W-3
Jewitt, Mrs M A	Mason, Miss Serena	Ross, Mrs Mary
Johnson, Mrs S	Mitchell, Kirk P	Roche, R J
Jacobs, Miss M B	Matthews, Rev J D	Rhodes, Mrs Eliz
John, Gopher, Ind Interpreter	Morris, Thos W	Rose, Dr Wm
	Myers, Dr	Ramsay, David
King, Mrs Julia	Morton, L M	Rowand, Chas L-2
Keith, Lt L G	Minor, Miss M S	Randals, Jas
Kingsbury, Thos	Murray, Jas C	Rogers, Chas
Kanderer, C	Murdock, L H	Ridgely, Lt L C
Lee, John D	Mason & Washington, Cols	Rathbone, Maj W R
Liles, Miss Mary		Reeler, Saml
Lay, Lt G W	McLean, Wm	Ringgold, Thos
Lee, Elisha	Magill, Mrs I R	Robinson, Col Wm or Mr Custis
Lodge, Mrs Rebecca	McDevitt, Joh	
Langtry, Henry	McLanahan, PdM T	Robinson, Mr Engi'r
Lusby, Jas	McKinna, Mrs	Reader, Richd
Lewis, Mrs Jane C	McMakin, Alex J	Robinson, Miss M
Lancaster, Mrs H	McDougall, W R-2	Stelle, Thos J
Lancaster, Basil	McIntosh, Mrs E	Smith, Miss Ann

Smith, Dr Sydney
Simmes, Miss Jane
Simms, Miss Ellen
Stow, Fred'k
Smith, Dr T L, USN
Small, David
Speer, Mrs Ann
Simms, Act Mid Rd
Smith, Granville B
Smith, Miss Mary A
Straub, Jos
Salomon, Wm
Sommers, S F L
Storer, Mrs Priscilla
Seiler, F W
Stokvis, A B
Sinnott, B H
Searight, Capt J D
Simonton, Col John
Stewart, John
Sanford, J
Saxton, Mrs Arabella
Sessford, John K

Taite, Miss Ann
Tate, Janet
Tucker, Mrs S M
Tasistro, L F-3
Turner, Geo
Tattnall, E F
Thompson, Miss J
Taylor, G W
Taylor, Patrick
Tucker, Enoch G
Thompson, Mrs H M
Throckmorton, [Pd Mid] C J
Varnum, Miss Mary
Vandergrift, H W
White, Chas
Wolf, Wm
Webb, Miss Frances
Welch, Jos
West, Lt R R
Woodall, Wm
Wilcox, Maj D
Walker, Mrs E M

Warren, Owen G
Wallace, Mrs H
Williams, Edw-2
Warren, Jas B
Worrall, A
Warren, Robt S
Wharton, Robt S-2
Wharton, Dr John O
Wilson, Thos N
Warner, L T
Wilcox, Randall
Wagner, John
Wheeler, Clark
Waller, Mrs M H
Wilkins, Jas
Wallace, John F
Williams, Jas-2
Washington G C & J T Mason-2
Yell, A-2
Young, Wm
Young, Miss Camilla

The island postage on all letters intended to go by ship must be paid, otherwise they remain in this ofc. –C K Gardner, P M

Proposals for wood will be received until Sep 1, for the furnishing & delivery on the wharf at the Penitentiary, in D C. –John B Dade, Warden

WED JUL 16, 1845
More victims of the steamboat **Marquette**, none of whom are known to have survived the dreadful catastrophe of Jul 1. Their names are: Jas F Nichols, embarked for Mills' Point, Ken; S L Littrell, for Lake Providence, La; J Taylor, for Louisville, Ken; J Melton, for Louisville, Ken; D White, for Smithland; & J Woodhall, for Cincinnati.

The Chicago Journal records the death of John Sampson, a merchant of Dixon, who was drowned in attempting to swim his horse across a small river. He was of the firm of Sampson & Dixon, Ill, & belonged to the late firm of Boyer, Murray & Sampson, of N Y.

Richmond, Va: Fire on Fri destroyed the stone-mason's shop of Mr Alvery Lake, the carpenter's shop of Mr B M Morris, & several other bldgs.

Thos Dryburgh Walker left his home in N Y on Sep 25 last, & has not been heard of since. He is a Scotchman, aged about 37, & is 5 feet 8 inches high; had T D M marked in blue ink on his arm. Any information regarding him left at 119 Mulberry st will be received with thanks by his afflicted wife.

St Louis Reporter of Jul 7. On Jul 4th 5 persons entered the house of Col Geo Davenport, on Rock Island, during the absence of his family, & shot him through the thigh, mortally wounding him, & then dragged him through the house until he told them where his money was, which they took, with his watch. They then tied him fast to an easy chair & left. One of the persons was known to Col Davenport by the name of Budd. The Col lived until Fri night, when he expired, after having given full particulars. [Jul 26 newspaper: Budd, the person arrested, though still in confinement, is now believed to be guiltless of the charge. It would have been as well had this increased reward been offered at an earlier day. –Reveille] [Nov 15th newspaper: Aaron Young, & 2 brothers named Long, were executed at Rock Island, Ill, on Nov 4, for the murder of Col Davenport. The rope on which Aaron Long was suspended broke, & he fell, striking his back on the beam below & laid insensible from the effects of the rope on his neck. When he recovered his senses & again led to the gallows, raising his hands he cried out: "The Lord have mercy on me! You are hanging an innocent man, & [pointing to his brother] there hangs my poor brother."]

Died: on Jul 14, in Wash City, after an affliction of 12 years, Mrs Sarah Ferguson, consort of Rev J B Ferguson, in her 62nd year. Her funeral will take place this afternoon, at 3 o'clock, from her late residence near Blagden's wharf, Navy Yard.

Died: on Jul 14, of a painful illness, Rachel Isabella, d/o Thos & Malinda Malloy, aged 2 years, 9 months & 4 days.

Desirable pew at auction: Pew #78, in St John's Church, owned by John B Jones, who has removed from the city. –A Green, auctioneer

Orphans Court of Wash Co, D C. Letters of administration on the personal estate of Mary Campbell, late of said county, dec'd. –Thos Woods, adm

Dissolution of the copartnership between Jos Jewett & P H King, under the firm of Jewett & King, by mutual consent on Jul 11. Jos Jewett having transferred all his interest to the subscriber. -P H King

My partners, Thos A Maguire & Wm Flinn, in a contract for furnishing paving stone on Pa ave, have, for a consideration, resigned all interest in said contract, & have assigned all their rights in the same to the undersigned. –John Purdon

Wanted to hire, 2 good servant women, one a house servent, & the other a washer & ironer. Servants from the country preferred. Apply to Thos Havenner, C st, between 4½ & 6th sts.

Wash Corp: 1-Ptn of Jas Laurie & others, for extension of the alley in square 226: referred to the Cmte on Improvements. 2-Ptn of Jos Frazer & others, praying an alteration of the alley in square 127: referred to the Cmte on Improvements.

THU JUL 17, 1845
The trial of Henry G Green, for the murder of his wife, was at Troy, N Y, during the whole of last week, without being concluded. Green had been married but a short time to a beautiful, affectionate, & confiding girl of 18, he being 22. He dosed her day & night with arsenic which he put into her coffee, her chicken broth, & her medicine, standing by her beside unmoved while the poison was agonizing her with pain. The victim herself, though apparently conscious that her husband was murdering her, took whatever he offered.

Metropolitan Ice Cream Saloon: A R Jenkins, of the Metropolis House, corner of Pa ave & Jackson alley.

The Alexandria Will Case was finally decided yesterday: this is the 4th trial of the same cause. Verdict: it is not the true last will & testament of said Geo Dent Alexander, as we believe the said Geo Dent Alexander to have been acting under the undue influence of said Geo Wise at the time of making the will in question.

Three sudden deaths on Tue from exposure to the sun & drinking too freely of cold water while much too heated: all natives of Ireland, viz: Denni Sullivan, aged about 25, from Castle Island, county Kerry. He was attended by Drs Miller & McClery. Michl Hone, aged about 60. Patrick Talty, a brother of Michl Talty, on 7th st, who lately arrived from Ireland. He was attended by Dr Dawes.

Mrd: on Jul 13, by Rev Mr Tarring, Mr John T Mortimer to Miss Martha Ellen Dix, all of Wash City.

Died: on Jul 3, at Bedford Springs, Pa, Jas F Conover, of Cincinnati. He was a native of Monmouth Co, N H. In 1820 he removed to Cheraw, S C, where he studied & practiced law; he was for a time the editor of the Cheraw Intelligencer. In 1829 he went to Cincinnati; edited the Cincinnati American from Feb to Dec, 1830; in Apr of 1835, he established the Cincinnati Daily Whig, & continued there until the spring of 1839; in 1841 & 1842, he, with J W Caldwell, of New Orleans, established the Cincinnati Gas Works, of which he was President at the time of his decease.

Mrd: on Jul 10, in Balt, by Rev Dr Wyatt, Capt Jos E Johnston, U S Topographical Engineers, to Lydia, d/o the Mon. Louis McLane.

Died: on Jul 1, in Raleigh, N C, in her 68th year, of a gradual decay of the vital powers, Mrs Jane Taylor, the venerable relict of the late Chief Justice Taylor, & sister of the late Judge Gaston.

Mr Wm J Shelton has retured from the editorial chair of the Charlottesville Advocate. Messrs Robt C Noel & Robt L Saunders have become proprietors of the paper, & engaged Mr Wm T Early as editor.

Geo W Humphreys, Dentist, has taken rooms over Mr Anderson's Book & Fancy store, between 11th & 12th sts, on Pa ave, where he will attend to all the duties of his profession.

On Jul 4, the last night of a military encampment near Lexington, Ky, Mr Thos J Watts, s/o Mr David Watts, of Fayette Co, was shot during a sham-fight, & instantly killed. He was a young man of great worth, & beloved in the circle of his acquaintances.

FRI JUL 18, 1845
Thos N Carr, Consul Genr'l to Morocco, & lady, were passengers in the splendid brig **Republic**, which sailed from N Y on Tue for Gibraltar. He will proceed from Gibraltar to Tangiers, the consular residence, in the U S frig **Cumberland**.

Wm Stewart, convicted some years since of the murder of his father, & now confined in the penitentiary, is hourly expected to die from a pulmonary affection, & has made a confession of all knowledge in his possession, of the most foul deed. It will not be published until after his death. –Balt Clipper [Jul 23rd newspaper: Wm Stewart died on Sat of consumption.]

Wm Ruck, a caulker, & a resident of N Y, was drowned on Sun, near the line between Brooklyn & Wmsburg.

The schnr **Oraloo**, bound from Boston to Da_nariscotta, was capsized in a squall on Sun, off Cape Elizabeth: Mrs Dunbar & a child were not saved. [Jul 28th newspaper: the aged lady drowned, who has been stated to be Mrs Dunbar, turns out to be Mrs Spear, mother of Dr Spear, of Boston City. She was going to visit her friends at the eastward.]

The only child of Mr Wm Richardson, of Snow Hill, Md, was scalded to death on Jul 13, during the absence of its parents at the funeral of a neighbor. He had been left in the care of the nurse & cook. Neglecting their charge, they left it in the kitchen alone, & found it in a tub filled with boiling water.

Drowned: on Tue, Wm H J Spear, s/o A J Spear, 275 Spring st, N Y, while bathing at Coney Island.

A drover named Jos English, from Ohio, was robbed on Thu, at Burlington, N J, of $1,300, the proceeds of his sales of cattle. He was robbed by 2 men while put up at the Temperance Hotel.

Sudden deaths in N J: John Clark, a native of Ireland, by apoplexy from drinking too freely of cold water while exposed to the sun; Fred'k Tombert, a German, drowned while bathing; Thos Gray & John Murray, both Irishmen, drowned at Belleville, while bathing; Edw McKinney, a boy, drowned.

Trial before the Superior Court at Northampton last week, Judge Dewey presiding. A man named Wells, losing his wife, had given one of his children to Mr & Mrs Nash, of Amherst, to bring up as their own. A change of circumstances in his family created a desire on the part of Wells to get possession of his child. Judge Dewey decreed that it should continue under the protection of its adopted rather than its natural parent.

Navy Dept-Orders, Jul 15. Cmdor R F Stockton, detached from the command of the steamship **Princeton**, & put on special duty. Cmder Fred'k Engle, to command of the steamer **Princeton**. Cmder Jas M McIntosh, ordered as inspector of provisions, at N Y.

Died: on Tue last, after an illness of but few days' duration, the Rev Chas Eden Browne, a member of the Balt Annual Conference of the Methodist Episcopal Church, appointed in Mar last to the charge of the Wash City Mission. He was in his 30th year, & has left an extensive circle of acquaintances.

2 farms at public auction: the excs of the late Jos J Hopkins, will sell the Farm on which the dec'd resided, being part of a tract called ***White Hall***, near the heart of South River, Anne Arundel Co, Md, containing 250 acs, & adjoining the lands of Jos Evans, Basil D Hall, & Capt Gantt. Improvements consist of a brick Mansion & commodious stables, barns, & tobacco houses. Adjoining the home-place is another farm called ***Lug Ox***, containing 175 acres more or less. This farm adjoins the lands of Polly Warfield & the late Gerard Hopkins. –Isaac Hoge, Saml Hopkins, excs

The Hasty Pudding Club of Harvard Univ propose to celebrate their 50th Anniversary by a supper at the U S Hotel in Boston on Aug 26 next. Cmte of Arrangements:

John C Warren	N L Frothingham	J Otis Williams, sec of
Caleb Stetson	Geo Putnam	cmte
Oliver W Holmes	Geo S Hillard	Boston, Jul 10, 1845
Chas T Russell		

SAT JUL 19, 1845

At West Stafford, Conn, on Jul 14, Mr Eber Buck, while securing the last tumble of hay, was struck dead by lightning.

A young man, Abraham Smith, in Bristol township, Pa, was lately attacked by a bull & gored to death. It appears he had been teasing the animal the day before.

Mr Jas Fish, a highly respectable inhabitant of Bedford, Westchester Co, was, last Mon, so severely injured by a stone falling upon his head, having been thrown by blasting a rock, that he died the next day.

Jos Arey, of Fayetteville, N C, on Jul 7, lost a fine boy by the explosion of some powder in a glass vessel with which he was playing.

A child of Mr Downs, aged about 3 years, while with his father in the factory of Mr Danl Abbott, in Southbury, Conn, a few days since, caught its clothes in the machinery & was drawn in & crushed to death before his father's eyes.

Four lads, belonging to the whaleship **Audley Clarke**, went to Conanicut Sunday in a sailboat. They commenced knocking each other's hats off in sport, when 2 of them were thrown overboard & drowned. One of the them was Otis Ball, aged 16, of New Shoreham; the other boy belonged to Providence.

Yesterday Mr Jas Glascow was seriously hurt on the brick bldg now being erected for Mr N Travers by G H Plant, on Pa ave, near 9th st. He was beginning the gable end of the bldg when the rafters fell, & crushed him against the wall. By the timely aid of friends, we learn that he is out of danger.

Died: on Jul 16, at his residence, near the Navy Yard, Bennett Biscoe, formerly of St Mary's Co, Md, but for the last 15 years a resident of Wash City, in his 65th year.

Died: on Jun 27, at **Rose Mount**, near Nottingham, PG Co, Md, Benj Skinner, in his 44th year.

Jas Haynes, plasterer, of Brooklyn, was drowned on Tue, in consequence of cramp while bathing.

Circuit Court of Wash Co, D C-in Chancery. Robt Ramsay against Ann McCormick & others. Trustee reported he had sold the south half of lot 6 in square 345, in Wash City, with improvements thereon, to Z Collins Lee, for $1,040; sale is hereby ratified.
—W Brent, clerk -J M Carlisle, trustee

A Funeral discourse for the late Rev Chas E Browne will be preached in the new Lutheran Church, corner of 11th & H sts, on Sun, at 4½ o'clock, by Rev Septimus Tuston. Public is invited to attend.

MON JUL 21, 1845
Terrible conflagration in N Y, on Sat: over 200 bldgs burnt-$10,000,000 of property destroyed-serious loss of life-tremendous explosion. Francis Hart, of Engine Co #22, was thrown over the bldg to the opposite side of the street, & escaped on his feet, scarcely injured. [See Jul 23rd newspaper.]

Northampton, Mass, Jul 15. Henry W Paine, of Oxford, an optician, said he was shot at by robbers in Wash a few weeks since, & was waylaid by 3 robbers last Wed, while on his way in a wagon from Worcester to Oxford. The story & the circumstances leave but little doubt that it is a self-robbery. -Gaz

Appointments by the Pres:
Gansevoort Melville, Sec of the Legation of the U S near her Britannic Majesty, in the place of Francis R Rives, resigned.
John Dougherty, Assist Engineer in the Revenue Marine, appointed a Chief Engineer, to supply the vacancy occasioned by the resignation of Thos W Faron.
Walker Anderson, Navy Agent, Pensacola, Fla, vice Jackson Morton, whose commission has expired.
Paschal Bequette, Receiver of Public Moneys for the District of Lands subject to sale at Mineral Point, Wisconsin, vice Robt W Lansing, removed.
Wm P Lynde, U S Atty for the Territory of Wisconsin, from Jul 22, in place of Thos W Sutherland, whose commission will on that day expire.
Wm Nelson, Consul for the Port of Panama, in place of Jeremiah A Townsend, recalled.
Geo H Goundie, of Pa, Consul for the city of Basle, in Switzerland, in place of Seth T Otis, recalled.
Jos Codwin, of N Y, Consul for the port of Glasgow, in Scotland, in place of Thos McGuire, recalled.
Thos W Gilpin, of Pa, Consul for the port of Belfast, in Ireland, in place of Jas Shaw, recalled.
Ramon L Sanchez, of Florida, Consul for the port of Carthagena, in New Granada, in place of Saml H Kneass, resigned.
Benj Sherman, Register of the Land Ofc at Ionia, Mich, vice Ira Porter, whose commission will expire Aug 6, 1845.
Jos B Browne, U S Marshal for the Southern District of Florida, the ofc having been vacated by his resignation.
Geo Center, Collector of the Customs at St Augustine, Florida, vice Augustus W Walker, removed.
Thos B Abrams, of Pa, Consul of the U S for the port of Mayaguez, in the island of Puerto Rico, in place of Gurdon Bradley, recalled.

The collection of rare & valuable paintings belonging to the late Jos Bonaparte, [Count Survilliers] & now the property of his grandson, will be sold at auction at Bordenstown, N J, in Sep next.

John Troubat, of the firm of Allibone & Troubat, drowned while bathing at Cape Island on Jul 16. He had left the city, in company with his sister, to spend the extreme hot weather at the Island.

Lewellyn, the eldest s/o Wilson C Fairfax, was drowned at Alexandria on Thu last. He was the pride of his parents, just ripening into manhood. How the accident happened is not known.

Alexandria Boarding School 22nd annual session will commence on Sep 8.
–Caleb S Hallowell & Brother, Principals, Alexandria, D C.

The cause of humanity will be served if any person will give information where Jas Gordon can be found. He is about 15 years of age, & left his home on Jul 18; & it is generally believed he went to Phil, Pa, or to N J. His parents are in the greatest distress, & any information respecting him will be gratefully & thankfully received.
–Geo Gordon, Wash, D C

Orphans Court of Wash Co, D C. . Letters of administration on the personal estate of Marcus C Buck, late of Wash Co, dec'd. –Wm M Buck, adm [Those having claims against said estate will present them to Chas S Wallach, Atty & Counseller, #6 west wing City Hall, Wash.]

Circuit Court of Wash Co, D C-in Chancery. Jas Robertson & others vs Clara F Forsyth & others. Ratify sale by Trustee of lots 5, 8, & 10, & part of 9, in square 27 in Wash City, with the appurtenances, to John Forsyth for $3,600. It is further ordered that the creditors of John Forsyth, dec'd, do, on or before the third Mon of Oct, file in this cause their respective claims, with the vouchers thereof. By order of the Court.
Test-Wm Brent, clk

A murder was committed last Fri night, near the residence of Gen Van Ness, by a person named Thos Cook upon Thos Naylor, a brother of Mr Alison Naylor, of Wash City, who keeps an extensive livery stable opposite Fuller's Hotel. Thos Naylor was very much intoxicated & incapable of making any resistance at the time. Witnesses had heard Cook make threats towards Naylor after a previous quarrel. Cook stroke the dec'd several times on the side of the head. Naylor's skull was fractured by the severe blows he received. Naylor was conveyed to jail.

Mr Davis, hackdriver, who was sun-stricken last Thu in the 1st Ward, died on Jul 18th & was interred on that day.

TUE JUL 22, 1845
Meeting of the Ofcrs of the 5th Regt U S Infty, held at *Fort Mackinac*, Mich, of which Capt Martin Scott was Pres & Lt Spencer Norvell Sec: resolved, that we have heard with deep regret of the demise of Capt Alex'r Johnston, late of said regt: a valuable ofcr: condolence to his relatives.

Martin Scott, Capt 5th Regt Infty
Jno Byrne, Assist Surgeon U S Army
Wm Chapman, Capt 5th Infty
John O'Brien, Chaplain U S Army

Henry Whiting, 2nd Lt 5th Infty
J P Smith, Brevet 2nd Lt 5th Infty
L T Jamison, Post Sutler
Spencer Norvell, 2nd Lt 5th Infty

A young Mr Boyd, s/o David Boyd, of Phil, was dreadfully injured on Thu at Cape May. He laid a wager of a bottle of wine to climb a pole. He ascended about 50 feet, & in descending quickly the friction burnt his hands, & caused him to fall 30 feet, which broke his back & displaced his bowels. His situation was so precarious as to prevent his removal, & it is supposed that his injuries are fatal.

Constable's sale: by virtue of 5 writs of fieri facias, issued by Thos C Donn, J P for Wash Co, D C, one at the suit of Dr Fred'k May, use of Mary Austin; one at the suit of Thos Lowe; & 3 at the suit of Henry Lee & Jas Esprey, trading under the firm of Lee & Esprey, against John H Smith: sale of lots 10, 11 & 12 in square 939; also, the life interest of said John H Smith in lots 13 thru 15 in said square: sale on Aug 10, on the premises, I will offer for sale for cash, at public auction, all the right, title, interest & estate of said John H Smith. –R J A Culverwell, Constable

Information wanted respecting a man & his wife by the name of Richd & Mary Conden, formerly, if not at present, residents of Balt, by their dghts, Sarah & Mary Conden. Any information respecting these persons would be thankfully received by their dghts, by addressing a few lines to W A Allen, Wash, D C.

WED JUL 23, 1845
The Nantucket Inquirer states that Capt Roberts, of the English sloop-of-war, was supposed to have been mortally wounded in the skirmish that took place in Mar at the Bay of Islands, New Zealand, between the English & the Natives. The Sgt of Marines & a number of the ship's company were killed.

New Orleans Tropic. [Maj] Wm H McCardle, the efficient Editor of the Tropic, has retired. The paper is to be conducted hereafter by Messrs F Sawyer, B F Flanders, & Chas E Hall.

John W Eaton, Representative of the town of Stoddard in the Legislature of N H, committed suicide by hanging himself on Wed last. He was elected Pres of the Wilton Railroad Company a few weeks since.

Marshall, Mich, Jul 8. On Jul 4, while firing the federal salute, the powder prematurely ignited, & the cannon went off while the gunners were in the act of removing the cartridge. John Carver had his arm mutilated & Wm Shaw had both of his arms mutilated. Both of Shaw's arms were amputated, but he only survived until Sunday. Carver's arm was amputated below the elbow, & he is doing well. Both were young unmarried men. –Statesman

American ship burnt at sea: the ship **Hoogly**, Capt Roubin, arrived at Havre on Jul 1, having on board Capt Crawford & the crew of the American ship **Ten Brothers**, of Waldoborough. The latter had fire on board which increased and Capt Crawford decided upon abandoning her on Jun 27th.

Conflagration in N Y-see Jul 21 newspaper. Augustus L Cowdrey was overwhelmed in the ruins of a house in New st at the time of the explosion of the saltpeter. He & a young man named Van Winkle had proceeded to the 3rd story with a hose. Van Winkle was blown through a window into the street, & experienced but little injury. Peter A Johnson, a porter, has left a wife & 3 children. A married lady, who was a sister of the wife of Ofcr Martin, was buried in the ruins of 42 Broad st. Adolph Von Groening, of the firm of Pavenstedt & Von Groening, 94 Pearl st, was blown up in the store 42 Broad st. Four men, heads of families, Jones, Johnson, May, & Barker, are said to be missing. Various business firms who were burnt out:

Adelphi House, Misses Constantine
Laurent Allien, merchant
Harriet Barker, boarding
Wm C Burdick, clerk
Alex Bertrand
Walter R Jones, jr, residee
Wm Sayer, steerage
Mrs Jacobs & Fidelia Blanchard, board
John C Cass, dwlg
Jas Donelson, res corner Morris, scorched
Henry Van Arsdale, Doctor
Millers, Ripley & Co, merchants
Hashie & Nicol, merchants
J F A Sandford, merchant
P Chouteau, jr, & Co, American Fur Co
Gay, Lusac & Co, French Plate Glass
Edw B & John Hayes, chairmakers
Owen Byrne, cider vinegar
Sevin & Brother, furniture & dwlg
Sarah Simes, boarding
Wm L Branch, furniture
Fred'k Burkelow, Dr [P O] residence
Oliver C Burnham, laces & silks, residence over
Mrs G B Miller & Co, tob't
Siffkin & Ironside, merchants
Staniford & Smith, furniture
Mrs Eliza Viall, boarding
W Spencer, cooper
L Kennedy, porter
Lowerre & Hawley, carpenters
Edw Carey, porter-house
John Coots, cider refiner
J S Nugent, com
Wm Deitering, tailor

Burlage & Hurter, com
David McLeod, carpenter
R S Robertson, clk
John Foster, carpenter
R Pyekman, coachmaker
J Sullivan, laborer
J Thomson, blacksmith
David Broderick, laborer
Wm Burger, carpenter
Timothy Collins, laborer
T Talbott, blacksmith
Nich Dimond, porter-house
P J Figueira & Co, wine mer
P N Searle, wine mer
Residence of Sabin
C & C G Sabin, stables
Chas Meletta, mer
Wm H Franklin, auct
Gerding & Kunkelman, mers
Chas E Quincy, mer
Robt M Penoyer, mer
David, Brooks & Co, com mer
W S Durbrow, sailmaker
Fox & Livingston, mers
Wm Neilson, wines
G S Stagg, mer
E H Ludlow & Co, aucts
Joshua Hilton, com mer
H Meterholtz, liquors
Eugene Borgouzin, com
H G Duvivier, broker
Woodward J Haven & Co, com mers
Lue Palmieri, importer
Geo Brady, mer
Barclay & Livingston, com mers
F Stirling, mer
Beckwith N Marvin, com mer
Herman C G Bade, mer
E Shannon, com mer
Coe, Anderson & Co, com mers
Chas Bellows, com mer
Robt Gracie, wines
Francis Echartre, broker

Emeil H Lecomb, mer
Chas Darbefueil, broker
Wm D Malthie, com mer
Achilles Bogoden, importer
Jas W Malthie, storage
John Brower, merchant
A Patterson, city weigher
W D Scott, broker
R C Stone, merchant
E Fieldler, importer
Thos Clark, porter
Lumley Franklin, broker & imp
John Clark, cabinet maker
Edw C Little, chairmaker
H S Hayward, wines
Jas Robinson, com mer
J Waydell, cooper
S E Weir, com
Jos D Pierson, cabinetmaker
T Warner, paints
W D Vredenburgh, painter
Wm B Fuller, paints
H L Routh & Son, com
Wm R Smith, mer
Alpheus J Lightburn, mer
Chas Brady, grocer
E R Nafey, blacksmith
J W Westervelt, State weigher
J D Halstead, cabinet
Francis Kelley, grocer & dwlg
Alex B McAlpin, mer
E V Price
Henry Butt, grocer
Philip Dutch, laborer
Wm H Creagh & Heydecker, com mers
Gustavus Drexel, accountant
Christian Heydecker, mer
Edw A Jee, com
Geo W Shields & Co, iron-mongers
J E Ward, metals
Hen McFarlan, iron manf's
H L Cotheal, do do
W Dubourdieu, cooper

T M McFarland, city weigher
Amzi Cook, charis
Michl Connor, carpenter
T Wall, grocer
G Warren, com
Wm C Maitland, com mer
S Coddington, metals
T B Coddington, metals
Jolin Michel, com
John D Kleugen, com
Geo W Kruger, Consul to Lubee
Henry Fisher, imp
C Struver, merchant
J C Zimmerman, Consul
Thos Braidwood, calico designer
M T Nicholson, broker
R M Picabia
Adolf Rodewald, mer
Nicholas Gloystein, mer
J C Zimmerman, sr, mer
E A Strong, in the rear
A Stoutenburgh, weigher
Jas Eckhoff, carpenter
Krentler E Buermeyer, porter-house
John Backer, tailor
Peter Mastick, shoemaker
Robt S Butters, hardware
Louis A Morin, wines
Jno B Timmerman, agent
A J Smith, imp of liquors
J Swinborne, merchant
Conrad Klingelhoefer, grocer, & house
Christopher Cochran, porter
Patrick Hibbotson, laborer
E Vincens, imp & dwlg
Nich Dalton, cot sampler
Pascal Kerney, painter
P Naylor & Co, metal roofers & plumbers
Martin Miller, shoemaker
Jos Blacklin, metal roofer
John Dufan, cooper
Asa Dow, dry good broker

E L Williams, dry goods
Asa Gardner, hotel
W Taggard, cotton press
John H Brown & Brothers
J B Lasala & Co, mers
J C Muller & Co, imps
John O'Neil, saddler
Wm H Guion, weigher
Wm Bloodgood, mer
Edw Bossauge, com
Wm H Leary, weigher
Leger Freres, imps
T D Ryan, merchant
David Newman, grocer
Wm H Meeks, lawyer
J Von Heydemarck, imp
Dickson & Co, mers
Jos Morrison, imp
Washington Meeks
Saml G Davis, mer
Edw Delany, porter
Ferdinand Holland, mahogany
Wm H Tuion, weigher
E A Strong
Jos Rhodes, imp
Chas Krutger, imp
E S Theband, broker
J Wilbur, com
Thos Scott, com mer
J P Beauville, imp
W Dovenor & Co, refiners
G Ashton, jr, imp
J Naylor & Co, mers
Danl Winn, laborer
Sarah Disbrow, boarding
Martin Doyle, porter
David McLeod's residence
Mrs Eliz Burr
J Carughan, blacksmith
Morris Earle's residence
Adam Klein, bootmaker
John Brower, residence
Tennis Quick

Chas H De Luze, mer
Louis P De Luze, consul from Switzerland
Julius Chun, imp
T T Edgerton
H Steffens, tailor
Horace R Hotchkiss, com
D L Suydam, mer
Victor Durand, com mer
W A Smetts, imp
Jos W Hale, com
P R Potter, dry goods
Jas J A Bruce, com

Danl Oakley & Sons, imp
J W Mulligan, jr, com mer
J C Robillar, com mer
Chas E Townsend, grain-the fire stopped here
Corner Exchange Place-H W Miller, porter-house
J H Vanderbilt, agent for Nor & Wor steamboat Co
Ellen C Traphagen, lodging house, owned by Mr Ray

Died: on Jul 21, in Gtwn, Mrs Mary Ellen Barker, in her 23rd year.

Died: on Jul 22, at Gtwn, D C, John Ignatius Davis, in his 25th year, s/o Ignatius David, late of Fred'k Co, Md, dec'd.

Circuit Court of Wash Co, D C-in Chancery. Richd Cruickshank, adm de bonis non of John Ott, cmplnt, against Mary Ott, the widow, Catherine Ott, the mother, Juliana Ott, Philip Mauro & Eliza his wife, Wm Riley & Catherine his wife, Jacob Ott, Maria Ott, Chas B Ott, John W Ott, heirs & devisees of David Ott, dfndnts. Bill is filed by the complnt, as administrator de bonis non of John Ott, & states that Ann Ott, his admx, had filed her bill in the said Court, that on or about Feb 15, 1815, the said John Ott sold lot 2 in square 379, in Wash City, with improvements unto the said David Ott, who entered into possession of the same, & died seised of part thereof; David Ott died insolvent as to his personal estate, & that the debt aforesaid is a lien on said premises. Ann Ott died; letters of adm d b n upon the estate of John Ott were granted to Robt H Beatty, who filed his bill of survivor in said suit; that on Jul 1, 1829, the Court, by decree passed in said cause, established the then cmplnt's lien upon said premises for the principal sum & interest, from Feb 18, 1815, & $55.67 cost, & authorized the sale of the same for payment thereof, by a trustee appointed for that purpose; that the said decree was returned duly executed, but before any further proceedings were had in the cause the said Robt H Beatty departed this life; that letters of adm d b n on the estate of the said John Ott have been granted to the complnt, & the object of the said bill is to revive the said cause, & to have the decree for sale of said premises for the payment of the said principal, interest, & costs, made absolute & carried into effect, or to have such other relief as is fit; & it appears that the dfndnt, Mary Ott, Catherine Ott, Juliana Ott, Philip Mauro & Eliza his wife, Wm Riley & Catherine his wife, Jacob Ott, Maria Ott, Chas B Ott, & John W Ott, do not reside within D C, but beyond the reach of the process of this court, & it is ordered that they appear in the said Court on or before the 4th Mon of Nov next, in person or by solicitor. -W Cranch -W Brent, Clerk -J Marbury for cmplnts

Medical Dept of the Columbian College: the Chair of Pathology & Practice of Medicine in this Institution having become vacant because of the death of Prof Sewall, the Faculty will defer nominating a successor until Aug. –W P Johnston, M D, Dean

For rent: 3 story brick house on Pa ave, between the Railroad Depot & the Capitol. Apply to Gregory Ennis, or at the Railroad Hotel.

Wash Corp: 1-Act for the relief of A C Kidwell: passed. 2-Ptn from Jas E Thumlert: referred to the Cmte of Claims. 3-Richd R Burr & John M Wright confirmed as police constables. 4-Ptn of Wm Easby & others: for grading & gravel for 22nd st: referred to the Cmte on Improvements. 5-Ptn of Chas Borremans, praying remission of a fine: referred to the Cmte of Claims. 6-Act for the relief of Wm A Scott: passed.

$2,000 wanted for a friend, for which the most satisfactory security will be given, & the interest paid monthly. –W Fischer

For sale: $3,000 Missouri 3% stock, with coupons, for sale. Inquire of Mr Davis, Teller of the Bank of the Metropolis.

Lost, in Gtwn, a leather pocketbook, containing $60; also, judgments against Fred'k Ludeke, for $45.61, & superseded by Jas Hicks; Henry W Edwards, for $8.51; W J Nevius, for $3.33½, superseded by C Hogmire; & a note of John Crumbough for $98.45, dated Jul 9, 1845, & endorsed to me. –Robt M Lauck, East of the market, on the canal, Gtwn.

$10 reward for lost silver watch, marked inside on the case the letters R H L V with ink. Having stopped at Douglas' Green-house, I may have dropped it in getting on my horse there. –Horatio E Berry, Gtwn

THU JUL 24, 1845
Gtwn Agricultural Implement Manufactory: long established manufactory: all bills must be settled previous to or at the expiration of 6 months. –Jos Libbey, Proprietor; Levi Davis, Agent

National Eating House. Will be served up this day an extra fine Sea Turtle, in soup, steaks, & otherwise. Also, Gumbo, made in the best possible manner.
–W Walker [100 pairs of Woodcock wanted immediately.]

A detachment of U S Dragoons under the command of Col Kearney reached **Fort Laramie** on Jun 14. The ofcrs & men were all well & in fine spirits. Some of the emigrants for Oregon reached Fort Laramie.

[See Jul 21 & Jul 23 newspapers on conflagration in N Y.] More victims of the explosion. Henry Medigos & Henry Rodman, both Germans, are missing. Medigos was a single man; Rodman has left a wife & children. A young married woman, a bride of 3 months, name understood to be Runyan, is missing. Peter Mahan, public Porter, & his wife, are supposed to be killed. A little son, 8 years of age, supposed to be their only child, escaped unhurt. He has not seen his parents since the fire. –Journal of Commerce

The trial of Henry G Green, at Troy, for the murder of his wife within a week after their marriage, terminated on Sat in a verdict of guilty, & he was sentenced to be executed on Sep 10 next. [See Jul 17th newspaper.]

Notice: by virtue of a writ of fieri facias, issued by Jos W Beck, a J P for Wash Co, D C, at the suit of Enoch W Smallwood, against the goods, chattels, lands & tenements, rights & credits of Robt H Clements: I will offer the goods & chattels of the same, on Jul 31, in front of the Centre Market. –Horatio R Maryman, Constable

Died: on Jul 19, in his 88th year, Jos O Andrews, a native of Great Britain, but for many years a resident in Wash City. His long life was one of great usefulness, upwards of half a century of it having been devoted to the instruction of youth in various depts of knowledge, by numbers of whom his memory is affectionately cherished.

Died: on Jul 20, at Balt, after an illness of several weeks, Robt Neilson, printer. He was one of those who defended Balt at North Point in 1814, & in the various relations of life he discharged his duty faithfully & honorably

Lost, in Gtwn, yesterday, a bundle of dry-goods, wrapped in a newspaper. Finder will be rewarded by leaving it at G & 20th sts, Wash, south of Mr Stott's Grocery. –Alex Ray

Household furniture at auction: on Thu, at the residence of the late Louis G Gassaway, 20th & N Y ave. -R W Dyer & Co, aucts

Matthew Mills, of Phil, has been fined by the Mayor of that city $100 for interfering with the dog-catchers.

At the last term of Court in Milwaukie, Geo W Barton was indicted & tried for robbing the U S mail, & putting the life of the carrier in jeopardy. Sentenced to 10 years in the county jail of Milwaukee until a State prison should be erected in the Territory, & then to be removed thereto.

FRI JUL 25, 1845
A barn of David Zeller, near Hagerstown, was struck by lightning during a thunder storm on Mon, & burnt to the ground. Mr Zeller's loss, who is a most worthy man, is upwards of $4,000.

Hartford Timers: the d/o Pres Totten, of Trinity College, fell from the cars as they were starting from Greenbush a day or 2 ago, & her arm was crushed badly from the shoulder to the wrist. Her father was waiting to receiver his child at the depot when the Springfield train arrived with the painful news.

Annual commencement of Gtwn College was held on Jul 24, 1845.
Degree of D D conferred on: Rev John McCaffrey, Pres of Mount St Mary's, Emmittsburg.
Degree of L L D conferred on: Baron Auguste Gabriel vander Straten-Ponthoz & Dr Wm E A Sikin, Md.
Degree of A M conferred on:
Mr Matthew F Maury, U S Navy   Mr Francis H Dykers, N Y
Mr Thos I Semmes, D C
Degree of A B conferred on:
John W Archer, Md   Peter C Howle, D C
John E Wilson, Md   Jas A Iglehart, Md
Nichlas S Knighton, Md   Waldeman de Bodisco, Russia
Medals or premiums conferred on: the 6 immediately above and the following:
Jas A Iglehart, Md   John V Livingston, N Y
Eliel S Wilson, Md   John Duncan, Ala
Robt E Doyle, N Y   Bennet R Abell, Md
L Tiernan Brien, Md   Claudius F Legrand, Md
John Nevins, D C   Geo A Dyer, Ky
Richd H Clarke, D C   John L Carroll, Md
Oliveria T Andrews, Va   Victor Forstall, La
Jas H Donegan, Ala   Jacob B Smith, Pa
Nicholas Snowden, Md   Francis G Dwight, Pa
Eusebius L Jones, D C   Geo W Arnold, Md
Henry D Powers, D C   Richd Woodward, D C
John C Longstreth, Pa   Pierre de la Croix, La
Polycarp Fortier, La   Chas Fulmer, D C
Chas De Blanc, La   Fred'k Sasscer, Md
Bernard G Caulfield-   John P Coke, Ky
Wash, D C   G Edmund Brent
Henry I Forstall, La   Wm L Higgins
Edw R Smith, N Y   Thos J Fenwick, Md
Clement Cox, D C   Chas H Pendergast, Md
Adrian Lepretre, La   Patrick Morgan, N Y
Andrew J Spalding, Md   Henry Mountz, D C
Chas Carroll, Md   Matthews Lancaster, Md
Francis M Hall, Md   Edw R Smith, N Y
Chas H Pendergast, Md   Nicholas Daunois, La

John F Ellis, Va	D Clinton Yell, Ark
Wm A King, D C	Adolphur Sabal, Ga
Julius Brou, La	J F Ellis, Va
Oscar Olivier, La	Peter Leonard, D C
Henry W Brent, Md	Martin P King, D C
Geo W French, Va	Wm A King, D C
John Gabaroche, La	Thos Dawson, D C
Jules Tete, La	Chas H Pendergast, Md
John V Livingston, N Y	Ignatius Langley, Md
Adolphus Sabal, Ga	Chas J Pye, Md
Alcide Buard, La	Washington A Young-Wash, D C
Alfred Peire, La	Dennis O'Donoghue-Wash, D C
Henry J Forstall, La	Arthur Jorda, La
Victor J Forstall, La	Geo Richie, Va
Eugene Forstall, La	Francis Baby-Lower Canada
Edwin F King, D C	Louis Turgeon-Lower Canada
Jos N Young, D C	Andrew Jackson Pageot-France

Col Josiah H Vose, commanding ofcr of the 4th Regt of U S Infty at the barracks below New Orleans, died of an affection of the heart on Jul 15.

Household & kitchen furniture at auction: on Aug 12, at the residence of Mr W J Burneston, on 7th st, near the Navy Yard: also, one Electrical Machine. Afterwards: I will sell the house & lot, being lot 26 in square 882. Title unquestionable.
–A Green, Auctioneer

There died recently at Unity, Maine, Mrs Hannah Chase, at age 106 years & 25 days. She left 10 children, 66 grand children, 160 great grand children, & 12 of the 5th generation. There were about 150 of her descendants present at her funeral, & 130 walked in the funeral train.

Accident on Mon last at Broadway, a small village on the line of the Morris canal, in Warren Co, N J. Mrs Eveland & her grand-daughter, were riding in a light wagon, when the horse took fright, & caused the wagon to come in contact with some obstruction, & they were thrown out & both instantly killed.

<u>Balt Academy of the Visitation, Jul 16, 1845: premiums awarded to the following young Ladies:</u>

E Jane Kernan, Wash City	Emily Chassaing, Balt
Zeline Billups, Balt	Mary J Millard, Md
Eliz M Combs, Md	Rosa Millard, Md
Anna M Combs, Md	Ellen A Manning, Md
Adeline Chassaing, Balt	Mary A Wade, Balt

Caroline M Hall, N H
Amanda C Sojourner, La
M Josephine Campbell, Md
Virginia Bunting, Balt
Catharine Merrick, Md
Josephine A Merrick, Md
Mary Grant Jackson, Va
Helen Fitzgerald, Balt
Martha Maddox, Md
Sally Maddox, Md
Anna M Spalding, Md
Mary Eliza Spalding, Md
Eliz Gosnell, Balt
Henrietta Clark, Balt
Frances Berryman, Balt
Amelia J Delmas, Balt
Ann Ellen Jenkins, Balt
Susan J Semmes, Md
Mary A Slater, Balt
Ann Louisa White, Balt
Mary M Fortune, Balt
Louisa Pochon, Balt
Mary A M Donnell, Balt
Priscilla Morgan, Md
Missouri Morgan, Md
Georgiana J Tufts, Balt
Adela Laroque, Balt
Josephine Barry, Balt
Anna Paca, Balt
Mary Rosina McManus, Balt
Mary Anastasia Byrne, Pikesville
Anna Lenning, Phil
Mary E Coad, Md
Emily Coad, Md
Sarah Clark, Balt
Mary E McHenry, Balt
Eliza Green, Md
Mary Dougherty, Balt
Josephine Sharkey, Balt
Araminta Fendall, Balt Co
Catharine Camalia, Md
Mary Elder, Balt
Virginia Denmead
Ann Priscilla Gough, Md
Garafilia Berryman, Balt
Mary E Heuisler, Balt
Frances A Baker, La
Emily Stuart, Md
Augusta D'Ouville, Guadaloupe
Augustine D'Ouville, island of Guadaloupe
Nadine P LeBrun, island of Guadaloupe
Victorine Sirati, Balt Co
Mgt A Murray, Balt
Victorine McLosky, Ala
Isabella McLosky, Ala
Mary Edmonia Pye, Md
Sally Ann Johnson, Md
Betsey Hillen Jenkins, Balt
Caroline L Baker, La
Eliz Grace, Havana
Polymnia Ducatel, Balt
Mary Eliz Wilcox, Pa
Mary A Boyle, Balt
Mary Keating, Phil
Alice Gloninger, Balt
Juliana De Cour, Pa
Caroline E Desilver, Phil
Virginia Thornton, Balt
Emily Marriott, Balt
Violetta Boyd, Eastern Shore of Md
Victoria Thompson, Ala
Mary W A Roper
Rebecca Hart
Catharine Schmuck, Balt
Juliana Hooper, Balt

For rent or lease: 2 story brick house on corner of E & 13th sts, & a new 3 story brick house adjoining it on 13th st. Apply to Mr Joel Downer, House-joiner, near the premises.

Cheap & good bricks for sale: having completed the re-creation of his Steam Brick Press, which was last year destroyed by fire, has made several kilns of excellent bricks in its new location on Tweny Bldgs Hill, N st, south of the Capitol. –J G Proud, jr

Three miles above Westport, Ky, on Sun, a man by the name of Moses Tristler was shot & died soon after. He declared several times while dying that he was shot by a woman called Martha Green. She had some time previously threatened to take his life.

Coroner's inquest was held on Wed last over the body of a man named Fagan, who was attacked with hemorrhage of the lungs, & who died in about 15 minutes after the attack.

Wm Mayo, colored man, was committed yesterday to the jail of this county for further examination. He is charged, on the oath of Bernard Cole, of Spottsylvania Co, Va, with stealing a negro woman & 2 children, the property of Francis Wyatt, of Fredericksburg, Va.

SAT JUL 26, 1845
For rent: 2 large new frame houses, on 23rd st near I west. Inquire of Saml Drury, with whom the keys are left, & who will show the premises, or to the owner.
–Jos Libbey, Water st, Gtwn

Orphans Court of Wash Co, D C. Letters of administration on the personal estate of John C Wallis, late of said county, dec'd. –Wm Bell

Lt O'Reilly, of the British Navy, has succeeded in illuminating a shot used in Capt Manby's apparatus, by means of which a communication in cases of shipwreck can be effected in the darkest nights with the greatest certainty. A fusee is fitted to the shot, &, when discharged, affords a splendid light, capable of withstanding the power of water. Objects within its range become visible, whereby the projector is enabled to see the direction of his aim, & the people on board distinguish the light, which is attached to the projectile, should it pass over any part of the rigging or yards aloft.

Boarding: at his residence, opposite the Intelligencer ofc, corner of 7th & D sts.
–John Macleod

Contributionship Insurance Co, N Y, Jul 19, 1845. As the severe fire in N Y C will doubtless cause uneasiness to the parties holding policies of this company: after all their losses are paid, we will still have a handsome capital remaining, & are continuting to do business. –J Smyth Rogers, Pres; Wm M Randolph, Agent, Washington.

Farm for sale near Alexandria. I am authorized to sell a handsome farm of 44 acs: improvements consist of a good dwg-house, of 11 rooms, with a pump of never failing water; a tenant's house, recently erected, hen-house, 4 stall stable, work-shop, or granary;

sheds, stalls for cows, sheep-pens. Any part of the stock, tool, & household furniture, may be had by the purchaser, & possession will be given at any moment. For further particulars, inquire of J F Callan.

Died: on Jul 24, Wm James, for many years a clerk in the Ofc of the Register of the Treasury, aged 45 years. His funeral is from the Church of Epiphany on G st, between 13th & 14th sts, on Sun at 5:30 p m.

MON JUL 28, 1845

Mr Geo Sandford, shoe manufacturer, residing at 409 High st, N J, was found on the grass, plat in the rear of his house, on Fri, with the arteries of his arm severed, & a razor lying beside him.

Gtwn College: this College is of considerable antiquity, having been established many years ago. In 1815 it was elevated to the rank of a University, with a power to confer degrees. It is Catholic, & under the management of the Jesuits. Youths of all denominations are freely admitted into this College, & no distinction is made between the Catholic & Protestant student. The annual Exhibition was held on Thu last: among who attended were the Pres & his Lady, Atty Gen Mason & his Lady, Mr Bodisco & his Lady & . the Archbishop Eccleston of Balt, & Bishop Fenwick of Boston. Also, Mr Wm S Archer, of Va, was there. Peter G Howle, was the author of a composition in verse, which reflected great credit on his talent. It's title was Monologue on the Potomac, & recited by W H Donoho. The Annual Address of the Philodemic Society, was by Geo Brent, a former graduate of the College.

Appointments by the Pres:
Chas Ward, of Maine, Consul of the U S for the island of Zanzibar, in the dominions of the Sultan of Muscat, in place of Richd P Waters, recalled.
John L Dawson, U S Atty for the western district of Pa, in place of Wm O'Hara Robinson, removed.
Cyrus Barton, U S marshal for the district of N H, in place of Israel W Kelley, whose commission has expired.
Henry Relves, of Gtwn, & Robt H Clements, of Wash, to be justices of the peace in Wash City, D C.
Henry Campbell, Postmaster at Rochester, N Y, in place of S J Andrews, removed.
Amos S Rathbun, Postmaster at Auburn, N Y, in place of W C Beardsley, removed.
Wm W Teall, Postmaster at Syracuse, N Y, in place of H Raynor, removed.
Robt Cochran, Postmaster at Erie, Pa, in place of Andrew Scott, removed.

Two citizens of Milledgeville, Ga, Mr J D Alleman & Mr John Hass, were severely injured on Wed by the premature discharge of a cannon which was being fired in honor of Gen Jackson's memory.

Mr Orrin Woodford, of West Avon, Conn, who has been regarded as a respectable man, & is a farmer of some property, on Tue last, in the most inhuman manner butchered his wife. He had been the user of ardent spirit pretty freely. She was a church member, a mild & pleasant woman. Woodford made no attempt to escape, but allowed himself to be bound by the neighbors, & was committed for trial.

S J Ober & R J Ryon have entered into copartnership, under the firm of Ober & Ryon, for a Grocery Business on the corner of 7th & Pa ave.

By virtue of an order of distrain from M A Queen, & to me directed, to levy & distrain on the goods & chattels found on the premises lately occupied by T J Airheart, on square 224 in Wash City, to pay rent in arrears due to said M A Queen, I have levied on the following goods & chattels, viz: a clock, bureau, dozen chairs, 2 mahg tables, 2 candlesticks, 4 pictures, & 1 pine table: sale on Aug 2, in front of the Centre Market-house, for cash. –Jno S Hutchinsons, Bailiff

Late from Texas: Hon K L Anderson, the Vice Pres of Texas, died of fever on Jul 10, in Montgomery Co.

TUE JUL 29, 1845
Was committed to the Jail of Fred'k Co, Md, Jul 25, as a runaway, a dark mulatto who calls himself Wm Bates, about 22 years of age. Says he belongs to Maj Coombs, of Fauquier Co, Va. Owner, if any, is to come & have him released, he will otherwise be discharged according to law. –Geo Rice, Sheriff of Fred'k Co, Md.

Circuit Court of Wash Co, D C. Oswald B Clarke has applied to be discharged from imprisonment under the act for the relief of insolvent debtors. –W Brent, clk

One Cent Reward for runaway, an indented apprentice to the tailoring business by the name of Wm C Drury, about 14 years of age, & thick set. –Wm A Richardson

Trustee's sale: by virtue of a deed of trust of Edw R Wheeler, executed for the benefit of his securities on his sheriff's & collector's bonds, & an order of Chas Co, Court as a Court of Equity thereon, I will sell at public sale, in front of the the Courthouse in Port Tobacco, Chas Co, Md, a number of likely young negroes, on Aug 5 next. –Robt S Reeder, Trustee

Prof Whiting, of the Univ of Michigan, died at Ann Arbor on Sun. We are sorry to hear that considerable sickness, or debility at least, prevails among the students in the University. –Detroit Adv of Tue

Thos Wallace, 12, was run over & killed at Newark, by the cars of the train from N Y, on Wed.

Fatal accident happened to Henry Somerville, 10, the s/o Jos Arey, of Fayettsville, N C, on Jul 7. He filled a cruet with powder, & turned it up to pour some of it on a coal fire. The consequence was an explosion of the whole, which wounded him in several places with the fragments of glass. He expired on Wed last.

Mrs Mary L Eliason will open a Boarding & Day School at her residence, corner of Prince & St Asaph sts, on Sep 8, for the instruction of young ladies. Alexandria is admirably located for an institution of this kind.

Amongst the losses by the great fire of Sat week, we are sure [says the Morning News] our readers will deplore the destruction of the plates of the large & beautiful work of Audubon, the ornithologist. His loss may probably be about $15,000 on plates, which are wholly uninsured.

Sale of very valuable real estate: by vitue of a decree of the Circuit Superior Court of Law & Chancery for Stafford Co, Va, at Jun term, 1836, in the cases of Bronaugh vs Bronaugh & others, & Browne vs Bronaugh & others, the undersigned Com'rs will offer for sale, at public auction, on Aug 29, 1845, before the Farmers' Hotel, in Fredericksburg, Va, a moiety of the tract of land called **Marlborough**, which formerly belonged to John W Bronaugh, dec'd: contains about 709 acs, in Stafford Co, Va. There is upon the estate an inexhaustible bank of the richest Marl. There are, besides, 2 valuable Fisheries; one, the **Tump**, has rented for $800; the other, the **Island**, for $300 per season. Adjoining this land is the well-known landing called **Thorny Point**, the terminus on the Potomac of the Richmond, Fredericksburg, & Potomac Railroad.
–Thos H Botts, Richd C L Moncure, Arthur A Morson, T B Barton, John W Bronaugh

Died: on Jul 28, after a short illness, Miss Agnes Hammill, in her 16th year. Her funeral will take place this afternoon, at 5 o'clock, from the residence of her mother, on D st.

Died: on Jul 26, Louisa Catherine, infant d/o Dr Thomas.

Household & kitchen furniture at auction: on Jul 31, on F st, near 14th st, at the residence of Mr Girault, who wishes to leave the city: his entire furniture. –A Green, Auctioneer

WED JUL 30, 1845
For sale or barter: first rate 1 or 2 horse Carriage, brass mounted, made to order of the best materials, which he has no use for; consequently a great bargain will be offered.
–Jenkin Thomas, Gtwn

By virtue of an order of distrain for rent in arrear due to the heirs of Jas Williams by John Hall, I will expose at public sale, for cash, on Aug 5, furniture & sundry articles.
–H R Maryman, Bailiff

By virtue of an order of distrain for rent in arrear due to Benj McQuay by Sarah Stroman, I will expose at public sale, for cash, on Aug 5, in front of the Centre Market-house, Wash City: one mahogany centre table. –H R Maryman, Bailiff

$100 reward for runaway from the estate of Walter Bowie, dec'd, on Jul 26, negro Solomon Sprigg, aged about 17 years. –Walter W W Bowie, Good Luck Post-ofc, PG Co, Md

Official: Navy Dept, Jul 26. Board of Naval Engineers have approved the following:

First Assistant Engineers:

Alex'r Birkbeck, jr	Danl B Martin	Jas Cochrane
Henry Hunt	Hiram Sanford	

Second Assistants:

Joshua Follansbee	Levi T Spencer	Naylor C Davis
John Alexander	Albert S Palmer	Danl Murphy
Jas Atkinson	Jesse S Rutherford	
Levi Griffin	Saml Archbold	

Third Assistants:

John M Middleton	Jas W King	Wm H Shock
Wm F Mercier	Jas R Drybergh	John Serro
Wm Taggert	Theodore Zeller	M M Thompson
Wm Luce	Robt Danby	

Circuit Court of Wash Co, D C-in Equity. Western Bank of Balt, vs Chas S Fowler, adm of Wm Prout, dec'd, John Hoover, & John B Steinberger. It is Jul 25, 1845, ordered by the Court, that the sales made & reported by Henry May, appointed trustee, be ratified & confirmed: report states that part of lots 19 & 20 in square 316, with bldgs & improvements, which were conveyed by Michl Hoover, jr & wife to the said John Hoover by deed dated Nov 17, 1827, was sold by said trustee to Chas Miller for $2,190. That the whole of lot 524, with improvements, was sold to Richd Wallach, for $1,070. That the north half of lot 21 in square 376, with improvements, was sold to Wm B Kibby, for $1,850. That all of that part of lot 8 in square 457, with a 3 story brick warehouse thereon, was sold to Chauncey Brooks & Alonzo Lilly, for $5,050. That part of a tract of land called *Jamaica*, lying contiguous to Wash City, containing, according to a recent survey made by Louis Carbery, county surveyor, 211 acres & 10 perches, with improvements, was sold to Chas Miller & John Little, for $161 per ac. That all that part of a tract of land contiguous to Wash City, know as *Port Royal*, conveyed by R Y Brent to said John Hoover for 21½ acs, which last mentioned land is part of a tract called *Jamaica*, contains, clear of the turnpike, almost 3 acres, & was sold by said trustee to John A Smith for $33 per ac. –W Brent,clk

On Jul 11, Miss Rosalie Huelbig/Huelrig, her mother, 2 sisters, & Miss Dressel, were drowned in the Kaskaskia river, which they attempted to cross on their way to Prairie du Long. Miss Huelrig left home that morning with a bridal party, to be married to Mr E H Kettler, who was waiting at his residence, some miles distant, to receive his bride. The father, Mr Huelbig/Huelrig, was nearly frantic with grief.

Mrd: on Jun 18, at Venice, John Randolph Clay, Sec of the U S Legation at St Petersburg, to Jane Tucker Macknight Crawford, d/o Wm Crawford, of Cartsburn, Edinburgh, Scotland.

Mrd: on Jul 24, by Rev Mr Engleston, Richd R Goldin to Miss Ann Catharine Coby, d/o the late Wm Coby, of PG Co, Md.

Died: on Jul 17, at Old Point Comfort, Col Wm Bolling, of Goochland Co, Va, in his 69th year.

Died: on May 9, of dysentery, on board the U S sloop-of-war **Boston**, at Montevideo, Lt Lovett, U S Navy.

Died: on Jul 26, in Gtwn, Eliza Austin, d/o the late R C Austin, of Gtwn, D C, & formerly of N Y, after a long sickness. A young lady, she died as she had lived, a Christian.

Obit-died: on Jul 22, in Gtwn, D C, John J Davis, in his 25th year. One short month ago the dec'd was in the full flush of life. He leaves his poor wife, now desolate in her wo, crushed by this cruel blow.

Wash Corp: 1-Ptn of Thos H Gilliss & others: for improvement of F st: referred to the Cmte on Improvements. 2-Ptn of Edw Mead, praying a remission of a fine: referred to the Cmte of Claims. 3-Act for the relief of John Shaw: passed. 4-Ptn of F A Russell, asking the reissuing of a certificate of a grocery license in lieu of one lost or mislaid: referred to the Cmte of Claims.

For rent: large frame house on the corner of 15th & M sts. Inquire on the premises of E Brannan.

THU JUL 31, 1845
Matthew Thompson killed himself accidentally in Jackson Co, Indiana, a few days ago, when the gun he was blowing in went off. He thought it was unloaded.

Peter Duffy, alias John Jones, attempted a brutal outrage on Clarissa Davis, but was rescued by some people who heard her screams. He was bailed on Sat in the sum of $1,500, & is now at large, while the poor girl is locked up in the prison as a witness.

Phineas Bradley, late Assist Postmaster Genr'l of the U S, known more familiarly as Dr Bradley, was born in Litchfield, Conn, Jul 17, 1769, & died at Wash City on Mar 1, 1845, aged 76 years. He was tall, a high forehead, dark thin hair, yet so long as to be tied behind, dress plain, & countenance habitually cheerful. For many years he resided at his country seat, 2 miles north of the Capitol, called *Clover Hill*. When Col Pickering was called by Washington to take charge of the Post Ofc Dept, Abraham Bradley,jr, an Associate Judge of Luzerne Co, [Where Col P exercised the ofc of Prothonotary,] was invited to accompany him to Phil as a confidential clerk. He married a very amiable Luzerne lady, Miss Smith, of Pittston, whose tastes & habits sympathized with his own. Dr Bradley was several years younger, having pursued the usual course of study, had entered on the practice of medicine, near the Painted Post, on the Chemung, in N Y, where he married Miss Jones, a lady eminentlay distinguished for pleasing manners & personal beauty. Soon after the removal of his brother, the Dr made Wilkesbarre his residence, his father living in Hanover, the adjoining township. The Post Ofc, needing additional aid, Dr Bradley accepted a situation in the Dept beside his brother. It may be said that the Post Ofc Dept was nursed & brought up & educated under the superintendence of Abraham & Phineas Bradley. Abraham was a book-man; had a farm near Wash City; & had a fine family of children. Dr Bradley enjoyed the gratifying success & unceasing attentions of his sons & their families. Though not a communicant, Dr Bradley was a constant attendant of the Presbyterian Church. His eldest son was W A Bradley.

Extensive sale of land: pursuant to the decree of the Circuit Superior Court of Law & Chancery of Fauquier Co, pronounced on May 14, 1845, in the cause of Fitzhugh vs Fitzhugh, on Aug 25 next, in front of the Court-house, will be offered for sale 3 valuable parcels of land, being those portions of the real estate of Thos Fitzhugh, dec'd, that were allotted by Com'rs Beale, Stovin, & Combs severally to the heirs of Wm Fitzhugh, of Geo Fitzhugh, & of Henry Fitzhugh, & are designated on the plot & survey of Wm McCoy, which accompanies the report of said Com'rs, as lots 4, 6, & 9. Lot 4 was allotted to the heirs of Wm Fitzhugh, contains 463+ acs, & is the house part of *Owl Run Farm*. Lot 6 was allotted to the heirs of Geo Fitzhugh, contains 267+ acs, & is the house part of *Ajax Farm*. Lot 9 was allotted to the heirs of Henry Fitzhugh, contains 333+ acs, being the south end of the *Page Land Farm*, & 87+ acres of the north end of *Ajax Farm*. On Sep 1, on the premises, will be sold 2 other parcels of land, being those portions of the said real estate of the said Thos Fitzhugh, dec'd, that were allotted as aforesaid to the heirs of Mary Fitzhugh & the heirs of Nicholas Fitzhugh, designated as lot 1 & lot 2. Lot 1 contains 322+ acs, & was allotted to the heirs of the said Mary Fitzhugh; lot 2 contains 369+ acs, & was allotted to the heirs of Nicholas Fitzhugh. These lots comprise the upper & middle parts of the *Mountain Run Farm*, in Culpeper Co, & lie near Stephensburg, in that county. The *Page Land, Ajax, & Owl Run Farms*, of which lots 4, 6, & 9 are parts, lie in Fauquier Co, contiguous to each other, about 9 miles from Warrenton. –Jas A English, auct

Union. I have taken Mr J T King as my copartner in the Hardware business. Call at the American Hardware Store, between 10th & 11th sts, Pa ave, & save one-third of your money. —C Woodward -Woodward & King

Trinity Church spire, in N Y, is at last free of scaffolding, & its beautiful proportions now sharply cut the blue sky. —Tribune

$75 reward for runaway negro Wm Dean, about 20 or 21 years of age. Also, $25, for the apprehension of negro woman Ann, about 19 years of age, the sister of Wm. I may be found at Mrs Tilley's boarding house on Missouri ave. —Matilda R Done

Appointments by the Pres:
Jas H McBride, Register of the Land Ofc at Springfield, Missouri, vice Joel H Hadan, removed.
Nicholas R Smith, Receiver of Public Moneys at Springfield, Missouri, vice Geo R Smith, removed.
Peter Dixey, Collector of the Customs at Marblehead, Mass, vice Jas Gregory, removed.
Jos T Pease, Collector of the Customs at Edgartown, Mass, vice Leavitt Thaxter, removed.

For rent: 2 story brick house, with basement, on 17th st, between H & I sts, in good order. To a good tenant the rent will be low. Inquire of Geo W Harkness, opposite the West Market, 1st Ward.

Left the Gold Mine of Mr Smith, in the lower end of Orange Co, on Jun 8, my negro man Dennis, about 21 years of age. I will give $100 for his apprehension if taken in Va or D C, or $150 if taken elsewhere. Any communication on the subject will be directed to me, at Somerville, Fauquier Co, Va. —Seth Combs

The Hon John Pope died suddenly at his residence in Wash Co, Ky, on Jul 12. He entered the U S Senate in 1807, & served for 6 years; served 2 or 3 terms afterwards as a Rep in Congress from his State; & was for a time, under the appointment of Pres Jackson, Govn'r of the then Territory of Arkansas.

Mrd: on Jul 13, at Hopewell Church, Chester district, S C, by Rev Mr Nowland, Wm F Davidson, of Charlotte, N C, to Miss Charlotte M Gooch, of Chester district.

Died: on Jul 29, of consumption, Richd Ashton, aged 23 years, in full assurance of blissful immortality.

FRI AUG 1, 1845
For rent: the subscriber offers a 2 story frame house, on F st, between 9th & 10th sts, containing 5 rooms, with a garret. Also, a carriage house large enough for 5 horses & 2 carriages. Apply to Simon Fraser, near the Mansion House.

Trustee's sale: by virtue of a deed of trust to me, dated May 18, 1841, recorded in Liber W B 87, folios 304 thru 307, of the Land Records of Wash Co: auction on Aug 15, all the west half of lot 2 in square 320, in Wash City, with a valuable 3 story brick dwlg & other improvements thereon: fronts on F st north. -Clement Cox, Trustee
-R W Dyer & Co, aucts

A Card. The undersigned, not being otherwise engaged at present, respectfully offers his services to the public as measurer of builder's work. Application at Residence, or through the Post Ofc, will be promptly attended to. –I Mudd, Md ave, near 12th st

For rent: the subscriber offers a 2 story frame house, on F st, between 9th & 10th sts, containing 5 rooms, with a garret. Also, a carriage house large enough for 5 horses & 2 carriages. Apply to Simon Fraser, near the Mansion House.

For rent: 3 story dwlg-house on 6th st, first north of the Unitarian Church. It is just finished. Apply to Mr Francis Mohun, at the new house adjoining the premises.

List of Letters remaining in the Post Ofc, Wash City, Aug 1, 1845.

Anderson, E H
Anderson, Jas M
Ackermain, J D
Angammarre, E
Atkinson, Jos, U S N
Anderson, Capt Jos, or his heirs
Anderson, Gen Alex-3
Armistead, Col John
Browne, Alex
Brown, M
Brooks, Mr
Beach, Elgin
Brown, Robt-2
Brown, J H, U S N
Birth, Mrs Rebecca M
Blanc, J
Bliss, Ashiel
Brook, Geo
Beck, Lemuel J
Bruff, John

Brown, John E
Birch, Mary Ann
Bruce, Mrs Catharine
Brown, Geo G
Boyd, Jas G T
Bryan, Miss Mary
Branagan, John-2
Bernard, John
Burcheyer, Saml
Bartley, Thos W
Bramnon, Rhea
Bartow, Mrs E L
Becraft, M
Bryan, Mrs Wm P
Bidermann, A
Boche, Richd
Baldwin, Wm
Beetley, Mrs Mgt
Burgrin, Mrs Julia-2
Bradley, Mrs Eliz

Berry, Christopher C
Blackwell, Miss E H
Burnett, Miss Barbara
Bartler, Jas
Bremer, John A
Broadrup, Geo
Boykin, Dr Francis M
Browning, Lt R L
Bowen, Leonidas
Chase, E P
Cross, Jos
Clark, R A & S Barnard
Clarke, Edw P
Clark, C C
Camp, Maj J G
Cook, John H
Cook, Sally
Clarke, Miss Sarah A
Cambird, Mrs Sarah
Clifton, Miss Adelaide-2
Ceocil, Miss Ann
Clemens, Josias
Crawford, Francis
Cliver, John
Connell, John, of Phil
Chichester, R M B
Coryell, Tunison
Colby, Capt John
Covert, Miss T H
Carter, Jas
Clinton, J G
Collins, Nancy S
Cooper, Saml
Cornish, Mrs Harriet
Cadwallader, E J
Crockett, Col G S
Campbell, Mary A
Collison, Thos W
Colquit, Walter T
Cherokee, Commission's
Cushing, Caleb
Courtney, Mrs E
Digges, Miss Jennette ELiz

Dix, Miss Mary C
Dodge, Joshua
Dove, Mrs
Dunn, Tim
Dodge, Stephen G
Delany, J W
Dogburn, Sylvester E
Daley, Jas
Dwyer, Patrick
Douglass, Henry
Davis, Richd
DeBlanc, Chas-2
Diesen, Rosa
Devens, Richd
Dornin, Thos
Davidson, Lt J W
Eichbaum, Wm
Edmonson, Jas
Evans, Edmund M
Everhart, E V
Fairfax, Lt A R
Forrest, John
Fulton, Mrs Ann M
Frazier, Dr Wm L
Fitzgerald, Pass Mid W B-2
Francis, Miss Alexina
Fletcher, Wm A
Francis, John
Freeman, Walter-2
Fletcher, Mrs B P
Goods, Miss Jane
Graves, Wm
Grason, Henry-2
Gleeson, Thos M-2
Goddard, H
Grindall, Edw
Gordon, Mrs L
Gramsley, M
Goodling, Eliz
Gittings, John S
Gilliss, G W
Glover, Saml T
Grenacker, Lewis

Geddes, Robt
Hill, Maria A
Hayne, Col Arthur P-3
Hughes, A K, U S N
Hide, John
Hall, Wm H
Hall, John
Hall, Miss Fanny W
Hall, Edw-4
Hall, Miss Louisa
Hooper, Chas S
Henderson, Mrs Nancy
Hammett, Dr
Holdin, John
Harrison, Miss Lucy A
Hurbert, Mr
Hamerack, Wm F
Hodgkin, John W
Hubbard, Capt Wm
Howard, Mary
Hitchcock, Jos
Hubbard, Capt Wm
Hilling, Walter B
Herrick, Joshua
Hosey, Miss Amanda
Harlan, S
Heide, Geo
Hanlon, John
Hernandez, Gen Jos
Hungerford, O J
Hamilton, Alex
Harrington, Prevost G
Hopkins, John
Hotchkiss, Gideon
Holandshead, John
Howard, Miss Emily
Johnson, Eliza
Johnson, Francis M
Johnson, Lester
Jackson, Rev Wm G
Jewitt, Miss Mary C
Jones, Miss Emilie
Jones, Mrs Mgt

Jones, Wm McCrabb
Johnson, Miss Marion
Kain, Miss Sarah
Knott, Mrs Catharine
Kuhn, Walter
Knight, Franklin
Kebel, Jacob
Kelly, Jas T
Kleekamp, Henry
Korponay, Gabriel
Lee, Saml
Leake, Nathan
Lee, John D
Larkin, Wm
Lister, John W
Lowry, Mrs A H
Lewis, Wm
Lawrence, Robt J
Legare, Miss Mary S-2
Leclair, Monsieur
Lavallete, Com E A F
Lewis, Saml L
Lewis, Jacob
Lamar, G B
Moore, Wilson D
Maus, Isaac R
Monk, Henry
Malahan, Thos
Martin, Thos
Miller, Mrs Mary E
Mortimore, Mary-2
Morris, Mrs Eliza Ann
Moses, Mrs Rosina
Myers, Mr
Maurice, chas
Murray, Mrs Mary
Mayers, John H
Meriwether, Geo W
Middleton, Miss K
Matthews, Henry
Mahoney, John J-3
McNeill, J & Chas Lyon
McDugall, Mrs Leah

McCollum, Jas
Maguire, Mrs Eliza
McNulty, Col C J
McGarr, John
Nourse, Henry M-2
Neale, Dr Robt
Nevitt, Capt J B-2
Nelson, John
Owens, Fenton
Oswell, Wm
Orgiazzi, Monsieur
Peak, Jas W
Poss, Gariel
Palm, Wm
Poole, Rev Wm C
Porter, Andrew
Piper, Col John
Philips, Thos
Persico, Signore
Pickett, J C
Perrie, Miss Susan
Perry, Miss Helen
Plummer, Fielder B
Peyton, Sallie
Parris, Virgil D
Queen, Mrs Ann
Quimby, A B
Quantrill, A R-2
Quantrill, Maj Thos
Quimby, Thos R
Roach, R J
Ricks, Jas Thos
Right, Miss Martha
Rall, Chas
Ruark, Mrs Eliz
Reiss, B
Rogers, Capt John
Riorden, Mr
Richardson, Wm
Rathbone, Maj W R
Ringgold, Mrs Ann
Reeder, Sarah
Robertson, Mrs E B

Robinson, A L
Randolph, Richd
Rennahan, M
Russell, J
Ridgley, Lt S C
Rowand, Chas L
Reading, Eliz
Reeside, Jas
Smith, Matilda R
Simmes, Miss Ellen
Scott, Saml T
Scott, Miss Maria R
Springs, Richd C
Schenck, Lt W S
Sheets & Co, Wm-2
Stone, Geo B
Slye, Mrs Mary P
Silcox, J
Sabin, H W
Spencer, Wm
Symington, Miss M S
Spigwill, Wm B
Simmons, David
Sewell, Jos
Spaulding, Mrs Mary
Stewart, Dr E H
Sanford, Hiram, U S N
Stewart, Miss J A F
Sturgess, Handy J
Slicer, M
Sampson, T W
Seddon, Jas A
Stoney, Edgar G-2
Snyder, Wm F
Storor, Capt G W-3
Stanly, Edw
Sherburne, John H
Tod, Capt John G
Thurler, Wm
Thompson, Geo C
Thompson, Mrs M
Thompson, Alex
Territt, Mrs Julia-2

Thornton, Mrs Harriet
Tyler, Mrs Ann
Thorburn, Miss Martha
Tiller, John
Thomas, Wm B
Ten Eyck, Anthony-4
Tranah, Miss Ann
Upton, Chas H
Vance, David C
Valentine, Mrs Louisa
Valentine, Mrs Deliha
Vandegrift, Henry W
Villagrand, Mr
Wright, Henry
Ward, Wm H
Wright, Geo
Wood, R
Wood, Miss Sarah
Wall, Capt Wm
Wolf, John S
White, Miss M Ann
Wood, Mrs Abbey C
Welch, Jos
Williams, mrs H B
Wesson, Miss Emeline
Wilkinson, Geo
Wilson, Thos
Walters, Capt Jas
Wilkinson, Miss E B
Watkins, Miss M A
Walker, Miss Lizzie
Wratcliff, Catharine
Woodworth, W W
Wharton, Robt S
Wallis, Wm
Waters, David S
Waldron, R R
Whalon, Jas
Wiley, Bernard-2
Wincard, Wm
Winser, Lewis
Wingard, Saml C
Wilson, Jas G
Wilson, Mrs Dr C L
Watson, Miss Mary A
Watson, John L
Wilson, Chas E
Willard, Wm H-3
Washington & Mason-3
Xaveria, Jose de-2
Young, Mrs R
Young, Miss Camilla
Yeatman, Arthur H

The inland postage on all letters intended to go by ship must be paid, otherwise they remain in this ofc. -C K Gardiner, P M

Naval: The U S ship **Mississippi** was to have sailed from the Charleston Navy Yard yesterday for the Gulf of Mexico. The following is a list of her ofcrs:

Capt Andrew Fitzhugh　　　　　　　　Cmder, Henry A Adams
Lts: Wm Smith, John C Carter, Wm A Parker, Francis S Haggerty
Acting Master: Henry Rodgers　　　　Assist Surgeon: Washington Sherman
Purser: Lewis Warrington, jr　　　　　Prof of Math: Mark H Beecher
Surgeon: A G Gambrill　　　　　　　　Chief Engineer: Wm Sewell, jr
Midshipmen: Oscar C Badger, John Walcutt, Thos S Fillebrown, Jas Wiley, John Wilkes, jr, Wm K Bridge, Francis Gregory, D A Cheever
1st Assist Engineers: D B Martin, Levi Griffin　　　　3rd Assist Engineers: J Follansbee, W F Mercier
2nd Assist Engineers: Danl Murphy, J R Dryburg　　　Capt's Clerk: Berkely Ward
　　　　　　　　　　　　　　　　　　　Purser's Clerk: Geo Hutchinson

We learn that a person named Hall dropped down yesterday in Gtwn & died suddenly in the street.

New Orleans, Jul 22, 1845. The 3rd Regt of Infty leaves tomorrow on the steamship **Alabama**, for the Bay of Aransas, near Corpus Christi, Texas, & letters or packages should be directed as above, in care of the Quartermaster in New Orleans. The following is a list of the ofcrs of the regt, & of the ground staff serving with it:

Lt Col: E A Hitchcock, Commanding Surgeon: N S Jarvis
Brevet Capt: P N Barbour, Adj Assist Surgeon: A W Kennedy
Capts: L N Morris, H Bainbridge, J Van Horne, G P Field
Lts:

J L Coburn	D T Chandler	J B Richardson	G C McClelland
W S Henry	S D Dobbins	W T H Brooks	H B Schroder
J H Eaton	B R Johnson	A W Bowman	J J C Bibb
L S Craig	W B Johns	C Sykes	
J M Smith	D S Irwin	C E Jarvis	
W H Gordon	D C Buell	J C McFerran	

The regt is 567 strong, [all included,] in perfect health, & eager to plant the stars & stripes on the banks of the Rio Grande.

SAT AUG 2, 1845
Washington High School: 3rd academic year will commence on the first Mon in Sept. –Edwin Arnold, A M, D C L, Principal

Emigrants from Europe & the Northern States can get bargains in lands in Va, near Wash City, & in the States of Ky & Ohio, & in the Territory of Wisconsin, by application to the owner & subscriber, residing near Alexandria, D C. Any letters addressed to him must be post paid. –Wm M McCarty

Very valuable Farm in Harford Co, Md, for sale: The subscribers offer, at private for the present, sale of their farm called *Moale's Success*, the residence of the late Saml G Smith: contains about 400 acs: on the western side of the head of Swan Creek, 4½ miles from Havre-de-Grace: 2 landings on the premises: dwlg-house is substantial & handsome, 48 feet front by 32 feet deep. Any further information can be obtained of John Jay, who will show the premises, or of the subscribers. –F F Smith, M M Smith, Hall's X Roads P O, Harford Co, Md.

Wilmington [Delaware] Journal: Dr Wm Gibbons died in this city on Fri last. [Dr Gibbons was the father of Chas Gibbons, of Pa, a member of the State Senate of Pa.] As a man of science & literature, he was eminent in a high degree, & his benevolent heart & gentle manners endeared him to all.

The 2nd Regt U S Dragoons, which has taken up the line of march for Corpus Christi, in Texas, numbers upwards of 500 men, besides some 60 public wagons, for transportation of supplies. The following are the names of the ofcrs: Field & Staff: Col J E Twiggs, Maj T T Fauntleroy, Adj H H Sibley; Capt O Cross, Quartermaster; Brevet Capt R A Arnold, Commissary of Subsistence; W L Wharton, Surgeon; Geo Buist, Assist Surgeon; A Geo Stevens, Topographical Engineer. Capts: W M Fulton, C Ker, Seth Thornton, C A May, N W Hunter, L P Graham, W J Hardee 1st Lts: O P Ransom, A Lowry, W H Saunders, Fowler Hamilton, O F Winship 2nd Lts: R P Campbell, Wm Steele, Lewis Neill, R H Anderson, Geo T Mason Brevet 2nd Lts: J H Whittlesey, Augustus Cook

The remains of 6 bodies in all have been recovered from the ruins of the late devastating fire in N Y. The bodies of Mr Cowdry & Mr Groening, both of whom are known to have perished, have not been recovered.

Stewarts-town, N C, Jun 15, while the children of a school were at play, lightning struck a tree & killed the following: Thos Overstreet-18; Richd Coe-14; & Henry Wade-16.

University of Virginia commences on Oct 1 & terminates on Jun 29th following. –Willis H Woodley, Proctor & Patron, Univ of Va

Died: on Wed, near Balt, of typhus fever, Francis Clark Meigs, the grandon of the late Francis Clark, of Wash City. The friends of his family are requested to attend his funeral from the Railroad Depot, on Sat, this morning, at half past 11 o'clock, without further notice.

Died: on Jul 12, Mrs Lucy F Smith, widow of the late Govn'r Smith, of Va, in her 73rd year. She had resided here for many years as the consort of Meriwether Jones, & more recently that of the lamented Gov Smith. She was the intimate friend & correspondent of the accomplished Wm Wirt. –Richmond Whig

For rent: residence on the corner of G & 6th sts: large & commodious. Inquire of Jas Owner, at the Genr'l Post Ofc, or of the subscriber. –H Allen

Trustee's sale: by virtue of a decree of PG Co Court, sitting as a Court of Equity, the undersigned trustees will offer at public sale, on the premises, on Aug 26, the valuable farm in PG Co, about 4 miles n e of Bladensburg, known as the property of Thos Wall, dec'd, late of said county, containing about 238 acs. Improvements are a good dwlg-house, a barn, & other necessary out-houses. –Jesse H D Wall, Washington, Jas T Wall, Trustees

MON AUG 4, 1845
Wm H McGuffey, of Cincinnati, has been elected Prof of Moral Philosophy & Political Economy, in the Univ of Va, in place of Geo Tucker, resigned, & Jno B Minor, of Albemarle Co, Va, appointed Prof of Law, in place of H St George Tucker, resigned.

The Hon Saml G Wright, a Rep elect to the next Congress from the second district of N J, died at Allentown on the 30th ult.

The London papers announce the death of the eminent barrister, Mr Adolphus, suddenly, on Jul 16. He distinguished himself as counsel of the prisoners at the trial of Thistlewood & the other Cato st prisoners.

The mail from Chestertown to Sandy Hill, N Y, was robbed by the carrier, Danl Hilliard, on Sun. He was arrested, making partial confession of the act, & fully committed for trial.

Circuit Court of Wash Co, D C-in Chancery, Mar term, 1845. Geo Parker vs Catharine W Hand, widow & excx, Catharine C Hand, & others, heirs at law of Jos W Hand, dec'd. The trustee in this cause having reported, on May 6, 1845, he sold all that parcel of ground in Wash City, being part of lot 11 in square 690, with 3 story brick bldg & appurtenances to the said piece or parcel of ground belonging, to Mrs Frances W Cook, she being the highest bidder, for the sum of $1,550, & that she complied with the terms of the sale. –Wm Brent, clk

St Louis New Era of Jul 25. On Jul 23, the steamer **Big Hatshee**, Capt Frisbee, bound from this place to Weston, burst her starboard boiler as she was shoving out from the landing at Herman. Badly wounded: Patrick Currigan, fire-man; Arthur Neal, of Callaway Co, passenger; Thompson Gaines, Saline Co, passenger; Harman Spellman, of Germany, & John Ryan, firemen; John Hammonds, of Van Buren Co, passenger; John Barber, of Bath Co, Ky, passenger; Wm Pulliam, passenger; Bolivar Foster, Callaway Co, passenger; Robt Carter, of Osage Co, passenger-all badly scalded & many will not survive. Slightly scalded: Zachariah Titus, Warren Co, Pa, passenger; Geo Carrico & wife, of Carroll Co, Mo; also a negro belonging to them; Thos Pearce, of Boone Co, Mo, passenger; Cornelius McGinis, Mason Co, Ky; E W Richardson, fireman, Summit Co, Ohio; Mrs Amelia Sparey, *Fort Leavenworth*. Escaped unhurt: Mrs Amelia Allen, Adair Co, Ky; John Juda & wife, Clark Co, Mo; Capt Bennett, Calloway Co, Mo; Winslow Turner, Pittsburg, Pa; Enos Taylor & wife, N Y; Capt Frisbee, Jas Miller, clerk; John Allen, pilot of the boat; & between 8 & 10 hands & firemen.

Rittenhouse Academy: the Annual Exhibition of the young gentlemen, under the tuition of Messrs Chas H & Jos E Nourse, was held in their neat & commodious edifice, on La ave last Thu afternoon. It is now 5 years since the academy was established; the number of their students averaged from 65 to 70 each year.

City Ordnances: Act for the relief of A C Kidwell: that $228.92 be appropriated, payable to A C Kidwell, to make good a deficiency in the appropriation for certain footways in the Second Ward.

TUE AUG 5, 1845
On Mon last, Mr Jas Rowland, near the Cross Roads, Middlesex Co, N J, fell while loading a saw log, & the log rolled upon him, causing his death. He was about 40, & left a large family.

U S Circuit Court at Boston, on Fri last: sentence pronounced on Peter Flowery, convicted of fitting out the schnr **Spitfire**, with intent to engage in the slave-trade. He was fined $2,000, & 5 years in the common jail.

Accident. On Jul 20, a horse, upon which the wife of Nathl Burris, near Vincennes, Indiana, was riding, stepped upon a hornet's nest. The insects immediately commenced stinging the horse, whereupon he reared & threw Mrs Burris, & then fell backward upon her, crushing her instantly to death.

Horse & Gig, harness, & furniture, at auction, by order of the Orphans Court of Wash Co, D C. Sale at Mr W Bell's dyeing establishment, near 4½ st, Pa ave, the personal effects of the late John C Wallis, dec'd, consisting of: horse & gig, harness, saddle, bridle, 4 trunks & contents, lots of clothing, silver watch, bookcase, & mattresses.
–A Green auctioneer

Three valuable farms for sale: subscribers, excs of the late Thos Parker, will sell at private sale the farm on which the dec'd resided, about 2 miles from Vansville, PG Co, Md, containing about 194 acs. Adjoining the home place, another farm of about 174 acs, & near the above farms, a small farm of about 50 acs. The farms all have convenient dwlg-houses & all necessary out-houses. Apply to Mr John Parker, who will show the premises. Inquire of Thos Parker, living in Wash. –Thos Parker, John Parker, excs

Appointments by the Pres:
Wm E Russell, Register of the land ofc at Danville, Ill, in place of John W Vance, whose commission will expire on Aug 24, 1845.
Geo P Manouvrier, of La, Consul for Pernambuco, Brazil, in place of G T Snow, recalled.
Stewart Steel, of Pa, Consul for Dundee, in Scotland, in place of Edw Baxter, recalled.
Joel Truuill, of N Y, Consul for the Sandwich Islands, in place of Alex'r G Abell, recalled.
Saml Haight, of La, Consul for the Azores, or Western Islands, in place of Chas W Dabney.

Alex'r J Bergen, of N Y, Consul for the island of Bermuda, in place of Wm Tudor Tucker, recalled.

Stephen S Levy, Postmaster at Lowell, Mass, in place of Jacob Robbins, removed.

Stephen R Mallory, at Key West, Florida, vice Adam Gordon, removed. [Ofc not specified.]

Abel C Pepper, U S Marshal for the district of Indiana, in place of Robt Hanna, whose commission has expired.

Wanted, a nice colored girl, about 15 years of age, as Nurse. Apply at Mrs Fischer's, Pa ave, near 12th st.

The undersigned informs that his son, John Edw Thompson, will be associated with him in his business as a Collector, Genr'l Agent, Scrivener, & Accountant.
–Wm Thompson & Son

Stray Cow: liberal reward for anyone who will return her to the subscriber, or give him information where she may be found. –B B French, East Capitol st, Capitol Hill

For sale or exchange for property in Wash City: desirable piece of property over Hunting Creek Bridge, being part of a tract known as the *West Grove* estate. There are about 51 acres in the tract. –F Forrest

WED AUG 6, 1845
Among the passengers who sailed from N Y in the steamer **Great Western** on Thu last for Liverpool was Gansevoort Melville, U S Sec of Legation to London.

Florida. H Carrington Cabell, formerly of Richmond, Va, & s/o Judge Wm H Cabell, has been selected as the Whig candidate for Congress, in place of Mr Levy, resigned; & Mr Wm H Brockenbrough, formerly of the Univ of Va, has been nominated for the same ofc as the Democratic candidate.

Appointments by the Pres:
1-Wm J Grayson, Collector of the Customs at Charleston, S C, reappointed; to take effect on Aug 6, 1845, when his present commission will expire. 2-Arthur R Crozier, Register of the Land Ofc at St Louis, Mo, vice Wm S Allen, removed. 3-John A Langlois, Receiver of Public Moneys, at Kaskaskia, Ill, vice Richd B Servant, removed.

Circuit Court of Wash Co, D C, Mar Term, 1845. Maria C French, admx de bonis non of Geo French, vs Jas Dundas, trustee, & the heirs of Geo French, dec'd. By decree passed, bearing the date of Jul 14, 1845, will be sold at public auction, a tract of land called ***Aaron***, containing or estimated to contain 340 acs, being the same lying on the eastern side of the Anacostia or Eastern Branch of Columbia. –David A Hall, Trustee
-A Green, auctioneer

Teacher wanted. A single gentleman, competent to teach Mathematics, & assist in the general duties of an Academy, in Upper Marlborough Academy. Applications to be made by letter, or personally after Sep 15, to the subscriber.
–H C McLaughlin, Principal of the Upper Marlborough Academy.

The undersigned notifies the creditors of the estate of the late Tully R Wise, dec'd, that he is now ready to distribute the assets in his hands belonging to it, on Aug 11, at the house of Maj Wm D Nutt, on Vt ave, a few doors from the residence of M St Clair Clarke. –John C Wise, Adm of T R Wise, dec'd

THU AUG 7, 1845
Orphans Court of Wash Co, D C. Letters of administration on the personal estate of Wm James, late of said county, dec'd. –Mary W James, admx

Othniel Looker, sen, died on Jul 23, at Palestine, Ill. He was born in N J, Oct 6, 1757, & served 5 years in the army during the war of the Revolution. He emigrated to Hamilton Co, Ohio, in 1804, & was elected to represent the people of that county in the Senate of Ohio in 1813. He was afterwards elected Speaker of the Senate, & after the resignation of Govn'r Meigs in 1814, became acting Govn'r of Ohio. He was an Associate Judge of Hamilton Co Court of Common Pleas for the term of 7 years.

Capt Benj Roper died at Salem, Mass, last week, in his 73rd year. He was a brave ofcr in the army of the late war, & commanded a company in Col Miller's Regt. He participated in the brilliant affair at Lundy's Lane, in the sortie from **Fort Erie**, at Chippewa, & several hard fought fields, & was frequently especially noticed in the official dispatches for his meritorious services & gallant conduct.

On Jul 17 the remains of Danl Boon, the celebrated Western pioneer, & those of his wife, were disinterred & removed from Warren Co, Missouri, & taken to Frankfurt, Ky, where they are to be re-interred, & a monument erected over them.

Died: on Aug 6, in Wash City, after a short illness, Mrs Ellen Hubbard Nalley, w/o Wm H Nalley, aged 18 years, 8 months & 18 days. Her funeral is this afternoon at 4 o'clock, at the residence of her father, Mr H Knowles, on D st.

On Sat last, on the Worcester Railroad, in Boston, near the depot, Mr Lewis Holmes, of East Weymouth, was thrown from the driver's seat of the stage & instantly killed, the wheels of the cars passing over his head. Other passengers in the stage were considerably bruised. The horses had become restless & backed upon the rails as the train was coming.

Country Seat for rent: the country seat of the late Jos Nourse, about 30 acs, on the heights of Gtwn: house has been fully repaired. The keys may be had at Mr Levis' store, on the turnpike road, nearly opposite the gate of the premises. Terms very moderate.
–Chas J Nourse

Tiber Mill for rent: situated within the limits of Wash City, & about a mile north of the Capitol. Information can be obtained by applying at Mrs Pearson's, near the mill.

FRI AUG 8, 1845
From the Georgia papers: Jas A Everett, of Houston Co, a few days ago, donated $8,000 to the Georgia Female College at Macon, which sum was necessary to relieve the College from debt.

St Vincent's Female Orphan Asylum, Jul 27, 1845, election held at the Rector's House of St Patrick's Church for managers of the asylum, & the following ladies were elected:

Mrs Newman, 1st Directress	Mrs Graham
Mrs Talbot, 2nd Directress	Mrs Blake
Mrs Ann S Hill, Treasurer	Mrs Riggs
Mrs Chas Hill	Mrs E A Lee, Sec
Mrs Stubbs	

Capt E G Colby, of the ship **Clarissa Andrews**, has been held to bail in Boston in the sum of $3,000 for putting out the eye of one of the crew by shooting him with a pistol. The seaman was in a state of phrenzy at some fancied wrong, & it became absolutely necessary to shoot him, in order to disarm him of an axe with which he threatened all on board.

Mr Peter Rose, the well-known cutler & manufacturer of surgical instruments, of 412 Broadway, formerly of William st, committed suicide yesterday, at Hoboken, by shooting himself through the heart with a pistol. He had reasons to apprehend that his family would come to want. His body was delivered to his son, who had been sent for, & it was conveyed to his late residence in this city. Mr Rose left a large family to mourn his untimely end. –Courier & Enquirer

Wash Corp: 1-The Cmte of Claims: asked to be discharged from the further consideration of the ptn of John N Ashton. 2-Ptn of Wilhelme Grupe: referred to the Cmte of Claims. 3-Ptn of Jas Maniken & others, for widening of the gutter on 9th st: passed. 4-Act for the relief of F A Russell: passed. 5-Nomination of W P Elliot, as Surveyor of the city: ordered to lie on the table. 6-Act for the relief of the heirs of Geo Adams, dec'd: ordered to lie on the table. 7-Same for the ptn of Mrs Ann Creamer.

SAT AUG 9, 1845
Very desirable & valuable property at private sale. The well known *Globe Hotel*, on the south side of Pa ave, & opposite the Union ofc: it has long been very profitably occupied as a hotel by Mr Jas Maher: the lot fronts 31 feet on Pa ave & runs back 70 feet: the house is commodious, containing 21 rooms, with excellent back bldgs & good yard. The property is now unoccupied & will not be rented, the owner determined to sell. The key can be had on application to Mr Jas Maher, or to the subscribers. –R W Dyer & Co, aucts

Valuable estate for sale: subscriber will sell *Bowieville*, lying in PG Co, Md, containing 500 acres of land: dwlg, built at great cost: has every necessary out-bldg: lies in the centre of that delightful region known as the Forest of PG. He will also sell a tract adjoining the above, containing about 250 acres of the same quality. The title to both of these tracts is unquestionable. –Robt Bowie, Good Luck P O, PG Co, Md

Private sale of the Iron Works known as the *Mary Ann & Augusta Furnaces*, at the base of South Mountain, 3 miles from Shippensburg, Cumberland Co, Pa: has a mansion house, & other out-bldgs. Also, for sale, 2 valuable Limestone farms, containing each about 300 acs: on one is a large stone house: on the other is a good plastered house: each with out-bldgs. The charter of the Carlisle Bank having expired on May 7 last, the Directors are under the necessity of winding up affairs of the institution; they, with Jacob M Haldeman, who owns an undivided interest in the above mentiond, will sell on moderate terms. Inquire of Mr Jos W Patton, in Carlisle. –Geo A Lyon, S D Henderson, Cmte of Carlisle Bank. –J M Haldeman, Carlisle

Notice: by virtue of a writ of fiera facias issued by Thos C Donn, J P for Wash Co, D C, at the suit of Andrew Stappar, against the goods & chattels, lands & tenements, rights & credits, of Peter Bartoni, to me directed: I shall his bay horse, on Aug 16, in front of the Centre Market. –H R Maryman, Constable

Appointments by the Pres:
David C Glenn, Receiver of Public Moneys for the district of lands subject to sale at Jackson, Miss, vice Isaac McFarran, resigned.
Rufus O Pray, Collector of Customs for the district of Pearl river, Miss, vice John J McCaughan, who delines the appointment.

Mrd: on Aug 7, by Rev H Myers, Mr Thos A Jameson to Miss Mary Henrietta Barkley, all of Chas Co, Md.

Mrd: on Jul 28, in Wash City, at the Wesley Chapel, by Rev Thos Sewall, of Balt, Prof Lorenzo D McCabe, of Athens, Ohio, to Miss Martha E, d/o Danl Sewall, of Farmington, Maine.

Died: on Aug 7, in Alexandria, Mrs Anna Maria Hardin, w/o Lauriston B Hardin, of the Navy Dept, in her 28th year. She faithfully fulfilled her duties as a dght, wife & mother. She died after an exceedingly protracted & distressing malady. Her funeral will take place from the residence of her father, Bernard Hooe, this afternoon, at 4 o'clock.

Died: on Aug 5, in great peace, at *Low Hill*, Fairfax Co, Va, Mary, consort of John Dulin, aged 61 years & & one day.

Died: on Aug 8, Rev Henry C Turner, Pastor in charge of Israel Church, after a short illness. His funeral is Sun at 3 o'clock, at the Israel Church.

Companies C & D, of the 4th Regt of U S Infty, reached St Louis on Jul 30, & took passage down the Mississippi, destined for Texas. They are under the command of Capts Graham & McCall.

The subscriber, who served in the 12th Regt of U S Infty during the last war, is desirous of information as to the present residence [if still living] of Lt Hughes & Ensign Parker, then attached to that Regt. Any person will communicate to the subscriber, addressed to Junior Post Ofc, Green Township, Scioto Co, Ohio, with such information as will enable him to correspond with either of the above gentlemen, will assist an old crippled soldier. –Wilson Sullivan

Murder & Arson: last Sun the store-room of Messrs Peterbaugh & Allison, [at Xenia, Ohio,] was consumed by fire. Jas Kenney, a clerk, who slept in the store, was found senseless, cut & bruised, & died that day. The other young man, Wm Steele, another clerk, who slept in the store, also died. His body was discovered in the cellar where it had fallen through.

Accident at East Boston: On Sat, John Davis, 9 years of age, was attempting to jump on the cars, & fell & was crushed to death. Mr Danl Crowley attempted to cross the railroad track, on Marginal st, in a wagon, regardless of the bell: the wagon was demolished, but the man & horse escaped uninjured.

On Sat last, while a party were hunting deer in Plymouth, Mass, Mr Jerome Purrington was accidentally shot & killed by Mr Augustus Holmes. Mr Purrington was from Rhode Island, on a visit to his father in Carver, & was one of the party.

Fatal accident at Columbia, Pa: on Sun last, Michl Schloat, a man employed in the warehouse of D Leech & Co, in a state of but partial consciousness, fell on the end of the iron brake handle of a railroad car standing against the side of the house; the handle, projecting upwards, passed entirely through his body. He survived until Monday.

MON AUG 11, 1845
Young Ladies High School: H H Smith, M A & Miss Abbie B Smith, Principals. The next quarter will commence on Sep 1: location, 11th st, between F & G sts. Reference: I have been acquainted for some time with Mr Smith & sister, & take pleasure in recommending their Seminary. –John C Smith, Pastor 4th Presbyterian Church

Notice: The subscriber, in the Hardware Business, has associated with him Chas A Buckey & John Marbury, jr: at the old stand under the firm of E M Linthicum & Co. –E M Linthicum, Gtwn

The 2nd Regt of the U S Dragoons, under command of Col Twiggs, took up the line of march for Texas from Nitchitoches on Jul 25. The Chronicle says that they are to be stationed at San Antonio de Bexar.

Writing & Stenography at his Academy on Pa ave, near 12th st. –W B Malcolm

Genteel furniture at auction: household & kitchen furniture: on Aug 13, at the residence of Mr Wm Benthall, on 1st st. –E S Wright, Auctioneer

The ***Ryland Chapel***, near the corner of 10th st & Md ave, was dedicated yesterday.

Died: on Aug 8, suddenly, in his 66th year, Jas Summers, formerly of Fred'k Co, Md, but for the last 13 years a resident of Wash, & at the time of his death a clerk in the Patent Ofc.

Died: on Aug 9, Mrs Rebecca Riffetts, aged 80 years. Her funeral is this morning, at 10 o'clock, from the residence of her son-in-law, Presley Simpson.

TUE AUG 12, 1845
Desiring to make room for an extensive supply of Fall & Winter Goods, we will offer any & all summer fabrics in store at prime cost. –Perry & Ashby

Richmond, Aug 11. On Fri last, during the storm, Eliza Ann Putney, d/o Mr Saml Putney, & Mary M White, d/o Mr P K White were struck dead by lightning. They were but 14 years of age, were at Mr White's house, on Union Hill, sitting in the basement on a sofa. Lightning struck the house, descended through the upper rooms, & a part went along the bell-wire to the front door, & some how it connected with the basement. They were the only dghts in their respective families. Each family had a son & a dght. Mr & Mrs Putney are now in the North. -Compiler

The subscriber informs his customers that they can now obtain, at very reduced prices, any article of dress goods that may be appropriately designated summer wear. –Geo W Adams, Pa ave, between 8th & 9th sts.

Virginia: At a Court held for Nelson Co, at the Court-house, on Jul 28, 1845: on the motion of Mary Stroud, one of the heirs & distributees of Jas Stroud, dec'd, & it appearing to the Court that 2 years have expired since letters of administration were granted upon the estate of said decendent to Wm Robinson; the Court orders that all persons who may have claims do exhibit the same for settlement within 3 months from this time; & that a copy of this order be published for 8 successive weeks in the Nat'l Intelligencer, & some newspaper published in Wilmington, Dela. –Sp Garland, Clerk. In pursuance of the foregoing order, the creditors of Jas Stroud, dec'd, [who, having removed from Delaware to Virginia, became a contractor on the James River & Kanawha Canal, & died in Nelson Co,] are to make known their claims as speedily as possible to the undersigned, acting for the administrator, at Charlottesville, Va.
–Wood & Watson, Attys

Positive sale of a valuable farm: by virtue of a decree of the Court of Chancery of Md, the undersigned Trustee will offer at public sale, on Sep 20, 1845, at Baldwin's Tavern, in Bladensburg, that Farm called *Clover Farm*, in PG Co, on the Good Luck road: contains about 273 acs; a good dwlg, barn, & other out-bldgs. It is at present occupied by Mr Weeden, who will show the premises. –M Courtney Jenkins, Trustee, Balt, Md.

Teacher wanted: subscriber wishes to employ a gentleman to reside in his family who is fully competent, from a through knowledge of Latin & Greek languages & the various branches of Mathematics, to prepare boys for college. Please forward certificates to the subscriber, near Queen Anne, PG Co, Md. –Wm Clark

Meeting of the Delegates appointed by the several counties composing the First Congressional District of Md, held on Aug 9, for nominating a suitable person to represent them in the next Congress of the U S.
Dr Hanson Penn, of PG Co, called the meeting to order, & Alex'r Kilgour, of Montg Co, was appointed Pres, & Jas McCormick, of Chas Co, Sec. Delegates called, when the following answered to their names:
Anne Arundel: Jas Kent, Dr S Gambell, Dr Lynch, D McBrogden, Alex'r Randall
Montgomery: Elisha R Griffith, Alex'r Kilgour, W M Stewart, Robt W Carter, Geo W Dawson, John Braddock, Saml D Waters, Dr Hardy, Jas Hawes, Thos Fawcett, Edw Daws, Rich J Bentley, Zedediah Gettings.
Calvert: Thos J Hillen
PG: Dr J M S Maccubbin, Thos J Marshall, Dr Hanson Penn, Dr Richd W Bowie, Richd L Ogle.
Chas Co: John D Freeman, Jonas Hawkins, Saml Cox, Jas McCormick
St Mary's: Richd H Reeder

From Europe: Earl Grey, father of the Reform Act, & for 4 years Prime Minister, died at his residence, Hewick Hall, on Jul 17, aged 81.

A boat, containing 8 men, swamped on Tue at the foot of Gordon falls, on the Penobscot river, & 4 drowned: Stephen White, Isaac Hall, Sampson Gulliver, & Mr Ferguson.

Died: yesterday, Mrs Eliz Noland, in her 84th year. Her funeral is this evening, at 4 o'clock, from the residence of her grandson, Jas H Collins, near the Long Bridge.

WED AUG 13, 1845
Mr O N Steele died at Athens, on Aug 7, in consequence of wounds received from the Anti-Rent Indians.

Murder of Oregon Emigrant: letter from Mr A W Russell, of Platte City, Missouri: giving information of the murder by Sioux Indians, of Mr Aldis A Robinson, of Tioga Co, N Y.

An inquest was held on Sat, at Alexandria, over the body of Mr Saml Sipple, who died suddenly on Thu. Verdict: he came to his death by the injudicious treatment of a Thompsonian practitioner.

Mrd: on Aug 4, at Rockville, Md, by Rev L J Gilliss, Henry Allen to Mrs Kitty Anne Grant.

Assignee's sale of 7,190 acres of land in Pa: in the matter of C S Fowler, a bankrupt. Auction on Sep 12, at the auction rooms of A Green, in Wash City: the tracts of land lie in the township of Montgomery, in Indiana Co, Pa, which were conveyed by patent, under the great seal of the said State in 1835. –David A Hall, Assignee of Bankrupts -A Green, Auctioneer

Money found on Mon last in the bldg occupied by the Post Ofc Dept, which the owner can have by giving a description thereof, & paying for this advertisement, by application to Rd Dement, of the Post Ofc Dept.

$1.00 reward: lost, on Aug 12, by a boy who was sent home with them, one rib-cross Breastpin, one Filegre wreath ditto, & chased finger Ring. Reward for returning the above to Peter McCardle, watchmaker, between 10th & 11th sts, on Pa ave, or Jos Huggins, jeweler, on F st.

THU AUG 14, 1845
Worthington G Snethen, Atty & Counsellor at Law: Missouri Ave, Wash, D C. [Ad]

House & lot on Pa ave for sale at public auction: by virtue of a deed of trust, executed on Apr 29, 1841, duly recorded in Liber W B 86, folio 220 to 224: sale of lot 15 in square 168; with improvements thereon, a small 2 story brick house. –Rd Smith, Trustee -R W Dyer & Co, aucts

French & English Boarding & Day School for Young Ladies, 6th st, corner of D st, Wash. Miss Cheshire has engaged several competent female teachers. The scholastic year commences on the first Mon of Sep.

Mrd: on Aug 12, by Rev Jas Knox, Mr Andrew Johnson to Miss Susan Ann Robinson, all of Wash City.

The Albany Journal says that the murder of Deputy Sheriff Steele was a cold-blooded assassination by a party of "Indians," in Delaware Co, N Y. It appears incredible that in a neighborhood of farmers, a hundred men could be got together, who, in broad daylight, in the presence of a crowd of spectators, could deliberately shoot down a fellow creature because he dared to do his duty. Actors & spectators, 'Indians' & whites, participated at this fiendish murder.

Died: on Jul 29, after a short illness, in the 2nd year of her age, Maria Louisa Dorsett, d/o T J & H Dorsett, of Anne Arundel Co, Md.

Died: yesterday, in his 55th year, Richd M Waring, for the last 5 years a resident of Wash City. His funeral is this afternoon, at 4 o'clock, from his late residence on Md ave, between 6th & 7th sts.

English & Classical School will be opened on Sep 1, at the Hall of the Wash Benevolent Society, G st, between 6th & 7th sts. The subscriber, a teacher of 14 years' experience, & late Principal of an Academy on the eastern Shore of Md, will devote his time exclusively to the duties of the School. –Francis S Dunham

FRI AUG 15, 1845

Mr Custis in N Y. The arrival of Geo Washington Parke Custis, the grandson of Mrs Washington & the adopted son of the great chief, with his Lady, after a lapse of 54 years since his first visit here, in his youth, with the Father of his Country, has been deemed an event of entraordinary interest. Mr Custis visited the house at the corner of Cherry st & Franklin square, in which Gen Washington first resided as Pres of the Republic. Letter: Lenox Place, N Y, Aug 7, 1845; 22nd st, near 8th ave. Invitation to spend Aug 9, at my residence with the Hon Custis & Lady, of Va. –Jno R Peters. The event. Venerable guests began to assemble: Alderman Peters [himself the s/o Gen Absalom Peters, a brave ofcr in the Rev army,] & his lady, d/o the Hon John Lovett, formerly a member of Congress, & an ofcr in the last war; Maj Popham, aged 93, aid in the Revolutionary war to Gen Jas Clinton, f/o De Witt Clinton; Mr John Battin, aged 92; John Van Buren; Judges Miller, Lynch, & Edwards; Dr Jas Manley, Thos Morris, [born in 1771,] A L Underhill, [1763,] Zuenis Quick, [1767,] Robt Cheesborough, [1776,] Jas Black, of Newark, [1767,] Cornelius Bogart, [1775,] Jacob Hays, [who carried a staff & was marshal of Gen Washington's inauguration,] Rev Dr Lyell, Dr Gilbert Smith, John

Mulligan, Elisha Whittlesey, [for many years member of Congress from Ohio,] Dr John W Francis, Rev Dr Mathews, Henry Talmadge, Danl B Talmadge, M M Noah, Hosmer Curtis, Geo B Thorp, Geo Hopkins, W Mandeville, J D Beers, Isaac Hopper, Dr Bliss, W Vermilye, Jos Weeks, Jos M Crane, Preserved Fish, Professor Griscom, Nicholas Dean, Abraham Van Nest, Geo Dummer, Abm R Lawrence, Richd M Lawrence, & others. Mr Custis, with his lady & only dght, Mrs Lee, with her oldest son, age 12 years, bearing the name of this grandfather, arrived & were received with the most cordial respect & enthusiasm. The father of Mr Custis was the only son of Mrs Genr'l Washington by a previous marriage, a gallant young ofcr of the war of Independence, who died from zeal & exposure in the cause, immediately after the surrender of Cornwallis. Mr Custis was adopted as a son by the Father of his Country, & made heir to some of his most valuable estates. Two sons of Dr Francis, were introduced to Mr Custis as the grandsons of Gen Marion, when Mr Custis, calling his own grandson, [who is also the grandson of Gen Henry Lee,] introduced the 3 to Maj Pophan. Maj Pophan had a badge with him once worn by Washington as Pres of the Cincinnati, an eagle set in diamond with a blue riband attached, & which is now worn by himself as occupying that ofc. We can hardly imagine a more interesting scene.

St Matthew's Church. Rev Mr Verhaegan, provincial of the Jesuits, will preach here on Aug 15: Assumption of the Blessed Virgin Mary. Divine service at 10 a m. –John P Donelan, Pastor

Letters remaining in the Post Ofc, Wash City, Aug 15, 1845.

Auld, Capt Hugh	Brown, Lt Wm H	Berry, Albert B-2
Armistead, Col John	Ball, Lt Wm H	Brosnahan, Cornelius
Anderson, John P	Bond, Mrs Laura E	Barclay, Dr J T
Aisquith, Wm	Brown, Simon-2	Brady, Alex
Ayars, Miss Anna A	Beall, Edw, U S N	Biewend, Rev Aug-3
Arnold, Miss Eliza A	Brent, Geo	Birchett, Richd T
Adams, A	Boman, Wm	Coombs, Dr Jas
Alexander, Edw F	Baker, Mrs Ellen	Chase, Miss Eliz
Abbott, Geo	Bowman, Hannah	Clarke, Oswald B
Ashton, Pass Mid H-2	Burnside, Jos	Childs, Mrs A
Broom, Robt H	Beverly, Col W B	Clay, John
Ball, John T	Baker, Mrs Catharine	Craig, Maj H K
Beach, Miss Jane C	Bunten, Miss C	Craigin, Dr C-2
Balch, Alfred	Baldwin, F P, U S N	Cotclazer, Jacob
Barnes, Geo W	Butler, Wm C	Caulkins, John H
Bright, R	Bradley, Maria	Cammann, J
Boyd, Thos	Braiden, Miss E	Calderwood, Thos
Brooke, Jas H	Bohrer, J S, U S N	Cropley, Wm S
Ball, Sydney	Belton, Miss Lucy	Carter, Robt, colored
Beall, Otho W	Bandel, Saml L	Canfield, J C

Chapman, Danl
Camow, David L
Chapple, Geo Thos
Colquit, W T-2
Diggs, Miss Jane E
Downes, Cmdor
Dodge, A C
Donaldson, Lt Jas L
Durand, E
Duvall, Andrew J
Daley, Jas
Daley, Mrs M A
Deneale, Wm H
Davis, Geo R
Dulany, Thos
Dolve, Geo
Duvall, Eli
Davis, Miss John L
Davidson, Lt John W
Dabney, W W
Eckardt, Thos
Espy, John
Edwards, John S
Elsworth, Mr stage con
Eckford, Jas
Elton, Prof R
Earhart, J T-2
Edward, Amory-4
Espy, Jas P-2
Flinn, Simon
Fletcher, Miss S A
Farish, Robt O
Foster, H J
Fulton, Wm S
Farley, Mrs Anna M
Farley, John
Fitzgerald, W B, U S N
Faron, jr, John, U S N
Graeve, Z
Groves, Capt Wm H
Gray, Rev Saml A-3
Green Gen Duff
Godrick, Jemima

Gallagher, Danl
Gater, Edw
Gorman, Peter
Gilbert, Monsieur
Giddings, Saml S
Goodye, Jos
Gilmer, Lt J H
Golden, Saml
Grimsley, Miss Marinda
Griffith, Wm A
Graham, Maj J D
Guegan, Henry
Humes, Geo
Hill, Miss
Hall, Wm H
Hall, Harvey
Hall, Hester
Hughes, A W
Hunt, Wm W
Hart, John
Hall, Miss Miranda
Hall, Edw
Hart, Noah H
Heide, Geo
Hodgkinson, Miss Mary
Hawkins, Chas G
Henderson, Chas A
Hanlenbeck, Mr
Haver, David
Hobtitz II, Jas H
Henshaw, J P R
Ingraham, Washington
Irons, Lt J F
Johnson, Mrs Caroline
Jordan, Willard
Jacobs, Loring
Johnston, Capt J E
Ingle, Henry
Johnson, A E
Jones, A D
James, G W
Keith, Cleveland-2
Keith, Mrs Eliza

King, Wm R
Keith, Lt I G
Kellmond, Wm
Kingsbury, Lt C P
Kidwell, John J
Kingsbury, Joanna
Kegan, John
Kervand, Monsieur
Korpunay, Gabriel
Kimball, F W
Lee, Miss Ellen
Lister, John W
Lemmons, David-2
Lewis, Mid R F R
Lamme, D S
Lowe, jr, Thos
Lawrence, Geo F
Loxey, R
Larkin, Wm
Little, Jas
Marks, Rev S A H
Mount, Thos L
Muntz, Mr
Manowvrier, F P
Mathias, G W
Moran, Jas
Middleton, Chas H
Middleton, Alex-2
Morgan, Geo
Macrae, Geo W
Monroe, Danl
Morsell, D K
Morgan, Rudolph S
Myers, Mrs Emily
Medary, M H
Menger, M R
Mayo, Mid Wm
Myerle, David
Mason, John
Minor, Col Geo
Miner, Benj
Mittrigger, C
Morgan, Washington

Milburn, Z F
Murray, Chas
Martin, Jas
McGrath, Jas
Maguire, Thos
McGregor, Jas
McIntosh, Mrs E J
McDevitt, John
McCardle, Maj W H
McElrach, H McD
McDougall, W R
Magee, Mary Ann
Nye, Thos C
Niles, Dr Nathl-3
Nicholas, Randall
Owings, Chas C
O'Regan, Jas
O'Leary, Miss Ellen
O'Bryon, B F
O'Brian, Mrs Susan
Price, Mr F
Prout, John
Peyton, Balie
Philips & Sampson
Philips, John
Purcell, Wm F
Pullen, Mrs Ann
Porter, Henry O
Parry, Alfred H
Porter, Rev Robt
Perry, Prof T H
Pendleton, E H
Parker, Francis E
Piper, Col John-4
Pollard, Maj Richd
Queen, Miss Mary
Quales, Benj
Rall, Leis-2
Rhet, R H
Rawling, Jas-2
Rathbun, Chas P
Renshaw, Corn Jas

Rogers, Col John
Robey, Townly B
Rustin, Thos
Robinson, Solon
Randolph, J B, U S N
Rinehart, Geo A
Reddy, Mrs Mary Ann
Rabit, Mrs Caroline
Simms, Mrs Cecelia
Sheels & Co, Wm
Smith, J Wightman
Smith, John Wilson
Speir, Robt
Sprigg, Osborn
Spears, John
Smith, Mrs Pauline
Smith, Miss Lizza
Smith, B M
Stone, M
Smith, D Hailes
Smith, Ashbel
Simmes, Miss Ellen
Simmes, John Francis
Simmes, Wm
Strong, Geo D-2
Stewart, Wm W
Sackett, Richd H
Shorter, C
Sharpless, Isaac
Simmons, Mrs Eliza
Scoville, J A
Sanaders, R M
Sisler, Mary-2
Storer, Capt Geo W-2
Thellerterger, Miss E T
Thomas, Col Jas
Tuzer, Mrs Julia A
Townsend, E
Taylor, Miss Eliza R
Thompson, John Thos
Thomas, M V
Thumblert, Mrs E

Thumblet, Jas E
Thompson, Mrs
Thompson, Mrs A
Talor, Arina
Trumbull, Maj Wm
Thomas, Wm H-7
Vondelehr, Geo
Ward, Wm H
Wright, Geo
Webb, John A
Wayne, Jas M
Waln, jr, Wm
Wade, John K
Wynne, Dr Jas
Ward, Geo W
Wood, Pliny
Ward, Mid Wm
Walch, Mrs
Weatherspoon, Jas
Wall, Wm H
Williams, Mrs Sarah
Williams, Mrs Francis
Williams, Miss Lucy
Warder, Miss S A-2
Williams, Rev Wm
Waters, David
Wilson, Mrs Cor L
Waters, Mr
Wilson, Wm
Williams, wm
Williams, Miss Ann-2
Wilkinson, Wm
Walter, T [Cherokee]
Walker, Carter
Woomer, C F, U S N
Yardy, John J
Young, Wilfed
Young, jr, Benj
Young, Miss Eliz
Zimmerman, Wm S

Mrs C McLeod's Academy, on H st, between 10th & 11th sts, will be re-opened on the first Mon of Sep.

Last evening, at the Arsenal on **Greenleaf's Point**, Albert Eiring, an artificer of the Ordnance Dept, employed in grinding percussion powder, to prepare it for charging percussion caps for muskets, when an explosion took place, in the laboratory where he was working. The bldg was demolished, & Mr Eiring was taken from the ruins in a dreadfully lacerated condition, so that no hopes can be entertained of his recovery. Dr Van Buren, of the U S Army, & Dr J F May, attended him. The poor man's left hand was blown off. [Aug 16th newspaper: Mr Albert Eiring, about 35, unmarried, died the same night about 9 o'clock.]

Miss Cynthia Browning, the Ky giantess, died at Flemingsburg, Ky, on Jul 30. She was 7 feet high.

Rev Lloyd Selby, local preacher of the Methodist Episcopal Church, was riding on horseback near the railroad, when the horse took fright, was caught by the iron forks attached to the engine, & was immediately killed. Mr Selby was so much injured that he died the following day. –Ellicott's Free Press

Died: on Wed, after a long & painful illness, Christopher O'Neale, in his 36th year. His funeral is this afternoon, at 3 o'clock, from his late residence, near the Navy Yard gate, Wash.

Died: on Aug 13, Rosina, w/o Henry Ingle, & d/o the late Archibald Chesire.

Wash Naval Lodge 4, Ancient York Masons, will meet this afternoon to pay the last tribute of respect to their dec'd Brother Christopher O'Neale, late member of that Lodge. –A G Herold, Sec

SAT AUG 16, 1845
Ofc of the Washington & Fredericksburg Steamboat Co, Richmond, Va, Aug 11, 1845. Persons having claims against the Company are to send them in without delay to Mr N Falls, late Pres of the Company, at Balt, for payment. –C W Macmurdo, Sec

The Newark Daily Advertiseer requests all persons of the name of Townley, & descendants of that name, to meet at Elizabethtown, N J, on Aug 21, to make arrangements for prosecuting their claim to a very large estate in England, which has been ascertained to have been left by will to heirs in this country.

The 7 year old son of Mr Eslinger, of Greenfield, Wisconsin Territory, was with his brother, when a dog sprang towards the younger boy, tore his head, throat & arms in a shocking manner. The boy soon expired.

Terrible accident at Alleghany, opposite Pittsburg, on Aug 12: the new Protestant Methodist Church in that city is lighted with gas, manufactured on the premises. Something had gone wrong with the apparatus & several members of the congregation assembled to repair it. The gas ignited from a candle, burst the gaso-meter, & set fire to the gas-house. Mr Herron, the Sexton, is very badly burnt-since dead. Mr Brown, a pedlar, living on Butler rd, badly burnt. Wm Karns, Postmaster of Alleghany, badly burnt. Mr Jas Russell, carpenter, had his head badly cut, & is dangerously burnt. Mr Issler, very badly burnt, supposed to be dangerous. Mr Henry Williams, Grocer, slightly burnt. The main body of the Church was uninjured. [Aug 18th newspaper: Mr Herring, Mr Oister, & Mr Russell, have since died of their injuries. They were all married men.]

Notice: By virtue of an order of distrain for house rent due to Thos Owens by John Saulsbury, I will expose at public sale, on Aug 21, goods & chattels of Saulsbury. –H R Maryman, Bailiff

Appointments by the Pres:
Robt Butler, to be Surveyor Genr'l of the Public Lands in Florida, in place of V Y Conway, from Sep 30 next, on which day the resignation of Conway will take effect.
Thos J Read, to be Postmaster at Louisville, Ky, in place of Littlebury H Mosby, removed.
Wm J Miller, Collector of the Customs for the district of Bristol & Warren, R I, vice John Howe, removed.
Nathl W Walker, Collector of the Customs at St Mark's, Florida, vice Wm W Ware, whose commission will expire on Sep 13, 1845.

The Monroe Railroad was sold at Macon, Ga, on Aug 5, by an order of court, for $155,100, & was bid off by J Cowles. Half of the purchase was on account of parties in N Y, & the balance for citizens of Macon.

Hagerstown News: An intemperate man named McAffee, living on the South Mountain, in Wash Co, took home a jug of whiskey, & 2 of his children, in the absence of the family, partook of it freely. On the return of the mother, she found her 2 children in the agonies of death, & in her presence died an awful death.

London Globe of Jul 19. Earl Grey died on Thu at his seat at Howick Hall, Northumberland: was a lineal descendant of the Greys of Werke-a very ancient Northumbrian family. The late Earl Grey was born Mar 13, 1764, & was in his 82nd year. By the death of his father, the Duke of Northumberland, Mr Grey, though not then of age, was invited to fill the vacancy in representing his native county: took his seat when he became of age. He is succeeded in title & estates by his eldest son, Lord Howick.

The French papers announce the death of Signor Artot, the fine player on the violin, who was here but a little while ago with Madame Cinti Damoreau. He died in France of consumption, at age 30 years.

I will sell at private sale 2 tracts of land in Montg Co, Md, about 6 miles from Rockville, containing in the whole about 700 acs. These lands adjoin the farm of Willy Offutt, & are owned by the heirs of Timothy Winn. One farm is called *Williamsburg*, 396 acs, with a comfortable dwlg-house. –Geo W Campbell, [Agent for the heirs:] living in Gtwn, D C

Mrd: on Jul 22, at St Mary's Church, Lancaster, Ohio, by Rev J M Young, Chas F Garaghty to Miss Maria, eldest d/o H H Hunter.

Died: on Aug 15, Mr Chas Bell, aged 79 years & 10 months. He was born in Va, but for upwards of 30 years past was a resident of Wash City. His funeral is tomorrow, at 5 p m, from the Baptist Church on 10th st.

MON AUG 18, 1845
Grass Cloth Skirts: just received, of 4 yards & yard wide, at 75 cents. For sale by John Allen, Pa ave, between 9th & 10th sts.

Sarah Parescho died at Beaufort, N C, a few days ago at the advanced age of 107 years. She was the mother of 4 generations.

Mrd: on Aug 14, by Rev Mr Donelan, Mr Thos Connelly, of Montg Co, Md, to Miss Sarah, d/o Richd Thompson, of Wash.

Died: on Jul 26, at Mrs Louisa Edelin's, in Chas Co, Md, after a long & painful illness, Mrs Eleanor Ann Edelin, w/o Eugenius F Edelin, in her 28th year. She has left a husband & son to bewail her loss.

Nat'l Institute. Newbern, N C, Jun 20, 1845. Sir: At the request of my brother, Robt S Moore, late of the U S Navy, I present one of the bolts to which Columbus was chained whilst imprisoned in the Island of St Domingo, previous to his being sent in chains as a prisoner to Spain. This bolt was obtained by Purser Moore whilst on a visit to St Domingo, in the U S ship **Vandalia**, during her late cruise, & is accompanied by a certificate of its identity from the Secretary & Interpreter of the President of that portion of the Island. I also send a copy of "the Newbernian" containing an account of the manner in which the bolt was obtained. –Verina S Moore. To: Francis Markoe, jr, Corr Sec Nat'l Institute [The death of our lamented young townsman, Robt S Moore, late Purser in the U S Navy, has been too recent to have been forgotten by any of us. Upon the death of Columbus, the iron bolt, with his journal & other papers, were forwarded to his relatives.]

Four persons have been arrested as participators in the last anti-rent murder: Henry D Wickham, Zera Preston, Isaac Burhans, & Richd Davis. Sheriff Moore has offered a reward of $300 for the apprehension of Warren W Scudder, who is concerned in the murder. Excitement in Delaware Co, still continues. [Sep 26th newspaper: Scudder has been traced to Steuben Co, & there caught & placed in custody to await his removal to Delaware.]

Mr & Mrs Michard will re-open on the first Mon in Sept their Day School for Young Ladies. The school-room is now on the east side of 19th st.

Wm Carr, who has acted for many years as a messenger, to carry & bring papers to the City Post Ofc Arsenal, has been missing from his quarters since last Thu.

Fire in a frame bldg, now being erected, on 3rd st, between G & Mass ave. The house was bldg for Mr Wm Dalton, hack-driver. It is thought the bldg was set on fire.

Valuable farm for sale: about 10 miles from Wash: contains 200 acs: with a good dwlg-house & other necessary out-bldgs. –Horatio Beall

TUE AUG 19, 1845
Mrs Genr'l Carrington will open Oct 1, in Richmond City, Va, a School for Young Ladies. Mrs Carrington is in faith a Presbyterian, & though warmly attached to the doctrines, worship, & discipline of the Church, she is no bigot, & has no wish to use any influence over her pupils for the purpose of proselytizing.

Genr'l Wm McDonald died Mon: in his 87th year. He was a soldier of the Revolution, & was for a long time an enterprising merchant of Balt. -Patriot

Fire at Boston, on Fri, in large stables attached to the City Tavern. Walls fell and 3 firemen were killed: Thompson, Roulstone, & Howard.

W T Smith, American Consul at Matagorda, Texas, was lately washed from his horse & drowned, in attempting to pass the Bayou between Indian Point & Pass Cavallo.

Mrs Dyson & Mrs Chalmers will open their Seminary for Young Ladies, in the Session room of the Baptist Church, on 10th st, between E & F st, on Sep 1 next.

Wash Corp: the nomination of Benj E Gittings, as Com'r of the 3rd Ward, was unanimously confirmed.

West River land for sale: about 200 acs: with a frame dwlg, sufficient for a small family, & all the requisite farm bldgs. For terms, apply to Dr Jas Cheston, West River, Md.

Teacher wanted in the Wash Academy, Somerset Co, Md. Cmte: Jas Stewart, Wm T G Polk, John H King

Detroit Adv: on Tue, below Point au Pelle, on lake Erie, the steamer **London** from Buffalo, & the steamer **Kent**, came in contact with a dreadful crash. Among those lost we reckon were:

Rev Jas E Quaw, of Redford, Mich
Mr Chauncey Osborn, of Genesee, N Y
Mr Jas Lowden, Ypsilanti, Mich
[79 were saved.]

Mr Seth Deming, of Berlin, Conn
Master Bruce Deming, of Galena, Wisconsin Territory

Died: on Aug 18, Mrs Eliz Nowlan, a native of England, aged 84 years. Her funeral is today at 4 p m. from the residence of Saml Drury.

Died: on Patterson's creek, 15 miles from Moorefield, Hardy Co, Va, John Berry, aged 101 years. He was a soldier of the American Revolution, & was engaged in the battles of Trenton, Monmouth, Brandywine, Germantown, Brooklyn Heights, & several others. In the memorable winter of 1777-8, he endured his portion of those extreme sufferings & privations which the army experienced when encamped at Valley Forge, & he was also present at the surrender of Lord Cornwallis, at Yorktown, in 1781.
[No date-appears recent.]

Died: on Aug 2, after a short & painful illness, Mrs E Muse, leaving a husband & a number of small children to mourn their irreparable loss.

WED AUG 20, 1845
Lucerne, Switzerland, Jul 24. M Leu, one of the leading members of the Jesuits party, was found dead in his bed: partisans declare that he was basely assassinated. His wife sleeping by his side, was alarmed by the report of the pistol, but saw no one. The affair is enveloped in great mystery.

Capitol Hill Female Seminary: Miss Taylor [who succeeded Miss Whitwell & Miss McCormick as Principal of this Institution] will receive pupils on Sep 1. Location: N J ave & south B st. References:

Rev Wm T Sprole	Silas H Hill	John S Meehan
Hon J Y Mason	Lewis H Machen	John P Ingle
Col S Burche	Wm Dundad	Jas Adams
Wm Dervick	Danl Gold	John Underwood

Mrs D H Burr's Seminary for Young Ladies: 9th & E sts, Wash, will re-open on the 2nd Mon of Sep.

Appointments by the Pres:
Fred'k Hall, Receiver of Public Moneys for the district of lands subject to sale at Ionia, Michigan, vice Thos Fitzgerald, resigned.
Chandler C Young, U S Atty for the Western district of Florida, in place of Walker Anderson, resigned.
Elihu Stout, Postmaster at Vincennes, Indiana, in place of Jas W Greenhow, removed.

Mrd: on Aug 14, by Rev Mr Sprole, Mr Jas L Cathcart to Miss Eliza J, d/o Jno D Barclay, all of Wash City.

Jas B Clarke has fitted up the store formerly occupied by Mr Wm C Orme, one door east of Gilman's Drug Store, with rich Cashmeres, Bonnet silks, Calicoes, Cotton, Shirtings, Merino Hosiery, & Irish Linen.

Died: on Mon last, suddenly, Wm Zebedee Kendall, s/o the Hon Amos Kendall, aged 22 years. His funeral will take place from his father's residence, 12th st near Pa ave, on Thu next, at 10 o'clock.
+
Wm Rufus Elliott was arrested last Mon, on a warrant issued by Justice Morsell, charging him with causing the death of Wm Zebedee Kendall, by shooting him with a pistol on Pa ave. It appeared that Mr Elliott, after firing the pistol at Mr Kendall & wounding Mr Baily, went in a hack to the house of Geo Parker, on C st, where he surrendered under the advice of his friends. At the close of yesterday's investigation the prisoner was reconducted to prison in custody of the Marshal. [Aug 22nd newspaper: Kendall's father arrived from N Y today at 2 a m. He desires that the unfortunate youth now at the bar of public justice may receive all the forgiveness consistent with the laws of his country. Mr Hoban said it was willful deliberate murder; Gen Jones said it was one of necessary self-defence. The funeral of the unfortunate Mr Kendall took place at 10 o'clock yesterday. The corpse was deposited in the ***Congress Burial Ground***. It was attended to the grave by relatives & friends.]

Orphans Court of Wash Co, D C. . Letters of administration on the personal estate of Henry C Turner, late of said county, dec'd. –Enoch G Bell

Notice: application has been made at the Mayor's ofc for a renewal of the bond given by the Com'rs of the Low Grounds, dated Apr 3, 1826, for lot 36 in square A, to David Munro, by virtue of a sale made by said Com'rs on that day of said lot to said David Munro, & from him to one Wm Wardell, & which said bond, by subsequent assignments, became the property of the late Dr Thos Sewall, dec'd, & has been lost or mislaid. This is to give notice a renewal will be granted to the subscriber. –Thos Sewall

Wanted a respectable middle aged woman, as child's nurse, one who can do plain sewing preferred. Apply to F Black, Md ave.

THU AUG 21, 1845
Raffle of splendid furniture at my Ware Room on 11th st: chances at $5 per chance.
–Wm McL Cripps

Trustee's sale of valuable Tavern & other property in Frostburg, on the Great Western Central Route: by decree of Alleghany Co Court as a Court of Equity, passed on Jul 11, 1845, appointing the undersigned trustees for the sale of certain portions of the real estate of Lucius W Stockton, dec'd, being in Alleghany Co: sale on Sep 20: the Tavern-stand & Stage-house in Frostburg, now occupied by Saml Cesana. A lot of ground fronting the Nat'l road, now occupied by F R Shepherd. A lot of ground & an extensive stable, opposite the Tavern. One other lot of ground in rear of the hotel.
–Wm Price, M Topham Evans, Trustees

For rent: 3 story brick house & store, 10th & Pa ave. Apply to Michl Sardo, 10th & H sts.

Orphans Court of Wash Co, D C. Letters testamentary on the personal estate of Richd M Waring, late of said county, dec'd. –Chas S Wallach, exc

Appointments by the Pres:
1-Jas McKissick, of Arkansas, to be Agent of the Cherokee nation of Indians west of the Mississippi, to take effect on Sep 13, 1845, on which day the term of service of the present incumbent will expire. 2-Robt Colyman, of Wash, to be Warden of the Penitentiary in the District of Columbia, from Sep 1, 1845, in place of John B Dade, whose resignation will take effect on Aug 31, 1845.

If John Elliott, who left his mother in 1826, at the Bay of Honduras, in the ship **Beard**, Capt Garvin, for London, will direct a letter to Mrs Feeny, Tallahassee, Florida, he will again hear from her.

Miss B A Rooker, assisted by her sisters, having taken a house on 12th st, near Md ave, known as the Island, propose opening a School for Young Ladies.

Letters received by the last English steamer contain the intelligence of the death of Col Saml Moore, of Balt, at the residence of his brother in Ireland, where he had been for some time past on a visit. The dec'd was an active participant in the battle of Balt in 1814, having been a field ofcr of the gallant 27th Regt, [which was in the hottest of the fight,] & received a severe wound in the action.

Died: yesterday, after a short & painful illness, Anna B Raikes, aged 7 years & 3 days. Her funeral is this afternoon at 4 o'clock, from the residence of her grandfather, Wm Darby, N Y ave, between 13th & 14th sts.

Died: on Aug 10, at his residence, Broad Creek, PG Co, Md, Dr Thos Clagett Lyles, in his 56th year. He has left an affectionate wife & loving offspring, lamenting their irreparable loss.

Died: Aug 16, of scarlet fever, Eliz Hannah, d/o John R Nourse, of Frostburg, Md. She was in her 9th year.

Household furniture, & piano forte, at auction: on Aug 27, in the Navy Yard, at the residence of the 1st Lt of the Yard, his household & kitchen furniture.
-R W Dyer & Co, aucts

Isaac Goodall, a Whig member of the Tennessee House of Reps from Smith Co, was killed in Gallatin, on Jul 17, by Mr Chas Pele Lewis, of that place. The affair grew out of a jesting remark about a poke stalk upon a tar wagon in the street. Both men, though differing in politics, were on friendly terms till that awful moment. Lewis has not been taken.

FRI AUG 22, 1845
Among the passengers in the ship **Hibernia** were Mr & Mrs Chas Kean, who will continue about a year in this country. Mrs Kean will be recollected as Miss Ellen Tree. They presented a brilliant appearance at the Theatre-Royal, Dublin, on Jul 29: the pit & galleries were overflowing.

Foreign Item. Mr John Ray, of London, who some time ago amassed a fortune of L60,000, began speculating with it in the stock exchange, lost all, & has died suddenly in a state of utter destitution. [No date-recent news.]

Mrd: on Aug 15, by Rev N Wilson, Mr John N Browning to Miss Alethia Ann Berry, all of Wash City.

Died: on Jul 30, after lingering for many weeks, at his residence in Fairfax Co, Va, Allan Macrae. The dec'd was the s/o John Macrae, formerly of Orangefield, near Dumfries, Va; was a gentleman of amiable & affectionate heart. During the late war with England he quitted the luxuries by which he was surrounded, &, joining a volunteer company, served a tour of duty at Norfolk with good repute. He also served for many years in the Post Ofc Dept, in which he contracted the disease which terminated his life. He leaves an afflicted family.

Died: on Aug 18, in Wash, Josephine Pulcharia, infant d/o John E & Mary E Neale, aged 21 months.

SAT AUG 23, 1845
Principal ofcrs of the State of Florida:
Govn'r-Wm D Mosely   Treasurer-Benj Bird
Sec of State-Jas T Archer   Private Sec to the Govn'r-Oscar Myers
Comptroller-N P Bemis   Atty Genr'l-Jos H Branch
Judges: Geo S Hawkins, Thos Baltzell, I H Bronson, Wm Marvin
Solicitors: Caraway Smith, Thos J Heir, Felix Livingston, R F Brantly
Clerk of the Supreme Court-M D Papy

Truman Phelps, of Catahoula, is the Whig candidate for Congress in the 2nd district, to fill the vacancy caused by the death of Mr Dawson. John H Harmanson, of Avoyelles, was nominated by the Locofocos.

Mr Nicholas P Trist, formerly U S Consul at Havana, has been appointed Chief Clerk of the Dept of State.

By an order of distrain for rent in arrear due to Simon Frasier to Chas Cooper, I will expose at public sale on Aug 28, in square 412, F st, between 8th & 9th sts, in Wash City, the following goods & chattels, to wit: a lot of cabbages, a lot of beets, a lot of corn, a lot of beans, & a lots of cucumbers. –H R Maryman, Bailiff

Letter to F Markoe, Corr Sec Nat'l Institute, from Capt J H Aulick, U S Navy: Navy Yard, Wash, Aug 19, 1845. The lithographic likeness enclosed, of our countryman, Mr Wm Wheelwright, who first introduced steam navigation in the Pacific Ocean, was sent to me a short time since by an American gentleman residing in Valparaiso, with a request that I would have it placed in some public institution of this capital, as that of a man who is an honor to his country. I beg it may be so honored. –J H Aulick

Appointments by the Pres:
1-J Geo Harris, purser in the U S Navy, to fill a vacancy occasioned by the death of Edw N Cox. 2-Livingston Dunlap, Postmaster at Indianapolis, Indiana, vice Saml Henderson, removed.

Died: yesterday, at his seat in PG Co, Md, Mr Wm Cooper, aged 72 years; a native of England, but for 40 years an inhabitant of the U S, nearly the whole of which time he resided in his city & neighborhood. He has left a mourning widow & several children to lament his loss. His funeral will take place from his late residence, at 10 a m tomorrow.

Died: on Aug 21, after a long & painful illness, Mrs Mary Ellen Farrar, in her 29th year. Her funeral is this afternoon at 2 o'clock, from the residence of her mother, Mrs Hurst, 3rd & L sts east.

Farm wanted: from 10 to 100 acs, with a comfortable dwlg-house & necessary out-bldgs, from 1 to 5 miles from Wash City. City property would be exchanged, in whole or in part. Apply to Richd Patten, Pa ave, between 10th & 11th sts.

For sale or rent, the Steam flour Mill at West Wheeling, west of the Ohio river, with a large warehouse. The brand Anchor Mills, West Wheeling, stand high. Apply to Thos H Glenn, St Clairsville, Ohio.

By order of the Orphans Court of Wash Co, D C, I shall sell on Aug 26, at the residence of the late Rev Henry C Turner, on 4½ st, between Md & Va aves, his household & kitchen furniture. –A Green, auct

MON AUG 25, 1845
The subscriber will render every account on his books on or before Sep 1 next, when he hopes that each & every one will be prepared to settle. Those not settled will be put in the hands of a collector. –R C Washington

Loss of life at Albany, N Y, on Thu, at the intersection of the Mohawk railroad with Broadway: the driver of a carriage containing Mr & Mrs Jacob Anthony, of Cohoes, & Mr Lyman, wife, & child, of Rochester, when warned of the approach of the train, which was in sight, attempted to cross the track. Mr Anthony was thrown & was unhurt, his wife was killed. One of the horses was killed. Fool-hardy recklessness! [Aug 29th newspaper: Geo Wilson, the driver of the carriage, has been arrested & held to bail on a charge of manslaughter, in having caused the death of Mrs Anthony by his conduct as driver on the occasion.]

The Emperor Nicholas has just entered on the 50th year of his age, & the 20th of his reign. His brother Alex'r did not attain that age, although he governed Russia for 25 years. Of 5 dghts & 4 sons of Paul, there remain only the present Emperor, his brother the Grand Duke Michel, 40 years of age, the Grand Duchess of Saxe Wiemar, & the Queen of Holland, the former 8 years, & the latter 5, older than Nicholas. The other 3 Grand Duchesses died in the prime of life. The Grand Duke Constantine died in 1831 at Siedlie, at the commencement of the Polish war. The Emperor Nicholas has had 7 children: 4 sons, Alex'r, Constantine, Nicholas, & Michel, & 3 dghts, one of which died last year, at the time of her father's return from London.

Sale of valuable real estate near the Nat'l Theatre: by deed of trust from Wm O'Neale to Wm A Bradley, Cashier of the Bank of Wash, or his successors, dated Nov 11, 1820, recorded in Liber W B #1, folios 148 & 149, in the land records of Wash Co, D C: sale on Sep 20, all that piece of ground in said city, being part of lot 2 in square 254, fronting on E st, where two 2 storied brick houses were erected by the said Wm O'Neale, together with all other improvements thereon. –Jas Adams, Cashier

$100 reward for runaway negro John. This negro was in my possession as Edw R Wheeler's trustee. -Robt S Reeder, Trustee, Port Tobacco, Md

U S vs W Rufus Elliott. Prisoner could not be admitted to bail on the serious charge preferred against him of causing the death of Wm Zebedee Kendall, & the prisoner was fully committed for trial at the Dec term of the Criminal Court. Justices decided he be required to give bail in the sum of $3,000 for his appearance at the same court to answer to the charge of assaulting with intent to kill Josiah R Bailey.

Died: on Aug 24, of intermittent fever, Mary Catharine Ratcliff, eldest d/o Lewis & Mgt Ratcliff, in her 13th year. Her funeral is tomorrow at 1 o'clock.

Fred'k Academy, Fredericktown, Md, will open Sep 1 & ends the last of Jul. There are 2 recesses, of a week each, one at Christmas, & the other at Easter. –A Ritchie, Sec

Copartnership formed this day, for the purpose of transacting the Dry Goods business in this city, under the firm of Carter & Washington. –Henry Carter, R C Washington

Upholstering & paper-hanging: at his old stand on 9th st, near Pa ave. –Geo Willner

Orphans Court of Wash Co, D C. In the case of Chas W Boteler, adm of Aaron Vancoble, dec'd, the adm has appointed Sep 10 for the final settlement of the estate. –Ed N Roach, Reg o/wills

Bldg lots for sale: square 563, fronting on N J & Mass ave, 2nd st west, & H st north, divided into bldg lots. Also, lot 29 in square 564, on Mass ave. A plot of square 563 is left at the auction store of R W Dyer & Co, & one is also with Mr Geo Klotz, who resides in square 564. -R W Dyer & Co, aucts

TUE AUG 26, 1845
At the late Commencement of Yale College the honorary degree of Master of Arts was conferred on Jas M Saunders, of Wash City.

Landon Female Seminary, Rev R H Phillips, Rector: will open on Sep 10: located in Fred'k Co, Md, within 3 miles of Ijamsville Depot, on the Balt & Ohio Railroad.

The Townley Estate in England, for which heirs are wanted, is said to be worth L4,000,000. There is a family in Md which traces its descent direct from the female branch of the Townely family of England.

The Misses Koones, dghts of Mr David Koones, intend opening a School in the row of bldgs east of the City Hall, on the 1st Mon in Sep, & will be glad of the patronage of their friends & the public generally.

The partnership existing between B K Sharetts & W H Brereton is this day dissolved by mutual consent. Saml Brereton will continue the grocery & shoe business at the old stand. –B K Sharretts, W H Brereton

Sale of household furniture at auction: on Aug 28, by virtue of the last will & testament of Richd M Waring, at his late residence on Md ave, between 6th & 7th sts. –Chas S Wallach, exc -Boteler, Donn & Co, auctioneers

Frescati for sale at public auction: this desirable estate, the estate of the late Judge Barbour: sale on Oct 6. My son will show the farm. –Frances T Barbour, Frescati, Orange Co, Va

Died: on Aug 22, at the residence of her father, on Capitol Hill, after a short illness, in her 15th year, Mary H Dundas, 3rd d/o Wm H Dundas, of the Post Ofc Dept.

Died: on Aug 22, in Wash City, after a long & painful illness of 4 years, Julia A Dement, d/o Walter Dement, of St Mary's Co, Md, in her 23rd year.

Died: on Aug 4, at Benton, Mississippi, of pulmonary consumption, Mrs Eliz L C Slade, consort of Thos P Slade, clerk of the Circuit Court of Yazoo Co, & d/o the late Edw S Lewis, dec'd, of Wash City, in her 28th year.

Notice to Capitalists. The subscribers offers for sale her undivided interest in the valuable Lead Mines of *Mine La Mote*, situated in Madison Co, Missouri. The tract contains 24,010 acs, & is a Spanish concession to the person whose name it bears, [who discovered it in 1720,] & was confirmed by special act of Congress in 1825. The estate of the late Dr L F Linn owns one-sixth of these mines, of which interest the subscriber is, by the will of her late husband, possessed of $1/3^{rd}$ thereof, in fee simple, & is at her unconditional disposal. –Eliz A R Linn, of St Louis

Farm for sale: the subscriber, having engaged in a business in Washington which will require his constant personal attention, offers for sale the farm on which he now resides: contains 125 acs, on Rock creek, about 2 miles from Gtwn: with a comfortable 2 story frame dwlg house. His father on the farm will show it to any person who may wish to examine it. –L J Middleton

For sale, a farm containing about 72¼ acs: with a comfortable frame house: located about 1 mile of the Eastern Branch bridge, on the main road, near the Good Hope Tavern. Also for sale, a large 2 story brick house on N J ave. Wanted, a small place containing about 20 acres of land, with a comfortable dwlg thereon. Apply to Richd I A Culverwell, Genr'l Agent & Collector.

Expecting to be absent from Wash City for some time, my son, Wm H Ward, is authorized to attend to my business, & receive all money payable to me during my absence. –Wm Ward

WED AUG 27, 1845
The Genesee Republican announces the death of Hon Thos L L Brent, formerly Charge d'Affaires to Portugal, & s/o the late Danl Carroll Brent, of Va.

$10 reward for runaway mulatto woman, Kitty Frazier, from 30 to 35 years old. She also took with her her baby, a little girl about 4 months old. –Stanislaus Blandford, near Piscataway, PG Co, Md.

John W Baden recently purchased of the executor of the late Richd M Waring the entire stock in trade of Waring, consisting of a general stock of American & Foreign Hardware & Cutlery, & will conduct the business at the old stand on Pa ave, near 6th st.

Mrd: on Aug 25, at Leesburg, Va, by Rev Mr Adie, Alfred B Thruston, of Wash, to Fannie C Gordon, youngest d/o the late Col Chas Magill, of Winchester, Va.

Died: yesterday, after a protracted & painful illness, Chas H Smoot, in his 25th year. His funeral is on Thu morning at 10 o'clock, from the residence of his father, Mr Saml Smoot, on K st, near Gtwn.

One of the Powder Mills belonging to Mr O M Whipple, on Concord river, about a mile from Lowell, has blown up, killing 2 men, Gardner Boynton, & Albert J Brown. They were each about 30 years of age. [No date-recent news.]

House hold furniture at auction: on Aug 29, at the residence of Mrs E Evans, corner of 8th st & N Y ave north, [the flag will designate the house.] -Wm Marshall, auctioneer

Household & kitchen furniture at auction: on Aug 29, at the house occupied by Mr John West, on the south side of Pa ave, near 6th st. Also, several pairs of fancy Canary Birds. -R W Dyer & Co, aucts

Wash Corp: 1-Ptn of Benedict Jost: referred to the Cmte of Claims. 2-Cmte of Claims asked to be discharged from the further consideration of the ptn of Wilhelm Grupe. 3-Ptn of C S Fowler, praying remission of a fine: referred to the Cmte of Claims.

THU AUG 28, 1845
A Montevideo letter of May 10 announces the death of Acting Lt Robt Poinsett Lovell, of U S ship **Boston**. He died of dysentery.

High School for Young Ladies at Balt: 77 North Liberty st, Balt, Md. –A N Girault, one of the Principals.

Mrs Mead's School, Shockoe Hill, Richmond, Va: will re-open on Oct 1 next. Reference is made to the following gentlemen, who have dghts or wards in the Institution: Right Rev Bishop Johns, Rev Dr Empie, Rev Mr Norwood, Jas E Heath, Jas A Seddon, Chas F Osborne, Richmond; Com Ap Catesby Jones, Judge J Y Mason, Wash; Nelson Page, Cumberland; Jas Galt, Fluvanna.

Dixon Land Ofc: the receipts into this ofc average about $1,000 per day since the opening of the ofc by the present Receiver & Recorder, principally from emigrants from Pa & Md, who have come with their families to make this delightful region of country their home. –Galena Sentinel

Died: on Aug 15, in Wash City, where she had been on a visit, Mrs Susan Cookendorfer, in her 84th year, a native of Gtwn, D C, & relict of the late Leonard Cookendorfer, of said town.

Lands of John Randolph of Roanoke, for sale: by virtue of a decree pronounced on Jun 4, 1845, by the Circuit Superior Court of Law & Chancery for Petersburg, in the suit of Braxton's exc of Coalter & others vs Randolphs exc & others, the Com'rs will, on Oct 6, that being the court day of Charlotte Co, at the court-house of said county, sell at auction, the lands hereinafter described, lying in said county, belonging to the estate of the late John Randolph, dec'd. *The Middle Quarter*: on which is the Mansion House of the late proprietor, contains 1,719 acs, so well known as scarcely to require description. *Hundley's & Bouldin's*: 2 contiguous tracts: together, 1,151 acres of land. *Gilliams*, another estate of Mr Randolph's, containing 391 acs. On the day following will be sold all the stock, including a number of the finest blooded horses, personal property of every description, on *Middle Quarter Estate*, on *Hundley's & Bouldin's*, & *Gilliam's*, & also *Lower Quarter* & *Ferry Quarter Estates*, in the same neighborhood.
–H L Brooke, R T Daniel, Com'rs

Six Cents Reward for runaway, Dennis Conley, an indented apprentice to the shoemaking business. I caution all persons against employing said boy, at the peril of the law.
–Jas Cull, near the Navy Yard.

FRI AUG 29, 1845
We learn that Mathew L Davis has been removed from the ofc of Deputy Collector at last. We are not at liberty to give the name of his successor. Amongst the removals are 3 of the Empire Club: McCleester, [Country McClusky,] John Austin, & Edw Gallagher. Rynders holds on yet. –N Y Express

A <u>Large Pipe</u>! One of the pipes intended for the Trinity Church organ, N Y, will contain 30 men.

Norfolk Herald: the battalion of artillery ordered from *Fortress Monroe* to join our army in Texas consists of companies G, E, I & D; 250 rank & file. The ofcrs are: Brevet Major John Monroe, Brevet Major Wm W Morris, Capt J B Scott, Assistant Surgeon J B Wells, 1st Lts-R Smeed, E Deas, J C Pemberton, E Bradford; 2nd Lts-M Lovell, E Whitting, J Gill, J P Johnstone, J R Reynolds. All the ofcrs attached to the battalion, now absent on detached service, are ordered to join their companies either at Norfolk or in Texas.

Norfolk Herald: orders changing the destination of the frig **Congress** from the Pacific to the Gulf of Mexico. The **Congress** is to relieve the ship **Potomac**, now in a leaky condition at Pensacola. This latter ship has been ordered to Norfolk, & her crew is to be transferred to the frig **Columbia**. Capt Stockton is to proceed to the Gulf of Mexico as soon as the **Congress** is manned. The following ofcrs have been ordered to this ship: Cmder, Saml F Du Pont; Lts: John W Livingston, J F Schenck, R L Tilghman, W S Drayton, H Eld, W Gwathmey; Master, V R Morgan; Surgeon, Saml Mosely; Passed Assist Surgeon, John S Whittle; Assist Surgeon, Chas Eversfield. A detachement of 30 marines, under charge of Lt Kinsing, for the frig **Congress**, arrived at Norfolk from Balt on Sunday. The schnr **On-ka-bye**, Lt Com't Sinclair, received orders on Monday to sail immediately for Texas.

French & Italian Languages: Mons S Charton intends to make Wash, Gtwn, & Alexandria the places of his labor & permanent residence. Day classes for ladies & evening classes for gentlemen are now forming. Apply to Mr Charton at Mrs Wise's, on F st, between 11th & 12th sts.

Notice: by virtue of an order of distrain for rent in arrear due to Sarah G Stewart by Thos Wright, I will expose at public sale on Sep 2, in front of the Centre market-house, in Wash City, for cash, the following goods & chattels: 1 bureau, 1 saddle, 1 desk, 3 tables, 15 chairs, 1 table cover, 1 stand, 2 pictures, a lot of books, 1 pair of andirons, a lot of crockery ware, 2 lamps, a lot of glass ware, 1 waiter, 1 tea-kettle, & 3 candlesticks. –Wm Cox, Bailiff

Wash City Ordinances:
1-Act for the relief of Wm A Scott: that the fine imposed on him, by judgment of R H Clements, for an alleged violation of an ordinance of the Corp relative to using firearms, the same is remitted, provided that the said Scott pay the costs of prosecution. 2-Act for the relief of F A Russell: that he be issued a new grocery license, his old one having been lost or mislaid. 3-Act for the relief of John Shaw: that the fine imposed on him by judgment of John D Clark, for a violation of the law relative to the protection of trees, is hereby remitted, provided the said Shaw pay the costs of prosecution.

Died: on Aug 26, at the Convent of the Visitation B V M, Gtwn, D C, Virginia, d/o Maj Gen Winfield Scott, U S Army, in her 24th year.

Collegiate School will reopen in the new bldg on 4½ st, between Pa ave & C st, Sep 1. –C W Feeks, Principal

SAT AUG 30, 1845
Orders were received here on Sat to fit out the U S frig **Columbia** now lying at the Gosport Navy Yard. We should like to see Cmdor Thoas Ap Catesby Jones appointed to the command of one of these vessels, in order to raise his broad pennant again in the Pacific. There is no better man to be found in the Navy for that important station at this crisis. –Norfolk Beacon of Monday.

Naval Intelligence: Capt Stockton is not to proceed in the frig **Congress** to the Gulf of Mexico. His destination is to be the Pacific; nor is his big gun to be transferred to the **Congress**.

The steamer **Alabama** left N Y on Thu week for Aransas Bay, with about 500 men on board, composed of 2 volunteer companies of Artl under command of Maj Gally & Capt Forng, & 6 companies of the 7th Regt U S Infty. Companies A & I, of the 3rd Artl, are ordered to Aransas Bay, Texas, & will sail in a few days from Charleston, S C.

A man named John Carr was run over by the cars at N Y on Tue. No person was to blame, as he was warned of the danger of crossing between the trains, but he persisted in crossing.

Valuable Gold Mines for Sale: the excs of the last will of testament of John Reid, sen, dec'd, will sell on the premises, in Cabarrua Co, N C, on Feb 5, the Gold Mine known as the *Reid mine*. The late proprietor never would permit any persons out of his own family to work the mine, & they were never were permitted to enter the lands he cultivated. There are about 750 acres in the tract. This Mine is 15 miles s e of Concord, N C. –Geo Barnhardt, John Reid, excs

The Misses Gaither will open school on Sep 1, in the house recently occupied by Miss Latimer. Terms, payable quarterly in advance, & made known at their room, on N Y ave, between 12th & 13th sts.

Gtwn Classical & Scientific Academy: conducted now more than 22 years by the subscriber, will be open again on Sep 1. –Jas McVean

Died: on Aug 29, after a long & severe illness, Mr Thos Williams, painter, in his 28th year. His funeral is this day at 4 o'clock, from his late residence on 2nd & G st north.

Died: on Aug 22, Ellen Roberta, infant d/o Jos O & Eliz Bower.

Died: on Jul 29, in Wash City, Fred'k Jacob, infant s/o Jos & Matilda Smith, of Balt.

Register's Ofc, Sussex Co, Delaware, Aug 25, 1845. In the matter of the last will & testament of Elijah Hastings, sen, dec'd. Ptns of review filed in the ofc of the Register, to wit: one by Peter Hasting of Elijah, dec'd, Jun 16, 1845, & one by Peter Hasting of Fred'k, dec'd, Aug 12, 1845. And now, to wit, this 25th of Aug, 1845, it appearing to the Register for the Probate of Wills & granting letters of administration in & for the county aforesaid by the ptns aforesaid, that Barney M Hasting, Elisha Hasting, Elijah Hasting, Jesse Outten & Mary Ann his wife, in right of said Mary Ann, Elias Hasting, Euphemia Hasting, Elijah Murphey & Amelia his wife, in right of said Amelia, Renatus Hasting & Nancy his wife, in right of said Nancy, Felty Hasting & Maria his wife, in right of said Maria, Winder Hasting of Archilus & Arena his wife, in right of said Arena, Noah Hasting, Elijah Murphey, Eliz Christopher, late Eliz Murphey, are parties interested, residing out of the State of Delaware. It is therefore ordered by the said Register that they appear at his ofc in Gtwn, on Sep 23 next: why the allowance of a certain instrument of writing, dated Dec 22, 1840, & purporting to be the last will & testament of the said Elijah Hasting, sen, dec'd, as & for his last will & testament, & granting letters testamentary thereupon should not be revoked & the said instrument be rejected.
–Peter Parker, Register

Household furniture at auction: on Sep 2, at the house next to the residence of the Hon J Q Adams, on F st, between 13th & 14th sts, part of the furniture of a person declining housekeeping. -R W Dyer & Co, aucts

Orphans Court of Wash Co, D C. Letters of administration on the personal estate of Christopher O'Neale, late of said county dec'd. –May A O'Neale, admx

MON SEP 1, 1845
Gen Scott returned to Wash on Thu from West Point, to attend to the duties of his ofc. He was not aware, until his arrival, of the melancholy domestic blow which awaited him in the sudden & unexpected death of his eldest & accomplished dght, Miss Virginia Scott, who died on Tue evening, in the convent at Gtwn, in her 24th year. A very intimate friend of the family, who witnessed the ofcs of the church, has given us an affecting account of the funeral ceremonies, which took place before the General's arrival. -Union

Letters remaining in the Post Ofc, Wash City, Sep 1, 1845.

Anderson, S J	Atkinson, Arch'd	Burns, Wm C-2
Archer, Wm S	Adams, John [col'd]	Beech, Silas, or M
Anderson, G N	Anderson, Col S K	Harrison
Abbott, Mrs	Andrews, Miss M M	Bibb, T P Attieus

Banks, Mr	Clark, Mrs Maria	Davies, Jas
Beck, Jos	Cook, John	Doniphan, T A S-3
Bearch, John	Chew, R M	David, Geo R
Beck, Lemuel J	Clark, Dr J J	Dulany, Capt Bladen
Brown, Fanny	Coile, John	Edwards, J
Brown, Miss Sarah	Codrick, Jos	Elderton, Somerset H
Brown, Miss S A	Crawford, Robt L	Eheler, Miss Amelia
Browne, Mrs Reb'ca	Cooper, Maj S U S A	Evans, Chester B
Brown, Thos B	Clinton, Jas G	Edwards, Miss Susan
Brown, Edw H	Clements, Miss Rach	Eminison, Miss Anna
Brown, Simon	Carusi, L	Emory, Lt Wm H
Brown, Peter H-2	Collins, Mrs Sarah W	Eaton, John
Brent, Dr A Lee	Colelaser, Danl P	Edwards, Amory-3
Brent, Wm L	Chapin, Chester H	Espy, Jas P-2
Baker, J	Cherry, Dr Geo	Espy, Mrs Mgt
Brady, Mrs	Colegate, Col John	Floyd, R J
Brayton, Thos R-5	Carroll, Miss V L	Flemming, Miss G
Baker, Mrs Ellen	Courtney, Miss Ann	Fowler, Jas J
Bancker, J W	Coffin, Isaac N	Fersaille, Monsieur
Bartow, Mrs E L	Crandel, Mrs Cath	Ferguson, Benj
Ballade, Mrs Col'bia	Cockrill, Miss N	Friday, Mrs P
Bunkley, Miss A-2	Colier, Jos	Gould, Stephen G
Baker, Jno of Salem	Caloman, Wm	Gaines, Geo S
Barney, Capt e G	Crossman, Capt	Griffin, John
Brandson, Anna	Day, Jas W	Godfrey, Wm
Burford, R P	Dix, John A	Garehur, Miss A A
Bower, Abraham	Dell, Col Chas L	Gerding, Geo F
Brereton, Mrs A	Day, Mrs Louisa	Gilmore, Edwin E
Barrette, Miss Ann	Dean, Miss Catharine	Griffith, Richd
Bielaski, Alex	Day, Wm	Gibson, Henry
Baker, Jos	Donelson, Edw	Gordon, Chas
Braiden, Miss E	Dustan, J C S	Giddings, Saml J-3
Bisher, Mrs Mary	Drummond, Miss A R	Grosshans, Adam
Boyden, Mr	Deroe, Jas	Gorman, Peter
Bowes, Henry M	Dickinson, Townse'd	Gadsden, Col Jas-3
Bailey, Dr	Dunlop, Miss Mary L	Hall, Jas
Berry, Wm F	Doran, Miss Cath'ne	Hall, Edw-3
Bartley, T W-2	Dimpiel, F J	Henck, Miss Caroline
Brion, Mrs Eliz	Davis, John	Hughes, Holker
Clarke, Miss M A	Dolan, Mrs P	Hatch, Lewis M
Clark, Miss Sarah G	Daniel, Moses	Hall, Levi A
Cree, Jas	Duvall, Marcellus	Hall, Miss Mgt
Clark, John	Davis, Mrs Eliz	Haight, Silas

Hicks, Chas
Hurlbert, Miss Vesta
Hasking, Miss Aria
Hunter, Wm H
Hartnett, Mrs P
Hannegan, E A
Hockrine, Nicholas
Hoover, Jacob
Hurlburt, H F-3
Harrison, Miss E
Hogan, Col Wm-2
Howard, Wm J
Hanscom, A H
Holtmeyer, J
Hutton, Isaac G
Hooper, Chas H
Harrison, Miss Sarah
Hoffman, Leonard
Hammack, Wm-2
Haller, Jacob
Isherwood, B F
Iglehart, Edw J
Ingraham, John
Jones, Wm
Johnson, Rachael
Johnson, Wm
Johnson, Thos
Johnston, Edw S-2
Jackson, E
Johnson, Miss R
Jerman, Mrs Ann E
Jackson, Geo C
Johnson, Jas J
King, C B-3
King, Thos
Kluk, Jos
King, Catharine
Kearney, Mrs J A
Kelly, John
Kegan, John
Keoble, Jacob
Lyles, Miss Mary
Logan, Mrs Harriet

Lashley, Robt
Loring, Mrs
Larnagan, Kennedy
Lasher, Thos
Lingebach, H
Laporte, E
Lowry, Miss Mary A
Littlejohn, Wm H
Ludlow, Augustus C
Lanam, Mrs Lucy
Loockerman, J T
Lachenmyer, Jos
Londen, dghts of Mary & Richd
Macke, Hy & Jos
Marsh, Jas B
Mine, Dr John
Mangum, W P
Mershan, Wm
Morgan, Washington
Melcher, Andrew D
Montgomery, Miss C
Mitchell, John R
Martin, Mrs Cecilia H
Malster, Wm
Mitchell, Patrick
Marshall, J
Maxwell, John
Moreland, Miss M E G
Marshall, Mrs Ellen
Mason, Mrs Hannah
Mozene, Jas
Mufhawn, Wm
Mussey, Thos
Milstead, Isaac
Morton, John S
Montgomery, Jas-3
Murdock, Jas H-5
Mason, John
Mandlebaum, Simon
Massoletti, Vincent-2
Muller, Michael
McCobb, Jas

McKay, Wm
McCrab, Mrs Jane
McFarren, Jas
McCullum, Jas
McMechen, Miss A B
McHenry, H
McClellan, Robt
McDuffee, Thos
Nevitt, Capt J B
O'Neal, Jas
Oyster, Wm F
O'Neal, Dr G P
Owens, Miss N W
O'Connell, Serg John
Owen, Eliza
Pierce, Richd
Peck, Henry
Paul, Fed'k
Pratt, Rev D D
Paine, A N
Price, Miss E H-2
Poland, L P
Parmelee, Dr S
Porter, H
Porter, Mid Henry O
Paris, Mr
Philips, Wm H
Parker, Montgomery
Petersen, Wm C
Parrott, Lt E G
Prettyman, Miss S E
Pambeauff, Col
Pendleton, W F-2
Padgett, Miss A
Piper, Mrs Louisa
Parker, Henry T
Queen, Mrs Eliza
Queen, Miss Charl'te
Queen, N L
Rose, Hugh R
Rich, David
Redman, Jos
Randolph, Mrs

Robinson, L B	Shippen, jr, Wm	Wayne, Justice
Reeler, Saml	Simpson, Miss Sarah	Wise, Saml
Robinson, Wm	Stephens, Thos A	Will, Miss H Eliza
Randolph, J B U S N	Stephens, Robt A-2	Wren, Geo W
Runnells, Mrs	Sopher, P	Wast, Chas
Rogers, Capt John	Stetson, Miss Mary A	Winne, Thos
Robinson, Mrs M A	Smallwood, Miss V	Wright, Chas J
Symms, Miss F H	Smallwood, Caroline	White, Mrs Harriet
Siecle, Augustus-3	Sizer, Henry-2	White, Wm
Scott, Mrs E B	Sanderson, John	Wise, Mrs Cath-2
Simms, Mrs Delila	Simpson, Michl T	Walker, David
Scott, Miss Mary A	Thomas, Capt W	Weaver, Mrs Cath
Semmes, Wm H	Thumblet, J E	Wilson, Fred'k
Sheets & Co, Wm-2	Taylor, Knowles	Wellner, Chas-2
Scot, Thornton	Thompson, Miss A	Williams, Mrs Sarah
Smith, Mrs Jane	Thompson, Wm of N Y	Wilson, Mrs F S-2
Smith, David	Tucker, Enoch G	Williams, Emeline
Smith, E T	Tyler, Robt	Waters, David
Smith, Thos	Tilghman, Miss J	Worseley, Miss M
Smith, Wm B	Tilghman, Henry	Williams, Wm
Smith, Jas	Thomas, Mrs Caro	Weaver, Mrs T G
Smith, Albert-2	Tolson, Henry	Williams, Mrs Wm H
Searight, Capt J B	Taylor, Robt A	Wickenshop, B
Shallenberger, E T	Taylor, H	Wadsworth, T M
Shorter, Chas W	Taylor, Col Geo	Wrixon, Rob S-2
Sullivan, P J	Taylor, Wm, of Point Coupee	Young, Mrs Amelia T
Stewart, Mrs Wm of Havana	Thomas, Wm H-4	Young, Miss Sarah V
Strader, Chas M	Weeks, Edw A-3	Young, jr, Ezekiel
Sluper, Lewis	White, Miss Ellen M	Yeatman, John H

Died: on Sat last, at his residence in Wash City, in his 83rd year, the Hon Buckner Thruston, Associate Judge of the Circuit Court of the U S for the District of Columbia. He was a native of Va, but emigrating to Ky, his fine abilities brought him into public life. He has left a large circle of descendants, relatives, & friends to cherish his memory. His funeral will take place at 11 o'clock this morning, from his house on 3rd st, to which the friends, of the dec'd are respectfully invited. [Sep 3rd newspaper: The remains of the venerable Judge were deposited in *Congress Burial Ground*: services of the Episcopal Church were read by Rev L Gilliss, assisted by Rev Mr Stringfellow. The following acted as pall-bearers: Hon Judge Cranch, Hon Judge Morsell, Hon Judge Dunlop, Gen Walter Jones, W W Seaton, Jas Henry, Jos H Bradley, John Marbury, Gen Roger Jones, & Gen Roger Weightman.]

First District School resumes on Sep 1: corner of G & 14th sts.
–J L Henshaw, Principal Teacher

Advices from the Sandwich Islands to May 16 have been received. The death of Haalilio, one of the King's envoys to the Goverments of France, England, & the U S, is announced.

Twenty six of the *Van Dieman's Land* prisoners had arrived at Honolulu in a whale ship, seeking passage for the U S.

Gtwn College, D C: will be resumed on Sep 15. –Thos F Mulledy, President

A German, about 35 years of age, who arrived at Balt on Thu by the Norfolk steamboat, & registerd on the books of the Exchange Hotel as G Kunkel, of New Orleans, committed suicide during the night by hanging himself to the bedpost. $330 in gold & in bank notes upon the Louisiana Banks were found on his person.

Western Academy will be resumed on Sep 1. –G J Abbot

TUE SEP 2, 1845
Anacostia Bridge, well known as Benning's Bridge, has just undergone a thorough repair, & is now in as complete order as any bridge on the Potomac or Eastern Branch. It is a mile & a quarter nearer to the Capitol from Marlborough Courthouse than any other bridge that crosses the Eastern Branch.

House & lot at auction: on Sep 4, on the premises, a new house, in square 513, between M & N sts: adjoining the Rev U S Ward's property. –A Green, auctioneer

Dissolution of the partnership lately subsisting between John Pettibone & De Vere Burr, of Wash City,
D C, under the firm of John Pettibone & Co: by mutual consent. John Pettibone will continue the business & has on hand a superior article of Butler Coal.
–John Pettibone, De Vere Burr

English Classical & Mathematical School, N Y ave, First Ward, will be resumed on Sep 2. –W S Graff

New Orleans, Aug 25. Yesterday 5 companies of Col Dakin's new Regt of Volunteers for Texas were reviewed in Lafayette Square by Genr'l Gaines, accompainied by his Staff. The Lone Star Guard, which organized in the 3rd Municipality on Sat, mustered at the same time, with several companies of the Irish Brigade, under command of Lt Carrigan. Gen Gaines addressed the gallant fellows. The whole body of 257 men marched through some of the principal streets & then separated. –Bee

Died: on the 27th ult, in Boydton, Mecklenburg Co, Va, Miss Henrietta, eldest d/o Edw R Chambers, in her 20th year. An afflicted family weeps over her tomb. Her memory will be precious to many.

Mrs Anne E Bronaugh, having taken a house in Gtwn, on 1st st, Cox's Row, will receive boarders.

For rent: with or without furniture, the large 3 story house on G st, now occupied by Mrs Dashiell as a boarding house. Possession can be given early in this month. Apply to John Douglas, jr, Florist & Seedsman, on 20th st north.

St Mary's Female Institution, Bryantown, Chas Co, Md: on Aug 19th awarding of premiums. The Academy is watched over by the venerable Rev Mr Courtney, Pastor of Bryantown. The following were rewarded by the Rev John P Donelan, of St Matthew's Church, Wash City, assisted by Rev Mr Courtney, Drs Queen & Boarman, & Edw Dyer, of Wash.

Mary F Neale, Chas Co, Md
Eleanor Downey, Chas Co, Md
Ellen Queen, Chas Co, Md
Rose E Boarman, Chas Co, Md
Mary J Boarman, Chas Co, Md
Ellen Rose Boarman
Julia Boarman, Chas Co, Md
Rebecca Adams, Chas Co, Md
Mary C Mudd, Chas Co, Md
Ann Downey, Chas Co, Md

Eleanor A Bryan, PG Co, Md
Mary C Hughes, Cahs Co, Md
Ann Maria Bowling, Chas Co, Md
Maria L Hamilton, Chas Co, Md
Agnes Courtney, Balt, Md
Rosalie Boone, Chas Co, Md
Mary Jane Hamersley
Maria L Hamilton, Chas Co, Md
Eleanor Downey, Chas Co, Md

Mrs Wilmer will re-open her school at Alexandria, D C, on Sep 15th.

The Richmond Institute, a school for young ladies will be opened in Richdmond, Va, on Oct 1, 1845, under the superintendence of Mrs Gen Carrington.

WED SEP 3, 1845
Appointments by the Pres:
John F Steele, of Pa, Purser, in place of Thos E Norris, of Md, resigned.
Benj M Bosworth, Surveyor & Inspector of the revenue for the ports of Warren & Barrington, in R I, vice Wm B Snell, removed.
John G Winston, Receiver of Public Moneys for the district of lands subject to sale at Lebanon, Ala, vice Levi W Lawler, whose commission will expire on Sep 13, 1845.
Hugh P Carpenter, Register of the Land Ofc for the district of lands subject to sale at Lebanon, Ala, vice Jacob T Bradford, removed.
John L Slaymaker, Postmaster at Galena, Ill, in place of Robt W Carson, removed.

Died: on Sep 1, at his place near Rock Creek Church, D C, Capt Wm G Sanders, aged 54 years, a native of Md, & recently a citizen of Florida. He was a gallant ofcr of the late war with Great Britain, & was taken prisoner under Col Boerstler at the Beaver Dams on Jun 24, 1813. As a volunteer in the late Florida war he was shot through the body in Feb, 1836, near **Camp Izard**, on the Withlacoochie, while at the head of a band of friendly Indians. This wound & exposure to the severities of climate in Canada & Florida, shattered his iron consitution & hastened his decease. Long will the poor in his neighborhood mourn in him a benefactor whose money & labor were freely expended in their behalf. His funeral will take place this morning at 10 o'clock at Rock Creek Church.

Mr Geo W Frederick died at Greensborough, Ala, on Aug 9, from the effects of a snake bite received 16 hours previously. He was in the water fishing when he was bitten. The snake was a water moccasin.

Died: on Sep 2, in Wash City, of gangrenous decay of the lower limbs, at the house of his son-in-law, Edw Wm Johnston, Josephe Jerome De Cressac Villagrand, a native of Magnac, in the kingdom of France, aged 69 years & nearly 6 months. [The Courer des Etats Unis, N Y, & Richmond Whig will please copy.]

Died: on Sep 2, in Gtwn, after a lingering illness, in her 57th year, Mrs Eliz, consort of Francis Dodge. Her funeral is this afternoon, at 5 o'clock.

Died: on Aug 23, at Richmond, Mrs Ann Hoop Barclay, w/o David Barclay, sen, in her 55th year. In all the relations this eminently good woman sustained, as wife, mother, mistress, & friend, her example was good, & worthy of close imitation.

Wash Corp: 1-Cmte of Claims: asked to be discharged from the further consideration of the ptn of Patrick Murphy. 2-Bill for the relief of M P Mohun: ordered to lie on the table.

Handsome household furniture for sale at the house of Mr John Douglas, on G st, near 15th, on Sep 9. –Boteler, Donn, & Co, Auctioneers

THU SEP 4, 1845
The Ebenezer Station of the Methodist Episcopal Church, in Wash City, has concluded to hold a Camp Meeting on the ground of Mr Selby Skaggs, 3 miles from this city, on the opposite side of the Eastern Branch of the Potomac, about 1 mile from Benning's Bridge, to commence on Sep 5. The ground is easy access either by land or water.

Miss H McCormick & sister have re-opened their school. Terms made known at their place of residence, on 4½ st, south side Pa ave, Mr Ward's row, next door to Dr Telnore.

Household furniture at auction: order of the Orphans Court of Wash Co, D C. Sale of a variety of furniture, being part of the personal property of the late John Brannan.
-R W Dyer & Co, aucts

Lumber at auction on Sat, in front of Mr C H James' store, 14th & Pa ave.
-R W Dyer & Co, aucts

During a severe storm in Chanango Co, on Aug 12, Elder Hart, of Smithville, a clergyman of the Baptist persuasion, was struck by lightning, & killed instantly. He was returning home, & was near there.

Mrd: on Sep 2, by Rev John Decker, Rev W B Crawford, of Perryville, Ky, to Miss Mary Ferral, of Bladensburg, Md.

FRI SEP 5, 1845
The present Pope, Gregory XVI, says the Journal des Debats, is the 25th successor to St Peter. He will complete his 80th year on the 18th of next month. He was raised to the Pontifical see on Feb 2, 1831. The College of Cardinals is composed of 55 members, 2 named by Pius VII, 7 by Leo XII, & 46 by Gregory XVI. The Dean of the Sacred College is Cardinal Padini, 87 years of age. Schwartzenburg is the youngest of the cardinals, scarcely yet 36 years of age. 61 cardinals have died since the accession of Gregory XVI.

Arrivals from the Oregon. The ship **Inez**, from the Sandwich Islands, arrived at New Bedford on Sun. Among the passengers were Dr J L Babcock, lady, & 2 children, & the Rev H W Perkins, lady, & 4 children, recently members of the Methodist Episcopal mission at Oregon.

There are 2 editions of the Bible printed in the reign of Henry VIII, one in 1539, & the other in 1541; both printed by Richd Grafton. Another Bible was printed by Robt Barker & John Bill, in London, 1640. An imperfect copy of the Bible, translated by Thos Matthew, folio, 1537, was sold in London lately for 100 guineas. This version was translated by the celebrated John Rogers, who was the first martyr in Queen Mary's reign. Thomas, in his History of American Printing, says the first edition of the Bible in English printed in America, was published by Kneeland & Green, of Boston, in small quarto, about 1750. Christopher Sauer, alias Sower, printed in 1743, at Germantown, an edition of the Scriptures in the German language.

Appointments by the Pres:
John T Pickett, of Ky, U S Consul for Turk's Island in place of Abraham Morrell, recalled.
Silas A Comstock, Naval Ofcr for the district of Providence, R I, vice Moses Richardson, removed.

Mrd: on Sep 2, by Rev L J Gilliss, Mr Edw D Willard to Miss Sarah E Hepburn, all of Wash City.

Died: on Sep 3, after a long & painful illness, Mary Jane, consort of Francis Barry, jr, in her 22nd year. Her funeral is this afternoon at 4 o'clock, from the residence of her mother, Mrs Lowe, near Blagden's wharf.

Died: on Sep 3, Sarah E Shreve, consort of Caleb H Shreve, of Wash City, & eldest d/o Mrs Maria Hearn, of Howard District, Md. [Baltimore Sun please copy.]

Died: on Sep 2, Wm Henry Cheshire, only child of Henry & Rosina Ingle, aged 11 months & 23 days.

The 2nd & 3rd Regts of Artl, the 4th Regt of Infty, & the Medical Staff of the Army have recently united in erecting, at West Point, a monument to the memory of Maj Dade & his command. It is placed on the brow of the hill near Kosciusko's garden. The workmanship reflects great credit on the artist, Mr Launitz, of N Y C. The American eagle surmounts the shaft, sustaining in his beak a laurel wreath. The inscription: To commemorate the battle of the 28th December, 1835, between a detachment of 108 U S Troops & the Seminole Indians of Florida, in which all of the detachement save 3 fell without an attempt to retreat. Erected by the 3 Regts & the Medical Staff, whose comrades fell on the 28th Dec, 1835, serving their country & honoring their profession. The remains of the dead repose near St Augustine, Florida. The 4th inscription give the names of the ofcrs who fell: Maj F L Dade, 4th Infty, from Virginia; Capt G W Gardiner, 2nd Artl, from D C; Capt U S Frazer, 3rd Artl, from N Y; Lt W E Bassinger, 2nd Artl, from Georgia; Lt R R Mudge, 3rd Artl, from Mass; Lt Kears, 3rd Artl, from N C; Lt R Henderson, 3rd Artl, from Tenn; & Assist Surgeon Gatlin, of the Medical Staff, from N C. Forty out of the 100 survived at the end of a first attack victors, in possession of the field, & it is believed that they might have effected a retreat to Tampa Bay, but they nobly resolved to remain to protect & defend their wounded men. After a few hours' interval the Indians, reinforced in numbers, &, mustering not less than 1,000 warriors, renewed the attack, & finally destroyed the whole party; this band of 40 evidently falling victims to their heroic devotion to their wounded comrades. Three wounded soldiers escaped to Tampa to tell the story. –A

Lands in Alexandria Co, nearly opposite Gtwn, for sale at public auction: under deed of trust executed on Mar 25, 1844, recorded in the Clerk's ofc, Alexandria Co, in Liber F #3, folios 132: sale on Sep 16, at the auction rooms of Mr Edw S Wright, Gtwn, those parts of sections 4, 5, & 9, & the whole section #15, conveyed by Gen John Mason to the Bank of the U S. –Rd Smith, Trustee -Edw S Wright, auctioneer

Commencement exercises at Harvard last week. The first class was graduated in 1642, 203 years ago. The whole number of graduates is 5,942, of whom 3,897 are dead, & 2,045 are living. The oldest graduate is Dr Ezra Green, of Dover, N H, of the class of 1765, a soldier of the Revolutionary Army, a surgeon on board the ship **Ranger** of 18 guns, commanded by John Paul Jones. In a few months he will attain his 110th year. In 1783 Hon Harrison Gray Otis was graduated, & was a classmate of Hon Ambrose Spencer, Judge of the Supreme Court of the State of N Y. In 1787, 4 years after, Hon John Quincy Adams, with whom Judge Cranch, of Washington, was a classmate. The next year we meet the name of Benj Abbott, L L D, who resided for 50 years over the Phillips Academy at Exeter, N H. We never had at once in those high places of honor 3 men more worthy than Danl Webster, Edw Everett, & Lewis Cass. In 1790 Hon Saml Crafts, Gov'r & Senator of Vt was graduated; & the same year the Hon Josiah Quincy.

$30 reward for runaway negro man David [Davy] Greenleaf; about 28 years of age. He has left a wife at Mr Robt Clarke's, & is likely lurking in the neighborhood.
–John Eversfield, living near Bladensburg, PG Co, Md.

SAT SEP 6, 1845
Battle of *King's Mountain*-copy of the original paper drawn up by the late Gen Jos Graham, father of the present Govn'r of N C, of Lincoln Co, N C, the county in which the site of the battle is located: the battle that led to the retreat of Cornwallis, then on his advance through Carolina. After the defeat of Gen Gates & the army under his command, on Aug 16, 1780, & the defeat of Gen Sumpter, 2 days later, near Rocky Mount, by Col Tarlton, the South was almost entirely abandoned to the enemy. Wm L Davidson, who had served as Lt Col of the regulars in the Northern army, was appointed Brig Gen of the militia in the Salisbury district, in place of Gen Rutherford, who was taken prisoner at Gates' defeat. After Gates' defeat, the attention of Lord Cornwallis was occupied with burying the dead & taking care of the wounded, & forwarding the great number of prisoners he had taken, to Charleston. By Sep 1 he had his arrangements made, & detached Col Ferguson over the Wateree with only 110 regulars, under command of Capt Dupiester, & about the same number of Tories, but with an ample supply of arms & other military stores. His forces later increased to upwards of 1,000 men. Col Chas McDowell, of Burke Co, on the approach of Ferguson, had gone over the mountain to obtain assistance, & was in consultation with Col John Sevier & Col Isaac Shelby as to what place should be persued. Col Shelby was to give intelligence of their movements to Col Wm Campbell of the adjoining county of Washington, Va. They met on the Wataga, Sep 30, & were joined by Col Benj Cleveland & Maj Jos Winston, from Wilkes & Surry Counties. They had between them 1,390 in number. The troops were led in the following order: to the right, Maj Winston, Col Sevier, Col Campbell, Col Shelby, & Maj McDowell; to the left, Col Hambrite, Col Cleveland, & Col Williams, of S C. A brisk fire was poured upon Ferguson's men. At length he was shot dead, & his whole command driven up into a group of 60 yards in length & not 40 in width. The British ofcr, Capt Dupiester, who took the command, ordered a white flag to be raised, in

token of surrender, but the bearer was instantly shot down. Col Hambrite was wounded & Maj Chronicle was killed. Col Williams, of S C, was also killed. The Whigs lost about 30 killed & 50 wounded. The enemy had about 150 killed & the rest taken prisoners. On the 8th a court-martial was held, & several prisoners who were found guilty of murder & other high crimes, were sentenced to be hanged. About 20 were executed. At the forks of the branch where Maj Chronicle & Capt John Mattocks were buried, a monument was erected. On the east side is the following inscription: Sacred to the memory of Maj Wm Chronicle & Capt John Mattocks, Wm Robb, & John Boyd, who were killed at this place on Oct 7, 1780, fighting in defence of America. On the western side of the monument, facing the battle ground: "Col Ferguson, an ofcr of his Britannic Majesty, was defeated & killed at this place, on the 7th of October, 1780."

Orphans Court of Wash Co, D C. Letters of administration on the personal estate of Buckner Thruston, late of said county, dec'd. –Th L Thruston, W A Bradley, adms

$100 reward for runaway negro, Wm, about 21 years of age, employed as a waiter. He formerly belonged to the estate of Mrs Mgt Doane, of Princess Anne, Somerset Co, Md, & has relatives there. I am authorized by his present owner, Miss Matilda Doane, to give the above reward if taken out of D C. I may be seen at the ofc of Jas Hoban, U S Dist Atty, east wing of the City Hall, Wash, D C. –G C Morgan, for the owner.

N Y: in the neighborhood of 37 Laurens st, yesterday, a woman was found with her throat cut almost from ear to ear. Her name was Canning, w/o Thos Canning, about 40 years of age, & the mother of 3 or 4 children. The woman was taken to the City Hospital, where her wounds will be properly attended to. She said she got into a quarrel with a woman, who came to hire rooms in the house, & who fled.

For rent: 2 story frame dwlg-house on I st, 3 doors east of 7th st. Apply at R D Spencer's Shoe Store, 7th st, near the premises.

House for sale or rent: 2 story brick house on E st, between 9th & 10th sts, end of the block known as Green's Bldgs, & at present occupied by Mr Thos J Williams. –A Coyle, Agent

For sale, the boat **La Belle Boat** & Boat-house, with oars, boat-hooks, cushions, & everything connected therewith. Apply to John Alexander, between 12th & 13th sts, Pa ave.

MON SEP 8, 1845
Examined before the Army Medical Board, lately in N Y, & the following were approved & recommended for appointment in the Medical Staff of the Army, viz: 1-John Frazier Head, M D, of Mass. 2-Lewis A Edwards, M D, of the District of Columbia.

At N Y on Wed the wall of an old bldg fell, burying workmen beneath its ruins. Henry McLaughlin & John Welsh were killed; Barney McLaughlin was severely injured & not expected to live.

Mrs Moseley & Mrs Oakes, of Boston, who were im imminent danger of drowning while bathing on Mon at Plum Island, Mass, were saved by the fortitude & energy of a d/o Mrs Oakes, who is only 12 years old. The dght put on her life preserver & swam to her relatives, [for the parties in danger were sisters,] & succeeded in saving them both.

Died: on Sep 3, at Cumberland, Md, Mr Robt N Johnston, formerly a resident of Wash City, & for many years disbursing Clerk in the ofc of the Clerk of the House of Reps. He had many warn friends here as well as in his native city of Balt.

Died: on Sep 4, Mrs Mary Ball, relict of the late Isaac Ball, of PG Co, Md, aged 66 years.

Died: on Aug 30, of cholera infantum, Arthur M, infant s/o Geo M & Jane Phillips, of Wash City.

By virtue of an order of distrain for rent in arrear due to Sarah G Stewart by John Thos Wright, I will expose at public sale on Sep 8, in Wash City, goods & chattels of Wright. –Wm Cox, Bailiff

By virtue of an order of distrain for rent due to Simon Frazure by Wm B Cook, I will expose at public sale on Sep 13, goods & chattels of Cook. –H R Maryman, Bailiff

By virtue of a writ of fieri facias, issued by Thos C Donn, a Justice of the Peace for Wash Co, D C, at the suit of Thos M Millburn, against the goods & chattels, lands & tenements, rights & credits of Wm W Whitmore: I will expose at public sale, on Sep 13, goods & chattels of Whitmore. –H R Maryman, Bailiff

Paris, Aug 16, 1845. Inauguration of the statue of Beethoven. Beethoven has been dead 18 years; he was born in 1770; grew deaf at age 26; retired to a village near Vienna; suffered much from dropsy; read chiefly Homer & Walter Scott; passionately admired Napoleon until the Imperial Crown was assumed; then he dedicated a compostion to the memory of the great man Bonaparte. The statue is of bronze; 12 feet high; erect; he holds in his right hand a pencil, & in his left an album, as if about to note down some rich musical idea. The expression, drapery, the details in general, are represented as admirable.

Local Item: on Thu a free negress, Jane White, was found dead in the 1st Ward: verdict- died by intemperance.

Servant girl wanted: a colored girl about 14 years of age. –H Stringfellow

Letter to Capt F A Tucker: **Mount Vernon**, Sep 2, 1845: from John A Washington. The rule prohibiting persons who come by water from landing at **Mount Vernon** was established by Judge Washington & has been continued ever since, though it has been set aside twice in the last 13 years. To allow all would render my residence here intolerable. If the Dauphin Guards wish to come by land, the privileges granted to other strangers will be extended to them, viz. to walk over the grounds to the tomb of Gen Washington; but I cannot consent to their landing upon my premises from the water. –John A Washington

TUE SEP 9, 1845
Mr Nathl Lamson, a land broker, committed suicide at N Y on Thu by discharging the contents of a pistol into his right temple. No cause can be assigned for the fatal act.

The Military Academy. Letter dated: New Hamburg, Dutchess Co, N Y, Jun 28, 1845: to the Hon Wm L Marcy, Sec of War. Discipline is very strict. Attendance at the Chapel is required on the Sabbath. The pay & subsistence of a cadet is $26 per month. The Commandant is Major Delafield. Annual graduation at West Point averages 35 or 40. The term is 4 years. Present 4 classes consist of numbers 41, 62, 44, & 57. The age of admission must range between 16 & 21; they demand at least 4 years preliminary education, & require an examination for the standard of admission. The location of this academy is remarkably happy-on the banks of the Hudson, nearly midway, within 4 hours' distance from either N Y or Albany. It is among the Highlands of the Hudson, which was a centre of the war of the Revolution, whose passes were selected by Washington & Geoge Clinton, & fortified as points of national defence. **Fort Putnam** & **Fort Clinton** are in ruins; they suffered ruthless dilapidation before the Gov't had acquired the right of property. –Jas Tallmadge

The Oldest Bible in the World. Among the curiosities at the Connecticut Historical Society, in Hartford, is a Bible printed in 1478, & which Dr Robbins thinks the oldest Bible in the world. It is a Latin version of the Bible; there were 3 editions of it printed in that language, in 1478, all in folio; one printed by Leonard Wilke, at Venice; another by Theoderic de Reynberg, & Reynold de Novimagis, [Spires,] also at Venice; & a third by Antony Koburger, at Nuremburg. Dr Robbins is wrong in supposing that the Bibles of 1478 are the oldest printed ones. The first edition was printed at Mentz in Latin [folio] by John Faust, soon after the year 1450, certainly before 1455; a second edition was also printed at Mentz in 1462; the third edition was printed at Augsburg 1466; the fourth at Reutlingen [in Wirtemberg] in 1469; the fifth, in 2 volumes, at Rome, in 1471; the the sixth, in Italian, at Venice, also in 1471. The value of the Bible in the Historical Society at Hartford, I would by no means depreciate. [Signed: ***]

For rent: large house on Pa ave, between 3rd & 4½ sts, & has been occupied by Mr Beers for 8 years as the American Hotel. –John Sinon

Died: on Sep 7, Richd Beckett, infant s/o Jas M & M E Peyton Torbut, aged 11 months & 22 days. [Wilmington, Delaware, papers please copy.]

Annapolis, Sep 6. The company of artillery which has been stationed at *Fort Severn* for several years past, under the command of Maj Gardiner, took its departure in one of the bay steamers on Wed last for *Fort Monroe*, Old Point Comfort, Va. This company has been ordered from Fort Severn to make room for the Naval school which is to open there on Oct 1. The ofcrs with the company are Maj J L Gardiner & Lts Drum & McCown. Assistant Surgeon King, who has also been attached to the command, proceeds hence to the Phil station. Capt Franklin Buchanan, of the Navy, has taken possession of the Gov't property at *Fort Severn*, with a view to its immediate preparation for the reception of the midshipmen who are to join the school on Oct 1. –Republican

Sudden death of David Henderson, of Jersey City, near his iron-works in Adirondack, N Y, on Wed. The hunter Cheeney & Mr Henderson were crossing the lake to fish, & while Cheeney prepared the fishing tackle, Mr Henderson took up Cheeney's pistol from one of the seats of the boat; as he was stepping on shore it went off, producing instant death. –N Y Commercial Advertiser [Sep 10th newspaper: Mrs Henderson & children were lodged nearby. Mr Henderson was a native of Scotland, but had resided many years in this country. He married a d/o Arcibald McIntyre, of Albany, & resided in Jersey City.]

School for Young Ladies, Portsmouth, Va. Mrs Comegys intends to open a School for Boarding & Day Pupils in Portsmouth, commencing on Oct 6 & closing the last of Jul. Those who become members of her family will excite the same solicitude, & receive the same zealous care in this respect as her own children.

Died: on Sep 8, at his residence in Wash Co, D C, Edw Dyer, late Sergeant-at-Arms of the U S Senate, in his 53rd year. He leaves a large circle of relatives & friends. To his widow & orphan children the loss is indeed irreparable. His funeral will move from his late residence at 3 p m on Sep 9, & proceed to St Patrick's Church, on F st, where the funeral service will be performed.

WED SEP 10, 1845
Trustee's sale of valuable lots: by virtue of an act of Congres, passed Jul 20, 1840, & of the decree of the Circuit Court of Wash Co, D C, made in the case of Lewis G Davidson's heirs, I shall offer at auction on Sep 22, the following lots in Wash City:
Lots 1 thru 8 in square 161
Lots 2, 4, 5, 6, 11, 12, 14, 15, 16, 20, & 21, in square 163
Lots 1 thru 8, & 16 thru 18, in square 127
Lots 4, 6, 7, 8, 11, 13, 15, 16, & 17, in square 168
Lors 2, 3, 4, & 19, in square 169
Lots 1 thru 5, in square 170
Lots 2, 4 thru 19, in square 165

Lots 1 thru 25, in square 183
Lots 1 thru 6, & 8 thru 16, & 18, in square 184
These lots are numbered according to Davidson's sub-division, & are in the neighborhood of the President's house. The sale will commence at square 163. Plats of the lots can be seen at the ofc of Mr Redin, Gtwn. –Sam G Davidson, Trustee

Hagerstown News: Mr Snively, the Whig candidate, is confined to his room by sickness. We learn that Mr Stotlemeyer, one of the Democratic candidates, is dangerous ill, & in the small village of Hancock, where these gentlemen reside, more thatn 60 persons are at present prostrated by disease-fevers we presume.

Letter received that Mr A H Everett, who went out in the U S ship **Columbus**, on his way to China, was expected to return from Rio to the U S in consequence of ill health.

Meeting of the "Defenders" of Balt in 1814: Dr Jas S Gunnell in the chair; Jas Lawrenson, Sec: on Sep 8, in the Chamber of the Board of Aldermen, Wash City. Cmte appointed to make arrangements for a reception.

Benj B French	Wm Fischer	Geo Cochran
A Woodward	Wm Thompson	Presley Simpson
Jos H Bradley	Wm H Gunnell	S S Colemen
Wm Gunton	Wm Easby	A Fuller
J W Maury	John Y Bryant	Marshal Brown
Jos W Beck	John C Rives	Enoch Tucker
Geo Parker	Wm B Magruder	

+
Immediately after the Citizen's Meeting, a call was made for the organization of a meeting of the Old Defenders; which being promptly responded to: Dr Jas S Gunnell, in the chair; Jas Lawrenson, Sec. Proposition by Capt de La Roche; motion by Jas C Wilson; announced Capts Thos Sangster & Geo F De la Roche as assistant marshals; & Mr John Allen was present.

Appointment by the Pres: Jas T Miller, Naval Ofcr for the District of Wilmington, N C, vice Jas Owen, removed.

Mrd: on Tue, by Rev Mr Stringfellow, Morven I McClery to Anna, eldest d/o Robt Keyworth, all of Wash City.

Mrd: last evening, by Rev Wm Matthews, Alfred T Agate to Miss Eliz H Kennedy, all of Wash City.

Firemen's Board of Control meeting at 7 o'clock, at Perserverance Hall.
-Geo S Gideon, Sec pro tem.

Died: on Sun last, Jas Thomas, s/o Geo Washington Cissil, in his 4th year.

Wash Corp: 1-Ptn of Jas Towles & John P Heiss: referred to the Cmte on the Canal. 2-Ptn of Allison Nailor, praying remission of a fine: referred to the Cmte of Claims. 3-Ptn of P L Lemar, praying remission of a fine: referred to the Cmte of Claims. 4-Ptn of John Purdy & others, for paving an alley: referred to the Cmte on Improvements.

Dissolution of the copartnership existing under the name of S E Smith & Co, is this day dissolved by mutual consent. Saml E Smith, Jas G Smith. [S E Smith will continue the business at the same place.]

National Hotel, Washington: formerly known as Gadsby's, but now generally called Coleman's Hotel, is now refitted, in first-rate order, for the reception of travelers or residents. –S S Coleman

Information wanted of Ebenezer Bray, a native of Maine, who left Wash City on Aug 26 for Balt; since which he has not been heard of by his family. Any information concerning him will be gratefully received by his afflicted wife, living on I st, between 6th & 7th sts. –Eliz Bray

THU SEP 11, 1845
University of Md: Wm E A Aikin, M D, Dean of the Faculty.

$100 reward for runaway negro man Andrew Jackson: about 24 years old. He was purchased a few years since of Wm Penquite, dec'd, in the neighborhood of Upperville, Fauquier, & may be lurking about there. –John Scott Payne, near Warrenton, Fauquier Co, Va

On Mon one of the orphan boys attached to the Asylum of St Vincent's Church, Balt, was killed by falling down the stairs, which having been just washed, were slippery. He fell upon his head. His name was Francis Creaney, & he is said to have been a great favorite with his teachers & fellow scholars.

Appointments by the Pres:
1-Wm Crosby, of Ohio, Consul for the port of Talcahuano, in Chile, in place of Paul H Delano, recalled. 2-Denis Prieus, Collector of the Customs for the District of New Orleans, La, vice Thos Barrett, removed.

Benj Harrison, in the employ of the Patterson Machine Co at Paterson, N J, was killed last Wed,
when a large rack of iron fell on him, causing almost instant death. He was about 30 years of age, & has left a wife & 2 small children.

Mrd: on Wed last, by Rev Mr Sprole, Wm Hogan, of Henderson, Rusk Co, Texas, to Miss Cornelia Virginia, d/o Jas B Holmead, of Wash City.

Died: yesterday, after a long & painful illness, Michl Quigley, in his 88th year. His funeral will take place at St Peter's Church, Capitol Hill, this afternoon, at 4 o'clock.

FRI SEP 12, 1845
Oakland School, near Burlington, N J: Prof E C Wines, Principal: there are 2 sessions of 5 months each: vacations are the months of April & October.

The subscribers are now prepared to furnish a variety of Coal: orders will be received at our store, 10th & E sts, Potomac Bridge. –J S Harvey & Co

The steamship **Great Western**, commanded by Capt B R Mathews, left Liverpool on Aug 23, & arrived at Sandy Hook on Tue, making the passage in 17 days. The number of passengers is 145. Among them are: Hon Mr Jenifer, U S Minister to Austria, & his Attache; Hon Mr Boulware, late U S Charge to Naples, supplanted by W H Polk; Hon C Hughes, do, Hague; J H Vernon, member of the British House of Commons from East Retford, & other distinguished individuals.

Mrd: on Sep 8, at *Prospect Hill*, D C, by Rev Wm Pinckney, John T W Dean, Associate Judge of the 2nd Election District Court of PG Co, Md, to Mary Cornelia, d/o Levi Sheriff, of the former place.

Delaware Express gives intelligence of the recent murder of Steele. Wm Sprague, a young man who was taken prisoner testified: on Aug 7, when Steele was shot, he had a 6 barrel pistol. I handed it to Richd Davis. I took the pistol home & gave it to my grandfather, & he put it in his chest; later I gave the pistol to my father. Chas Knapp was examined, as did also E S Edgerton; Ephraim Sprague, father of the first witness, corroborated his testimony. P P Wright, testified; his evidence is sustained by that of Chas Hathaway. It seems, therefore, to be established, that the Indians fired upon & murdered Steele, without even the poor excuse that, in self-defence, he had fired upon them. The number of prisoners now under arrest is 144. Among those taken, the correspondent of the Albany Argus says, is a Mr Jonathan Ferguson, taken on Dry Brook. He is 74 years of age, was treasurer of an anti-rent association, & has executed Indian deeds. He confesses being disguised as an Indian at Clovesville. [Oct 6th newspaper: John Van Steenburgh, indicted for the murder in having been concerned in the affair in which Sheriff Steele lost his life, has resulted in a verdict of guilty.] [Oct 15 newspaper: Delhi, Oct 11: trial of Edw O'Connor, alias Powhatan, for the murder of under Sheriff Osman N Steele ended. John Van Steenberg to be hung on Nov 29. Danl W Squires to be confined in the State prison in Clinton Co for the term of his natural life. Moses Earle to be confined in the State prison for life. Zera Preston: State prison for life. John Phonix, aged 21; John Burtch, aged 22; John Lathan, 45; Wm Reside, 24; Isaac L

Burhans, 23; each sentenced to 7 years in the State prison. Calvin Madison: State prison 10 years. Wm Brisband: State prison 7 years. Danl Northrop: State prison for life-could be pardoned in 2 or 3 years. Chas T McCumber: State prison 7 years. Wm Joscelyn: State prison 2 years. Robt Scott: fined $500. John Davis: fined $100. Darius Travis, Augustus Kettle, Edwin Mason, Barbour Stafford, Henry L Russell, Zadoc Pratt Northrop, John Whitson, jr, Jas Clayton, Smith Sanford, & Alonzo Sanford, all young men, mostly under 21 years of age: sentence suspended, & prisoners allowed to go at large. Henry D Wickhan: sentence suspended; & gave bail to appear at next Oyer & Terminer. Francis F Scott: sentence suspended. The Court adjourned sine die.]

For rent: 2 story brick dwlg, with 6 rooms: located on G st, near the War Dept, now in occupancy by Dr Robbins, of the Land Ofc, who will show the premises. Apply to Judson Mitchell, Gtwn

SAT SEP 13, 1845

Ogdensburgh Republican gives the names of 26 of the *Van Dieman's Land* prisoners who had returned to Honolulu on their way to the U S, & among others those of John Thomas & Edw A Wilson, formerly of the St Lawrence County, & who were taken prisoners at the Wind Mill, opposite Ogdensburg, in the affray of the autumn of 1838. Robt G Collins, the only remaining prisoner from St Lawrence Co, who was released at the same time, in Apr, 1844, does not appear as being with them.

Mrs Minor, having recently taken the house lately occupied by Mr John S Skinner, on F, between 6th & 7th sts, is now prepared to accommodate boarders.

Mr Luther Faulkner, formerly known as a dry goods merchant in Boston, of the late firm of Faulkner & Reed, dropped down dead in an apoplectic fit, in Beacon st, on Sunday.

On Fri last, Elias Hubband, s/o Judge Hubbard, Andrew Lake, Jacob Matthews & son-age 12 years, & a Mr Reed, all of Flatlands, Long Island, started by Jamaica Bay on a sailing expedition. When off Rockaway beach, the boat, in a flaw of wind, capsized, & all were lost, with the exception of Reed, who clung to the baot upwards of 14 hours. He is now in critical situation. –N Y True Sun

Died: on Aug 9, at her residence, in Arkansas, Mrs Ann Conway, aged about 75 years. She has left a numerous & affectionate family: a native of Va, she was an early emigrant to the Great West, where she had found but the rude wilderness & its ruder denizens, & to experience with pride the elevation of several of her sons to high honor among their fellow-men in the noble country of which she was a pioneer. Among her sons were the late Hon Henry W Conway; ex-Govn'r Jas S Conway; Gen E N Conway, at present Auditor of Arkansas; Hon Wm Conway, Judge of the Circuit Court for the Batesville district; Dr John R Conway, of Hotspring Co; & Fred'k R Conway, at present Surveyor Genr'l of Illinois & Missouri.

Mrd: on Sep 10, at Bloomsbury, Balt Co, Md, by the Most Rev Archbishop Eccleston, assisted by Rev Mr Coskry, Mr Wilmer Shields, of the U S Navy, to Agnes, 2nd d/o the late Henry Vernon Somerville.

Died: on Fri week, at the residence of her mother, Mrs White, in Wheeling, Mrs Mary, w/o the Hon Lewis Steenrod. Her numerous acquaintances will recall her as a kind & gentle remembrance of the past.

From the Boonsboro' [Md] Odd Fellows: an affray occurred at the campmeeting near Hagerstown, on Thu, between some blacks & several white men, which resulted in the death of Jos Merchant, a white man, 45 years of age.

A young man, Francis Davenport, a messenger employed on Gay's Express, between Boston & N Y, disappeared very mysteriously on Fri last, & has not since been heard of. He had with him a package of bills containing $2,500 for the Suffolk Bank of Boston, in New England notes. He had another package containing $1,658. He had been employed only a month: reward of $400 for his apprehension.

Late Barbadoes papers state that Jas Yearwood, druggist, & H D Buchanan, planter, were mortally poisoned by drinking some liquid which was supposed to be bitters, with a small infusion of gentian & quinine. Mr John Crone, planter, suffered dreadfully, but there were hope of his recovery.

State of Md, Wash Co, to wit: on application, it is ordered by Wash Co Orphans' Court, Jul 29, 1845, that Andrew Cline, adm of Francis Storkwell, late of said county, dec'd, give notice in the Nat'l Intelligencer, for 6 successive week, to the absent heirs of said dec'd to produce in said Court the evidence that they are the legal reps of said dec'd. –Jas Wason, Reg o/wills for Wash Co, Md

Law School. Having derived great advantage to my health from traveling this summer, I propose to open a Law School in Richmond, Va, to be conducted on the plan pursued by me at the Univ of Va. –Henry St Geo Tucker

MON SEP 15, 1845

Judge Jos Story died on Wed, at his residence in Cambridge. His disease was stoppage of the intestines, or internal strangulation, which 2 years ago caused the death of Hugh S Legare, Atty Gen of the U S, then on a visit to Boston. Jos Story was born in 1780; graduated at Harvard Univ in 1798; appointed Assoc Justice of the U S by Pres Madison in 1811.

Saml Bragg was arrested at Troy on Sat charged with forging a set of pension papers by which he had obtained from the Pension Agent, at Albany, about $400 on a pension due a poor woman in Schaghticoke.

Mr John B Gough, the well known advocate of Temperance, arrived in this city from New Haven on Sep 5, & stopped at the Croton Hotel. He has not been seen or heard of since. Leave information with E D Hurlbut & Co, 84 South st, or Holbrook, Nelson & Co, 37 Pine st, will be gladly received. –N Y Com Adv

The bones of Adolphus Van Groning, of the firm of Pavenstadt & Groning, who was buried beneath the ruins of 42 Broad st, N Y, at the time of the great fire, were recovered on Wed, & recognized by his partner by means of his pantaloons.

Died: on Aug 24, at Detroit, Mich, Mrs Sylvia E Larned, wid/o Gen Chas Larned, dec'd, in her 50th year. She was affectionately devoted to her children & friends.

Naval Storekeeper's Ofc: Navy Yard, Wash, Sep 13, 1845. Sealed proposals will be received to furnish a good vessel to take on board-one set of water tanks.
–J M Selden, Naval Storekeeper

Copartnership between Jas A Burch & Jas H Chezum, Carpenters, has dissolved.
–Jas H Chezum

TUE SEP 16, 1845
The proprietor of the U S Agency & Notarial Ofc has removed from Pa ave to F st, near 14th, opposite J Kennedy's Boodstore, & next door to the residence of Gov Parris, 2nd Comptroller. –Edmund F Brown, Notary Public, Com'r of Deeds for Illinois.

All persons having claims against Wm Cooper, late of PG Co, Md, are to present them to the subscriber for payment, properly authenticated, on or before Nov 30th.
–Sarah Cooper, excx

Boat lost: stolen, on Sep 13, the brig **Ariel**, lying at anchor off Alexandria, a new small boat, supposed to be taken by the steward of the brig, as the captain's watch with $28 in money is also missing. Suitable reward for the delivery of the boat to the brig at Gtwn or to the subscribers. –F & A H Dodge, Gtwn

Letters remaining in the Post Ofc, Wash City, Sep 15, 1845.

Anderson, Geo A	Brent, Wm L	Brice, Miss Sophia G
Allen, Wm	Barnes, Mrs Maria S	Blood, Caleb H-2
Adams, Miss Eliza	Brown, Mrs Rebecca	Barnes, Sally
Abrengelh, Adolp's	Bush, John	Black, Patrick
Ashley, Jas	Broome, Jas	Bell, Miss Martha A

Branch, John
Bibb, T P Atticus-4
Bibbs, Anthony-3
Brown, L S
Brown, Maria
Brown, J P
Brown, Benj
Brown, Miss M
Brown, John
Beard, jr, Maj j-2
Bowen, Miss C J
Barclay, Jas
Boutcher, Mrs
Bohrer, J S U S N
Bishop, David J
Boarman, Mrs M L
Breasarer, W J
Bingham, Capt D H
Bradley, Newton
Burgess, C H
Brannan, R
Bowman, R J
Barry, Robt G
Bogardus, C S-2
Brady, Mrs Alice
Babbitt, Sam F
Baker, Wm B
Bansketi, Thos
Bradfield, Sarah J
Bettas, Sylvester-2
Barrette, Mrs Ann
Barras, F
Bauskett, Col John
Bogert, Jacob
Broadrup, Geo-2
Barry, David
Berry, Wm
Blackford, John A
Burgess, Miss H
Besancon, Gen-2
Brayton, Tho R-6
Brayton, Rufus
Butterworth, S F-1

Cooke, Capt H H-3
Combs, John C
Coumbe, John T
Clarke, Miss L
Cyssell, H Alfred
Cavanaugh, Mr
Clement, John
Cherry, Dr G W
Claiborne, L A-2
Carroll, Miss B
Collier, Jos
Coakley, Geo W
Caulfield, B G
Cooper, Saml
Cartwright, Jos
Carew, Col John E
Campbell, D R
Cushman, Chas C
Cushing, Caleb
Clifford, Nathan-2
Curtis, Thos J
Chilton, Lt R H
Diehl, Henry
Dix, J A
Dent, G W
Dick, John
Dougalss, Henry
Duvall, Miss P W
Daley, Jas
Dickson, Angus-2
Dana, G W
Davis, Saml
Dickson, Town'd-9
Donelson, A J-2
Emmons, Wm-5
Evans, J H
Eaton, E D
Evans, Chester B-2
Elliott, Lynd
Edmonds, Mrs M
Forbes, Saml C
Fowler, Robt B
Ferraile, Peter

Ferrye, Susan
Fullerton, P H
Ferguson, Saml
Foster, Fred'k
Follett, F-2
Guy, Wm B
Geer, Calvin
Green, Geo
Gee, Nicholas
Gray, Rev Sam-4
Gordon, E
Gaston, Miss
Graily, David
Graminger, John
Griffith, Philomon
Garner, Mrs Caro
Guffan, Pedre
Guadagul, Mrs E-2
Geier, Philip
Geringer, John
Gansevoort, Lt G
Hunt, Dr R F [found]
Hall, Maj Wm M
Hicks, Mrs E E
Hill, Mrs Ann
Horst, Chas
Hall, Mrs Silva
Hall, F X
Hall, Mrs Cath
Hall, Edw-3
Hallowell, Prof B
Hooper, Geo K-2
Harris, J G, U S N-2
Humphreys, Mrs S D
Hardern, Enoch
Hogarth, Mrs F L
Hardison, John
Herlet, Wm
Holland, Mrs E
Hooper, Chas-3
Hodson, Thos J
Holkins, Chas
Heitmuller, Anton

Hardy, J Le Chev'r
Hammond, J R
Hewitt, Danl
Hucking, Mrs Ame
Harman, Saml C
Hebard, John
Hoffman, D
Hamilton, Alex M
Harris, Groyner
Haley, Mrs Eliz
Hitchcock, Josiah
Hopkins, Colum-2
Hanna, Francis
Hannegan, Ed A-4
Ireland, Mrs E A
Jones, Miss R M
Jone, Eliza
Joice, Polly [col'd]
Jones, Thos H
Johnson, Mrs C
Jaquer, John J
Jacobs, Loring
Johnson, Wm
Johnson, Geo W
Johnston, Capt E J
Jackson, Miss Char'e
Jimeson, Miss Jo'e
King, Benj F
Klunk, Chas
Keith, Mrs Eliza M
Kaufmann, Hern
Klimkiewiez, Mrs A
Kennison, Nch'h-3
Love, Miss P A
Lee, Henry
Long, Col G
Little, Jos
Lindner, Ludwig
Lancaster, Ignatius
Lewis, C
Lassiter, Miss E S
Lucker, Miss Ann
Leonard, Michl

Lewis, Henry H
Lanergan, Ken-2
Mill, John
Mills, Thos J
Mead, Edmund
Mattinger, Wm
Muller, Danl
Manford, Stan'e R
Marshall, J
Myer, Franklin S
Massolette, J R
Moulton, Mrs R
Murdock, Miss R
Mershan, Wm
Myers, Mrs Ann S
Masterson, Mrs C
Mitchell, John H
Morgan, Rudolph S
Myer, Geo W
Marshall, Geo C
Martin, Miss Maria
Macy, J B
Mereer, J [col'd]-2
Murfey, John
Montgomery, Jas -2
Mason, Mrs John-2
Martin, John-2
Martin, Jos
Mason, jr, John
Mercer, Chas F-3
Murdoch, Jas H-3
Morrison, Alex
McKeon, John-3
McGinnis, Mrs Ro
McNamara, John
McIntosh, Jas T
McGilton, Cath
McHenry, H
Norment, Saml T
Navy Yard, U S
Norman, J A-2
Norris, Mrs Cath
Orme, Wm C

Owens, Miss M W
O'Rourke, Jas
O'Reily, Henry
Ogden, Mordecai-7
Pearce, Lt
Page, Wm
Payne, Lt Col M M
Payne, W W-2
Pearce, John A
Pearce, Dutee J
Perkins, Miss Caro
Palmer, Miss Cath
Patison, Henry
Perry, Wm
Perry, Robt
Posey, Miss Mar A
Peterson, Mrs Bar'
Pawling, Jos H
Pettrick, Mr
Procilton, Geo
Poland, L P
Philips, Mrs Eliz
Perkins, J of Lou-2
Pleasants, Henry-2
Pleasants, Jos B
Parrott, Lt E G-2
Phoenix, Thos
Quantrill, A R
Quantrill, Mr
Rupp, Solomon
Read, John
Rich, David
Rich, Lt J C
Root, Henry
Ricks, Jas Thos
Reed, Miss Mary A
Rose, Francis A
Roche, Robt J
Reeder, Miss Sarah
Randolph, Lt J B-2
Robinson, Wm
Russell, Mrs Jane
Reinhard, Michl

Redman, Jos	Stewart, Wm A	Wise, M M
Ranson, Joel L	Sullivan, Mrs Har't	Wood, John
Rutledge, Fred'k	Spaulding, Joshua	Wise, Henry A, U S N
Robertson, Miss J E	Spradley, Mary	Whitlock, Wm D
Rowen, Mrs Anne	Saltmarsh, Orlandso	Warren, Horace-2
Smith, John S	Schuyler, G L	Walker, Wm S
Smith, Goe Clinton	Siebel, Geo C	Wallington, Miss A F
Smith, Thos of Ohio	Sewall, Miss Caro	Winchell, Hiram
Scott, Sam T	Stuteley, Matilda	Watson, Miss Mary
Simms, Miss J –2	Spencer, Mr	Williamson, Henry
Sloan, Jas	Steward, Miss Sarah	Williams, Marion S
Sheels, Wm & Co	Sanford, Jas	Williams, Jas
Smoot, Mrs Eliz	Smallwood, Dennis	Williams, Wm S
Steele, Augustus	True, Loring B	Walker, Henry N
Smith, John	Todd, W H	Wiley, B
Swartze, Dr	Torre, P Della	Woodcock, Bancroft
Smith, C D	Thriff, Jas W	Willoughby, Jas D
Smith, Wm B	Thomas, Capt J R, USN	Wilford, J C
Smith, Mrs Mary	Truscott, John	Williamson, John-2
Smith, Mrs Sarah J	Turner, Henry	Wilson, Mrs Betsy
Smith, Wm	Trouman, Miss Julia	Walker, S P-3
Smith, John Ch'r-2	Tippett, Edw D	Wharton, Robt S
Smith, Mary Ann E	Tumbler, Mrs E	Williams, W
Smith, Robt	Travers, John	Warrington, Widow
Stinson, John C	Thomas, John D	Weasner, Jas
Sherman, S G	Turner, Jas P	Young, Notley
Sewall, Dr Thos	Van Dewater, H-2	Young, jr, Ezekiel
Seymour, Thos H	Wight, O C	Young, sen, Benj
Swearer, Miss Cath	Wells, Chas W	Young, A
Simmons, Mrs Eliz	Wood, Miss Mary	-C K Gardner, P M
Sinclair, John-2	Wiel, W	

Mrd: on Aug 19, in St Mary's Church, Newton Lower Falls, Mass, by Rev Mr Baury, Mr Alex H Rice to Miss Augusta E, d/o Mr John McKim, of Wash.

Mrd: on Aug 28, in Schenectady, N Y, by Rev John Williams, Mr D B Hagar, Principal of Canajoharie Academy, to Miss Mary B, d/o Mr John McKim, of Wash.

Died: on Sun last, after a protracted illness, Mr Griffith Coombe, in his 78th year. He was a native of Delaware, but was one of the first & most active & enterprising founders of this city. He was long a member of the Church of Christ on earth, & died in the hope of a blessed immortality. His funeral will be from his late residence, near the Eastern Branch, at 10 o'clock this morning. [A paper in Smyrna, Delaware, will please notice the above.]

Died: on Sep 9, suddenly, Henry Baldwin Bomford, y/s/o Col Geo Bomford, U S Ordnance.

Agency for Pensions & Other Claims: Wm S Allison: ofc Callan's bldgs. Also, for sale or rent: desirable dwlg in Gtwn. Also, for sale, a farm of about 175 acs, near the Gtwn & Rockville Turnpike Road.

WED SEP 17, 1845
For rent, an excellent basement room, calculated for an ofc, on F st, adjoining the store of the subscriber. Inquire of A Carothers, F & 11th sts.

Household & kitchen furniture at auction: on Sep 24, at the residence of John K Townsend, on N Y ave, near 9th st. –A Green, auctioneer

The brig **Albert**, of Boston, arrived at Phil on Sun from Bahia, in charge of an ofcr of the U S brig **Bainbridge**. The **Albert** has been sent home at the instance of Alex'r H Tyler, U S Consul at Bahia, on the charge of being engaged in the slave trade, between the Coast of Africa & Brazil, in conjunction with brig **Washington**'s barge, late of Phil. The first ofcrs & crew of the **Washington**, barge have been brought home prisoners in the **Albert**. Capt Woodbury, late master of the **Albert**, effected his escape prior to her sailing.

The brig **Canton**, of Brunswick, Maine, from Havre de Grace, bound to Boston, collided with the steamer **Georgia** on Tue last. She was off Poplar Island: 3 men drowned-Elijah Jordan, foreigner, Wm Woods, of Md, aged about 17 or 18 years, & Nathl Lunt, of Maine. The captain's name is Given. –Balt Sun

On Fri E C Davidson, of Marion, Ohio, was robbed at Balt, while at the Theatre, of a pocket-book containing $7,000. He was returning home from Pa, where he had disposed of a drove of cattle. No clue as to the perpetrator of the act.

The connexion in the Livery Stable Business heretofore subsisting between the undersigned has been this day dissolved by mutual consent. B O Shekell & Jas P Gannon are alone authorized to receive debts due the undersigned on account of said business. –B O Shekell, Jas P Gannon, Wm Smithea

Wash Corp: 1-Cmte on Improvements: referred the ptn of Peter Gorman, in relation to Pa ave: laid on the table. 2-Ptn from S S Coleman & others in relation to the law regulating taverns: referred. 3-Ptn of Andrew Noerr & others, for a curbstone in front of square 291: referred to the Cmte on Improvements. 4-Ptn of Jos Stephenson, praying to be reimbursed certain taxes erroneously paid: referred to the Cmte of Claims.

Medical Society of D C will meet this afternoon at the City Hospital, at 3 o'clock. –Jos Borrows, Rec Sec

Mrd: on Sep 16, by Rev Mr Bean, Ferdinand E Hassler, of Cape Vincent, N Y, to Betty B, eldest d/o Saml Hanson, of Wash City.

Died: yesterday, suddenly, in Wash City, Mrs Helen Nicholson, consort of Maj Aug A Nicholson, of the Marine Corps. Intelligence of this event cannot but be most painful to her friends who hear of it.

Died: yesterday, at his residence, in Wash City, after a long & painful illness, Dr Geo Washington May, in his 58th year. He was a native of the city of Boston, & a graduate of Harvard, but the prime & manhood of his life had been spent in Wash City, where he practiced medicine with high reputation. His funeral is this evening, at 4 o'clock, from his late residence.

Died: on Sep 5, at his residence in Tuckerton, N J, after a short illness, the Hon Ebenezer Tucker, in his 88th year. He has an extensive acquaintance & a numerous circle of friends & relatives who will cherish a remembrance of his virtues. He served in the war of the Revolution under Genr'l Washington, & shared in the battle of Long Island. He held several appointments of honorable trust during the Revolution, & was appointed the first collector of the revenue for the port of Tuckerton, N J, which situation he held for many years. He received from Gen Washington the appointment of postmaster for the same place, & continued to hold the ofc under every succeeding President with the exception of John Quincy Adams, during whose term Judge Tucker was called by the people of his district to represent them in the Congress of the nation.

Orphans Court of Wash Co, D C. In the case of Jacob Bigelow, adm of Francis Cazeau, dec'd: settlement of said estate on Sep 23. –Ed N Roach, reg/o wills

Female wanted to attend a lady. A woman who is strong enough to lift a lady affected with paralysis, & who is handy with her needle, may find a place by applying at the residence of Dr T P Jones, F st, near the Patent Ofc. No one need apply who cannot bring a very satisfactory character for sobriety & quietness.

THU SEP 18, 1845
$100 reward for runaway negro boy Willis Carroll, about 18 years old. He was raised by Mr Jas Mallikin, about 5 miles east of me, where he has relations. –Jos K Roberts, *Rose Mount*, living near Bladensburg.

Houses to rent: 3 story brick house on Capitol Hill. Apply to Mr Hill, near the premises. Good 2 story brick on B st. Apply to Mr Brashear, grocer, on Pa ave, adjoining the railroad ofc. A first rate 2 story brick, corner of G & 12th sts. –Saml Burche

Horse & Carriage for sale: any person wishing to purchase a one-horse carriage, nearly new, & an excellent family horse, with harness complete & in perfect order, may examine the same at the stable of Mrs Dixon, on F st, between 11th & 12th sts, where terms of sale will be made known by the owner.

Household & kitchen furniture at auction: on Sep 22, at the late residence of the late Hon B Thruston, on 3rd st, between Pa ave & C st. –A Green, auctioneer

Ex-Pres Van Buren, accompanied by his youngest son, & Mr Paulding, late Sec of the Navy, arrived at Charlestown on Mon week, on a visit to Com Nicholson.

Mr J C de Figaniere E Moras, the Minister resident of Portugal here, has been created by her Majesty the Queen of Portugal, the Commandeur de Figaniere e Moras, Knight Comder of the Order of Conception. -Union

Mr Taylor & Mr Harrison, brothers-in-law, of Harrodsburg, Ky, fought a duel a few days since at 10 paces distant. Harrison at the first fire was shot through the body & was mortally wounded, although alive at the last dates.

A young man, Chas E Goodwin, of Balt Co, after some difficulty with Mr Thos D Cockey, near Cockeysville, went to Cockey's house last night & deliberately shot him, causing a dangerous if not fatal wound. Prof N R Smith, of this city, was sent for, who dressed the wounds. A reward of $200 for the arrest of Goodwin. –Balt Patriot

New Orleans, Sep 9. Arrival of U S troops from Detroit, via the river, on their way to Texas. List of Ofcrs of the respective companies: Capt E R Smith, commanding Company H, 5th Regt; Capt L Lynde, of Company F; Capt J L Thompson, of Company D; Capt C C Sibley, of Company E; Surgeon R C Wood; 1st Lt R B Marcy, A C S & A A Q M; 2nd Lt G Deas, Adj; 1st Lt H J Whipple, of Company G; 1st Lt N B Russell, of Company H; 2nd Lt S H Fowler, of Company F; 2nd Lt P Lugenbeel, of Company D; 2nd Lt M Rosencrantz, of Company E; Brevet 2nd Lt T J Wood, Topographical Engineer.

Washington [N C] Whig announces the death of Mr Jeremiah Cherry, aged 79. On hearing of his death, his neighbor, Mr N Brown, an aged & feeble old gentleman, went to take a last look at the corpse of Mr Cherry, & while doing so, fell dead by its side.

Hunter Hill, a tailor by trade, assassinated Maj Robt R Smith, of this county, last night. He was stabbed a short distance from the Washington Hotel. Maj Smith died this morning. The relatives of the dec'd offer a reward of $500 for the arrest of Hill. Major Smith has left a wife & 2 interesting children, & a large circle of friends to lament his untimely end. –Suffolk, Nansemond Co, Va, Sep 14, 1845 [Oct 25th newspaper: Hunter Hill, who killed Maj Smith, at Suffolk, Va, has been sentenced to be hung on Jan 2 next.]

Mrd: on Sep 16, by Rev John P Donelan, Mr Wm P Drury to Miss Mary Eliz Lenman, all of Wash City.

Mrd: on Sep 17, by Rev S A Roszel, Henry Carter, of Wash City, to Miss Susan Fentz, of Balt.

Mrd: on Sep 4, by Rev Edw D Bryan, of Rye, N Y, Wm Bryan, of Peoria, Ill, to Jane G, d/o the late Robt Evans, of Lancaster, Pa.

Mrd: on Sep 10, at Mount Holly, N J, by Rev Geo Y Morehouse, Hon Alex Ramsey, of Dauphin Co, Pa, to Anne Earl, d/o Hon Michl H Jones, of Newtown, Bucks Co.

Died: on Sep 15, Rev Peter S Schreiber, Pastor of St Vincent de Paul's Church, Balt, in his 43rd year, after an illness of 10 days.

Died: on Sep 12, in Cumberland, Md, Fred'k Deems, in his 72nd year. He was one of the original settlers of Cumberland, & supported throughout his life a character without spot or blemish. He is a brother to Col J Deems, of Balt, & was in the Md line during the late war. He has been a teacher in Cumberland for upwards of 45 years, & has taught father, son, & grandson. Peace to his ashes.

The friends & acquaintances of the Family are to attend the funeral of the late Mrs Helen Lispenard Nicholson, w/o Maj Nicholson, of the Marine Corps, this Thu, at 12 o'clock, without further notice.

FRI SEP 19, 1845
A French gentleman, named Hardy, was drowned on Mon near the Narrows, below the Telegraph Station, N Y harbor, while bathing. Mrs Hardy ran into the water, but he was beyond reach. The body was recovered a short time later, & efforts made to restore animation, without avail.

Jas Benson, one of the proprietors of the Carlton House, N Y, died on Tue, aged 45 years & 5 months. He formerly commanded the steamboats **Saratoga**, **North America**, & **Erie**, from 1827 to 1839.

$100 reward for runaway negro man Henry Diggs, about 23 years of age. My residence is Pickawaxon, Chas Co, Md. –Peter W Crain

Orphans Court of Wash Co, D C. Letters testamentary on the personal estate of Edw Dyer, late of said county, dec'd. –Henrietts H Dyer, excx

Nashville Whig announces the death of Gen Richd Cheatham, of Springfield, Tenn, who died at White's Creek Springs, on Tue last, after an illness of 11 days. He died with fever; was in his 47th year, & in the midst of his usefulness as a parent, a neighbor, & a citizen.

Gospel Banner: Maj Gen Henry Sewall, a veteran patriot of the Revolution, & a patriarch in the social state, died at his residence in this town, on Thu of last week, aged 93 years. He was in the whole revolutionary struggle, having entered the army in 1775, & continued till the peace of 1783. He was personally acquainted with Washington, to whose staff he was for a time attached. There are letters now in his house written him by Washington in friendly correspondence after the war was over.

A new weekly newspaper has just been established in N Y by Messrs Geo W Wilkes & Enoch E Camp, called "The National Police Gazette." It is intended to furnish a regular police record, embracing notices of thieves & offenders, & a register of all stolen property coming into the possession of the police ofc.

Died: on Sep 14, in her 73rd year, Mrs Mary Travers, a native of Scotland, but for the last 35 years a resident of D C.

Subscriber wishes to engage a lady to teach the thorough branches of an English education, the French language, & piano forte. Address the undersigned, Pomonkey, Chas Co, Md. –Robt Brawner

Valuable real estate on C st for sale: the residence of Robt N Johnson. –Jos H Bradley

The Globe, published by Casper C Childs & edited by Levi D Slamm, made its first appearance this morning.

On Wed Mr Jas H Shreve, on 7th st, was offered for sale a small horse, by a young lad, about 16. Suspecting the horse was stolen, Mr Shreve detained the horse, but was unable to detain the lad.

John J Joyce has removed to G & 13th sts, & is ready to serve the public with Groceries.

Vicksburg, Miss, Sep 1. John F Buckhardt, a young music teacher, recently arrived from Germany, was on Fri walking home with a lady to whom he was giving music lessons on the organ at the Episcopal Church. They were met by the husband of the lady, H C Coons, who for many years had been resisting a suit for a divorce which his wife has commenced against him in La. An altercation occurred & Burkhardt stabbed Coons 4 times, but it is thought he should recover.

SAT SEP 20, 1845
Mr Henry Lee descended the well of Mr Slifer, near Charlestown, Va, on Fri last, to ascertain the cause of the impurity of water, but without using any precautionary measure to test the character of the air. After his descent, he got into the bucket to come up, but before reaching the top he fell to the bottom & was instantly killed.

City property to be sold for taxes on Dec 13 next. –A Rothwell, Collector
Ault, Henry, heirs of: 1842 thru 44: $31.05
Acton, Osborn: 1842 thru 1844: $7.57
Bealle, Beverley W: 1841 thru 1844: $57.14
Baum, Chas: 1840 thru 1844: $102.83
Brent, Geo: 1842 thru 1844: $10.37
Barclay, Jas & J Simpson: 1842 thru 44: $21.54
Bowling, Robt: 1842 thru 44: $60.00
Boulanger, Jos: 1842 thru 44: $138.90
Burke, Mary P & Susan D Anderson: 1842 thru 44: $106.97
Billing, W W, heirs of: 1838 thru 44: $321.98
Bates, Wm: 1842 thru 44:$88.12
Coote, Clement T: 1835 thru 44: $347.00
Carroll, Danl: 1842 thru 44: $450.53
Clarke, Edw W: 1841 thru 44: $24.64
Crawford, David: 1842 thru 44: $9.63
Carson, Geo: 1842 thru 44: $1.20
Cross, Geo: 1842 thru 44: $1.62
Chancey, John S: 1841 thru 44: $25.38
Clements, John: 1842 thru 44: $49.32
Clephane, Louis, heirs: 1841 thru 44: $33.10
Clarke, Ruth Ann: 1842 thru 44: $48.99
Cooper, Wm, jr: 1843 & 44: $11.56
Cross, Eli, heirs of: 1841 thru 44: $50.06
Cammack, Wm: 1842 thru 44: $18.86
Donohoo, Dolly Ann: 1842 thru 44: $23.08
Duedney, John: 1842 thru 44: $11.89
Dashiel, Sarah E: 1841 thru 44: $129.33
Durr, Wm: 1842 thru 44: $31.60
Drummond, Lewis D: 1841 thru 44: $3.91
David, Richd: 1842 thru 44: $3.00
Essex, Josiah: 1842 thru 44: $109.11
Eckloff & Wagler: 1842 thru 44: $62.44
Forrest, Jos: 1841 thru 44: $$276.01
Frederich, Mary: 1842 thru 44: $66.68
Foyles, Thos, heirs of: 1842 thru 44: $6.93
Fletcher, Thos: 1840 thru 44: $48.92

Frazier, Thos: 1842 thru 44: $29.25
Grant, Geo W, heirs of: 1843 & 44: $6.94
Gawronski, U M & F X Hall: 1842 thru 44: $33.96
Glasco, Kno, heirs: 1842 thru 44: $38.83
Gorman, Jno B, heirs: 1840 thru 44: $10.19
Gardiner, Jno, heirs: 1842 thru 44: $34.88
Greenleaf, Jas: 1841 thru 44: $33.29
Garretson, Remsen, & others: 1842 thru 44: $25.22
Golding, Richd R: 1841 thru 44: $123.58
Gratiot, Chas: 1842 thru 44: $226. 40
Harper, Andrew: 1842 thru 44: $19.36
Hatch, Anselm: 1842 thru 44: $4.05
Hibbs, Chas: 1842 thru 44: $65.28
Houck, John: 1842 thru 44: $9.01
Haswell, N B: 1841 thru 44: $6.99
Hindman, Wm: 1842 thru 44: $5.52
Homans, Danl: 1842 thru 44: $28.32
Hubbard, Eleanor: 1842 thru 44: $8.10
Harkness, G W: 1841 thru 44: $55.49
Hoban, Jas & Alex'r Diamond: 1841 thru 44: $17.59
Houston, John H: 1841 thru 44: &
Houston, John H & Moses Young's heirs: 1841 thru 44: total-$27.36
Hammond, M A B: 1842 thru 44: $9.48
Handy, Mary G: 1841 thru 44: $42.29
Hughes, Thos: 1842 thru 44: $33.82
Hogan, Thady, heirs: 1842 thru 44: $49.21
Kedglie, John: 1842 thru 44: $88.10
Kervand, Lazaree: 1842 thru 44: $82.14
King, Henry: 1842 thru 44: $26.76
Lewis, Thos, & Isaac T Elwood: 1843 & 44: $42.48
Lewis, Thos: 1842 thru 44: $47.72
Lindenberger, Anne E: 1842 thru 44: $91.79
Lindsay, Adam: 1840 thru 44: $3.99
Lawrence, John: 1842 thru 44: $5.58
Lawrence, Eliz: 1842 thru 44: $6.32
Lambert, Morris' heirs & Thos Cissel: 1842 thru 44: $43.65
Marshal, John & others: 1842 thru 44: $28.26
Mackall, Leonard: 1842 thru 44: $4.96
Mitchell, Jos: 1842 thru 44: $31.70
Mullikin, John: 1842 thru 44: $16.65
Moore, John, heirs of: 1842 thru 44: $17.01
Murphy, Martin: 1840 thru 44: $214.83
McGlue, Owen, heirs of: 1837 thru 44: $22.20

Morrow, Wm: 1835 thru 44: $168.76
McGill, Wm, heirs of: 1842 thru 44: $20.29
Mantz, Peter: 1841 thru 44: $6.54
Nicholson. Augustus A: 1842 thru 44: $126.75
Nicholson, Peter: 1841 thru 44: $7.15
Niles & Horton: 1842 thru 44: $4.70
Oswald, John H, heirs of: 1842 thru 44: $24.64
Peter, David, heirs of: 1840 thru 44: $12.58
Parrot, Richd, heirs of: 1840 thru 44: $3.12
Poor, Mary S: 1842 thru 44: $35.82
Prentiss, Wm H: 1843 & 44: $39.03
Prout, Wm, heirs of: 1841 thru 44: $36.58
Peter, America P: 1842 thru 44: $3.75
Peter, Ann: 1842 thru 44: $2.77
Peter, Eliz: 1842 thru 44: $7.44
Peake, Dr H: 1842 thru 44: $6.94
Peter, Mary: 1842 thru 44: $1.93
Reynoldson, Catharine E: 1842 thru 44: $13.35
Roberts, John: 1842 thru 44: $14.25
Richey, Jas: 1838 thru 44: $3.45
Ridgley, E M, & Sophia Plater: 1841 thru 44: $1.44
Sands, R C & Z Hazle: 1841 thru 44: $20.71
Sanders, Edw J: 1841 thru 44: $36.30
Scott, Geo: 1841 thru 44: $56.99
Speake, Mary Ann: 1842 thru 44: $27.23
Semmes & Murray: 1842 thru 44: $39.45
Smith, Richd, in trust: 1842 thru 44: $18.90
Smith, Richd: 1842 thru 44: $9.44
Smallwoon, Saml N, heirs: 1836 thru 44: $8.46
Smith, John A: 1840 thru 44: $64.64
Sheriff, Mary C: 1842 thru 44: $116.43
Travis, Levin, & wife: 1840 thru 44: $41.32
Tyler, Chas: 1842 thru 44: $11.64
Tryson, Geo W: 1841 thru 44: $2.24
Tousard Lewis: 1842 thru 44: $2.04
Tucker, Micajah: 1835 thru 44: $2.80
Towles, Jas: 1841 thru 44: $233.80
Waller, A B: 1840 thru 44: $2.53
Walker, Fielder: 1840 thru 44: $11.21
Wright, Jas, heirs: 1840 thru 43: $14.11
Wilson, John A, heirs: 1841 thru 44: $138.59
Walter, Jas D: 1842 thru 44: $59.06
Wormly, Mary: 1842 thru 44: $3.34

Walker, Wm B: 1842 thru 44: $15.63
Woodward, Wm: 1842 thru 44: $20.52
Wilson, Jas & Thos: 1842 thru 44: $5.95
Withers, John & Geo Johnson: 1842 thru 44: $113.54
Young, Benj: 1841 thru 44: $210.57

Appointments by the Pres:
A D Mann, of Ohio, Consul of the U S for the port of Trieste, in place of Geo Moon, recalled.
Jas McDowell, of Botetourt Co, Va, Consul for the port of Londonderry, in Ireland, in place of Jas McHenry, dec'd.
Dillon Jordan, Collector of the Custome at Pensacola, Florida, vice Robt Mitchell, removed.
Edw C Doran, of Vincennes, Indiana, to be a purser in the navy, in place of Philo White, resigned.

The Hon R E B Baylor, writing from Austin, Jul 30th, to a gentleman in Alabama, mentions his brother's death. His brother, Walker B Baylor died suddenly & unexpectedly. Mr Rivers, late of Tennessee, having a revolving pistol in his hand, the hammer slipped through his fingers, causing the pistol to fire, & shooting my brother through the heart. A nephew standing by exclaimed, 'You have killed my uncle!" Mr Rivers suffered greatly from agony of mind, on account of this occurrence.

A man named Huffnar drowned himself in the Ohio Canal on Aug 7, in consequence of his wife's tongue giving him no peace at home.

A gentleman, who was among the passengers by the Pilot Line, from N Y to Phil, on Tue, accidentally fell overboard while landing from the steamboat **New Philadelphia**. The only clue to his name is that on his baggage, which is Capt R de Luteen, N Y. This gentleman is known as being the author of a series of letters upon the subject of fortifications, published in the Home Journal some time since.

Fall Fashions: Josiah Dixon, Merchant Tailor, Coleman's Nat'l Hotel, 6th & Pa ave. [Ad]

Public sale on Sep 30, on the premises, the farm now occupied by Mr Geo Semmes, nearly opposite the Navy Yard, the stock, farming utensils, & the crop, together with the principal part of the household furniture. The creditors of Geo Semmes are requested to present to me their claims. [No name given.]

$150 reward for runaway negro Edmund. He left with a negro man of John S Payne's, who lives adjoining me, & calls him Andrew Jackson: both about 26 years old.
–Arthur M Payne, Warrenton, Fauquier Co, Va

P W Browning, Merchant Tailor: under the U S Hotel, Wash City. [Ad]

MON SEP 22, 1845
A Duel Stopped. New Orleans Picayune: Miss Mary Ann Golden was yesterday arrested on the affidavit of Miss Mary Rodgers, charged with sending the latter a challenge.

Naval Intelligence: The U S brig **Perry**, Cmder John S Paine, arrived at Norfolk on Thu in 39 days from Rio Janeiro. Her ofcrs are:
John S Paine, Cmder   Lt, Horace N Harrison
Acting Lts-2: Thos M Crossan & John C Howell
Acting Master, H McLaughlin   Acting Purser, Jas Tilton
Acting Surgeon, J D Miller
Midshipmen-3: Walter W Queen, E E Stone, C M Mitchell;
Capt's Clerk, H R Weightman   Acting Carpenter, Jas C Ferguson
Acting Boatswain, Wm Bergen   Acting Master's Mate, Jas Lown
Acting Gunner, Wm Collins

Ofcrs of the U S frig **Brandywine** at Norfolk from Rio de Janeiro:
Cmdor Foxall A Parker
Lts-7:
Timothy A Hunt   R B Pegram
J B Marshand   Catesby Ap R
Wm T Muse   Jones
A Ludlow Case   Wm E Boudinot
Acting Master: Augustus McLaughlin   Purser: D McF Thornton
Lt Marines: Archibald H Gillespie   Chaplain: Geo Jones
Fleet Surgeon, Geo Blacknall   Sec: A R Bogardus
Assistant Surgeons-2: A F Lawyer & R W Jeffery
Cmdor's Clerk: R Leroy Parker   Purser's Clerk: Pollard Webb
Midshipmen-11:
Jas H   John P Jones   Wm H   Stephen D
Somerville   Allan McLane   Murdaugh   Spence
Wm L Powell   Thos Young   John Laurens
Wm H Wever   Wm DeCoven   E D Denny
The frig **Brandywine** has been absent from the U S 28 months, during which time she lost 18 men by sickness & 2 by casualities.

Appointment by the Pres: Russell G Hopkinson, collector of the customs for the district of Vt, to take effect on Oct 1, 1845, vice Archibald W Hyde, resigned.

House to let: 3 story brick house at the corner of 3rd & Missouri ave. Apply to Mrs M Coyle 2nd house east of 3rd st on Pa ave.

Newark Advertiser: Lt Stephen Don, of the U S Navy, died suddenly at Newark on Fri. He left his lodgings at the Park House in ordinary health on Thu, for a visit to the township of Livingston, & died in his bed at the house of Mr John Squier, the next morning. He returned a few months since from a 3 years' cruise in the Mediterranean; & has been many years an able, honored, & efficient ofcr.

Trustee's sale of valuable lots: by deed of trust dated Jul 15, 1844 & recorded in Liber W B 108, folios 510 thru 513, in the land records of Wash Co, D C: part of lot 3 in square 343; also, lot 4 in subdivision of lot 5 in square 518. –John Pickrell, Trustee –R W Dyer & Co, aucts

Household, kitchen furniture, leather, & shoe finding, at auction: on Sep 23, at the residence & store of Mr Pilling, south side of Pa ave, between 9th & 10th st: an excellent lot of furniture. –A Green, auctioneer

$20 reward for runaway negro woman Kitty Francis, about 25 years of age. Apply to Jas Shaw, agent for Mrs Pearson, Brentwood, near Washington.

Died: on Sep 19, at Alexandria, D C, of typhus fever, Eliz, eldest d/o John M Johnson, Postmaster of the House of Reps of the U S, in her 14th year.

Died: at her residence at **High Point**, D C, in her 57th year, Mrs Mary H Semmes. The life of this excellent lady was most exemplary. For her servants she manifested a deep interest, ever mindful of their temporal comfort. She died in the communion of the Episcopal Church. [No death date given-recent.]

Died: on Sep 16, at the residence of Saml Fitzhugh, Miss Mary Hodnett, aged 63 years. The dec'd was a native of Ireland, but resided in Wash City with her borther, Mr Jas Hodnett, [formerly a clerk in one of the public Depts,] for more than 30 years. For the last 30 years she has been a member of the Episcopal Church under the pastorship of Rev Dr Hawley. Though without a relative in this country to mourn her loss, she was followed to the grave by many sympathizing friends.

TUE SEP 23, 1845
Trustee's sale: deed of trust from Jas W Rowland & Eliza his wife, executed on May 31, 1842, & recorded in Liber J B B #2, folios 328 thru 331, of the land records of PG Co: sale on Sep 25, of a tract or parcel of land called **New Birmingham Manor**, in said county, & is the same land which formerly belonged to the late Richd Snowden, containing 240 acs, more or less. Description of the land is unnecessary. –John M Donn, Trustee, Washington

Journal of Commerce: a few days since, a large tumor was taken from the shoulder of Mrs Dunn, w/o the Princiapl of the Academy at Hempstead, L L, without pain, she having been put in a mesmeric sleep.

Public sale of valuable land near Wash City: by several deeds: sale on Oct 22, of a large tract of land in Wash Co, D C, comprising the whole of a tract called **Bayly's Purchase**, & part of a tract called **Fortune Enlarged**, containing about 1,350 acs. The land has been divided into 20 lots, varying from 24 to 120 acres each. The deeds referred to are the following, viz: Dec 21, 1793, Wm Berry Warman to Jas Greenleaf; recorded among the land records at Wash Co, in Book A, folio 464. Mar 21, 1796, Jas Greenleaf to Geo Simpson, in trust; recorded in Liber C, #3, folios 160. Mar 23, 1797, Geo Simpson to Henry Pratt et al; recorded in Liber C, #3, folio 154. Jun 26, 1797, J Greenleaf et al to H Pratt et al; recorded in Liber C, folio 192. Feb 28, 1798, N Maddox, sheriff, to Wm H Dorsey et al; recorded in Liber D, #4, folio 60. Jul 30, 1803, Wm H Dorsey et al to H Pratt et al; recorded in Liber I, #9, folio 568. Oct 17, 1838, H Pratt, surviving trustee, to B Tilghman, & deed endorsed, dated Oct 18, 1837, B Tilghman to H Pratt, J Dundas & C S Miller, in trust; recorded in Liber W B, #71, folio 111.
–Jas Dundas, Surv'g Trust -A Green, auct

$100 reward for runaway negro man Remus Carter, about 45 years of age. –Wm Z Beall, near Upper Marlborough, PG Co, Md.

Christian & Curad Finsart, a man & his wife, who occupied a small shanty about 8 miles from Buffalo, N Y, were killed last Sat by the falling of a large tree, which was blown across their cabin,

To let: very handsome & commodious front & back parlor sleeping-room, on Pa ave, above 9th st. Inquire at J Visser's Fancy Store, Pa ave, above 9th st.

Our esteemed fellow-citizen, the Hon Danl Jenifer, late Minister to the Court of Vienna, is at present on a visit to the seat of Gov't. We are happy to see him return home from his long absence in excellent health.

On Sat week the remains of Danl Boone & his wife, which had been previously removed from their former resting place in Missouri, were reinterred in the cemetery at Frankfort, Ky, with imposing public solemnities. Mr Senator Crittenden was the orator on the occasion.

House for sale or rent: a 2 story brick house on E st, between 9th & 10th sts, being in the east end of the block known as Green's bldgs, & at present occupied by Mr Thos J Williams. –A Coyle, Agent

The Hon John Hunter, of Hunter's Island, a large proprietor of lands in Delaware Co,

N Y, has ordered a deed to be made out granting 200 acres of land to Mrs Steele, the widow of the Deputy Sheriff who was killed by the Indians in the execution of his duty. [Nov 24 newspaper: Gov Wright, it is said in the N Y Tribune, resolved to commute the sentence of death against Von Steenbergh & O'Conner, the murderers of Sheriff Steele, to one of imprisonment of life.]

Mrd: on Sep 18, in Wash City, by Rev Mr Tarning, Mr Leonidas Bowen to Miss Mary Ann Larcombe, all of Wash.

Died: yesterday, at Balt, Benj I Cohen, after a long illness. He was a native of Va, but for a long time was a prominent citizen of Balt, & well known throughout the country as a member of the former banking-house of J I Cohen, jr, & Brothers. At the time of his death he was Pres of the Board of Stock Brokers.

Died: on Sep 11, at Dover, Ky, Mrs Eliz G Greer, d/o Arthur Fox, & w/o Wm P Greer, formerly of Wash City. She died with Christian resignation & without a struggle, assured of a peace which this world cannot give nor take away.

Reward: my large Sorrel Horse got loose from his fastening, near the lower bridge, Gtwn, & went off with saddle & bridle on. He is well known both in Gtwn & Wash. I will give a suitable reward for his delivery to me at Mr J Libbey's lumber yard. –J Van Reswick

Cmte to make arrangements for the reception of the "Defenders of Balt in 1814:"
Benj B French	Wm Fischer	Geo Cochran
A Woodward	Wm Thompson	Presley Simpson
Jos H Bradley	Wm H Gunnell	Saml S Coleman
Wm Gunton	Wm Easby	A Fuller
J W Maury	John Y Bryant	Marshall Brown
Jos W Beck	John C Rives	Enoch Tucker
Geo Parker	Wm B Magruder	

For rent: 2 stores on Pa ave, near Gadsby's Hotel. –Edw Simms

Instruction in German: Dr Emil Preusser, recently from Germany, & late of Cuba, would devote his leisure to instruction in the German, French, Spanish, & ancient languages. Card left at the National Zeitung, 7th & La ave, will meet with his attention. Reference is made to: Thos W Pairo, near the Treas Dept; Alfred Schucking, Treas Dept; J G Klenck, Editor Nat'l Zeitung.

WED SEP 24, 1845
Paint Store: C st, Todd'd Bldg. –O Whittlesey

Official: Information from C W Dabney, late U S Consul at Fayal, Azores, of the death of Wm Riggs, on Jul 22 last. Mr Riggs had discharged the duties of consular agent at Terceira for 39 years preceding his death. Information from the same source received of the death of Hiram Nelson, of West Vienna, N Y, on Jul 28 last.

Meeting of the Sons of New England: held at Todd's Concert Hall on 20th st, David A Hall, chairman, & Jesse E Dow, sec. Resolution by J Bigelow: cmte appointed: Maj Geo Bender, J Bigelow, R Farnham, Wm Brown, N C Towle. Bender declined to serve, on account of his official duties. Mr Geo J Abbott to fill the vacancy. E L Child added to the cmte.

Wash Corp: 1-Cmte of Claims: asked to be discharged from the futher consideration of the ptn of John Shaw. 2-Ptn from Jas Fitzgerald: referred to the Cmte of Claims. 3-Ptn of Susan Norris: referred to the Cmte of Claims. 4-Ptn from E Brooke & others: referred to the Cmte on Improvements. 5-Ptn of John Ousley & others for improvement of the west front of 13th st: referred to the Cmte on Improvements. 6-Ptn of Abraham Cook & others: setting curbstone, squares 564 & 566: passed.

Races over the National Course will begin on Oct 20, & continue for 3 days. –Wm Holmead, Proprietor

Strayed or stolen from 7th & L sts: a Gray Horse: $10 reward. –John Walker

Lumber. The subscribers have entered into copartnership, under the name of O J Preston & Co: 14th st bridge. –O J Preston, L Stowell

For sale: 130 panels of board fencing: apply to the subscriber, living near the Six Bldgs. –Thos Lundy

THU SEP 25, 1845
Household & kitchen furniture at auction: on Oct 1, at the residence of Dr J G Coombes, on E st, between 11th & 12th sts, near the steamboat wharf; also a cooking stove, nearly new. -R W Dyer & Co, aucts

Great Attraction. Public sale of 3 or 4 finest full-bloodied Durham Calves. They are from the herd of Chas B Calvert, at his splendid farm of Riversdale, near Bladensburg, PG Co, Md. They will be exhibited, with their dams, at the stable of Mr Levi Pumphrey. -R W Dyer & Co, aucts

Mr Benj Mifflin has retired from the Phil Pa, of which he was one of the original proprietors, & his interest has passed to A Boyd Hamilton, who with Mr B Parry, will conduct the paper. The Pennsylvanian is a Locofoco paper, & is one of the ablest of those of that party.

Published on Mon last, for sale in the book-shops of N Y C: "The Lives & Opinions of Benj Franklin Butler, U S Atty for the Southern District of N Y, & Jesse Hoyt, Counsellor at Law, formerly Collector of Customs for the port of N Y, with anecdotes or biographical sketches of Stephen Allen, Geo P Barker, Jacob Barker, Jas Gordon Bennett, Saml R Betts, Isaac W Bishop, F P Blair, Walter Bowne, C C Cambreleng, Moses I Cantine, J I Coddington, W H Crawford, Edwin Croswell, John W Edmonds, Azariah C Flagg, Lorenzo Hoyt, Jeromus Johnson, Isaac Kibbe, Cornelius W Lawrence, Isaac Q Leake, Chas L Livingston, Edw Livingston, Wm L Marcy, Mordecai M Noah, Thaddeus Phelps, Elijah F Purdy, Roger Skinner, Peter W Spicer, Saml Swartwout, Enos T Throop, Henry Ulshoeffer, John Van Buren, Martin Van Buren, Prosper M Wetmore, Campbell P White, Levi Woodbury, Silas Wright, Saml Young, & their friends & political associates: by Wm L Mackenzie."

Mrd: on Sep 18, by Friend's Ceremony, at the residence of Jos H Miller, Alexandria, Gerard H Reese, of Balt, to Sarah Jane Janney, of the former place, d/o the late David Janney.

Mrd: on Sep 22, at Stephen's Church, Balt, by Rev Jno N McJilton, Wm Morgan Shuster to Miss Eliz M Gardiner, both of Wash City.

Died: on Sep 23, after a long & severe illness, Mrs Martha Ann, w/o Francis C Labbe, in her 52nd year. Her funeral is today at 4 o'clock, from the residence of her husband, on Pa ave, between 14th & 15th sts.

Died: on Sat last, at Buffalo Spring, Mecklenberg Co, Va, whither he had gone for the improvement of his health, Mr Robt Tweedy, of Wash City, in his 57th year. His funeral will be from his late residence, corner of 12th & G sts, this morning, at 9 o'clock.

Died: on Sep 23, of typhus fever, Sarah Isabella Fenwick, eldest d/o the late Robt W Fenwick, aged 16 years. Her funeral is this day, at half past 10 o'clock, from the corner of 4½ & I sts.

Died: on Sep 24, Mary Adelaide, d/o Horatio King, aged 4 years & 10 months. Her funeral is today, at 4 o'clock, from the residence of her father, on Capitol Hill.

Died: Sep 19, at his residence in Prince Wm Co, Va, of congestive fever, Col John Hooe, in his 51st year.

Died: on Sep 9, at Woodville, near Milledgeville, Georgia, Mrs Catherine M Grantland, w/o Hon Seaton Grantland, & d/o the late Capt Geo Dabney, of Hanover Co, Va.

Died: on Aug 26, at *Oak Hill*, Fairfax Co, Va, Meade Fitzhugh, in his 52nd year.

Died: on Sep 2, at the residence of his mother, in King George Co, Va, Mr Smith Moxley, aged about 33 years.

Died: on Aug 17, in Nashville, Tenn, Capt Jos B Boyd, late Lt of the 3rd Regt of the U S Artl, after an illness of 3 weeks, in his 26th year-a brave & gallant ofcr, who graduated at West Point in 1839, & served for 3 years with credit & honor in the Florida campaigns. He has left many warm friends, both in & out of the Army, who loved him for his stirling virtues, & deeply regret his loss.

Died: on Aug 5, at the residence of her son, in St Louis, Missouri, Mrs Dorcas Bayliss, of Fauquier Co, Va, in her 70th year. Her illness, though a short duration, was most painful, but she bore her sufferings with that Christian fortitude which had characterized her life, & died in the hope of a blessed immortality.

Died: on Sep 7, at his residence, [*Ardus Cottage*,] Accomack Co, Va, John C Kellam, in his 53rd year, after a protracted illness of 6 weeks, which he bore with Christian fortitude. [Delaware Journal please to copy.]

Death of a venerable Jerseyman. The Sussex Register reports the death of Jos Sharp, on Sep 14, at his residence in Vernon in that county. He was an actor in the stirring scenes of the Revolution; & about 50 years ago was elected a member of the Legislature from Sussex Co, a position he held for 15 years.

For rent: the large 2 story brick dwlg near the corner of I & 7th sts, adjoining the residence of A Rothwell. A good tenant the rent will be at the reduced price of $240 per annum. Possession immediately. Apply to Messrs R W Dyer & Co, aucts, or the subscriber, on 8th st, between E & F sts. –Jane M Dyer

FRI SEP 26, 1845
Maryland Election: candidates for Congress:

Whigs	Locos
John G Chapman	H G S Key
Jacob Snively	Thos Perry
John Wethered	T W Ligon
John P Kennedy	Wm F Giles
Henry E Wright	Albert Constable
Edw Long	Jas L Martin

Sentence on Duelists: at St Louis, Missouri, at the last term of the Criminal Court, on Sep 15. Mr S W Wilson, Mr Barr, & Mr J B Colt, each sentenced to 10 days in the county jail. –St Louis Republican

From New Zealand: Capt Pierce, of the whaling ship **General Pike**, arrived at New Bedford on Sat from the South Pacific Ocean. He brought with him an English family, consisting of John Florance, his wife, & 2 dghts, 20 & 22 years of age, to whom he had afforded a refuge & protection on board of his vessel from the exterminating warfare of the natives of Vangaroa, New Zealand. Mr Florance's property had been wholly destroyed by the natives.

Stoves! Stoves! Stoves! J H Nevett, opposite Fuller's Hotel, Pa ave: just received & for sale.

For sale or rent: 2 houses & lots on 8th st, between L & M sts. –J F Callan, E & 7th sts.

By virture of a deed of trust from Thos Magnier to me, dated Oct 3, 1838, I shall offer for sale, on Oct 1, in front of the premises, the following property in Wash City, D C: lot 6 in the original division of the square #458, known & described in the subdivision of the heirs of Wm Whetcroft, & recorded in a book kept by the Surveyor of Wash City, for that purpose, as lot #4. –Benj Burns, Trustee

Fatal Rencontre: the Platte Argus of Sep 5 says: on Wed last, Mr Notley C Young was killed by Col Jas M Estill, on the farm of Mr R Culver, in Clinton Co, Missouri. They were in one of the fields, when Mr Young was met by Col Estill, who called on him to make sone retraction, which he refused. The Col then discharged the rifle, & almost immediately the shot-gun, the contents of both took effect, & Mr Young fell, spoke a few words, & expired. [Mr Young formerly resided in this neighborhood, where he has left many friends to lament his premature death.]

Rev Alonzo Potter was on Tue last consecrated Bishop of the Episcopal Church of the diocese of Pa. Bishop Chase presided, assisted by Bishops Brownell, Doane, Hopkins, McCoskey, Lee, & Freeman. Bishop Hopkins preached the sermon.

The U S Marshal for this district [Mr Barnes] was in town on Fri, & arrested Wells Southworth & Saml Leonard, of West Springfield, through a warrant charging them with violating the new post ofc law, in running or establishing a private express mail between this town & West Springfield. They gave bail for their appearance at the U S Circuit Court in Boston, on Oct 15.

Groceries: Geo & Thos Parker. Superfine flour just landing from schnr **Dodge**.

Mrd: on Sep 11, by Rev Father Parris, B F Thomas, of the St Louis Bar, to Jane, d/o Chas Chambers, of St Louis Co.

Mrd: on Sep 23, by Rev Philip D Lipscomb, Mr John Pitts White, of Wash City, to Miss Sarah Miranda, eldest d/o Mr Jas Pitcher, of Anne Arundel Co, Md.

Died: yesterday, in Wash City, John Thomas, aged 5 years & 8 months, & Eliz Jane, aged 4 years, children of Jos & Eliz Smith. Their funeral is this afternoon at 3 o'clock, from C st, between 13th & 13½ sts.

Died: at the residence of Maj Dimick, **Fort Constitution**, Portsmouth, N H, Mrs Olive Rindge Waldron, aged 68 years.

$5 reward for a large Buffalo Cow that strayed on Sep 22. –D W Middleton, Pollard's Row, near City Hall

SAT SEP 27, 1845
The Chesapeake & Ohio Canal Company have entered into a contract with Walter Gwynn, Wm Beverhout Thompson, Jas Hunter, & Walter Cunningham for the completion of the Canal to Cumberland within 2 years from this time, & the agents of the State of Md have approved the contract.

Appointments by the Pres:
1-Henry G Hubbard, of N Y, Consul for the port of St John's, in the island of Puerto Rico, in place of O S Morse, recalled. 2-Philo F Barnum, Postmaster at Bridgeport, in Connecticut, in place of Isaac Sherman, removed.

Mormon troubles: war between the Mormons & anti-Mormons of Illinois. The Nauvoo Neighbor states that upwards of 40 houses & out-houses had already been burnt in Green Plains & Lima districts. On Sep 16 an anti-Mormon, Franklin A Worrell, a merchant of Carthage, & a lt of a volunteer company, was shot dead by a party of Mormons.

Wm Gray, British Consul for the State of Va for the last 27 years, has retired from that ofc. He left Norfolk on Fri for Nova Scotia, where he intends to spend the winter. He was an attaché to the British Consulate at Norfolk in 1800.

Late from Corpus Christi, Texas. Explosion of the boilers of steamer **Dayton** on Sep 12, when about half way between Corpus Christi & St Jos' Island: 11 persons were killed, including Lts Berry & Higgins, of the 4th Regt of Infty. Names of the rest are not stated.

The residence of Mrs M B Bratton, of Bath Co, Va, was destroyed by fire last week. It is presumed that mice gnawed on lucifer matches & ignited them.
–Charlestown Republican

Mrd: on Sep 25, by Rev J P Donelan, Mr Abram Cook to Miss Mary Cornelia Ayton, all of Wash City.

Mrd: on Sep 23, at Governor's Island, N Y Harbor, by Rev John McVickar, Chaplain U S Army, Lt S S Anderson, 2nd Regt U S Artl, to Harriet, d/o Mr John Tisdale, of that place.

Decision of the Court Martial at the Naval Asylum, Phil, for the trial of Lt R E Johnson, was approved by the Sec of the Navy. The charges were substantially 3: oppression, disrespect to his superior ofcr, & fraud. They acquit him of every charge which reflected upon his honor as a man or conduct as a gentleman, but convict him of severity & a breach of discipline, for which they sentence him to suspension from duty for a period of 6 months. –Phil Ledger

Family tutor/teacher: desires a situation as teacher in a family in one of the Southern States. Please address A B Weston, jr, Boston, Mass, post paid.

MON SEP 29, 1845
The Newark Advertiser says that a lad of 18, John Shields, who had been paying attentions, which it appears were not acceptable, to a girl [Mary] living in Catharine st, in Newark, shot himself before the door of her father's house on Sat night last. He was a native of Ocmagh, county Tyrone, Ireland, where his father holds a Gov't ofc.

The U S ship **Preble** arrived at N Y on Thu from a cruise of upwards of 12 months on the coast of Africa & adjacent islands, & last from Porto Grande, Island of St Vincent, Cape de Verds. The ofcrs of the **Preble**:

Thos W Freelon, Cmder
Chas W Pickering, Lt
M C Watkins & G V Fox, Acting Lts
Jas H Moore, Acting Master
Midshipmen-5:
Homer C Blake   T H Carter
Robt A Mear   J P Hall
Saml Drew, Boatsman
Benj Benker, Gunner
C C P Parker, Capt's Clerk

Andrew D Crosby, Purser
S Wilson Kellogg, Passed Assist Surgeon
Jas Hamilton, Assist Surgeon

C C Hunter

T D Burham, Purser's Clerk
J Moore, Acting Master's Mate

List of invalid & other ofcrs who have returned home in the **Preble** as passengers:
Lts: V Harvey   J Hartstene   J A Doyle   M C Marine
J S Neville, Passed Midshipman   A S Byrens, Midshipman
E D Chenowith, Midshipman
Mr W H Blow, late Naval Storekeeper's Clerk at Porto Praya
Mr J B Peach, late Capt's Clerk of the U S ship **Jamestown**

Improvements & extension of the city of Washington are observed by every one who passes through the metropolis. *Washington* will soon be a great city, in size, population, & in wealth. -Alexandria Gaz

Richmond, Ky, Sep 22, 1845. The Hon John White, ex-Speaker, is dead. He left his home in ill health about a week since, to attend to his duties as Circuit Judge, & returned home to the bosom of his family. He was sick today, confined to bed, until he terminated his existence by shooting himself through the head. [Oct 3rd newspaper: Pecuniary embarrassment is assigned as the cause. He has left an amiable wife & several interesting children.]

Whig nominations as the candidates for Govn't & Lt Govn'r: Stephen Vickery, of Kalamazoo, & John M Lamb, of Lapeer.

Cecil Whig: Danl Lord, of Phil, has purchased 2 Elk Forges, with 971 acres of land attached, for $18,000. He intends to carry on an extensive cotton factory. Mr Fisher has purchased the *Tyson's Mills*, on Big Elk Creek, & he likewise intends to start a cotton factory.

Ellen Nelson, a married woman, was arrested at N Y on Thu, on a charge of murdering her mother, Margaret Williams, aged 70. They are Irish, & lived at 50 Orange st. During a quarrel on Mon, the dght struck her mother in the head with a broomstick. The next morning her mother was found dead in bed.

Saml Waters, of Chester Co, Pa, was killed on the Columbia railroad on Sat, in attempting to get on a burden car.

N Y-on Sep 22, Ofcrs Leonard & Brown, of N Y C, arrested Hunter Hill on board the schnr **Fair**, at Rawson's wharf, Brooklyn, charged with assassinating Maj Robt R Smith, of Suffolk, Nansemond Co, Va, & then fleeing to this city. He is to be delivered over to the authorities of Va for trial. –Courier & Enquirer

Mrd: on Thu last, by Rev J Van Horseigh, Mr Lucien Clavaditcher, from Switzerland, to Mrs Rosalia Bihler, of Wash City.

Aeolian Pianos for sale: Wm Pratt, Prof of Music, King, near Wash st, Alexandria, has received several of Nonns & Clark's superior Pianos; also, one with the Aeolian or Organ attachment, with all the improvements. It combines 2 perfect instruments in one, organ & piano, which can be played together or separately, at the will of the performer, with the organ swell. He will sell them at the price charged at the factory.

Died: on Sat last, after a prolonged illness of some years, Miss Ann Moss, d/o the late Philemon Moss, in her 29th year. Her funeral is this afternoon at 2 o'clock, from the residence of her brother, Mr Philip Moss, on 8th st, near the Navy Yard gate.

For rent: storehouse & cellar now occupied by the subscriber. Apply to Edw S Wright, Bridge st, Gtwn.

Wash City: Union Row: erection of 3 handsome dwlgs at F & 7th sts by Mr Jacob Gideon. Another has been added by Mrs Michl Shanks & another by Mr Geo S Gideon. We understand these houses have been erected by Messrs Jos Bryan & Chas F Wood, carpenters, & Mr Thos Lewis, bricklayer.

TUE SEP 30, 1845
The Curiosities of Heraldry, by Mark Antony Lower, an elegant 8vo volume, published in London during the present year, is a good book full of interesting & useful information. Camden says surnames began to be taken up in France about the year 1000; & in England about the time of the Conquest.

Valuable real estate for sale: by virtue of the last will & testament of the late Walter B C Worthington, the subscriber, as exc, will sell, on Nov 4, the estate formerly owned by Mr Fielder Bowie & Brooke Beall, lying on the Patuxent river, PG Co, Md, containing about 900 acs, it being a part of the real estate of which the said Walter B C Worthington died seised & possessed, being about 3 miles from Nottingham & 7 from Upper Marlborough, & adjoining the lands of Richd D Burroughs, Eleazer Talbert, Col Truman Cross, & John K Pumphrey. Improvements are a commodious Dwlg House, & all necessary out-bldgs, in complete order. Persons can apply to Mr Geo Atcherson, the manager on the estate, or the subscriber. At the same time will be offered another tract of land, 137+ acs, in PG Co, adjoining the lands of Jas E S Hollyday, Edmund Key & Jos N Baden: known as ***Tayman's Land***, on which are 2 tobacco houses. Also, another tract of land, containing 100 acs, being part of Mattaponi, formerly owned by Benj Mackall, adjoining the lands of Leonard H Early, the late Benj Skinner, & John L Waring. Also, an unimproved lot in the village of Nottingham, about three-quarters of an acre. Also, the schnr **Saml 1st**. –M B Carroll, exc of W B C Worthington, Nottingham

Orphans Court of PG Co, Md: ordered by the Court that Michl B Carroll, exc of Walter B C Worthington, dec'd, give the notice required by law to the decd's creditors to exhibit their claims. –Jas Harper, Reg o/wills for P G Co, Md. [This is followed by the notice required: W B C Worthington, of PG Co, Md. –Michl B Carroll, exc.]

Latest London & Paris fashions, just received: Christian Eckloff, Merchant Tailor. Call & see, at his stores, opposite Brown's Hotel & between 12th & 13th sts, south side, Pa ave. –C Eckloff

The Texan Expedition against Mier-Journal of Gen Thos J Green, with the subsequent imprisonment of the author, his sufferings, & final escape from the Castle of Perote: 1 volume with many engravings. –F Taylor

The Bordentown [N J] Palladium of Sep 17 states that the sale of Paintings & Statuary, the collection of the late Jos Bonaparte, Count de Survilliers, took place this day at the Mansion, & was well attended; the bidding were spirited, & the paintings may be considered as having sold well. Some of the principal pieces, with the prices obtained:
Toilet of Venus, by Natoire: $325.
A Calm-Morning Scene, by Jos Vernet: $950.
Two Lions & Fawn, by Rubens: $2,300.
Landscape, with Mountain Scenery, Waterfall, & Cattle in foreground, by S Denis: $725.
Landscape, Italian Scenery, Bay of Naples, Cattle at Fountain in foreground, by Denis: $1,000
A Dutch Fair, by Francis Frank: $250.
The Entrance into the Ark, by Bassano: $225.
Herodias receiving the Head of John the Baptist, by Guercino: $400
Scene near Naples, by Vernet: $550.
Hawk among Chickens, by Sneyders: $160.
Magdalen & two Cupids, by Vienne: $200.
The Lion caught in the Net, by Rubens: $1,800.
Visitation of St Anna, by Sebastian del Plombo: $300
Passage of the river Po by the French Army, by Boguet: $125.
Royal Stag Hunt, by Jacques Savery: $100.
Massanissa & Sophonisba, by Philip de Champagne: $200.
Christ breaking bread with his two disciples Emaeus, by Gherardo Delle Notti: $171.
Marble Bust of Pauline, sister of Napoleon, by Canova: $250.
Young Diana & Hound, a fine piece of sculpture, by Bartolme: $380.
Antique bronze casting, Stork & Frog, from the ruins of Pompeii: $130.
Antique bronze Hawk & Animal from the ruins of Pompeii: $130.
Medici Vase of Phorphyre, 3 feet 1 inch high, do, slightly damaged: $200.

$10 reward for a lost $100 note on the Bank of Wash. –John Wagner, Looking Glass & Picture Frame Store, opposite the old National Theatre.

Mr Reuben Rowley, an elderly gentlemen from Wrentham, Mass, left his home on Fri, & took the Stonington cars to the steamer **Massachusetts** for N Y. He had $27,800 in bank bills. During the passage a man who gave his name as Mr Southgate, engaged him in conversation. He offered Rowley a peach, when he accepted & ate. The peach caused Mr Rowley to be seized with violent stomach pains & caused him to fall into a deep sleep. On awakening he found his money had been stolen. Mr Rowley is a wealthy man. He offers a reward of $3,000 for the arrest of the rogue & the recovery of the property.
-Herald

Rocking Chairs: 100 just received: for sale at $3 each. –H J Gould & Co, La ave, between 6th & 7th sts.

To let: store & small dwlg attached, on Pa ave, at present occupied by John Sheahan as a fruit sotre. Also, for sale, in the rear of the above store, on B st, a brick house & lot occupied by B H Shad as a refectory. -Jos Follansbee, Capitol Hill

Mrd: on Sep 16, by Rev J T Wheat, Hon A V Brown, Govn'r elect of the State of Tennessee, to Mrs Cynthia Saunders, of Davidson Co. –Nashville Banner

Died: on Sun, at the residence of Wm Selden, on N Y ave, in Wash City, Mrs Sarah Anne Hunter, in her 74th year. Her numerous friends & heart-stricken relatives should bow with resignation to the heavy stroke. Her funeral will take place this morning, at 11 o'clock, at the house of Mr Selden, where the friends of the family are invited to attend.

Died: on Sep 27, Mr Geo Saml Mulloy, in his 19th year, of 5 days' sickness of brain fever. His funeral is today at 4 P M, at his mother's, C st & Delaware ave, Capitol Hill.

WED OCT 1, 1845
From Oregon: letter from an emigrant published in the Fayette [Mo] Democrat: Dr McLaughlin, who has charge of **Fort Vancouver**, & is Govn'r of the Hudson Bay Co in the west, has treated the 2 last emigrations with a great deal of kindness. He has furnished them with boats to bring their families, good, & wagons, down the Columbia; lent all that wished to borrow seed-wheat, & charges them 6 bushels on the 100 until they can raise crops.

Schuyler Strong, one of the most distinguished members of the Illinois Bar, put a period to his existence at his residence in Springfield a few days since.

John Nelson jumped overboard from the steamer **United States**, on Sep 22, about 15 miles from Cleveland & was drowned. He lived near Sandusky, & went on board at Huron in charge of his wife, who was taking him to his friends in the State of N Y. Capt Whitaker immediately put about & made search for him, but, as quite a sea was running, without success.

Notice: All persons are forewarned from trespassing upon my enclosures, with dog or gun, from & after this date, as the law will be put in force against all such, without respect to persons. –Thos N Wilson, Montgomery Co, Md.

Eliz M Peart, a Minister of the Society of Friends, proposes holding a meeting for public worship this evening, at 7 o'clock, in Friends' Meeting-house on I st.

Trustee's sale of valuable house & lot on 12th st: by deed of trust from Henry D Cooper & wife to me, dated Sep 3, 1844, recorded in Liber W B, #112, folios 62 thru 66, in the land records of Wash Co: sale on Nov 1, for cash, on the premises, all that piece or parcel of ground on 12th st west, known as lot G, in Buist's subdivision of lots 1 thru 9, of Davidson's subdivision of square 318, together with the bldgs & improvements thereon. The house is a new brick house, next to Buist's garden. The title believed to be good. –Chas S Wallach, Trustee -Boteler, Donn & Co, auctioneers

List of letters remaining in the Post Ofc, Wash City, Oct 1, 1845.

Apenwall, Col	Baker, Mrs Eliz	Collins, Mrs Ann
Aers, Miss Anna	Burcher, Miss N E	Carter, Rob M
Abell, Mrs Eliz	Bulfinch, Stephen G	Colston, Mr T
Adams, Geo	Barrett, Jas	Chilton, Lt R H
Bright, Henry	Babcock, Chas W-2	Catlett, Mr
Beard, John-2	Blackson, Miss M	Coston, John
Brooke, Miss Ann E	Besaneon, Gen L A-4	Capers, Maj L G
Beard, Lewis	Blackford, J A	Chapman, R
Bart, R R	Burgess, Henderson	Crozier, John H
Brooks, Miss A E	Boulware, Wm	Cullom, A
Bird, W Smith	Bronough, Robt	Christian, Miss M Muge
Balch, A	Bailey, Jessee	Done, Miss M R
Blair, Miss Rebecca	Baily, Thos H	Dix, John A
Bray, Mrs Eliz	Baillie, Miss Mgt	Day, Passed Mid J S
Black, Jas	Burchett, Mr	Diggs, Miss Louisa
Boyd, Saml	Butler, Jas	Dennison, Edw H
Boyd, Stephen	Benedict, Mr	Downing, Jas
Beale, E F-U S N	Bailey, R S	Dewley, Robt
Brook, Miss Mary A	Bowen, Geo Y	Davis, Richd-2
Bibb, T P A-3	Bowman, Rob J	Douglass, L W
Bibbs, Anthony-2	Barrow, jr, Alex	Devaughn, L
Brown, Miss M E	Bogert, Jacob	Duyley, Wm
Brown, Edw W	Ballade, Clementine	Davidson, Geo W
Brown, Wm Linn-2	Baldwin, Mrs Lydia	Davis, Miss Jouretta
Brown, J N, U S N	Cripps, Wm	Delahay, M H
Brown, Jas P	Chase, Miss Eliz	Dickinson, Towns'd
Brown, Robt-2	Clar, John	Dyer, Kinsey
Brooms, Robt	Clack, Franklin H	Dunawin, Jas E F
Brown, Miss Mary	Cook, John G	Dunsmore, Mr S
Brown, Milton	Crane, Wm R	Dander, E
Bryant, Jas W-2	Cocke, Wm M	Dawson, John B
Bennett, Jas H	Crawford, Rob L	Eld, Lt Henry-2
Bishop, Wm H	Clary, Wm	Edwards, Wm W
Barrett, Mrs Eliz	Carroll, Miss Harriet	Eigler, Jacob-2

Edwards, Capt O E
Eberhart, John
Evans, Mrs Matilda
Evans, Chester B
Edwards, Amory-2
Evans, E B
Estep, Mrs Catherine B
Evans, Miss Lucy M
Fox, Geo
French, Miss Mary G
Free, J D
Forster, Wm
Fouman, Dr
Fagan, Miss Mary A
Fitzgerald, Miss M E
Fitzgerald, Wm D
Fairfax, Chas-2
Foreman, Geo
Fisher, David
Fletcher, Miss Ellen
Fardy, John
Gray, Rev S T
Galt, Capt P H
Gillott, Jos
Gardner, C T
Grodon, F
Goutier, Jos
Gaeno, Saml
Gebower, Christopher
Grindell, Miss H
Gentry, M P
Giddings, Sam S
Gillott, Miss
Holt, H Dr-2
Hill, Geo
Hawl, Miss M
Hart, Dr Moses
Hughes, Mrs Ann
Hatch, Darant
Hill, Chas
Huel, G W V
Hall, Wm
Hall, Miss Caroline

Hall, Edw
Hall, Geo F
Hurlert, Miss V N
Hinton, Mrs C J
Herbert, Miss Ellen
Hagarty, Wm
Henson, Mrs Celia
Howard, J M
Henry, Geo W V
Holbrook, B A
Hopkins, Lt Ed
Hanson, Josiah H
Hazard, Robt R
Hewbert, Miss R
Hansford, Wm
Haislep, Henry
Hutchison, Martha
Hanson, John M
Hoover, David
Hubert, Edw H
Herbert, Geo
Hernandez, Gen J M-6
Haxtion, Wash M-2
Irwin, Wm H
Jones, P
Jones, A D
Jones, Geo W
Johnson, Thos-2
Johnson, Charlotte
Jackson, Miss L
Johnson, Andrew
Keith, Mrs Eliza M
King, Chas
Keobel, Jacob
Klimkiewiez, Mrs A L
Kennedy, S W
Kenny, Henry T
Kelly, Michl
Lay, Lt Geo W-2
Lord, Mary
Love, Miss P A-2
Lunt, Miss Ann
Loveless, Jas A

Lucas, Miss M A
Linwood, Miss A
Lefler, Shep'd
Langley, Geo T
Lewis, Maj M G
Laidlow, Peter
Leonard, M G
Lamkin, John
Lewis, Geo W
Lowrie, Walter
Lewis, Mrs S E
Lockeb, Mrs Polley
Mills, Jas L
Mounts, Geo W
Martin, Miss C
Minor, Richd
Monroe, Mrs A F
Morgan, Rudolh S
Middleton, Theo-2
Milburn, Thos
Matthews, Geo
Mackey, Owen
Mullin, Mrs Naancy
Murray, Miss C
Mussey, Osgood
Milstead, Isaac
Miller, W N
Miller, R E
Marcadel, Petro
Mendez, Francisco
Mason, Miss Emily V
Mason, Miss Laura
Morgan, G W-2
Mershon, Wm-3
Mitchell, Jas
Mitchell, Gen John
Macy, John B-2
Murgotrey, Thos
Martin, Barclay
Magrudger, Lt
McGrath, Miss E J
McLean, A C
Macabee, Eliz

Macrae, Geo W
McFadden, Saml
McLemore, Col J C
McPherson, Mrs E
McFarren, Isaac P-2
McCarty, John
Norn, Edwin J
Nourse, A
Norris, Ralph W-2
Nelson, John
Osburn, Robt
O'Bryon, Miss H
O'Brien, John
Plant, Jas K
Paine, Miss Mary
Page, Wm L
Page, Benj
Payne, W W
Parker, Com F A
Pickering, Chas-2
Petrie, Lemuel W
Parker, Mrs R
Patterson, Mrs M
Pfeifer, John M
Palmer, Richd
Parris, V D-2
Prather, Isaac
Patterson, Thos
Peyton, Jos H
Quantrill, Maj T
Queen, Mid W W
Ricks, Jas S
Rogge, Henry
Rice, Geo W
Runnells, Mrs
Riley, Mrs Eliz
Ratcliffe, Mrs
Robinson, E W
Ratcliffe, Lewis
Ramsay, Miss M A
Robinson, J Welsey
Rainbow, John-2
Reader, Wm A

Reinburg, Lewis
Simms, Miss Jane
Smith, Miss M A
Smith, Wm
Stoub, F
Shanks, Michl
Scott, Mrs Ann
Sheets & Co, Wm
Smith, Wm T
Smith, F O J
Sip, Hezekiah
Smith, Geo Clinton-3
Smith, Miss Sarah S
Smoot, Chas H
Smith, Mrs Martha
Smith, Thos J S
Simmes, Miss F
Shawk, Abel
Shields, Com W F-2
Sanger, Richd
Stetson, Miss S W
Stanford, W H
Stansbury, A J-2
Sansardine, Mous'r
Sanford, C O
Scroggins, Miss M E
Strother, Francis
Sperling, Mrs Mary
Steiner, Miss M J
Stewart, W T
Shryock, Chas W V
Stewart, Com Chas
Southern, Richd
Shoemaker, Miss M J
St Clair, Geo
Stutely, Matilda
Sartoro, Lt L C
Stewart, W A
Stitcher, Miss Ruth
Starkey, Isaac G
Stewart, W–2
Smallwood, Rd-2
Sanford, G A

Sibrey, Wm
Staunton, F P
Tribe, Powhatan Red
Men-10
Tribe, Anacostia R M
Turner, Miss Mary
Tansil, Lt R
Tozer, Mrs Julia A
Tilton, Jas
Thompson, Mrs A
Thomas, Wm
Townley, J D
Thomas, Maj C-2
Thomas, Benj
Tilley, Chas
Taylor, Wm
Thompson, Mrs H P
Thompson, Mrs E
Thompson, Sam B
Talmadge, N P-2
Valentine, Jacob
Walsh, Jas W
Ward, Henry
White, Dr P S
Wolf, Wm
Wright, J T
Wise, John H-3
Wade, John
Wright, Capt J T
Ward, Geo W
Williams, J L-2
Waters, Miss S A
Warren, Henry
Walker, Saml
Walters, Capt Jas
Washington, Mrs M
Webster, Jas
Walker, David
Walker, S G
Warren, John W
Walker, Mrs C
Walker, S P-2
Young, W

Household & kitchen furniture at auction: on Oct 14, near 7th st south, in the house formerly occupied by W A Bradley, his entire stock, which is of the best quality.
–A Green, auctioneer

Wash Corp: 1-Cmte on Improvements: was referred the ptn of Silas H Hill. 2-The Board resumed the consideration of the ptn of Benedict Jost. 3-Ptn from Franklin Little & others: referred to the Cmte on Improvements. 4-Cmte discharged from further consideration of the ptn of S H Smith & others. 5-Ptn of G C Grammer, for his relief: ordered to lie on the table. 6-Bill for the relief of M P Mohun, reconsidered. 7-Ptn from John Peters: referred to the Cmte of Claims. 8-Communication from Peter Gormon, respecting the excavation & removal of gravel from certain streets in the 4th Ward: referred to the Cmte on Police.

Court of Inquiry convened last Wed at the Navy Dept, consisting of the following ofcrs, viz: Cmdor M E Perry & Cmders Ogden & Stribling, with P Barton Key, as Judge Advocate. The investigation involves the truth of cerain charges brought against Lt McLaughlin, of the U S Navy, while in command in the Florida squadron, which charges are contained in a printed letter addressed to the Sec of the Navy by Lt Tunsill, of the U S Marine Corps. Witnesses already examined: A O Dayton, 4th Audiror, Mr Etheridge, Lt John Rodgers, Chas H Winder, & others. We understand that Lt McLaughlin, unaided by counsel, attends the Court of Inquiry from day to day.

Tiber Mill for rent: situated within the limits of Wash City, about a mile north of the Capitol; possession can be had immediately. Apply for information at the residence of Mrs Pearson, near the Mill.

TUE OCT 2, 1845
The Art of Dancing & Waltzing: Mr L Colton teaches all the latest steps: school in the U S Hotel.

Household & kitchen furniture, & shower-bath, at auction: on Oct 4, at the residence of Wm Harper, at the corner of 9th & D sts, opposite the residence of Dr Dawes.
–A Green, auctioneer

Strayed from the residence of B M Berry, on Capitol Hill, a large red Setter Dog: suitable reward.

The undersigned having administered on the estate of John F Thiel, who died Sep, 1842, in Gtwn, D C, would hereby inform the legal heirs of said estate, whose residence is unknown to him, that he has funds in his possession, being the proceeds of said estate, which will be paid to them on their appearing & substantiating their claims.
–Wm Grindage, Adm, Gtwn

Orphans Court of Montgomery Co, in the Commonwealth of Pa. In the matter of the partition or valuation of real estate of Archibald Maguire, late of Whitemarsh township, in said county, dec'd. And now, to wit: Aug 18, 1845, the return of the inquest making partition or valuation of the real estate of said Archibald Maguire, dec'd, was duly confirmed by the Court, nisi eo die. The Court, on motion of D H Mulvany, atty for petitioners, grant a rule upon all the heirs & legal reps of Maguire, dec'd, to appear at an Orphans' Court to be held at Norristown, in Montg Co, on Nov 17, then & there to accept or refuse to take the said real estate at the valuation thereof made, or show cause why the same should not be sold according to law. -Wm Rossiter, Clerk Orphans' Court

Family horse for sale: sound horse for $50 cash, or he will take dry goods, groceries, or wood to that amount for him. Inquire at Wm Green's printing ofc, on 9th st, between D & E sts.

A number of the citizens of Charleston, S C, have presented to Wm Ogilby, late British Consul for N C & S C, a service of plate, in testimony of their appreciation of his services.

Richmond [Va] Times: Mr Jas H Jurey, a merchant of this city, was arrested & committed, on Sat last, relative to alleged fraudulent transactions.

Mrd: on Sep 30, by Rev Wm Pinckney, Dionysius Sheriff, of PG Co, Md, to Margaret M, d/o Marmaduke Dove, of Wash.

Died: on Oct 1, Rev Stephen Chapin, D D, aged 67 years. His funeral is Fri, at 10 a m. at his late residence, near Benning's bridge.

Died: on Sep 24, Rosealbert Deatly, d/o John S & Catherine A James, aged 11 months & 14 days.

To let: one of the houses in the Six Bldgs. Apply to Saml Drury, opposite, or to M Adler, agent.

FRI OCT 3, 1845
Appointments by the Pres:
Wm McNair, Register of the Land Ofc for the district of lands subject to sale at Fayette, Mo, vice John B Clark, resigned-to take effect on Sep 30, 1845.
Alfred W Morrison, Receiver of Public Moneys for the district of lands subject to sale at Fayette, Mo, vice J W S Mitchell, resigned.

Col Thorne, who was for many years resident at Paris, arrived at N Y on Mon, in the packet ship **Zurich**, from Havre. He is accompanied by his family, 16 in number, & does not return to Europe. –True Sun

From Texas: it is ascertained that the following persons have been elected to the 10th Texan Congress: Archibald McNeill, for Montg Co; Dr C McAnelly, for Harris; Gen W S Fisher, for Galveston; J P Hudson, for Fayette; R M Williamson, for Washington; & S W Perkins & W B P Gaines, for Brazoria.

Mr David Taylor, a respectable citizen of La Grange, was killed a few days ago while attempting to break a wild horse, by becoming entangled in the rope attached to the horse's neck. –From Texas

Annual Commencement of the Columbia College was held yesterday. Order of Exercises: Prayer by the Pres. Orations by

R M Barker, Bedford Co, Va
C B Jennett, Halifax, Va
S C Boston, Somerset Co, Md
Alfred J King, Cave Spring, Ga
W L Childs, Wash
J B Pleasants, Richmond, Va
W Cunningham Hunter, Newbern, N C
P H Winston, Fayettsville, N C.

Degree of A B conferred on:
Geo Exoll, of Va
Wm M Pratt, of Ky
Wm H Jones, of Va
Jas M Saunders, of D C
Geo Pearcy, of Va

Honorary Degree of A M conferred on:
S J Wheeler, of N C
Rev Danl Eldrige, of Ohio
Rev Norman W Camp, of Mississippi
Rev Wm Brand, of Indiana
Rev Geo C Chandler, of Indiana
Rev Jos Banvard, of Mass

Honorary Degree of M D conferred on:
R H Worthington, of N C

Degree of A B conferred on the following gratudates of Hamilton Theological & Literary Institution, N Y:

R Jeffrey
E W Pierce
H M Campbell
E N Jenks
J B Tombs
F Ketcham
J B Saxton
J J Stoddard
O G Wheeler
G M Lawton
T Swaine, jr
J N Loomis, jr
A Taylor
& that of A M upon B F Taylor

Railroad Accident: the train on the Camden & Amboy Railroad, from Phil, on Tue, ran over a cow & was thrown off the track. A passenger, John O'Brien, was killed, & several others [all, with him, standing on the platform outside of a car or cars] were severely injured, among whom were Mr Nugent, of Phil, & Mr Talbot, of New Rochelle. The brakeman also had his thigh broken.

Mrd: on Wed last, by Rev Mr Tarring, Benj G Tompkins, of Poplar grove, Mathews Co, Va, to Miss Juliet Latimer, of Wash City.

Died: on Oct 1, Maj Jos Forrest, aged 77 years. This venerable gentleman was descended from one of the most ancient families in Md, & leaves behind him a large circle of friends & relatives. He possessed a mind of uncommon strength & discrimination, stored with a large share of practical information, & with an almost intuitive knowledge of the world in which he had been permitted so long to sojourn. He died at his residence in Wash, in the bosom of his devoted family. His funeral is today, at 3 o'clock.

SAT OCT 4, 1845
A burden train of cars from Harrisburg to Carlisle ran off the track on Tue last, & Mr Souder, of Hagerstown, was instantly killed. He was employed as an agent on the road.

Caution: I forewarn all persons that I will not pay any debts hereafter contracted unless it is by myself in person, or my written order. -T M Milburn

For rent: a large 3 story brick bldg, corner of I & 20th sts, opposite the West Market. –A H Mechlin, 4th Auditor's Ofc

Large Boarding-house for rent: the subscriber offers for rent the dwlg part of his large 3 story brick house, east of Coleman's Nat'l Hotel, on Pa ave. Apply to Mr E Lacy, at his shoe store, on the premises, or to Lewis Johnson, G & 11th sts.

Valuable house & lot in the village of Bladensburg for sale, now occupied by Dr Hanson Penn. Apply to A Green, auctioneer, Concert Hall, Wash.

A R Jenkins infroms that the Bowling Saloon will be closed until further advices. It will be fitted up in Oriental style for the approaching Congressional campaign. He is determined to keep pace with the spirit & taste of the age.

Cmdor Bolton was detached from the command of Port Captain of the Naval Station at Norfolk on Wed, in conformity with the general order of the Dept abolishing the ofc of Port Captain. A salute was given to Com Bolton from the ship **Pennsylvania** on his leaving her.

Mrd: on Thu last, by Rev G W Samson, Thos B Brown, of Cambridge, Mass, to Laura E, eldest d/o Andrew Rothwell.

Mrd: on Oct 2, in Gtwn, D C, by Rev Wm Hamilton, of Balt, Dr Chas H Cragin, of Wash, to Mary, d/o Saml McKenney, of Gtwn.

Died: on Sep 29, at his residence, near Port Tobacco, Chas Co, Md, John Tayloe Key, the oldest s/o H G S Key, a young gentleman beloved & respected.

Died: on Sep 26, at the residence of her father, in Emmittsburg, Md, Miss Ann Frances Motter, in her 19th year. She completed her education at St Joseph's Academy, near Emmittsburg, about 2 years since. She died of congestive fever, after an illness of but a few days.

MON OCT 6, 1845

The Queen of England accepted an invitation from the King of the French to visit him at Chateus d'Eu, & proceeded in the Royal steamer **Victoria & Albert**, to the little harbor of Treport, where she landed. When she approached the French shore, it was found that the small steamer which had formerly carried the Queen from the royal yatch could not now be employed due to the low state of the tide. The only way in which Louis Philippe could get on borad the royal yatch was by getting into a bathing machine, by which he was carried so far as to enable him to get on board his own barge, & thence the royal yatch; & the queen would remain for some hours on board, or take the same rather undignified manner of reaching the shore. The Queen of England thought she might adopt the mode of getting on shore that brought the King of the French on board; & thus it happened that Queen Victoria & King Louis Philippe got on shore together in a bathing machine. The Queen was handed into the barge by the King, & followed by Prince Albert, the Prince of Joinvile, Prince Augustus of Saxe Coburg, & M Guizot.

Encyclopaedia Britannica, 21 vol. 4to Edinburgh copy, new edition, much enlarged & improved beyond all preceeding onces. Lowest price in England 37 pounds 16 shillings sterling, unbound. Can be supplied here in best Russia binding, for $200, which is much lower than it had been offered before in the U S.
-F Taylor, Bookseller, Wash

Appointments by the Pres:
1-Jas Dunlop, of D C, as one of the Assist Judges of the Circuit Court of the U S for said District, in place of Buckner Thruston, dec'd. 2-Wm Patterson, Register of the Land Ofc for the district of lands subject to sale at Clinton, Missouri, vice Abraham B Morton, removed.

Col Edw Milford, formerly of N Y, where he had charge of the American Hotel, & recently proprietor of the hotel at the bay of St Louis, was killed at New Orleans on Sep 23. He fell from the 3rd floor of where he was staying.

Mrd: on Oct 2, in Immanuel Church, Newcastle, Delaware, by Rev Mr Billopp, Henry H Lockwood, Prof U S Navy, to Anna, d/o the Hon Jas Boots, Chief Justice of the State of Delaware.

Mrd: on Oct 5, by Rev Mr Tarring, Mr Saml C Espey to Emily Ann, d/o Fielder Burch, all of Wash City.

Died: yesterday, Geo Scott, after an illness of about 2 weeks. His funeral is today at 10 a m, from the residence of his father on Capitol Hill.

Died: about Sep 10, at his residence, on the Bayou Gross Tete, in the Parish of Herville, La, where his death is universally lamented, Dr John Carroll Brent, aged 48 years, & formerly, for many years, a resident of Wash City.

Died: on Aug 25, at Elverton Hall, PG Co, Md, in her 35th year, Mrs Mary E Young, w/o Notley Young, after a protracted & lingering pulmonary affection, which she yielded to with Christian fortitude & resignation. -B

Sons of Temperance meeting this day at 3 o'clock, at the Hall on C st.
–Z K Offutt, Grand Scribe

TUE OCT 7, 1845
$20 reward: strayed away, & lost or stolen, 3 head of fat Cattle, from my slaughter-house on North Capitol st, on Sep 27. The whole amount will be given for the return of the 3.
–P Crowley

House & lot at auction: on Oct 10: part of lot 5 in square 771, with improvements-2 story frame dwlg, near Mr Mattingly's wharf. –A Green, auctioneer

Jefferson College will commence on the 1st Mon in Nov next, & terminate on the last Thu of Mar ensuing.
Located 7 miles from the National road on one side & 18 from Pittsburg on the other. A line of stages passes daily through the village in each direction. Faculty:

Robt J Breckinridge, D D, Pres
Jas Ramsey, D D, Prof of Hebrew
Wm Smith, A M, Prof of Greek
A B Brown, A M, Prof of Belles Lettres & Latin
Henry Snyder, A M, Prof of Mathematics
S R Williams, A M, Prof of the Physical Sciences
Robt W Orr, A M, prof of Civil Engineering & Natural History
Jas P Sterrett, A B Tutor

-Jas McCullough, Sec of the Board of Trustees

To let: a new 3 story brick house on the corner of 16th & K sts: within 2 squares of the Pres' House & the public Depts. –John Alexander, Pa ave, between 12th & 13th sts.

Mrd: on Thu last, by Rev Chas A Davis, Nathan W Fales to Miss Eliza Shanks, all of Wash City.

Mrd: on Oct 5, by Rev Mr Murray, Mr Hugh F Pritchard to Miss Harriet W Meredith, all of Wash City.

Mrd: on Oct 5, by Rev G W Samson, Mr Wm Starr to Miss Harriet Johnson, both of Wash City.

Mrd: on Oct 6, by Rev Mr Stringfellow, Gilbert Rogers, jr, of Balt, to Miss Delia, d/o Capt F Black, of Wash City.

Mrd: on Oct 1, in Phil, by Rev Mr Suddards, in Grace Church, Greer Brown Duncan, counselor at law, of New Orleans, to Miss Mary Jane Cope, d/o Herman Cope, of Phil.

Died: on Oct 4, in Gtwn, Imogen, infant d/o Imogen & John Taylor, of Windsor, King Geo, Va.

Election of the School Com'rs & Police Magistrates-Washington:
School Com'rs:
G Abbot	Peter Force	Geo Watterston	Ignatius Mudd
Thos Hartley	Thos Donoho	N C Towle	Isaac S Miller
Rob Farnham	John Marron	R M Coombe	Thos Blagden

Police Magistrates:
Saml Drury	W Thompson	Enoch	Jas Crandell
Saml Smoot	B K Morsell	Smallwood	Jas Marshall
John D Clark	R H Clements	Edw Mattingly	
J L Smith		Nathan Brady	

WED OCT 8, 1845
Wm B Kincead appointed State Judge of the 19th district of Ky, in place of the late Judge John White.

Fire broke out in Lowell on Fri in Warren st, in the premises occupied by Deacon W Goding, glue & picker maker. Damage to the amount of $30,000.

Mrd: on Mon, in Wash City, by Rev G W Samson, Mr John W Faulconer to Miss Eliz Waring, both of Essex Co, Va.

Died: on Oct 2, Louis, infant s/o Wm H Nalley, aged 3 months & 26 days.

Wash Corp: 1-Ptn of Jos Stephenson & others, praying for footways on F st: referred to the Cmte on Improvements. 2-Cmte on Improvements: ptn of Thos H Gillis was read twice. 3-Cmte of Claims: bill for the relief of Henry S Wood, reported the same without amendment.

Paris Millinery: will be opened on Oct 10, at Mrs S Parker's, on Pa ave, between 9th & 10th sts.

PG Co, Md: I certify that Saml S Suit, of said county, brought before me a stray bay horse; branded Y on the left shoulder. Given under my hand, Jno T W Dean, Justice of the Peace. To John B Brooke, Clerk of PG Co Court: The owner is to prove property, pay charges, & take him away. –Saml S Suit, living at Bladensburg.

THU OCT 9, 1845
Delhi, Oct 3, 1845. Anti-rent trial: Mr Gordon, counsel for Moses Earll, tendered a plea of guilty of manslaughter in the first degree: he stands indicted for murder. Earll is now an old man, 65 years of age, has no children, his family is his wife, now 80 years of age, & an adopted dght. Danl W Squires, indicted for murder, also interposed the same plea. He is a middle aged man & a deacon in the Baptist Church. Wm Brisbane, indicted for murder, plead guilty of manslaughter in the 2nd degree. He is a Scotchman of little or no education; but having a fluency of language. He will leave behind 8 children, the eldest not yet 12 years of age, when he goes to the State prison.

Appointments by the Pres:
Jas E Saunders, Collector of the Customs at Mobile, Ala, in place of Collier H Minge, removed.
Jas G Lyon, U S Marshal for the southern district of Alabama, in place of Wm Armistead, removed.

Breach of marriage promise just closed in the Wayne County Common Please: suit was brought by Miss Mary Fleming vs Thompson Eckart, & resulted in a verdict of $2,250 for the plntf. –Cleveland Herald

Capt John Nelson, a soldier of the Revolution who lately died at Louisville, Ky, was the capt of the 1st steamboat which ever ascended the Missouri river. He was only 25 years of age-says the St Louis Republican.

Died: on Oct 8, of consumption, after a much protracted illness, Mr Benj Kinsley, aged 57 years, a native of Lincolnshire, England, but for the last 28 years a resident of Wash City. His funeral will take place at his former residence on the Navy Yard, at 2½ p m, on Sun next.

Died: on Oct 3, Mrs Sarah Dade Hunter, w/o Gen John C Hunter, of Fairfax Co, Va, aged 70 years.

For rent: 3 story brick house on Capitol Hill, adjoining the residence of Judge Cranch. Apply to the subscriber, at whose house the key is kept. –Wm Brent

Washington College, Washington, Pa: commencement on Sep 23. Orations by:

Jos White, Wash Co, Pa
A G Fergus, Eliz, Pa
G W Miller, Claysville, Pa
Chas Menager, Gallipolis, Ohio
Alex'r M Jacob, Wheeling, Va
John Y Calhoon, Hookstown, Pa- [Unavoidably absent]

Robt Niccolls, West Newton, Pa
H Byers Kihns, Greensburg, Pa
Andrew Hopkins, Wash, Pa
Lyman W Potter, New Lisbon, Ohio
R N Waterman, Blairsville, Pa

Bachelor of Arts conferred on:

W Mitchell Baird, Wash, Pa
John J Brown, Kingwood, Va
John W Chandler, N Y
Jas Cummins, Wheeling, Va
Wm R Erskine, West Alexandria, Pa
Jas R Hughes, Wellsville, Ohio
Robt Johnston, Wellsville, Ohio
M E Johnston, Wellsville, Ohio
John B Krepps, Brownsville, Pa
J S B Koontz, Wash, Pa
Spencer H Lamb, Memphis, Tenn
Robt C McGinley, Westmoreland Co, Pa

G H Oliver, Wash Co, Pa
W S Patterson, New Lisbon, Ohio
Byron Porter, Bridgewater, Pa
Nicholas N Pumphrey, Wellsburg, Va
Wm Reed, Calcutta, Ohio
J C Robinson, Gallipolis, Ohio
Edwin H Stow, Beaver, Pa
A G Stringer, Parkersburg, Va
Wm H Templeton, Chester Co, Pa
Jack Twyford, Accomac, Va
David S Wilson, Wash, Pa

Master of Arts conferred on: [All graduates of this institution.]

Wm Colmery	Louis C H	Josiah M Pugh
Silas Condit	Pinney	Cyrus Cummins
Jas Dinsmore	W J Wills	John Marple

Honorary degree of Master of Arts conferred on:

Thos Bakewell, of Pittsburg, Pa   R H Koontz, of Wash, Pa
Prof John Neely, vicinity of Wash City

Honorary degree of Dr of Laws was conferred on the Hon Richd Biddle, of Pittsburg.

Boarding: Mrs H T Weightman: her house is on south side of E st, between 9th & 10th sts.

House to let: 3 story brick house on Pa ave, lately occupied by J W Pilling.
–Nicholas Callan, Genr'l Agent

Valuable property at public auction: on Nov 10, part of lot 6 in square 459, with a good 2 story brick house; fronts on 6th st, between C st & La ave. It was sold on Sep 9 last, under a deed of trust from John Emerick & wife to the subscribers, & the purchaser at the sale having failed to comply with the terms, it will now be sold at his risk & expense on the day above mentioned. –Lewis Johnson, Nicholas Callan, jr, Trustees
-R W Dyer & Co, aucts

FRI OCT 10, 1845
Died: on Sun, at New Haven, Conn, Mrs Mary Dwight, at the advanced age of 91, widow of Pres Timothy Dwight. Since his decease, which is now 28 years, she has resided in New Haven, universally respected.

Fall Millinery: Miss Jane E Briscoe, next door to the dry goods store of D Clagett, & over the store of Lewis & Holland, announces that she has just returned from the North with extensive Millinery.

Rocky Mountains, Oregon, & North California: Capt J C Fremont's Narrative of his tour is now in press & will be sale on Oct 13, at Mr C S Fowlers, 7th st; also at the store of Mr W H Winters, Tobacconist, Pa ave.

$300 reward for runaway negro men, Richd-26 & Mick-24; & at the same time Emanuel, who was hired to Mr Greg, in the Quaker Settlement in Loudoun. These 2 are brothers, & Dick of the same family. They have a mother & aunt, mulatto women, who have been liberated, & have resided for some time at the North, one formerly in the service of the Hon C C Cambreleng. –Thos Triplett, Fauquier Co, near Middleburg, Loudoun Co, Va.

<u>Irving Association: gentlemen elected ofcrs of the Association:</u>
John E Norris, Pres   Edw Warner, Sec
T S Donoho, V Pres   J T King, Treas

Jane Brooks, alias Butler, a colored woman, died suddenly yesterday in the hospital of the Wash Almshouse. She died of apoplexy, induced by habitual intemperance.

Asbury Tyler, colored, was committed to jail last Tue charged with stealing 7 silver table spoons & 2 silver spoons, the property of Mr John L Fowler, of Wash City. Prisoner said he sold the spoons, & were only in part paid by the purchaser, Mr Voss, on Pa ave. Mr Voss denied the statement of the prisoners.

Shop tools at auction-Oct 22nd: by 2 deeds of trust from E H Roper to the subscriber: sale at the workshop of E H Roper, on E st, between 12th & 13th sts. –John Ball, Trustee -R W Dyer & Co, aucts

Household & kitchen furniture at auction: on Oct 13, near the Navy Yard gate, the personal effects of the late Christopher O'Neale, dec'd. –Mary A O'Neale, Admx -A Green, auctioneer

SAT OCT 11, 1845
The Bordentown *Bonaparte Estate*: The Prince will reserve for himself the park & house, which cover about 700 acres of land. –N Y Express

Jas T Vermillion, of Fairfax Co, Va, was most inhumanly murdered by a negro man, whom he had apprehended as a runaway, near his residence, Pleasant Valley, Fairfax Co, on Oct 7, while he was in the act of carrying him before a magistrate. Said negro is supposed to be the property of Wm Brawner, of Prince Wm Co, Va.
–H W Thomas, Atty for Commonwealth, Fairfax Co, Va.

Trustee's sale of valuable farm: by deed of trust from Jacob Payne to me, dated Aug 10, 1844, recorded in Liber W B #115, folios 38 thru 41, in land records of Wash Co, D C: sale on the premises, on Oct 21, all that piece or parcel of land in said county, the same being parts of tracts called **White Haven & St Phillip's & Jacob**, containing 57 acres & 35 perches, with a good new dwlg house & necessary out-bldgs: lies 2 miles from Gtwn, on the Tenallytown road. –Jas A Lenman, Trustee -A Green, auctioneer

C S Fowler, Store on 7th st: Importer of China & Queensware. [Ad]

Mrd: on Oct 9, by Rev John P Donelan, Mr John Sommers to Miss Mary Ellen Wood, all of Wash City.

Mrd: on Oct 8, in Phil, by Rev Thos Brainard, John E Kendall, of Wash City, to Miss Ellen Tree, of the former place.

Died: on Oct 10, after a short illness, John Alex'r Brightwell, aged 43 years. His funeral is from his late residence, L & 9th sts, this Sat, at 11 o'clock.

Died: on Oct 9, suddenly, Mrs Eliz Biscoe, w/o the late Bennett Biscoe, in her 65th year. Her funeral is from her late residence, on the Navy Yard, on Sat, at 10 o'clock.

Unitarian Church: The Rev Jos Angier, of Milton, Mass, will preach at this Church tomorrow at 11 o'clock.

By virtue of a writ of fieri facias, issued by Wm Thompson, a J P in Wash Co, D C, at the suit of Wm F Austin, use of Jas Riordan, against the goods & chattels of Chas Kiernam, I have seized & taken one hackney-carriage & a lot of harness, property of said Chas Kiernam: sale on Oct 18, in front of the Centre Market-house, in Wash City.
–H R Maryman, Constable

MON OCT 13, 1845
Mr Howell, an elderly citizen of this county, lost his life on Sat last, in Scarritt's Prairie, when walking near a dry tree to which fire had been set, a large limb fell on him, breaking one of his legs, & he was unable to move. He remained until the fire seized him & brought him to a painful end. His wife reached the fatal spot, but he lived only a few minutes. –Alton [Ill] Telegraph

Mrd: on Oct 7, in N Y, at the Church of the Ascension, by Rev J M Wainwright, D D, the Rev G Thurston Bedell, [Rector of that Church,] to Julia, d/o the late Jas Strong, all of that city.

Died: on Fri, at his residence, in Alexandria, after a protracted illness, Mr Thos Swann, a highly respectable citizen, in his 56th year.

Died: on Oct 11, at the residence of her son-in-law, Richd Patten, Mrs S Hamilton, aged 92 years. Her funeral is this day at 11 o'clock.

Died: on Oct 8, in Alexandria, in his 64th year, Chas I Catlett, of Loudoun Co, Va, & formerly for many years a merchant of Alexandria, distinguished for his activity, enterprise, & strict integrity.

A new church is intended to be erected for the use of the German Catholics of Wash City. Gen Van Ness has offered the bldg cmte a valuable & suitable lot for that purpose near the corner of 5th & H sts.

Pierce's Linnman Hill Nursery located in the suburbs of Washington:
-Mr Joshua Pierce, proprietor

Orphans Court of Wash Co, D C. In the case of Wm N W Noell, adm of Lawson I Noell, late of the State of Alabama, dec'd, the adm & Court appoint Oct 31 for the final settlement of the said estate. -Ed N Roach, reg/o wills

Valuable lots & houses for sale at public auction: by deed of trust executed by the late Jos Forrest, on Feb 2, 1838, & at the request of some members of his family, the subscriber will offer, on Oct 23, on the premises, north part of lot 1, & lot 13 in square 104.
–Rd Smith, Trustee -R W Dyer & Co, aucts

TUE OCT 14, 1845
Thos Trice, editor of the Banner, published at Wmsport, Wash Co, Md, died on Thu week, in his 51st year.

New paper at Nashville: the Orthopolitan, a daily paper edited by Wilkins Tannehill, a veteran writer. -Louisville Journal

Mrd: on Sep 25, at Pittsfield, Mass, by Rev Mr Hague, of Boston, Capt Chas H Bigelow, of the Corps of Engineers, to Harriet C Briggs, d/o the Hon Geo N Briggs, Govn'r of the State of Mass.

Mrd: on Wed last, at Raleigh, N C, by Rev Dr Mason, Duncan K Macrae, U S District Atty, to Miss Virginia Henry, d/o Louis D Henry.

Died: on Oct 11, Jas Rustiage, in his 75th year, a native of this place.

Died: on Aug 26, at his residence, *Yates' Hope*, Chas Co, Md, Edw B W Barber, in his 41st year, after a painful illness of about 3 weeks, with congestive fever. He lived as he died, without a murmur & without reproach. He has left a large circle of relatives & friends to mourn his premature death.

Died: on Oct 2, at the residence of her father, Dr Luke P Barber, sr, St Mary's Co, Md, Rebecca W Barber, after a short illness. She died in the triumph of faith.

Died: in Elizabethtown, Canada, after a residence of 55 years in Canada, Ruth Judson, relict of the late Silas Judson, aged 99 years, 6 months & 9 days. She was the mother of 4 children, grandmother to 37, great grandmother to 125, & 16 of the 5th generation. On the morning of her death she arose from her bed without complaint; about 9 o'clock she complained of pain, & said she would rather die than live, as she was persuaded all would be well with her, & at 2 o'clock she breathed her last.

Beverly Allen, a member of the St Louis bar, died in N Y on his way home from a visit with his family to the south of France & Italy, whither he had been in search of health.

Houses for rent: 2 brick houses on Gay st, in Gtwn: one at Gay & Montgomery sts, lately occupied by Mr Chas G Wilcox; the other now occupied by Mr Jos McCorkle, & 2 doors from Col Saml Humphreys. –W S Nicholls

Lot at auction: deed of trust from Richd McCloskey to the subscriber, dated Sep 7, 1843: sale on the premises, Oct 22: part of lot 3 in square 450, fronting on L st north, between 6th & 7th sts. -R W Dyer, Trustee -R W Dyer & Co, aucts

$10 reward for either strayed or was stolen, from the commons of Wash, a Bull Calf. Information may be left with G C Grammer, Pres of the Patriotic Bank, on 7th st, or to C H Burgess, Sexton, Trinity Church.

WED OCT 15, 1845
Dr A Baker, convicted of the murder of Danl Bates, was executed in Clay Co, Ky, on Fri week.

Cheap Groceries: John J Joyce, corner of 13th & F sts. [Ad]

Reading, Pa, last week: a s/o Mr Wm Yohn, 7 years old, died from a distressing case of hydrophobia.

Wash Corp: 1-Ptn of Richd Cropley: referred to the Cmte of Claims. 2-Ptn of Jas W Watson, praying remission of a fine: referred to the Cmte of Claims. 3-Ptn of Jos Downing & others for a curbstone on L st: referred to the Cmte on Improvements.

Letters remaining in the Post Ofc, Wash, Oct 15, 1845.

Anderson, Mr
Arzevedo, J da costa
Allen, Richd-2
Atkins, Miss Cha'lte
Alexander, Mrs Jane
Addison, Rev W D
Acheson, David-3
Beck, Lemuel J
Birth, Jas
Burch, W T
Brown, Clagett
Barns, Mrs Sarah
Bruce, Mrs Sandy
Brown, Mary Jane
Bangs, Jas C
Baird, Rev Robt
Bell, Mrs Susan
Burt, Edmund
Brown, Mrs Sophia
Bruce, Miss Mary A
Ball, Mrs Ann C
Ball, Miss Sydney
Blood, C H-2
Bievand, Rev A
Bartlett, W H
Bohrer, Mid J S
Boilevin, Auguste
Burgevin, Mrs Julia
Burcher, Miss A E
Bagby, Robt B-2
Berry, W L
Bogily, Francis
Butler, Mrs Charity
Burnside, Jos A
Barbarin, Francis N
Brigham, E T
Butler, Miss Ann M
Butler, M E

Brannan, John
Bartin, Miss Cha'lte
Babcock, Chas W
Broadrup, Geo-2
Braxton, Carter M
Bryan, Joel N-2
Besaneon, Gen L A
Bradfield, Mrs S J
Chase, Miss Eliz
Cook, Trueman-2
Chew, Danl B
Clarke, Oswald B
Craig, Dr John E
Clarke, Miss Mary A
Clarke, John
Chase, Saml H-2
Carpenter, Mrs H A
Clements, John T
Carroll, Miss Bridget
Cantwell, John
Coldwell, John H
Cowan, John F
Chilton, Mrs Robt H
Collins, Mrs N J
Conway, Miss Louisa
Chamberlin, C T
Curtis, Henry B
Clifton, Miss Ad'lde
Campbell, Miss S C
Crosby, R
Coffin, Isaac N
Cooper, Mark A-2
Daniel, Mrs
Darne, Lt A C H
Dixon, Mrs Mary
Davis, Jos
Davis, Addison
Dickinson, Judge T-2

Douglass, J C, U S N
Denham, Aaron
Dyer, Kensy
Desau, Francis
Downing, Miss H A
Deford, Chas
Davis, Maj Thos
Duvall, John P
Eldred, Allen
Ellis, Vespasian
Emerson, Chas
Emmons, Wm
Ennis, J T
Estis, R
Estcourt, J B-2
Eaton, Nathan
French, Edmund F
Fitzgerald, Wm B
Ferguson, John-2
Fitzhugh, John W
Ferguson, Benj
Fowler, Mrs Jane
Flaherty, John P
Freeland, Mrs Sarah
Fawble, David
Fowler, Philip W
Fister, Mrs Adeline
Gray, Rev Saml T
Green, Jas
Gould, Stephen G
Gray, John
Green, Maj N T
Gaines, A W-2
Griffith, Wm H
Gardner, Edw F
Grayson, Henry
Gilman, David W
Gormley, Miss Mary

Golden, J A
Graham, J D
Gillott, Mrs
Gilbert, M J
Griffin, Jas
Gilpin, Wm
Hyde, Geo
Hall, Edw
Hurst, John T
Holt, W C
Hughes, Mrs Marg't
Holt, Mrs Susan J
Hayne, Col A P-4
Huger, T V, U S N
Hamilton, Gen Jas
Hitcherson, Saml
Hurlbert, Henry F
Harvey, Capt
Hawley, Miss H A
Humbert, Madam A
Haislep, Henry
Hambleton, Mrs L
Hanna, Francis
Hurlbert, J P
Hernitz, Dr S
Hinman, Davis
Howard, Mrs V E
Harris, Jane
Happer, Mrs M E S-2
Hinkley, Mrs A P
Hartsline, Lt H F
Henry, Dr B, U S N
Hamilton, Mathias
Hurbert, Wm
Heaton, David F
Hernandez, G J M-4
Ingle, Randolph
Iardella, Chas
Jones, John W
Johnson, Dr Jos-3
Johnson, Geo
Jenkins, Miss M E
Jenkins, Miss Eli'th

Jeniter, Danl
Jackson, Miss M J
King, Chas-2
Kirk, Miss Mary H
Kerr, Geo
Kennison, Nebe'h-2
Knoblock, Fred'k
Kenyon, Thos
Kenner, Alex'r
Kelly, Miss Ann-2
Kelly, Miss Eliza
Kelly, C D
Locke, John
Locky, A K
Lilly, S W
Luckett, David W
Lowry & Dork
Lemmon, Mr
Lusese, Miss Am'da
Lemmon, Wm H
Landing, Mrs Maria
Lowry, Robt
Lewis, Dr John B
Ludlow, A C
Latimer, Jos T
Loveless, Jas A
Lindley, Adam
Larkin, Ann, trustee
Leffler, Shepherd
Lansing, P
Mount, Miss Virg'a
Murgatroys, Thos
Morrice, Mrs M A
Millett, Danl C-2
Millett, Miss Jos'ne
Mitchell, Jas D
Morris, Dr Jno M
Morrison, Jas H C
Metcalfe, Orrick-3
Manning, Ignatius
Miller, Capt M S
Murray, p'd mid A
Mershon, Wm-2

Mulloy, Thos
Mason, Gen J T-2
Mason, jr, Capt J-4
Mason, jr, Mrs John
Maltzan, Baron
McIntosh, Jas T
McLemore, Col J C
McDonald, Col A
Mackey, Philip
McKimm, Jas
McLaughlin, Randal
McFarran, Isaac
Nourse, Dr Amos
Noeth, T G
Newly, F A
Naylor, John
Norris, Miss Virg'a
Newcomb, Capt F D
Nalle, Thos B, U S N
Owen, Mrs Ann-2
O'Reilly, Henry
Osborn, Franklin J
Owens, John S
O'Conner, E
O'Sullivan, John L
Pease, Judge
Paine, Henry M-2
Payne, - W
Prescott, E S
Philips, Wm H
Pastorius, F
Philips, Eliz
Pullen, Jas
Purdy, S M
Porter, Mid'n H O
Pickett, John T-2
Porter, Lt Wm D
Queen, Mid'n Wal-2
Queen, Mrs
Reden, Wm
Rhett, R B
Rhett, Lt Thos G
Russell, Mrs Susan

Rodrick, Hugo	Slacum, G W	Vanhorn, Capt
Riley, Mrs Mgt	Sutherland, Jas	Van Ney, Chas
Rohrer, Henry	Sylvester, G S-2	Vanderhoost, Mid E
Robinson, G	Stanton, John C	Wright, John T
Rogers, Mrs John C	Stoner, M M	Ward, John L
Rodgers, Mrs M A	Stoneall, Thos H-2	White, Allison
Ridgeley, Com C G	Sauper, Miss E A	Walsh, Wm
Randolph, J B, U S N-2	Spencer, Miss S J	White, Harriet
Rainbow, John-2	Shirtliff, Jonas	Woodruff, David
Scott, Lewis Allain	Slidell, John	Wander, Miss S A
Slye, Mrs Mary P	Stansbury, A J-2	Weaver, Jas G
Shott, Geo Thos	Stewart, Henry	Waterhouse, E G
Semimes, Mrs M O	Tait, Mrs Ann	Wilson, Chas G
Shawk, Abel	Thorn, John	Wrixon, Robt J
Smith, Wm	True, Loring B-6	Walback, Lt J J
Smith, Mrs Martin S	Thibadeaux, B	Wilson, Jonathan
Sheets & Co, Wm	Thompson, A	Warren, Miss R
Stelle, Thos	Terrinet, A P	Watson, John B
Stone, Mrs Caroline	Turner, Danl	Wallis, J E
Smith, John W	Timberlake, Lewis	Williams, Rev Wm
Scott, John	Thomas, Wm H	Wilkins, John
Swayne, Wm P	Thomas, Jas	Walker, S P-2
Schwartz, Dr	Townley, J D	Yost, J S-3
Smith, Geo L	Thompson, Wm B	Young, Notley-2
Speckman, John	Underwood, Miss C	Yates, Andrew J
Stewart, Chas W	Vance, Jos	Zimmerman, Saml-2

Mrd: on Oct 13, in Wash City, by Rev Mr French, Mr Wm McDermott to Miss Josephine Emily, d/o the late J Bender, of Boston.

Trustee's sale of blooded stock: sale on Oct 17, on the **Kendall Race Course**, Balt, [which contains 100 acres of land,] all the right, title, & interest which Peyton R Johnson has in the unexpired lease,] of 4 years from Jan 1 next,] from the Canton Co, in the above Race course, & grounds thereto attached, with all the household & kitchen furniture now in the Tavern House attached to said Race Course. Also, the following blooded Stock, viz: Nobleman, Kanawha, Bay colt Victor, & half of bay colt. Also, one negro boy, Isaac, about 13 years old, slave for life, a first rate Race Rider. –Thompson & Gover, auctioneers

Bacon Stall, #41 Centre Market: ware-room on 9th st, between D & E sts. –Jas Tucker

Dr David Moore, for many years a member of the Legislature from Madison Co, & Speaker of the House of Reps of Alabama, died in Huntsville, on Sep 23, aged about 60 years.

Mrd: on Tue, at Balt, by Rev G D Purviance, Michl L Ross, of Hagerstown, Md, to Lauretta, d/o the late Andrew Hazlehurst, of Wash City.

Mrd: on Oct 7, at the residence of Hon Geo S Catlin, in Windham, Conn, by Rev Mr Nichols, John T Reid to Mary Louisa Clack, grand-daughter of the late Mr Justice Thompson, of the U S Supreme Court. [Oct 17th newspaper: correction-Mrs Clack is the daughter of Judge Smith Thompson, dec'd, not the grand-daughter. This was an error of the pen.]

Died: on Oct 14, Master John Crowell Cox, in his 15th year. His funeral is today at 12 o'clock, from his mother's residence.
+
Master J C Cox, s/o Mrs Cox in C st, a youth of 16, was unhappily killed yesterday afternoon by the accidental discharge of his fowling-piece, whilst gunning in the slashes, near the Railroad.

The Small-Pox. Batavia, Genesee Co, N Y, Oct 11th letter: Henry Hawkins, a member of the State Senate, & formerly of the firm of Hawkins & Blodget, at Alexander, is dead. He was buried yesterday; & the report is, that there were 12 new cases yesterday. The stores & taverns are closed at Alexander, & the street leading to that place fenced up.

Steel goods, combs, & brushes: also Perfumary. –Lewis Clephane, Pa ave, 3rd door east of 10th st. [Ad]

Sale of *Harwood*: this property, with all improvements, about 15 miles from Balt, on the Gunpowder river, was sold at Balt Exchange on Oct 11, by Messrs Wever, Poulterer & Co subject to a mortgage of $10,000 to J F Strohm, for $2,400. The property formerly belonged to Robt Oliver, dec'd, & more recently to A Ruff, dec'd. -American

Obit-died: on Sep 14, 1845, ater a short illness of 3 days, Eliza R, eldest d/o the Hon Philip Triplett, in her 19th year. She was the most affectionate of dghts & kindest of friends. –Owensboro, Ky -A Friend

Wish to employ a Journeyman barber, white or colored. Apply to John Chaner, D st, between 7th & 8th sts.

FRI OCT 17, 1845
Fresh arrival of Dry Goods: corner of 8th st. –Wm R Riley [Ad]

European Literature: from Tait's Magazine: Memoirs of Lady Hester Stanhope: it places without doubt, the craziness, if not absolute insanity of Lady Hester in the latter years of her life. She was the grand-dght of the great Chatham, & the d/o the eccentric & democratic Earl of Stanhope. Lady Hester was the eldest of the 3 dghts of the sister of Wm Pitt. Lady Hester early lost her mother-& got a stepmother. She was very precocious, the genius of the family, & the favorite of her father & his guests. The Memoirs are as related by herself in conversations with her Physician.

For rent: 3 large lots of land in the northern part of Wash City, & back of the Franklin Row. Upon one is a small dwlg-house, stable, & a well of good water.
–Mrs Mary A Cox, living on C st.

Army Genr'l Order: Gen orders #47: Headquarters of the Army, Adj Gen Ofc, Wash, Oct 15, 1845. Announce the death of a honored veteran, Brevet Brig Gen W K Armistead, Col of the U S 3rd Regt of Artl, who departed this life on Oct 13, after a protracted illness, at Upperville, Va. Gen Armistead entered the Army as 2nd Lt of Engineers more than 42 years ago: for many years he was the chief of the Corps of Engineers, whence he was transferred to the head of a marching regt, &, as a genr'l ofcr, had, for a campaign, [1840-41,] the chief command in the war against the Florida Indians. –R Jones, Adj Gen

Boots & Shoes: Thos Bayne, H st, Navy Yard. [Ad]

Valuable real estate at auction: by authority vested in me as adm de bonis non, with the will annexed, of the late Andrew Scholfield, I will sell, on Nov 7: all of square 863, with a commodious Cottage House: on Md ave & 6th sts. Also, lot 7 in square 576, with a 2 frame tenements that rent readily: on Md ave. Title is believed to be indisputable.
–Benj Waters, adm d b n -A Green, auct

Died: on Oct 4, at the Navy Yard, Pensacola, in his 62nd year, Chas D Brodie, Naval Constructor, U S Navy, while superintending the repairs of the frig **Potomac**. On the 2nd he was struck with an apopletic fit, which hurried him to his grave. He lived "to love your neighbors," which drew to him many a warm friend.

SAT OCT 18, 1845
Thos R Gerry died at New Rochelle, on Oct 6, after an illness of 72 hours. He was the s/o the venerable Elbridge Gerry, formerly V P of the U S. In early life he entered the U S Navy, & was esteemed as an ofcr of great promise. After a service of 3 years in the ship **John Adams** as 1st Lt, duty to his family induced him to resign his commission to the great regret of the Gov't. He married the d/o the late Peter P Geolet, of N Y. He was a devoted husband, father, & friend.

For rent: well known tavern & fruit store, on Pa ave, between 4½ & 3rd sts. Apply at the premises. –Martin Murphy

Orphans Court of Wash Co, D C. In the general matter of the real estate of the late Lewis G Davidson. Saml G Davidson, Trustee, having reported the following sales, namely:

Square 165:
To Richd Smith: lot 2: at $432.18
Richd Smith: lot 17 at $213.04
Richd Smith: lot 18 at $219.84
Wm Grindage: lot 7 at $259.35

Wm Grindage: lot 8 at $279.45
Geo J Abott: lot 9 at $234.00
Cornelius Cox: lot 13 at $289.60

Square 127:
Jos Frazer: lot 4 at $316.11¼
Joe Frazer: lot 5 at $338.72¼
John M Moore: lot 18 at $380.35

Rich Cruikshank: lot 8 at $276.36
Rich Cruikshank: lot 9 at $276.36

Square 126:
Jas J Abert: lot 7 at $337.28

Jas J Abert: lot 8 at $337.28

Square 163:
Wm B Lewis: lot 15 at $59.40
Hanson Gassaway: lot 19 at $61.65

Nicholas Callan: lot 12 at $142.23

-Nathaniel Pope Causin -Teste: N Roach, Reg/o wills

The Last Scene. The actor Booth is seriously ill at Boston, & is now under medical treatment. His services on the stage of life are drawing to a close, we fear, & he will soon finish his last scene. –N Y Express [May 20th newspaper: Booth, the tragedian, has recovered from his illness.]

The N Y Enquirer says that Rev Chas W Whitall, of New Orleans, is now lying at the hospital, in N Y, in a very critical & hopeless condition, from recently falling into the hold of a vessel in which he had taken passage for New Orleans. We believe several relatives reside in this vicinity. [Dec 1st newspaper: Rev Mr Whitall sailed from N Y for his home on Thu, having entirely recovered.]

Female teachers wanted: Trustees of Everettsville Female Academy wish to employ 2 unmarried ladies, who have experience in teaching. Everettsville is in a small village in Wayne Co, N C. Address J C Slocumb, Sec, Waynesborough, Wayne Co, N C, post pd.

Valuable Tanyard at auction: by decree of the Circuit Court of Wash Co, D C: sale on Nov 19, of the Tanyard at the conrer of Fayette & 2nd sts, long known as **Baker's Tanyard**: comprises lots 78 thru 81, fronting 138 feet on Fayette, & 180 on 2nd st, containing 24,840 square feet, in Threlkeld's addition to said town. Improvements are a 2 story brick warehouse, a brick bark-house, etc. –E S Wright, auct

Mrd: on Oct 9, by Rev John J Murray, Mr Geo Branzell to Miss Martha Ann Rose, all of Wash City.

Died: on Oct 15, at Alexandria, Mr Thos Vowell, one of the oldest inhabitants of that town, of which he has been a resident about 57 years, & filled many respectable situations with credit.

Died: on Oct 5, in Gtwn, Mrs Mary Meatherall, after a few days' illness, of bilious fever, in her 30th year, leaving a husband & 2 infant children to mourn her loss.

Orphans Court of Wash Co, D C. Letters of administration on the personal estate of Geo Scott, late of said county, dec'd. –Wm A Scott, adm

MON OCT 20, 1845
Excellent household furniture at auction: on Oct 27, at the residence of Mrs Hewitt, corner of 6th & D st, her household & kitchen furniture. -R W Dyer & Co, aucts

Freemen's Vigilant Temperance Association of Wash: Resolved, that, entertaining a high respect for the character & usefulness of John B Gough as a man & a successful temperance lecturer, we have learned with deep regret that, by an act of treachery on the part of some enemies of our holy cause, he has been led to violate his pledge. We have read the statement of J B Gough of the occurrences of his fall. We do fully sympathize with J B Gough & family. –Jas Rawlings, Rec Sec

Mechanical Riflemen: meeting this evening, at 7 o'clock. –Thos Caton, Sec pro tem

Edw McCubbin, barber & hairdresser, at the 3 story house erected on the site of his former stand: Temple of Fashion, #1, on 8th st, near Pa ave.

Young Pointer Dog lost: suitable reward. –Geo C Whiting, 6th & F sts.

Capt West, wounded by the explosion on board the steamer **Dayton**, of which he was acting as clerk, has died of his wounds, as also some 2 or 3 others, from the same cause, one a cabin boy & another a U S soldier.

TUE OCT 21, 1845
For rent: 3 story brick house in Carroll's Row, on Capitol Hill. Inquire of Ben E Green, Jas Adams, at the Bank of Wash.

The anniversaries of the victories of the American troops in the Revolutionary war over the British armies commanded by Genr'ls Burgoyne & Cornwallis were celebrated at Dedham, Mass, on Fri last. A volunteer company, got up at Cambridge, attended the field under Capt Coy, of the Mass Guards, who personated the character of Gen Washington. While going through some maneuvers, Capt Cox was shot from his horse; the several shots have been removed. At a late hour yesterday, fears were entertained for Mr Coy's life. Mr Eaton, of the same company, was shot at the same time. -Atlas

Wash Co, D C: I certify that Owen Connolly brought before me, as strays, trespassing on the premises of E Fenwick, of said county, a gray horse & a gray mare. –T C Donn, J P [Owner is to come forward, prove property, pay charges & take them away. –Owen Connolly]

Trustee's sale of valuable real estate in Chas Co, Md: by virtue of a decree of Chas Co Court sitting as a Court of Equity, passed on Sep 5, 1845, the subscribers, as trustees, will offer at public auction, on Nov 20 next, at *Hardbargain*, in Pacowaxen, Chas Co,] the late residence of Nathan Harris, dec'd, the following valuable real estate, being the same of which the said Nathan Harris died seized & possessed, viz: *Hardbargain*, containing 678 acs: with a 2 story brick dwlg & every necessary out-house. Also, *Borrough Hall*, in the neighborhood of *Hardbargain*, adjoining *Milton Hill*, the residence of Mr Hamilton, & *Mount Tirza*, the residence of H R Harris, with the mill-seat attached, containing 300 acres of land, more or less. Also, another portion of the same real estate, called *Brick House tract*, being part of *James' Purchase & Harris' Lot*, containing 200 acs, more or less: with a very large old brick dwlg. –Benj G Harris, Henry R Harris N B: the Trustees would inform the public that there are 7 minors interested in this real estate, the oldest of whom is about 13 & the youngest about 18 months, with about 2 years between the ages of each child. –B G Harris, H R Harris]

In Equity: Aug Term, 1845. John B Lawson, Trustee of Thos Lloyd, vs Robt Teachum & Mary O his wife, Wm Nottingham, Mary A Nottingham, & Margaret Nottingham. The object of this suit is to procure a sale of the real estate of Wilfred Nottingham, late of Chas Co, dec'd, to pay the debts due the complainant & others. The bill of complaint of complainant states that on Dec 1, 1842, Thos Lloyd, of Chas Co, Md, executed to the cmplnt a deed of trust of all his property for the benefit of his creditors, & by virtue of said deed of trust there came into the hands of the cmplnt 2 single bills of said Nottingham which were due to said Lloyd, & the said Nottingham has died since the execution of said bills, & has not left enough of personal property to pay his debts, due to the cmplnt as aforesaid, & to others; that the personal property has been exhausted in the payment of the debts of Nottingham, & that Nottingham died seised of certain real estate, in Chas Co, Md, leaving the following heirs at law, to wit: Mary O Teachum, Wm Nottingham, Mgt Nottingham, chldn of Wm Nottingham, brother of the said Wilfred Nottingham; & that Mary A Nottingham, widow of said Wm Nottingham, is living, & prays a decree of the real estate of said Wilfred Nottingham for the payment of the claims of the cmplnt & others, & a summons having issued to the Sheriff of Chas Co, & a return having been made that the respondents cannot be found. Dfndnts to appear in this Court on or before the 3rd Mon in Mar next. –A C Magruder. –W Mitchell, Clerk

Died: on Oct 12, at the residence of her mother, in Prince William Co, Va, Maria Louisa, y/d/o the late Wm French, after a painful illness of less than 4 days.

Died: on Oct 10, at *Locust Grove*, PG Co, Md, in his 20th year, Henry Digges Manning, eldest s/o Mrs Martha Manning. The dec'd was an obedient son, a kind brother, & good in all the relations of life. -H

Orphans Court of Wash Co, D C. In the case of Edw M Linthicum, adm of John W Deeley, dec'd: final settlement of decd's estate on Nov 7 next.
–Edw N Roach, reg/o wills

WED OCT 22, 1845
Silver vase [upwards of 3 feet in height] presented to Henry Clay, by the Gold & Silver Artisans of N Y C. As a tribute of their respect for the faithful & patriotic manner in which he has discharged his high public trusts, & especially for his early & untiring advocacy of "Protection to American Industry." Cmte: Wm Adams, M G Baldwin, A G Peckham, Edw Y Prime, Danl Carpenter, David Dunn

At the recent Agricultural Fair in Burlington, Vt, Mr L Chase presented for premium 3 pretty female children, 2½ years old, born at birth! The cmte awarded him $14.

In Chancery-Circuit Court of Wash Co, D C. Maria C French, adm de bonis non of Geo French, vs Jas Dundas & others. David A Hall, the Trustee, appointed to sell the real estate in the bill, sold a tract of land in said county called *Aaron*, containing 340 acs, to Henry Naylor, for $8.50 per ac, making the sum $2,890. –W Brent, clerk

Fatal disaster on Sep 12 on board the steamer **Dayton**, killing instantly Lt Higgins & Lt Berry, of the 4th Infty, 2 sergeants, 6 of the ofcrs & crew of the boat, & wounding others. Lts Graham & Gordon escaped with their lives.

Mrd: on Oct 16, at *Mount Ida*, near Alexandria, D C, by Rev E R Lippitt, John J Lloyd, of Balt, Md, to Eliza Armistead, d/o the late Dr Wilson Cary Selden, of Loudoun Co, Va.

Died: on oct 21, after a short illness, Mr Wm Martin, in his 71st year. His funeral is this afternoon, at 2 o'clock, from the residence of his son, Mr John Martin, near the Steamboat wharf on 11th st.

Dissolution: of the firm of Whitaker & Co, by mutual consent. –M M Teprell, John T Whitaker The subscribers will continue the business at the old stand, Pa ave & 15th st.
–G Brooke, M M Teprell

Wanted to hire, a servant woman for a small family. Good wages will be given. Inquire at Hall & Magruder's Shoe Store.

$100 reward for runaway mulatto boy Wm Henry Ringold, about 24 years of age.
–Jesse Brown, of Brown's Hotel

THU OCT 23, 1845
Household & chamber furniture at auction: on Oct 25, at the residence of Mr Richd Harrington, at the Navy Yard. –A Green, auctioneer

The Phil North American paper has passed into the hands of Messrs Geo R Graham & Alex'r Cummings.

Mr Levi C Frost, keeper of the City Temperance Lunch, at Providence, R I, committed suicide on Sat by shooting himself.

Mrd: Oct 16, by Rev Mr Eggleston, Mr Alfred C Belt to Miss Agnes McGill, both of Wash City.

Mrd: Oct 21, by Rev Dr Muller, Mr Wm H Campbell, of Gtwn, to Miss Louisa F Desaules, of Wash City.

On Sat, Chas Simeon was caught between 2 coal cars near Pottsville, while in the act of fixing the coupling, & was instantly killed.

New Goods, Hardware & Cutlery: English & Muncaster, Bridge st, Gtwn.

Orphans Court of Wash Co, D C. Letters testamentary on the personal estate of Griffith Coombe, late of said county, dec'd. –Mary Coombe, Jas G Coombe, excs

FRI OCT 24, 1845
St Louis, Mo. Conviction of Col Geo Davenport's murderers: Burch, Baxter, the 2 Longs, & Young, for the murder of Davenport, on Jul 4 last. On Sat they were sentenced to be hung on Nov 29. –Republican

Wash Corp: list of the ordinaries & taverns in Wash City, the names of the persons to whom licenses have been granted, the names of those who have certified the act to regulate taverns & ordinaries have been complied with by the persons obtaining the said licenses.
License issued to:
A Favier, square 119, 19th st
Benedict Jost, square 168, Pa ave
M Gilbert, square 291, E & 13th sts
Thos J Earhart, square 224, F st
Jeremiah Sullivan, square 225, 15th st
Andrew Hancock, square 292, Pa ave
Geo McCauley, square 225, Pa ave
Wm Creutzfeldt, square 292, Pa ave
L Gallabrun, square 225, Pa ave
Peter Jones, square [blank]
A Fuller & Co, square 225, Pa ave & 14th
Jas Maher, square 256, 13½ & E sts
Abraham Butler, square 234, F st
Jas Davis, square 348, D & 10th sts
Saml S Coleman, square 491, Pa ave

Thos Baker, square 431, 8th & D sts
Benj O Sheckell, square 461, 7th st
Jesse Brown, square 450, Pa ave
John H Clarvoe, square 461, F st
Jas Long, square 460, 8th st
P A Desaules, square 431, 7th & K sts
C F Zackman, square 455, 7th st
Wm Benter, square 491, Pa ave
Michl Talty, square 432, 7th st
Patrick Moran, square 575, Pa ave
John Douglas, square 490, La ave
John H Eberbach, square 407, 8th & E sts
Chas Peesch, square B, Pa ave & 4½ st
Andrew R Jenkins, Res 10, Pa ave
Jas s Hall, square B, Pa ave
John C Cook, square 461, 7th st
Jas Cuthbert, Res 10, Pa ave
B H Shadd, Res 12, B st

Jewett & King, square B, Pa ave
John West, square 461, Pa ave
Wm Dipple, square 461, 7th st
Wm Feeny, square 437, 7th st
John Foy, square 378, D st
Martin Murphy, Res 10, Pa ave
John Donovan, Res 12, Pa ave
H W Sweeting, square 490, C st
Tyler & Birch, Res 10, Pa ave
John West, square 461, 7th st
Wm Gadsby, Res 10, Pa ave & 3rd st
J W Smith, square 453, 7th & I sts
Andrew Rupert, square 729, East Capitol st
Jas Casparis, square 688
R H Harrington, square 930, 8th st

Premises examined & certified by:

W G Bitner
Saml Stott
Matthew Bouvet
Saml Redfern
Thos Smith
A Hoover
Chas H Smoot
J Schwartz
Geo Krafft
Chas H Schneider
Jas Kelly
Jacob Brodbeck
John France
N Travers
E Simms
Jas McColgan
C Eckloff
Geo A M Randall
Abraham Butler
Allison Nailor
John C Rives
Wm Dowling
Wm Drury
Jas Larned

Jas Anderson
Wm B Laub
Jas H Causten
W W Corcoran
S W Handy
Wm Flenner
C P Sengstack
Jas M McColgan
J T Davis
Wm Morow
John France
Geo A W Randall
Fred'k Reitz
Wm Dowling
Geo Lamb
M P Callan
P Kinchy
Jas Maher
A Fuller
Abraham Butler
R Wimsatt
Jas E Thumlert
K H Lambell
Jas Mitchell

J W Martin
Jos Stephenson
Robt Cruit
E Evans
Jas Laurie
E Stephens
John C Rives
Michl Nourse
McClintock Young
Jos S Wilson
John M Krafft
Wm Orme
Garret Anderson
Michl R Combs
Geo McDuell
Reuben Patton
Benj Beall
John W Maury
Alex Lee
J Pepper
John M Johnson
Lemuel Harbaugh
Michl Talty
Raphael Jones

C Utermuhle	A F Kimmell	Chas Lee Jones
J H Eberbach	J H T Werner	Jas Long
W H Harrover	Ch Lee Jones	E Lindsley
S Hyatt	Jacob Acker	A J Duvall
Walter Clarke	R Burdine	B H Duvall
Chas Stott	Ernest Guttschlich	T F Semmes
Jos Peck	B F Middleton	P Thyson
Urias Hurst	Peter F Bacon	D S Waters
John H Clarvoe	Rachel Johnson	Beverly W Beall
A Coyle	Owen Connolly	G Ailier
Z D Gilman	W T Steiger	J Wheeler
R G Briscoe	J B Moore	John A Lynch
Jos Beasley	Fred Cuillipp	Edmund Reilly
B O Sheckell	Andrew Small	Jas B Phillips
J Emerich	E Lindsley	Hugh Lochrey
Levi Pumphrey	C Utermohle	Jas Lynch
Wm Ward	S Masi	D Homans
R C Washington	Robt Keyworth	W W Stewart
Thos Baker	J C McGuire	Wm J Wheatly
Leonard Harbaugh	S P Franklin	J D Waller
Jos Harbaugh	O Connolly	C K Gardner
Geo Sweeny	J Fitzgerald	Simon Brown
Jas Caden	J McDermott	C W Stewart
J H Goddard	Geo Parker	Philip Otterback
Thos Magill	W G W White	Jas Tucker
Fred Bates	P W Browning	Wm M Ellis
Peter Callan	Edw Simms	Jas Rhodes
Wm Jacobi	John M Johnson	Jos M Padgett
Jacob Saufferly	Isaac Beers	Adam Gaddis

By whom recommended: The above and the following:

Fred'k Schneider	E Lacy	Jas Caden
Jas Lusby	R C Washington	Stanislaus Murray

Spontaneous combustion: yesterday fire was discovered at the lime-houses of Mr W H Gunnell & Messrs Ward & Collard, at 6th & Mo ave: damaged amounted to $200. No insurance.

Mrd: on Oct 21, at the residence of Francis Lowndes, Gtwn, D C, by Rev S G Gassaway, Mr Horatio E Berry, of Gtwn, to Mrs Martha Louisa Manning, of Jefferson Co, Va.

Mrd: on Oct 23, by Rev Mr Tarring, Mr Danl H Cady to Miss Rebecca Adams, of Wash City.

Wash Co, D C: I certify that John Bettinger brought before me as an estray, a dark bay Horse, trespassing on his premises. Said horse formerly belonged to & was sold by him about 2 years since, but knows not to whom he now belongs. –J I Stull, J P [Owner is to come forward, prove property, pay charges, & take him away. -John Bettinger]

A sum of money was found in the store of R Estep on Oct 21; owner can have said money by calling on the subscriber & describing the same & paying for this advertisement. –J D Marr, L, between 6th & 7th sts

Auction: without reserve, 217 acres of land on Rockville & Wash Turnpike: immediately opposite *Silver Spring*, the farm of F P Blair. Also, 460 acres of land on Rock Creek: partly in this District & partly in Montgomery County, about 5 miles from Washington. Sale on Nov 17, at Conrad's Tavern, in Tennallytown, about 3 miles above Gtwn. –Wm Thos Carroll, Wash

SAT OCT 25, 1845
For rent: 2 story brick dwlg house on 7th st. Apply to Mrs Cheshire, on 6th st.

A party of Indian Chiefs, of the Pottawatamie tribe, from Council Bluffs, east of the Missouri river, are now in Wash City, accompanied by Richd S Elliott, who has been for some years Gov't agent in that region. They desire to have a full investigation & settlement of their business with the Gov't.

Mrs Hannah Gouge died in N Y last Sunday, aged 109 years, 11 months & 15 days. This lady, it is said, has seen & held converse with each & every Pres of the U S, besides many other dignitaries of lesser magnitude.

H Craft, Genr'l Land Agent: Holly Springs, Mississippi. Attends also to paying taxes, examining lands & land titles. Refer to:

Henry Anderson, Holy Springs	John C Wright, Cincinnati
Goodman & Means, Memphis, Tenn	Chas Butler, N Y
Danl Revenel, Charleston, S C	A Porter, Savannah, Ga
Judge Bryan, of Alabama, Wash.	Hon Washington Poe, Macon Ga

Valuable Albemarle Estate at Auctin: on the premises, on Dec 10, the estate called *Dunlora*, the late residence of Col Saml Carr, containing 443 acs, within 2 miles of Charlottesville, Va. Improvements consist of a large & elegant brick dwlg, & all necessary outhouses. –Geo Watson Carr

For rent: 3 story brick, on Pa ave, between 12th & 13th sts, with a good store room. Also, a 3 story brick on Bridge st, Gtwn. Apply to Nicholas Travers.

Orphans Court of Wash Co, D C. Letters testamentary on the personal estate of Stephen Chapin, late of said county, dec'd. –H L Chapin, exc

Died: on Thu last, of consumption, Mrs Susanna Collins, w/o Mr Thos Collins, in her 40th year, leaving a disconsolate husband & several small children. Her illness was of long duration, & borne with Christian fortitude. Her funeral is from her late residence on 8th st, between G & H sts, on Sun at 2 p m.

Died: on Sep 27, 1845, at Kilmarnock, Lancaster Co, Pa, after an illness of 12 days, Mrs Susan B Crittenden, w/o Geo W Crittenden, & d/o Rev Addison Hall.

Somerville Whig: Two brothers, sons of Peter Teats, near Cokesbury, went hunting on Sat last; the gun of the foremost brother discharged, it contents lodging in the head of the other, who expired immediately. Still another: case reported by the Boston Traveller: a s/o Saml Topliff, only 13. The ball of a pistol in the hands of a playmate entered his throat, but striking the button on his shirt collar, it is supposed, its force was impeded, & thus providentially his life was saved.

A company, under the charge of Miles W Goodyear, has left Independence for the mountains, to build a kind of fort & cultivate a portion of ground, more as an experiment than anything else, & if possible, make it a sort of half-way house between Independence & Oregon & California, where the companies may stop & refresh themselves & obtain supplies. He has 6 or 8 men going with him. –St Louis Republican

MON OCT 27, 1845

Edw C Cabell, Whig, has been elected the Rep to Congress from the new State of Florida by a majority of some 200 votes over W H Brockenbrough, his Locofoco competitor.

Boilers in the steam floring mill of Messrs J & E Walsh, in St Louis, burst on Wed, so badly scalding the first engineer, Mr Wm Freeland, that he died in about 3 hours.

Mrd: on Oct 16, at Warrenton Female Seminary, N C, by Rev C McRae, Mr Julius Wilcox, of Warrenton, to Miss Sarah A, the only d/o the Rev Noah Nichols, of Cuttingsville, Vt

Ofc of the Board of Health: Oct 23, 1845. A few cases of small-pox having recently occurred in our city, it has been deemed expedient to call public attention to the fact in order to induce those who have not been vaccinated to have it done without delay. Those who choose can have the operation performed gratuitously by calling at the City Hospital, where the resident physician will be in attendance at all hours. A bldg for the accommodation of small-pox patients has been provided in the neighborhood of the Almshouse, where those who cannot be taken care of at their respective residences will be received. –Harvey Lindsley, Pres Board of Health

Farrar's Bowling Saloon, on Missouri ave, between 4½ & 6th st, re-opened.
–John M Farrar

TUE OCT 28, 1845
T Chaner, Barber, D st, between 7th & 8th sts, has for sale Corosale Oil, which is superior for cleaning the hair & preventing it becoming gray, & is very useful for improving the hair of children.

Boots & Shoes: Call at A Hoover's, Pa ave, opposite the Seven Bldgs.

Wm H Nalley has again opened his Bookbinding establishment on Pa ave, next door to Jackson Hall.

Valuable real estate at private sale: the subscriber has in his hands for sale several thousand acres of the best limestone Land in Wash Co, Md. Lands are divided into farms, ranging from 120 acres to 300 acres each, in said county. Upon each tract are large Barns. I have also for sale 37,000 acres of Western Land, in Michigan, Illinois, Missouri, Ky, Ohio, & Indiana. –W B Clarke, Atty & Agent, Hagerstown, Md

Qunicy Whig: Mr Backenstos, the Sheriff of Hancock Co, who was arrested at Nauvoo by Gen Hardin, & taken to Quincy, charged with the murder of Worrel & McBratney, was examined before Judge Purple, & held to bail for his appearance at the Hancock Circuit Court in the sum of $3,000.

On Tue, above Marietta, on the State road, C F M Garnett, the state engineer, had both legs broken & mangled, & the conductor, whose name we did not learn, had one leg entirely cut off. This is the account & we fear it is not exaggerated. –Georgia Chronicle

Bargain for someone: 620 acres of first rate Cumberland river Bottom land for sale: in Livingston Co, Ky, 6 miles from the town of Smithland. I will sell the above for cash, or I will take in payment negroes or freehold property in the District of Columbia. Call on Milton Garrett, residing on F st, near the Observatory, or at Stall #66, Centre Market, Wash.

Beautiful residence for sale: lately erected on Capitol Hill by Mr J Martin for his family. The house is near the Capitol corner of 1st & C sts: just finished & built in the best style. Mr Martin is desirous of selling it, or exchanging it for other property. Apply to A Green, Auctioneer & Commission Merchant, Concert Hall.

Mrs Poulton has just received her latest London & Paris fashions: residence-10th st, 3 doors below Pa ave.

Splendid real estate for sale at public auction in Loudoun Co, Va: by direction of the last will & testament of John Nixon, dec'd: sale on the premises, on Dec 25 next, all the real estate of said dec'd, containing about 900 acres of first-rate Loudoun land, divided into 2 farms: one called *Nixon's Mills*, containing 619 acs: lies about 4 miles s w of Leesburg; adjoins the lands of Joel Nixon, Wm Hall, Peter Cost, & others; improvements are all nearly new: a large 2 story brick dwlg, 52 feet in front by 32 feet deep; together with necessary out-houses. Also another farm, about 3/4th miles south of this one, containing about 270 acs; improvements on this farm are indifferent. Also, one unimproved Lot in Leesburg, fronting King st, containing half an acre. –Eli Janney, Thos Nichols, Benj F Taylor, excs of John Nixon, dec'd.

Died: on Oct 26, after a severe illness of 14 days, Thos Elliot, a promising youth, in his 9th year, s/o Jonathan & Eliz Elliot, Capitol Hill.

Circuit Court of Wash Co, D C-sitting in Chancery. Thos Carbery & Wm Jones, excs of Rachel Coombe, dec'd, vs Jas B Frere & Robt Reynoldson. Bill filed in this cause is as follows, viz-that the said Jas B Frere, being indebted to the said Rachel Coombe in her lifetime, in 1836 gave her his promissory note for $500, dated Nov 12, 1836, at 12 months after date, with interest, which is filed in the cause; & in order to secure the payment of the note, he executed a deed dated Nov 12, 1836, by which he conveyed to Robt Reynoldson, his heirs & assigns, lot 10 in square 86, with bldgs, & the reversions & remainders, rents, issues, & profits thereof, & all the estate, right, title, interest, property, claim, & demand whatsoever of him the said Jas B Frere, both at law & in equity, or otherwise howsoever, of, in, to, or out of the same, upon trust, in case the said Jas B Frere, his heirs, excs, adms, or assigns, should fail to take up & pay off the said note at maturity, with interest thereon, or expenses which might be due thereon, then & in that case the said Robt, on the request of said Rachel, her excs, adms, or assigns, should advertise the said property & sell it at public auction, to satisfy the said debt, interest, & costs; that the note is unpaid; the said Rachel hath died, having first made her will & appointed the cmplnts her excs; they have proved the will; the said Robt Reynoldson hath removed from this District, & they have been unable to ascertain where he now is; & praying for the removal of said Robt & the appointment of another trustee in his place, & for the sale of the property to satisfy the said debt. In default of his appearance & answer, the Court will proceed to decree in the premises. By order of the Court: Wm Brent, Clerk

Public Sale: virtue of a decree of Chas Co Court, sitting as a Court of Equity: sale on Feb 24, 1846, in Port Tobacco, the real estate upon which John Hamilton now resides, called *Prospect Hill*, supposed to contain 128 acs, being in said county. Sale requires the payment of $300 cash on the day of sale or ratification, the purchaser give bonds, with such security as the trustee shall approve, for the payment of the residue in the following installments: such portion as the Court may award to the said John Hamilton, as tenant by courtesy, in equal instalments of 1, 2, & 3 years, with interest till paid; & such portion as shall be awarded to the several infant children of the late Edw L Hamilton of the proceeds of said sale, to be paid to the several infants as they shall severally arrive at age, or on the day of their several marriages, with interest, to be annually paid to their several guardians. Possession will be given on Jan 1, 1847. The lands cannot be sold under said decree for a less sum than the appraised value-$16 per ac. –Geo W Matthews, Trustee

WED OCT 29, 1845
Boarding: Mrs M A Williams, south side of Pa ave, between 9th & 10th sts.

Official: headquarters Army of Occupation, Corpus Christi, Oct 11, 1845. On Oct 9, 5 companies of the 5th Infty, under Lt Col McIntosh; 2 companies of the 8th Infty, under Capt Montgomery; & 1 company of the 7th Infty, under Brevet Maj Seawell, arrived at St Joseph's island. All in good health. The news from the frontier continues still to be of a pacific character.

The U S storeship **Lexington** arrived at Aransas Pass on Oct 4, from N Y, having on board 7 companies of U S Artl, under command of Maj Ewing-ofcrs & men being generally in excellent health.

Fatal Accidents. 1-On Sat last, the 3 year old s/o Rev Mr Fort, was killed by falling from the terrace of the Patapsco Hotel, at Ellicott's Mills. 2-On Mon a middle-aged man, Mr Hasler, was drowned by falling into the mill race of the Patapsco flouring mill. He was a stranger there. 3-As the up-train of cars on Tue was passing Hooksett Falls, N H, a boat containing 3 sons of Mr Whitney, of H, drowned when the boat upset. The youngest was 5 years old, & the oldest 10.

Circuit Court of Wash Co, D C-in Chancery. Richd Smith et al, cmplnts, v Moreau Forrest, Zachariah Forrest, David B Denham & Josephine his wife, Julia Forrest, Richd H Carter & Mary W his wife, Richd E De Butts, Jos A Forrest, ___ Locke & Sarah D his wife, & others, heirs at law of Jos Forrest, dec'd, dfndnts. Bill charges that the said dec'd, Jos Forrest, became bound by written agreement during his life to execute a deed of trust to the cmplnt Smith, as trustee to secure a debt owing to the other cmplnts, for lot 12 in square 104, of Wash City, but died intestate without doing it, & the legal title therein descended at his death to his heirs at law, made dfndnts, subject to the obligation aforesaid; & under said obligation said Richd Smith has made contracts for the sale of the premises, with the engagement to perfect his title. The objects of the bill are to obtain from the heirs & reps of said deceased the execution of a deed of trust in conformity with said agreement, & so as to enable him to fulfil said contracts of sale, & for general relief. It is represented that the above named dfndnts reside out of D C, & it is, by the Court, ordered that they do, on or before the 4th Mon of Mar next, be & appear in Court.
–W Brent, clerk

Fatal rencontre at Yazoo, Miss, on Oct 5, between Mr Saml Swisher, keeper of the Eagle Hotel, & Col F A Bailey, a planter, which terminated in the death of Bailey.

A little d/o Mr John H Gardner, of Mass, was choked to death on Wed last by eating chestnuts. A physician was sent for, but before he arrived the child was dead.

Yesterday Mr Fred'k Speisser had a pumpkin that weighed 56 pounds in our Centre Market. This mammoth vegetable was raised on the farm of Mr Roderick McGregor, in PG Co, Md.

Boarding: Mrs Hannah Wells has taken the house lately occupied by Mrs Tully Wise, on F st, between 11th & 12th sts. The house has been thoroughly repaired, & the rooms are large & comfortable.

Situation for a Foundry. The subscriber offers for sale, or upon a long lease, a situation for a Cannon Foundry on the largest scale. It is upon the *Arlington Estate*, immediately opposite to Wash City, & bordering on the Alexandria Canal. Also, for sale, or upon long leases, sites for Factories of any description, for a mile in extent, bounded by the Canal & the Potomac river; for all of which water-power can be had of 37 feet. –Geo W P Custis, *Arlington House*, near Alexandria, Oct 27, 1845.

The Rev A Biewend, Minister of the German Lutheran Church, is prepared to give instructions in the German language. Apply at his residence, Green st, Gtwn, 3rd door north of Bridge st, nearly opposite Rother's vinegar depot.

THU OCT 30, 1845
We deeply regret to learn that the illness of the d/o the Hon Geo Bancroft, Sec of the Navy, has proved fatal. She died at Phil. -Ibid

The subscriber offers, on behalf of the Texas Association, 320 acres of land, the one moiety of a section, to be surveyed by the Association, for $8, to any family who may settle thereon from any part of the U S, or Europe, by Jul 1, 1846; after which time but 200 acres will be given to each family. The lands lie on both sides of the Trinity, above the mouth of Cedar Creek. Dr Danl Rowlett, residing on Red river, near Bonham, is the sub-agent of the Association; Col E L Ripley Wheelock, of Wheelock, Robertson Co, for the part of the above grant west of that river. Messrs T E Lindenberger & Co are the agents of the subscriber at New Orleans, & an agent will be provided at Galveston in due time. –Chas Fenton Mercer, Original Grantee & Chief Agent of the Texas Association, New Orleans, La, Aug 20, 1845.

Mrd: on Tue, by Rev John C Smith, John Scott Cunningham to Miss Eliz Brockett, all of Wash City.

The frig **Congress** proceeded to Hampton Roads on Sat last, preparatory to her departure for the Pacific. List of her ofcrs:

Cmdor R F Stockton   Cmder Saml F Dupont
Lts-6:
John W   Theodore P   Richd L
Livingston   Green   Tilghman
Jas F Schenck   A P V Gray   E G Parrott
Fleet Surgeon, Saml Mosley   Master, Van Rensalaer Morgan
Passed Assist Surgeon, John S Whittle   Cmdor's Sec, J Parker Norris
Assist Surgeon, Chas Eversfield   Cmdor's Clerk, Geo Hyde
Purser, Wm Speiden   Purser's Clerk, Constantine Sargent
Chaplain, Walter Colton 1st Lt Marines, J Zeilin
Passed Midshipmen-7:
Edw F Beale-Acting Master]   M K Warrington
John Guest   Chas H Baldwin
Wm H Thompson   Maurice Simons
Jas M Duncan
Midshipman-6:
Saml B Elliott   Benj F Wells
Theodoric Lee   Josiah S Byers
Archibald H Waring   Wm Mitchell

Gunner, Chas Cobb   Sailmaker, John Peck
Carpenter, John Southwick

Passengers to the Sandwich Island:
Anthony Ten Eyck, U S Com'r to the Sandwich Islands, lady, & children
J Turrills, Consul, lady, & family

Will be offered for private sale until Nov 6, when, if not sold, will be publicly sold for cash: a beautiful country seat, containing 50 acs, on the Turnpike leading from 7th st to Wash, to Rockville, 7 miles from Wash, & is also bounded by a good country road leading from Tennallytown. Improvements are a good 2 story frame house, with necessary out-houses. The land is near the farm of F P Blair. For further information call upon Mr Judson Mitchell, in Gtwn. –Empson B Davidson

Elegant & extensive property for sale: late residence of Mr Armfield, on Prince st, in Alexandria: the house is brick, built of the best materials: out-houses of brick, covered with metal. The flower-garden extends from Patrick to Henry st; the vegetable-garden is large & productive. –Wm D Nutt, at the Treas Dept

Household furniture at auction: by deed of trust, executed from B M Smoot: will be sold on Nov 6, at the 2 houses lately occupied by her in F st, between 13th & 14th sts, all the furniture of that large Boarding Establishment. -R W Dyer & Co, aucts

Appointments by the Pres: 1-Wm Monroe, Register of the Land Ofc for the district of lands subject to sale at Clinton, Mo, vice Wm Patterson, dec'd. 2-Thos Hartley Crawford, as Judge of the Criminal Court for D C, in place of Jas Dunlop, resigned. 3-Wm Medill, of Ohio, as Com'r of Indian Affairs, in place of Thos Hartley Crawford, resigned.

An extraordinary surgical operation in a liver complaint was lately performed by Dr J P Tarbell, of N Y C, by opening the side of the patient & removing the diseased portion of the liver. The patient was a middle aged man, who had suffered severely for many years, & latterly had given up all hopes of recovery.

Died: on Oct 29, Mr Wm Degges, in his 57th year. His funeral will take place from his late residence, on 20th st, between E & F sts, on Fri, at 3 o'clock.

Died: on Oct 25, in Gtwn, at the residence of her son-in-law, Matthew McLeod, Mrs Mary Manning, aged 63 years, after a painful & protracted illness, which she bore with Christian fortitude.

Died: at *Greenleaf's Point*, in Wash City, Herman Kaiser, aged 28 years. [No date- recent.]

For rent: 3 story brick house on 26th st, between 7th & 8th sts north. Apply to Wm J Brown, on the premises; Jos F Brown, at the Capitol.

FRI OCT 31, 1845
Wash Corp: 1-Act for the relief of Wm J Geffers: passed. 2-Ptn of J Martin: referred to the Cmte of Claims.

Boston: on Oct 27 Coroner Pratt was called to the house near Mt Vernon st, to examine the body of Mrs Bickford who was lying on the floor dead, her throat having been cut. Mrs Bickford has a husband living in Maine, is said to have been connected to this city with a man named Albert J Tirrell, of Weymouth. Ofcrs have been dispatched for him. He is a married man, & has 2 children, & inherited some property. He was recently indicted for adultery, but the matter was compromised by the interference of his wife & friends. –Daily Advertiser

On Fri at *Fort Pickering*, 3 little boys, John, Oceola, & Tecumseh, sons of Mr J A Turley, Mr John Morris & Mr Nevil, were sought for by their parents. They were buried alive in dirt, recently fallen down the bluff. They were all dead. –Memphis [Tenn] Eagle

Alex'r Prince, former postmaster at Hamburg, Erie Co, N Y, had plead guilty to an indictment for embezzling letters as postmaster, & been sentenced to the State prison for 10 years.

Among the passengers in the ship **Great Western** at N Y from Liverpool, were the Hon Reverdy Johnson, lady, & family, of Balt, & Dabney S Carr, U S Minister at Constantinople.

By virtue of a writ of fieri facias issued by John H Goddard, J P for Wash Co: public sale for cash, on Nov 6, opposite the Centre Market-house, one sorrel mare & one bay horse, seized & taken as the property of David Cushwa, & will be sold to satisfy a judgment in favor of John G Hewes. –R R Burr, constable

Mrd: on Oct 29, at *Kalorama*, by Rev Mr French, Cmder John S Paine, U S Navy, to Ruth Theodora, d/o Col Bomford, U S Army.

Mrd: on Oct 28, by Rev Mr Eggleston, Mr Wm Conner, of Alexandria, to Miss Rebecca Prather, all of Wash City.

Died: in Gtwn, D C, Stephen Rawlings, in his 42nd year. [No date-appears recent.]

A white chicken with 4 legs is now in the possession of Mr Richd Cruit, of Gtwn. The bird was raised in PG Co, Md. The chicken is alive & well.

SAT NOV 1, 1845
Just received & for sale at Jos H France's Cigar store, a very superior lot of imported Cigars, not to be equaled by any in this city. Wholesale & retail dealer in Cigars, Tobacco, & Snuff, 7th st, between D & E sts, sign of the Indian, 2 doors from the Intelligencer Ofc.

Mrs S H McGragor, the talented lady who has met the smiles of an enlightened public for the last 4 years, will lecture at Todd's Concert Hall this Sat, on the science of Phrenology, examine the heads of Ladies & Gentlemen in public, & tell their predominant passions. She will perform Vocal & Instrumental Music, & practical illustrations in Magnetism, provided there can be a subject selected. Admittance 25 cents, to examine the head 50 cents.

For rent: 2 large brick houses on 10th st, between D & E sts. Apply to F Masi & Co, Pa ave, between 9th 10th sts.

John W Bronaugh has engaged in the business of Grocer & Commission Merchant, one square west of the Market space, on the south side of the Canal, Gtwn.

Auction Goods: Thos T Barnes has just opened a very extensive assortment of goods, bought at the Northern auctions very low, & will be sold at a very small advance: includes cloths, woolen cloaking, linseys, flannels, curtain musline, woolen carpenting, & figured Crumb Cloth.

Orphans Court of Wash Co, D C. Letters testamentary on the personal estate of Benj Kinsley, late of said county, dec'd. –Jas T Smull, exc

Mr Wm J Brown, a Rep in the last Congress from Indiana, has been appointed 2nd Assist Postmaster Genr'l, in place of Wm Medill, of Ohio, now Com'r of Indian Affairs. -Union

Norfolk correspondent of the Phil North American says: Cmdor Parker, it is understood, is to have the Boston Yard, Cmdor Perry the West India station, & Cmdor Jones the African squadron. The flag-ship **Congress** to be of the Pacific station, & Cmdor Bolton is to go to the Mediterranean. The orders for the return of the frig **Cumberland** have been revoked; she will finish her cruise, & be relieved by the flag-ship of Cmdor Bolton.

Appointment by the Pres: Robt L Longhead, of Pa, Consul of the U S for the port of Londonderry, in Ireland, in place of Jas McDowell, declined.

John M Auley, aged 55, an only son of honorable parents, & a graduate of Princeton College, died in the Poor House of Orange Co, N Y, on Oct 21. He was in the army during the war.

A man whose name is supposed to be Chas C Foote, about 45 years of age, fell down & died suddenly on board the steamboat **Buffalo**, just as she left Detroit for Buffalo, a few days since.

List of letters remaining in the Post Ofc, Wash, Nov 1, 1845.

Angel, Thos or Jno	Brown, Mrs Reb C	Bailey, Jesse
Allen, Mrs Eliz	Bonn, Philip	Butler, Miss Maria
Armstrong, Capt Jas, U S N	Bibbs, Anthony	Baker, D B
	Brown, Wm Linn	Braiden, Miss Eliz
Adams, Geo	Brown, Geo	Bogety, Francis
Antrim, A J	Brent, Wm L	Buffington, G W & A S
Brown, Wm D	Brent, Jas Robt	Bryann, Thos E
Blood, C H-3	Bathan, John	Ballade, Mrs Col'ba
Bontz, Henry	Bachman, Rev Dr J	Bevens, John L
Bell, Jacob E	Barnard, Edw	Byers, S
Brooke, Gideon	Baker, Mrs Ellen	Bradford, Prof
Berth, Jas	Benedict, W B, U S N	Carr, Geo Watson

Cross, Jos-2
Crain, Miss M C-2
Chase, Miss Eliz
Chase, T B
Crown, Jeremiah
Cole, John
Coe, Saml A
Crump, Geo W-4
Carter, Miss Eliza F
Coffin, Isaac N
Cunningham, Gen W
Cooper, Lloyd N
Chenney, Jas W
Collins, Jane B
Collins, Mrs Nancy J
Cooper, Miss Harr't
Chaney, jr, Thos
Clements, Col R E
Corbin, P Mid T G
Chaney, Mrs S Ann
Clement, John
Cridler, Isabella
Cochran, Mrs Ann
Comstock, Nathl
Collins, P McD-3
Cushman, C C-2
Clements, Alban
Dodge, Joshua
Day, Q W
Duke, Lt Nathl W
Dutton, G U S Eng
De Koven, Pd Md W
Dyer, jr, Mid Chas
Donley, Miss W A
Donovan, Michl
Downing, Jas R
Dailey, O A
Davis, Wm
David, Jas
Dougherty, John
Dugan, Miss Julia A
Duvall, gen J P
Dixon, Jas

Doniphan, Dr
Davis, W W
Ewing, Col G W-2
Evans, Edwin G
Emann, Saml
Ennis, Jas A
Enos, A W
Estis, R
Emack, Wm
Eustis, Geo
Everett, Lt Col Geo
Evans, B A
Ennis, John F
Eaton, Gen Lewis
Edelin, Capt Jas
Ford, S P
Fease, Geo
Fales, Mrs Eliza
Fay, Henry C
Freasure, Mr
Ferguson, Wm
Faron, Edw
Farry, J L U S A
Forret, H F
Freeman, John D
Fowler, Jas J
Fletcher, Mrd Han'a
Fischer, A A
Fobey, Addison F
Fowler, Rob B
Fenwick, Jas S
Fitzhew, John
Green, Gardner-2
Gray, Rev S T
Galt, Capt P H
Graeff, Miss A M
Giberson, Gilbert
Gibson, Nathl-2
Gaither, John
Gordon, Chas
Gordon, D S
Goodrich, Wm
Horn, E J

Harte, Edw
Heath, Robt
Hill, Miss Eliza
Hall, Edw
Hodge, Wm
Hunt, Lt Col T F
Hawkins, Chas G-2
Hurlbert, Henry F
Hopkins, Mrs A M
Hooper, Chas H
Hooper, Mrs Cath
Hickey, Miss A O
Hinman, David-2
Hoffman, Josiah
Hipkins, John
Henry, Miss
Heyden, C W
Herbert, Geo
Harper, Wm
Hockrote, A G
Hunter, Jas
Harrison, Maria L
Jourdan, Jas
Jeffrey, Dr R W
Jefferis, Thos
Johnson, Lewis F
Jenkins, Fanny
Johnson, F W-2
Jackson, Mrs M A-3
Jackson, Geo C-2
Jenifer, Danl-3
King, Mrs C C
King, Jos W
King, Wm
Keabel, Jacob
Kennard, John H
Kevill, Lawrence
Lee, Capt R C
Lodge, Rebecca
Lewis, Thos
Lister, John W
Lewis, Reeve
Luther, Mrs Sarah

Little, Mrs C	Norris, Wm	Ringgold, Fred'k
Lockerman, Jere'h	Nally, Miss Mary C	Randolph, J B-U S N-2
Lowry, Geo W	Nelson, Chas N	Randolph, Peyton
Lucas, Miss Eliza	O'Brien, P W	Richardson, Ira
Leffler, Sheppard	O'Neil, Geo P	Ryder, Rev Jas
Lairy, Mrs Jane	O'Sullivan, Timothy	Smith, Mrs Lucinda
Ledyard, Monsieur	O'Reilly, H O	Smith, Miss Cath'e
Loeihtel, Andrew	Osgood, John A	Smith, Mrs Ellen
Merritt, Henry	Officer, Thos	Smith, Geo Clinton
Matthews, David	Pool, Rev Wm C	Scott, Wm H
Maxwell, Francis	Post, Waldon B	Smith, Miss Lizzy
Monroe, Mid A	Pratt, Lt W C	Smith, Mrs John H
Menger, M B	Pratt, Saml	Shap, W D
Mergoun, Robt	Pierce, Richd	Smith, Henry
Morrison, J H C	Plumber, Mrs E	Smith, Jas
Mister, Capt Isaac	Perry, Wm	Sheets, Wm & Co
Molloy, Francis P	Pedlar, Peter	Symms, Miss Fanny
Manning, J H	Prindell, Mary Jane	Smith, Miss Fannie L
Martin, David	Parket, Geo W	Stark, Rev Dr
Merz, Aquilin	Perrie, Mrs Sophia	Smith, Geo
Mitchell, Dr J W S	Pickett, Miss Ann J	Smith, Robt
Mitchell, John	Pierre, Wm	Scott, Wm
Moran, Wm E	Pinkney, Rev Wm	Smith, Wm M-2
Morrison, Mrs Ma'a	Pleasants, Hes [col]	Smith, Miss Caroline
Mason, Mrs J T	Parker, F A U S N	Suarez, Leonardo S-2
Macy, John B-3	Queen, Col Nicholas	Spencer, John C
Mattingly, Y J	Quimby, Thos R	Stanton, W C
Marino, Lt M C	Rich, Lt D C	Sanders, Geo N
Martin, Barkley	Rhett, Lt Thos G-2	Simmons, Wash
Miller, T M	Ricks, Jas T-2	Seely, John M
Miller, Rev J W	Rose, H R	Sutton, Miss M L
Miller, Royal E	Rhodes, Jos W S	Somerville, W T
Marcy, Lahan-2	Robey, Miss M C	Stewart, Mrs Lucy
Mulloy, Wm A	Robinson, Jas W	Spradley, David
Mason, John T-2	Roberson, Hannah F	Seiler, F W
Mackey, Philip	Rigdon, Miss Anna	Sommers, Miss Eliza
Magee, Mrs Arab'a	Robinson, E W-2	Snodgrass, John
McLean, John	Robins, Mrs C C	Sickels, Fred E-3
McLauchlin, B L	Rollett, Edw	True, Loring B
McCarty, Wm	Richmond, Miss M	Thrift, Miss R M
McIntosh, Robt L-2	Ransom, Robt F	Thompson, Miss J E
McCarty, Robt	Russell, Otis F	Tully, Myles M
McCorkle, J W-3	Ruffield, Miss Louisa	Tilghman, Wm M-2

Tenney, Miss Mary	Westcott, Rev W A	Wethby, Thos
Terore, Miss Eliza	Whealer, Miss Julia	Warren, Jas B
Truscott, John	Wilson, Edw	Waters, D S
Thomkins, Mrs M A	Woodrock, B	Wilson, Micajah
Tolson, Edw	Wilson, Mrs Jas T	Weaver, Mrs C M
Taylor, Stark B	Watson, Miss M E	Williams, John W
Thornton, D U F, U S N	Wallace, Geo W	Winters, Miss Mary
Taylor, Henry C	Walker, Saml W	Whitlock, Wm D-2
Underwood, Miss K	Whistler, Geo W	Warren, Miss R
Wright, Chas J	Williams, Rev Wm	Wilson, Thos
West, Chas	Washington, Simon	Whitmore, H C
Ward, Saml	Warren, Henry	Young, Miss Tracenia
Wise, John	Watterson, H M	Young, Wm [color]
Ward, W	Wallace, John	Young, Richd
Ward, Henry	Walters, Capt Jas	

The inland postage on all letters intended to go by ship must be paid, otherwise they remain in this ofc. -C K Gardner, P M

Just received: the Author's Daughter, a Tale, by Mary Howitt, price 25 cents. Memoirs of An American Lady, by Mrs Grant, price 30 cents. Cries of N Y, with 15 illustrations, by F S Osgood, price 25 cents. Harpers' Bible, #41, price 25 cents. –G Brooke & Co, right on the corner of Pa av & 15th st, Wash.

Attempt yesterday to rob Dr J C Hall, on Pa ave, & possibly set the house on fire. Dr Hall gave the alarm & the rascal made his escape. The hope is the villain will be speedily discovered & arrested.

Mrd: on Oct 29, by Rev Smith Pyne, T B Huger, of Charleston, S C, to Mariamne, y/d/o the late Richd W Meade, of Phil.

Mrd: on Oct 21, by Rev A L Hitselberger, Walter J Doyle to Miss Celestia E Reardon, eldest d/o Henry B Reardon, of Wash City.

Died: at the residence of T Washington Gough, Richd Forrest, aged 25 years, s/o Gen Jas Forrest, late of St Mary's Co, Md, dec'd. [No date-recent.]

Died: on Oct 17, at the residence of his father, Dr Richd McSherry, at Martinsburg, Va, Wm Du Bourg McSherry, in his 21st year, a young gentleman of great worth, whose sudden death is a severe bow to his numerous relatives & friends.

Died: at Portsmouth, N H, John Haven, aged 79, an upright merchant & a true gentleman. [No date-lately.]

Died: on Sep 26, in camp, at Corpus Christi, Texas, after a painful illness, contracted at Key West, Lt Jas Overing Handy, of the 8th Regt U S Infty, aged 22 years, s/o the late Thos Handy, of Newport, R I.

MON NOV 3, 1845
Monseigneur Clement de Droat Wischering, Archbishop of Cologne, expired at Munster on Oct 14.

Mr Jos Myers, residing near Mercersburg, Franklin Co, Pa, met his death a short time ago, by falling from a hay loft through a hatchway on a fork handle, which penetrated his body & caused his death in 20 hours.

At Liberty, Indiana, a few days since, Mr Archibald Ested struck Mr Haslem over the head with a chair, killing him instantly. Mr Ested gave himself up, & was held to bail in the sum of $2,000.

The Common Council of Boston has passed an order offering a reward of $1,000 for the apprehension of Albert J Tirrell, charged with the murder of Maria Bickford. [Nov 5th newspaper: Albert J Tirrell, the Boston murderer, was arrested on Sun, & passed over the Long Island Railroad on Monday for Boston. He is supposed to have been taken in N J or Phil.] [Nov 7th newpaper: the man arrested was not Tirrell, but another criminal.] [Dec 18th newpaper: Albert J Tirrell was arrested at New Orleans on Dec 5: he was arrested on board a ship from N Y, where he had shipped under the assumed named of Wm Dennis.]

On Oct 24, the towboat **Persian** was towing up to New Orleans the ships **Thos B Wales** & **Tyrian**, & both her boilers exploded, scalding the following: C Crowley, 1st engineer- dangerously; Geo Clinton, the mate, Mr Wagner, the carpenter, J Arnold, the pilot, & Wood, the steersman, [a colored man,] slightly scalded. Three of the firemen have since died, one named Donohoo, the others not known. [Nov 8th newspaper: Captain of the **Persian** has been held to bail in the sum of $2,000 for his appearance before the Dist Court of La, to answer charges relative to the catastrophe.] [No name given for the Capt.]

Mr Douglass Houghton, State Geologist of Michigan, was drowned near Eagle river, Lake Superior, during a violent snow storn on Oct 13. He had 4 men with him, 2 of whom were also drowned. Most of his papers were saved. Although a young man, he had acquired a very respectable rank among the scientific men of the country, & was endeared to a large circle of friends & acquaintances.

Crawford Burnett & his wife Lavinia have been sentenced to be hung at Fayetteville, Arkansas, for being accessories to the murder of Jonathan Sibley. The deed was committed by their son & his cousin.

Inquest was held over the dec'd remains of Mr Lazarus Maddox, at his residence near Dublin, on Fri last, Verdict: death by blow supposed to have been inflicted by his wife & son. The latter, Geo Maddox, was immediately arrested & lodged in the county jail to await his trial. –Somerset [Md] Herald

The New Judge of the Criminal Court, Thos Hartley Crawford, of Pa, will take his seat upon the bench in the Court of Alexandria Co this morning, when the Nov term commences its session. He desires to reside in Alexandria, & it will give pleasure to our whole community.

Died: on Nov 1, Saml Harrison Smith, in his 74th year. His funeral is this day, at half-past 1 o'clock, from his late residence.

The large brick mill, occupied for the manufacture of cotton goods by Chas Richmond, at Taunton, Mass, was destroyed by fire on Thu.

A fire broke out in the wooden factory at Union Village, Wash Co, N Y, on Sat, & destroyed the factory & its contents; also a chair & pail factory, owned by Calvin Fenton.

Circuit Court of Wash Co, D C: in the case of Thos W Morris & his wife Caroline M, [late Calvert,] against Chas B Calvert, exc of Geo Calvert & others, Richd S Coxe concluded the argument on the part of the cmplnt. Jos H Bradley & Gen Jones addressed the Court on the other side. No decision made as yet.

New bldgs in Wash City: 1-Commodious dwlg at the corner of 4½ st & La ave, a place of residence for Philip R Fendall. Erected by Mr Douglas, carpenter, & Messrs Cassell & Wise, bricklayer. 2-Two large 3 story houses, recently erected on the east side of 6th st, near the Unitarian Church, one for Thos Blagden, the other for Mr Francis Mohun. These houses are already occupied by Purser Stockton & Mrs Cheshire. They were built by Mr Peter Heavener, bricklayer, & Mr F Mohun, carpenter. 3-Opposite, & adjoining the dwlg of Mr Hewitt, there is being erected for Mr Alex'r Lee an extensive dwlg by Mr W G Deale, carpenter, & Mr Lowe, bricklayer.

John Williams, [Sailor Jack-had one arm] came to his death suddenly on Nov 2, 1845, at the dwlg of a colored man, named Burgess, on Canal st. He had been cared for by the colored people for several days.

A young & healthy woman wants a situation as Wet Nurse. She can come well recommended. Apply to Mrs Catherine Thompson, living near Coleman's Tan-yard, near the lower bridge, Gtwn.

China, Glass, & Queen's Ware: T A Lazenby, Bridge st, next door to Union Bank, Gtwn. [Ad]

TUE NOV 4, 1845
Gen Geo Gibson & Maj T P Andrews appointed to confer with the Delegation of Pottawatamie Indians now in Wash City upon matters between them & the U S.

West Chester [Pa] Village Recorder: Jesse Kersey, long know as a minister of the Friends' Society, passed away on Oct 25, at an advanced age. For many years he has been physically very infirm, & rarely appeared in public. His fame had spread to both sides of the Atlantic; & in England, as elsewhere.

On Tue last the dwlg house of Mr Noah Brown, about 1½ miles east of Edinburgh, Ohio, was discovered to be on fire, & the house & 2 of Mr Brown's children were consumed by the flames. –Wayne Co Standard

Wm Smith, the Mormon Patriarch, had addressed a long letter to his brethren, in which he dissuades them from listening to the counsel of Brigham Young, & his associates at Nauvoo.

The Hon John A Bryan, late U S Charge d'Affaires to Peru, arrived at New Orleans on Oct 25 from Havana, on his return home. He left Lima on Sep 7, at which time all was quiet there.

A few days since, Miss Eliza Baker, housekeeper of Rev Mr Huntoon, while lighting a camphene lamp, the lamp exploded setting fire to her clothing. She was so burnt that she died the next day. –Boston Jour

Mr Hiram Tharp, of Morristown, N J, was dangerously injured on Thu last by falling off a ladder while painting a house. He fell about 30 feet. Although dangerously wounded, he is recovering. -Jerseyman

Mrd: on Sunday last, by Rev Mr Wilson, Mr Wm J Matlock, of Wash, to Miss Eliz Kelly, of the Eastern Shore, Md.

Mrd: on Nov 2, by Rev Mr Bean, Mr T P Venable to Miss Mary J O'Donall, all of Wash City.

Mrd: on Oct 9, in Circleville, Ohio, by Rev Jas Britton, B F Brannan, late of Wash, to Mary E, d/o the late Rev Jos Doddridge, of Va.

Died: on Oct 9, at Richland, his residence, in Boone Co, Missouri, Dr A W Rollins, formerly of Richmond, Ky, in his 63rd year.

Died: on Oct 30, at his residence, in Middletown, Chas Co, Md, after a few days' illness, Terance Duffy, a native of Ireland, but a resident of Md for the last 27 years, highly esteemed by a large body of friends & acquaintances.

WED NOV 5, 1845
Franklin Ins Co, Wash.
Directors:
J H Bradley	Dr J M Roberts	Dr J C Hall	Chas Bradley,
J Boyle	Jas McCleary	W A Bradley	Sec
J F Callan	A Coyle	W J McDonald	
W Lenox	J P Ingle	G C Grammer,	
	S H Hill	Pres	

Capt Thos Duling, tried in the U S Dist Court at Phil on a charge of serving on board the brig **Washington's Barge**, on the Coast of Africa, while that vessel was engaged in the slave-trade, has been acquitted.

Gen Gideon Foster, a veteran of the Revolution, died on Sun last at his residence in Danvers, Mass, at the advanced aged of 96.

C Buckingham has for sale a Fire Engine complete, made in the best manner, with copper box. Inquire at the subscriber's, on C st, between 10th & 11th sts. He still continues the Black & Whitesmith's business.

THU NOV 6, 1845
The Village Register [Salem, Ohio] tells that a suit for damages for breach of marriage promise just closed in the Wayne Co Common Pleas. The suit was brought by Miss Mary Fleming vs Thos Eckhart, & resulted in a verdict of $2,250 for the plntf.

One of the early pioneers of Cleveland, Ohio, died on Oct 31. Abraham Hickox died at age 81: visited the then wilderness site of the city of Cleveland in 1807, & in 1809 removed there with his family from Connecticut. He was a mechanic & many well remember the sign, "Uncle Abram works here," on the brow of the hill, now the head of Superior st. It was changed to where the Weddell House now towers.
-Evening Herald

Drowned himself in Monmouth, N H, on Wed of last week, Bezer L Story. He had been married but 6 weeks before, & his wife had left him in consequence of a dispute about the disposition of her property.

Pamell, who shot & killed Bland, in a drunken mock-duel at Cincinnati some time since, had his trial in the Court of Common Please last week, & was acquitted by the jury.

Troy Whig of Sat mentions the death of Lt J Russell Soley, 4th Regt of Artl, & an Aid-de-Camp to Gen Wool, who died on Fri at the residence of Dr Brinsmade, in Troy, of disease of the brain. Lt Soley had been for some time a resident of that city. He was a fine young man, only 29 years of age.

Wash Corp: 1-Ptn of Jas Williams & others, for a gravel footway on 4th st: referred to the Cmte on Improvements. 2-Bill for the relief of John Donovan: reported the same without amendment. 3-Ptn of Wm J Bronaugh: Cmte of Claims asked to be discharged from its further consideration. 4-Cmte of Claims: bill for the relief of P L Leman: read twice. 5-Ptn of John F Caho, praying permission to move a frame bldg within 24 feet of a brick stable: referred to the Cmte on Improvements. 6-Cmte of Claimss: adverse to the ptn of Robt Farnham. 7-Bill for the relief of Wm J Geffeir: referred to the Cmte of Claims.

Valuable improved property in Montg Co, Md, for sale at public auction. Under authority of a deed of trust executed on Aug 17, 1842, by John Poole & Ann R Poole his wife, recorded in Liber H S #11, folios 262 & 266, in the land records of said county: sale on the premises, near to Colesville, Md, part of a tract called *Peach's Lot*, being part of a tract called *Beaver Dam*, & part of a tract called *Snowden's Manor Enlarged*, containing 54 acres 2 roods & 34 perches, more or less. Also, all that tract of land called *Fine Meadows*, it being part of 2 tracts of land, one called *Saint Winoxberg*, & the other *Poplar Point*, containing 34 acres 16 perches, more or less. Also, all that tract or parcel of land called *Addition*, being part of a tract called *Good Luck*, containing 3 acres 1 rood & 17 perches, more or less. Also, part of the *Second Addition to Culver's Chance*, formerly the property of Milberne Semmes, containing 100 acs, more or less; together with the bldgs & improvements on the said several tacts, reserving, however, to Edw Dawes, his heirs & assigns forever, all the rights & privileges to a mill-race as described in a certain deed from Richd Smith & others to John Poole, dated Aug 15, 1842. The sale will take place on Nov 27 at 12 o'clock. –Rd Smith, Trustee

Mrd: on Oct 21, at Gap-View, Jefferson Co, Va, by Rev Dr Jones, Benj Franklin Washington, of Charlestown, to Georgiana Hite, d/o Jas L Ranson.

Died: on Sunday, in the city of Albany, N Y, Angus McDuffie, aged 54 year & 8 months. He was formerly sheriff of Albany Co, agent of the Sing Sing State Prison, & at the time of his death was captain of the special police. He was respected for his personal qualities.

House for rent: on Dec 1 next, the new 3 story brick house, now occupied by Amos Kendall, on 12th st, between Pa ave & E st. Inquire of David Munro, near the premises.

FRI NOV 7, 1845
Died: on Nov 3, at Alexandria, Mrs Sarah L Waters, w/o Thos A Waters, after a protracted illness of pulmonary disease.

The Sons of New England: meeting of the citizens of Wash disposed to form a Society to commemorate the early history of New England, was held on Nov 3: David A Hall, acting Chairman; N C Towle, Sec. Association to be called" The New England Society of the District of Columbia."

Sun-Nov 3. Mr C Aisquith, a mechant of Charlestown, Jefferson Co, Va, was accidentally killed when his gun went off, discharging its contents in his head. He was attempting to get on his horse at the time.

Rev Dr Beaseley died at his family residence in Elizabethtown on Sat, aged 68 years, leaving a large family circle to mourn his loss. He was formerly Provost of the Univ of Pa, but he several years since retired from active service. –Newark Adv

Boston papers: Leopold Herwig, the well-known violinist died, suddenly. He led the first oveture at the concert of the Philharmonic Society, Boston, Sat last, but returned to his residence at an early hour in consequence of a slight indisposition. He had a second attack, which proved fatal. He had some time past been afflicted with a disease of the heart.

Annapolis Star: Jonas Green died after a lingering illness of several years, at the age of 66. He was for many years the editor & proprietor of the Md Gazette, the first newspaper printed in the Province of Md. [No date-recent news.]

At the late Circuit Court, Whiteplains, Westchester Co, N Y, Miss Conklin, a lady rising 40 years of age, obtained a verdict of $4,000 against Mr Addison Hill, of about the same age, for breach of promise of marriage.

Mrd: Nov 4, by Rev J Hoffman Waugh, Thos P Morgan to Caroline, d/o Townshend Waugh, all of Wash.

Mrd: on Nov 4, at the First Presbyterian Church, by Rev Dr Parker, of Phil, the Rev Chas H Ewing, of Phil, to Miss Charlotte Eliz, d/o Jery L Page, of Fairfax Co, Va.

Mrd: on Oct 30, by Rev Jas T Johnston, Henry W Davis to Constance, d/o the late Wm C Gardner, all of Alexandria.

Died: on Oct 9, at Paris, David Bailie Warden, aged 67 years. He was Sec of the U S Legation in France, nearly 40 years of age, when Gen Armstrong was Minister, & was appointed U S Consul at Paris, which ofc he held for several years. He was a member of the French Academy & it is believed he was a native of Ireland.

Household & kitchen furniture at auction: on Nov 7, at the residence of Martin Murphy, on Pa ave. –A Green, auctioneer

Female Union Benevolent Society: meeting on Nov 4, in the Presbyterian Church, 4½ st.
Directresses:
Mrs Laurie
Mrs O B Brown
Managers:
Mrs W A Bradly
Mrs Anderson
Mrs Cox
Mrs L Powell
Mrs Easby
Mrs Tucker
Mrs John Davis
Mrs E Stelle

Mrs M St C Clarke
Mrs Mills

Mrs Purdy
Mrs Milburne
Mrs Doct Bradley
Mrs Lyons
Mrs Col Munroe
Mrs Macomb
Mrs Conly
Mrs Drake

Mrs J F Webb, Sec
Mrs Jos Ingle, Treas

Mrs Morton
Mrs F Hall
Mrs Rice
Miss M Moore
Miss Lucy Stott
Miss Rebecca Lowry
Mrs King

On Sunday last, the steamboat **Columbus**, on her regular trip from Balt to Richmond, ran foul of the small schnr **John Roberts**, of Va, Somerset Co, Va, in which 2 men, Wm Larmer & Wm Garret were knocked overboard. Larmer drowned; Garrett was only saved by having his hand caught, which was shockingly crushed.

At Pittsburg on Mon, a young man J T Bradford, employed as a shearer at the Kensington Iron Works, became caught in the cogwheels of some of the rolls & was killed. He was a native of Somershetshire, in England, about 24 years of age, & bore a most excellent character.

For rent: house near the corner of F & 20th sts, lately the residence of Maj Jos Forrest, dec'd. Apply to Bladen Forrest, at his ofc, near Gen Van Ness', or at his residence, Cox'r row, Gtwn.

SAT NOV 8, 1845
New Periodical & Cheap Publication Store, Pa ave, 2nd door from corner of 12th st, Wash. -Wm Thomson

On Fri, as a little child of Mr Geo Adams, about 3 years of age, was playing in the yard of his dwlg, in Camden Co, N J, it was suddenly set upon with great fury by one of Mr Adam's hogs, &, before effectual assistance could be rendered, was literally torn to pieces, & immediately killed. An older sister, in attempting to rescue the child, was also seized by the hog, & had her arm seriously mangled.

Danl Mogarth, a murder, was executed in Van Wert Co, Ohio, on Nov 3.

A Swindler. Benj F Waters, a carriage manufacturer of South Hadley, Canal Village, recently left for parts unknown, leaving a host of deluded creditors to mourn his exit. He decamped his liabilities were $25,000 to $35,000, the fruits of which he must have taken with him. –Boston Cour

Our esteemed fellow-citizen Christopher Hughes is on a visit to Wash City. We are glad to see this worthy gentleman return home in firm health, from a 30 years' service of his country abroad.

Mr David G Yost, one of the oldest & most worthy citizens of Hagerstown, Md, committed suicide last Wed by shooting himself. Pecuniary embarrassment, producing much distress of mind, & partial derangement, is assigned as the probable cause which led to this fatal act.

Wisconsin Territory District Court, Fond du Lac Co, May Term, 1845. Satterlee Clark, jr, & Frances E Clark, vs Satterlee Clark, senior. Eastman, for plntfs. Martin, for dfndnt. In the matter of the ptn for com'rs to be appointed in inquire into the insanity of Satterlee Clark, senior, the Court appoint Henry Conklin, Geo McWilliams, & Warren Chase com'rs to inquire into the insanity of said Satterlee Clark, senior. Oct 14, 1845. It is considered & adjudged by the Court that the report be & the same is hereby quashed, & the petitioners, Satterlee Clark, jr, & Frances E Clark, pay the costs of the proceedings. I, Isaac Brown, Clerk of said District Court, do hereby certify that the above is a true copy of the record in the above entitled cause. –Isaac Brown, Clerk

Mrd: on Nov 6, by Rev W G Eggleston, Mr Richd G Hyatt to Miss Margaret A, d/o Mr Jas Lawrenson, all of Wash City.

Mrd: on Nov 4, by Rev Mr Tarring, Mr Wm J Douglass to Miss Sarah Virginia Darnes, all of Wash City.

Charlestown, Va, Nov 7. On Thus, Mr Henry Brown, the agent of the Winchester Railroad at Harper's Ferry, his son Wm, & Mr Henry Gasker, with several others, were engaged in pushing an iron car, laden with coal, when a porton of the trussel work at the bridge over the road leading to the Shenandoah river gave way, precipitating all engaged, with the car, & burying them beneath the coal. Wm Brown & Mr Gasker were killed, & Henry Brown was taken much injured, & his recovery doubtful.

MON NOV 10, 1845
Appointments by the Pres:
1-Jas Clarke, Govn'r of the Territory of Iowa, in place of John Chambers, removed.
2-Jos S May, Postmaster at Apalachicola, in Florida, in place of Geo F Baltzell, resigned.

The Shawneetown Gaz states that all the persons who were lost by the recent collision of the steamboat **Lady Madison** & the steamboat **Plymouth**, on the Ohio river, were German emigrants. Some 25 or 30 are missing. [No names were given.]

Mechanical Riflemen monthly meeting this Mon, at half past 7. –W F Connell, sec

Exercise & Economy: only 6¼ cents for 30 balls at Farrar's Bowling Saloon, & for rent a warm room attached to the Saloon, suitable for keeping snacks, & confectionery, on moderate terms. –John M Farrar, Missouri ave, near 6th st.

Pilot boat **Fell's Point**, which left the port of Balt a considerable time ago, has not since been heard from, & feared she has been lost, with all hands on board, some 8 or 9 souls.

TUE NOV 11, 1845

French's Hotel, Norfolk, Va: having reached that period of life which renders retirement agreeable, I offer for sale my interest in the above Hotel. This hotel was built in 1837 by a Joint Stock Co & incorporated by an act of the Legislature in 1832. It contains about 80 rooms. The largest Naval depot in the Union is here. -Wm French

Jas Powers was about to be tried in Salem last Wed for a crime punishable with death, when, to the surprise of all, the prosecution was withdrawn, the girl whom he had injured having become his wife that morning, & thus by law was encapable of testifying against him.

The steamer **Confidence** arrived at Hannibal, Mo, on Oct 25, with about 200 Pa Germans on board. They are from Westmoreland & Beaver counties, & from 500 to 600 more are expected from the same counties during the present season. They are all going to Shelby Co, Mo, where the united colony will make about 3,000 souls. They have been settling there for a year past.

Gen Chas Cuvellier, an old & respectable citizen of New Orleans, died in that city on Fri week. He was a resident of 30 years' standing, & for 20 years had commanded the Louisiana Legion. He had been Recorder of the 3rd Municipality, & Superintendent of the Public Schools in the 1st Municipality.

Fire at Wilmington, N C a short time since: owners of the bldgs destroyed: Jas Bradley, estate Julius Walker, Danl B Baker, Gen Dudley, estate Thos Cowan, Thos H Wright, Thos Cowan Griffith, J McRee, John Iver McMillan, John Brown, Wm N Peden, P K Dickinson, Mrs Lord, sr, John Walker, Richd Bradley, Nicholas N Nixon, Mrs H Urquhart, Dr Jas R McRee, Wm Love, jr, Wm Distrac, estate Wm J Harris, Joshua G Wright.

Recent accident at Ware, Mass: Mr Chancey L Root, engaged in erecting 2 new & large mills for the Otis Manufacturing Co, was with 3 of the men in his employ, & all were precipitated from the 5th floor, falling about 45 feet. Mr Root died the next morning. It is thought the others will recover.

For rent: 2 story brick dwlg-house on 5th st, & now occupied by Mr John D Butler, who will leave in a few days. Apply to Henry L Carlton, in Bladensburg, or to Saml Clark, Surgeon Dentist, 11th & Pa ave, Wash.

Pittsburg [Pa] Gaz: Beware of a Villain. Some 10 years since a fiend in human form, named John G B Robinson, age 39 years, came here from N Y, where he left a wife & child. Here he married a highly respectable young lady, whom he has now left with 2 children, after robbing her of several thousand dollars, entrusted to establish him in business. One of his aliases is Edwin Robinson. –G

Mrd: on Nov 6, by Rev J N McJilton, of Balt, John R Piper, M D, & Mary L Cheshire, of Wash City.

Died: on Nov 5, at Middleburg, Va, Martha Frances Campbell, eldest d/o Saml Campbell.

Died: on Nov 10, at the residence of his brother, Richd Henry Hall, in Balt, Osborne Sprigg Hall, for many years a Clerk in the Treasury Dept, at Wash, aged 48 years. His funeral is Nov 12 at 11 o'clock, from the residence of his brother, on Howard st.

WED NOV 12, 1845
On Nov 4 Mr Artemas Richardson, of Keene, N H, was sporting with a dirk-knife in a bar-room, when he accidentally stuck it into his thigh, cutting the main artery, & bled to death immediately.

On Sun week, a gentleman, Thos Davis, a passenger in the schnr **Dorchester**, from Great Wycomico river, Northumberland Co, Va, was accidentally knocked overboard by the boom, & sunk before assistance could reach him. The body has not yet been recovered. -Patriot

Medical Notice: Dr Wm A McDowell, with a view of directing his attention more especially to diseases of the chest, will hereafter practice his profession, from Nov 15 to May 15, in New Orleans, & from Jun 1 to Nov 1 in Louisville, Ky.

For rent: convenient cottage, on 9th st, near N Y ave. Inquire of John C Harkness, N Y ave, one door west of the Rev John C Smith.

For rent: 3 story brick house on Pa ave, & 4 ½ st. Apply to Geo Watterston, Capitol Hill. –C B Hamilton

$100 reward for runaway negro Richd Neale, 25 years of age; ran away from the residence of Noble S Braden, 5 miles west of Leesburg, Loudoun Co, Va. Thos Rogers, Deputy of A Gibson, late Sheriff of Loudoun, Va, & administrator of Geo M Chichester.

Members of the Cincinnati of Maryland: [Name & rank; term of service; dismission; residence]
Maj Gen Wm Smallwood; 7 y 10 mo; dis army 1785; Chas Co
Govn'r Wm Pace; ele'td 1783; [blank]; Annapolis
Brig Gen:
Mordecai Gist; 7 y 10 mo; Dissolu'n 1783; Balt
Otho H Williams; 7 years; Spe res'n 1783; Balt
Jno Gunby; 7 years; Dissolution; Somerset Co
J Carroll Hall; 5 years; Reformed 1781; Harford Co
Jno H Stone; 3 y 3 mo; Resigned 1779; Annapolis
Lt Col:
Saml Smith; 3 y 6 mo; Resigned 1779; Balt
John E Howard; 7 years; Deranged 1783; Balt
Tench Tilghman; 6 years; Dissolution; Balt
Levin Winder; 7 y 10 mo; Dissolution; Somerset Co
Nathan Ramsey; 5 years; Reformed 1781; Annapolis
Thos Woolford; 7 years; Reformed 1783; Dorchester Co
Moses Rawlins; 4 years; Resigned 1779; Wash Co
Major:
John Swann; 6 y 11 mo; Dissolution; Balt
John Lynch; 7 years; Dissolution; Balt
John Eccleston; 7 y 10 mo; Dissolution, Dorchester Co
Henry Hardman; 7 y 5 mo; Dissolution; Fred'k Co
David Hopkins; 8 years; Dissolution; Anne Arundel Co
John Gale; 6 years; Dissolution; Somerset Co
Wm Brown; 7 years; Dissolution; Annapolis
John Carlisle; 7 years; Dissolution; Harford Co
Benj Brooks; 7 years; Reformed 1783; PG Co
Thos Lansdale; 7 years; Reformed 1783; PG Co
Wm D Beall; 7 years; Reformed 1783; PG Co
John Davidson; 7 years; Reformed 1783; Annapolis
Jon Sellman; 7 years; Deranged 1783; Annapolis
Capt:
Jacob Brice; 7 y 4 mo; Dissolution; Annapolis
Jas Smith; 6 y 10 mo; Dissolution; Annapolis
John Gassaway; 7 years; Dissolution, Annapolis
Chas Richmond; 5 years; Dissolution; Annapolis
Rich Anderson; 7 years; Dissolution; Montgomery Co
Henry Gaither; 7 years; Dissolution; Montgomery Co
Lloyd Beall; 7 years; Dissolution; Montgomery Co
Edw Oldham; 7 years; Dissolution; Balt Co
Wm Reilly; 6 y 8 mo; Dissolution; Balt Co
Jas W Gray; 7 years; Dissolution; Dorchester Co

Walter Muse; 7 years; Dissolution; Dorchester Co
Wm Bruce; 7years; Dissolution; Chas Co
John Mitchell; 7 years; Dissolution; Chas Co
Edw Hall; 6 years; Dissolution; Queen Anne's Co
P Fitzhugh; 5 years; Dissolution; Queen Anne's Co
John Smith; 7 years; Dissolution; Fred'k Co
J Winchester; 7 years; Dissolution; Fred'k Co
Richd Dorsey; 7 years; Dissolution; Balt
Jno Sprigg Belt; 7 years; Dissolution; PG Co
Perry Benson; 7 years; Dissolution; Talbot Co
Edw Prall; 7 years; Dissolution; Harford Co
A Hoops; 7 years; Dissolution; Phil
Geo Handy; 7 years; Dissolution; Somerset Co
Gass Watkins; 7 years; Dissolution; Anne Arundel Co
Thos Mason; 7 years; Dissolution; Caroline Co
Geo Hamilton; 7 years; Cecil Co
Fran Revelly; 6 y 10 mo; Dissolution; Culpeper, Va
Paul Bentaloe, Com'r of late Pulaski's legn; [term of service-blank]; Reformed 1781; Balt
Jos Smith; 5 y 6 mo; Reformed 1781; Balt
Alex Furnival; 3 y 7 mo; Reformed 1779; Balt Co
J Hamilton; 6 years; Reformed 1783; Balt Co
Benj Price; 7 years; Reformed 1783; Wash Co
A Tannehill; 5 years; Reformed 1781; Wash Co
Michl Boyer; 5 years; Reformed 1781; Fredericktown
Jonathan Morris; 7 years; Reformed 1782; Fredericktown
Wm Lamar; 6 years; Reformed 1782; PG Co
I Williams; 7 years; Reformed 1783; PG Co
Ed Spurvier; 7 years; Reformed 1783; Anne Arundel Co
John Kilty; 6 y 8 mo; Reformed 1783; Anne Arundel Co
Ed Dyer; 6 years; Reformed 1783; Fred'k Co
Philip Reed; 6 years; Reformed 1783; Kent Co
Jas M Lingan; 4 y 6 mo; Reformed 1781; Montgomery Co
David Lynn; 6 y 6 mo; Reformed 1783; Montgomery Co
Rezin Davis; y 6 mo; Reformed 1783; Hagerstown
Jas Ewing; 6 years; Reformed 1783; Somerset Co
Jas W Gray; 7 years; Reformed 1783; Dorchester Co
Alex Trueman; 7 years; Reformed 1783; Annapolis
Saml McPherson; 6 y 10 mo; Reformed 1783; Chas Co
Jas Somerville; 7 years; Reformed 1783; Calvert Co
Jas Bruff; 6 years; Reformed 1783; Queen Anne's Co
Richd Waters; 6 years; Deranged 1785; Somerset Co
Mount Bailey; 3 years; Resigned 1778; Fred'k Co

A McAlister; 4 years; Resigned 1781; Balt
John Hughes; 6 years; Resigned 1781; Harford Co
Jas Peale; 3 y 6 mo; Resigned 1781; Queen Anne's Co
Lts:
John K Lowe; 3 y 10 mo; Dissolution 1783; PG Co
Thos Rousel; 6 years; Dissolution 1783; PG Co
Philip Hill; 4 years; Dissolution 1783; PG Co
Thos Bowie; 7 years; Dissolution 1783; PG Co
Thos Boyd; 4 years; Dissolution 1783; PG Co
Jos Cross; 2 y 2 mo; Dissolution 1783; PG Co
Isaac Rawlins; 4 years; Dissolution 1783; Chas Co
Saml Hanson; 6 years; Dissolution 1783; Chas Co
Edm Compton; 5 y 6 mo; Dissolution 1783; Chas Co
Thos A Dyson; 2 y 3 mo; Dissolution 1783; Chas Co
M McPherson; 3 y 10 mo; Dissolution 1783; Chas Co
Henry Clements; 3 y 10 mo; Dissolution 1783; Chas Co
Thos Beatty; 2 y 2 mo; Dissolution 1783; Fred'k Co
Nath Borrham; 2 y 1 mo; Dissolution 1783; Fred'k Co
Benj Fickle; 3 y 10 mo; Dissolution 1783; Fred'k Co
John D Cary; 2 y 2 mo; Dissolution 1783; Fred'k Co
Joshua Rutledge, 4 years; Dissolution 1783; Balt
Clem S Kennet; 5 years; Dissolution 1783; Balt
J W McFadden; 1 y 9 mo; Dissolution 1783; Balt
Saml Edmeston; 3 y 10 mo; Dissolution 1783; Balt
Jacques Baginer; 6 years; Dissolution 1783; Annapolis
Henry Gassaway; 3 years; Dissolution 1783; Annapolis
Wm Pendergrast; 4 years; Dissolution 1783; Annapolis
Henry Baldwin; 5 y 5 mo; Dissolution 1783; Anne Arundel Co
Basil Burgess; 2 y 3 mo; Dissolution 1783; Anne Arundel Co
Isaac Hanson; 4 years; Dissolution 1783; Anne Arundel Co
Zedekiah Fourd; 6 y 2 mo; Dissolution 1783; Cecil Co
John Sears; 3 y 10 mo; Dissolution 1783; Cecil Co
J Brevitt; 3 y 5 mo; Dissolution 1783; Balt Co
Nathan Wright; 7 years; Dissolution 1783; Dorchester Co
C Ricketts; 6 years; Dissolution 1783; Montgomery Co
Isaac Rawlins; 5 years; Dissolution 1783; Caroline Co
W Goldsborough; 2 years; Dissolution 1783; Talbot Co
Anthony Harris; 4 years; Dissolution 1783; Calvert Co
D Luckett; 5 years; Dissolution 1785; Chas Cl
Wm Smoots; 3 y 10 mo; Reformed 1783; Chas Co
H H Chapman; 1 y 10 mo; Reformed 1783; Chas Co
Thos Price; 6 y 11 mo; Reformed 1783; Chas Co
Geo Winchester; 5 y 9 mo; Reformed 1783; Fred'k Co

Robt Denny; 7 years; Reformed 1783; Balt
Adam Jamieson; 6 years; Reformed 1783; Balt
Saml Beall; 1 y 6 mo; Reformed 1783; Montgomery Co
John Truman; 5 years; Reformed 1783; Annapolis
John Lynn; 4 years; Reformed 1784; Wash Co
E Hall, jr; 4 years; Resigned 1781; Cecil Co
Jas G Heron; 3 y 8 mo; Resigned 1780; Cecil Co
John J Jacob; 4 y 3 mo; Resigned 1781; Wash Co
Jas Brano; 3 y 4 mo; Resigned 1781; Talbot Co
Osborn Williams; 3 y 1 mo; Resigned 1780; PG Co

Surgeons & Physicians:
Jas Craik, phys; 6 years; Reformed 1783; Chas Co
D Jenifer, phys & Surgeon to Gen Hosp; 5 y 6 mo; Reformed 1782; Chas Co
Wm Kiltz; 5 years; Reformed 1783; Anne Arundel Co
Richd Pindell; 6 years; Dissolution; Elk Ridge
Ezekiel Haynie; 4 years; Dissolution; Somerset Co
Levin Denwood; 6 years; Dissolution; Somerset Co
Walter Warfield; 6 years; Dissolution; Fred'k Co
T Marshall; 3 y 6 mo; Resigned 1783; PG Co
Jas Mann; 3 years; Resigned 1782; Balt

Surgeon's Mates:
Saml Y Keene; 2 y 5 mo; Dissolution; Queen Anne's Co
Elisha Harrison; 1 y 6 mo; Dissolution; Anne Arundel Co
John L Elbert; 2 y 8 mo; Dissolution; Talbot Co
Gerard Wood; 1 y 6 mo; Reformed 1783; Chas Co

Dwlg-house to let: on corner of B & 3rd st east, formerly occupied by the late Edw Ingle. Apply to D W Middleton, or to John P Ingle, exc

Died: on Nov 8, at the residence of her father, Mr A H Boucher, in Gtwn, Mrs Chloe Ann Crow, aged 23 years, consort of John T Crow. Her numerous relatives & friends, who, scarce 9 months since, witnessed, with high hopes for the long enjoyment of its blessings, her change from the single to the wedded state of life, have, in this still more important & sad change of her being, much more reasonable hopes of her happiness-happiness not in word, but in the true promise of Heaven. She died trusting & believing only in Him who giveth what the world cannot give.

Wesley Scott was committed for trial for taking a draft to the Bank of the Metropolis, representing himself as Mr Offut, & got money for it. He had gotten a letter from the postofc in Gtwn, telling them there that he was Mr Offut. [Nov 17th newspaper: Scott fully committed for trial at the Dec term of the Criminal Court.]

Army General Orders: Genr'l Orders #50: War Dept, Adj Gen Ofc, Wash, Nov 5, 1845.
Promotions & appointments in the Army made by the Pres of the U S since the promulgation of Genr'l Orders #31, of Jul 7, 1845.
Promotions: 2nd Regt of Dragoons:
Brevet 2nd Lt Jos H Whittlesey to 2nd Lt, Nov 3, 1845.
3rd Regt of Artl:
Lt Col Wm Gates, to be Col, Oct 13, 1845, vice Armistead, dec'd.
Maj Francis S Belton, 4th Artl, to be Lt Col, Oct 13, 1845, vice Gates, promoted.
4th Regt of Artl:
Brevet Maj John L Gardner, Captain 4th Artl, to be Major, Oct 13, 1845, vice Belton, promoted.
1st Lt Raphael C Smead, to be Captain, Oct 13, 1845, vice Gardner, promoted.
2nd Lt Francis N Clarke, to be 1st Lt, Oct 13, 1845, vice Smead, promoted.
2nd Lt Geo W Getty, to be 1st Lt, Oct 31, 1845, vice Soley, dec'd.
Brevet 2nd Lt Danl H Hill, of the 3rd Artl, to be 2nd Lt, Oct 13, 1845, vice Clarke, promoted.
Brevet 2nd Lt John H Grelaud, of the 1st Artl, to be 2nd Lt, Oct 31, 1845, vice Getty, promoted.
3rd Regt of Infty:
1st Lt Jos L Coburn, to be Capt, Nov 3, 1845, vice Cotton, resigned.
2nd Lt Oliver L Shepherd, to be 1st Lt, Nov 3, 1845, vice Coburn, promoted.
Brevet 2nd Lt Robt Hazzlitt, of the 4th Infty, to be 2nd Lt, Nov 2, 1845, vice Shepherd, promoted.
4th Regt of Infty:
Lt Col Wm Whistler, of the 7th Infty, to be Colonel, Jul 15, 1845, vice Vose, dec'd.
Brevet 2nd Lt Christopher C Augur, of the 2nd Infty, to be 2nd Lt, Sep 12, 1845, vice Higgins, dec'd.
Brevet 2nd Lt Franklin Gardner, of the 7th Infty, to be 2nd Lt, Sep 12, 1845, vice Berry, dec'd.
6th Regt of Infty:
Capt Benj L E Bonneville, of the 7th Infty, to be Major, Jul 15, 1845, vice Hoffman, promoted.
7th Regt of Infty:
Major Wm Hoffman, of the 6th Infty, to be Lt Col, Jul 15, 1845, vice Whistler, promoted.
1st Lt Roger S Dix, to be Capt, Jul 15, 1845, vice Bonneville, promoted.
1st Lt Richad C Gatlin, to be Capt, Sep 30, 1845, vice Dix, appointed paymaster.
2nd Lt Jas R Scott, to be 1st Lt, Sep 30, 1845, vice Gatlin, promoted.
Brevet 2nd Lt Ulysses S Grant, of the 4th Infty, to be 2nd Lt, Sep 30, 1845, vice Humber, promoted.
Breve 2nd Lt Jos H Potter, of the 1st Infty, to be 2nd Lt, Oct 21, 1845, vice Quimby, resigned.

8th regt of Infty:
Brevet 2nd Lt Theodore L Chadbourne, of the 2nd Infty, to be 2nd Lt, Sep 10, 1845, vice Darne, resigned.
Brevet 2nd Lt Edmunds B Holloway, of the 4th Infty, to be 2nd Lt, Sep 26, 1845, vice Handy, dec'd.

Appointments: Quartermasters' Dept:
1st Lt Morris S Miller, 3rd Artl, to be Assist Quartermaster, with the rank of Capt, Sep 13, 1845.

Pay Dept:
Roger S Dix, Capt of the 7th Infty, to be paymaster, Sep 30, 1845, vice Davies, resigned.

7th Regt of Infty:
Thos R Quimby, of Maine, to be 2nd Lt, Aug 1, 1845.

CASUALTIES:
Resignations-6:
Capt John W Cotton, 3rd Infty, Nov 3, 1845.
Capt Dixon S Miles, of the 7th Infty, as Assist Q M, [only,] Sep 30, 1845.
Capt Roger S Dix, as Capt of the 7th Infty, & Assist Q M, Sep 30, 1845.
2nd Lt Alex'r C H Darne, 8th Infty, Sep 10, 1845.
2nd Lt Thos R Quimby, 7th Infty, Oct 21, 1845.
Paymaster Chas Davies, Sep 30, 1845.

Deaths-6:
Brevet Brig Gen Walker K Armistead, Colonel of the 3rd Artl, at Upperville, Va, Oct 13, 1845.
Col Josiah H Vose, 4th Infty, at New Orleans barracks, La, Jul 15, 1845.
1st Lt Jas R Soley, 4th Artl, at Troy, N Y, Oct 31, 1845.
2nd Lt Thaddeus Higgins, 4th Infty, near Corpus Christi, Texas, Sep 12, 1845.
2nd Lt Benj A Berry, 4th Infty, near Corpus Christi, Texas, Sep 12, 1845.
2nd Lt Jas O Handy, 8th Infty, at Corpus Christi, Texas, Sep 26, 1845.

The ofcrs promoted & appointed will join their proper regts, companies, & stations without delay; those on detached service, or acting under special instructions, will report by letter to the commanding ofcrs of their respective regts & corps. By order: R Jones, Adj Gen

Memoranda: Re-appointments:
Benj F Larned, re-appointed paymaster in the army, from Nov 24, 1845, when his present appointments will expire.
Thos J Leslie, re-appointed paymaster in the army, from Nov 27, 1845, when his present appointment will expire.
St Clair Denny, re-appointed paymaster in the army, from Oct 15, 1845, when his former appointment expired.

Transfers:
Maj W B Cobbs, of the 5th Infty, to the 4th Infty.
Maj T Staniford, of the 4th Infty, to the 5th Infty.
Brevet Maj S Cooper, Capt 4th Artl, from Company D to Company A.

Mrd: on Nov 6, by Rev Chas A Davis, Mr Chas W Harding, of Va, to Miss Margaret Ann Tarlton, of this place.

Mrd: on Oct 16, at Brentsville, by Rev Robt Leachman, Mr Johnston Cockrell to Miss Emina A, d/o Richd Weedon, all of that place.

Died: on Nov 3, at Mount Pleasant, in Chas Co, Md, Mrs Jane Ann Sheirburn, in her 22nd year.

THU NOV 13, 1845
Banker's Weekly Circular, N Y, Nov 11, 1845: list of Banks in the U S, with the names of their Presidents & Cashiers, amount of capital, & discount on their circulation. –J Smith Homans, 295 Broadway, N Y

Homoeopathy: Dr Jonas Green, late of Phil, offers his professional services: residence is on C st, near 3rd st.

A member of Congress & family can be very comfortably accommodated in a small private family, on 17th st, with a parlor & 2 bedchambers. They are the same rooms occupied by the Hon Geo P Marsh & family during the last session. Apply to Jesse E Dow.

For sale: a new 3 story brick house, fronting on L st, between 9th & 10th sts. Inquire of the subscriber on the premises, or of Lt S M Gillis, F st, near 18th st west. Also, for sale, lot 2 in square 263. –Geo Gilliss, agent

The death of Thos Miller, of Powhatan, Va, which took palce on Nov 2, has deprived the State of an old & valued public servant. He was as guileless in private as in public life. –Richmond Whig

The law of Connecticut allows or compels the Court to grant <u>divorces</u> where either husband or wife are habitually intemperate. At the late session of the Supreme Court in New Haven Co, no less than 13 divorces were granted.

While 2 men, employed in Bissell's iron works at Alleghany City, Pa, were standing near a tap-box, the vehicle was upset & the molten ore exploded. Mr Richd Kemp lost both his eyes, & Mr Thos Boyd, had his left arm burnt to the bone. It was thought that both of them would die. [No date-a news item.]

To Let: 2 rooms opposite Fuller's City Hotel, Pa ave, for many years occupied by Mr Templeman as a Book & Stationery Store. Apply to Mr Saml W Handy, a few doors east of the premises, with whom the key is left, or to Thos Cookendorfer.

Mrd: on Nov 6, at Ellenborough, St Mary's Co, Md, by Rev Mr Johnson, Dr Thos J Franklin, of West River, Anne Arundel Co, to Josephine, y/d/o Col Jos Harris.

Mrd: on Oct 30, by Rev Jas T Johnston, Henry W Davis, to Constance, d/o the late Wm C Gardner, all of Alexandria.

Mrd: on Nov 6, by Rev John C Smith, Mr J H Sturgess, of Phil, to Mary Ann, d/o the late John Espey, of Gtwn.

Died: on Nov 2, at Phil, of congestive fever, Mrs Ann Baker, in her 51st year, w/o the late Dr Baker, of PG Co, Md.

Died: on Oct 23, at the residence of Dr Davezac, in New Orleans, Francis I Jones, aged 40 years, 7 months & 17 days, a native of Somerset Co, Md.

FRI NOV 14, 1845
Orphans Court of Wash Co, D C. Letters testamentary on the personal estate of Saml H Smith, late of said county, dec'd. –J B H Smith, exc

By virtue of a writ of fieri facias, issued by John H Goddard, a J P for Wash Co, D C: I shall expose to public sale, on Nov 18, at G & 6th sts, Wash City, 32 bundles of shingles, taken as the property of Abraham Clarke, & will be sold to satisfy a judgment in favor of Zachariah Dove. –R R Burr, Constable

Circuit Court of Wash Co, D C-in Chancery. Sarah E Craven, Elijah R Craven, David S Craven & Rebecca J his wife, John Jones & Lydia his wife, Saml Jefferson & Ann his wife, vs Wm Craven. Bill: by the will of John Craven, dec'd, the real estate of said John, to wit, parts of lots 11 & 12 in square 118, & improvements, in Wash City, became vested in the dfndnts, Sarah, Elijah, David, Thos, Lydia, & Ann, & the dfndnt Wm, in the respective proportions set forth & specified in the bill; that the share of the dfndnt Wm therein in one-seventh of two-thirds of the said real estate; that the said Wm is absent in parts unknown, & hath not been heard of for a long time; that the said estate cannot be divided without great loss to all concerned: that it cannot be sold without the aid of Chancery, for that otherwise no disposition can be made of the share of the said Wm Craven, against whom, as against an absent dfndnt, the bill prays the usual order of publication; & that the said real estate may be sold, & the proceeds distributed according to the rights of the parties. –W Brent, clerk -Carlisle, Solicitor for cmplnts

Wm C Woodbridge, author of the Modern School Geography, & a member of the Geographical Society of Paris, Frankfurt, & Berlin, died at Boston, on Sunday last, 50 years of age.

The large collection of curiosities in the Phil Museum were sold on Sat at Sheriff's sale. The sole purchaser was Edmund Peale, of Balt, & the aggregate amount abtained was about $13,000. Mr Peale intends removing the collection to the Masonic Hall in Phil, where it is to remain permanently.

At N Y, on Tue, a bldg on Cedar st, occupied on the lower floor by Wm Scott & Isaac Dittenhoeffer, dry-goods dealers; on the 2nd floor by R T Wilde, straw goods; & on the 3rd by Ellis & King as an umbrella factory, was destroyed by fire, together with a large quantitiy of straw goods & dry goods.

On Tue, as the engine from Worcester was proceeding to Hopkinton, it came in collision with a hand-car, which was used in examining the road, under the charge of David Melvin, who was instantly killed. It being quite dark, the engineer was unable to see the car until he came in contact with it.

Dr Richd F Cooke, of Hoboken, N J, was drowned on Nov 7, when the boat he was trying to save that when adrift, filled with water & sunk. An excellent swimmer, he was suddenly jerked under. –N Y Sun

Mrd: on Nov 10, by Rev W T Sprole, Hon T Dickinson, of La, to Miss M Ramsdill, of Wash City. [See Nov 15th newspaper.]

Died: on Wed last, in his 45th year, Chas Longdon. His funeral is today at 10 o'clock, at his late residence on G, between 11th & 12th sts.

Died: on Nov 12, Mrs Sophia Emmerich, in her 56th year. Her funeral is today at 3 o'clock, from the residence of Mr C Weber, near the Protestant Church, N Y.

The undersigned informs that he has taken the Wharf & Warehouse formerly occupied by Messrs Smith & Proud, adjoining the lumber-yards of Mr Blagden, where has for sale a good assortment of Fire Wood; also, lime, sand, corn & oats. –F M Jarboe

A writer in the Cincinnati Atlas is very warm in his praises of Mr John A Collins, of Steubenville, Ohio, a passenger on board the steamboat **Madison** at the time of her recent collision on the Mississippi with the boat **Plymouth**. He rescued his fellow creatures from a watery grave.

New organ lately erected in the Presbyterian Church, Gtwn: it is 15 feet in height, & of the Grecian order of architecture; has 12 stops, 6 on the great organ, & 6 on the swell. The organ was manufactured by Mr Jas Hall, of Balt.

New England Society: meeting on Nov 10 at Concert Hall: ofcrs elected:

David A Hall, Pres	N C Towle, V P	Jesse E Dow, Rec Sec
Geo Bender, V P	Geo J Abbott, Corr Sec	R Farnham, Treas
Executive Board:		
Theophilus Fisk-Chairman	T P Trott	Chas Gordon
	J O'Brien	P C Johnson
J L Henshaw	E Warner	Philando Gould
Jas Larned	Jas Adams	S L Harris
J J Greenough	R P Stow	

SAT NOV 15, 1845
Oliver H Smith, late U S Senator, has refused, under any circumstances, to be the Whig candidate for the Govn'r of Indiana.

From an official letter from Com Smith, of the U S frig **Cumberland**, Thos N Carr has been formally received at Tangier as Consul-Gen of the U S for the empire of Morocco.

The frig **Columbia** & brig **Dolphin**, the former for Brazil, & the latter for the coast of Africa, dropped down to Hampton Roads on Thu, preparatory to sailing for their respective stations. Ofcrs of the **Columbia**:

Cmdor Lawrence Rousseau   Cmder Robt Ritchie
Lts-6:
John H Marshall   Richd Wainwright
Gabriel G Williamson   Jas D Johnson
Wm P Griffin   Wm S Drayton

1st Lt of Marines, Wm E Stark   Acting Master, John S Taylor
Fleet Surgeon, B R Tinslar   Assist Surgeon, Alex Y P Garnett
Purser, Dudley Walker   Cmdor's Sec, Richd Gatewood, jr
Chaplain, Thos R Lambert   Master's Mate, Richd P Robinson
Passed Assist Surgeon, Jas O'Conner Barclay

Passed Midshipmen:
H K Stevens   Thos G Corben
Paul Shirley   H K Davenport
Edw T Nicholls   A K Hughes
Midshipmen-4:
J M Brooke   Wm R Mercer
Henry Willis   John L Langhorne
Cmdor'd Clerk, Gilbert H Smith   Gunner, Wm B Brown
Capt's Clerk, Geo F Lindsay   Carpenter, Jas Meads
Purser's Clerk, Chas C Swett   Sailmaker, Geo P Blackford
Boatswain, Wm Hoff

Ofcrs of the **Dolphin**:
Cmder John Pope
1st Lt D F Dulany
2nd Lt L B Avery
Assist Surgeon John T Mason
Acting Master A Reid

Purser, Ed C Doran
Passed Midshipman Wm F Spicer
Midshipman Copeland C Jones
Capt's Clerk, J C Means

Augustus A Adams, a tragedian of some celebrity, attempted to commit suicide on Mon at his boarding-house in Prince st, while suffering from delirium tremens. He is not expected to survive.

Mr Andrew Snyder died at Intercourse, Lancaster Co, Pa, on Nov 4, in his 113th year of his age. He was a soldier of the Revolution, & a highly respectable citizen; & was perhaps the oldest man in Pa.

Union Hotel, Gtwn, D C. The subscriber having leased this old established house for a term of years, is now prepared to receive permanent boarders or transient travelers. –Geo H Holtzman

The Columbian: his new bldg on the corner of 8th & E sts, is now prepared for reception. The Restaurant attached is at all times prepared to furnish families with all dishes desired. –J H Eberbach

New Dry Goods from N Y: R L Smallwood & Co, Between 9th & 10th sts, Pa ave, Wash.

Mrd: on Nov 13, in Wash City, by Rev G W Samson, Mr John Majors to Miss Eliz Ann Ward, both of Wash City.
+
Mrd: also, by the same, Mr Isaac F Ruster to Miss Eliza N Samson, both of Wash City.

Mrd: on Nov 11, at Phil, by Rev R Newton, Mr Jas Skirving, of Wash City, to Miss Caroline H McEwen, of Phil.

Mrd: on Nov 10, by Rev W T Sprole, Hon T Dickinson, of New Orleans, to Miss Martha Ramsdill, d/o Mrs B Chambers, of Wash City.

Died: on Oct 28, in Fredericktown, Md, Mrs Mary Magdalen Balderson, consort of Mr John Balderson. She was the d/o Mr Jacob Fauble, one of the earliest settlers of Fredericktown. In her life were exemplified the virtues that adorn a Christian mother, in her death those consoling hopes that smooth the path to the tomb. May she rest in peace! -C [See Nov 14th newspaper.]

MON NOV 17, 1845
In 1802 [says Mr Robt Mills] the Smallpox vaccination was introduced into Charleston by Dr David Ramsay, within 4 years after Dr Jenner had published its efficacy in preventing the smallpox; & this loathsome disease has been, comparatively speaking, eradicated in the State.

Our title to Oregon rests on : discovery, settlement, & continguity. The explorations of Perez & Heaceta, Spanish navigators, were made in 1774 & 1775; that of Van Couvre, English, in 1791. Capt Grey's discoveries by sea, & Sir Alex'r Frazer's by land, amount to nothing, because neither of them acted by authority of their Gov'ts. Lewis & Clark's explorations by land, are equally valueless, because the lower part of the Columbia river was not open to discovery-being already known. The only attempt at settlement there was made by Mr Astor in 1811, not by the authority of the Gov't, however.

List of letters remaining in the Post Ofc, Wash, Nov 15, 1845.

Allen, Jas	Butler, Miss F N	Drane, Rev Dr R B
Ashton, Psd Mid Henry	Butler, Miss Sarah	Davis, Wm M
Armstrong, B W	Braiden, Miss E	Donawin, Jas E
Alexander, Sandy	Bonnett, Mrs Peter	Dunlap, Francis H-2
Alexander, Mrs J A	Barton, Roger	Dunben, Mrs Eliza
Aldrich, Mrs Dr	Clark, Rev M M-2	Dorsey, Arthur
Andrew, Chas	Clark, Col Edw	Dorsey, Alfred
Beale, E F	Chase, L B	Dugan, Miss Julia A
Blythe, Calvin	Clark, L B	Dyer, Mary Ellen
Burch, Miss Eugenia	Cook, Mrs Sarah	Duval, Mr, late of Richmond
Burch, R E	Carr, Miss Louisa	Dement, John E
Ball, Mrs Ann	Croggon, Chas	Dutton, G, Capt U S Engineers
Ball, Miss M D	Cunningham, Robt	
Beall, Miss Mary A	Cooper, Lloyd N	Espy, Mrs Mgt
Brook, Geo	Cooper, G W	Espy, Prof Jas P
Brown, W Linn	Callender, S C	Espey, John
Brown, Wilson	Conoway, Wm	Ennis, Gregory
Bibb, T P Attieus	Coston, Augustus	Eaton, Lewis
Bibbs, Anthony-3	Cullin, Wm	Evans, Saml
Bridge, E T-3	Chatman, Benj	Estep, Mrs Catharine
Bryan, John A-2	Cridler, Isabella	Ellis, Chesselden
Brishbuy, Augustus	Chisner, Mr	Eshleman, Isaac-2
Borlvin, Jean	Carpenter, Edw	Evans, jr, S
Butler, Wm	Caldwell, John H	Edmundson, Mrs
Burges, Miss Ann	Cameron, Eli-3	Estiss, R
Benedict, Prof U S N	Cummins, Ord Ser John	Enos, Alonzo H
Blacknall, Dr Geo	Digges, Charlotte	French, Thos
Bonton, Miss C	Day, J W	

Finch, Mrs Mary E
Fisk, Jas
Frost, Edw N
Faas, Harman
Fertney, Edwin
Fisher, Wm
Fenwick, Edw
Fenwick, Mrs M C-2
Fletcher, Miss Ellen
Ferguson, Benj C S
Frazier, Rayson
Farley, T
Greene, Max J-2
Gray, A B-4
Gwinn, Mr, U S N
Gale, Willard
Guy, Wm B
Green, Noah
Guion, E P
Greenleaf, Abel
Griffith, Philip
Glascock, Enoch
Godran, Miss F
Gardner, Wm Ford
Griffith, Jas T
Hunt, Col T F
Holmes, Christian
Hall, Jas C
Hall, Mrs Clarissa
Heath, Rob, of N O
Hodge, Wm
Hill, Richd
Hall, Joshua W
Hill, John C
Hillyer, Rev J F—2
Hillard, Christian
Heaton, D F
Hanne, David
Henrie, Geo W V
Howlin, Mark
Hogan, John
Hickman, J C
Hussey, J G

Hyatt, C C
Heydon, C W
Howison, Jas R
Harris, Herbert
Harris, Tabitha
Harris, Miss M E
Holiday, Wm
Hitchcock, Dr C M
Hooper, Chas-3
Hutchinson, Miss A
Isherwood, B F
Jacobs, Presley
Jasper, Wm
Jenkins, Miss M E
Jarvis, John
Jameison, Mrs E R
Jackson, Miss M
Jones, Thos C
Jones, Jas
Jack, Miss Mary
Johnson, Chas
Johnson, Mrs R
King, Thos
Kuhland, Claus
Kinningham, Jas
Kaiser, H
Korner, Dr G P
Lane, Anthony
Lane, Ambrose A
Lowe, Mrs Eliz
Lunt, Mrs Sarah
Leffler, Shepherd
LeRoy, Miss Emma
Leseur, Francis
Luckett, David W-2
Moore, R B
Meigs, Mrs M
Mann, Jos-2
Miles, Prof Phiny
Muse, Lt W T-2
Mount, Thos C
Mount, Jas W
Mount, John W

Munn, Lt S E
Merritt, P J
Martin, g N
Morris, Geo W
Miller, Miss Ann
Munson, Ira
Morgan, Stephen
Magruder, Fielder
Marin, Lt M C
Mitchell, John G
Minor, Mrs M T
Martin, Thos
Meyhefer, Peter
Middleton, C H
Mayberry, Mrs J
Marcy, L
Meacham, Gaylor
Matthews, Michl or Saml
Matthew, Matthew
Matthews, David-2
Matthews, Henry
Morgan, Geo
McBride, Miss C
Magee, Hugh
Matabee, Miss E-2
McCobb, jr, Parker
McRae, D R
McGonegal, Alex
McKeever, Alex
McGragor, Mrs S
McGurk, Owen
Maguire, T A
Maguire, Thos F
McNulty, Col C J
McFarren, Col I
McFarland, Robt
McNamee, Jas L
McDonald, Capt J
Norris, Ralph
Nevit, Luciana
O'Hare, Mrs Kitty
Owen, John

O'Connell, Miss R
O'Neall, Timothy
Paine, Com John S
Peachy, J B
Porter, John
Preston, Asa
Plummer, J W, U S N
Possa, Miss Martha
Porter, Rev Robt
Powell, John A
Quinn, Felix
Quimby, Thos R
Quessenbury, Mrs Jackson T
Quinter, Jos R
Reed, David G
Rice, Geo W
Ricks, J T
Ross, Jas
Rust, Robt B
Randall, Miss M A
Reckless, Jos
Redden, Wm
Raynolds, Lt Wm
Randolph, W E E-3
Reeder, Richd
Richmond, Ephraim
Rogers, Col John A
Slamm, T L
Smith, John W
Smith, Geo S
Scott, Miss Ellen
Stone, Alex W-2
Shields, Wm
Smith, John H
Scott, Wm L-2

Shiek, John
Scott, A F
Smith, Mr
Shanks, Michl
Simms, Richd
Stelle, Thos
Smith, Andrew A
Stowbriski, Count
Sinclair, Chas N
Salmon, Miss Ellen
Summers, J T
Stewart, Emily
Saunders, Alex
Sinclair, John
Stewart, Mrs C
Segar, Jos
Sauer, John H
Saltmarsh, A D
Sutton, Miss M S
Seymour, Wm
Sibley, A H
Stewart, W W
Thorn, John
Turpin, Mrs E A H
Thomas, Binah
Tyler, Danl
Turner, Eli
Thompson, Mrs
Tucker, John T
Turner, Lt Thos
Tallmadge, N p
Tuffey, John
Townsend, J K
Turner, Mrs Eliza
Thompson, Mrs A
Turner, Mrs Ann

Vallentine, Wm
Wade, Miss Olivia
Woods, D W
Ward, Geo W
Welch, Abraham
White, Harriet
Winn, Mrs R-2
Walback, Col J B
Williams, Mrs S
Wilson, Minard
Wilson, Mrs D C
Wrixon, Robt
Watrons, J C
Walker, Jos T
Woodward, W A
Wallis, Wm
Whittle, L N
Wilson, Chas
Waters, David S
Williams, Mrs M
Walker, David
Watson, Miss M
Walker, Jas J
Washington, Mrs M
Warters, Mrs S A
Wilhelm, H
Whitney, A
Walker, Wm S
Whittock, Wm D
Williams, Wm
Warner, Walter
Williams, W J
Whittlesey, Chas
Young, Jas
Young, Miss Emma

The island postage aon all letters intended to go by ship must be paid, otherwise they remain in this ofc. -C K Gardiner, P M

Lt Cooke, of the U S Dragoons, who was a passenger in the steamer **NewYork** from Galveston for New Orleans disappeared from the vessel. In the morning he was no where to be found, & must have gone overboard. Lt Cooke came up recently from the camp at Corpus Christi, in consequence of ill health.

Amateur premiums for fruit: Peaches: E G Emack, Col J Brooks, Dr J H Bayne, G W Riggs, W Cammack, John Kedglie, Dr C B Hamilton, Geo Thomas-from J F Callan's orchard, Anthony R Frazer, John M Donn, Joshua Peirce. Plums: Geo Shoemaker. Pears: Jos L Smith, Mrs Seaton, Jos F Caldwell, A Favier. Quinces: Col Jas Thompson. Melons: G W Riggs, J A Smith, Joshua Pearce. Grapes: Joshua Pearce, Mrs Seaton, John F Callan. Apples: Mrs Seaton, R Farnham, C W Boteler, Jos Gales, Dr N Young.

Some weeks since, Geo Wells attempted to murder Mr Lewis A Hall, at Monroe, Mich. Wells has been sentenced to the State prison for 20 years. He is only 22 years of age, & very respectfully connected.

The court-house at *Tazewell*, in Marion Co, Ga, was destroyed by fire on Nov 4, together with all the records, books, & papers belonging to the sheriff & the clerks of the several courts. No doubt that the fire was the work of an incendiary.

The Hudson st Pond at Albany was the scene of a very distressing casualty last Thu. Wm Clarke, employed in grading the upper end of Hudson st, drove his team to the pond for the purpose of washing. The bank sunk & the wagon, horses & driver sunk to rise no more. –Evening Journal

Alarming & repeated incendiaries: attempt on the livery stable of Mr Dennis Pumphrey, on Fri. Attempt to set fire to the carpenter shop of Mr Wm C Mohun. John Webster, a stone-mason by trade, was arrested on Fri & lodged in the watch-house on suspicion of setting fires.

Died: on Nov 15, Robt Fielder, s/o Saml D & Matilda S King, aged 3 months & 8 days.

TUE NOV 18, 1845
Wash, Nov 14, 1845. All those whose claims against the personal effects of the late Cmdor Danl T Patterson have been admitted by the Orphans Court of Wash Co, D C, will be pleased to apply for the final dividend declared by the Court on the estate.
–Rd Smith, Atty for the admx

Rochester Democrat: the Hon Chas H Carroll was seriously injured by the upsetting of a stage, near Wooster, Ohio, about 2 weeks ago. He is still much indisposed.

$25 reward for the recovery of a trunk with its contents, which was lost on yesterday in Gtwn. Contains $90 in gold, $160 in silver, & $10 in paper money; also a note drawn by Christopher O'Hare for $22, payable to Saml Shreve. –Saml Shreve, on 7th st between L & M sts.

I wish to engage, as governess to my 3 children, a lady who can teach music & the usual branches of a good English education. My residence is healthy. The number of children to be taught will not exceed 7. –Benj T Johns, M D, Charlotte Hall, St Mary's Co, Md.

Military & Civic Ball will be at Carusi's Saloon on Dec 2. Cmte of arrangements:

Lt J P McKean	Jas G Ellis	F J Waters
Lt J B Philips	Wm McCarty	Wm E Morcoe
Serg H Richey	Jas Booth	Geo Becker
Serg Jas Kelly	Jas Power	Andrew J Joyce
Serg E Varden	S H Warner	Judson Warner
Wm H Clark	Lt J F Tucker	P H King
H W Sweeting	Richd Brown	Thos Sessford
Jas Y Davis	John S Marl	Jas W Allen
John Mead	Wm Morgan	Jas H Mead
M E Bright	Jas Bouseau	Francis Columbus

Tickets $2, to be obtained at the following places: Todd's Hat Store; Dulany's & Morgan's Drug Stores; Farquahar & Knoblock's, corner of 7th & H sts; Danl Kealey's near the Navy Yard; G M Sothoron's Drug Store, Gtwn; & at the door on the evening of the Ball.

Mrs D H Burr's Boarding & Day School: the services of Mr Vaas, late from Germany, have been engaged. A gentleman of extraordinary attainments on the Piano Forte. Apply at the seminary, corner of E & 9th sts.

Trustee's public sale: by decree of Chas County Court, in equity, the undersigned, as trustee, will sell on the premises, Dec 11, the real estate upon which the late Geo R Spalding resided, & of which he died seised & possessed, called **Oak Grove**, & part of **Boswell's Enclosure**, supposed to contain about 53¼ acs, in Chas Co, Md. Upon it is a good brick dwlg & all necessary farm houses & out-bldgs. –Geo Brent, Trustee

By 2 writs of fieri facias, issued by John H Goddard, a J P for Wash Co, D C: I shall sell, for cash, on Dec 22, at the store-house on 7th st, between F & G sts, goods & chattels,]subject to rent in arrears]: taken as the property of Calvin Goddard, & will be sold to satisfy a judgment due Seth Hyatt, as also one due to Thos Purcell.
–Jas M Wright, Constable. –A Green, auctioneer

Furnished House for rent: 3 newly finished houses on D, between 9th & 10th sts. Apply at Selby Parker's, Perfumery & Fancy Store, between 9th & 10th sts, Pa ave.

Died: on Nov 15, Washington Given, in his 20th year.

Died: on Nov 16, in Wash City, Mrs Theresa Luchessi. The members of St Matthews Sodality are requested to attend the funeral at St Matthew's Church this day, at 10 o'clock A M.

Died: on Sat before last, in Upper Marlborough, Md, after an illness of a few days, Eli S Baldwin, Sheriff of PG Co, in his 44th year, leaving a disconsolate widow & 3 young children, & a large circle of relatives & friends, to mourn his loss.

Society for the erection of a Statue to Henry Clay: meeting on Oct 30, 1845, at Richmond, Va. Clay statue of Henry Clay: Mr Joel T Hart to be the Sculptor selected for the purpose; money subscribed for the purposed to be placed in the hands of Mr Wm H Macfarland, Treas, to be lent out by him only on good landed security. –Lucy Barbour, Pres; Julia Leigh, Sally B Fay, Louisa Carrington, V Ps; Eliza M Riddle, Assist Treas. [Letter to Mrs Lucy Barbour. Madam: Mr Hart is a Kentuckian; a poor man, whose life was spent in common labors till he was lately drawn from humble employments by the force of his native genius. He has produced a bust of Mr Clay, & Mr Clay did not sit for this likeness more than 2 hours. Mr Healy, the celebrated painter, expressed praise & admiration of it. –J J Crittenden]

Mrd: on Nov 16, at the U S Hotel, by Rev G W Samson, Mr Saml P Hackett to Miss Clara Woolfolk, both of Louisa Co, Va.

WED NOV 19, 1845
In Spain the question of the marriage of the Queen & her sister, the Infanta Maria Luisa Fernanda, is still the order of the day. The Madrid papers announce as certain that the marriage of the latter with the Duke of Montpensier was definitively settled during the interview at Pampeluna between the French princes & the royal family of Spain. As to Queen Isabella II, her choice is not yet fixed. Queen Victoria warmed espoused the cause of Prince Leopold of Saxe-Cobourg. –F Gaillardet

By writ of venditioni exponas, I will expose to sale at public auction, on the premises, on 1st st, near B st, on Capitol Hill, Wash City, on Nov 26, for cash, one frame Blacksmith Shop, late the property of Wm McCarthy, seized & taken in execution at the suit of Vandora Mallion. –H R Maryman, Constable

Nat'l Convention for Abolishing Capital Punishment: met at Phil: ofcrs of this body: Hon Geo M Dallas, Pres. V Ps: Horace Greely, of N Y; Robt E Hornor, of N Y; Danl Neall, of Pa; J E Snodgrass, of Md; Jacob Harsen, of N Y; Wm H Johnson

For sale: large 3 story brick house on La ave, next to 6th st. Inquire on the premises of E Guttsclich.

Mr Arunar Mason, of the firm of Mason & Son, was killed at the machine shop of Howe & Goddard, in Worcester, on Fri of last week, by coming in contact with the machinery. [Nov 20th newspaper: Mr Asa Mason was between 50 & 60 years of age.]

Mrd: on Nov 17, by Rev Mr Pinckney, Mr John Cooper to Miss Rebecca Ferrall, both of PG Co, Md.

Died: on Nov 18, at the residence of Mr Jas H Lowry, on I, between 17th & 18th sts, Mr John H Gibbons, in his 28th year. His funeral is this afternoon at 3 o'clock.

Died: on Nov 14, at the residence of her father, in Montgomery Co, Md, Mary, y/c/o Henry & Mary Bradley, aged 2 years.

The Lt of the U S Infty who was lately killed by the falling of a spar from the brig **Ontario**, at Corpus Christi, Texas, was a graduate of West Point, named Merrick, of Ohio.

We recorded a few days since the death of Wm Byrnes, one of our most respectable & influential merchants. We add the name of C Suydam, of the house of Doremus, Suydam & Nixon. He was ill but a few days. His disease was bilious fever. –N Y Express

A s/o Gen J B Harvie, of Richmond, was severely, if not fatally, wounded on Sat, by the accidental discharge of his gun. Mr Archibald Brenner, of St Peter's Parish, S C, met his death last week by a similar accident.

Wash Corp: 1-Ptn from Eliz Abbot & others: referred to the Cmte on Improvements. 2-Ptn of Patsey N Walker for permission to erect a wharf at the end of 11th st west: referred to the Joint Cmte on Wharves. 3-Ptn of Jacob Wachter, asking the remission of a fine: referred to the Cmte of Claims. 4-Ptn of Henry Ellis & others, asking construction of certain flag footways in the 3rd Ward: referred to the Cmte on Improvements. 5-Act for the relief of Wm J Geffers: reported the same without amendment. 6-Act for the relief of John Shaw: referred to the Cmte of Claims. 7-Act for the relief of P L Leman: passed.

THU NOV 20, 1845
Capt Wm E Conklin, lost his 3 year old son, on Sunday, when he ate, the previous day, a cake of paint, such as is sold in small boxes for painting water colors. The poison took a hold upon him. –Balt Sun

Dr Elijah Pratt's Patent Artificial Nipple: Patented Jul 4, 1845: offered to the public, in cases where the nipple is entirely wanting, it being inverted, or where it has sloughed or come off by the child's nursing upon it. In Wash he has permission to refer to Drs H Lindsly & F Howard. For sale by Chas Stott, Agent for the District.

The farm owned by Hon B C Howard, in Howard District, Md, containing 400 acs, was lately sold for $20,000 cash. Purchaser, Reuben M Dorsey, whose property it adjoins.

Jeremiah Genung, aged 22 years, s/o Mr Thos Genung, died at Morristown, N J, on Sun last, in having accidentally shot himself.

Valuable land at auction: by deed of trust, for certain purposes, from Robt Widdicombe & Mary S Widdicombe his wife, dated Apr 6, 1844, & recorded in the Clerk's Ofc at Alexandria Co, in Liber F, #3, folio 57: sale on Dec 3, in Wash City: subdivision #10, one of the subdivisions of land, in Alexandria Co, D C, inherited by John Mason of his father Geo Mason, of *Gunston*, & has been subdivided by survey & plot of Lewis Carberry, containing 56 acres 1 rood & 6 perches, more or less, with all & singular the bldgs, rights, privileges, & appurtenances unto the same belonging.
–Azariah Fuller, Trustee -R W Dyer & Co, aucts

Valuable farm at private sale: the farm on which I now reside, formerly the property of Saml Pumphrey, dec'd: containing 550 acs, 5 miles from Rockville, & adjoining the farms of Thos J Bowie, Otho Magruder, Thos Worthington, & Wm G Robertson. The improvements are a log dwlg-house, 40 feet in length; necessary out-bldgs-all new, as the old were some time since deatroyed by fire. There are also 2 other dwlg houses & necessary out-houses. –Wm Pumphrey

Very Valuable Property at Auction: on Dec 8, the following property, belonging to the estate of the late Dr Marcus C Buck: part of lot 1 in square 351, with a 2 story brick bldg: fronts the Mall, between 10th & 11th sts, & adjoins the residence of Nicholas Tastit. Also, lots 20 & 21 in square 534, fronting on south B st, between 3rd & 4½ sts. These lots belong to the same estate. -R W Dyer & Co, aucts

Chancery sale: decree of the Court of Chancery at Franklin, Tenn, at its Oct term 1845, in the cause between Chas I Love's exc & Wm M Gwinn, dfndnt: I will expose to sale on Dec 27, at the Court-house in Nashville, the Iron Works lying in Perry Co, known as *Cedar Grove Furnace*, with upwards of 8,800 acres attached. Ore is inexhaustible, having been analyzed by Dr Troost. –Benj Litton, C & M

Neward [N J] Daily Advertiser, Nov 17. We mourn the loss of another honored Jerseyman in the death of the Hon J P S Maxwell. He died at the residence of Judge Robeson, [his brother-in-law,] in Belvidere, on Fri, after a 6 weeks' illness of typhus fever, aged about 40 years. He was a native Jerseyman, completed his classical education at Princeton College-graduated in 1823, studied law in the ofc of Chief Justice Hornblower, in this city, & was admitted to the Bar in May, 1827. He removed to Belvidere, Warren Co, which has since been his place of residence.

Groceries, wines & liquore: P Tiernan & Son, #4 south Chas St, below Balt st, Balt.

Mrd: at Pittsburg, Pa, by Rev Dr Heron, J Watson Spring, [s/o the Rev Dr Spring, of N Y C,] of New Orleans, to Mary O H, d/o Hon Harmar Denny, of Pittsburg. [No date-appears recent.]

Mrd: on Nov 11, at Martinsburg, Va, by Rev W B Dutton, Burr Powell Noland, of Loudoun Co, to Susan Chapline, eldest d/o the late John K Wilson.

Died: on Nov 7, at his residence in Duanesburgh, N Y, Col Wm Augustus Steuben North, only s/o the late distinguished Gen Wm North.

Died: on Nov 13, at the U S Naval Hosp, near Norfolk, Va, where he had been confined by a painful illness for the last 13 months, Lt Robt Dulton Taylor, of the U S Marine Corps, aged 29 years.

The undersigned intending to move to the country, wishes to sell his Tavern stand, called the Northern Liberty Hotel, 7th st, opposite the Patent Ofc.
–Chrfr Zachmann, Northern Liberty Hotel

FRI NOV 21, 1845
Furnished house to rent: in Pollard's Row, near the City Hall. Inquire of C Bestor, at the Patriotic Bank.

Farm land for sale: about 160 acs, part of the *Glenn Ross Farm*, in Montgomery Co, Md, 7 miles from Wash City: tract is susceptible of being divided into 2 farms.
–J C Lewis, Genr'l & Land Agent, 7th st.

John Edgar, Professor of Music: will give lessons in Music upon the Piano forte & other instruments. He refers to the following gentlemen, in whose families he has been teaching for 3 or 4 years: Judge B Tucker, Prof Wm & Mary College; Prof Saunders, Prof Millington, Prof Minagorode, Prof Dew, Dr Peachey, Dr Mercer, Dr Waller, Dr Cole, & Rev Mr Hodges. Apply at Fischer's Music Store.

Mr Oliver Haley, of Penobscot, Maine, who was believed was drowned last summer in Penobscot Bay, his boat having been found upset & the man missing, was not drowned, after all, but has recently returned to his friends, & will probably take the administration of his estate into his own hands, another person having commenced it. It appears he was found in distress by an outward bound vessel, taken on board & carried to England, whence he has returned.

Lts Jas W Abert & Wm G Peck, of the U S Topographical Engineers, arrived at **Fort Gibson** on Oct 22, with a party of 40 men, & a train of wagons & mules. Lt Abert parted from Capt Fremont at Brent's Fort, on the Arkansas, on Aug 15.

The new schnr **H M Johnson**, of Castine, Maine, dragged her anchors & went ashore on Little Deer Isle, on Nov 4. Next morning, in carrying off an anchor, the boat was upset & Capt John Boss & Mr Staples were drowned.

The barque **Mary**, of & from London for St Andrews, N B, went ashore near Moose river, Trescott, Me, on Nov 4, & went to pieces. The 2nd mate, Barrett, was drowned.

Accident at the Chemical Works, near Roxbury & Boston, on Mon, by the falling of a staging inside a large chimney: Mr Lakin was found to be dead. Mr Morehead who fell about 155 feet had his arm broken. Mr Peirce, the master-mason, was very badly hurt.

Mrd: on Nov 6, at St John's Church, New Brunswick, by Rev J B W Gray, Maj John Harris, of the U S Marine Corps, to Mary, only d/o Wm Gray, late Her Britannic Majesty's Consul for the State of Va.

For rent: 2 story brick dwlg house on N J ave, recently occupied by Thos L Thruston. Terms made known by the subscriber, near the U S Hotel, Pa ave. –Jas Fitzgerald

SAT NOV 22, 1845
St Peter's Church, Capitol Hill: Rev Mr Early, of Gtwn College, will preach tomorrow, at 11 o'clock.

Wheeling Times: Capt J Chester Reid, of the U S Army, & late Aid-de-Camp to Gen Gaines, committed suicide at Wheeling on Nov 18, at the U S Hotel, where he had taken lodgings the preceding Mon, on his arrival from Cincinnati. He succeeded on the 3rd trial in blowing a ball throught his right temple, which killed him instantly. He had a letter from Gen Gaines, accepting his resignation as one of his aids. He had also a sword, presented to his father by the Legislature of N Y for honorable service in the last war, & by his father presented to him in 1841. He had about $80 with him & some luggage. He was about 35 years old. [Dec 8th newspaper: The remains of this ill-fated ofcr, & the benevolent cares of the excellent Messrs Mitchel & Caldwell, at whose house he died, will be faithfully treasured in the memory of his friends.]

Mrd: on Nov 20, by Rev Mr Matthews, Mr Henry Alex'r Clarke to Miss Mary E Rumpff, all of Wash City.

Mrd: on Thu last, by Rev Mr Evans, Mr John H Stevenson to Miss Mgt Harris, all of Wash City.

Mrd: on Sun last, by Rev Wm Coombes, Mr Edwin R Violett to Miss Harriet Baggett, all of Alexandria.

Mrd: on Nov 16, by Rev F S Evans, Mr Jas w Shiles to Miss Mgt Musgrove.

Mrd: on Nov 13, in Richmond, Va, by Rev Wm Norwood, Adolphus Frederick, 3rd s/o the late John Gifford, of Bromley, Shropshire, to Mary Ann, only d/o Chapman Johnson, of Richmond.

Died: on Nov 21, in Wash City, Mr Geo Kendrick, in his 45th year. His funeral will take place on Sun, at 2 o'clock, from his late residence, near the steamboat landing.

MON NOV 24, 1845
Memphis Convention held on Nov 13: cmte reported the following ofcrs:
Pres: Hon John C Calhoun, of S C
V Ps:
Dr J Overton, of Tenn
Col John Hanna, of Ky
Col W Strong, of Ark
Gen Roger Barton, Miss
Capt H H Shreve, Mo
Hon O T Morgan, La
Maj A Black, of S C
Secretaries:
C T M Noland, of Ark
J G Harris, of Tenn
A B Chambers, of Mo
A V S Lindsley, Tenn

Gen L White, of Ill
Dr R Sneed, of N C
J L Hawkins, of Ia
Gen A C Dodge, Iowa
B B Minor, of Va
Gen Gaines, of La

J D B De Bow, of S C
F A Lumsden, of La
T B Drinker, of Ohio

Jas Boyd was hung at Westchester, Pa, on Fri last, for the murder some time since of a boy under very aggravated circumstances.

Prof Gouraud has disposed of his Niagara Falls property to Gen Chas M Reed, of Erie, Pa, who intends to carry out the project originated by Mr Rathbun, & build a public house at the Falls 2nd to none in the West.

New Bldgs. Mr Utermoehle has erected 2 good 3 story brick bldgs on 9th st, between D & E sts: erected by Mr R W Griffith, bricklayer, & Messrs Gregory & Shaeffer, carpenters. Messrs Masi & Co erected two 3 story dwlgs on 10th st: Mr Peter Heavenner, bricklayer, & Messrs Clement & Gallant, carpenters. Mr Richd Dement erected a 3 story dwlg on 2nd st, between C & D sts. Mr Dement has also raised his old residence a story higher. The new bldg is to be warmed by a furnace to be erected by Mr Skirving, sen. Mechanics employed: Mr Balaam Birch, carpenter; Messrs Heavenner & Irons, bricklayers; Mr John Stallings, painter; Mr Jeffers, plasterer; & Mr Skirving, jr, tinner. Along 7th st, a new brick 2 story bldg completed & now occupied by Messrs Moorhead & Brown, as a grocery store. Bldg was erected by Mr Harrover, by Peter Heavenner, bricklayer, & Mr Wood, carpenter. Mr C Schussler erected a 2 story brick bldg, which he now occupies, on the east side of 7th st: bldg erected by Mr Plant, bricklayer. On the same side of this street is erected one of the most spacious bldgs in this city-The Odd Fellows Hall: a credit to Mr Wm G Deale, the superintendent, Mr Jerome Digges, Messrs Emory & Gault, Messrs J T Walker & Job Mills, & all the other workmen employed in the erection of it. Nearby is a 1 story brick bldg, lately rebuilt & now occupied by Mr Mattingly as a hat store. Mr Whitmore also occupies a new store-as a shoemaker. Mr R Semmes occupies a new bldg contiguous to Mr Mattingly's, as a law ofc. Mr John F Callan erected a 2 story brick bldg, near E st, on the site of his Greenhouse. On E st is the 3 story brick bldg now in erection for Mr John F Callan, by Geo H Plant, bricklayer, & Messrs Harkness & Barker, carpenters. Returning into 7th st, is the brick 3 story bldg erected for Mr J Shreeve, & now occupied as a commodious tavern by Mr J W Smith: erected by Mr Wilkerson Williams, bricklayer, & Mr Thos Jarboe, carpenter. Above I, near N Y ave, are five 3 story brick houses, uniformly built for Mr Wm Utermoehle, by Mr Jerome Digges, bricklayer, & Mr Josiah Essex, carpenter. On the Old Almshouse square, a 3 story brick bldg was erected for Mr Caleb Shreve, by Mr Wilkerson Williams, bricklayer, & Mr Jarboe, carpenter. In D st, between 7th & 10th sts, are 3 handsome brick houses, having 3 stories, & lately erected for Mr Selby Parker, by Mr Wm H Parker, contractor & carpenter, Mr Wroe, bricklayer, Messrs R J & W Brown, plasterers, & Mr Ignatius King, painter. Mr Peter Force is now erecting a 3 story bldg on the north side of D st, & near his printing ofc; intended for a printing ofc, to be occupied by Mr Wm Q Force: Mr Plant is the bricklayer, Mr Holliday, the carpenter. Two brick dwlgs are being erected on the north side of D st for Mr J K Plant, cabinet-maker, by Messrs Ball & Anderson, bricklayers. Opposite side of the street is a neat brick dwlg erected not very long ago for Mrs Bihler. On the west side of 8th st, Messrs Clarke & Briscoe have lately erected 3 handsome 3 story brick houses; the basement of one is occupied by Mr Edw McCubbin as a hair-dressing & shaving establishment Bldgs are being erected for Messrs Clarke & Briscoe by Mr Lewis, bricklayer, & Mr J G Robinson, carpenter. Adjoining, on the same side of the street, Mr Saml Kirby erected a large 4 story brick bldg, which is now occupied by him as a furniture warehouse & manufactory: erected by Mr Ray, bricklayer, & Mr Towles, carpenter. Mr Owen Conolly, who keeps the Farmers' Hotel, at 8th & D sts, just erected a back bldg to his house. On 9th st, between D st & Pa ave, Mr Geo Savage just completed a handsome & substantial brick bldg, intended by him for a store & dwlg: Mr T Hickey, bricklayer, & Mr Davy, carpenter.

Gov Wright, it is said in the N Y Tribune, resolved to commute the sentence of death against Von Steenbergh & O'Conner, the murderers of Sheriff Steele, to one of imprisonment of life.

All persons are forewarned from taking sand, stone, or materials of any kind from the road which leads out of Wash, from North Capitol st, throught Wash Co towards Bladensburg, or from the public side of the enclosures contiguous thereto, under the pains & penalties of law. –J Brooks, Supervisor, Wash Co

TUE NOV 25, 1845
The copartnership existing between the undersigned as contractors for the completion of the eastern division of the Chesapeake & Ohio Canal, has been dissolved, by the withdrawal of Walter Cunningham & the transfer of his interest to the other members of the firm. The firm will be under the style of Gwynn & Co, at Cumberland, Md. –Walter Gwynn, W Beverhart Thompson, Jas Hunter, Walter Cunningham

St Mary's School, Raleigh, N C: Right Rev L S Ives, Visiter. Rev Albert Smedes, Rector: winter term will commence on Nov 11 & continue till Apr 15.

Naval Intelligence. Cmdor Nicholson has been relieved from the command of the Charlestown Navy Yard by Cmdor Foxhall A Parker.

The mansion residence of Wm P Preston, in Balt Co, about 7 miles from the city of Balt, was destroyed by fire last Sat.

Four steamboats belonging to the People's Line were sold: -the *Gazelle*, to Henry Green, for $6,000; the *Utica*, to Peter Taggert, for $18,000; the *Diamond*, to J E Coffee, for $6,000; & the *New Jersey*, to J R Vandewater, for $24,000.

The Caesarian operation was successfully performed, on Sun week, at Fredericksburg, Va, by Dr Brodie S Herndon, of that place, in the presence of Drs Browne, Wallace, Wellford, & McGuire. The patient is doing well & in a fair way to recovery.

Rev Geo Bourne, employed in connexion with the Christian Intelligencer in Boston, expired suddenly on Fri, at the ofc, as is supposed, of an affection of the heart.

Robt Layton, alias S G Warren, convicted at Charleston, S C, for forgery, has been sentenced to be hanged. It is thought that the pardoning power will be interposed in his case.

Mrd: on Nov 20, by Rev S G Gassaway, Mr P J De Voss, of Petersburg, Va, to Emilie, d/o Wm S Nicholls, of Gtwn, D C.

Mrd: on Nov 23, in Chas Co, Md, by Rev Mr Todd, Wm T Barton, of Va, to Marion Eliza, d/o the Hon Danl Jenifer.

Chas Ellet, jr, a celebrated engineer of Phil, has within a few days past, in company with Maj C B Stuart, of Rochester, inspected the localities in the vicinity of Niagara Falls, with a view of a suspension bridge across the Niagara river. Cost estimated by Mr Ellet at $200,000.

Phoenix Hotel, Lexington, Ky. John G Chiles, late of Harrodsburg, announces that he has purchased the above & invites the public to give him a call.
+
Having sold the Phoenix Hotel, of which I have been the proprietor for the last 12 years, to Mr John G Chiles, I take pleasure in recommending him. –John Brennan

Notice to non-resident Ky land owners. The subscriber has removed to Frankfort from Culpeper Co, Va, & tenders his services to such persons as have interests in lands in Ky. –Geo Mason Green, Frankfort, Ky

Notice: Stephen Rawlings, on Aug 6, 1845, conveyed all his books, book accounts, judgments, & notes then due him, & caution making payment except to them. –Briscoe & Clarke

On Sunday fire was discovered in Mr Coote's brew-house, near Blagden's wharf, in Wash City. The adjoining dwlg occupied by Mr Hickey was destroyed. Mr Antoine Grinder & Mr Walter Pumphrey, were seriously injured while exerting themselves to save the property in the brew-house. Mr Pumphrey had his leg broken & Mr Grinder had his shoulder & side very much bruised. The property was not insured.

WED NOV 26, 1845
We regret to learn of the death of Dr Albert B Dod, Prof of Math in Princeton College, N J. His early death is a loss to the college, to the church, & to the country. [Nov 29th newspaper: Prof Dod died on Nov 20. Condolences to his afflicted family by the Cliosophic Society, Princeton College.]

Thu, Nov 27, being set apart by the City Authorities as a day of general Thanksgiving, the several ofcs in the City Hall will be closed on that day.

A lady in Balt has received a letter from her son, an ofcr on board the brig **Bainbridge**, dated Rio de Janeiro Aug 13. They had just returned from a cruise of 3 months, all well.

Late Havana papers mention the death of Matanzas of Alfred Kruger, a native of the U S, who has lived for many years in the Island of Cuba, &, as engineer, had the direction of the first railroad in Havana, afterwards that of Sobanilla, & recently he superintended the one to Colisco.

On Fri, Mr Bogardus, of Albany, N Y, while driving his wagon in Lydius st, his horse took fright, & struck down Mrs Stephenson, 73 years of age. She expired in the afternoon; Bogardus lies in a critical state. -Albany Argus

Ofcrs attached to the brig **Truxton**, at Norfolk, from Port Prays, Cape Verde:
Henry Bruce, Cmder
1st Lt, Simon Frasier Blunt
2nd Acting Lt, Henry A Clemson
Acting Master, Selim E Woodworth
Purser, Geo F Cutter
Surgeon, Silas Holms
Passed Midshipman, I Blakely Creighton
Midshipmen: Wm T Truston & Robt Patten
Purser's Clerk, Jos L Curry
Passenger, Passed Midshipman Jas H Spotts

Jas McCaffrey, who murdered David Hessler, in Huntingdon Co, Pa, had been sentenced to death. Dexter Wells, who shot Robt Headden, at Greenville, S C, is to be hung on the 3rd Fri in Feb next.

Mr Manson Hicklin was killed near Paris, Ky, on Fri week, by the accidental discharge of his fowling piece whilst he was out in search of game.

Fatal affray on Wed last, near Uniontown, Pa, between Hayden P Bliss & his brother-in-law, Mr Evans, which resulted in the death of the former, whose head was shockingly mangled with a corn-cutter in the hands of the latter.

Mr Thos Powell, a resident of Berkeley Co, Va, was found drowned, near a fish pot of his, in the Potomac river, on last Wed. He was engaged in trapping.

In the bar of the St Louis Exchange, at New Orleans, on Nov 17, a fatal rencontre took place, by which Capt Jos Carson lost his life instantaneously, a pistol having been fired at him by Mr J M Wadsworth, the ball passing through the heart. Mr Wadsworth immediately surrendered himself. The affair was over a previous difficulty between the parties. [Dec 24th newspaper: jury returned with a verdict of not guilty.]

Dr Wm Reilly, of Snow Hill, Md, was accidentally killed on Sun last, while riding out on professional business, when his horse took fright & threw him from his sulky. He was a young man much respected.

Mrd: on Nov 20, by Rev Mr Merriken, Mr Geo H Ish to Miss Eliz M, d/o the late Francis Adams, all of Loudoun Co, Va.

Mrd: on Nov 20, at *Poplar Grove*, Chas Co, Md, by Rev Mr Abercrombie, John H Smoot, of Gtwn, to Mgt E, d/o the late Jas Morton.

Died: on Oct 28, at Paris, Mrs Clara B Catlin, the w/o Geo Catlin, the eminent traveler. None knew her but to love, none named her but to praise. Galignam's Messenger, Oct 29, 1845.

Orphans Court of Wash Co, D C. Letters of administration on the personal estate of Stephen Rawlings, late of said county, dec'd. –J R Thompson, adm

New Cash Clothing & Tailoring Establishment: on Pa ave, 3rd door from 3rd st, under Gadsby's New Hotel. I have engaged the services of Mr W H Wimsatt, well known in Wash as a fashionable cutter. –Rudolph Massey

Valuable farm for sale: about 100 acres, having a good frame dwlg & necessary outbldgs. Apply to J C Lewis, Genr'l & Land Agent, 7th st.

Wash Corp: 1-Ptn of Collin Bayless: referred to the Cmte of Claims. 2-Ptn of Enoch Ward, praying remission of a fine: referred to the Cmte of Claims. 3-Ptn of Eliz G Delany, praying the remission of a fine: referred to the Cmte of Claims. 4-Ptn of Wm R Goldin & others, owners of omnibuses in Gtwn, praying a reduction of the cost of licenses: referred to the Cmte on Police. 5-Bill for the relief of John Donovan was taken up & passed.

THU NOV 27, 1845
Three children of Mr Wallace, the oldest 5 years of age, were burnt to death at Paper Mill village, N H, on Nov 17. Their mother had just placed them in bed & stepped across the street to a neighbor's, & the fire is supposed to have communicated to the bed clothes from her lamp.

The Hon Thos A Davis, Mayor of the city of Boston, died at his residence in Brookline, on Sat last. His severe illness & rapid decline, from a period some weeks previous to that on which he offered the resignation of his ofc, had led his friends to apprehend this event. –Daily Advertiser

Mrd: on Tue, by Rev John C Smith, Dr R Finley Hunt to Mrs Catharine A Crandall, d/o the late Capt John McKnight, of Alexandria.

Mrd: on Nov 19, by Rev Geo Adie, Robt Henderson, of Leesburg, Va, to Eliz L, d/o Jas L Hawkins.

Mrd: on Nov 24, by Rt Rev Bishop Lee, S Abbott Lawrence, of Boston, to Sally Cresson, d/o the late Nathan Bunker.

Died: on Nov 24, at Dumfries, Va, Mrs Margaret Dulaney, aged 55 years, after a few days' illness. Her death will be severely felt by her numerous relatives & friends. She had long been a devoted member of the Methodist Church.

Died: yesterday, after a very short illness, Josephine Slicer, y/c/o Thos & Eliz Havenner, aged 8 years. Her funeral is today, at half past 2 o'clock, from the residence of her parents on C st.

Mr Bradley Pease died some months since in Louisiana, leaving about $4,000, for which there is no claimant. He is said to have been from Vermont, & has a sister living near Lake Champlain. If the heirs don't get the money the State will.

A few days ago Mr Christopher Sewell, of Boston, a chemist, a young man of good parts, died from the effects of an inveterate habit of smoking cigars. He frequently consumed 30 a day, & died from the rupture of a small blood-vessel.

For rent: 2 story brick house on Pa ave, between 12th & 13th sts. Inquire of V Blanchard, next door, or of Anne Blanchard, 8th st, opposite the Genr'l P O.

SAT NOV 29, 1845
Capt Chas Vanderford, an old & respected merchant of Cheraw, S C, was killed in his own store on Nov 13th by a young man named Angus Taylor, who was immediately seized & imprisoned.

Orphans Court of Wash Co, D C. Letters of administration on the personal estate of Hermann Kaiser, late of Wash Co, dec'd. –Sophia Kaiser, admx

A house occupied by John Turpin as a tavern, located in the rear of the Balt & Ohio Railroad Depot, at Balt, was destroyed by fire yesterday. Edw Parks, of Somerset Co, Md, & formerly captain of a bay craft, was burnt to death, having been asleep in a room from which he could not escape.

An intelligent & industrious young man, Jos Green, of Crawford, Orange Co, N Y, was killed on Nov 14, by the accidental discharge of a gun in his own hands.

Culpeper Court-house, Nov 26, 1845: 5 o'clock, Wed morning. The centre of Culpeper Court-house is now wrapped in flames. The fire caught at the Fairfax Hotel, kept by Saml Decamp, & is now spreading with tearful rapidity. Bayle's store, H Schackelford's house & ofc, & the Masonic Hall, are already consumed. Maj Hill's house has just caught.

Reminiscences of Washington. I knew the days when the bar was graced by the talents & eloquence of Mason, the 2 Keys, Swann, Jones, & Law. I see the Chief Justice Cranch, now silvered over with the frost of near 80 winters, but with faculties still unimpaired by time. Francis S Key was a man of a high order of talent. His mind was inventive, imaginative, & yet logical. His beautiful lyric, the Star-spangled Banner, written in the meridian of life, showed that he could not wholly abandon his first love. The first jail in Wash was a small brick edifice of 3 rooms, which stood on a lot adjoining the Bath-house on C st: recently been pulled down. The first man who committed murder in Wash was imprisoned in this jail, & afterwards executed. He murdered his wife. He was defended by Augustus B Woodward. He was exceedingly eccentric, & built a kind of ofc in the woods, which then covered the space between the Capitol Hill & Navy Yard. Mr Woodward was afterwards appointed a Judge in the Territory of Michigan. The subsequent history of the murderer is courious-his countrymen had caused his body to be interred near that of the dght of a poor but respectable widow of this city, who became so deeply afflicted at the circumstance that some of her friends undertook to disinter the murderer's body, which they deposited in what were then called the Slashes-now nearly covered with fine bldgs & gardens. When the disinterment became known, his body was carried back & deposited in its first resting-place. The poor widow became inconsolable, & again the body was removed, & placing it with the lid downwards, the body fell out, & was buried where it had been left by those who had taken such an interest in his fate. The coffin for several years served as a bridge over a small gully where the body of the guilty man was finally interred. -W

On Tue last, at Appomatox Court-house, Wm Jas McDearmon, deputy sheriff of that county, & a most estimable citizen, was killed by Coleman C May, atty-at-law, formerly of Staunton, who has been for some months a resident of Appomattox. May made his escape & has not been arrested. –Lynchburg Virginian

The Albany Evening Journal announces the death at Nassau, Rensselaer Co, on Nov 19, of Maj Abijah Bush, aged 91, a soldier of the Revolution, who served honorably through several campaigns.

Mrd: on Nov 27, by Rev Wm Parsons, Mr Thos H Parsons, of Balt, to Miss Julia Lawrence, of Wash City.

Mrs B Sprigg is prepared to receive boarders in Green's Row, fronting the Capitol, east.

Parlor & chamber for rent: house is on 4½ st, between Pa ave & C sts. Inquire of Jas Williams, Pa ave, 4 doors west of 4½ st.

Household & kitchen furniture at auction: on Dec 3, at the residence of Mrs Weaver, Pa ave. –Wm Marshall, auctioneer

John Mills, Fashionable Bootmaker, Coleman's Hotel, #1 6th st, Wash.

MON DEC 1, 1845
Boarding: Mrs Mary Ann Whitfield, from Pa, has taken the house formerly kept by Mrs Buck, next door to Messrs Semmes, Murray & Semmes, wholesale grocery store, near 4½ st, south side Pa ave, where she is prepared to take a mess of members of Congress, yearly or transient boarders.

Mrs E T Arguelles is prepared to accommodate a mess of Members, with or without families: 2 doors east of Congress Hall.

Boarding: at the house formerly kept by Mrs Pittman, on 3rd st. –I Beer

C Weber & A Pons respectfully inform the Ladies & Gentlemen of Wash that they will attend balls, parties, etc, with a well organized band of scientific musicians. Orders may be left at Mr Kinchy's, Pa ave; Mr Krafft's, corner of 18th & Pa ave; Mr Weber's, 2 doors from the Protestant Church, Navy Yard; or at Mr Pons', near Col Henderson's residence, Navy Yard.

For rent: houses on F st, lately occupied by Mrs Smoot. Apply at the subscriber's residence, near the City Hall. –J Hellen

Strayed upon the premises of Jas Little, near the Congress Burying-ground, a black Buffalo cow. Owner to identify property, &, after paying expenses, besides the cost of this advertisement, to remove the same.

Rev Jas Caldwell, to whose memory a monument has lately been erected at Elizabethtown, N J, was the Chaplain of the Army of the Revolution while occupying N J; he went also to the Northern lines, was high in the confidence of Washington, who made him Commissary. In the early part of the struggle his wife was shot by a refugee, who fired at her as she was at prayer with her children. A like fate was his, he being shot at Elizabethtown Point while receiving a young lady who had come under a flag of truce from N Y.

Railroad accident on Nov 15, when the passenger car on the Madison & Indianapolis railroad ran off the track. The conductor, Mr John Lodge, was crushed to death when the car fell upon him.

The dwlg-house of Wm Cobs, of ***Poplar Forest***, Bedford Co, 7 miles from Lynchburg, Va, [known as the former residence of ex-Pres Jefferson, by whom the bldg was erected,] was burnt to the ground on Fri last. The disaster was occasioned by sparks falling upon the roof from the chimney, which had taken fire.

Mr Jas Cameron, one of the earliest settlers of Iowa, committed suicide on Nov 10 by shooting himself. Cause, pecuniary losses.

List of letters remaining in the Post Ofc, Wash, Dec 1, 1845.

Adams, Mrs M	Beetley, Mrs M	Dulin, Rev E S
Alvee, Wm	Bentley, Dr M A	Dickson, Mrs Sarah
Alexander, Mrs J A	Bremer, E	Douglass, Lewis O
Appich, G	Bohrer, J S, U S N	Dulaney, Thos
Able, Miss Mary A	Ballade, Mrs C-4	Duritz, Jas R
Armstrong, Maj W	Brodie, Chas D	Dehass, W
Alston, Jas T	Bagby, Robt B	Drummond, Miss A
Allen, Gen Jas	Bagby, Travis	Duvall, Gen J P
Brooks, J C	Crump, Geo W	Drayton, Lt W S
Bell, Miss M Ann	Cole, Penelope	Dowell, Mr
Bives, Mrs Mary A	Clark, Rev M M	Davis, Miss L A
Brown, Mrs R	Cooke, Miss M E	Drummond, Miss V
Beck, A S	Chase, Saml B	Duman, Eliza
Brown, Clarke S-2	Clarke, Thos	Durham, Rev C
Brown, Wilson-2	Carter, Mrs S A E	Dahlingrausen, M V
Bell, Otho B	Cowen, Mrs J F	Davis, Mrs Anna
Brown, Chas B	Crawford, Adam	Davis, Jos
Brooks, Miss T	Conner, Rev C C	Edds, John
Beard, Lewis	Cunningham, Robt	Ellis, Mrs Harriet
Brooks, Hannah	Curvin, Jas	Ellis, Miss H W
Barnes, Geo W	Cooper, Maj S	Edmonds, Mrs M B
Bell, Colonel	Carter, Mrs Eliza F	Eckardt, T
Bonn, Philip	Conner, Michl	Evans, jr, Saml
Bibbs, Anthony-4	Chezum, Jas H	Edwards, J S
Bibb, T P Atticus	Collins, Jane R	Echleman, Isaac S
Berry, Miss L R	Cabell, Dr R H-2	Evans, B A H
Buckley, Miss M	Cummin, Mrs M A B	Edelin, Capt Jas-4
Bradley, Alex	Cordova, Jacob D	Egleton, jr, John
Bolding, Mrs	Capin, R S, U S N	French, Michl
Bennette, P	Crandell, Mrs C	Fridel, Madame
Berry, Miss L R	Capron, Capt John	Finch, John S
Bentley, A	Cockrell, Ann	French, J W
Bieuvand, Rev A	Dade, Miss Caroline	Farran, Jas J
Berry, Geo M	Drane, Robt J T	Fleurot, E G
Burress, Wilson A	Dunn, Henry F	Fraser, Thos
Brearuire, W S	Duff, Jas	Fowler, Jas Wm
Boshley, John	Davis, Mrs Mary G	Fisher, Wm S, of Texas
Barney, Pass Mid S C	Dickson, Jas	Fisher, Wm T
Bankhead, Col Jas	Dyer, Miss E	Frazer, Wm

Feister, Reuben	James, Chas K	Mason, Gen John
Francis, Miss Alex	Jackson, Saml A-2	Merschel, W-4
Gwinn, Dr W M-2	Jordan, Jas W	Mattingly, T J
Gaines, Mad M	Jackson, Miss M-2	Mason, Miss F A
Gray, A B	Jackson, Williby	Murdock, Mrs J B
Graham, Wm S	Keech, Alex	Miller, Capt M S-2
Gathrel, Mrs Ruth	Knip, Julius	Middleton, Francis
Gilpin, Wm	Kerfooh, Mrs E A	Myer, Franklin S
Gaston, Miss C J	Kingsbury, Thos	Miller, Miss L E-2
Gladding, Miss D	Kelly, Wm	Moran, Dison
Golding, Ellen	Kershaw, John	Mapie, John H
Griswold, Dewitt C	Kable, Jacob	Miller, Jesse
Galbert, Mgt	Kendels, Mrs Nancy	McGregor, Miss L
German, N T	Kapriz, Jermais	McMackin, Alex J
Goodman, John	Loocke, Mrs M A	McClintoe, John
Gibson, Dr John	Lack, Mrs	McNamee, J L
Hall, Edw	Lane, Ambrose A	McGray, Rossana
Howe, J C	Lee, Richd	McDuffee, Thos
Haire, Michl	Lowry, Wm H	Macfarland, Robt
Hanna, Mrs Christian	Leturner, Mrs E	McAlister, J K-2
Hall, Mrs	Leonard, Mrs Isabel	McCabral, Thos
Hill, Lt B H	Leighton, Miss J	McColey, T
Hodge, Wm	Lucus, Miss M A	McDonnell, Miss
Hall, Sprigg	Leggett, Miss S J	McGuire, Thos
Hall, Jas-2	London, G L	McLester, W W-4
Hill, Chas-2	Lasley, John D	Newsom, Matilda
Hill, Francis H	Lefler, Shepherd	Norris, Miss Maria
Harris, Herbert	Mills, Saml	O'Neal, Michl-2
Harrington, Miss A M	Marks, Isaac D	O'Brien, Dennis J
Heckrotte, A G	Moore, Jas J	Officer, Thos-2
Henderson, Miss A	Moore, Geo F	O'Connell, Miss R B
Hoffman, J H	Mount, Mrs M A	Osnabruck, M
Howert, John	Macy, John B-5	Ottman, Solomon
Hinton, Dr Jos B-2	Marchiavella, Cor'dt of N Y Herald	Pope, A
Hickman, Maj E W-2		Paine, Miss E C
Hickman, Mrs P J	Markle, Jas B	Pool, Rev Wm C
Hamilton, Josiah	Martin, Miss J M	Page, Dr F B
Hogan, John	Marlor, Henry E	Parks, Montgomery
Harris, Capt of Ark	Millstead, Robt A	Payne, Miss D
Ingler, Jos	Morgan, Capt G W	Paine, Henry
Isherwood, Robt	Mattock & Becker	Poindexter, Rev A M
Jackson, Alphonse-2	Minor, Miss M E	Pettit, Miss Ann
Jones, Mrs Sarah	Millard, John	Proctor, Mrs P

Porter, Geo A	Simms, Miss Frances	Thomas, J D
Patterson, Henry	Slacum, Geo W	Verdin, M
Pendleton, jr, W C	Stewart, Wm W	Viers, Mrs E
Piper, Col John	Sinclair, John	Wright, S M
Plowman, Jesse	Scoville, Jos A	White, Mathias
Patterson, B	Stinger, Mrs R	Wolf, Miss Barbara
Philips, Mrs C-2	Samuel, M L	White, Saml H
Quimby, Lt T R-2	Sherman, Mrs M	Wood, Abigail C
Root, Jos M	Samuels, Wm	Warner, Lt W H
Rind, M P & Burts	Spalding, J H	Warner, Sergt W
Rian, Mrs	Siphax, Mrs E	Wiggin, Benj
Reed, Jas D	Stevens, Matthews	Watson, John L
Rowan, Jos T	Stockton, Gen John	Williams, N L
Russell, Ignatius	True, Loring B	Waters, David S
Rusha, Henry	Thom, Lt Geo	Walker, Wm S
Russell, Mrs	Taylor, Mrs K L	Washington, Mrs M
Reintzel, Anthony-2	Tracy, Philomon	Watson, Obadiah
Rollins, Wm	Taylor, Henry	Winston, Stephen P
Shaw, Mrs M A	Thomas, Henry	Wrigley, J
Stone, Mrs C m-2	Tschieffly, A G-2	Whittlesey, Elisha
Soule, Geo W-2	Toppin, Mrs Emily	Webster, Jas
Smith, Saml	Turpin, W H	Wheeler, Wash'n
Stout, J	Thompson, John H	Whitney, A-2
Smith, F O J	Thornton, D M, U S N	Williams, Wm
Shield, John R	Tasistro, Fitzg'd-2	Walker, S P-3
Smith, Mrs M R	Tompkins, Richd	Williams, Jos L
Smith, Geo Clinton	Tucker, E G	Wimpsatt, Wm
Smith, Miss R M	Thompson, Alex	Young, Mrs Coleman
Smith, Miss Ann	Taylor, R j-2	

Thom Thumb, the celebrated American dwarf, Col Chaffin, 20 years old, & only 27 inches high, making him the smallest man in the world, will be exhibited 4 days more at the Odeon Hall, 4½ st & Pa ave, on Dec 1 thru Dec 4. Admittance 25 cents, children 12½.

The New Orleans Bee of Nov 20: the steamer **Montezuma**, from Pensacola arrived yesterday, & brought from *Fort Pickens* Companies H & F, of 1st Regt of Artl, Capt Van Ness, Capt Nauman, Lt W H French, Assist Quartermaster, Lts Haskins, Ricketts, & Brannon, the former company stationed at *Fort Pike*, the latter at *Fort Wood*.

Died: on Sat, in Wash City, Mrs Sarah Boyce, aged about 83 years, a resident of Wash City for upwards of 40 years. Her funeral is from her late residence at her son-in-law's, Mr Geo Collard, on 4th st, near the Navy Yard, this day, at 1 o'clock.

Died: on Nov 29, in Wash City, after an illness of 4 months, Mr John Drudge, in his 33rd year.

Eliz J Speed, a respectable lady of Norwich, Chenango Co, N Y, a few nights since left her room, having dressed herself with great care, went to the canal, & drowned herself. She had been for some time engaged in marriage to a young man, who, she was convinced, intended to desert her.

Howard District [Md] Free Press: Will of the late Nicholas Worthington: value of estate nearly a quarter of a million of dollars, is, with the exceptions named, left to his 3 grandchildren, 2 of whom are boys. An estate of 400 acres is left to their father, son-in-law of Mr Worthington, who is also appointed guardian of the divisions. To one of his grandsons are left 4 farms, 6 to another, & to his grand-dght 2. He also created 3 money-trusts of $15,000, $20,000, & $10,000 respectively; the 2 larger amounts in behalf of his eldest grandson, who is to take the name of Nicholas Worthington when of age. Nearly all the property reverts to him or his heirs at the death of the other legatees. All the slaves belonging to the dec'd are manumitted, with the exception of 5 superamuated negroes, who are to live upon either of 2 estates mentioned, as they may choose, & who are to be supported without labor the remainder of their lives. The slave of 16 years of age are to be free in 6 months; the younger slaves when they attain age 16-until then are the property of their mothers. Big Airy is free from the day of his death; the children of Dorcas are free at 11 years of age; the children of Little Airy are free at 11. His slave Chas receives his freedon immediately & a legacy of $500. To 16 of his negroes he has left 150 acres of land in Carroll Co, to be equally divided among them. To Little Bill he leaves $20 a year for 10 years. To 7 of his negroes a legacy of $40 each. To 14 of his negroes he leaves a legacy of $30 each.

Miles Grey has been sent to the penitentiary in Alabama for challenging a man to mortal combat.

Mrd: on Nov 27, by Rev Smith Pyne, in Wash City, Chas P Chouteau, of St Louis, Mo, to Julia A, y/d/o Gen Chas Gratiot.

New Bldgs-Wash: Well finished brick dwlg on north side of Pa ave, between 2nd & 3rd sts: 3 story dwlg, erected for Mr John Purdy, by Mr Plant, bricklayer, & Messrs Harkness & Barker, carpenters. Mr Morrow has erected a brick bldg not far from this bldg: erected by Mr P Mackey, bricklayer, & Mr Cooper, carpenter. Jackson Hall is next, yet unfinished: being erected by Mr Jones, bricklayer, Mr Curran, carpenter, & Messrs Emory & Gault, granite cutter. Mr Kell, formerly of Alexandria, has just erected on Pa ave, a 3 story brick bldg: erected by Messrs Mills & Stanton, bricklayers, & Messrs Smith & Sears, carpenters, both of Alexandria. On north side of Pa ave, between 8th & 9th sts, Mr N Travers has erected a neat 2 story brick bldg, now occupied by Mr Norbeck, confectioner, who was burnt out some time ago. The bldg was erected by Mr Plant, bricklayer, & Mr Borland, carpenter. At the corner of D & 10th sts, Mr John Moore just completed a large & commodious 3 story brick bldg, which is occupied by Mr R W Dyer, auctioneer, as a sale-room & furniture warehouse: the bldg now rented by Mr Dyer, was erected by Mr G H Plant, bricklayer, & Mr H Harvey, carpenter. Next door, Mr Dougherty, marble cutter, has lately erected on 10th st, a brick bldg which he occupies as a sales & work-room for marble mantel pieces & other articles. On Pa ave, between 12th & 13th sts, Mr N Travers erected a handsome 4 story bldg: erected by Mr Plant, bricklayer, & Mr Curran, carpenter. At Pa ave, on 14th st, Mr Fielder Burch has erected a good 2 story bldg, in which is a spacious bowling saloon: erected by Mr Plant, bricklayer, & Mr H Clark, carpenter. Between 14th & 15th sts, on Pa ave, Mr Thos Carbery erected a large brick bldg 4 stories high: first floor has 2 stores, Mr Hand as a lottery ofc, the other by Messrs Flenner & Co, merchant tailors. Bldg erected by Mr Plant, bricklayer, Mr Curran, carpenter. We arrive at two 3 story brick houses, the one built by Mr Lemuel Williams for a dwlg & ware room, the other by Mr R W Bates for a dwlg & store. They have slate roofs, & were built by Mr W H Parker, carpenter, Messrs Gregory & Shafer, & E S Wroe, bricklayers. A 3 story brick house has been built for Mr Murry on I st & Pa ave: bldg has a tin roof: erected by Mr Edwards, carpenter, & Mr Peter Heavenner, bricklayer. A large brick stable & coach-house has been built on H st for Mr Robt Earle, by Mr Wm Wilson, carpenter, & Mr Fielder Magruder, bricklayer. A 3 story brick dwlg & store has been built on Pa ave, for Mr A Hoover, by Messrs McLain & Acker, carpenters, & Messrs E & S Wroe, bricklayers. Mr Saml Stott has built a 3 story brick dwlg on I & Pa ave: erected by Messrs Harkness & Barker, carpenters, & Mr John Taylor, bricklayer. On H st, between 17th & 18th sts, 2 frame houses have been erected by Mr Swartz. The 2 story brick bldg on H st was built by Mr Jos Frazer, carpenter. Mr Saml Duvall built a 3 story brick bldg on H st, between 17th & 18th sts: erected by Mr Wm H Digges, carpenter, & Messrs E & S Wroe, bricklayers. Mr T H McGlue built, near the above, two 2 story brick houses: by Mr Thos Lewis, bricklayer, & Mr J Frazer, carpenter. A 2 story frame bldg has been built near the above by Mr R Knowles, carpenter. Mr Holland built a 2 story brick dwlg on 17th st, near Pa ave: Mr Geo Deal, carpenter. Mrs Alexander built a 3 story brick dwlg, with a slate roof, on 16th st, between I & K sts. Mr Jas Carrico has built a 3 story brick bldg between I & K sts. Mr B H Smith has erected a 3 story brick bldg on H, between 15th & 16th sts, for private residence: bldg has a tin roof. Mr Alex'r Borland has erected a 2 story frame house on 15th st.

On Fri last Maj G Tochman, now a member of the Bar of N Y, was admitted to practice law as an Atty & Counsellor of the Circuit Court for D C. He has been retained by the heirs of Gen Thaddeus Kosciusko to attend legal suits pending in that Court. The assets which Gen Kosciusko left in this country, & which are claimed by his heirs, the descendants of his 2 sisters, amount, according to the last account of the administrator, to about $42,000. He has also left valuable real estate in Ohio near Columbus. The heirs commenced the suit in 1825. Their former counsel were the dec'd Messrs Swann & Sampson.

For rent: a fine house on 10th st, near the avenue. Inquire of Edwin Green, Pa ave, corner 11th st.

The Penitentiary at *Greenleaf's Point*, of which Mr Robt Coltman has lately been appointed Warden, was visited a few days ago, & found to be in admirable order. There are 57 prisoners-3 are female, 1 white & 2 colored. In the boot & shoemaking dept, where most of the male prisoners labor, work of an excellent kind is made, & a regular supply of boots & shoes are kept up. Good brooms & substantial wheelbarrows are also manufactured in other parts of the prison.

The Wash Light Infty elected Richd France, Cmder of the company, to fill the vacancy occasioned by his resignation about 18 months ago, when he left Wash City.

TUE DEC 2, 1845
Mr Saml H Smith, who died in this city on Nov 1, in his 74th year, was the s/o Jonathan Bayard Smith, of Phil, a distinguished Whig of the Revolution. Our first recollection of Mr Smith is of his having opened a Printing-ofc in 1796, on Chestnut st, Phil, from which he issued the New World, a morning & evening newspaper. In Phil was a weekly paper by Mr Jos Gales [purchased by him from Col John Oswald, of Revolutionary memory] by the title of The Independent Gazetteer. Mr Smith effected a purchase from the proprietor, who had other plans in view. Mr Smith changed the title to The Universal Gazette, & issued the first number on Nov 16, 1797. In the autumn of 1800, Mr Smith transferred his residence & business to Wash City; he began the publication, thrice a week, of a new paper titled The National Intelligence, the first number of which was issued on Oct 31, 1800. On Sep 1, 1810, Jos Gales, jr, s/o the above named gentleman, became the proprietor. At age 38, assisted by his accomplished & excellent wife, the rearing & instruction of his children, with his cottage, a hundred or two acres of land, he never realized all his wishes. In 1813 he was induced to accept from Pres Madison the responsible ofc of Com'r of the revenue. He discharged this trust until the abolition of the ofc. Later he took the post of Pres of the Bank of Wash. This briefly sketches the outlines of the history of Saml Harrison Smith.

Cow lost-$4 reward. Return to the subscriber, W B Burgman, corner of 12th & C st south.

The Hon Elisha Whittlesey declines being a candidate for the ofc of Govn'r of the State of Ohio.

Boarding: handsome suite of rooms, located on Missouri ave, between 4½ & 6th sts, at Mrs Mary Connor's.

Alexander, Emperor of all the Russias. The Emperor Alexander was not only the eldest son but also the eldest child of the Emperor Paul, & Dorothy of Wirtemberg, grand niece of Fred'k the Great, Maria so entitled as Empress. Sophia Dorothy, of Wirtemberg, the 2nd wife of the Emperor Paul, & Mother of Alexander, & the reigning Emperor Nicholas, was born Oct 25, 1759, & was d/o Fredk'k Wm, Grand Duke of Wirtemberg, & Frederica Dorothy, of Bradenburg, who was herself dght of Sophia Dorothy Maria, sister of Fred'k the Great. Before her marriage, contracted at Berlin, but consummated in Russia Oct 25, 1776, the Grand Duchess joined the Greek Church, under the name of Maria Foederowna. [Taganrock, 18th Nov old style] 30th new style-Elizabeth writes of the condition of her husband, Alexander, to Dear Maman.] Alexander died the following day, Dec 1, 1825. I hope that I shall not long survive. In this hope she was not long left to languish; its consummation came in about 2 years. –Wm Darby

$50 reward for runaway, my negro man Washington Bransome, about 19 years of age. –Henry D Hatton, **Hatton's Hill**, near Piscataway, PG Co, Md.

Shooting match in South Scituate, Wed: Otis Torry, s/o Geo Torry, accidentally discharged a musket into his own breast, in the act of drawing it towards him, by grasping the gun near the muzzle. –Boston Whig

Died: on Nov 15, in the city of Balt, after a short illness of inflammatory rheumatism, Chas Russell Geisinger, aged 15 years, a highly promising s/o Capt D Geisinger, of the U S Navy.

Capt Thos Sangster, a soldier of the late war, respectfully presents himself to the Senate of the U S, as a candidate for the ofc of Sergeant-at-Arms of that honorable body.

Clement T Coote acknowledges the prompt & perservering efforts of the Anacostia Fire Co, from the Navy Yard Hill, who arrested the destruction of his dwlg-house, brewery, & malting establishment by fire a few days since, & deeply deplores that they were unavailing, & that the conflagration destroyed property for which he was once offered $20,000.

WED DEC 3, 1845
Supreme Court met Dec 2, 1845, at the Capitol. Present: Hon Roger B Taney, Chief Justice
<u>Associate Justices:</u>   Hon Jas M Wayne   Hon Saml Nelson
Hon John McLean   Hon John Catron   Hon Levi Woodbury
Jas Shields & Albert T Bledsoe, of Wash, Fred P Stanton, of Tenn, & J Van Buren, of N Y, were admitted attys & counselors of this Court.

Music, Pianos, & Fancy Goods: the subscriber has removed his establishment from Alexandria to Wash City, south side of Pa ave, between 10th & 11th sts. –Richd Davis

Mrd: on Thu last, by Mr Ege, Mr Jas Henry Jones to Miss Eliza P, d/o Geo Adams, all of Wash City.

The Hotel Picayune, Wash City: on Pa ave, next house but one to Jackson Hall. –John Cotter

Criminal Court-Wash: Grand Jury:

Peter Force, Foreman	Chas R Belt	Thos Blagden
Henry C Mathews	Geo Thomas	Robt White
Geo W Young	Robt S Patterson	Edw M Linthicum
Henry Haw	Chas A Burnett	John Austen
John Mason, jr	Thos Thornly	Richd Jones
John F Cox	Jacob Gideon	John P Ingle
Thos Brown	Washington Berry	Geo Parker
Joshua Pearce	Isaac Clarke	Wm I Stone

Jas W Sheahan, Henry M Nourse, & J Martin were admitted as Attys & Counsellor of this Court.

Mrs Crossfield can accommodate 4 or 5 gentlemen with board. Her residence is on 10th st, between Pa ave & C st.

THU DEC 4, 1845
Naval Court Martial: sentence pronounced upon Capt Voorhees, who commanded the frig **Congress** in the Rio de la Plata, & captured the Buenos Ayrean squadron: dismissal from the service, with a recommendation of the Court to the mercy of the Pres, who commuted the sentence to 5 years' suspension, without pay or emolument. It is some time since so severe a sentence has been pronounced. –U S Gas

Fire in the town of Petersburg, Va, last Sat: the tobacco factory of Mr Jas Orr was destroyed; dwlg-house occupied by Mr E H Osborne, also destroyed.

Fashionable Dressmaking: Mrs Lansdale has changed her place of residence to the corner of 10th & E sts. -Catharine Lansdale

Mrd: on Nov 25, in St Mary's Co, Md, by Rev Mr Woodley, Arsenius J Harvey, of Wash, to Mgt F, eldest d/o John H Bean, of the above county.

Died: on Oct 29, at the City Hospital, Mr Anthony Rentzill, formerly a clerk in the State Dept, & a native of Gtwn, D C, aged about 45 years.

Boarding: Miss Shonnard, at the Elliot Bldgs, near the U S Hotel.

Vertical Water-Wheel invented by Mr G Hotchkiss, shown at the last Fair, of Broome Co. A mill near Talladega, belonging to Robt Jamison, now cuts with this wheel over 300 clips in a minute. Hon Roger L Gamble, late Member of Congress from Ga, examined it in operation at Mr Dove's mill, in this county-Augusta, Feb 19, 1845.

Criminal Court-Wash. 1-Saml Fearson, jr, found guilty for an assault on Saml Adams, of Gtwn. Fined $10. 2-Chas Fearson found guilty for an assault on Saml Adams. Fined $10. 2-Isaiah Stewart & Wm Stewart, found not guilty for being concerned in a fireman's riot on Sep 27, 1844.

Henry Lacy, an aged & infirmed free negro, was seated by the fire, when a cotton quilt around him took fire, &, owing to his entire helplessness, he was unable to remove himself, & perished.

Wash Corp: 1-Cmte of Claims: asked to be discharged from the further consideration of the ptns of Collin Bayless, of Susan Norris, of Richd Cropley, & of Jas E Thumlert: & they were discharged accordingly. 2-Bill for the relief of A C Kidwell, was committed to the Cmte of Claims.

FRI DEC 5, 1845
Music on the Piano: Mrs Eliz B Scott will resume giving lessons on & after Dec 1. Miss Scott has had considerable experience as a Teacher in several Seminaries South & West. She can be found at Mrs Slye's Boarding-house, on 10th st, nearly opposite the residence of Mr Peter Force.

Boarding House & Restaurant: on Pa ave, between 9th & 10th st, directly opposite Marshall's auction rooms. His endeavors to please will continue to him that patronage which has been so liberally extended during the last 20 years of his residence in the District. –Sedley Woodward

Lost, on Dec 2, between my residence, on F, near 7th, & Pumphrey's stable, corner of 6th & C sts, a pair of gold Spectacles, thin rims. Suitable reward for returning them to me. –Moses Poor

Supreme Court of the U S: Wm F Giles, of Md, Jas D Westcott, jr, E C Cabell, & John A Rockwell, of Florida, & Gaspard Tochman, of N Y, were severally admitted attys & counselors of this Court.

Mrd: on Dec 1, at Chester, Queen Anne Co, [Eastern Shore of Md,] by Rev Mr King, Henry May, of Wash City, to Henrietta, only d/o W H DeCourcy, of the former place.

Goshen butter & cheese, buckwheat, mackeral, preserved ginger.
–S Jacobs Ratcliff, 6th & H sts.

J F Browne begs to inform his friends, the elite of musical taste, that he will visit Wash the 3rd week of this month with an elegant assortment of Harps, & will be happy to attend any favors for repairs. Communications may be sent to Mr Fischer's Stationers' Hall, Pa ave. –J F Browne, Maker & Importer of Harps, 231 Broadway, N Y

An old store remodeled, [Gilman's late Todd's] fitted out in a modern & elegant style. About 13 years' experience in his profession warrants him in the assertion that what he does will be well done. –Z D Gilman, Druggist

The 29th annual meeting of the American Colonization Society will be held in Wash City on Jan 20th in the Colonization Rooms. –W McLain, sec

SAT DEC 6, 1845
Coal! Best quality Anthracite Coal for furnaces, grates, & stoves. For sale by B M Deringer, Yard at the foot of 17th st, on Tiber creek.

Servants for sale: by order of the Circuit Court of Wash Co, D C: sale on Dec 10, on the premises of Gen Semmes, near the Navy Yard Bridge, 8 or 10 likely & valuable servants, of both sexes. –John H Bayne, Comm of Geo Semmes. N B: 2 farms will also be leased for the term of 3 years.

Mrd: on Thu, by Rev John C Smith, Mr John Cook to Miss Virginia Burch, all of Wash City.

Mrd: on Dec 2, by Rev Mr Tarring, Henry F Read, of Mississippi, to Martha M M Robinson, of D C.

Classical & English Seminary: H st, between 9th & 10th sts. The school has been here 18 years. -C Strahan

For sale: excellent house, suited for a large family, with out-houses complete. Large square in the neighborhood of the Patent Ofc. –Geo Sweeny, Genr'l Agent, 7th st west

Groceries & store fixtures at auction, at the store of Mr Lowry, 7th st, between K & L sts. –A Green, auct

MON DEC 8, 1845
The estate of the late Nicholas Worthington, of Anne Arundel Co, will pay to the State of Md nearly $7,000, under the law taxing legacies & collateral inheritances 2½ %, supposing the estate not to exceed in value $250,000.

Criminal Court-Dec 5. 1-The case of the U S vs Ignatius Grimes, charged with stealing $26 belonging to Danl Chew: jury returned a verdict of guilty. Mr Ratcliffe gave notice to move for a new trial, based on new evidence discovered favorable to the prisoner, who is said to have borne a good character. 2-Geo Seitz found guilty of an assault upon J A Ratcliff & Thos Donaldson, constables, for resisting them in the discharge of their duties. 3-Perry Biggs was found guilty of an assault & battery. Dec 8-Riot cases: 4-Jas Freer found guilty for an assault & battery upon Elias Barnes, J H P O'Neil, & Kinsey Dyer-watchman. Fined $24 in all & 2 weeks in jail. 5-Joshua Lloyd: guilty for an assault upon Messrs Freer & Hines: sentenced-a fine of $4. 6-John E Dement: guilty for an assault on Silas Moore, constable, while in the discharge of is duty: fined $10 & costs.

The trial of Caleb J McNulty, ex-clerk of the House of Reps, charged with embezzlement of the public money, is fixed for next Wed. Mr Carlisle is retained for the defence.
+
Columbus, Ohio, Dec 2. Mac made his escape at Jacktown, & at last accounts, not been heard from. He was in company with the Sheriff & one of his bail, had left for Washington, much against the inclination of the former. [Dec 9th newspaper: Mr McNulty had arrived in this city, & was ready for trial, and Mr Carlisle, counsel for Mr McNulty, publicly contradicts these unfounded statements of his absconding.]

Election for Mayor of the city of Boston is appointed to take place this day: candidates-Josiah Quincy, jr, Whig; John T Heard, Democrat; Wm S Damrell, Native.

A pilot, John Lane, killed himself in Cincinnati on Sat last, by hanging himself.
–Balt Patriot

A large 3 story warehouse in Portland, Maine, owned by Mr Thos Chadwick, filled with fish, oil, & colverseed, fell in, a few days since, with a tremendous crash. The goods were owned by Messrs L & W S Dana, & Hall & Conant. Loss not much, except the bldg.

New Bldgs-Wash. Two 2 story brick bldgs & store lately built for Mr F S Walsh, druggist & apothecary, on 8th st east, between K & I sts: Mr T Van Reswick, carpenter; Mr Thornton C Hickey, bricklayer. Two 3 story bldgs for stores & dwlgs built on K st, east of 8th st, by Mr Robt Clark, for himself. Mr H Fowler, bricklayer. Large warehouse & store built at the foot of 11th st, near the Navy Yard, for Mr Philip Otterback: Mr Benj Bean, carpenter. Edifice for the Methodist Protestants is now in progress at the corner of Va ave & 5th st. Bldgs cmte, Messrs Wm D Acken, P M Pearson, & Geo Collard. Architect & carpenter, Mr Geo Collard. We come into 2nd st & 7th st, where Mr Acker had lately erected, near the brick dwlg of Mr Richd Dement, 2 brick bldgs. 2 dwlg were erected by Mr Lewis, bricklayer, & Mr Jos Bryan, carpenter. Mr Bradford was the plasterer. In 7th st, a 3 story bldg was erected for Messrs Queen, which is now occupied by them as a grocery store. On the opposite side of the street Messrs T Havenner & Son, have raised the bldg occupied by them as a bakery & a dwlg. This brick bldg, which is 3 stories high, is a decided improvement. In F st, between 9th & 10th sts, we find a 3 story brick bldg, erected for Mrs Burns by Mr G H Plant, bricklayer, & Mr Harvey, carpenter. On F st Mr John Ferguson erected a 3 story dwlg: Mr Jones, bricklayer; Messrs Jones & Lansdale, carpenters. Mr Robt Cruet erected on 14th st, near F st, 2 good brick dwlgs. Messrs Gregory & Shafer, bricklayers; Mr Willet, carpenter. Mr Isaac C Smith has erected on 12th st, near F st, a 3 story brick dwlg: Mr G H Plant, bricklayer; Messrs Hilton & Clampet, carpenters. Mr G W Uttermoehle has erected a 3 story brick bldg on E st, near 12th st: Mr Collins, bricklayer; Mr Childs, carpenter.

Died: on Dec 4, in PG Co, Md, after a short but painful illness, Saml Childs, aged 12 years.

Fire in Benton, Miss, on Nov 17 consumed the law ofcs of Mr Holt, Judge Burrus, Judge Battaile, Maj Michie, & Wm Battaile. The law library of Judge Battaile was entirely destroyed.

Geo Norbeck has again resumed the Confectionary business, in the new store between 9th & 10th sts, Pa ave. Also, a well selected assortment of Toys.

TUE DEC 9, 1845
$10 reward for lost green silk net purse, has his name engraved on the clasp, containing a bond of the Corp of Alexandria for $500, a check from a Boston Bank on the Bank of the Metropolis for $100. Finder will receive the reward by leaving it at the store of B L Jackson & Brother, merchants, near the Centre Market, Wash. –J C Herbert, Beltsville

Subscriber offers for sale, or in exchange for negroes, a tract of woodland, containing 500 acs, in Clermont Co, Ohio, 12 miles from Deerfield. Title indisputable. Address the subscriber, residing at Greensborough, Ga: Sterling H R Gresham.

Public sale: order of the Orphans Court of PG Co, Md: sale at the late residence of Walter B C Worthington, dec'd, [known as the *Fielder Bowie Farm*,] on Dec 16, all the personal estate of said dec'd, [except so much as is specifically bequeathed,] consisting of 55 valuable negroes, of both sexes; horses, mules, cattle, carriage, hay, fodder, crop of tobacco, farming utensils; threshing machine-Cheneworth's, & barrels of fish. Sale of that portion of the personal estate of said dec'd which is upon the *Valley Farm* will be resumed on Dec 23. –Michl B Carroll, exc of W B C Worthington, dec'd.

$100 for runaway negro man Wilson Thomas, about 23 years of age. He has a mother at Mr Alfred Wills', near Port Tobacco, & connexions in the neighborhood.
–Jos E Simms, near Bryantown, Chas Co, Md.

WED DEC 10, 1845
Criminal Court-Wash. 1-John Campbell & Chas Kreamer, convicted of riot: fined $5 each. 2-Chas Kreamer, convicted of an assault upon Ofcr Little: fined $5. 3-Wm Barton, free negro, guilty of stealing wearing apparel above the value of $5: guilty of grand larceny: sentenced to 1 year & 4 months at labor in the penitentiary. 4-Geo Washington Barker, free negro, guilty of stealing wearing apparel of the value of $30, the property of Peter Barnes. Sentence: imprisonment at labor in the penitentiary for 1 year & 8 months. 5-Geo Seitz, convicted of assaults upon J A Ratcliff & Thos Donaldson, constables, sentenced to pay a fine of $15 in each case. 6-*In the case of the U S vs Jas Baker, charged with burglariously entering the bedroom of Mr Masterson, at Coleman's Hotel, on Jul 7, & concealing himself under the bed, the jury found a verdict of acquittal, it being proved that the name of Mr Masterson was charged in the indictment & presentment, to be Wm M Masterson, & not Wm W Masterson, which is the right name. The trial of Baker will take place tomorrow. 7-Case of the U S vs Chas Scrivener: found not guilty for an assault upon John Collins. 8-Jas Williams, free mulatto, tried for stealing a watch the value of $25, the property of Chas Bradford. Jury had not returned their verdict. [*Dec 11th newspaper: Jas Baker, charged with a burglary at Coleman's Hotel on Jul 7, 1845, was found guilty.]

For rent: the upper part of my store-house, now occupied by Miss F St Clair as a millinery-store, will be for rent on Jan 1 next. –G W Adams, Pa ave, between 8th & 9th sts.

Wash Corp: 1-Bills for the relief of Geo McDuell & for the relief of P L Leman were referred. 2-Ptn from Jane Fagans: referred to the Cmte of Claims. 3-Bill for the relief of Henry Hoffman & others: being considered.

Senate-Dec 9: Sergeant-at Arms: on the first ballot, Mr Robt Beall received 40 votes, Mr Coyle 4, Mr Dade 1. Mr Beall was therefore elected. 2-Assist Doorkeeper: on the 4th ballot, Mr Isaac Holland received 25 votes, Mr Salisbury 22 votes; scattering 2 votes. Mr Holland was elected.

Mr C P Van Ness, late Collector of the port of N Y, has settled his accounts with the Treas Dept, & received a receipt for the balance due the Gov't, being forty-seven cents in a running account of some twenty millions of dollars.

Dr H K Burroughs-Whig, was elected Mayor of the city of Savannah on Mon week.

Alex'r Graham, long the editor & proprietor of the Easton Gaz, Md, died on Mon of last week in his 56th year.

The Augusta [Georgia] Chronicle announces the death of Mr Jas Fraser, Pres of the Bank of Augusta, who died on Fri, after a severe illness of 4 days from paralysis. He had been a citizen of Augusta for near half a century, & in all the relations of life maintained the character of a just man.

The trial of Mrs Van Valkenburgh, in Fulton Co, N Y, for the murder of her husband by poisoning, in Mar last, has come to a close. It was proved that she had purchased arsenic a short time before the dec'd was taken ill. Jury found her guilty, & the sentence of death was immediately passed upon the wretched woman by Judge Willard. The day appointed for the execution is Jan 24 next.

Mrd: on Dec 7, by Rev Dr Muller, Mr Henry Kuhl to Miss Mary E Fowler, all of Wash City.

Mrd: on Sun last, by Rev Mr Van Horseigh, Mr Francis M Jarboe, formerly of St Mary's Co, Md, to Miss Harriet McJilton, of Wash City.

Died: at Phil, Benj C Wilcocks. Pursuits of a mercantile character led him at an early age to China, where he resided for many years. For considerable time he was the Consul of the U S for the port of Canton. He returned to the U S in 1828, & continued to reside in his native city until the close of his benevolent life, on the first of the present month. His virtues were deeply felt & justly appreciated.

Rev Thos Robinson, a local preacher of the Methodist Episcopal Church, residing near the head of Severn river, met an untimely death, on Sat week. He was thrown into the water by the upsetting of a small boat, but managed to reach shore by swimming, but in so exhausted a condition from the intense cold, that he died shortly after being taken to a house close by. He was a devoted Christian. –Annapolis Republican

St Charles Hotel, corner of Pa ave & 3rd st: the subscribers announce they have become the lessees of the above hotel, known as the property of Chas Lee Jones. The establishment is new & furnished with neatness & elegance. There is a Restaurant attached. –Brown & Raff

House of Reps: 1-Ptn of Mgt Gwinup, of Hamilton Co, Ohio, praying for a pension. 2-Ptn of Richd Harryman Lee, for a pension. 3-Ptn of Patrick Smith, for a pension. 4-Ptn of Elijah Foster, for a pension. 5-Ptn of Stacy Lamphire, for a pension. 6-Ptn of John R Williams, of Detroit, Mich, praying for payment of damages incurred by the loss of property during the late war with Great Britain. 7-Ptns of Enoch Perkins, Mgt Corwin, & Eliz Ellis, for pensions. 8-Ptn of Judith Worthen, for arrears of pension. 9-Ptn of Saml Corry, for invalid pension. 10-Ptn of Col Jehiel Tuttle, for an invalid pension. 11-Ptn of Wilmer Shields, in behalf of the heirs of Thos Shields, late purser in the U S Navy, praying for a pension. 12-Ptn of Capt ohn Martin, of Detroit, for arrears of pension. 13-Ptn of H D Johnson, for compensation for services rendered as Judge Advocate. 14-Ptn of Danl Sampson, for compensation for loss of sight in the service of the navy. 15-Ptn of

A J Locke & others, inhabitants of Charlestown, for abolishing the liquor ration in the navy. 16-Claim of John Otis, taken from the files. 17-Claims of Geo Hollenback, Geo B Hollenback, Elsey Ackley, P Cunningham, Wm Brook, & Wm Harris, taken from the files. 18-Ptn of Timothy Cook, of Mass, for an increase of pension. 19-Ptns of Alex'r H Everett & Matthew Tasker, of Massachusetts, were taken from the files & referred to the appropriate cmtes. 20-Memorial of the widow of the late Lt Col Wm H Freeman, of the U S Marine Corps, complaining of injuries & injustice received by her husband in his lifetime at the hands of public ofcrs, which he moved to refer, without reading, to the Cmte on Naval Affiars, & that it be printed. Mr Adams stated the hardships complained, were, in fact, a complaint of improper conduct on the part of high ofcrs of the Gov't, which he thought ought not to be passed over lightly by the House, & declined to withdraw the motion to print. It was agreed to.

THU DEC 11, 1845
House of Reps:: 1-Ptn of the heirs of Philip R Rice, dec'd, formerly of King Wm Co, Va, & late of Bracken Co, Ky, praying compensation for a vessel lost in the service of the U S in the Revolutionary war. 2-Ptn of Andrew Ferguson, for increase of pension. 3-Ptn of David Sage, for an invalid pension. 4-Ptn of the heirs of Silas Duncan, for a navy pension. 5-Ptn of Michl Johnson, praying for payment for provisions furnished the army at Plattsburg in 1814. 6-Ptn of Jos Watson, & that the accompanying papers now in the ofc of this House be withdrawn therefrom. 7-Ptn of G T Beyer, for indemnity of property taken by the British during the late war. 8-Ptn of Robt Brady, for indemnity for the loss of the schnr **Eagle**, taken from him for the public service in 1813. 9-Ptn of David Myale, for remuneration for services, in promoting the manufacture of domestic water-rotted hemp. 10-Ptn of Robt Sewall, for indemnity for property destroyed by the British during the late war. 11-Ptn of John Pettibone & others, for the benefit of an act extending a patent right. 12-Ptn of Henry M Shreve, for compensation for the use of his snag-boat. 13-Ptn of Satterlee Clark, for settlement of his public accounts. 14-Ptn of J W Simonton & others, for compensation for the use & occupation of Key West for public purposes. 15-Ptn of G F De la Roche, for the payment of certain expenses incurred while in performance of certain public duties. 16-Ptn of Bates & Lacon, for indemnity for illegal seizure of iron.

The Annual Address before the Agricultural Society of Newcastle Co, Delaware, this year, was delivered by Dr Jos E Muse, of Dorchester Co, Md.

The partnership formerly existing between the subscribers is this day renewed, in Wash City, to continue until Oct 21, 1848. –J Smith Dodge, L Parmele

$5 reward for a watch-seal lost: an English Gold Watch-seal, with a blood stone, on which is cut a strap & buckle in a circle, with the motto "Old Virginia never tire," & the initial M. Above reward will be paid by leaving it at the store of Seraphim Masi.

To let: 2 story brick house at 21st & H sts, with stable on the premises. Apply next door to M Adler, agent.

The Cheapest & most splendid pictorial paper of the day. Hewett's Excelsior & N Y Illustrated Times. Publisher, H W Hewett. Artist,T H Matteson. Editor, C F Hoffman. Will be published once a fortnight at the ofc, #2 Astor House, at 12¼ cents per copy, or $3 per annum, in advance.

Pension, Land, & Genr'l Agent, at Wash, D C: ofc on 10th st, 5 doors north of Pa ave. –Geo M Phillips, late of the Treasury Dept; charges moderate.

Farm to let: small farm containing about 50 acs, with dwlg house & necessary out-bldgs. I will sell the above & take city property in exchange at fair prices. Apply to Nathan Leake, 13th st, between F & G.

A lad, Desilvau, residing near Brockville, Canada, came to his death Nov 26 by accidentally falling on a clasp-knife which he held open in his hand while at play on ice.

Mr John Connor, in jumping from the cars of Woburn, Mass, on Sat, fell upon the track & had both his legs severed by the wheels of the cars. He is a most respectable citizen of Lowell, & is a man of some property.

Newburyport Herald: Horace Banning, a young man, employed some time in the Essex cotton mill, was ran over by the railway train between Rowley & Ipswich & killed. He may have jumped off the cars while they were in motion, or fell off the platform. [No date-recent news item.]

On Sat, Mr Hayden, of South Newmarket, N H, was riding in a sleigh, in company with his wife & child, & another lady. At the railroad crossing he stopped his horse. The animal became frightened & the sleigh came in contact with the engine & was smashed to atoms. Mrs Hayden & the child were killed instantly. The other lady was considerably injured, but Mr Hayden escaped unhurt.

Senate: 1-Ptn of Titian R Peale, praying indemnification for losses sustained by the wreck of the U S ship **Peacock**, at the mouth of the Columbia river. 2-Ptn of Catlin, Peoples & Co, to be indemnified for property destroyed by the Creek Indians in 1836. 3-Bill for the relief of Pierre Menard & others, sureties of Felix St Vrain. 4-Also, a bill for the relief of Pierre Menard, Antoine Peltier, & Jos Placy. 5-Bill for the relief of Wm Elliot, jr.

Mrd: Tue last, by Rev Septimus Tuston, Mr John W Nicholls to Miss Martha E Walker, both of Gtwn, D C.

Died: on Dec 10, after an illness of several weeks, of a complication of diseases, Thos R Hampton, in his 45th year. He was a native of Prince Wm Co, Va, & for the last 8 or 9 years has resided in Wash City, & been a Clerk in the Treas Dept. His funeral is from his late residence, on E st, near the steamboat wharf, this morning at 11 o'clock.

Died: on Dec 10, in Wash City, in her 67th year, Mrs Margaret Callan, relict of the late Nicholas Callan. Her funeral is this afternoon, at half past 3 o'clock, from her late residence, on F st, near 15th st.

Died: on Dec 9, after a short illness, Mrs Isabella Martin, in her 60th year. Her funeral is from her late residence, at 3 o'clock this afternoon.

FRI DEC 12, 1845
The venerable John Cotton Smith died at his residence in Litchfield Co, Conn, on Dec 7, in his 71st year. He was at the time of his death Pres of the American Bible Society; nearly half a century ago was one of the Reps in Congress from Conn: also served Connecticut in the capacity of Govn'r.

Phil papers announce the death of Cmdor Jesse D Elliott, of the U S Navy, who died at his residence in that city on Wed, in his 63rd year. He had been afflicted with a dropsical affection for 5 or 6 months previous to his decease.

Wm Smith, formerly a Rep in Congress from the State of Va, was on Wed last elected Govn'r of Va for the term of 3 years, commencing on Jan 1 next.

Thos G Broughton, the senior editor of the Norfolk Herald, fell from the steps of his dwlg a few days ago-having slipped on account of the sleet, & fractured the bone of his left leg just above the ancle. The injury may confine him to his house for a considerable time.

Naval: The U S schnr **Flirt** left Norfolk on Mon for Hampton Roads, & was to go to sea with the first wind. Lts John P Gillis & Wm Ronckendorff go out as passengers in the **Flirt**, to join the Pacific squadron.

Mr W H Jamison, a native of Va, & formerly a Passed Midshipman in the U S Navy, was found dead on the pavement in front of the Merchant's Hotel, at Charleston, on Tue. He arrived there the previous day from Pensaacola, where he had received his discharge, owing to the bad state of his health. It is supposed that he accidentally walked out of the window of his room, as there was no cause to believe he contemplated suicide.

The Sag Harbor Corrector says that the wife of Wm Sherwood died in that village on Sat from the effects of fright experienced at the late great fire at that place.

The body of Mr Bowers, a Superintendent on the White Water Canal, was found in one of the locks of that work last week, near Connellsville, Ohio. When last seen he had five or six hundred dollars in Canal money in his possession; when found only a few dollars were on his person.

The Quebec Canadian of Nov 26 mentions the death of the Rev C Belanger, Roman Catholic missionary at Somerset. When returning from a visit at one of his missions, he lost his way in crossing a swamp, & with 2 companions, perished of cold. The dec'd clergyman was but 32 years of age.

Senate: 1-Memorial from Edwin Bartlett, of N Y, praying relief for losses on U S bonds: referred to the Cmte on Finance. 2-Message received on the death of the late John B Dawson, of La, a member of the House: he had suffered much during the last winter, confined to his chamber for several weeks; he died on Jun 16 last, surrounded by his family & friends, at his residence in La. In the last 2 years Louisiana has mourned the loss of 3 of her distinguished sons: Porter, Bossier, & Dawson. Mr Dawson was Maj Gen of the Militia, & was distinguished as an active, gallant ofcr; he was Judge of the Parish Court of the Parish in which he resided.

House of Reps: 1-Bill for the relief of Wm McCauley. 2-Bill for the relief of Isaac Barker. 3-Ptn of the artists of Boston, that Congress would purchase Stuart's portraits of the 5 first Presidents of the U S. 4-Ptn of Ebenezer Atwill, of Mass, for remuneration for losses, were taken from the files & referred to the appropriate cmtes. 5-Ptn of Pearson Freeman, praying for an additional pension. 6-Ptn of Sarah C Wenwood, for compensation for Revolutionary services rendered by her father. 7-Ptn of Saml Allen, late Collector of Bristol, R I. 8-Ptn of Elisha Dyer & others, for an appropriation to clear out & deepen Providence Harbor. 9-Ptn of Saml Gladding, for drawback duties on sugar. 10-Ptn of Philip Allen & others, for indemnity for French spoliations. Ptn of Audley Clarke & others, for the same. 11-Ptn of David Melville, adm of Benj Fry. 12-Ptn of Eliphas C Brown, for an invalid pension. 13-Ptn of Z King, for compensation for services. 14-Ptn of Asa Sprague, for relief. 15-Ptn & papers of Thos Brownell. 16-Ptn of Fred'k Gibbs, of Oneida Co, N Y, praying for a pension in consideration of services in the army of the U S in the Revolutionary war. 17-Ptn of Saml Cochran, of Vernon, Oneida Co, N Y, praying for a pension in consideration of disabilities incurred in the service of the U S in the war of 1812. 18-Ptn of Wm Randall, of Northumberland Co, Pa, asking for a pension. 19-Ptn & documents of John P Schuyler, of Lycoming Co, Pa, for a pension. 20-Memorial of Alex'r M Cumming, of Princeton, N J, late mail contractor, praying for an equitable adjustment of his accounts for services rendered. 21-Ptn of Geo Taylor, for indemnity on account of French spoliations prior to 1800. 22-The papers in the cases of John W Hackett, Peter Shaffer, the heirs of Wm Arnold, dec'd, John Stone, Wm McCauley, & Isaac Barton, were withdrawn from the file of the House & severally referred. 23-Mr Ramsey asked & obtained leave to withdraw the ptn & papers of Jane Fertenbaugh.

Criminal Court-Wash: Jas Williams, John H Butler, Asbury Tyler, & John Suter, free negroes, were all found guilty, & with the exception of Butler, for whom a new trial was moved, were sentenced to the penitentiary. Jas Barker, convicted of burglary, & Thos Maling & Benedict Howard, both of whom plead guilty to charges of larceny, were also sentenced to the penitentiary.

Mrd: on Dec 3, at Easton, Pa, by Rev Dr Gray, the Rev Ninian Bannatyne, co-pastor elect of the F st Presbyterian Church, of Wash City, to Amelia A, d/o the late Rev David Bishop, of the former place.

Mrd: on Dec 9, at *Locust Grove*, Montgomery Co, Md, by Rev Wm Pinkney, Benj Beall, of Wash City, to Miss Susan Ann, y/d/o Michl Connelly.

Died: on Dec 10, after a long & painful illness, Saml Handy, formerly a Clerk in the Treas Dept, in his 74th year. His funeral is from his late residence, corner of 4½ st & Va ave, this day, at 12 o'clock.

Excellent farm for sale low: private sale of the Farm formerly Jas Clagett's, in Montg Co, Md: contains 241 acres of land: dwlg house is old, the barn a fine large one, & a tolerably good stable. I will sell the entire farm for $2,700 cash. –L N Norton, Gtwn, D C, Agent for Rev J J Bowden, N Y.

Mr Jos Cummings, a citizen of Evansburg, in this county, lost his life on Thu, while attempting to repair the water-wheel of a bark-mill, his head became crushed, & he died instantly. –Meadville [Pa] Rep

Circuit Court of Wash Co, D C-sitting in Chancery. Ex parte Geo Semmes, a lunatic. The creditors of the above lunatic are notified to exhibit their claims, with the evidence in support thereof, to me, at my ofc, on or before Dec 20 next. –Clement Cox, aud

SAT DEC 13, 1845
House of Reps: 1-Announce the death of Dr Jos H Peyton who died on Nov 12 last at his residence in Tennessee. He was the best of husbands & fathers, & Heaven permitted him to breathe his last surrounded by the cherished objects of his tenderness & affection. The House tenders to the surviving widow & relatives of the dec'd the expression of sympathy on this afflicting bereavement. 2-Ptn of Geo Hickman, praying for a pension, for disabilities received as a soldier in the late war. 3-Ptn of A M Kitzmiller, clerk to the commanding ofcr at Harpers Ferry, praying an increase of his salary. 4-Ptn of Chas M Gibson, praying for compensation for a wagon captured by the Indians in Florida. 5-Ptn of Jas L Loyd, praying for an increase of his pension on account of wounds received during the late war while in the service of the U S.

Mrd: on Nov 27, at Smithfield, Montgomery Co, Va, by Rev Mr Wilmer, Mr Geo H Gilmer, atty at law of Pittsylvania Co, to Miss Jane G, d/o the late Gov Jas P Preston.

Ladies' Seminary, Providence, Fairfax Co, Va: Mrs Dr Baker will open her School on Jan 5, 1846, after a vacation of 2 weeks, in the new & commodious house, near the Episcopal Church.

For sale: 2 servant women from the country. They are good plain cooks, washers & ironers, & will be sold low for cash. Inquire of Wm H Richards, south B st, between 6th & 7th sts, who is authorized to sell. -Wm Richards

Old man Burnett & wife, were executed at Fayetteville, on Sat last. Not a soul went forward to bid them adieu, nor did they take farewell from each other or of the world. There were probably between 2,000 & 3,000 people there. Young Burnett, the son, in prison on the morning of the execution, appeared unconcerned about the destiny of his father & mother. –Van Buren [Ark] Whig

On Sat we announced the death of Mr Jean Baptiste Rochebrun who had died of a terrible stroke of apoplexy. A physician declared him dead. When they were about to consign him to his coffin, it was discovered that he was warm in the region of the heart. He was immediately carried to bed, & all proper remedies were applied to revive him, but it was too late, & he parted from sleep to death. He was buried yesterday at 11 o'clock. –New Orleans Courier

MON DEC 15, 1845
Church of the Ascension: another new edifice, on H st, between 9th & 10th sts, lately erected by the Episcopalians, under the pastoral care of Rev Levin ___. The following mechanics of Wash City employed in the erection & completion of the bldg: Mr Saml Fowler, builder; Messrs Butt & Berry, carpenters; Mr Thos Lewis, bricklayer; Mr Phillips, plasterer; Messrs Stanley, Iddings, & Henderson, painters; Mr John H Boyd, upholsterer; & Mr W H Harrover, stove & furnace builder. The fresco painting is by Mr Ernst Dreyer, of Balt. The bldg is 54 by 85 feet. [Dec 17th newspaper: the front of the bldg, the geometrical stairs, & the pulpit, were constructed exclusively by Mr John W Ferguson, & the work reflects great credit on the mechanical ability of that gentleman.] [Dec 22nd newspaper: Church was open for public worship on Dec 14: service read by Rev L S Gillis, rector; service by Rev M Atkinson, of St Peter's Church, Balt; sermon by Rev Thos M Clarke, Rector of St Andrew's Church, Phil. Maj Gen Scott & the Hon Mr Berrien were among the distinguished persons in the congregation. The Organ built by Mr F Knauff, of Phil, was played admirably. The vestry of the Church: Anthony Holmead, Capt L M Powell, Wm A Bradley, Jas J Randolph, John A M Duncanson, Basil Magill, Saml Butt & B K Sharrett.]

List of letters remaining in the Post Ofc, Wash, Dec 15, 1845.

Auld, Wm H	Baltimore, Wm C	Drummond, Mrs H
Alston, Jas T	Baley, Jas C	Dekay, Richd
Allen, Edmund C	Bainbridge, Capt Wm P	Delany, Miss S
Alexander, Sandy-2	Bradford, Mrs Jane	Dawson, Aaron
Allen, Gen Jas	Carr, Dabney S	De Hart, Cap U S A
Birth, Jas W	Clay, C C	Dinnies, A J
Brown, John	Clark, Jos	Dalton, G, U S E
Burch, John D	Crate, Monsieur	Durall, Gen J P-3
Bruce, Com Henry	Carr, Saml M	Dickinson, T
Buck, Wm M	Coale, Wm-2	Eaton, Levi C
Brown, Carter	Cross, Mrs Eliza	Evans, Miss M
Been, Seth	Clyde, C G	Edwards, Rev Dr J
Butt, Mrs Reb M	Cox, Jas	Ennis, Gregory
Brook, J C –2	Curry, Mary	Eder, H M
Ball, Miss Caroline	Cockrill, Wm	Eadie, Andrew
Brown, Absolem	Collins, Mrs C	Edelm, Capt J-6
Brooks, John G	Collins, Mrs N J	Fry, John B-2
Barnes, A	Chilton, Mrs R H-2	Ford, Addison J
Brooks, Theresa	Crampsey, John T	Fales, Wm R
Bell, Robt	Coffin, Jared	Foster, H J
Brooks, Col Ed	Conner, E	Fuller, Wm A-2
Bruning, Henry	Cochran, Mrs F S	Fellows, Miss A
Bissell, Geo H	Cooper, P F	Feller, Johannes
Borchers, Henry O	Clement, John	Frisley, Mrs
Baker, John	Cassedy, Mrs M	Feeny, Mrs Ann
Bishop, Wm H	Callahan, Edw	Forsyth, Jas H
Bowie, R J-3	Crosby, Jessee	Frazer, Jas A
Barbour, J S	Chancy, John	Feagans, Benj
Baldwin, Dr J	Cadwallader, J-2	Fowlers, Henderson
Bidleman, Danl	Coleman, J, col'd	Fraley, T F
Butler, Henry	Comstock, Allen	Fowble, David
Bowen, W W	Coburn, Mrs H	Gray, Rev S T
Bishop, Dr W S-2	Creighton, J B	Green, C K
Bryan, Benj	Chapman, Alex	Graves, Saml
Bergel, Signund-2	Caldwell, John	Grave, L
Baker, Mrs Ellen	Campbell, Maria	Greer, A P
Blansherd, John	Coffin, Isaac N	Glenn, Mrs Eliza
Bronough, Mrs A	Donoho, C	Gray, John
Bartlett, Nelson	Dumas, J C	Gwinn, Dr W M-5
Bohrer, Mid J S	Donnelly, Mrs S	Guthrie, Abelard
Berry, Mrs A R	Davis, Wm	Goodman, C S
Baldwin, Harvey	Deneale, Miss J J	Graefly, Chas

Gunnell, Wm G
Gillooly, Thos
Gillespie, Lt A H
Gilbert, M, Ohio
Goddard, Saml H
Grefer, Ludwig
Gibson, John W
Greason, Wm
Garwood, Jas
Goodwin, A L
Gaither, John
Gorman, Peter-9
Griffith, Philemon
Hale, Wm
Hughes, Jos B
Hall, Edw
Hill, Clement
House, Prof R E
Hill, Geo
Hodge, Wm
Hurst, Wm B
Hall, A G
Hokes, Henry
Hall, Mrs Clarissa
Holmes, Christian
Howe, John C
Hammond, a F-2
Hayden, Miss H E R
Hassard, Thos
Hedger, Henry
Hunter, Miss M A
Hoover, Miss S
Holcomb, L C
Harper, Wm R
Handy, Col Levin
Handley, Mrs B
Hoffman, Martin
Hoffman, Miss S
Hilton, Miss J A
Hodgkin, Mrs E F
Harper, Judge
Hollenback, G W
Hummbert, Maad A

Henderson, J, Miss
Holinsar, Count
Hoffman, Josiah
Hamilton, W B
Headman, Andrew
Harris, J Geo
Harris, S G-5
Harford, Wm
Healey, John
Hernandez, J M
Joy, Arad
Jones, Mr
Jackson, J E
Jordan, Mrs M A
Johnson, Col Jas
Johnston, John
Johnson, Col F W
Jamaison, Miss M E
Jamaison, Elias
Jackson, Warren
Jackson, Saml A
Jervis, John H
Jacobs, Col H
Kelly, Michl
Kehgslenburg, Rev E
King, Miss Mary
Kerr, Geo
Kemp, Wm A
Kent, Jos
Keech, Alex
Knapp, Capt
Lord, Francis B
Long, Edw
Lunt, Miss Eliza
Low, Peter
Low, Miss Eliza
Lee, John-2
Lee, Saml
Lewis, Reeve-2
Lucas, Miss Martha
Ladreyh, C
Landen, Thos
Little, David

Latreat, Mrs E
Lauman, Geo
Lewis, Thos, or Caroline P
Larned, A S
Linding, Wm
Loving, Lansford
Mills, Wm
Mount, Mrs M A
Mead, Edw
Moore, M
Mills, C H
Mahon, John D
Merritt, P G
Mitchell, Miss M G
Mitchell, K P-2
Meredith, J
Mitchell, J
Mecker, G W-2
Miller, Horatio
Murphy, Mr T
Mason, Lewis E
Myers, Mrs A S
Merritt, Mrs M
Mower, Saml-2
Minor, Col Wm
Miller, Lt L S
Matthews, Elvira
Milburn, Thos
Marshall, Clem
Martin, Thos-2
Mason, jr, John
McLean, John
McLean, Wm
Mackey, Philip
McCobb, jr, Parker
McBee, Miss Eliza
Macabee, Wm
McArthur, Moses
MacKubin, C N
Macomber, Capt B
McPherson, W H
Mckenny, Col J F

McIntire & Co, C	Redman, Jos	Upperman, C E
McIntire, Mrs S	Swann, F T	Umphries, Miss A M
McEndre, Mrs M	Smoot, L R	Venner, Mrs H
McCormick, Miss S	Smith, Rev M H-2	Welsh, Wm
North, M L, M D	Stark, Henry	Ward, Miss M
Nugent, Benj H	Smith, S, Maine	White, Saml C
Neville, John S-2	Smith, Miss M E	Wick, Mrs L
Nuttall, E G-3	Scott, Wm H	Woodcock, B
Newcomb, Dr	Scott, Miss E	Williams, Mrs M
Newby, F A	Speekes, Jas	Wallis, J C
O'Neill, Geo P-2	Sims, L H	Williamson, D
Orr, Gen R	Smith, Miss Lizzy	Wilson, Henry
O'Hara, Col	Stewart, Mrs L	Weasner, T H
O'Brien, Mrs A	Sargent, H B	Wheeler, S H-2
O'Brien, D	Spencer, Miss S J	Wilson, Jas G
Pierce, Saml	Semmes, Jos	Walker, Jas-2
Pool, Rev W C	Sergeant, John	Wrixon, R S
Page, Geo A	Sanford, Miss J H	Williams, Mrs E H
Pope, John-4	Spellman, Benj	Wiggin, Benj-3
Pleasants, H, col'd	Seaver, M C W	Watson, S L
Pleasants, Jos B-2	Strider, T P	Watson, S F
Poindexter, A M-2	Sanders, G N-3	Wagoner, Mrs C
Pettitt, Richd-2	Tee, Wm	Williams, S S
Parkhill & Duvall	Thrift, J W	Williams, Miss A
Patterson, Geo S	Tannell, Mrs E B	Watson, Miss M R
Pringle, Mrs R	Thornbury, John	Wescott, J B
Proctor, Mrs E	Thompson, H E	Winder, Dr
Quimby, Lt T R	Thompson, John	Woodside, H C
Root, Wm	Terrett, Lt G H	Walker, Sent John
Rhea, Capt Allen	Taylor, Alfred	Williamson, J B
Rice, G W-3	Thompson, E H	Williams, Mrs M A
Redden, Wm	Thomas, Col S	Waters, David S
Raymond, L H	Taylor, David	Webber, Capt J A
Rowand, C L	Towers, Mrs C F	Young, Dorsey
Rawlings, Jas	Thompson, Mrs E	Yong, Dr B B
Rhyen, Mrs	Taylor, H	Younger, Sally
Robertson, Miss E A	Truxton, Mid W T	Young, Miss T
Ringgold, Lt C	Tucker, John T	Young, Miss E T
Russell, Mr	Thomas, Wm	Zabriskie, Col J C
Richardson Ira	Taylor, Miss M	

The inland postage on all letters intended to go by ship must be paid, otherwise they remain in this ofc. -C K Gardner, P M

The President's Message was conveyed from Wheeling to Cincinnati, 250 miles, in 15 hours & 45 minutes, including a detention of 2 hours & 50 minutes.

Two of the Nauvoo Saints were arrested in Burlington, Iowa, on Nov 20 for passing counterfeit money. Their names were Cyrus Chase & Rufus Adams. They were both committed for trial.

Rev Jonathan Brooks, preacher of the N J Methodist Conference, died at his residence in Bridgeton, on Nov 26, aged 87 years. During 41 years he was connected with the Methodist Church in N J.

Five months have now elapsed & the fire kindled on Jul 19 in N Y C is still burning; the smouldering ruins still send up a volume of smoke to remind the passer-by of the great fire; while the great vacancy occasioned by the destruction of bldgs is fast disappearing.

Obit-died: in Surry Co, Va, in her 22nd year, after a lingering & distressing illness of 3 months, Miss Julia Hargrave, of Petersburg, Va. Her friends stood around her bedside, to pay the last sad offices of affection.
[No date-a current notice.]

Naval Court Martial for the trial of Passed Midshipman Bissell, & such others as may be brought before it, was convened on Thu on board the U S ship **Pennsylvania**, in Norfolk harbor. Ofcrs who compose the Court:

Cmder Stribling	Cmder Rudd	Lt Bushrod Hunter
Cmder Armstrong	Lt Upshur	Lt A Pennock, Judge
Cmder Farragut	Lt Manning	Advocate

-Beacon

Mrd: on Dec 11, in Wash City, by Rev Mr Eggleston, Wm B Hurst, formerly of Annapolis, Md, to Julia A Perrie, formerly of Chas Co, Md.

Mrd: on Dec 11, in Wash City, by Rev Mr Bevand, Mr Jas Casparis to Miss Christine Hitz, d/o Mr John Hitz, jr, both of Wash Co, & natives of Switzerland.

Died: Mrs Julia Powell, w/o Col John Hare Powell, of Phil, suddenly, & has left a large family of children to deplore her loss. Mrs Powell was a native of N Y, d/o the gallant Col Deveau of the Revolution. As a dght, wife, & mother, her example is above all praise. She was intimately connected with some of the oldest & most respectable families in N Y. –Even Gaz [No date-a current notice.]

TUE DEC 16, 1845
Teacher wanted: the Trustees of Primary school #5 will receive proposals for a Teacher to take charge of said School for the ensuing year. It is located near the village of Bryantown, Chas Co, Md. By order of Trustees: Robt L Burch.

Senate: 1-Ptns of Wm Nicholls, Wm Butterfield & Hugh W Dobbin, praying for pensions. 2-Ptn of Clara D Cobb, widow of Thos Cobb, for a pension. 3-Ptn of Talcott Reed, a teamster in the Revolutionary army, for a pension. 4-Ptn of Oliver J Morgan, praying the right of pre-emption to a certain tract of land in La. 5-Ptn of Wm B Keene, praying to be confirmed in his right of pre-emption to a tract of land. 6-Ptn of Elijah White, praying compensation for property stolen from him by Indians, within the limits of the U S, while bearing communications from the local authorities of Oregon to the seat of the Genr'l Gov't; & for compensation while acting as Indian agent west of the Rocky Mountains. 7-Ptn of W B Robson, for indemnity for French Spoliations prior to 1800. 8-Ptn of Jas Robinson & wife, for a pension. 9-Communication from Wm Greer, proposing to execute the printing for the Senate. 10-Ptn of Geo Taylor, praying indemnity for French spoliations prior to 1800. 11-Ptn of Jas Morgan, asking a pension. 12-Ptn of Benj D Hewitt, for a pension.

Lansford Stallings, sheriff of Cherokee Co, Ala, was murdered at Cedar Bluff on Dec 4, by Saml S Hinton, whom he had arrested. Hinton shot Stallings in the street, killing him almost instantly. At the same time he shot a Mr A G White, whose life is despaired of. Hinton fled, & a reward of $500 is offered for him.

Ohio Giant Girl: Miss Hannah Crouse is 5 feet 2 inches high, weight is 300 pounds, & is 11 years old. She is exhibiting herself for her livelihood & education. She may be seen at the Concert Hall, admittance 25 cents, children half price. She is accompanied by her sister & brother-in-law.

Died, at the residence of her son, T H Ward, of this county, Mrs ___ Ward, in the 111th year of her age. Mrs Ward witnessed many of the exciting scenes of the Revolution, & had for many years drawn a pension as the widow of a Revolutionary soldier. –Richmond [Ky] Chroniclae [No date-current article.]

Mrd: on Dec 13, at the U S Hotel, by Rev Geo W Samson, Mr Nathan C Wildman to Miss Sarah F Wilson, both of Petersburg, Va.

Died: on Mon, after a protracted illness, Mrs Sophia Clarke, aged 52 years, formerly of PG Co, Md, but for many years a resident of Wash City. Her funeral will be from her late residence on Md ave, near 12th st, on Tue, at 2 o'clock.

Died: on Dec 14, Jas C White, of Harlow, Essex Co, England, but for the last 30 years a resident of D C, in his 55th year. His funeral is this afternoon, at 3 o'clock.

Died: on Nov 28, suddenly, at the Merchants' Hotel, Charleston, S C, Passed Midshipman Wm Henry Jameson, only s/o Capt Jameson, U S Navy. The dec'd, in consequence of delicate health, had left his vessel at Pensacola, & was on his way to join his young wife & infant dght in Va, intending on his arrival to resign his appointment in the Navy & devote himself to agricultural pursuits & domestic enjoyments. He had for some years been subject to an affection of the heart. Although he died among strangers, it was in the sunny South, the land of kindness, hospitality, & chivalry. His funeral arrangements were taken charge of by Capt Richd S Pinkney, U S Navy, an old friend & mess-mate of his father.

Mr Wm B Willis, of N Y, who some time since recovered $1,000 damages for injury sustained on the Harlem Railroad, obtained a verdict a few days ago for $1,840, the first trial having been set aside on motion of the defendant.

WED DEC 17, 1845
Senate: 1-Ptn of Caleb Green, late clerk of the District Court for the Western District of La, praying an allowance of office rent. 2-Ptn of W W Hubbell, praying that experiments may be directed by law to be made to test the utility of his invention of an explosive concussion shell to be used for military purposes. 3-Memorial of Mary Reeside, excx of Jas Reeside, dec'd, praying the payment of a sum of money found to be due to her late husband by the verdict of a jury in a suit against him by the U S. 4-Memorial of Villeneuve Le Blanc, praying the confirmation of his title to a tract of land in La. 5-Bill introduced for the relief of John S Russworm, heir & legal rep of Wm Russworm, dec'd.

House of Reps: 1-Ptn of Wm Gump, praying for a pension in consideration of injuries received while in the service of the U S in the last war. 2-Ptn of Mrs Judith Keith, praying for a pension on account of her husband's services in the Revolution, equal to her rights under the pension system. 3-The papers of Nathl Mills & others, of Justin Jacobs, of Sarah Scovel, & of the children of Ichabod Peck, for pensions: referred to the appropriate cmtes. 4-The papers of Cornelius A Reeves, of N J, asking for a pension, were withdrawn from the files: & referred to the cmte on Invalid Pensions.

Criminal Court-Wash. Thos Hays & Saml Hays, indicted for an assault upon Albert B Berry, were found guilty, & sentenced to pay a fine of $5 each & to suffer 2 weeks in the county jail. 2-Jas W Garner was found guilty of an assault upon Geo A Davis. Mr Norris, counsel for the accused, moved for a new trial. 3-Jas Herbert, free negro, was found guilty of stealing a horse, saddle, & bridle: sentenced to 2 years in the penitentiary. 4-Eliz West, free mulatto, guilty of stealing jewelry of the value of $80: sentenced to 2 years in the penitentiary.

Mr B B French's stable & Woodhouse were destroyed by fire on last Mon night. We regret to learn that Mr French's horse was burnt to death & his carriage destroyed. Loss about $700.

Wash Corp: 1-Bill for the relief A C Kidwell & the bill for the relief of Geo McDuell: passed. 2-Ptn of Louisa Collins, praying remission of a fine: referred to the Cmte of Claims. 3-Act authorizing Patsy R Walker to erect a wharf opposite to the west corner of square 355, on the Potomac river, was read twice.

On Nov 22, the prairie about 9 miles north of Monticello, Clark Co, Mo, was set on fire, & spread rapidly. The family of Mrs Kyle reside on this prairie. Mrs Kyle, an old lady, the mother-in-law of the Hon Amos Kendall, accompanied by her son, endeavored to save the fence surrounding the farm. She was soon enveloped in the flames, & the son, in endeavoring to save her, perished with her. There were no negroes on the premises. –St Louis Register

Rezin Moxley was frozen to death last week by exposure to cold. He was about 70 years of age. -Howard District Free Press

Capt Barnett, an aged citizen of Elk Neck, Cecil Co, Md, choked himself so that he died on Tue last while eating his dinner.

Died: Dec 9, at Rochester, N Y, Mrs Sophia Rochester, wid/o the late Col Nathl Rochester, aged 77 years.

Thos Hickey, a German, froze to death on Sat, near his residence, on the west side of Will's Creek, near Cumberland, Md. He was found in the morning still alive, but died shortly after being removed to his residence. –Cumberland Civilian

I certify that Thos J Barcley, of PG Co, Md, brought before me as an estray trespassing upon his enclosures, a gray horse. Given under my hand, Jno T W Dean, Justice of the Peace [Owner is to prove property, pay charges, & take him away.
–Thos J Barclay, living near Bladensburg.]

THU DEC 18, 1845
Montgomery Co Court, [Md,]-Nov Term, 1845. On the ptn of Alex'r C H Darne, adm of Wm Darne, dec'd, it is order that the Auditor of this Court state an account of the costs & expenses incurred in the execution of a commission issued out of said Court on Dec 2, 1833, on the ptn of Levin Campbell, for the division of the real estate of Alex'r Campbell, late of said county, dec'd; & that the heirs at law of the said Alex'r Campbell show cause to this Court on or before the first Mon of Mar, 1846, why said costs & expenses should not be paid to the several persons to whom the same may be due & payable, out of a fund arising from the sale of the said real estate, made in pursuance of a decree of this Court of the payment of the debts of the said Alex'r Campbell, & remaining in the hands of the trustee appointed to make such sale. -T H Wilkinson, Nicholas Brewer, Saml T Stonestreet, Clerk, of Montg Co Court. [On Feb 16, 1846, at

10 a m, at my ofc in Rockville, I shall proceed to state the amount directed by the foregoing order, when & where they may attend if they think proper.
–L A Dawson, Auditor of Montgomery County Court.

Senate: 1-Ptn of Lydia Lush, widow of Stephen Lush, dec'd, a Revolutionary soldier, asking a pension. 2-Ptn of Simon Summers, an ofcr of the Revolutionary army, praying to be allowed commutation pay.

The subscriber wishes to hire by the year a Slave Woman, who can be recommended as a good cook, washer, & ironer, & of good moral character. Liberal wages will be given; or he would purchase such a woman at a fair price. Apply to D English, jr, Gtwn.

FRI DEC 19, 1845
Senate: 1-Memorial of Amos Kendall, praying compensation for losses sustained by him, & expenses incurred, from a prosecution against him while Postmaster Genr'l by certain mail contractors. 2-Memorial from Pierre Chouteau & others, the reps of Julien Dubuque, praying confirmation of certain land titles. 3-Ptn of John Binns, praying the aid of Congress in his publication of an edition of the Declaration of Independence. 4-Memorial of Eliz Ripley, only surviving child & rep of Eleazer W Ripley, asking remuneration from the Gov't on account of verdicts rendered in the District Courts of Louisiana. 5-Ptn of Henry Simpson, surviving administrator of Geo Simpson, dec'd, praying indemnification for losses on a loan negotiated with the U S in the year 1813. 6-Memorial of Thos McClellan & others, of Portland, Maine, praying indemnification for French spoliations prior to 1800.

Mrd: on Dec 16, at Norfolk, Va, by Rev Upton Beall, Mr Richd D Cutts, of Wash, to Miss Martha I Hackley, d/o the late Col Richd S Hackley.

Died: on Dec 16, Mary E, y/d/o John & Mary Espey, aged 12 months & 15 days.

Ball for the benefit of the Poor will be given at the Eastern Masonic Hall, on Dec 26.
Cmte of Invitation & Reception:

D M Comb	Capt John McCauley	Jas Boiseau
Thos Thornly	Wm Quigley	Wm J Barry
R H Harrington	Thos P French	
Cmte of Arrangement		
Jos Van Reswick	John F Tucker	Chas Hooper, Ballet
Jas T Clarke	Thos Venable	Master
Jas Daley	V T Hancock	-Wash Navy Yard
John W Thompson		

A son of Mr Wm Stevens, of Phil, about 14 years of age, was run over by a frightened horse on Tue & killed on the spot.

Wash, Dec 18, 1845. I forwarn all persons from receiving a note made by Saml Williams, of Balt, to me. The note is drawn for $425 payable in 12 months, with interest. This note, with $13 in cash, one dollar of which in silver, was enclosed to me in a letter by Rev W Hamilton, of Balt, & delivered by him into the hands of Mr J Dixon, of Gtwn, at the Balt Railroad Depot, with a request that it might be left for me at the store of Mr E Tucker, to whose care it was directed. Mr Dixon, however, forgot to leave the letter at Mr Tuckers, but on the same day placed it in the care of a person by the name of Cole, who drives an omnibus, with a special request that he should leave it at Mr T's store, stating that it contained some valuable enclosures. Cole says he lost it, & therefore I have been thus particular, lest some innocent person should be imposed upon by said note.
–Jas M Hanson

Confectionary: on Bridge St, Gtwn, D C. –Wm Emmert

SAT DEC 20, 1845
House of Reps: 1-An act to amend an act for the relief of Geo Mayfield, approved Jul 7, 1842. The bill was referred to the Cmte on Private Land Claims. 2-Bill introduced for the relief of Jeremiah Moors; & a bill for the relief of Chas McKenzie. 3-Ptn of Thos Underhill's heirs, praying for remuneration for damages done to the farm & bldgs of the said Underhill by the 9th Regt of the Virginia troops in the Continental service in the year 1776. 4-Ptn of the administrator of Bolitha Laus, praying for the payment of damages sustained by the non-fulfilment of a contract on the part of the U S for bricks for the bldg of the fort at Old Point Comfort. 5-Ptn & documents of Jesse Biddle, a soldier of the last war, praying for a pension. 6-Ptn of Mrs Mary Wicks, of Jessamine Co, Ky, wid/o Wm Wicks, dec'd, praying that her claim to a pension during life may be made to commence on Mar 1, 1842. 7-Ptn of Edith Ramsey, wid/o John Ramsey, a Revolutionary soldier, praying for the benefit of the pension laws. 8-Memorial of John Hutchinson, praying to be allowed a pre-emption right to a tract of land. 9-Ptn of the legal reps of Sidney Bay, dec'd, praying for the payment of certain loan ofc certificates. 10-Ptn of the legal reps of Francis Ware, dec'd, for the payment of a lost final settlement certificate. 11-Ptn of the legal reps of Richd Frothingham, dec'd, praying for the payment of a certain note & balance. 12-Ptn of Franklin Whitney, praying that he may be renumerated for loss sustained in consequence of an error of the Com'r of Patents. 13-Ptn of Ebenezer Blake, a Revolutionary soldier, for compensation for losses sustained in the service of his country. 14-Ptn of Orinda Cooper for a pension. 15-The papers of Job Hawkins were taken from the files & referred to the Cmte on Revolutionary Pensions. 16-The papers of John C McLaughlin were referred to the Cmte of Claims. 17-The ptn & papers of Mrs Lavinia York were referred to the Cmte of Claims. 18-Ptn of Elias Carpenter for a Revolutionary claim. 19-Ptn of Eliz Betts, praying for a pension. 20-Ptn of the legal reps of Saml Mifflin, dec'd, for the payment of a loan. 21-Ptn of Mrs Rodolphine Claxton, praying for the extension of an act renewing certain naval pensions for the term of 5 years. 22-Ptn of R A Clements, adm of J N Mullican, praying compensation for work

done on the nat'l road, in the State of Indiana, with accompanying papers. 23-Ptn of Jesse Johnson, praying that money paid by him to the Register of the Land Ofc at Crawfordsville may be refunded. 24-Ptn of Edw Fitzgerald, Purser in the U S Navy. [No details.] 25-Ptn of Enoch Dobbins, praying for a pension in consequence of injuries received in the service of the U S as a subaltern ofcr of the Ky militia during the late war with Great Britain. 26-Ptn of Benj Balch, of Mass, & his associates, praying for an incorporation of a Nat'l Life Ins Co, to be located in the District of Columbia. 27-Memorial of Eliz H Dixon, wid/o Wm Dixon, praying for the confirmation of her claim to a tract of land. 28-Ptn of Cmdor Thos Ap Catesby Jones, praying remuneration for services & a reimbursement of expenses incurred in holding intercourse with the chiefs of the Sandwich & other of the South Sea islands in the years 1826 & 1827. 29-Ptn of the widow of John Stith, praying to be Relieved from the fulfillment of a contract entered into between the said John Stith & the U S for the purchase of a tract of land in Northumberland Co, Va.

Rich China Dinner, Dessert, & Tea Sets & Vases: the subscriber, intending to resign business in a few months to the younger branches of her family, is anxious to dispose of her present stock. –Sarah Tyndale, 219 Chestnut st, Phil.

All persons indebted to the subscriber will please make payment; any person having claims against him will please present them. –S Holmes, Grocer, 7th st

Mrd: on Dec 18, in Wash City, by Rev J P Donelan, M Pierre Ferrailles to Mile Marie A Martin, all of France.

Mrd: Dec 18, by Rev Mr Wilson, S L Cole, formerly of Burlington, Vt, to Adelia A English, of Wash City.

MON DEC 22, 1845
U S vs Caleb J McNulty, indictment for embezzlement. Gentlemen who testified in his behalf: J E Miller, Byron Leonard, Thos Winne, David Tod, Judge Burchard, judge of the Ohio Supreme Court, Govn'r Vance, Govn'r Corwin, now Senator from Ohio, Senator Allen, Hon A G Thurman, Hon A G Parrish, Col Medill, Gen McDowell, Mr Ranson, Judge Haywood, Col Sawyer, member of Congress, Mr Robinson, Editor of the Cincinnati Enquirer, Mr G N Ayres, Mr Giddings, Mr Geo B Wallace, Mr Converse, [McNulty's father-in-law,] Mr Turner, & Gen Kephard. Arguments will commence this morning. [Dec 25th newspaper: Jury returned a verdict of not guilty. This trial has lasted an entire week.]

The court of Boston has tried the case of Hatch & wife for injuries against the Western Railroad Co: the verdict awarded $1,500 damages!

The Hon Michl C Sprigg died very suddenly at his residence in Cumberland, Md, on Dec 8. He retired in his usual health; about midnight he was attacked with a severe headache, & in a few hours breathed his last. He has repeatedly represented Alleghany Co, in the Legislature, & was formerly the Pres of the Chesapeake & Ohio Canal Co, & had held other public responsible ofcs.

Accident at the freight depot of the Nashua & Concord Railroad in Lowell, on Fri, by which Mr Dudley Heath, the freight-master was killed. He was about 25 years of age, a native of Alexandria, N H, & has left a wife, but no children. He had been freight-master only about 6 weeks, & was an efficient & valued ofcr.

Orphans Court of Wash Co, D C. On the ptn, filed in this Court this Dec 2, 1845, as Roman Estko, Hyppolitus Estko, Louisa Estko, [Sarbut,] & Martina Estko, John Zolkowski, Caroline Zolkowski, Brigida Zolkowski, Anna Zolkowski, & Helena Zolkowski, & Wladislaus Wankowiez & Hyppolitus Wankowiez, claiming to be next of kin & distributees of Thade [or Thadeus] Kosciusko, praying that the decision of this Court, heretofore made, admitting to probate a paper-writing propounded by Kosciusko Armstrong as the last will of said Thadeus Kosciusko, be again examined, & that the matters thereof be again heard by this Court. It is ordered that the said case be again examined & heard, & that notice be given to the said Kosciusko Armstrong to appear in this Court on or before the 3rd Tue of Jan next, in person or by solicitor, to show cause why the said probate of the said will shall not be set aside, & that the said paper-writing therein propounded by him as the last will of said Thadeus Kosciusko be declared null & void. –Nathl Pope Causin -Edw N Roach, Reg/o wills

New Orleans Times of Dec 10: Parish Court: charges impeaching the integrity of Rice Garland, one of the Judges of the Supreme Court, submitted to an investigation before Judges Maurian & Collens. This is the only instance on record of a similar crime having been committed by an American Judge. [We are sorry to state that an attempt was made yesterday, by Judge Garland, to drown himself in the river. He threw himself from the deck of the steamboat **Sultana**, at the foot of St Louis st. He was providentially rescued by the intrepidity of a sailor on board.]

City Ordnance-Wash. 1-Act for the relief of John Donovan: fine imposed on him for a violation of an ordinance relative to keeping open taverns, be & the same is remitted: provided he pay the costs of prosecution. 2-Act for the relief of A C Kidwell: to be paid the balance due, the sum of $41.74 for laying flag footways. 3-Act for the relief of P L Leman: that the fine imposed for an alleged violation of an ordinance relative to dogs, be & the same is remitted: provided he pay the costs of prosecution. 4-Act for the relief of Geo McDuell: to be paid the sum of $16, for filling up certain low grounds in C st; the same having been done by order of the Board of Health. 5-Act for the relief of Wm J Jeffers: to be refunded the sum of $8.75, being the amount paid by him for a huckster's license on Jun 5, 1845.

Wm Grupe, Confectioner, on the north side of Pa ave, 3rd door west of 4½ st: all sorts of confectionary, German & French toys, jewelry, & Fancy articles, at very moderate rates.

For rent: large frame dwlg house on the corner of 6th & H sts. Also for rent, 2 small cottage dwlgs. Inquire of Jas B Phillips, Mass ave, Northern Liberties.

To the People of Capitol Hill-for your convenience I have opened a little Dry Goods Store in your midst. Will you support it? It is only a square east of N J ave, on south B st. –John Hitz

TUE DEC 23, 1845
Senate: 1-Ptn of John Clark, a soldier of the last war, asking for a pension. 2-Memorial of Richd S Coxe, of Wash City, asking compensation for services while employed as counsel for the Genr'l Post Ofc Dept. 3-Ptn of Nathl Haggatt, praying the confirmation of a private land claim in Louisiana. 4-Memorial of Stephen May, praying the reimbursement of the costs & expenses of a suit against him by the U S, as surety for a delinquent postmaster. 5-Memorial of Jas S McIntosh, an ofcr in the Navy, praying compensation for the performance of duties while acting in a higher grade of service. 6-Memorial of Ann Mix, wid/o Merrine P Mix, dec'd, an ofcr in the Navy, praying the purchase by the Gov't of a patent right taken out by her late husband for an invention of a manger stopper for chain cables.

Notice: the situation of Assistant Teacher in the Upper Marlborough Academy is now vacant, & applications for the place will be received until Dec 26. Salary is fixed at $350 per annum, payable sem-annually. Applications to Jno B Brooke, Pres, Upper Marlborough, Md.

Nominations for Chaplain of the House of Reps: 3rd ballot:
*Rev A A Muller   *Rev Wm M Daley
Rev Wm A Milburne-105   *Rev T H Stockton
Rev Wm Sprole-63   *Rev Mr Matthews
*Rev Septimus Tuston   *Rev C Dickson/Dixon
Rev R R Gurley-8   *Rev Mr Hovey
Rev Champe C Connor-10   *Rev Mr Dewey
*Rev Geo W Maley   *The remainder withdrawn.
Rev Milburne was declared duly elected a Chaplain to Congress on the part of the House of Reps for the present session.

Died: on Dec 29, at Mr Peter Ottoback's, Chas Hunger, aged 29 years, a native of Germany, but for the last 12 years a resident of Wash.

Died: on Dec 21, at the Navy Yard, James R, infant s/o Jas & Eliz Dickerson, aged 1 year, 10 months & 7 days.

Died: on Dec 7, at the residence of Mrs Coleman, Cumberland Co, Va, John Baptist Thomson, of Chas Co, Md, in his 21st year. To his friends & acquaintances his death came with an appalling sadness.

WED DEC 24, 1845
Senate: 1-Ptn of Emeline Owens, wid/o the late Col J T Owens, aksing relief for losses sustained by her from the ravages of the U S soldiers during the Black Hawk war in 1832. 2-Memorial of John Crowell, late Indian agent of the Creek nation, asking further allowances in the settlement of his accounts. 3-Ptn of Archibald Smith, of Florida, for the remuneration of damages sustained in consequence of a suit against him by the U S. 4-Ptn of Col Robt Butler, of Tallahassee, for remuneration for private property applied for public use. 5-Ptn of Mrs Susan McCullogh, for a pension. 6-Ptn of Chas Fletcher, of Lancaster, for a mail route to the Pacific Ocean. 7-Memorial of Henry Etting, a purser in the navy, praying to be indemnified for expenses & losses incurred in a suit against the Commercial Bank of New Orleans for recovery of public moneys deposited in said bank. 8-Ptn of David D Porter, praying for a pension for Mrs Edmund Porter, the wid/o a dec'd naval ofcr. 9-Ptn of Danl R Baker, a soldier in the last war, asking a pension. 10-Ptn of Clara H Pike, wid/o Zebulon M Pike, dec'd, late an ofcr in the U S army, praying compensation for the services of her husband, in exploring the Mississippi river, & the southern part of the Territory of Louisiana; & another ptn of Mrs Pike, praying the restoration of her name to the pension list; both of which were refered to the Military Cmte. 11-Ptn of Amos Holton, praying the settlement of his accounts: referred to the Cmte of Claims. 12-Ptn of Wm Moore, of Littlefort, Lake Co, Ill, for relief. 13-Ptn of Jas Wyman. [No details.] 14-Ptn of Gideon Walker, with additional evidence. 15-Ptn of Asa Armington. [No details.] 16-Ptn of Francis Remmil, for a pension.

New & Amusing Games: for sale-Stationer, Pa ave, between 11th & 12th sts. –Wm F Bayly

PG County Lands. Marlborough Gaz: the farm belonging to the estate of the late W B C Worthington, on the Patuxent river, Md, near Nottingham, containing 900 acs, was sold at public sale on Tue last for $16,501.00-being a fraction under $18.33 1/3 per ac. Purchaser: L H Early. On Tue, Robt Bowie sold about 630 acres of *Bowieville farm*, in the Forest of PG Co, to Mr Wm L Berry, at $40 per ac.

Three children of Mrs Robinson, a widow lady, were burnt to death at Rochester, N Y, Thu last: 2 boys aged 8 & 5, & a little girl 3 years of age. They were sleeping in the upper part of the bldg.

At Phil, on Wed, a young man, Matthew Shaw, was killed when a large grindstone burst, while revolving at a rapid rate.

Marshall L Chapin, of Long Meadow, Mass, aged 16, & John Dresser, aged 8, were drowned when they fell through the ice on the Skungamung river, on Fri. They belonged to the East School, Pond Hill, Conn.

Died: on Dec 20, very suddenly, in his 43rd year, John Holmes Offley, s/o the late David Offley, of Smyrna. His funeral is this morning, at 10 o'clock, at his late residence, in Gtwn.

Died: on Dec 16, in Wash City, Thomas, eldest s/o Fielder & Sarah Burch, in his 25th year.

Mortality from Cancer. Died, in the town of Schaghticoke, N Y, on Dec 2, of cancer in the throat, Eleanor, aged 7 years, & on Dec 7, of the same disease, Catharine, aged 20 years, & the same day, of the same disease, Caroline, aged 5 years, all daughters of Phillip & Eleanor Strunk. Also, on Dec 6, of the same disease, Jos Henry, aged 1 year, s/o Phillip H & Eveline Strunk. The 3 latter were buried on Dec 6, all at one time, from one house. Thus their afflicted parents buried out of their sight 3 children & 1 grandchild in the short period of 5 days.

Wash Corp: 1-Ptn of Thos N Davis, for remission of a fine: referred to the Cmte of Claims. 2-Ptn of John P Stallings, for remission of a fine: referred to the Cmte of Claims. 3-Cmte of Claims asked to be discharged from its further consideration of the ptn of Louisa Collins: agreed to. 4-Bill for the relief of Henry Hoffman & others: referred to the Cmte on Improvements.

For rent: a house on 12th st, near Franklin row, occupied by Mr Hungerford; possession given on Jan 1 next. Inquire of Mr Hungerford, in the house, or of-Alex Borland.

THU DEC 25, 1845
Lt Rankin, one of the companies of U S Artl, stationed at St Augustine, [East Florida,] a very promising young ofcr, was riding on horseback on Wed, contemplating a visit to a friend near the city, when the horse started with him, &, the bridle-rein breaking, Lt Rankin was thrown violently against one of the trees in South Broad st. His head struck the tree, a concussion of the brain was caused, & up to last evening, lay in a very precarious situation. He was on a temporary visit to his family & friends in this city. –Savannah Georgian, Dec 19 [Dec 29th newspaper: Lt Jas L Rankin has since died. He was a native of Mercer Co, Pa, where his parents now reside.]

Mammoth Christmas Plum Cake, weighing 500 pounds may be seen at the confectionary store of the subscriber on Dec 24. After the exhibition, it will be cut up to suit purchasers. –Geo Krafft, 18th & Pa ave

New England Society of the City of Wash commemorated the founding of the first colony of New England: landing of the Pilgrims on Plymouth Rock. Mr David A Hall, Pres of the Society. On Dec 22, 1620 many landed on a shore unknown to them

The Caroline [Md] Pearl announces the death of Thos Wheeler, member elect from Caroline Co to the House of Delegates. He died on Dec 15, at his residence in Caroline Co.

The wife of Jos Hill, aged 65 years, of Sussex Co, N J, was bitten in the hand a short time since by a hog, causing a wound which spread through the entire arm, until the malignant virus entered the vitals, terminating her suffering by death on Thu last.

Died: on Dec 23, James M McArann, s/o John & Mary Ann McArann, in his 13th year.

Died: on Dec 8, at his residence, in Harrison Co, Va, Mr Job Goff, at the advanced age of 86 years. He was a native of the State of R I; coming to manhood during the contest between these Colonies & the mother country, he was one of those who freely took up arms in defence of the struggling cause of liberty. He served 3 years in his native State in the war of the Revolution. He subsequently removed to Vt, thence to N Y, & afterwards, more than 44 years ago, to the place of his late residence & of his death.

For sale: valuable fishery & farm: near the mouth of Aquia creek, known as the *Tump*, not more than a half a mile from the Steamboat Landing & Railroad Depot, on the route from Wash to Richmond. Also, a farm containing about 750 acs, being part of the old *Marlborough Estate*, on the Potomac, within 3 hours of Alexandria, Gtwn, & Wash. For terms apply to Messrs Wm Fowle & Sons, Alexandria, D C, or to the subscriber, Falmouth, Va. –J B Ficklin

SAT DEC 27, 1845
Wm Hickling Webber, age 16 years, s/o Capt John A Webber, U S Army, was instantly killed by a fall from the mizzen topsail yard of the ship **Woodside**, at the mouth of the Hoogly river, in Sept.

Miss Schuyler, a niece of Gen Stephen Van Rensselaer, was killed in Albany on Mon, while riding in a sleigh, by being run against by a pair of runaway horses attached to a farmer's sleigh. The pole of the sleigh struck Miss Schuyler in the side & caused her death almost instantaneously.

The Trustees of Primary School #8 wish to engage for 1846 a Tutor. Address the subscriber, post paid, at Port Tobacco, Chas Co, Md: salary $530 per annum. F B F Burgass, Treas Primary School #8

Miss Lucy Mary Evans purposes opening a school on Jan 6, for a few scholars. She has been for the last 20 years or more a member of the Episcopal Church of Wash. Terms made known by application at the residence of Wm Rowe, on 10th st, between G & H sts.

Horse stolen from the farm of Wm D Bowie, PG Co, Md, on Wed. $50 will be given for the horse & apprehension of the thief. –Richd H Beall, at Wm D Bowie's, PG Co, Md.

Wm Thomas, aged about 10 years, was saved from drowning on Tue when he broke through the ice in Spring Gardens, Balt. A negro man caught him by the hair & succeeded in extricating him.

Balt County Court: on Wed: the case of John Rider charged with the murder of John Combes, in Balt Co: verdict was justifiable homicide, & Rider was acquitted & homorably discharged: self-defence.

Mrd: on Dec 23, by Elder T D Herndon, Wm F Dowell, of Fauquier, to Miss Senorah A, eldest d/o Peter Gooding, of Fairfax, Va.

Died: on Dec 25, suddenly, at Jenkins' Metropolis House, Geo Hawkins, [colored,] one of the attendants of the establishment, aged 35 years. The cause of his death originating from cutting his corns 3 days before his decease. He was a sober, polite, & intelligent servant, & an honest man. His colored friends are invited to attend his funeral tomorrow, at 3 o'clock p m.

Rev Jas G Hamner, of Balt, will preach in the 2nd Presbyterian Church, N Y ave & H st, tomorrow at 11.

MON DEC 29, 1845
New Paper: the N Y Morning Telegraph, edited by Simeon De Witt Bloodgood, first issue-Dec 25.

The dwlg-house of Mr Wm Mangum, in Maury Co, Tenn, took fire on Dec 5, burning up 2 of his sons, one about 4 & the other about 6 years old, together with his household furniture. A similar calamity at Redbank township, in Armstrong Co, Pa, on Dec 9, by which 4 sons of Mr McClellan were burnt to death, the eldest being 18 years & the youngest 7 years old. They were sleeping in an upper room of a log-house.

Elisha Blackman, said to be the last survivor of the Wyoming massacre, [Jul 3rd, 1778,] died at his residence in Hanover, Wyoming Valley, on Dec 4, in his 89th year.

Senate: 1-Ptn of the reps of Geo W Corliess, dec'd, an ofcr in the Revolutionary war. 2-Ptn of Zadock Huntley, a Revolutionary soldier, asking a pension. 3-Ptn of Richd Kidd & Benj Kidd, for the payment of the residue of their judgment against Saml Swartwout, late Collector of N Y. 4-Ptn of Jonathan Little, praying the re-payment of certain duties illegally extracted on a cargo of silk twist imported in 1839. 5-Ptn of the legal reps of Mountjoy Bayly, a dec'd Revolutionary ofcr, asking interest on his commutation pay. 6-Ptn of Ruth Ralsom, of Dover, for the renewal of a lost bounty land warrant. 6-Ptn of Ambrose Davenport, for compensation for military services during the last war with Great Britain. 7-Bill for the relief of Mary McCrea, wid/o Col Wm McCrea: referred.

Dress & Water-proof Boots: Call & see, between Colemam's & Brown's, next door to Tucker & Son's, Pa ave. –S Hagerty

House of Reps: 1-Ptn of Mrs Ann Royall, the wid/o a Revolutionary soldier, praying for a pension. 2-Ptn of Ann Clayton, praying for an increase of pension. 3-Ptn of Saml Bump, of Licking Co, Ohio, praying for a pension. 4-Ptn & papers of Moses Segur were referred to the Cmte on Revolutionary Pensions. 5-Ptn of Caroline E Sanders, excx of Wm G Sanders, formerly a sutler in the U S Army, praying additional compensation for bldgs destroyed by order of an ofcr of the U S Army. 6-Ptn of Jas Green for pension as a midshipman in the Virginia State Navy from 1777 to 1781. 7-Ptn of John B Wingerd for compensation for services in the ofc of First Comptroller of the Treasury. 8-Ptn of Rosana Moore, praying for a pension in consideration of the services of her husband during the Revolutionarywar.

Meeting of the Ofcrs of the 7th Regt of the U S Infty, at camp near Corpus Christi, Texas, convened on the death of Lt Col Wm Hoffman, of that regt, on Nov 26, 1845. Lt F N Page, Adj 7th Infty, called to the chair. Resolved: our condolence to the bereaved widow & relatives of the dec'd. He lived a virtuous life.

Murders. Louisville Journal of Mon last: in one of the hotels in that city, Jas Hawthorn was struck by Jos Croxton as he was sleeping in a chair, with sufficient force to break his neck & kill him. Croxton made his escape. Wm Hall & Thos Good, renewed their quarrel in a public house in Cincinnati on Mon last, which ended in Good killing Hall with a knife.

A steam-boiler in the box factory of Messrs W & O Tirrell, at Boston, exploded on Wed, killing Mr Wm Tirrell, a son of one of the firm, & Mr Wm Ford, both of them young men.

Mrd: on Dec 23, by Rev Mr Tarring, Mr John T King to Miss Virginia A Atwell, all of Wash City.

Mrd: on Dec 23, in Richmond City, Va, by Rev Mr Norwood, Jas A Seddon, Rep in Congress from Richmond district, to Sarah Bruce, d/o the late Jas Bruce, of Halifax Co.

Died: on Dec 26, in Balt, Henry Payson, who was among the oldest residents of Balt, was in his time a distinguished & fortunate merchant, & was among the most esteemed of that venerable race who, by long residence, general usefulness, & great enterprise, are entitled to be called the Fathers of the City.

Died: on Dec 13, at Gorham, Maine, A M Hamlin, about 24 years of age, & recently of Wash City. He left here a few months since in feeble health, & returned to his home & friends in Maine, having previously attached himself to Beacon Lodge #15, I O O F, held in this place. Members of Saccarappa Lodge #11, Maine, watched by his bed, & smoothed the pillow of a dying brother.

Criminal Court-Wash. Since the trial & acquittal of McNulty, on one of the indictments against him, nothing has been done in Court relative to the other indictments for embezzlement & misappropriation of the public money. McNulty remains in prison to await the decision which may be made in these cases.

Criminal Court-Wash. 1-Jas Black, a white man, found guilty for stealing new books, the property of a book-vendor: sentenced to 1 year in the penitentiary. 2-Thos Gardiner, [white] found guilty for breaking into the house of Eliz Mattingly, near Gtwn, in Nov last, with a felonious intent: moved for a new trial. 3-Thos Stewart, [white,] also found guilty of the same offence. 4-Trial of Wm J Dowling, alias Wm J Brown, alias Wm C Brown, charged with burglary & arson. He was found in the cellar of Dr Hall's dwlg, on Pa ave, & made a furious attack upon the Dr on Oct 29 last. He was tried on 2 other indictments: burning the house of Mr Henry Thorn, on Nov 8 last; stealing small articles the property of Mr Thorn. Jury found him not guilty of arson, & guilty of larceny. He broke into the house of Mr I F Mudd with intent to steal; stole carpenter's tools, over the value of $5, the property of Mr Knowles: jury found him guilty in both cases. For burglary at Dr Hall's: he is to suffer 4 years & 6 months in the penitentiary; for burglary at Mr Mudd's: 3 years in the penitentiary; for larceny at Mr Knowles': 1 year in the penitentiary. 5-On Sat John Tennant was indicted for an assault & battery upon John Paxton, of Gtwn, in Sept last: found guilty. Dfndnt was sentenced to pay a fine of $25. 6-The trial of Thos Cook, charged with the murder of Thos Naylor, is fixed for this day.

TUE DEC 30, 1845
Mrs Maria Brooks, the authoress of Zophiel, died on Nov 11 last, at Matanzas, Cuba, from the debility consequent upon a severe fit of sickness. She was about 50 years old; born at Medford, in this State, & for a considerable period resided in this city. From the Boston Courier.

The Hon Jas Thomas, formerly Gov'r of Md, died at his residence in St Mary's Co, on Christmas Day, in his 62nd year, of typhoid fever, with which he lingered a long time. -Patriot

Senate: 1-Ptn from J L Cathcart, exc of Jas J Cathcart, dec'd, for indemnification of losses sustained by the illegal seizure & detention of himself & cargo by the French in 1803, while acting as Consul Genr'l to the Barbary Powers. 2-Ptn of J H Causten, the assignee of John B Hogan, for compensation as com'r to investigate frauds on the Creek Indians in 1835 & 1836. 3-Ptn of Wm H Hildreth, to be reimbursed for merchandise advanced to com'rs to locate the Sac & Fox Indians west of the Mississippi. 4-Ptn of Hannah Branch, asking a pension. 5-Ptn of Reuben Mills, asking a pension. 6-Ptn of Reuben Mills, asking a pension. 7-Ptn from Eliz Saila, wid/o a dec'd Revolutionary soldier, praying a pension. 8-Ptn of Col John Carter, of Gtwn, asking permission of Congress to bring certain slaves into the District. 9-Ptn of Richd Elliott, for a pension.

By a letter dated Minden, Parish of Claiborne, Louisiana, Nov 24, we learn that Gen Wimberly, an old & respectable citizen of that parish, was killed by his son James. We have not heard the particulars of this act. We fear it was the result of a long life of recklessness & crime on the part of the son.

Mrd: on Dec 23, at **Fort Johnston**, N C, by Rev Dr Drane, Lt D P Woodbury, of the U S Engineer Corps, to Catherine R, d/o Lt Col Thos Childs, U S Army.

Died: Dec 7, near Rome, Ind, Jacob Kopler, a Revolutionary soldier. He was born in Lancaster Co, Pa, on Apr 23, 1739, & would have been 107 had he lived to Apr 23 next.

Died: on Dec 2, at Savannah, Georgia, Mrs Maria H Sibley, w/o Capt E S Sibley, U S Army, y/d/o the late Judge Cuyler, of that city.

Died: on Dec 29, in Cob Neck, Chas Co, Md, Mrs Eliz Loretto McWilliams, leaving a husband & 4 small children to mourn their loss.

WED DEC 31, 1845
Mrd: on Dec 29, at the **Highlands**, by Rev Mr Gallagher, Theodore Mosher, of Gtwn, to Mary, d/o Robt Y Brent, of Montgomery Co, Md.

Senate: 1-Memorial of N Kuykendall, praying compensation for extra services in carrying the mail. 2-Ptn of Eliz Gassaway, widow, asking for a pension. 3-Ptn of Abigail Reeves, asking for a pension. 4-Ptn of Peter Gorman, asking for additional compensation due for gravelling the road from the Capitol to the **Congress Burying Ground**. 5-Ptn of Harriet Ward, wid/o a dec'd naval ofcr, praying a pension. 6-Ptn of the heirs of Lt Crocker Sampson, dec'd, praying for scrip on a bounty land warrant.

7-Ptn of the heirs of Nicholas Barrs, dec'd, asking for a title to a tract of land in Louisiana. 8-Ptn of Saml Knight, jr, praying a pension for injuries received while in the service of the U S, in the erection of a monument on Stag Island, in the State of Maine. 9-Cmte on Pensions: to inquire into granting 5 years' pay to Mrs Mary Jane West, wid/o Lt Jas West, who died in public service in 1839.

New Paper: the N Y Morning Telegraph, edited by Simeon De Witt Bloodgood, first issue-Dec 25.

A

Aaron, 316, 414
Abbot, 68, 348, 399, 458
Abbott, 54, 157, 286, 325, 344, 353, 380, 450
Abell, 24, 41, 296, 315, 390
Abercombie, 126
Abercrombie, 467
Abert, 151, 411, 461
Able, 471
Aborn, 258
Abott, 411
Abrams, 207, 287
Abrengelh, 363
Acerman, 74
Acheson, 123, 406
Acken, 31, 248, 481
Acker, 417, 475, 481
Ackerly, 270
Ackermain, 307
Ackley, 485
Acosta, 100, 278
Acre's Hollow, 214
Acton, 58, 372
Adams, 11, 40, 44, 53, 61, 69, 71, 74, 75, 82, 90, 94, 108, 110, 114, 116, 135, 142, 156, 158, 172, 173, 183, 206, 207, 215, 231, 255, 311, 318, 321, 325, 332, 337, 344, 349, 353, 363, 368, 390, 412, 414, 417, 427, 437, 450, 451, 466, 471, 478, 479, 483, 485, 494
Adcock, 247
Addison, 71, 74, 113, 162, 171, 213, 258, 406
Addition, 435
Adela, 3
Adie, 246, 340, 467
Adler, 84, 394, 486
Adolphus, 314
Aers, 390
Afton, 265

Agate, 358
Agner, 252
Agnew, 24
Aiken, 125, 177, 216
Aikin, 359
Ailier, 417
Airheart, 301
Aisquith, 128, 129, 325, 436
Ajax Farm, 204, 305
Akars, 31
Alber, 248
Albert, 278
Albertson, 256
Aldama, 71
Alden, 82
Aldrich, 30, 56, 220, 452
Alerson, 278
Alexander, 3, 11, 34, 49, 64, 125, 140, 143, 188, 223, 278, 283, 303, 325, 354, 398, 406, 452, 471, 475, 491
Algoma, 212
Alleman, 300
Allen, 2, 13, 28, 33, 34, 35, 40, 44, 45, 56, 62, 65, 77, 88, 94, 102, 108, 113, 121, 126, 177, 191, 200, 236, 239, 244, 272, 289, 313, 314, 316, 323, 330, 358, 363, 381, 405, 406, 427, 452, 456, 471, 488, 491, 500
Allibone, 288
Allien, 290
Allison, 211, 320, 367
Allouez, 222
Alston, 471, 491
Alvee, 471
Alves, 163
Alvey, 5, 278
Alvin, 100
Ambler, 245
Ames, 35, 49
Ammen, 147
Anderson, 7, 25, 75, 77, 95, 126, 155, 156, 174, 188, 257, 278, 284, 287, 291, 301, 307, 313, 325, 333, 344,

363, 372, 385, 406, 416, 418, 437, 441, 463
Andre, 31
Andrew, 452
Andrews, 18, 19, 44, 78, 88, 180, 272, 295, 296, 300, 344, 433
Andross, 184
Angammarre, 307
Angel, 427
Angier, 403
Ann, 444
Anthony, 219, 337
Antrim, 427
Apenwall, 390
Appich, 76, 471
Appleton, 152, 189, 264
Archbold, 303
Archer, 26, 296, 300, 336, 344
Archibald, 255
Ardasr, 197
Ardus Cottage, 382
Arey, 286, 302
Argais, 278
Arguelles, 470
Arlington Estate, 423
Armfield, 424
Armington, 503
Armistead, 59, 164, 307, 325, 400, 410, 414, 445, 446
Armstead, 279
Armstrong, 63, 100, 101, 147, 156, 172, 272, 274, 275, 427, 436, 452, 471, 494, 501
Arnold, 12, 13, 16, 32, 103, 259, 260, 278, 279, 296, 312, 313, 325, 431, 488
Arthur, 173, 243
Artot, 330
Arvin, 278
Arzevedo, 406
Ashby, 69, 321
Ashdown, 197
Ashford, 96, 267
Ashley, 32, 363

Ashmead, 100
Ashton, 249, 259, 260, 292, 306, 318, 325, 452
Astor, 93, 452
Atcherson, 387
Atkins, 406
Atkinson, 66, 256, 303, 307, 344, 490
Atwell, 55, 507
Atwill, 49, 488
Atwood, 122
Audubon, 302
Augur, 445
Augustin, 254
Auld, 325, 491
Auley, 427
Aulick, 60, 92, 199, 217, 336
Ault, 372
Austen, 478
Austin, 41, 68, 110, 154, 289, 304, 341, 403
Averill, 96
Avery, 48
Avondale, 167
Awalt, 103
Ayars, 325
Ayres, 500
Ayton, 385

B

Babb, 163
Babbitt, 364
Babcock, 351, 390, 406
Baby, 297
Bache, 100, 126, 151, 220
Bachman, 427
Back, 104
Backenstos, 420
Backer, 292
Backus, 79, 255
Bacon, 7, 20, 121, 215, 235, 236, 417
Bacques, 175
Bade, 291
Baden, 207, 340, 387

Bagby, 47, 406, 471
Baggeld, 47
Baggett, 462
Bagley, 266
Bagmam, 157
Bagot, 65
Bailey, 1, 142, 266, 269, 338, 345, 390, 423, 427, 442
Baillie, 390
Baily, 29, 232, 238, 333, 390
Bainbridge, 113, 312, 491
Baird, 195, 401, 406
Baker, 4, 33, 36, 41, 44, 56, 247, 256, 279, 298, 325, 345, 364, 390, 405, 416, 417, 427, 433, 439, 448, 483, 490, 491, 503
Baker's Tanyard, 411
Bakewell, 141, 401
Balch, 325, 390, 500
Balderson, 451
Baldridge, 88
Baldrige, 45
Baldwin, 38, 45, 59, 88, 136, 173, 233, 258, 259, 260, 307, 322, 325, 390, 414, 424, 443, 457, 491
Baley, 491
Ball, 18, 25, 104, 279, 286, 325, 355, 402, 406, 452, 463, 491
Ballade, 345, 390, 427, 471
Ballard, 27, 38, 247
Balser, 256
Baltimore, 491
Baltzell, 176, 336, 438
Bancker, 345
Bancroft, 82, 101, 181, 266, 270, 273, 423
Bandel, 325
Bangs, 406
Bankhead, 471
Banks, 279, 345
Bannatyne, 189, 489
Banner, 251
Banning, 486

Bannister, 121
Bansketi, 364
Banvard, 395
Baptist, 254
Barbarin, 406
Barber, 90, 314, 405
Barbour, 18, 187, 312, 339, 457, 491
Barclay, 9, 71, 187, 202, 207, 215, 291, 325, 333, 350, 364, 372, 450, 497
Barcley, 497
Bardin, 252
Barker, 22, 24, 78, 139, 224, 290, 293, 351, 381, 395, 463, 474, 475, 483, 488, 489
Barkley, 319
Barnaclo, 162
Barnard, 96, 427
Barnes, 25, 152, 157, 205, 261, 325, 363, 383, 427, 471, 481, 483, 491
Barnett, 25, 497
Barney, 261, 265, 345, 471
Barnhardt, 19, 343
Barns, 406
Barnum, 79, 92, 188, 384
Baron, 144
Barour, 94
barque **Hecla**, 162
barque **Mary**, 461
Barr, 47, 383
Barrand, 147
Barras, 364
Barret, 248, 249
Barrett, 24, 67, 255, 279, 359, 390, 461
Barrette, 345, 364
Barrington, 126, 238
Barrow, 111, 390
Barrs, 510
Barry, 4, 40, 163, 279, 298, 352, 364, 498
Bart, 390
Bartin, 406
Bartler, 308
Bartlett, 406, 488, 491

513

Bartley, 217, 307, 345
Bartolme, 388
Barton, 118, 295, 300, 302, 452, 462, 464, 483, 488
Bartoni, 319
Bartow, 225, 279, 307, 345
Bartruff, 254
Bascom, 97
Bass, 2, 32
Bassano, 388
Basset, 78
Bassett, 15, 95, 153, 258, 259, 260
Bassinger, 352
Batchelder, 44, 59, 82
Batchellar, 7
Bates, 11, 101, 112, 120, 159, 193, 197, 202, 206, 225, 233, 301, 372, 405, 417, 475, 485
Bathan, 427
Battaile, 482
Battin, 324
Batty, 55
Baum, 372
Baury, 366
Bauskett, 364
Baxter, 100, 315, 415
Bay, 499
Bayard, 90, 100, 207, 225
Bayle, 468
Bayless, 467, 479
Bayley, 191
Bayliss, 382
Baylor, 375
Bayly, 7, 37, 503, 507
Bayly's Purchase, 378
Bayne, 62, 279, 410, 455, 480
Beach, 154, 216, 307, 325
Beale, 204, 253, 305, 390, 424, 452
Beall, 144, 154, 172, 218, 236, 254, 278, 325, 331, 378, 387, 416, 417, 441, 444, 452, 483, 489, 498, 506
Beallair, 256
Bealle, 372

Bean, 27, 112, 133, 161, 209, 248, 260, 368, 433, 478, 481
Bearch, 345
Beard, 240, 364, 390, 471
Beardsley, 300
Beaseley, 436
Beasley, 417
Beatty, 35, 293, 443
Beauville, 292
Beaver Dam, 435
Becher, 214
Beck, 168, 295, 307, 345, 358, 379, 406, 471
Becker, 456
Beckett, 357
Beckley, 41
Beckner, 103
Becraft, 307
Bedell, 266, 404
Bedford, 258
Bee, 272
Beebe, 210
Beech, 344
Beecher, 311
Beeler, 32
Been, 491
Beender, 253
Beers, 103, 157, 161, 325, 356, 417
Beers', 103
Beethoven, 355
Beetley, 307, 471
Beirne, 121, 216
Beker, 275
Bel Air, 90
Belair, 254
Belanger, 488
Belcher, 49
Belknap, 16
Bell, 22, 28, 29, 31, 36, 40, 74, 76, 89, 140, 196, 226, 299, 315, 330, 333, 363, 406, 427, 471, 491
Bellows, 291
Belmonti, 254

Belt, 160, 172, 253, 263, 415, 442, 478
Belton, 325, 445
Bemis, 336
Bender, 155, 277, 380, 408, 450
Benedict, 144, 390, 427, 452
Benedictine monastery, 150
Benker, 385
Bennett, 97, 118, 381, 390
Bennette, 471
<u>Benning's Bridge</u>, 348
Benns, 23
Benson, 24, 25, 174, 370, 442
Bent, 89
Bentaloe, 442
Benter, 226, 416
Benthall, 321
Bentley, 322, 471
Benton, 46, 75, 122, 142
Bequette, 287
Berandon, 269
Bergel, 491
Bergen, 196, 316, 376
Berkeley, 33
Bernard, 190, 274, 307
Berret, 268
Berrien, 490
Berry, 2, 48, 59, 84, 110, 112, 123, 168, 206, 218, 228, 241, 246, 265, 277, 279, 294, 308, 325, 332, 335, 345, 364, 384, 393, 406, 414, 417, 445, 446, 471, 478, 490, 491, 496, 503
Berryman, 147, 206, 227, 298
Bert, 214
Berth, 427
Bertrand, 290
Besancon, 364
Besaneon, 390, 406
Bester, 114
Bestor, 86, 133, 270, 460
Bettas, 364
Bettinger, 418
Betts, 89, 233, 381, 499
Bevan, 279

Bevand, 494
Bevens, 427
Beveridge, 7, 254
Beverly, 325
Beyer, 485
Bibb, 312, 344, 364, 390, 452, 471
Bibbs, 364, 390, 427, 452, 471
Bickford, 95, 425, 431
Bickner, 104
Biddle, 78, 168, 193, 233, 401, 499
Bidermann, 307
Bidlack, 269
Bidleman, 491
Bielaski, 345
Bieuvand, 471
Bievand, 406
Biewend, 325, 423
Bigelow, 74, 368, 380, 404
Bigger, 111
Biggs, 481
Bihler, 32, 256, 386, 463
Bill, 351
Billing, 372
Billingslea, 42
Billopp, 397
Billups, 297
Binda, 188
Bingham, 21, 195, 364
Binney, 99, 230
Binns, 498
Birch, 25, 29, 38, 307, 416, 462
Birchett, 325
Birchmore, 30
Bird, 17, 53, 85, 172, 336, 390
Birdsall, 128
Birkbeck, 303
Birkhead, 49
Birth, 307, 406
Biscoe, 140, 286, 403
Biser, 91
Bisher, 345
Bishop, 97, 279, 364, 381, 390, 489, 491
Bispham, 13

Bissell, 36, 94, 133, 134, 447, 491, 494
Bitner, 416
Bives, 471
Black, 30, 99, 100, 144, 203, 324, 333, 363, 390, 399, 462, 508
Blackburn, 25, 189
Blackford, 100, 364, 390, 450
Blackford Estate, 165
Blackler, 75
Blacklin, 292
Blackman, 506
Blacknall, 28, 376, 452
Blackson, 390
Blackwell, 60, 63, 308
Bladon, 114
Blagden, 109, 166, 231, 399, 432, 449, 465, 478
Blaine, 186
Blair, 100, 205, 217, 220, 258, 381, 390, 418, 424
Blake, 44, 78, 92, 159, 318, 385, 499
Blakely, 466
Blakesle, 77
Blanc, 307
Blanchard, 109, 154, 290, 468
Bland, 209, 434
Blandford, 340
Blanding, 49, 56
Blannerhasset, 27
Blansherd, 491
Bledsoe, 50, 477
Bleeker, 279
Blen, 254
Blessington, 181
Bliss, 59, 307, 325, 466
Blodget, 45, 77, 89, 94, 409
Blood, 363, 406, 427
Bloodgood, 292, 506, 510
Bloom, 95
Blount, 45, 193, 258
Blow, 385
Blunt, 466
Blythe, 180, 452

Boarman, 137, 349, 364
boat **Belle of Nashville**, 44
boat **Fell's Point**, 439
boat **La Belle Boat**, 354
boat **Plymouth**, 449
Boche, 307
Boda, 34
Bodine, 148
Bodisco, 234, 296, 300
Bodkin, 191
Boerstler, 350
Bogardus, 28, 364, 376, 466
Bogart, 324
Bogert, 364, 390
Bogety, 427
Bogily, 406
Bogoden, 291
Boguet, 388
Bohlayer, 116, 139
Bohrer, 223, 259, 260, 325, 364, 406, 471, 491
Boilevin, 406
Boiseau, 47, 498
Bold, 7
Bolding, 471
Bolend, 279
Bolling, 304
Bolton, 396, 427
Boman, 325
Bomford, 81, 128, 143, 208, 367, 426
Bonaparte, 166, 182, 288, 355, 388
Bonaparte Estate, 402
Boncher, 58
Bond, 325
Bonds, 279
Bonn, 427, 471
Bonnedeau, 57
Bonnett, 452
Bonneville, 445
Bonton, 452
Bontz, 427
Booker, 271
Boon, 5, 212, 317

Boone, 144, 173, 207, 277, 349, 378
Boonsboro, 108
Booth, 261, 265, 411, 456
Boots, 397
Borchers, 491
Borgouzin, 291
Borland, 475, 504
Borlvin, 452
Borremans, 294
Borrham, 443
Borrough Hall, 413
Borrows, 5, 12, 138, 181, 368
Boshley, 471
Boss, 188, 461
Bossauge, 292
Bossier, 488
Boston, 45, 56, 88, 395
Boswell's Enclosure, 456
Bosworth, 349
Boteler, 169, 185, 187, 222, 278, 338, 339, 350, 390, 455
Botts, 302
Boucher, 444
Bouck, 46
Boudinot, 28, 376
Boudinots, 65
Boulanger, 372
Bouldin, 67, 230
Boulware, 360, 390
Bourne, 464
Bouseau, 456
Boutcher, 364
Boutwell, 203
Bouvet, 416
Bouvett, 131
Bowden, 489
Bowen, 52, 279, 308, 364, 379, 390, 491
Bower, 344, 345
Bowers, 488
Bowes, 345
Bowie, 12, 50, 99, 105, 119, 144, 147, 303, 319, 322, 387, 443, 459, 491, 503, 506

Bowieville, 319
Bowieville farm, 503
Bowling, 75, 250, 349, 372
Bowman, 312, 325, 364, 390
Bowne, 381
Boyce, 57, 165, 473
Boyd, 23, 45, 80, 175, 207, 279, 289, 298, 307, 325, 354, 382, 390, 443, 447, 462
Boyden, 345
Boyer, 176, 281, 442
Boykin, 308
Boyle, 2, 130, 203, 211, 235, 298, 434
Boynton, 340
Brackenbridge, 47
Brackenridge, 167, 186, 279
Braddock, 322
Braden, 440
Bradfield, 364, 406
Bradford, 97, 101, 113, 265, 342, 349, 427, 437, 481, 483, 491
Bradley, 11, 77, 83, 126, 191, 213, 223, 245, 248, 279, 287, 305, 307, 325, 337, 347, 354, 358, 364, 371, 379, 393, 432, 434, 437, 439, 458, 471, 490
Bradly, 437
Brady, 71, 168, 211, 216, 291, 325, 345, 364, 399, 485
Bragg, 363
Braiden, 325, 345, 427, 452
Braidwood, 292
Brainard, 1, 33, 59, 403
Brainerd, 82
Bramme, 67
Bramnon, 307
Bramson, 63
Branagan, 307
Branch, 78, 290, 336, 364, 509
Brand, 395
Brands, 259
Brandson, 345
Brandt, 279

Brannan, 178, 236, 279, 304, 351, 364, 406, 433
Brannon, 473
Brano, 444
Bransome, 477
Brantly, 336
Branzell, 411
Brashear, 236, 241, 368
Brashears, 196
Bratton, 384
Brawner, 154, 371, 403
Braxton, 279, 341, 406
Bray, 359, 390
Brayton, 345, 364
Breamen, 279
Brearley, 36
Brearly, 258
Brearuire, 471
Breasarer, 364
Breckenridge, 233
Breckinridge, 257, 398
Breese, 78
Bremen, 203
Bremer, 308, 471
Brennan, 465
Brenner, 458
Brent, 5, 18, 93, 117, 123, 134, 136, 163, 205, 211, 223, 264, 279, 296, 297, 300, 303, 325, 340, 345, 363, 372, 398, 400, 427, 456, 509
Brereton, 164, 212, 265, 339, 345
Brevard, 11
Brevett, 174
Brevitt, 443
Brewer, 497
Brewster, 141
Brice, 174, 363, 441
Briceland, 205
Brick House tract, 413
Bridge, 452
Bridgeman, 67
Bridges, 161
Bridget, 76

Bridgewood, 199
Bridgman, 225
Brien, 296
brig **Albert**, 367
brig **Ariel**, 363
brig **Bainbridge**, 367, 465
brig **Brookline**, 84
brig **Brothers**, 66
brig **Canton**, 367
brig **Daniel Webster**, 3
brig **Dolphin**, 450
brig **Faith**, 52
brig **Harbringer**, 261
brig **Montevideo**, 100, 247
brig **Ontario**, 458
brig **Peggy Stewart**, 237
brig **Perry**, 376
brig **Pioneer**, 112
brig **Republic**, 284
brig **Truxton**, 147, 466
brig **Washington**, 367
brig **Washington's Barge**, 434
Briggs, 13, 103, 139, 141, 207, 262, 276, 404
Brigham, 257, 406
Bright, 145, 224, 325, 390, 456
Brightwell, 403
Brinkerhoff, 33
Brinley, 182
Brinsmade, 435
Brion, 345
Brisband, 361
Brisbane, 400
Briscoe, 27, 28, 219, 402, 417, 463, 465
Brishbuy, 452
Bristol Manor, 111
Britain, 176
Briton, 142
Brittingham, 56
Britton, 200, 433
Broadrup, 308, 364, 406
Brockenbrough, 316, 419
Brockett, 67, 423

Brodbeck, 416
Broderick, 118, 291
Brodhead, 78
Brodie, 410, 471
Bronaugh, 13, 82, 302, 349, 426, 435
Bronough, 45, 106, 390, 491
Bronson, 336
Brook, 279, 307, 390, 452, 485, 491
Brooke, 100, 166, 174, 199, 208, 264, 325, 341, 380, 390, 400, 414, 427, 430, 450, 502
Brooks, 110, 126, 135, 141, 165, 193, 226, 257, 274, 291, 303, 307, 312, 390, 402, 441, 455, 464, 471, 491, 494, 508
Broom, 258, 325
Broome, 363
Brooms, 390
Brosnahan, 325
Brou, 297
Broughton, 487
Brower, 291, 292
Brown, 17, 21, 25, 29, 30, 35, 42, 50, 52, 54, 55, 75, 84, 85, 97, 98, 99, 103, 104, 112, 118, 120, 121, 122, 128, 132, 144, 156, 161, 170, 175, 189, 190, 196, 201, 212, 256, 257, 267, 279, 292, 307, 325, 329, 340, 345, 358, 363, 364, 369, 379, 380, 386, 389, 390, 396, 398, 401, 406, 414, 416, 417, 425, 427, 433, 437, 438, 439, 441, 450, 452, 456, 463, 471, 478, 484, 488, 491, 507, 508
Browne, 285, 287, 302, 464, 480
Brownell, 74, 383, 488
Browning, 46, 100, 160, 199, 220, 308, 328, 335, 376, 417
Bruce, 195, 293, 307, 406, 442, 466, 491, 508
Bruff, 174, 307, 442
Bruneau, 83
Bruning, 491
Brunner, 55

Bruton, 206
Bryan, 27, 65, 77, 82, 93, 98, 147, 156, 215, 307, 349, 370, 387, 406, 418, 433, 452, 481, 491
Bryann, 427
Bryant, 121, 215, 358, 379, 390
Bualison, 95
Buard, 297
Buchan, 86, 149
Buchanan, 26, 36, 56, 60, 62, 82, 92, 101, 137, 195, 233, 237, 357, 362
Buck, 76, 182, 193, 273, 286, 288, 459, 470, 491
Buckey, 321
Buckhalter, 125
Buckhardt, 371
Buckhart, 91
Buckingham, 218, 434
Buckler, 167
Buckley, 191, 471
Buckman, 112
Budd, 160
Buehler, 97
Buel, 30
Buell, 95, 312
Buermeyer, 292
Buffington, 427
Bugbee, 83
Buist, 3, 313, 390
Buit, 60
Bulfinch, 390
Bull, 183, 279
Bullen, 266
Bullitt, 110
Bulloch, 275
Bullock, 259, 260
Bump, 507
Bunker, 221, 467
Bunkley, 345
Bunten, 325
Bunting, 298
Burch, 4, 93, 192, 263, 363, 398, 406, 415, 452, 475, 480, 491, 495, 504

Burchard, 500
Burche, 85, 166, 180, 209, 215, 332, 368
Burcher, 390, 406
Burchett, 390
Burcheyer, 307
Burdeck, 30
Burdick, 290
Burdine, 417
Burford, 224, 345
Burgass, 506
Burger, 291
Burges, 452
Burgess, 127, 172, 276, 364, 390, 405, 432, 443
Burgevin, 406
Burgman, 476
Burgoyne, 412
Burgrin, 307
Burham, 385
Burhans, 331, 361
Burke, 180, 372
Burkelow, 290
Burlage, 291
Burnap, 152
Burneston, 189, 279, 297
Burnett, 2, 279, 308, 431, 478, 490
Burnham, 290
Burns, 158, 222, 344, 383, 482
Burnside, 325, 406
Burr, 60, 61, 152, 225, 248, 292, 294, 332, 348, 426, 448, 456
Burress, 471
Burrill, 176
Burris, 315
Burroughs, 110, 199, 387, 483
Burrus, 482
Burryl, 244
Burt, 406
Burtch, 360
Burton, 79, 109
Bush, 363, 469
Bushe, 138
Buskirk, 227

Buthmann, 5
Butler, 60, 65, 92, 96, 101, 122, 157, 231, 239, 258, 279, 325, 329, 381, 390, 406, 415, 416, 418, 427, 440, 452, 489, 491, 503
Butt, 248, 291, 490, 491
Butterfield, 47, 495
Butters, 292
Butterworth, 279, 364
Buzzard Point, 58
Byers, 424, 427
Byington, 68
Byrens, 385
Byrne, 289, 290, 298
Byrnes, 264, 458

C

Caballero, 221
Cabell, 316, 419, 471, 479
Cabin John Mill, 76
Caden, 417
Cadwallader, 308, 491
Cady, 154, 225, 417
Caho, 435
Cahoone, 100
Calder, 213, 223
Calderwood, 325
Caldwell, 47, 60, 114, 283, 452, 455, 461, 470, 491
Calhoon, 401
Calhoun, 75, 210, 462
Calimes, 44
Call, 233
Callaghan, 216
Callahan, 246, 491
Callan, 62, 69, 90, 102, 150, 168, 186, 197, 235, 244, 248, 262, 300, 383, 401, 411, 416, 417, 434, 455, 463, 487
Callender, 452
Calley, 161
Calloway, 314
Caloman, 345

Calvert, 4, 17, 63, 64, 186, 252, 267, 279, 380, 432, 442
Camalia, 298
Cambird, 308
Cambloss, 78, 210
Cambreleng, 381, 402
Camden, 387
Cameron, 213, 452, 471
Cammack, 135, 188, 222, 372, 455
Cammann, 325
Camow, 326
Camp, 308, 371, 395
Camp Izard, 350
Campbell, 2, 26, 29, 31, 44, 45, 46, 48, 69, 127, 128, 178, 206, 279, 282, 298, 300, 308, 313, 330, 353, 364, 395, 406, 415, 440, 483, 491, 497
Candler, 87
Canfield, 325
Cannan, 69
Cannell, 178
Canning, 168, 354
Cannon, 243
Canova, 388
Canthron, 103
Cantine, 381
Cantwell, 406
Capers, 390
Capin, 471
Capron, 471
Carberry, 459
Carbery, 2, 180, 196, 211, 235, 303, 421, 475
Carew, 364
Carey, 237, 290
Carleton, 16, 60, 179, 271
Carlin, 148
Carlisle, 272, 286, 441, 481
Carlock, 277
Carlos, 242
Carlow, 3
Carlton, 440
Carman, 53

Carothers, 195, 367
Carpenter, 15, 46, 96, 121, 126, 152, 181, 193, 349, 406, 414, 452, 499
Carr, 49, 55, 92, 162, 206, 216, 284, 331, 343, 418, 426, 427, 450, 452, 491
Carrico, 139, 145, 169, 314, 475
Carrigan, 348
Carrington, 20, 269, 316, 331, 349, 457
Carroll, 42, 171, 182, 195, 198, 225, 227, 246, 258, 276, 296, 345, 364, 368, 372, 387, 390, 406, 418, 455, 482
Carson, 67, 78, 176, 349, 372, 466
Carter, 17, 26, 43, 78, 91, 136, 199, 221, 240, 244, 308, 311, 314, 322, 325, 338, 370, 378, 385, 390, 422, 428, 471, 509
Cartwright, 102, 364
Carughan, 292
Carusi, 209, 345
Caruthers, 45, 72, 82, 108
Carver, 290
Cary, 96, 443
Case, 376
Casery, 233
Casey, 92
Cash, 114
Casparis, 416, 494
Cass, 290, 353
Cassaway, 149
Cassedy, 279, 491
Cassell, 432
Cassin, 199, 217, 247
Castner, 91
Catesby, 39, 208, 341, 343, 376, 500
Catharine, 102
Cathcart, 81, 264, 333, 509
Catlett, 133, 279, 390, 404
Catlin, 409, 467, 486
Caton, 195, 412
Catron, 477
Caudle, 218
Caulfield, 296, 364
Caulkins, 214, 325

Causin, 157, 184, 191, 196, 411, 501
Causten, 219, 416, 509
Cavanaugh, 364
Caville, 19
Cazeau, 368
Cedar Grove Furnace, 459
Center, 287
Ceocil, 308
Cesana, 334
Chadbourne, 446
Chadwick, 481
Chaffin, 473
Chalker, 34
Chalmers, 331
Chamberlin, 406
Chambers, 63, 279, 349, 384, 438, 462
Chamblin, 279
Champagne, 388
Champer, 25
Chancey, 372, 439
Chancy, 491
Chandler, 56, 67, 190, 312, 395, 401
Chaner, 409, 420
Chaney, 35, 428
Channing, 233
Chantrey, 32
Chapin, 144, 191, 254, 345, 394, 419, 504
Chapline, 460
Chapman, 78, 100, 121, 150, 271, 279, 289, 326, 382, 390, 443, 491
Chappell, 55
Chapperton, 1
Chapple, 326
Charles, 24, 108, 156, 208, 225
Charlton, 240
Charton, 342
Chas II, 70
Chase, 279, 297, 308, 325, 383, 390, 406, 414, 428, 438, 452, 471, 494
Chassaing, 297
Chateau, 81
Chatfield, 93

Chatham, 410
Chatman, 452
Cheatham, 371
Cheeney, 357
Cheesborough, 324
Cheever, 71, 77, 87, 89
Cheeves, 72
Cheneworth, 482
Chenney, 428
Chenowith, 385
Cherokee, 308
Cherokee Indians, 49
Cherry, 183, 279, 345, 364, 369
Chesebro, 235
Cheshire, 164, 324, 418, 432, 440
Chesire, 328
Chesley, 173
Chester, 345
Chestnut Hill, 73
Cheston, 331
Chetwynd, 181
Chevere, 176
Chew, 65, 73, 220, 345, 406, 481
Chezum, 363, 471
Chichester, 308, 440
Chickasaw, 77
Child, 276, 380
Childs, 325, 371, 395, 482, 509
Chiles, 465
Chilton, 364, 390, 406, 491
Chipman, 168
Chisholm, 199
Chisner, 452
Chittenden, 161
Choate, 149
Choctaws, 84
Choteau, 2
Chouteau, 78, 290, 474, 498
Christ Church Cemetery, 204
Christian, 390
Christmon, 33
Christy, 60
Chronicle, 354

Chun, 293
Chunn, 69, 202
Church, 94
Church of the Ascension, 490
Churchill, 238, 273
Cissel, 373
Cissil, 359
City, 100
City Hospital, 122
Clack, 390, 409
Clagett, 2, 18, 41, 86, 118, 140, 144, 174, 192, 222, 233, 263, 335, 402, 406, 489
Clagget, 130
Claiborne, 364
Clairborne, 149
Clamfit, 36
Clampet, 482
Clampit, 37, 279
Clapp, 56
Clar, 390
Clare, 73
Clark, 8, 17, 18, 26, 27, 28, 48, 123, 140, 151, 152, 154, 168, 222, 266, 279, 285, 291, 298, 308, 313, 322, 342, 345, 386, 394, 399, 438, 440, 452, 456, 471, 475, 481, 485, 491, 502
Clarke, 2, 28, 29, 38, 56, 79, 99, 104, 119, 131, 144, 148, 157, 197, 248, 296, 301, 308, 317, 325, 333, 345, 353, 364, 372, 406, 417, 420, 437, 438, 445, 448, 455, 461, 463, 465, 471, 478, 488, 490, 495, 498
Clarvoe, 279, 416, 417
Clary, 132, 168, 390
Claude, 205
Clavaditcher, 386
Claxton, 219, 227, 233, 499
Clay, 75, 183, 304, 325, 414, 457, 491
Clayton, 361, 507
Cleary, 170
Cleave, 121
Clemens, 308

Clement, 364, 428, 462, 491
Clements, 137, 142, 168, 175, 201, 295, 300, 342, 345, 372, 399, 406, 428, 443, 499
Clemson, 466
Clephane, 148, 372, 409
Cleveland, 353
Clevenger, 208
Clifford, 364
Clifton, 308, 406
Cline, 362
Clinton, 75, 78, 143, 308, 324, 345, 356, 431
Clitz, 272
Clive, 181
Cliver, 308
Cloud, 18
Clover Farm, 322
Clover Farms, 278
Clover Hill, 305
Cloverfields, 43
Clyde, 491
Clymer, 185, 258
Coad, 298
Coakley, 364
Coale, 491
Coalter, 206, 341
Coast, 81
Coates, 257
Cobb, 31, 424, 495
Cobbett, 240
Cobbs, 446
Cobs, 470
Coburn, 243, 244, 312, 445, 491
Coby, 304
Cochran, 279, 292, 300, 358, 379, 428, 488, 491
Cochrane, 151, 303
Cocke, 32, 53, 390
Cockey, 369
Cockrell, 252, 471
Cockrill, 345, 491
Coddington, 292, 381

Codrick, 345
Codwin, 287
Coe, 291, 313, 428
Coffee, 464
Coffin, 139, 140, 141, 345, 406, 428, 491
Coger, 187
Cogswell, 22
Cohen, 40, 266, 379
Coile, 345
Colborn, 147
Colburn, 87
Colby, 120, 308
Coldwell, 406
Cole, 19, 40, 48, 99, 116, 117, 126, 155, 180, 299, 428, 460, 471, 499, 500
Colegate, 345
Colelaser, 345
Colemam, 507
Coleman, 8, 10, 25, 48, 81, 105, 136, 157, 166, 190, 217, 274, 359, 367, 379, 396, 415, 432, 470, 483, 491, 503
Colemen, 142, 152, 279, 358
Coleridge, 208
Colhoun, 259, 260
Colier, 345
Colker, 199
Collard, 135, 152, 417, 473, 481
Collens, 501
Collier, 154, 364
Collins, 160, 206, 272, 279, 291, 308, 345, 361, 376, 390, 406, 419, 428, 449, 471, 482, 483, 491, 497, 504
Collis, 24
Collison, 308
Colmery, 401
Colp, 232
Colquit, 308, 326
Colquitt, 78
Colston, 390
Colt, 36, 44, 383
Coltdoff, 112
Coltman, 39, 127, 215, 476

Colton, 37, 393, 424
Columbus, 129, 224, 240, 243, 330, 456
Colwell, 41
Colyman, 334
Comanches, 250
Comb, 498
Combe, 207
Combes, 506
Combs, 19, 154, 204, 238, 255, 297, 305, 306, 364, 416
Comegets, 67
Comegys, 357
Comens, 276
Commerford, 228
Compton, 174, 443
Comstock, 351, 428, 491
Conant, 481
Conclean, 279
Conden, 289
Condit, 401
Condy, 25
Cone, 51, 98, 140, 156
Congar, 144
Congress Burial Ground, 333, 347
Congress Burying Ground, 509
Congressional Burial Ground, 54
Congressional Burying Ground, 66, 213
Conklin, 139, 436, 438, 458
Conley, 341
Conly, 279, 437
Connell, 308, 439
Connelly, 330, 489
Conner, 426, 471, 491
Connolly, 266, 413, 417
Connor, 199, 292, 476, 486, 502
Conolly, 463
Conover, 283
Conoway, 452
Conrad, 418
Constable, 382
Constantine, 290
Converse, 45, 62, 88, 500

Conway, 51, 188, 193, 329, 361, 406
Coodey, 63
Cook, 6, 74, 79, 83, 254, 279, 288, 292,
  308, 313, 314, 345, 355, 380, 385,
  390, 406, 416, 452, 480, 485, 508
Cooke, 47, 364, 449, 454, 471
Cookendorfer, 341, 447
Coolidge, 225
Coombe, 187, 245, 366, 399, 415, 421
Coombes, 197, 380, 462
Coombs, 42, 224, 301, 325
Coones, 200
Coons, 371
Cooper, 75, 122, 142, 150, 158, 207,
  248, 275, 308, 336, 345, 363, 364,
  372, 390, 406, 428, 446, 452, 458,
  471, 474, 491, 499
Coote, 144, 152, 179, 372, 465, 477
Coots, 290
Cope, 399
Copeland, 210, 279
Coppee, 272
Coppel, 41
Corben, 450
Corbin, 428
Corbould, 32
Corcoran, 2, 163, 194, 228, 242, 416
Cordova, 471
Core, 190
Corliess, 507
Cornell, 203, 228
Cornish, 279, 308
Cornwallis, 332, 353, 412
Corrigan, 279
Corry, 484
Corser, 3, 89
Corson, 44
Corwin, 279, 484, 500
Coryell, 308
Coskery, 47
Coskry, 362
Cospar, 197
Cost, 421

Coston, 390, 452
Cotclazer, 325
Cotheal, 291
Cottage, 227
Cottage farm, 59
Cotter, 478
Cotton, 445, 446
Couch, 44
Coulter, 97
Coumbe, 364
Count of Survilliers, 182
Courtney, 308, 345, 349
Coutant, 276
Couts, 179, 271
Coval, 239
Cover, 223
Covert, 167, 308
Cowan, 163, 233, 406, 439
Cowdrey, 66, 105, 290
Cowdry, 313
Cowen, 471
Cowles, 95, 329
Cox, 3, 7, 35, 67, 68, 71, 96, 133, 145,
  170, 180, 213, 226, 235, 249, 268,
  279, 296, 307, 322, 336, 342, 355,
  409, 410, 411, 412, 437, 478, 489, 491
Coxe, 21, 56, 217, 220, 266, 432, 502
Coy, 412
Coyle, 4, 119, 178, 354, 376, 378, 417,
  434, 483
Crabb, 234, 265
Craft, 418
Crafts, 353
Cragin, 396
Craglievich, 183
Craig, 312, 325, 406
Craighead, 265
Craigin, 325
Craigmiles, 45, 89
Craignilas, 69
Craik, 444
Crain, 77, 370, 428
Crampsey, 202, 491

Cranch, 152, 205, 230, 293, 347, 353, 400, 469
Crandall, 467
Crandel, 345
Crandell, 14, 399, 471
Crandle, 109
Crane, 144, 325, 390
Crate, 491
Craven, 448
Crawford, 55, 141, 207, 239, 244, 252, 270, 290, 304, 308, 345, 351, 372, 390, 425, 432, 471
Creagh, 291
Creamer, 318
Creaney, 359
Cree, 279, 345
Creel, 1
Creery, 171
Creighton, 147, 466, 491
Crerar, 12
Cresson, 467
Creswell, 251
Creutzfeldt, 415
Cridler, 428, 452
Crim, 260
Cripps, 334, 390
Crittenden, 272, 378, 419, 457
Crocker, 4, 165
Crocket, 50
Crockett, 279, 308
Croggon, 452
Croix, 296
Crommett, 276
Crone, 362
Crooks, 279
Croome, 160
Cropley, 325, 406, 479
Crosby, 359, 385, 406, 491
Cross, 16, 60, 62, 308, 313, 372, 387, 428, 443, 491
Crossan, 376
Crossfield, 478
Crossman, 345

Croswell, 381
Crouse, 495
Crout, 212
Crow, 58, 151, 152
Crowell, 503
Crowley, 73, 170, 220, 320, 398, 431
Crowly, 115
Crown, 23, 428
crows & blackbirds, 12
Croxton, 507
Crozier, 33, 45, 62, 88, 218, 316, 390
Cruet, 482
Cruickshank, 293
Cruikshanks, 157
Cruit, 416, 426
Crumbough, 294
Crump, 428, 471
Crutchell, 118
Cruttenden, 72
Cuillipp, 417
Cull, 216, 341
Cullin, 452
Cullom, 390
Culver, 15, 383
Culverwell, 131, 263, 289, 339
Cummin, 127, 245, 279, 471
Cumming, 488
Cummings, 415, 489
Cummins, 401, 452
Cunningham, 164, 384, 395, 423, 428, 452, 464, 471, 485
Cupid's, 224
Curran, 474, 475
Currie, 279
Currigan, 314
Curry, 99, 179, 466, 491
Cursier, 32
Curtis, 83, 161, 325, 364, 406
Curvin, 471
Curwen, 45, 88
Cushing, 25, 167, 308, 364
Cushman, 364, 428
Cushwa, 426

Cusick, 213
Custis, 66, 279, 280, 324, 423
Cuthbert, 416
Cutler, 16
Cutter, 149, 466
cutter **Colonel Harney**, 7
cutter **George M Bibb**, 91
Cutts, 133, 153, 156, 498
Cuvellier, 439
Cuyler, 259, 260, 509
Cyssell, 364

D

d'Naubunne, 174
D'Ouville, 298
Dablon, 222
Dabney, 315, 326, 380, 381, 491
Dade, 209, 276, 281, 334, 352, 471, 483
Dahlingrausen, 471
Dailey, 10, 428
Dakin, 348
Daley, 308, 326, 364, 498, 502
Dallas, 51, 81, 259, 260, 457
Dallecarlia, 114
Dalrymple, 9, 233
Dalton, 4, 11, 23, 84, 101, 292, 331, 491
Damoreau, 330
Damrell, 481
Dana, 93, 364, 481
Danby, 303
Dander, 390
Danforth, 95
Dangerfield, 280
Daniel, 63, 98, 99, 145, 156, 210, 255, 341, 345, 406
Daniels, 274
Dant, 27
Darbefueil, 291
Darby, 334, 477
Darling, 215
Darlington, 47, 113
Darnal, 219
Darne, 406, 446, 497

Darnes, 438
Darragh, 279
Dashiel, 372
Dashiell, 26, 349
Datcher, 29
Daunois, 296
Daurcited, 100
Davenport, 96, 209, 282, 362, 415, 450, 507
Davezac, 448
David, 291, 345, 372, 428
Davidson, 33, 56, 117, 157, 174, 227, 244, 265, 272, 306, 308, 326, 353, 357, 358, 367, 390, 411, 424, 441
Davies, 265, 345, 446
Davis, 2, 6, 14, 19, 28, 44, 45, 56, 68, 74, 75, 78, 88, 96, 101, 112, 116, 122, 130, 139, 141, 143, 154, 176, 179, 186, 207, 210, 215, 220, 222, 225, 243, 246, 257, 258, 264, 271, 273, 279, 289, 292, 293, 294, 303, 304, 308, 320, 326, 331, 341, 345, 360, 361, 364, 390, 398, 406, 415, 416, 428, 436, 437, 440, 442, 447, 448, 452, 456, 467, 471, 477, 491, 496, 504
Davisson, 251
Davy, 463
Dawes, 262, 279, 283, 393, 435
Daws, 322
Dawson, 260, 297, 300, 322, 336, 390, 488, 491, 498
Day, 27, 106, 194, 259, 260, 279, 345, 390, 452
Dayton, 57, 106, 157, 258, 393
De Blanc, 296
De Bow, 462
De Bree, 147
De Butts, 422
De Cour, 298
de Grasse, 181
De Grasse, 30
de Kalb, 143
De Korponay, 55

De Koven, 28, 428
De la Roche, 485
De Luze, 293
De Rochambeau, 30
De Selding, 154
De Voss, 464
Deal, 475
Deale, 85, 248, 432, 463
Dean, 105, 172, 276, 306, 325, 345, 360, 400, 497
Dearman, 274
Deas, 39, 342, 369
Deatly, 394
DeBlanc, 308
Decamp, 468
Decatur, 99
Decker, 274, 351
DeCourcy, 479
DeCoven, 376
Deeble, 223
Deeley, 414
Deems, 370
Defenders, 358
Deford, 406
Degges, 197, 425
Dehass, 471
Deitering, 290
Dejen, 118
Dekay, 491
Delafield, 356
Delahay, 390
Delamater, 26
Delaney, 21
Delano, 16, 359
Delany, 292, 308, 467, 491
Delarue, 239
Dell, 45, 53, 88, 345
Delmas, 298
Demarest, 239
Dement, 51, 126, 163, 323, 339, 452, 462, 481
Deming, 261, 332
Denby, 25

Deneal, 279
Deneale, 326, 491
Denham, 47, 62, 126, 406, 422
Denis, 388
Denman, 47
Denmead, 162, 298
Dennis, 431
Dennison, 390
Denny, 175, 376, 444, 446, 460
Dent, 23, 78, 140, 171, 174, 283, 364
Denwood, 173, 444
Depew, 45
Dephant, 57
Deringer, 36, 480
Deroe, 345
Derringer, 279
Dervick, 332
Desau, 406
Desaules, 416
Deshler, 225
Desilvau, 486
Desilver, 298
Devaughan, 64
Devaughn, 390
Deveau, 494
Devens, 308
Dever, 141
Devine, 67
Dew, 460
Dewdney, 54
Dewey, 285, 502
Dewley, 390
Dexter, 91, 118, 219, 248
Diamond, 373, 464
Dibble, 147
Dibrell, 251
Dick, 364
Dickens, 28
Dickerson, 6, 39, 179, 503
Dickey, 180
Dickins, 62, 227, 278
Dickinson, 48, 83, 163, 177, 250, 258, 279, 345, 390, 406, 439, 449, 451, 491

Dickson, 56, 71, 203, 292, 364, 471, 502
Didlake, 44
Diehl, 364
Diesen, 308
Diffenbach, 114
Digges, 216, 218, 308, 414, 452, 463, 475
Diggs, 171, 190, 326, 370, 390
Dillard, 3, 126
Dillingham, 279
Dillon, 80, 146
Dilworth, 30
Dimick, 384
Dimond, 291
Dimpiel, 345
Dinnies, 491
Dinsman, 163
Dinsmore, 19, 401
Dipple, 139, 416
Disbrow, 292
Distrac, 439
Dittenhoeffer, 449
divorces, 447
Dix, 27, 279, 283, 308, 345, 364, 390, 445, 446
Dixey, 306
Dixon, 33, 78, 83, 119, 136, 142, 157, 279, 281, 341, 369, 375, 406, 428, 499, 500, 502
Doane, 49, 354, 383
Dobbin, 50, 495
Dobbins, 103, 312, 500
Dobson, 37, 173, 277
Dobyns, 122
Dod, 465
Dodd, 161
Doddridge, 433
Dodge, 34, 38, 69, 84, 144, 202, 279, 308, 326, 350, 363, 428, 462, 485
Dodson, 251
Dogburn, 308
Dolan, 345
Dole, 100, 156

Dolve, 326
Don, 377
Donaldson, 40, 120, 243, 279, 326, 481, 483
Donawin, 452
Done, 306, 390
Donegan, 296
Donelan, 14, 57, 167, 180, 183, 202, 221, 325, 330, 349, 370, 385, 403, 500
Donelson, 24, 80, 194, 290, 345, 364
Doniphan, 18, 22, 84, 345, 428
Donley, 428
Donn, 27, 28, 29, 47, 131, 135, 137, 169, 185, 187, 206, 263, 278, 289, 319, 339, 350, 355, 377, 390, 413, 455
Donnell, 298
Donnelly, 491
Donnet, 51
Donoho, 168, 255, 300, 399, 402, 491
Donohoo, 236, 263, 372, 431
Donovan, 70, 207, 255, 266, 416, 428, 435, 467, 501
Door, 13
Doran, 345, 375, 451
Doremus, 458
Dornin, 308
Dorr, 119, 121, 254, 262
Dorrand, 279
Dorrett, 3
Dorsett, 170, 324
Dorsey, 41, 175, 378, 442, 452, 459
Doty, 193, 252
Doubleday, 128
Dougalss, 364
Dougherty, 168, 287, 298, 428, 475
Doughty, 4, 33
Douglas, 193, 294, 349, 350, 416, 432
Douglass, 50, 76, 201, 212, 248, 262, 279, 308, 390, 406, 438, 471
Dove, 6, 7, 99, 207, 216, 236, 308, 394, 448, 479
Dovenor, 292
Dow, 134, 215, 292, 380, 447, 450

Dowell, 471, 506
Dowlan, 112
Dowling, 19, 40, 197, 416, 508
Downer, 298
Downes, 231, 247, 326
Downey, 349
Downing, 390, 406, 428
Downs, 189, 199, 217, 286
Dowsing, 67
Doyle, 127, 292, 296, 385, 430
Drago, 242
Drake, 147, 197, 437
Drane, 452, 471, 509
Drayton, 147, 342, 450, 471
Dressel, 304
Dresser, 504
Drew, 16, 127, 385
Drexel, 291
Dreyer, 490
Drinker, 462
Drudge, 474
Drum, 357
Drummond, 345, 372, 471, 491
Drury, 20, 111, 168, 180, 197, 207, 248, 249, 299, 301, 332, 370, 394, 399, 416
Drybergh, 303
Dryburg, 311
Dryburgh Abbey, 86
Du Pont, 342
Dubant, 245, 255
Duboise, 13
Dubourdieu, 291
Dubuque, 7, 498
Ducatel, 298
Duchess of Nassau, 65
Duckett, 80, 105, 119
Duckworth, 236
Dudley, 8, 24, 51, 53, 439
Dueany, 253
Duedney, 372
Duer, 11, 21
Dufan, 292
Duff, 56, 471

Duffey, 46, 82
Duffy, 60, 304, 434
Dugan, 428, 452
Dujardin, 205
Duke of Wellington, 217
Dulaney, 468, 471
Dulany, 326, 345, 451, 456
Dulin, 320, 471
Duling, 434
Duman, 471
Dumas, 491
Dummer, 325
Dunawin, 390
Dunbar, 30, 123, 207, 284
Dunben, 452
Duncan, 188, 190, 200, 279, 296, 399, 424, 485
Duncanson, 69, 130, 153, 490
Dundad, 332
Dundas, 316, 339, 378, 414
Dunger, 9
Dunham, 53, 324
Dunlap, 336, 452
Dunlavy, 96
Dunlop, 48, 345, 347, 397, 425
Dunlora, 418
Dunn, 308, 378, 414, 471
Dunsmore, 390
Dunton, 125
Dunyea, 56
Dupiester, 353
Duponceau, 52
Dupont, 424
DuPontarie, 279
Duportaile, 143
Duralde, 240
Durand, 7, 74, 293, 326
Durbrow, 291
Durham, 181, 188, 471
Duritz, 471
Durr, 372
Dustan, 345
Dutch, 291

Dutcher, 29
Dutton, 452, 460
Duval, 452
Duvall, 22, 55, 60, 81, 89, 118, 171, 172, 247, 253, 326, 345, 364, 406, 417, 428, 471, 475, 493
Duvivier, 291
Duyley, 390
Dwight, 61, 69, 296, 402
Dwinell, 74
Dwyer, 308
Dyer, 22, 23, 26, 28, 65, 68, 72, 86, 88, 92, 100, 102, 109, 117, 121, 123, 126, 145, 146, 148, 150, 159, 160, 161, 163, 169, 172, 173, 179, 191, 201, 203, 207, 212, 214, 224, 226, 229, 235, 245, 253, 276, 295, 296, 335, 338, 340, 344, 349, 351, 357, 370, 377, 380, 382, 390, 406, 412, 428, 442, 452, 471, 475, 481, 488
Dykers, 296
Dyson, 331, 443

E

Eaches, 67, 84
Eadie, 491
Eakin, 250
Earhart, 326, 415
Earl, 254
Earl of Abergavenny, 181
Earl of Buchan, 86
Earl of Effingham, 109
Earl of Egremont, 181
Earl of Mornington, 109
Earle, 292, 360, 475
Earll, 400
Early, 284, 387, 461, 503
Easby, 11, 229, 277, 294, 358, 379, 437
Eastern Hill, 216
Eastman, 3, 142, 438
Easton, 22, 55, 89, 190
Eaton, 2, 15, 100, 290, 312, 345, 364, 406, 412, 428, 452, 491

Eberbach, 72, 114, 197, 205, 237, 416, 417, 451
Eberhart, 391
Eby, 236
Eccleston, 171, 300, 362, 441
Echartre, 291
Echleman, 471
Eckardt, 326, 471
Eckart, 400
Eckel, 84
Eckford, 326
Eckhard, 66
Eckhart, 434
Eckhoff, 292
Eckloff, 9, 218, 372, 387, 416
Econchattimico, 13
Ector, 207
Edds, 471
Edelen, 192
Edelin, 330, 428, 471
Edelm, 491
Eder, 491
Edes, 71
Edgar, 193, 205, 237, 460
Edgerly, 174
Edgerton, 293, 360
Edmeston, 443
Edmiston, 172
Edmonds, 91, 243, 364, 381, 471
Edmondson, 267
Edmonson, 308
Edmundson, 452
Edmunson, 67
Edward, 254, 326
Edwards, 32, 39, 105, 110, 168, 169, 256, 272, 294, 324, 326, 345, 354, 390, 391, 471, 475, 491
Edwin, 192, 428
Eells, 63
Efflin, 38
Egan, 72, 148
Ege, 478

Eggleston, 191, 259, 264, 415, 426, 438, 494
Egleton, 471
Eheler, 345
Eichbaum, 308
Eigler, 390
Eiring, 328
Elbert, 444
Eld, 342, 390
Elder, 298
Elderton, 345
Eldred, 406
Eldredge, 25
Eldreds, 5
Eldrige, 395
Eliason, 302
Ellery, 33
Ellet, 465
Ellett, 269
Elliot, 60, 89, 248, 318, 421, 486
Elliott, 2, 18, 19, 45, 47, 77, 88, 333, 334, 338, 364, 418, 424, 487, 509
Ellis, 4, 6, 11, 19, 150, 240, 244, 297, 406, 417, 449, 452, 456, 458, 471, 484
Ellison, 205
Ellson, 188
Ellsworth, 27, 102, 162, 180, 185
Elsworth, 326
Elton, 326
Elwood, 129, 373
Ely, 61
Emack, 72, 146, 428, 455
Emann, 428
Emerett, 253
Emerich, 417
Emerick, 401
Emerson, 26, 27, 406
Emery, 268
Eminison, 345
Emmerich, 38, 79, 449
Emmerick, 73
Emmert, 499
Emmons, 22, 69, 223, 364, 406

Emory, 208, 345, 463, 474
Emperor Alexander, 477
Emperor Nicholas, 234, 337, 477
Emperor of Russia, 61, 65
Empie, 341
Encyclopaedia, 397
Engle, 240, 285
Engleston, 304
English, 2, 204, 285, 305, 415, 498, 500
Ennis, 23, 36, 84, 90, 139, 180, 294, 406, 428, 452, 491
Enochs, 55
Enos, 25, 46, 428, 452
Ephrata, 119
Ericsson, 26, 27
Erskine, 401
Ervin, 143
Eshleman, 452
Eslinger, 328
Espey, 398, 448, 452, 498
Esprey, 263, 289
Espy, 238, 326, 452
Essex, 139, 372, 463
Estcourt, 406
Ested, 431
Estep, 133, 227, 251, 391, 418, 452
Estes, 13
Estey, 95
Estill, 383
Estis, 406, 428
Estiss, 452
Estko, 501
Etheridge, 393
Etting, 503
Eustis, 179, 233, 271, 428
Eutaw House Hotel, 278
Evans, 4, 8, 34, 35, 42, 47, 74, 79, 102, 160, 168, 176, 200, 213, 285, 308, 334, 340, 345, 364, 370, 391, 416, 428, 452, 461, 462, 466, 471, 491, 506
Eve, 5
Eveland, 297
Eveleth, 17

Everett, 1, 9, 101, 111, 193, 219, 235, 318, 353, 358, 428, 485
Everhart, 308
Everly, 56
Ever-May, 265
Eversfield, 342, 353, 424
Everts, 256
Ewing, 25, 172, 197, 422, 428, 436, 442
Exoll, 395

F

Faas, 453
Fagan, 4, 112, 299, 391
Fagans, 483
Fagg, 267
Faherty, 73
Fainam, 30
Fairfax, 147, 259, 260, 288, 308, 391
Faiter, 47
Fales, 398, 428, 491
Fanning, 21
Fant, 47
Fardy, 391
Farish, 326
Farley, 228, 326, 453
Farmer, 150, 264
Farmington, 82
Farnham, 380, 399, 435, 450, 455
Farnsworth, 35, 44, 65, 89, 96
Faron, 101, 287, 326, 428
Farquahar, 456
Farquhar, 14, 100, 203, 275
Farragut, 494
Farran, 471
Farrar, 226, 336, 420, 439
Farrelly, 272
Farrer, 33
Farrington, 13, 45, 106
Farris, 11
Farry, 272, 428
Fassett, 27
Fauble, 451
Faucett, 78

Faulconer, 399
Faulkner, 361
Fauntleroy, 313
Faust, 356
Favier, 64, 192, 415, 455
Fawble, 406
Fawcett, 32, 322
Faxon, 179
Fay, 81, 428, 457
Feagans, 491
Feaman, 89
Fearson, 132, 479
Fease, 428
Feeks, 343
Feeny, 334, 416, 491
Feister, 472
Feller, 491
Fellows, 491
Felty, 344
Fendall, 79, 100, 258, 261, 298, 432
Fenn, 167
Fenner, 104, 279
Fenton, 432
Fentz, 370
Fenwick, 6, 18, 22, 30, 62, 109, 117, 235, 296, 300, 381, 413, 428, 453
Ferdinand VII, 242
Fergus, 401
Ferguson, 14, 15, 54, 187, 197, 207, 248, 262, 266, 282, 323, 345, 353, 360, 364, 376, 406, 428, 453, 482, 485, 490
Fernanda, 457
Ferraile, 364
Ferrailles, 500
Ferral, 351
Ferrall, 458
Ferrers, 70
Ferry Quarter Estates, 341
Ferrye, 364
Fersaille, 345
Fertenbaugh, 488
Fertney, 453
Fesch, 166

Fetters, 57
Fichet, 151
Fickle, 443
Ficklen, 231
Ficklin, 45, 88, 505
Field, 94, 312
Fielder, 455
Fielder Bowie Farm, 482
Fieldler, 291
Figueira, 291
Fillebrown, 100, 199, 311
Finch, 95, 453, 471
Fine Meadows, 435
Finley, 56, 137, 175
Finsart, 378
fire, 494
Firth, 186
Fischer, 7, 18, 19, 75, 76, 258, 294, 316, 358, 379, 428, 460, 480
Fish, 286, 325
Fisher, 47, 55, 89, 104, 127, 208, 218, 219, 234, 292, 386, 391, 395, 453, 471
Fisk, 127, 134, 450, 453
Fiske, 61, 163
Fister, 406
Fitch, 40, 45, 56, 77, 89, 225
Fithian, 279
Fitton, 199
Fitzgerald, 66, 207, 209, 298, 308, 326, 333, 380, 391, 406, 417, 461, 500
Fitzhew, 428
Fitzhugh, 62, 204, 305, 311, 377, 382, 406, 442
Fitzpatrick, 216
Fitzsimons, 258
Flagg, 46, 381
flag-ship **Congress**, 427
Flaherty, 406
Flanagan, 121
Flanders, 289
Flaugeac, 270
Fleet, 145, 245
Fleming, 100, 182, 279, 400, 434

Flemming, 41, 345
Flenner, 416, 475
Fleschman, 238
Fletcher, 23, 120, 192, 277, 279, 308, 326, 372, 391, 428, 453, 503
Fleurot, 24, 471
Flinn, 282, 326
Flint, 239, 268
Flint Hill, 35
Florance, 383
Flowers, 218
Flowery, 221, 226, 315
Floyd, 125, 345
Fluzel, 70
Fobey, 428
Foederowna, 477
Fogg, 131
Foley, 264
Follansbee, 9, 303, 311, 389
Follett, 364
Foot, 13
Foote, 15, 427
Forbes, 122, 190, 235, 364
Force, 7, 130, 399, 463, 478, 479
Ford, 13, 42, 103, 147, 172, 174, 207, 218, 279, 428, 491, 507
Foreman, 391
Forng, 343
Forrest, 8, 25, 92, 199, 217, 235, 247, 264, 308, 316, 372, 396, 404, 422, 430, 437
Forret, 428
Forstall, 296, 297
Forster, 95, 391
Forsyte, 67
Forsyth, 75, 146, 233, 266, 288, 491
Fort, 422
Fort Atkinson, 30
Fort Brady, 98
Fort Clinton, 356
Fort Constitution, 384
Fort Crawford, 98
Fort Erie, 217, 317

Fort Gibson, 46, 85, 164, 461
Fort Hill, 27
Fort Howard, 98
Fort Jesup, 103
Fort Johnson, 118
Fort Johnston, 509
Fort Laramie, 189, 294
Fort Leavenworth, 189, 314
Fort Mackinac, 289
Fort Monroe, 357
Fort Pickens, 473
Fort Pickering, 425
Fort Pike, 473
Fort Putnam, 356
Fort Scott, 131, 146, 273
Fort Severn, 357
Fort Smith, 104, 234
Fort Stoddard, 115
Fort Vancouver, 389
Fort Wayne, 98, 107, 222
Fort Wood, 473
Forthingham, 3
Fortier, 296
Fortress Monroe, 11, 245, 342
Fortune, 298
Fortune Enlarged, 378
Foster, 7, 217, 291, 314, 326, 364, 434, 484, 491
Fouman, 391
Fountain, 42
Fourd, 443
Foutoute, 196
Fowble, 491
Fowle, 200, 505
Fowler, 6, 9, 14, 16, 189, 194, 197, 229, 232, 266, 303, 323, 340, 345, 364, 369, 402, 403, 406, 428, 471, 481, 484, 490
Fowlers, 402, 491
Fox, 58, 291, 379, 385, 391
Foy, 416
Foyles, 372
Frailey, 21, 68

Fraley, 491
France, 263, 279, 416, 426, 476
Francis, 55, 87, 308, 325, 377, 472
Francisco, 121
Frank, 388
<u>Franking Privilege</u>, 270, 273
Franklin, 33, 116, 119, 133, 258, 291, 417, 448
Franks, 210
Fraser, 129, 181, 307, 471, 483
Frasier, 336
Frazer, 10, 283, 352, 411, 452, 455, 471, 475, 491
Frazier, 340, 354, 373, 453
Frazure, 355
Freasure, 428
Frecklin, 1
Fred'k the Great, 477
Frederich, 372
Frederick, 350
Free, 391
Freeland, 197, 406, 419
Freelon, 385
Freeman, 8, 102, 113, 114, 206, 279, 308, 322, 383, 428, 485, 488
Freer, 144, 481
Fremont, 77, 128, 402, 461
French, 56, 60, 94, 114, 140, 168, 170, 194, 197, 212, 216, 245, 252, 266, 297, 316, 358, 379, 391, 406, 408, 413, 414, 426, 439, 452, 471, 473, 496, 498
Frere, 59, 421
Freres, 292
Frescati, 187, 339
Friday, 345
Fridel, 471
Fridenberg, 211
Friend, 205, 252
frig **Bainbridge**, 158, 199
frig **Brandywine**, 28, 34, 376
frig **Columbia**, 4, 342, 343, 450

frig **Congress**, 100, 199, 217, 220, 266, 342, 343, 424, 478
frig **Constitution**, 113
frig **Cumberland**, 5, 284, 427, 450
frig **Java**, 113
frig **Missouri**, 74
frig **Potomac**, 410
frig **Raritan**, 100
frig **Savannah**, 63
frig **Urania**, 162
Frisbee, 314
Frisley, 491
Frizzell, 105
Frogge, 1, 44, 88
Frost, 113, 160, 197, 415, 453
Frothingham, 285, 499
Fruit Hill, 200
Fry, 44, 488, 491
Fugitt, 47
Fuller, 40, 116, 130, 253, 288, 291, 358, 379, 415, 416, 447, 459, 491
Fullerton, 364
Fulmer, 216, 296
Fulton, 82, 88, 233, 279, 308, 313, 326
Furgason, 251
Furgerson, 105
Furnival, 442
Furr, 113

G

Gabaroche, 297
Gadberry, 150
Gaddis, 417
Gadsby, 109, 115, 234, 359, 416
Gadsden, 345
Gaeno, 391
Gaffield, 169
Gaillardet, 457
Gaines, 314, 345, 348, 395, 406, 461, 462, 472
Gaither, 65, 174, 248, 343, 428, 441, 492
Galabrun, 152
Galbert, 472

Gale, 205, 238, 441, 453
Gales, 62, 254, 455, 476
Gallabrun, 415
Gallagher, 6, 63, 202, 326, 341, 509
Gallaher, 267
Gallant, 462
Gally, 343
Galoway, 279
Galt, 85, 174, 341, 391, 428
Galvin, 126
Gambell, 322
Gamble, 479
Gambrill, 311
Gannon, 367
Gansevoort, 364
Gantt, 42, 220, 225, 232, 285
Garaghty, 330
Gardiner, 149, 167, 248, 260, 311, 352, 357, 373, 381, 454, 508
Gardner, 1, 24, 47, 118, 180, 242, 262, 281, 292, 366, 391, 406, 417, 423, 428, 430, 436, 445, 448, 453, 493
Garehur, 345
Garesche, 142
Garland, 322, 501
Garner, 364, 496
Garnett, 174, 420, 450
Garret, 437
Garretson, 27, 77, 146, 373
Garrett, 279, 420
Garrick, 242
Garrison, 98, 156
Garvin, 334
Garwood, 492
Gasker, 438
Gassaway, 136, 165, 172, 174, 268, 295, 411, 417, 441, 443, 464, 509
Gaston, 252, 284, 364, 472
Gater, 326
Gates, 104, 143, 244, 353, 445
Gatewood, 450
Gathrel, 472
Gatlin, 352, 445

Gatton, 105
Gaubert, 40
Gault, 463, 474
Gautier, 139, 147, 178, 185
Gawronski, 373
Gay, 290
Gay,, 165
Gayle, 22, 67
Gazelle, 464
Gebower, 391
Geddes, 309
Gee, 364
Geer, 364
Geffeir, 435
Geffers, 425, 458
Geier, 364
Geisinger, 4, 199, 247, 477
Geissenger, 217
Gelvert, 56
Genois, 57
Gentry, 22, 77, 89, 391
Genung, 459
Geolet, 410
George, 74
Gerard, 74
Gerding, 291, 345
Gerfuson, 207
Geringer, 364
German, 212, 472
German Catholics, 404
Gerry, 214, 410
Gettings, 322
Getty, 445
Ghiselin, 111
Gibbons, 142, 312, 458
Gibbs, 488
Giberson, 428
Gibson, 92, 120, 154, 174, 208, 240, 254, 345, 428, 433, 440, 472, 489, 492
Giddings, 41, 279, 326, 345, 391, 500
Gideon, 235, 358, 387, 478
Gifford, 462

Gilbert, 131, 137, 161, 279, 326, 407, 415, 492
Gildea, 29
Giles, 382, 479
Gill, 48, 216, 241, 342
Gillchrest, 248
Gillespie, 28, 376, 492
Gillette, 144
Gilliams, 341
Gillis, 22, 60, 72, 100, 399, 447, 487, 490
Gilliss, 21, 76, 77, 83, 304, 308, 323, 347, 352, 447
Gillooly, 492
Gillott, 391, 407
Gilman, 76, 244, 258, 333, 406, 417, 480
Gilmer, 66, 233, 326, 490
Gilmor, 249
Gilmore, 201, 345
Gilpin, 26, 135, 287, 407, 472
Girardeau, 78
Girault, 302, 341
Gisborough Manor, 163
Gish, 41
Gist, 143, 171, 175, 176, 441
Gittings, 308, 331
Given, 367, 456
Givens, 272
Gladden, 252
Gladding, 472, 488
Gladman, 57
Gladmon, 129
Glasco, 373
Glascock, 453
Glascow, 286
Glasgood, 77
Glasgow, 142
Glasscock, 25
Gleeson, 308
Glem, 95
Glenn, 165, 279, 319, 337, 491
Glenn Ross Farm, 460
Globe Hotel, 319

Gloninger, 298
Glover, 143, 308
Gloystein, 292
Gobrecht, 14
Gobright, 218, 222
Goddard, 17, 61, 135, 185, 200, 248, 308, 417, 426, 448, 456, 458, 492
Godfrey, 345
Goding, 399
Godran, 453
Godrick, 326
Godwin, 43
Goethe, 265
Goff, 254, 505
Goffe, 184
Goggin, 66
Goggins, 79
Gold, 332
Golden, 326, 376, 407
Goldin, 183, 200, 304, 467
Golding, 373, 472
Goldsborough, 279, 443
Gollady, 122
Gomillion, 176
Gooch, 306
Good, 507
Good Luck, 435
Goodall, 335
Goode, 76
Goodenough, 45, 88
Gooding, 506
Goodling, 308
Goodlow, 279
Goodman, 51, 418, 472, 491
Goodrich, 133, 428
Goodrick, 279
Goods, 308
Goodwin, 369, 492
Goodye, 326
Goodyear, 48, 419
Gordon, 6, 27, 42, 70, 100, 157, 159, 162, 182, 197, 216, 288, 308, 312, 316, 340, 345, 364, 400, 414, 428, 450

Gordy, 67
Gorham, 162, 165, 258
Gorman, 279, 326, 345, 367, 373, 492, 509
Gormley, 406
Gormon, 393
Gosnell, 298
Gouge, 418
Gough, 42, 93, 298, 363, 412, 430
Gould, 168, 173, 178, 236, 240, 345, 389, 406, 450
Goulding, 37
Goundie, 287
Gouraud, 462
Goutier, 391
Gove, 44, 88
Gover, 279, 408
Gow, 112
Gowins, 22
Grace, 97, 298
Gracie, 291
Graddys', 103
Graebe, 24
Graeff, 428
Graefly, 491
Graeve, 279, 326
Graff, 120, 168, 195, 265, 348
Graffan, 19
Grafton, 91, 118, 126, 128, 351
Graham, 50, 74, 146, 147, 170, 240, 249, 279, 313, 318, 320, 326, 353, 407, 414, 415, 472, 483
Graily, 364
Graminger, 364
Grammer, 2, 62, 132, 141, 187, 197, 207, 223, 237, 249, 279, 393, 405, 434
Gramsley, 308
Granberry, 18
Grandison, 246
Granger, 170, 272
Grant, 33, 113, 190, 323, 373, 445
Grantland, 381
Grason, 308

Gratiot, 373, 474
Grave, 49, 491
Graves, 75, 176, 181, 308, 491
Gray, 87, 122, 173, 246, 261, 285, 326, 364, 384, 391, 406, 424, 428, 441, 442, 453, 461, 472, 489, 491
Gray,, 491
Grayson, 100, 279, 316, 406
Greason, 492
Greaton, 144
Greble, 178
Greeland, 142
Greely, 457
Green, 3, 5, 26, 27, 31, 38, 51, 56, 57, 62, 67, 77, 89, 93, 98, 99, 115, 129, 136, 137, 142, 143, 145, 146, 148, 152, 153, 157, 160, 168, 186, 187, 196, 202, 210, 211, 224, 232, 234, 235, 236, 237, 279, 283, 295, 298, 299, 326, 337, 348, 351, 353, 364, 367, 369, 377, 378, 388, 394, 396, 402, 406, 410, 412, 420, 424, 428, 436, 447, 453, 464, 465, 468, 476, 491, 496, 507
Greene, 122, 453
Greenfield, 115
Greenhow, 333
Greenleaf, 27, 160, 215, 353, 373, 378, 453
Greenleaf's Point, 10, 28, 328, 425, 476
Greenman, 6
Greenough, 450
Greenwood, 93, 230
Greer, 40, 178, 229, 379, 491, 495
Grefer, 492
Greg, 402
Gregg, 113
Gregory, 224, 306, 462, 475, 482
Gregory XVI, 351
Gregson, 120
Grelaud, 445
Grenacker, 308
Gresham, 482

Grey, 200, 322, 329, 452, 474
Griffen, 205
Griffin, 39, 279, 303, 311, 345, 407, 450
Griffith, 237, 322, 326, 345, 364, 406, 439, 453, 462, 492
Griggsby, 279
Grigsby, 58
Grimes, 19, 211, 278, 481
Grimshaw, 187
Grimsley, 326
Grindage, 393, 411
Grindall, 135, 308
Grindell, 391
Grinder, 465
Griscom, 325
Grist, 151, 237
Griswold, 233, 472
Groat, 235
Grodon, 391
Groening, 290, 313
Gromath, 176
Gronough, 33
Grosshans, 345
Grosvenor, 41
Grotius, 48
Groton, 56
Grover, 220, 240
Groves, 326
Grundy, 75
Grupe, 197, 207, 318, 340, 502
Guadagul, 364
Guegan, 326
Guensey, 214
Guercino, 388
Guest, 424
Gueydan, 274
Guffan, 364
Guild, 262
Guillon, 56
Guillou, 147
Guion, 292, 453
Guizot, 397
Gulliver, 323

Gump, 1, 45, 88, 496
Gunby, 172, 441
Gunnell, 161, 191, 358, 379, 417, 492
Gunston, 459
Gunton, 3, 178, 358, 379
Gurley, 17, 129, 206, 502
Gurney, 58
Guthridge, 6
Guthrie, 39, 56, 252, 491
Guttschlich, 233, 417
Guttsclich, 457
Guy, 47, 187, 364, 453
Guyther, 222
Gwathmey, 342
Gwinn, 453, 459, 472, 491
Gwinup, 484
Gwynn, 384, 464

H

Haalilio, 348
Haas, 72
Hackett, 246, 457, 488
Hackley, 67, 498
Hadan, 306
Haden, 16
Hagan, 185, 267
Hagar, 366
Hagarty, 391
Hagerty, 507
Haggatt, 502
Haggerty, 311
Hagner, 122
Hague, 404
Hahn, 258
Haight, 315, 345
Haines, 165, 210, 279
Haire, 472
Haislep, 391, 407
Haldeman, 319
Hale, 5, 123, 179, 293, 492
Haley, 81, 365, 460
Halford, 167
Haliday, 126, 215

Hall, 11, 12, 19, 22, 48, 65, 69, 99, 101,
  146, 147, 160, 163, 175, 190, 191,
  199, 212, 221, 228, 230, 236, 252,
  279, 285, 289, 296, 298, 302, 309,
  312, 316, 323, 326, 333, 345, 364,
  373, 380, 385, 391, 407, 414, 416,
  419, 421, 428, 430, 434, 436, 437,
  440, 441, 442, 444, 449, 450, 453,
  455, 472, 481, 492, 505, 507, 508
Hallam, 235
Halleck, 127, 128
Haller, 346
Hallet, 247
Hallett, 199, 217
Hallowell, 123, 288, 364
Halsey, 46, 125
Halstead, 291
Halsted, 13, 45, 46, 88
Hambleton, 72, 407
Hambrite, 353, 354
Hamerack, 309
Hamersley, 349
Hamill, 280
Hamilton, 2, 14, 48, 66, 103, 149, 163,
  172, 174, 190, 220, 232, 258, 280,
  309, 313, 349, 365, 380, 385, 396,
  404, 407, 413, 421, 440, 442, 455,
  472, 492, 499
Hamiton, 90
Hamlet, 77
Hamlin, 508
Hammack, 346
Hammett, 309
Hammill, 302
Hammond, 38, 95, 128, 193, 365, 373,
  492
Hammonds, 314
Hamner, 506
Hampden, 184
Hampton, 487
Hanchett, 3
Hancock, 415, 498
Hand, 65, 84, 143, 314, 475

Handley, 280, 492
Handy, 25, 42, 60, 110, 137, 190, 261, 271, 373, 416, 431, 442, 446, 447, 489, 492
Hanlenbeck, 326
Hanley, 11
Hanlon, 309
Hanly, 60
Hanna, 140, 223, 316, 365, 462, 472
Hanna,, 407
Hanne, 453
Hannegan, 346, 365
Hanscom, 280, 346
Hansford, 16, 391
Hanson, 174, 215, 228, 271, 273, 279, 280, 368, 391, 443, 499
Happer, 407
Harbaugh, 187, 193, 198, 207, 236, 416, 417
Hard, 88
Hardbargain, 413
Hardcastle, 174
Hardee, 313
Harden, 25
Hardern, 364
Hardin, 103, 256, 320, 420
Harding, 447
Hardison, 364
Hardman, 173, 441
Hardy, 322, 365, 370
Hare, 270
Harford, 492
Hargrave, 494
Harker, 171
Harkness, 161, 167, 193, 197, 215, 229, 249, 306, 373, 440, 463, 474, 475
Harlan, 309
Harman, 365
Harmanson, 336
Harnden, 21
Harney, 234
Harper, 42, 56, 373, 387, 393, 428, 492
Harpff, 39

Harrell, 39
Harrington, 309, 415, 416, 472, 498
Harris, 42, 110, 162, 173, 224, 232, 278, 280, 336, 364, 365, 407, 413, 439, 443, 448, 450, 453, 461, 462, 472, 485, 492
Harris' Lot, 413
Harrison, 13, 17, 75, 109, 120, 140, 192, 208, 209, 211, 215, 233, 237, 245, 269, 275, 276, 280, 309, 344, 346, 359, 369, 376, 428, 444
Harrover, 152, 417, 463, 490
Harsen, 457
Hart, 4, 33, 34, 47, 48, 237, 287, 298, 326, 351, 391, 457, 491
Harte, 428
Hartley, 55, 244, 399
Hartman, 253
Hartnett, 346
Hartshorn, 173
Hartsline, 407
Hartstene, 385
Hartwell, 274
Harvey, 14, 34, 45, 51, 62, 82, 107, 156, 157, 197, 214, 360, 385, 407, 475, 478, 482
Harvie, 16, 458
Harwood, 42, 409
Hascall, 122
Hashie, 290
Haskell, 19
Hasking, 346
Haskins, 473
Haslem, 431
Hasler, 422
Hass, 300
Hassard, 492
Hassler, 368
Haste, 200
Hastings, 344
Haswell, 101, 373
Hatch, 13, 27, 57, 136, 272, 345, 373, 391, 500

Hathaway, 274, 360
Hatherston, 174
Haton, 103
Hatton, 180, 477
Hatton's Hill, 477
Haven, 94, 291, 430
Havenner, 183, 283, 468, 481
Haver, 326
Haw, 2, 171, 235, 478
Hawes, 272, 322
Hawkins, 39, 50, 96, 103, 115, 171, 187, 252, 322, 326, 336, 409, 428, 462, 467, 499, 506
Hawl, 391
Hawley, 21, 29, 171, 290, 377, 407
Hawthorn, 507
Haxtion, 391
Hay, 62, 145
Hayden, 486, 492
Hayes, 95, 114, 274, 290
Hayne, 169, 172, 309, 407
Haynes, 286
Haynie, 444
Hays, 25, 100, 120, 200, 234, 251, 254, 274, 275, 277, 324, 496
Hayward, 39, 291
Haywood, 103, 500
Hazard, 274, 391
Hazle, 183, 374
Hazlehurst, 409
Hazzard, 39
Hazzlitt, 445
Heaceta, 452
Head, 47, 77, 115
Headden, 276, 466
Headman, 492
Healey, 492
Healy, 7, 183, 457
Heard, 481
Hearn, 352
Heath, 123, 143, 247, 341, 428, 453, 501
Heaton, 95, 407, 453
Heavener, 432

Heavenner, 462, 463, 475
Hebard, 101, 365
Hebb, 181
Hebert, 116, 128, 271
Heckrotte, 472
Hedge, 66
Hedger, 492
Hedges, 232
Heide, 309, 326
Heinsman, 33
Heir, 336
Heislip, 105
Heiss, 359
Heitmuller, 364
Helfrick, 194
Hellen, 143, 232, 247, 470
Hempstead, 50
Henck, 345
Henderson, 21, 120, 161, 206, 275, 280, 309, 319, 326, 336, 352, 357, 467, 470, 472, 490, 492
Henley, 264
Henn, 225
Henning, 225, 267
Henrie, 453
Henry, 55, 121, 312, 347, 391, 404, 407, 428
Henry VIII, 351
Henshaw, 156, 222, 326, 348, 450
Henson, 60, 76, 77, 87, 89, 391
Hepburn, 352
Herbert, 91, 104, 223, 391, 428, 482, 496
Herbisso, 57
Hereus, 39
Herlet, 364
Hermitage, 145
Hern, 62
Hernandez, 20, 92, 280, 309, 391, 407, 492
Herndon, 67, 464, 506
Hernitz, Dr, 407
Herold, 328

Heron, 444, 460
Herrick, 279, 309
Herring, 329
Herrison, 57
Herrod, 264
Herron, 329
Hershey, 196
Hervey, 103
Hervus, 54
Herwig, 436
Heseltine, 123
Hessler, 466
Hetzel, 271
Heuisler, 298
Hewbert, 391
Hewes, 426
Hewett, 96, 486
Hewitt, 60, 136, 365, 412, 432, 495
Heydecker, 291
Heydemarck, 292
Heyden, 428
Heydon, 453
Heyward, 110
Hibbotson, 292
Hibbs, 76, 373
Hichock, 11
Hickey, 428, 463, 465, 481, 497
Hicklin, 466
Hickman, 453, 472, 489
Hickney, 11
Hickox, 434
Hicks, 102, 139, 252, 294, 346, 364
Hicks', 102
Hide, 309
Hiess, 78
Higgins, 24, 161, 259, 260, 263, 275, 296, 384, 414, 445, 446
High Point, 377
Highland, 218
Highlands, 509
Hilbus, 170
Hildebrand, 57
Hildreth, 509

Hill, 17, 67, 68, 80, 96, 133, 144, 149, 164, 167, 171, 173, 215, 236, 257, 276, 279, 309, 318, 326, 332, 364, 368, 369, 386, 391, 393, 428, 434, 436, 443, 445, 453, 472, 492, 505
Hillard, 285, 453
Hillary, 173
Hilleary, 241
Hillen, 298, 322
Hillhouse, 128
Hilliard, 314
Hilling, 309
Hillyer, 78, 453
Hilton, 36, 37, 248, 255, 279, 291, 482, 492
Hindman, 373
Hinds, 255
Hines, 251, 256, 277, 481
Hinkley, 230, 407
Hinman, 121, 407, 428
Hinton, 144, 391, 472, 495
Hipkins, 428
Hitchcock, 309, 312, 365, 453
Hitcherson, 407
Hite, 435
Hitselberger, 430
Hitz, 248, 494, 502
Hixon, 155
Hoban, 78, 255, 258, 261, 333, 354, 373
Hobart, 30
Hobbema, 166
Hobbs, 25
Hobtitz, 326
Hocker, 239
Hockett, 45
Hockrine, 346
Hockrote, 428
Hodge, 60, 453, 472, 492
Hodges, 97, 205, 460
Hodgkin, 309, 492
Hodgkins, 135
Hodgkinson, 326
Hodgson, 3

Hodnett, 377
Hodson, 10, 364
Hoff, 450
Hoffman, 170, 180, 279, 346, 365, 428, 445, 472, 483, 486, 492, 504, 507
Hogan, 14, 209, 346, 360, 373, 453, 472, 509
Hogarth, 364
Hoge, 25, 285
Hogg, 26, 34
Hogin, 267
Hogmire, 294
Hokes, 492
Holandshead, 309
Holbrook, 363, 391
Holcomb, 238, 492
Holden, 63, 94
Holdin, 309
Holding, 243
Holiday, 453
Holinsar, 492
Holkins, 364
Holland, 86, 120, 123, 132, 147, 236, 238, 255, 292, 364, 402, 475, 483
Hollenback, 233, 485, 492
Holliday, 463
Hollidge, 249
Hollingsworth, 80
Hollinsworth, 45
Hollister, 30, 44, 177
Hollohon, 28, 29
Holloway, 146, 446
Hollyday, 387
Holmead, 54, 137, 186, 280, 360, 380, 490
Holmes, 5, 33, 74, 180, 218, 222, 226, 227, 228, 233, 235, 236, 264, 285, 317, 320, 453, 492, 500
Holms, 466
Holt, 391, 407, 482
Holtmeyer, 346
Holton, 44, 503
Holtzman, 143, 222, 451

Homan, 40
Homans, 1, 45, 64, 106, 155, 373, 417, 447
Homer, 355
Hone, 283
Hong, 154
Hood, 217, 269
Hooe, 67, 151, 152, 168, 320, 381
Hooper, 172, 226, 298, 309, 346, 364, 428, 453, 498
Hoops, 442
Hoover, 4, 73, 75, 196, 303, 346, 391, 416, 420, 475, 492
Hopkins, 122, 200, 259, 260, 285, 309, 325, 365, 383, 391, 401, 428, 441
Hopkinson, 15, 376
Hopper, 325
Horback, 15
Horn, 180, 279, 428
Hornblower, 91, 459
Horner, 67, 183
Hornor, 457
Hornsby, 251
Horst, 364
Horton, 103, 123, 243
Hosey, 309
Hotchkiss, 293, 309, 479
Houck, 373
Hough, 32, 69, 210
Houghton, 431
House, 492
Houseman, 148
Houston, 120, 169, 226, 280, 373
Hovey, 502
Howard, 12, 25, 124, 157, 168, 172, 180, 187, 207, 208, 218, 222, 248, 250, 279, 309, 331, 346, 391, 407, 441, 458, 459, 489
Howe, 66, 96, 143, 154, 248, 329, 458, 472, 492
Howell, 19, 116, 207, 376, 403
Howert, 472
Howick, 329

Howison, 60, 113, 453
Howitt, 430
Howland, 36, 122
Howle, 60, 296, 300
Howlin, 453
Hoy, 180
Hoyt, 95, 97, 381
Hubband, 361
Hubbard, 61, 79, 83, 136, 276, 309, 317, 361, 373, 384
Hubbell, 496
Huber, 203
Hubert, 391
Hucking, 365
Huddleston, 65
Hudson, 3, 24, 67, 225, 395
Huel, 391
Huelbig, 304
Huelrig, 304
Huffnar, 375
Huger, 407, 430
Huggins, 60, 242, 323
Hughes, 24, 47, 48, 182, 191, 202, 205, 211, 259, 260, 279, 309, 320, 326, 345, 349, 360, 373, 391, 401, 407, 438, 443, 450, 492
Hughlette, 275
Hugo, 172
Hugunin, 28
Hull, 233, 264
Hulse, 19, 126
Humber, 445
Humbert, 407
Humes, 255, 326
Humphrey, 25, 120, 279
Humphreys, 32, 99, 100, 160, 284, 364, 405
Hundley, 106
Hundley's & Bouldin's, 341
Hunger, 502
Hungerford, 279, 309, 504
Hunley, 122

Hunt, 2, 5, 28, 38, 40, 60, 115, 271, 303, 326, 364, 376, 388, 428, 453, 467
Hunter, 39, 47, 64, 77, 94, 149, 313, 330, 346, 378, 384, 385, 389, 395, 400, 428, 464, 492, 494
Huntington, 121, 143
Huntley, 507
Huntoon, 433
Huntsacker, 104
Huntsman, 97
Hurbert, 309, 407
Hurdle, 221
Hurlbert, 346, 407, 428
Hurlburt, 346
Hurlbut, 363
Hurlert, 391
Hurst, 120, 147, 168, 336, 407, 417, 492, 494
Hurter, 291
Huskisson, 32
Husler, 123
Hussey, 12, 279, 453
Huston, 121
Hutchins, 20, 280
Hutchinson, 153, 256, 311, 453, 499
Hutchinsons, 301
Hutchison, 93, 267, 391
Hutton, 193, 346
Hyatt, 54, 67, 417, 438, 453, 456
Hyde, 376, 407, 424
Hynson, 259, 260, 280

I

Iardella, 127, 242, 280, 407
Icard, 44, 82, 107, 155
Iddings, 490
Iglehart, 64, 296, 346
Ijams, 269
ill, 468
Inch, 141
Ingallas, 271
Ingalls, 128, 179
Ingersoll, 147, 238, 258

Ingle, 2, 187, 207, 213, 249, 326, 328, 332, 352, 407, 434, 437, 444, 478
Ingler, 472
Ingraham, 326, 346
Ireland, 365
Irish, 35
Irons, 326, 462
Ironside, 290
Irwin, 38, 240, 312, 391
Isabella, 3
Isabella Furnace, 165
Ish, 466
Isherwood, 280, 346, 453, 472
Island, 280, 302
Israel, 97, 280
Issler, 329
Ives, 122, 162, 464
Ivey, 53
Ivory, 15

J

Jack, 196, 453
Jackson, 7, 26, 33, 57, 60, 66, 75, 99, 100, 119, 121, 122, 136, 145, 146, 183, 199, 231, 232, 233, 236, 237, 238, 242, 256, 258, 270, 298, 300, 306, 309, 346, 359, 365, 375, 391, 407, 428, 453, 454, 472, 482, 492
Jacob, 401, 444
Jacobi, 417
Jacobs, 13, 45, 69, 71, 89, 280, 290, 326, 365, 453, 492, 496
Jamaica, 303
Jamaison, 280, 492
Jameison, 453
James, 136, 238, 300, 317, 326, 351, 394, 472
James I, 269
James' Purchase, 413
Jameson, 319, 496
Jamesson, 147
Jamieson, 175, 444
Jamison, 275, 289, 479, 487

Janeson, 38
Janney, 254, 381, 421
Jaqueline Hall, 245
Jaquer, 365
Jarboe, 23, 449, 463, 484
Jarrett, 35
Jarvis, 312, 453
Jasper, 453
Jay, 312
Jaynes, 15
Jee, 291
Jefferis, 428
Jeffers, 100, 178, 253, 463, 501
Jefferson, 52, 61, 80, 90, 188, 227, 448, 470
Jeffery, 376
Jeffrey, 28, 395, 428
Jeffries, 205, 263
Jell, 206
Jenifer, 258, 360, 378, 428, 444, 464
Jeniter, 407
Jenkins, 16, 17, 47, 100, 103, 126, 217, 221, 283, 298, 322, 396, 407, 416, 428, 453
Jenks, 266, 395
Jenner, 452
Jenners, 146
Jennett, 395
Jerman, 346
Jerome, 166
Jerrold, 218
Jervey, 135
Jervis, 492
Jesuits, 127, 300, 325, 332
Jett, 35
Jewell, 213, 223
Jewett, 101, 234, 282, 416
Jewitt, 280, 309
Jillard, 175
Jimeson, 365
John, 280, 407
Johns, 216, 312, 341, 456

Johnson, 10, 20, 30, 39, 59, 61, 71, 74, 75, 82, 87, 88, 99, 101, 105, 129, 136, 141, 144, 147, 169, 186, 206, 210, 215, 225, 228, 231, 233, 249, 252, 253, 254, 256, 258, 267, 271, 273, 280, 290, 298, 309, 312, 324, 326, 346, 365, 371, 375, 377, 381, 385, 391, 396, 399, 401, 407, 408, 416, 417, 426, 428, 448, 450, 453, 457, 462, 484, 485, 492, 500
Johnston, 12, 106, 122, 200, 225, 271, 273, 280, 284, 289, 294, 326, 346, 350, 355, 365, 401, 436, 447, 448, 492
Johnstone, 342
Joice, 365
Joiner, 81
Jone, 365
Jones, 10, 28, 30, 35, 39, 61, 65, 66, 71, 75, 92, 95, 103, 110, 118, 122, 123, 125, 129, 141, 143, 145, 158, 159, 174, 179, 180, 188, 193, 208, 215, 216, 219, 223, 251, 254, 260, 266, 271, 273, 277, 278, 280, 282, 290, 296, 304, 305, 309, 313, 326, 333, 341, 343, 346, 347, 353, 365, 368, 370, 376, 391, 395, 407, 410, 415, 416, 417, 421, 427, 432, 435, 446, 448, 451, 453, 469, 472, 474, 478, 482, 484, 492, 500
Jorda, 297
Jordan, 121, 172, 201, 224, 326, 367, 375, 472, 492
Joscelyn, 361
Joseph, 141
Jost, 340, 393, 415
Jouett, 238
Jourdan, 428
Joy, 492
Joyce, 371, 405, 456
Juda, 314
Judd, 240
Judson, 24, 95, 190, 405
Judy, 122

Juler, 68
Julien, 236
Junkins, 126
Jurey, 394

K

Kable, 472
Kahl, 220
Kain, 309
Kaiser, 425, 453, 468
Kalorama, 426
Kanderer, 280
Kane, 231
Kapriz, 472
Karch, 253
Karns, 329
Kaufman, 132
Kaufmann, 365
Kaufmans, 103
Kavanagh, 233
Keabel, 428
Kealey, 456
Kean, 335
Kearney, 61, 92, 126, 189, 199, 217, 247, 294, 346
Kears, 352
Keating, 298
Kebel, 309
Kedglie, 216, 217, 373, 455
Keech, 254, 472, 492
Keefe, 76
Keeler, 5
Keene, 444, 495
Keeney, 128
Kegan, 326, 346
Kehgslenburg, 492
Kehoe, 131
Keith, 280, 326, 365, 391, 496
Ke-ke-no-kush-wa, 98
Kell, 474
Kellam, 382
Kellar, 221
Keller, 27, 89, 102, 123, 236

Kelley, 214, 291, 300
Kellmond, 326
Kellogg, 385
Kelly, 11, 19, 110, 166, 176, 195, 200, 216, 309, 346, 391, 407, 416, 433, 456, 472, 492
Kelse, 240
Kelso, 15
Kelty, 174
Kemble, 100, 242
Kemp, 447, 492
Kemper, 10
Kendall, 22, 26, 60, 62, 97, 185, 250, 333, 338, 403, 435, 497, 498
Kendall Race Course, 408
Kendels, 472
Kendrick, 462
Kennard, 428
Kennedy, 88, 96, 121, 130, 252, 264, 290, 312, 358, 382, 391
Kenner, 407
Kennet, 443
Kennett, 176
Kenney, 320
Kennison, 365, 407
Kennon, 233
Kenny, 391
Kent, 252, 322, 492
Kenyon, 407
Keobel, 391
Keoble, 346
Kephard, 500
Keppler, 6, 151
Ker, 45, 261, 313
Kerfooh, 472
Kerlin, 63
Kernan, 297
Kerney, 292
Kerr, 201, 407, 492
Kersey, 433
Kershaw, 472
Kervand, 326, 373
Keswick, 39

Ketcham, 395
Kettle, 361
Kettler, 304
Kevill, 428
Key, 2, 21, 78, 92, 382, 387, 393, 397, 469
Keys, 469
Keyworth, 40, 221, 358, 417
Kibbe, 381
Kibby, 303
Kidd, 507
Kidwell, 266, 294, 315, 326, 479, 497, 501
Kiernam, 403
Kiernan, 27
Kihns, 401
Kilgour, 322
Killmon, 201, 236, 241
Kilman, 248
Kilty, 442
Kiltz, 444
Kimball, 326
Kimmell, 10, 166, 417
Kincaid, 226
Kincannon, 113
Kincead, 399
Kinchy, 416, 470
Kinckle, 71
King, 10, 15, 16, 17, 18, 38, 44, 59, 71, 86, 89, 121, 148, 154, 194, 211, 213, 215, 234, 240, 258, 265, 280, 282, 297, 303, 306, 326, 332, 346, 357, 365, 373, 381, 391, 395, 402, 407, 416, 428, 437, 449, 453, 455, 456, 463, 479, 488, 492, 507
King's Mountain, 353
Kingsbury, 280, 326, 472
Kingston, 141
Kinkle, 45, 72, 82, 108
Kinney, 95, 96, 97
Kinningham, 453
Kinsing, 342
Kinsley, 83, 400, 427

Kinsman, 25, 266
Kirby, 203, 463
Kirk, 217, 246, 407
Kirkwood, 10
Kisley, 210
Kitchum, 199
Kitzmiller, 489
Kleekamp, 309
Kleiber, 248
Klein, 292
Klenck, 379
Kleugen, 292
Klimkiewicz, 58
Klimkiewiez, 365, 391
Kline, 252
Klingelhoefer, 292
Klopfer, 105
Klotz, 338
Kluk, 346
Klunk, 365
Knap, 103
Knapp, 176, 360, 492
Knauff, 490
Kneass, 287
Knight, 10, 95, 115, 309, 510
Knighton, 296
Knip, 472
Knoblock, 407, 456
Knott, 232, 309
Knowles, 262, 317, 347, 475, 508
Knox, 3, 143, 153, 176, 324
Koburger, 356
Koch, 219
Koones, 338
Koontz, 401
Kopler, 509
Korner, 453
Korponay, 55, 309
Korpunay, 326
Kosciusko, 58, 61, 276, 352, 475, 501
Krafft, 157, 241, 416, 470, 505
Kramer, 141
Kreamer, 483

Krebs, 171
Krepps, 401
Krofft, 15
Kruger, 292, 465
Krutger, 292
Kuhl, 484
Kuhland, 453
Kuhn, 309
Kunkel, 348
Kunkelman, 291
Kurtz, 71, 196, 235, 253
Kuykendall, 509
Kyle, 497

L

L'Estrange, 180
L'Hommedieu, 256
L'Infant, 199
la Fayetts, 143
La Glaise, 274
Labbe, 381
Labranche, 240
Lacey, 14, 15, 78, 92
Lachenmyer, 346
Lack, 472
Lacon, 485
Lacy, 255, 396, 417, 479
Ladd, 247, 259, 260
Ladreyh, 492
Lady, 430
Lafayette, 74, 107
Lafayette., 32, 59, 82
Lafon, 152
Lafontaine, 150, 162, 235
Laguire, 197
Laidlow, 391
Laird, 92, 146
Lairy, 429
Lake, 281, 361
Lakemeyer, 218
Lakin, 280, 461
Lamar, 172, 309, 442
Lamb, 386, 401, 416

Lambell, 10, 416
Lamberson, 141
Lambert, 45, 53, 82, 102, 108, 155, 373, 450
Lambeth, 157, 204
Lamkin, 391
Lamme, 326
Lamphire, 484
Lamson, 356
Lanam, 346
Lancaster, 137, 184, 280, 296, 365
Landen, 492
Landers, 199
Landing, 407
Landry, 188
Landsdale, 173
Lane, 25, 109, 169, 453, 472, 481
Lanergan, 365
Laney, 91
Langdon, 258
Langhorne, 100, 238, 450
Langley, 49, 79, 86, 297, 391
Langlois, 316
Langtry, 137, 280
Langworthy, 225
Lanman, 233
Lanoux, 21
Lansdale, 441, 478, 482
Lansing, 218, 287, 407
Lapon, 76
Laporte, 346
Larcombe, 379
Large Pipe, 342
Larkin, 130, 166, 224, 309, 326, 407
Larmand, 202
Larmer, 437
Larnagan, 346
Larned, 84, 187, 207, 218, 363, 416, 446, 450, 492
Laroque, 298
Larrabee, 1
Lasala, 292
Lasher, 346

Lashley, 346
Laskey, 156
Lasley, 472
Lassiter, 365
Latham, 47, 113, 238
Lathan, 360
Lathrop, 113
Latimer, 343, 396, 407
Latreat, 492
Latruitte, 257, 278
Laub, 416
Lauck, 294
Laudner, 194
Lauman, 492
Launitz, 352
Laurens, 28, 376
Laurie, 21, 37, 41, 130, 189, 283, 416, 437
Laus, 499
Lauson, 112
Lavalette, 208, 260
Lavallete, 309
Law, 51, 53, 469
Lawler, 349
Lawrence, 92, 93, 122, 216, 231, 309, 325, 326, 373, 381, 467, 469
Lawrenson, 358, 438
Laws, 55
Lawson, 20, 33, 139, 187, 208, 243, 413
Lawton, 395
Lawyer, 28, 376
Lay, 95, 280, 391
Laycock, 212
Layton, 464
Lazenby, 433
Le Blanc, 496
Le Breton, 63
Lea, 25
Leach, 33, 122
Leake, 309, 381, 486
Leaman, 207
Lear, 21
Leary, 292

Leatherbeury, 202
Leavenworth, 36, 49, 55, 56, 89
Leavitt, 16, 35
Lebengood, 11
LeBrun, 298
Leclair, 309
Lecomb, 291
Leddon, 257
Ledyard, 1, 66, 93, 429
Lee, 28, 80, 103, 115, 128, 137, 143, 144, 167, 190, 206, 227, 229, 250, 251, 263, 274, 280, 286, 289, 309, 318, 325, 326, 365, 372, 383, 416, 424, 428, 432, 467, 472, 484, 492
Leech, 195, 320
Leffler, 266, 407, 429, 453
Lefils, 122
Lefler, 391, 472
Legare, 233, 309, 362
Leggett, 472
Legrand, 296
Lehlman, 180
Lehman, 37
Lehmanowski, 8
Leigh, 457
Leighton, 472
Leland, 180
Leman, 435, 458, 483, 501
Lemanowski, 8
Lemar, 359
Lemmon, 407
Lemmons, 326
Lemon, 280
Lenman, 178, 197, 213, 370, 403
Lenning, 298
Lenox, 3, 68, 92, 167, 234, 434
Lenzler, 90
Leonard, 125, 151, 297, 365, 383, 386, 391, 472, 500
Lepretre, 296
LeRoy, 453
Leseur, 453
Leslie, 446
Lester, 126, 137, 280
Lettiere, 162
Leturner, 472
Levin, 43
Levis, 318
Levy, 267, 316
Lewin, 254
Lewis, 2, 8, 26, 27, 75, 107, 129, 132, 137, 145, 151, 156, 161, 164, 197, 225, 233, 236, 267, 280, 309, 326, 335, 339, 365, 373, 387, 391, 402, 407, 411, 428, 452, 460, 463, 467, 475, 481, 490, 492
Lewson, 104
Libbey, 71, 249, 294, 299, 379
Libby, 79
Lieberman, 262
Light, 203
Lightburn, 291
Lightfoot, 47
Ligon, 382
Liles, 280
Lilly, 167, 303, 407
Limetz, 238
Lincoln, 20, 25, 95, 143, 272
Lindenberger, 169, 373, 423
Linding, 492
Lindley, 407
Lindner, 365
Lindsay, 176, 373, 450
Lindsey, 94
Lindsley, 2, 110, 187, 200, 417, 419, 462
Lindsly, 12, 122, 235, 273, 458
Lingan, 176, 442
Lingebach, 346
Linkens, 48
Linkins, 170
Linn, 176, 233, 339, 390
Linnean Hill, 186
Linsley, 258
Linthicum, 71, 76, 196, 321, 414, 478
Linton, 114
Linwood, 155, 391

Lipscomb, 40, 55, 384
Lister, 309, 326, 428
Litchfield, 67
Littell, 6
Little, 52, 60, 66, 166, 170, 179, 213, 229, 248, 271, 291, 326, 365, 393, 429, 470, 483, 492, 507
Littlejohn, 346
Litton, 459
Littrell, 281
Lively, 251
Livingston, 74, 134, 258, 291, 296, 297, 336, 342, 381, 424
Lloyd, 50, 96, 116, 126, 189, 219, 413, 481
Lochrey, 417
Locke, 122, 134, 224, 407, 422, 485
Lockeb, 391
Lockerman, 429
Lockert, 152
Lockhart, 151, 168
Lockwood, 397
Locky, 407
Locust Grove, 414, 489
Locust Hill, 149, 187
Lodge, 280, 428, 470
Loeihtel, 429
Logan, 102, 239, 346
Londen, 346
London, 472
Long, 282, 365, 382, 416, 417, 492
Longacre, 14
Longdon, 449
Longhead, 427
Longs, 415
Longstreet, 128
Longstreth, 296
Loocke, 472
Loockerman, 346
Looker, 317
Loomis, 136, 280, 395
Looney, 63
Looser, 271

Lord, 264, 391, 439, 492
Loring, 241, 243, 346
Lotall, 114
Lott, 155
Lotz, 56
Love, 5, 365, 391, 439, 459
Loveless, 34, 391, 407
Lovell, 340, 342
Lovett, 31, 304, 324
Loving, 492
Low, 147, 259, 260, 492
Low Hill, 320
Lowden, 244, 332
Lowe, 40, 44, 61, 110, 145, 172, 278, 289, 326, 352, 432, 443, 453
Lower, 387
Lower Quarter, 341
Lowerre, 290
Lown, 376
Lowndes, 112, 119, 417
Lowrey, 225
Lowrie, 391
Lowry, 23, 171, 238, 309, 313, 346, 407, 429, 437, 458, 472, 480
Loxey, 326
Loyd, 489
Lucas, 12, 48, 245, 391, 429, 492
Luce, 21, 60, 100, 303
Luchessi, 457
Lucker, 365
Lucket, 173, 176
Luckett, 14, 246, 267, 407, 443, 453
Lucky Hit, 206
Lucus, 472
Ludeke, 294
Ludlow, 291, 346, 407
Lufborough, 2, 235
Lug Ox, 285
Lugenbeel, 369
Lumsden, 462
Lundy, 380
Lunt, 367, 391, 453, 492
Lusac, 290

Lusby, 280, 417
Lusese, 407
Lush, 498
Lusk, 102
Luteen, 375
Luther, 219, 428
Lybrand, 97
Lyell, 324
Lyles, 114, 335, 346
Lyman, 95, 96, 224, 337
Lynch, 120, 173, 225, 322, 324, 417, 441
Lynde, 287, 369
Lynn, 174, 442, 444
Lyon, 252, 319, 400
Lyons, 229, 437

M

M, 144
Macabee, 391, 492
Maccubbin, 322
Macdonald, 200
Mace, 16, 25
Macfarland, 457, 472
Machen, 332
Machin, 257
Mackall, 373, 387
Mackay, 30
Macke, 346
Mackee, 14
Mackenzie, 17, 52, 266, 381
Mackey, 280, 391, 407, 429, 474, 492
Macknight, 304
Mackubin, 180
MacKubin, 492
Macleod, 250, 299
Macmurdo, 188, 328
Macomb, 54, 75, 116, 163, 233, 437
Macomber, 492
Macrae, 326, 335, 392, 404
Macy, 365, 391, 429, 472
Maddox, 4, 11, 19, 31, 92, 216, 280, 298, 378, 432

Madison, 80, 156, 217, 258, 276, 361, 362, 476
Maertens, 136
Magar, 222, 248
Magee, 262, 327, 429, 453
Magill, 14, 100, 280, 340, 417, 490
Magnetic Telegraph, 129
Magnier, 383
Magruder, 48, 105, 118, 187, 219, 255, 257, 259, 358, 379, 413, 414, 453, 459, 475
Magrudger, 391
Maguire, 29, 246, 282, 310, 327, 394, 453
Magurder, 207
Mahan, 161, 295
Maher, 63, 116, 121, 129, 319, 415, 416
Mahon, 92, 492
Mahoney, 309
Maitland, 292
Majo, 221
Major, 244
Majors, 451
Malahan, 309
Malcolm, 321
Maley, 502
Maling, 489
Mallet, 153
Mallikin, 368
Mallion, 457
Mallory, 316
Malloy, 282
Maloy, 135, 137, 140
Malster, 346
Malthie, 291
Maltzan, 407
Manby, 299
Mancy, 182
Manders, 31
Mandeville, 325
Mandlebaum, 280, 346
Manford, 365
Mangers, 174

Mangum, 346, 506
Maniken, 318
Mankin, 129, 230
Manley, 324
Mann, 25, 40, 72, 104, 375, 444, 453
Manning, 77, 216, 280, 297, 407, 414, 417, 425, 429, 494
Manouvrier, 315
Manowvrier, 326
Mantz, 374
Manuyette, 262
Mapie, 472
Marbury, 173, 213, 245, 264, 321, 347
Marcadel, 391
March, 280
Marchand, 28
Marchiavella, 472
Marcy, 63, 82, 101, 124, 181, 208, 356, 369, 381, 429, 453
Marin, 453
Marine, 385
Marino, 429
Marion, 144, 325
Markle, 472
Markoe, 234, 330, 336
Marks, 280, 326, 472
Marl, 456
Marlborough, 302
Marlborough Estate, 505
Marlor, 472
Marple, 401
Marquis of Devonshire, 181
Marquis of Lansdown, 61
Marquis of Westminister, 109
Marr, 72, 250, 418
Marrast, 25
Marriott, 298
Marron, 207, 399
Marryatt, 48
Marsh, 49, 96, 346, 447
Marshal, 373
Marshall, 12, 39, 75, 112, 116, 136, 137, 154, 168, 171, 200, 202, 229, 261, 263, 269, 322, 340, 346, 365, 399, 444, 450, 469, 492
Marshand, 376
Marshll, 211
Marsteller, 277
Martin, 5, 33, 41, 46, 92, 179, 180, 264, 266, 280, 290, 303, 309, 311, 327, 346, 365, 382, 391, 408, 414, 416, 420, 425, 429, 438, 453, 472, 478, 484, 487, 492, 500
Martinez, 15, 221
Marvin, 291, 336
Mary Ann & Augusta Furnaces, 319
Maryborough, 109
Maryman, 27, 28, 29, 86, 111, 135, 137, 140, 179, 180, 183, 295, 302, 303, 319, 329, 336, 355, 403, 457
Masa, 280
Masi, 88, 417, 426, 462, 485
Mason, 2, 15, 43, 65, 81, 82, 84, 92, 101, 109, 137, 149, 168, 172, 187, 193, 199, 233, 235, 255, 271, 280, 300, 311, 313, 326, 332, 341, 346, 352, 361, 365, 391, 404, 407, 429, 442, 451, 458, 459, 469, 472, 478, 492
Massey, 467
Massi, 201
Massolette, 365
Massoletti, 280, 346
Masterson, 280, 365, 483
Masterton, 56
Mastick, 292
Mastondon, 268
Matabee, 453
Mather, 139
Mathews, 235, 325, 360, 478
Mathias, 326
Matlock, 433
Matteson, 486
Matthew, 351, 453
Matthews, 39, 49, 53, 79, 103, 181, 190, 194, 280, 309, 358, 361, 391, 422, 429, 453, 461, 492, 502

Mattinger, 365
Mattingley, 10
Mattingly, 398, 399, 429, 463, 472, 508
Mattock, 472
Mattocks, 354
Mauduit, 146
Maurian, 501
Maurice, 309
Mauro, 293
Maury, 2, 22, 190, 215, 235, 265, 296, 358, 379, 416
Maus, 309
Maxcy, 233, 234
Maxwell, 24, 143, 346, 429, 459
May, 12, 22, 92, 102, 127, 137, 142, 159, 187, 207, 223, 277, 289, 290, 303, 313, 328, 368, 438, 469, 479, 502
Mayberry, 453
Mayell, 96
Mayer, 223
Mayers, 259, 309
Mayfield, 208, 499
Mayo, 208, 260, 299, 326
Mazeen, 222
Mazine, 241
McAffee, 329
McAin, 125
McAlister, 443, 472
McAlpin, 291
McAnelly, 395
McArann, 280, 505
McArn, 138
McArthur, 200, 492
McAvoy, 55
McBee, 492
McBlair, 39, 43, 137
McBratney, 420
McBride, 306, 453
McBrogden, 322
McCabe, 319
McCabral, 472
McCaffrey, 296, 466
McCall, 320

McCalla, 78, 81
McCallion, 143
McCamant, 107
McCannon, 247
McCardle, 289, 323, 327
McCarthy, 457
McCarty, 39, 67, 94, 103, 159, 207, 312, 392, 429, 456
McCaughan, 319
McCauley, 199, 216, 217, 247, 415, 488, 498
McCauslen, 11
McCleary, 434
McCleester, 341
McClellan, 346, 498, 506
McClelland, 10, 81, 182, 193, 202, 210, 217, 275, 312
McClenahan, 35
McClery, 283, 358
McClintoe, 472
McClinton, 126
McCloskey, 405
McCloud, 44
McCluney, 238
McClung, 50, 113
McClury, 25
McClusky, 341
McCobb, 126, 346, 453, 492
McColey, 472
McColgan, 416
McCollum, 310
McComas, 11
McConnell, 96, 120
McCorkle, 100, 405, 429
McCormick, 8, 132, 148, 197, 254, 286, 322, 332, 350, 493
McCoskey, 383
McCown, 357
McCoy, 161, 174, 204, 305
McCrab, 346
McCrea, 92, 507
McCubbin, 220, 226, 412, 463
McCulloch, 87

McCullogh, 177, 503
McCulloh, 62, 98
McCullough, 398
McCullum, 346
McCully, 43
McCumber, 361
McCurry, 18, 20, 93, 249
McDaniel, 144
McDearmon, 469
McDermott, 55, 118, 152, 169, 408, 417
McDevitt, 280, 327
McDonald, 171, 331, 407, 434, 453
McDonnell, 472
McDonogh, 254
McDonough, 120
McDougall, 143, 280, 327
McDougle, 244
McDowal, 122
McDowell, 74, 353, 375, 427, 440, 500
McDuell, 72, 416, 483, 497, 501
McDuffee, 346, 472
McDuffie, 208, 435
McDuffy, 256
McDugall, 309
McElrach, 327
McElroy, 210
McElvain, 272
McEndre, 493
McEnery, 211
McEwen, 451
McFadden, 392, 443
McFaden, 195
McFadon, 175
McFarlan, 291
McFarland, 97, 110, 145, 292, 453
McFarlane, 45, 60, 82
McFarran, 319, 407
McFarren, 346, 392, 453
McFaul, 24
McFerran, 312
McGahey, 122
McGarr, 310
McGaughey, 264

McGavock, 131
McGee, 48
McGehee, 231
McGill, 189, 374, 415
McGilton, 365
McGinis, 314
McGinley, 401
McGinnis, 365
McGlue, 249, 373, 475
McGonegal, 453
McGowly, 141
McGragor, 426, 453
McGrath, 327, 391
McGray, 472
McGregor, 142, 144, 327, 423, 472
McGrew, 195
McGuffey, 314
McGuire, 255, 287, 417, 464, 472
McGunnigle, 130, 166, 224
McGurk, 453
McHenry, 258, 298, 346, 365, 375
McIlhany, 251
McIntire, 187, 201, 207, 493
McIntosh, 13, 24, 45, 62, 82, 106, 143, 147, 155, 186, 209, 280, 285, 327, 365, 407, 422, 429, 502
McIntyre, 357
McJilton, 381, 440, 484
McKaraher, 144
McKay, 346
McKean, 19, 81, 83, 137, 456
McKee, 91
McKeever, 453
McKelden, 137, 197, 248
McKelly, 203
McKelsey, 30
McKenney, 396
Mckenny, 492
McKenzie, 499
McKeon, 131, 365
McKibbin, 252
McKim, 366
McKimm, 407

McKinna, 280
McKinney, 210, 212, 285
McKissick, 334
McKnight, 33, 147, 225, 229, 230, 467
McLain, 135, 475, 480
McLanahan, 259, 260, 280
McLane, 9, 28, 58, 235, 266, 284, 376
McLaren, 142
McLauchlin, 429
McLaughlin, 21, 28, 33, 55, 64, 73, 74, 82, 101, 317, 355, 376, 389, 393, 407, 499
McLean, 86, 179, 188, 280, 391, 429, 477, 492
McLellan, 137, 228
McLemore, 392, 407
McLeod, 99, 111, 233, 291, 292, 328, 425
McLester, 472
McLosky, 298
McMackin, 472
McMakin, 280
McMan, 210
McManus, 298
McMechen, 346
McMillan, 439
McMillen, 55
McNair, 45, 82, 106, 155, 394
McNamara, 365
McNamee, 227, 453, 472
McNeil, 118, 126
McNeill, 309, 395
McNelly, 53
McNerhany, 29, 152
McNulty, 20, 255, 270, 310, 453, 481, 500, 508
McPherson, 2, 101, 165, 172, 173, 190, 193, 232, 235, 392, 442, 443, 492
McQuay, 303
McQuillan, 17, 232
McRae, 186, 203, 212, 419, 453
McRea, 122
McRee, 439

McRoberts, 233
McSherry, 430
McTavish, 208, 250
McVean, 132, 343
McVickar, 385
McWilliams, 12, 102, 164, 438, 509
Meacham, 11, 453
Mead, 304, 341, 365, 456, 492
Meade, 39, 206, 430
Meads, 450
Means, 418, 451
Mear, 385
Mears, 103, 234
Meatherall, 412
Mechan, 100
Mecker, 492
Medary, 256, 326
Medigos, 295
Medill, 118, 425, 427, 500
Meehan, 332
Meeks, 292
Megarey, 195
Meigs, 313, 317, 453
Melcher, 346
Meletta, 291
Melton, 274, 281
Melville, 268, 287, 316, 488
Melvin, 449
Menager, 401
Menard, 89, 486
Mendenhall, 20
Mendez, 391
Menger, 326, 429
Mercer, 100, 149, 187, 365, 423, 450, 460
Merchant, 23, 252, 362
Mercier, 303, 311
Meredith, 399, 492
Mereer, 365
Mergoun, 429
Meriwether, 309
Meriwether, Geo W, 309
Merriam, 227

Merrick, 171, 298, 458
Merrifield, 270
Merriken, 466
Merrill, 127, 272
Merritt, 48, 429, 453, 492
Merriwether, 43
Merry, 122
Merschel, 472
Mershan, 346, 365
Mershon, 391, 407
Merz, 429
Metcalf, 90
Metcalfe, 407
Meterholtz, 291
Meyhefer, 453
Miami Canal, 238
Michael, 58
Michard, 331
Michel, 292
Michie, 482
Mickle, 59
Mid, 326
Middle Quarter, 341
Middle Quarter Estate, 341
Middleton, 77, 93, 153, 236, 303, 326, 339, 384, 391, 417, 444, 453, 472
Mifflin, 198, 258, 380, 499
Milburn, 37, 54, 113, 327, 391, 396, 492
Milburne, 437, 502
Miles, 7, 33, 221, 446, 453
Milford, 397
Mill, 365
Millard, 297, 472
Millburn, 355
Miller, 6, 12, 17, 22, 37, 41, 49, 64, 72, 73, 89, 90, 92, 94, 97, 118, 120, 122, 170, 187, 199, 207, 212, 216, 233, 247, 254, 256, 278, 283, 290, 292, 293, 303, 309, 314, 317, 324, 329, 358, 376, 378, 381, 391, 399, 401, 407, 429, 446, 447, 453, 472, 492, 500
Millers, 290
Millett, 407

Millikin, 96, 97
Millington, 460
Millis, 95
Mills, 65, 86, 113, 145, 295, 365, 391, 437, 452, 463, 470, 472, 474, 492, 496, 509
Millstead, 472
Milnes, 191
Milnor, 138, 203
Milstead, 346, 391
Miltimore, 227
Milton, 3, 68
Milton Hill, 413
Minagorode, 460
Mine, 346
Mine La Mote, 339
Miner, 208, 326
Mines, 35
Minge, 252, 400
Minnigerode, 80
Minor, 53, 78, 85, 180, 280, 314, 326, 361, 391, 453, 462, 472, 492
Missourium, 219
Mister, 429
Mitchel, 8, 28, 461
Mitchell, 44, 59, 82, 94, 98, 108, 127, 174, 176, 229, 240, 251, 280, 346, 361, 365, 373, 375, 376, 391, 394, 407, 413, 416, 424, 429, 442, 453, 492
Mittrigger, 326
Mix, 19, 71, 502
Mixter, 122
Moale's Success, 312
Mobley, 103
Moffett, 216
Mogarth, 437
Mohum, 147
Mohun, 79, 207, 307, 350, 393, 432, 455
Molloy, 429
Mom, 115
Moncure, 302
Monk, 309

Monroe, 145, 156, 264, 326, 342, 391, 425, 429
Montgomery, 20, 165, 272, 346, 365, 422
Moody, 56
Moon, 375
Moore, 1, 11, 41, 59, 63, 67, 75, 76, 104, 108, 111, 151, 152, 168, 170, 173, 190, 221, 240, 257, 280, 309, 330, 331, 334, 373, 385, 409, 411, 417, 437, 453, 472, 475, 481, 492, 503, 507
Moorhead, 463
Moors, 35, 499
Moran, 36, 65, 84, 90, 101, 106, 326, 416, 429, 472
Moras, 369
Morcoe, 456
Morehand, 97
Morehead, 461
Morehouse, 370
Moreland, 346
Morell, 116, 124
Morgan, 144, 164, 176, 205, 226, 236, 267, 275, 296, 298, 326, 342, 346, 354, 365, 391, 436, 453, 456, 462, 472, 495
Moriarty, 211
Morin, 292
Morley, 192
Mormon, 384
Mormons, 216
Morow, 416
Morrell, 44, 82, 107, 140, 155, 243, 351
Morrice, 407
Morril, 82
Morris, 4, 11, 46, 66, 82, 141, 144, 170, 172, 233, 258, 268, 280, 281, 290, 297, 309, 324, 342, 407, 425, 432, 442, 453
Morrison, 40, 49, 60, 103, 292, 365, 394, 407, 429
Morrow, 17, 19, 63, 84, 87, 164, 374, 474

Morse, 23, 38, 45, 129, 168, 280, 384
Morsell, 2, 65, 135, 168, 235, 267, 326, 333, 347, 399
Morson, 302
Mortimer, 283
Mortimore, 309
Morton, 118, 126, 280, 287, 346, 397, 437, 467
Mosby, 329
Moseley, 267, 355
Mosely, 25, 336, 342
Moses, 118, 309
Mosher, 124, 245, 509
Mosley, 424
Moss, 101, 387
Mott, 280
Motte, 128
Motter, 397
Moulton, 365
Moultrie, 143
Mount, 326, 407, 453, 472, 492
Mount Air, 216
Mount Holl, 370
Mount Holly, 187
Mount Ida, 414
Mount Pleasant, 65
Mount Tirza, 413
Mount Vernon, 70, 75, 83, 356
Mountain Run Farm, 204, 305
Mountjoy, 1
Mounts, 391
Mountz, 280, 296
Moury, 252
Mower, 492
Moxley, 382, 497
Mozene, 346
Mudd, 307, 349, 399, 508
Mudge, 352
Mufhawn, 346
Muhlenburg, 143
Mulledy, 348
Muller, 22, 144, 170, 218, 228, 254, 259, 292, 346, 365, 415, 484, 502

Mulligan, 293, 325
Mullikin, 373
Mullin, 280, 391
Mullowney, 206
Mulloy, 389, 407, 429
Mulvany, 394
Muncaster, 415
Mundy, 256
Munk, 259
Munn, 453
Munro, 238, 333, 435
Munroe, 163, 437
Munson, 453
Muntz, 326
Murdaugh, 28, 376
Murdoch, 365
Murdock, 173, 280, 346, 365, 472
Murfey, 365
Murgatroys, 407
Murgotrey, 391
Murphey, 344
Murphy, 5, 12, 87, 110, 232, 303, 311, 350, 373, 410, 416, 436, 492
Murray, 39, 108, 147, 153, 179, 183, 208, 209, 212, 236, 275, 280, 281, 285, 298, 309, 327, 374, 391, 399, 407, 411, 417, 470
Murrell, 176
Murry, 111, 475
Muse, 28, 172, 332, 376, 442, 453, 485
Musgrove, 462
Mussey, 346, 391
Myale, 485
Myddleton, 269
Myer, 365, 472
Myerle, 326
Myers, 32, 40, 53, 141, 152, 167, 176, 189, 194, 213, 237, 241, 260, 280, 309, 319, 326, 336, 365, 431, 492
Myrick, 276

N

Naar, 240
Nafey, 291
Naile, 280
Nailor, 359, 416
Nalle, 407
Nalley, 317, 399, 420
Nally, 429
Napoleon, 355
Nappertandy, 74
Nash, 137, 194, 228, 285
Nat'l Theatre, 84
Natoire, 388
Naudain, 73, 252
Nauman, 473
Naval Ofcrs, 231
Naylor, 84, 113, 180, 229, 230, 288, 292, 407, 414, 508
Neal, 38, 314
Neale, 10, 11, 56, 58, 189, 197, 211, 234, 237, 310, 335, 349, 440
Neall, 457
Nealy, 15
Neely, 45, 69, 82, 86, 401
Neff, 23
Neill, 313
Neilson, 291, 295
Nelson, 67, 149, 175, 188, 202, 246, 287, 310, 363, 380, 386, 389, 392, 400, 429, 477
Nethaway, 214
Nevett, 186, 383
Nevil, 425
Neville, 385, 493
Nevins, 296
Nevit, 453
Nevitt, 68, 310, 346
Nevius, 91, 294
New Birmingham Manor, 377
New England Society, 436
New Jersey, 464
Newby, 493
Newcomb, 188, 407, 493
Newcombe, 51
Newell, 251, 255

Newhall, 19
Newly, 407
Newman, 43, 158, 197, 199, 207, 219, 292, 318
Newmayer, 20
Newsom, 472
Newton, 106, 230, 261, 451
Niccolls, 401
Nicholas, 327
Nicholason, 164
Nicholls, 196, 405, 450, 464, 486, 495
Nichols, 180, 246, 266, 276, 281, 409, 419, 421
Nicholson, 9, 30, 42, 78, 186, 259, 260, 292, 368, 369, 370, 374, 464
Nickleson, 197
Nicol, 290
Niles, 10, 124, 132, 257, 327, 374
Nix, 197
Nixon, 143, 260, 421, 439, 458
Nixon's Mills, 421
Noah, 325, 381
Noble, 11
Noel, 67, 284
Noell, 171, 404
Noerr, 367
Noeth, 407
Noland, 18, 90, 323, 460, 462
Nollner, 26
Nonns, 386
Noonan, 67
Norbeck, 14, 474, 482
Norman, 1, 365
Norment, 365
Norn, 392
Norris, 13, 19, 24, 120, 174, 201, 349, 365, 380, 392, 402, 407, 424, 429, 453, 472, 479, 496
North, 95, 98, 156, 460, 493
Northrop, 361
Norton, 489
Norvell, 153, 193, 289
Norwood, 341, 462, 508

Nott, 32
Notti, 388
Nottingham, 413
Nourse, 7, 23, 34, 83, 84, 86, 88, 109, 113, 114, 129, 179, 219, 235, 310, 314, 318, 335, 392, 407, 416, 478
Novimagis, 356
Nowlan, 332
Nowland, 54, 306
Noyes, 48, 102
Nugent, 290, 395, 493
Numbers, 94
Nunn, 103
Nutt, 424
Nuttall, 493
Nutting, 104
Nye, 87, 327

O

O'Barron, 185
O'Blemis, 19
O'Blenis, 238
O'Brian, 327
O'Brien, 3, 77, 280, 289, 392, 395, 429, 450, 472, 493
O'Bryon, 327, 392
O'Callaghan, 90
O'Connell, 346, 454, 472
O'Conner, 379, 407, 450, 463
O'Connor, 202, 360
O'Donall, 433
O'Donoghue, 169, 297
O'Flanagan, 58
O'Hara, 493
O'Hare, 453, 455
O'Leary, 327
O'Neal, 84, 252, 346, 472
O'Neale, 181, 328, 337, 344, 402
O'Neall, 454
O'Neil, 233, 292, 429, 481
O'Neill, 213, 493
O'Regan, 327
O'Reilly, 299, 407, 429

O'Reily, 365
O'Rourke, 365
O'Sullivan, 169, 407, 429
Oak Grove, 456
Oak Hill, 382
Oak Ridge, 111
oak tree, 70
Oakes, 355
Oakey, 166
Oakley, 293
Oaks, 50
Oatland, 99
Ober, 236, 263, 301
Ochiltree, 259
Odell, 126
Officer, 429, 472
Offley, 504
Offut, 444
Offutt, 151, 222, 330, 398
Ogden, 365, 393
Ogilby, 394
Ogle, 90, 322
Ogleby, 135
Oglethorpe, 52
Oister, 329
Oldham, 174, 441
Ole Bull, 221
Oliver, 28, 30, 401, 409
Olivier, 297
Olmsted, 149
Onderdonk, 6
Oo-tah-cau-hur, 85
Orendorff, 1, 55, 74
organ, 449
Orgiazzi, 310
Orme, 19, 29, 34, 38, 48, 71, 232, 248, 333, 365, 416
Ormes, 241
Orndorff, 172
Orr, 398, 478, 493
Orton, 280
Orvis, 1, 44, 88
Osage Chief, 239

Osage Indians, 250
Osborn, 95, 332, 407
Osborne, 121, 341, 478
Osburn, 91, 392
Osgood, 8, 120, 214, 429, 430
Osnabruck, 472
Ostrander, 274
Oswald, 374, 476
Oswell, 310
Otis, 52, 238, 287, 353, 485
Ott, 293
Otterback, 17, 170, 211, 417, 481
Ottman, 472
Ottoback, 502
Ottolengui, 79
Ould, 71, 196
Ousley, 170, 380
Outten, 344
Ovenshine, 210
Overman, 149, 151, 152
Overstreet, 44, 313
Overton, 462
Owen, 38, 130, 151, 236, 264, 346, 358, 407, 453
Owens, 74, 121, 187, 310, 329, 346, 365, 407, 503
Owings, 327
Owl Run Farm, 204, 305
Owner, 260, 313
Oyster, 16, 346

P

Pace, 441
Packard, 146, 280
packet-boat **Juniata**, 180
Padgett, 346, 417
Padini, 351
Pagaud, 206
Page, 11, 24, 39, 122, 142, 341, 365, 392, 436, 472, 493, 507
Page Land Farm, 204, 305
Pageot, 297
Paigh, 34

Pain, 72
Paine, 287, 346, 376, 392, 407, 426, 454, 472
Pairo, 15, 262, 379
Palm, 280, 310
Palmer, 39, 42, 79, 96, 193, 256, 280, 303, 365, 392
Palmieri, 291
Pamell, 434
Pandeput, 66
Papy, 336
Paradise, 277
Paradise Lost, 3
Pardee, 32
Parescho, 330
Paris, 346
Parish, 1, 139, 235
Park, 52, 103
Parke, 26, 91, 142, 241, 324
Parker, 2, 13, 14, 28, 32, 34, 65, 97, 103, 115, 125, 138, 141, 143, 161, 219, 222, 223, 225, 235, 236, 241, 273, 280, 311, 314, 315, 320, 327, 333, 344, 346, 358, 376, 379, 383, 385, 392, 400, 417, 427, 429, 436, 453, 456, 463, 464, 475, 478
Parket, 429
Parkhill, 493
Parkhurst, 95
Parks, 162, 165, 468, 472
Parmele, 485
Parmelee, 346
Parmenter, 101, 122
Parris, 25, 310, 363, 384, 392
Parrish, 500
Parrot, 374
Parrott, 42, 346, 365, 424
Parry, 327, 380
Parsons, 143, 216, 280, 469
Partlow, 79
Partridge, 20, 27, 34, 37, 73
Pastaer, 121
Pastorius, 407

Paterson, 43, 143, 359
Patison, 365
Patrick, 87
Patten, 18, 337, 404, 466
Patterson, 8, 76, 87, 90, 114, 169, 245, 246, 258, 291, 359, 392, 397, 401, 425, 455, 473, 478, 493
Pattison, 259, 260
Patton, 187, 207, 319, 416
Patty, 42
Patuck, 19
Paul, 205, 346
Paulding, 23, 147, 214, 369
Paulet, 63
Paulus, 253
Pavenstedt, 290
Pawling, 365
Paxon's Church, 70
Paxton, 45, 508
Payne, 74, 87, 133, 156, 212, 275, 359, 365, 375, 392, 403, 407, 472
Payson, 508
Payton, 49, 121
Peabody, 52
Peach, 257, 385
Peach's Lot, 435
Peachey, 460
Peachy, 11, 454
Peacock, 125, 278
Peak, 310
Peake, 374
Peale, 443, 449, 486
Pearce, 2, 49, 90, 92, 314, 365, 455, 478
Pearcy, 395
Pearl, 56
Pearson, 262, 318, 377, 393, 481
Peart, 389
Pease, 87, 306, 407, 468
Peavey, 238
Peck, 139, 143, 346, 417, 424, 461, 496
Peckham, 167, 414
Peckworth, 156
Peddecord, 86, 116, 120, 130

Peden, 439
Pedlar, 429
Peel, 269
Peerce, 207
Peeree, 116
Peesch, 416
Pegram, 28, 376
Peirce, 114, 242, 455, 461
Peire, 297
Pelham, 112, 155, 243
Peltier, 486
Pemberton, 342
Pendergast, 173, 296, 297
Pendergrast, 443
Pendleton, 141, 149, 187, 247, 327, 346, 473
Penfield, 84
Penn, 52, 68, 110, 171, 215, 322, 396
Penniman, 163
Pennington, 13, 28
Pennock, 45, 494
Pennoyer, 192
Penoyer, 291
Penquite, 359
Penrose, 118, 120, 121, 158, 169
Peoples, 486
Pepper, 115, 178, 201, 241, 243, 263, 316, 416
Pepperell, 8
Perez, 452
Perkins, 11, 95, 213, 351, 365, 395, 484
Perrie, 23, 310, 429, 494
Perry, 39, 74, 112, 202, 208, 260, 280, 310, 321, 327, 365, 382, 393, 427, 429
Persico, 310
Peter, 374
Peterbaugh, 320
Peters, 63, 72, 124, 131, 275, 324, 393
Petersburg Intelligencer, 141
Petersen, 346
Peterson, 49, 365
Petrie, 392
Pettibone, 245, 348, 485

Pettigrew, 96, 178, 207
Pettit, 180, 261, 264, 472
Pettitt, 493
Pettrick, 365
Peugh, 116
Peyton, 111, 189, 310, 327, 392, 489
Pfeifer, 392
Phelps, 93, 133, 177, 270, 336, 381
Philippe, 138, 183, 397
Philips, 2, 103, 280, 310, 327, 346, 365, 407, 456, 473
Phillipps, 250
Phillips, 35, 56, 116, 180, 200, 214, 231, 235, 275, 277, 338, 355, 417, 486, 490, 502
Philpot, 42
Phoenix, 365
Phonix, 360
Physie, 169
Picabia, 292
Pickerell, 280
Pickering, 122, 305, 385, 392
Pickett, 97, 280, 310, 351, 407, 429
Pickrell, 81, 377
Pierce, 20, 100, 113, 149, 168, 180, 186, 235, 346, 383, 395, 404, 429, 493
Pierre, 429
Pierrepoint, 186
Pierson, 62, 280, 291
Piggott, 28
Pike, 6, 22, 104, 503
Pile, 115
<u>Pilgrims</u>, 505
Pilling, 52, 377, 401
Pillings, 249
Pinchback, 60
Pinckney, 258, 360, 394, 458
Pindell, 172, 444
Pine, 44
Pinkerton, 96
Pinkney, 29, 211, 231, 429, 489, 496
Pinney, 401
Piper, 310, 327, 346, 440, 473

Pitcher, 272, 384
Pitkin, 71
Pitman, 15
Pitt, 410
Pittman, 470
Pittsburg in Ruins, 141
Placide, 162
Placy, 486
Plant, 248, 286, 392, 463, 474, 475, 482
Plater, 374
Platt, 74
Pleasant Hill, 197
Pleasants, 261, 267, 365, 395, 429, 493
Pleasnats, 137
Plimpton, 83
Plombo, 388
Plowden, 18, 253
Plowman, 473
Plumber, 429
Plume, 232
Plummer, 39, 310, 454
Plumsill, 277
Pochon, 298
Poe, 42, 418
Poindexter, 472, 493
Poinsett, 75
Point Breeze, 182
Poland, 346, 365
Pole, 109
Polhemus, 238
Polk, 51, 57, 81, 92, 101, 114, 137, 195, 269, 278, 332, 360
Polkinghorn, 280
Polks, 263
Pollard, 95, 158, 327
Pomeroy, 193
Pomonkey, 18
Pomroy, 3
Pons, 470
Ponthoz, 296
Pool, 429, 472, 493
Poole, 196, 204, 310, 435
Poor, 120, 143, 275, 374, 479

Pope, 92, 306, 351, 451, 472, 493
Pope Gregory XIV, 242
Pope Gregory XVI, 150
Popham, 324
Poplar Forest, 470
Poplar Grove, 467
Poplar Point, 435
Port Royal, 303
Porter, 35, 74, 92, 100, 182, 220, 233, 256, 272, 287, 310, 327, 346, 401, 407, 418, 454, 473, 488, 503
Posey, 171, 365
Poss, 310
Possa, 454
Post, 104, 196, 429
Poston, 248
Pottawatamie, 418
Pottenger, 94
Potter, 112, 155, 164, 252, 280, 293, 383, 401, 445
Pottinger, 10, 18, 25
Potts, 197
Poulterer, 409
Poulton, 48, 420
Powell, 28, 191, 235, 254, 280, 376, 437, 454, 466, 490, 494
Power, 151, 456
Powers, 42, 296, 439
Powhatan, 360
Pownil, 209
Prall, 442
Prather, 72, 84, 129, 133, 249, 392, 426
Pratt, 10, 16, 139, 346, 378, 386, 395, 425, 429, 458
Pray, 319
Prentiss, 101, 374
Prescott, 22, 407
President Elect, 80
President's Message, 494
Preston, 56, 69, 154, 265, 331, 360, 380, 454, 464, 490
Prettyman, 346
Preuss, 154

Preusser, 379
Prevost, 113
Price, 63, 74, 107, 108, 118, 125, 155, 173, 210, 280, 291, 327, 334, 346, 442, 443
Prieus, 359
Prim, 15
Prime, 414
Primrose, 238
Prince, 92, 426
Prince Leopold, 457
Prindell, 429
Pringle, 493
Printup, 228
Printz, 142
Pritchard, 225, 399
Procilton, 365
Proctor, 88, 472, 493
Prospect Hill, 360, 421
Prother, 103
Proud, 299, 449
Prout, 112, 178, 229, 303, 327, 374
Provest, 36
Public Baths, 177
Pugh, 401
Pulaski, 442
Pulcharia, 335
Pullen, 327, 407
Pumphrey, 41, 74, 221, 230, 380, 387, 401, 417, 455, 459, 465, 479
Purcell, 327, 456
Purdon, 282
Purdy, 92, 122, 139, 161, 221, 359, 381, 407, 437, 474
Purkis, 64, 77, 89
Purple, 420
Purrell, 40
Purrill, 178
Purrington, 320
Purviance, 237, 409
Putnam, 64, 82, 86, 143, 144, 285
Putney, 50, 77, 89, 321
Pye, 297, 298
Pyekman, 291
Pyne, 41, 60, 151, 219, 234, 244, 430, 474

Q

Quales, 327
Quantrill, 280, 310, 365, 392
Quaw, 332
Queen, 9, 68, 146, 216, 274, 301, 310, 327, 346, 349, 376, 392, 407, 429, 481
Queen Isabella II, 26, 457
Queen of England, 397
Queen Victoria, 217, 242, 457
Quessenbury, 454
Quick, 292, 324
Quifaro, 269
Quigley, 139, 164, 360, 498
Quigly, 210
Quimby, 280, 310, 429, 445, 446, 454, 473, 493
Quincy, 113, 291, 353, 481
Quinn, 454
Quinter, 454
Quirk, 132

R

Rabbitts, 103
Rabit, 327
Radcliff, 248
Radford, 272
Raff, 484
Raikes, 334
Rails, 104
Rainbow, 392, 408
Raison, 172
Raley, 57, 84
Rall, 310, 327
Ralsom, 507
Ramsay, 7, 8, 41, 280, 286, 392, 452
Ramsdill, 449
Ramsey, 17, 33, 45, 82, 107, 175, 212, 274, 370, 398, 441, 488, 499
Randall, 171, 322, 416, 454, 488

Randals, 280
Randolph, 17, 18, 46, 75, 92, 202, 236, 259, 260, 299, 310, 327, 341, 346, 365, 408, 429, 454, 490
Rankin, 504
Rannihill, 176
Ransom, 259, 313, 429
Ranson, 260, 366, 435, 500
Rantoul, 118
Ratary, 189
Ratcliff, 40, 47, 241, 275, 338, 479, 481, 483
Ratcliffe, 92, 137, 243, 392, 481
Rathbone, 191, 280, 310
Rathbun, 73, 300, 327, 462
Raub, 94
Raulet, 107, 155
Rawling, 327
Rawlings, 176, 239, 412, 426, 465, 467, 493
Rawlins, 441, 443
Rawls, 240, 252
Rawson, 386
Ray, 196, 335, 463
Raymond, 493
Rayner, 73
Raynolds, 3, 454
Raynor, 300
Read, 208, 240, 259, 260, 329, 365, 480
Reader, 280, 392
Reading, 310
Reardon, 274, 430
Reckless, 454
Rector, 206
Redden, 454, 493
Reddy, 327
Reden, 407
Redfern, 60, 205, 214, 416
Redin, 117, 169, 213, 223, 358
Redman, 346, 366, 493
Reed, 57, 67, 148, 164, 176, 188, 239, 258, 361, 365, 401, 442, 454, 462, 473, 495

Reeder, 37, 301, 310, 322, 338, 365, 454
Reeler, 280, 347
Rees, 243
Reese, 46, 108, 381
Reeside, 13, 89, 310, 496
Reeve, 180
Reeves, 496, 509
Reid, 173, 259, 343, 409, 451, 461
Reid mine, 343
Reilly, 112, 171, 417, 441, 466
Reily, 100, 172
Reinburg, 392
Reinhard, 365
Reintzel, 473
Reiss, 310
Reitz, 9, 37, 416
Relves, 300
Remick, 121
Remmil, 503
Remsen, 373
Rennahan, 310
Renshaw, 327
Rentzill, 478
Reside, 360
Retreat, 115
Revelly, 173, 442
Revenel, 418
Reybold, 176
Reynberg, 356
Reynolds, 23, 144, 210, 342
Reynoldson, 421
Rhea, 45, 69, 89, 177, 272, 493
Rhet, 327
Rhett, 237, 272, 407, 429
Rhind, 259, 260
Rhodes, 17, 53, 125, 127, 170, 229, 280, 292, 417, 429
Rhyen, 493
Rian, 473
Ricaud, 148
Rice, 44, 210, 224, 239, 280, 301, 366, 392, 437, 454, 485, 493

Rich, 1, 3, 13, 45, 54, 82, 88, 106, 155, 211, 265, 346, 365, 411, 429
Richards, 13, 104, 490
Richardson, 133, 134, 192, 211, 249, 284, 301, 310, 312, 314, 351, 429, 440, 493
Richey, 272, 374, 456
Richie, 297
Richmond, 95, 96, 172, 429, 432, 441, 454
Rickets, 175
Ricketts, 277, 443, 473
Ricks, 310, 365, 392, 429, 454
Riddle, 50, 77, 89, 252, 457
Rider, 506
Ridgate, 194
Ridgeley, 408
Ridgely, 71, 124, 199, 217, 280
Ridges, 65
Ridgley, 310, 374
Ridgway, 28, 123
Ridout, 249
Riffetts, 321
Rigdon, 60, 429
Riggin, 80
Riggs, 96, 235, 242, 318, 380, 455
Right, 310
Rigsby, 246
Riley, 97, 122, 131, 201, 210, 261, 293, 392, 408, 409
Rind, 473
Rinehart, 327
Ring, 214
Ringgold, 7, 169, 280, 310, 429, 493
Ringold, 414
Riordan, 7, 115, 403
Riorden, 310
Ripley, 290, 498
Risley, 50
Ritch, 2
Ritchie, 45, 59, 82, 186, 338, 450
Rivers, 375
Rives, 111, 205, 235, 287, 358, 379, 416

Roach, 24, 31, 51, 120, 157, 169, 183, 310, 338, 368, 404, 411, 501
Roane, 186
Robb, 354
Robbins, 76, 80, 95, 114, 164, 177, 233, 316, 356, 361
Roberson, 14, 429
Roberts, 40, 45, 54, 69, 82, 89, 108, 122, 155, 156, 163, 197, 252, 259, 260, 276, 289, 368, 374, 434
Robertson, 99, 146, 205, 248, 288, 291, 310, 366, 423, 459, 493
Robeson, 8, 459
Robey, 180, 327, 429
Robillar, 293
Robins, 429
Robinson, 6, 15, 96, 103, 114, 147, 171, 188, 248, 280, 291, 300, 310, 322, 323, 324, 327, 347, 365, 392, 401, 408, 429, 440, 450, 463, 480, 484, 495, 500, 503
Robson, 495
Roby, 109, 208
Roche, 160, 280, 358, 365
Rochebrun, 490
Rochester, 497
Rock Creek Church, 77, 249
Rockwell, 83, 113, 136, 479
Roddy, 22
Roden, 251
Rodewald, 292
Rodgers, 259, 260, 311, 376, 393, 408
Rodman, 147, 295
Rodney, 206
Rodrick, 408
Roe, 41, 109, 214
Roemmele, 218
Roerts', 98
Rogers, 30, 46, 47, 56, 95, 129, 230, 280, 299, 310, 327, 347, 351, 399, 408, 440, 454
Rogge, 392
Rohrer, 408

Rollett, 429
Rollins, 13, 433, 473
Romyn, 255
Ronckendorff, 100, 206, 487
Rooker, 334
Root, 203, 365, 439, 473, 493
Root Beer, 151
Roper, 37, 298, 317, 402
Rosburgh, 173
Rose, 75, 125, 137, 280, 318, 346, 365, 411, 429
Rose Hill Farm, 76
Rose Mount, 286, 368
Rose Valley, 246
Rosecrants, 271
Rosencrantz, 369
Ross, 46, 57, 63, 67, 93, 164, 263, 280, 409, 454
Rosser, 188
Rossiter, 394
Roszel, 370
Rother, 423
Rothwell, 129, 207, 372, 382, 396
Roubin, 290
Roulstone, 331
Rousel, 443
Rousseau, 450
Routh, 291
Roux, 18, 20, 93, 249
Rowan, 233, 473
Rowand, 280, 310, 493
Rowe, 506
Rowen, 366
Rowland, 315, 377
Rowles, 38, 166, 206
Rowlett, 423
Rowley, 7, 388
Rowse, 174
Royall, 30, 94, 507
Royer, 234
Ruark, 310
Rubens, 388
Ruck, 284

Rudd, 494
Ruff, 409
Ruffield, 429
Rumpff, 461
Rumsey, 13, 102
Runnells, 347, 392
Runyan, 295
Rupert, 416
Rupp, 365
Ruppert, 189, 226
Rush, 147
Rusha, 473
Russell, 2, 3, 8, 11, 17, 24, 33, 45, 46, 78, 88, 89, 124, 154, 272, 285, 304, 310, 315, 318, 323, 329, 342, 361, 365, 369, 407, 429, 473, 493
Russworm, 11, 22, 54, 496
Rust, 122, 128, 154, 179, 202, 271, 454
Ruster, 451
Rustiage, 405
Rustin, 192, 327
Ruth, 202
Rutherford, 303, 353
Rutledge, 174, 258, 366, 443
Ryan, 246, 292, 314
Ryder, 429
Ryland, 158
Ryland Chapel, 321
Rynders, 341
Ryon, 48, 168, 236, 263, 301

S

Sabal, 297
Sabin, 291, 310
Sackett, 272, 327
Safford, 15, 95, 96
Sage, 485
Saila, 509
Saint John, 56
Saint Vrain, 89
Saint Winoxberg, 435
Salisbury, 483
Salmon, 454

Salomon, 281
Saltmarsh, 40, 366, 454
Saltonstall, 184
Saluda, 103
Salzwedel, 2
Sample, 264
Sampson, 281, 310, 475, 484, 509
Samson, 39, 93, 135, 144, 176, 183, 209, 221, 241, 257, 259, 261, 396, 399, 451, 457, 495
Samuel, 473
Samuels, 5, 185, 473
Sanaders, 327
Sanborn, 53
Sanchez, 287
Sanders, 7, 149, 153, 207, 350, 374, 429, 493, 507
Sanderson, 78, 256, 347
Sandford, 80, 197, 205, 290, 300
Sands, 126, 374
Sanford, 154, 281, 303, 310, 361, 366, 392, 493
Sanger, 392
Sangster, 110, 358, 477
Sankey, 164
Sansardine, 392
Santa Anna, 52, 112
Sappintgon, 42
Sarbut, 501
Sardo, 334
Sargent, 424, 493
Sartoro, 392
Sasscer, 296
Sauer, 351, 454
Saufferly, 417
Saulsbury, 329
Saunders, 1, 49, 90, 130, 147, 149, 190, 210, 284, 313, 338, 389, 395, 400, 454, 460
Sauper, 408
Savage, 36, 54, 55, 68, 151, 222, 246, 463
Savery, 388

Sawkins, 114
Sawyer, 238, 289, 500
Saxton, 30, 281, 395
Sayer, 290
Scaggs, 278
scarlet fever, 185
Schackelford, 468
Schaeffer, 40, 41
Schaeffer-Bernstein, 194
Schaffer, 55
Schaumburg, 128, 129
Scheel, 14
Schenck, 310, 342, 424
Schiefflin, 94
Schiller, 265
Schlegel, 242, 253
Schley, 228
Schloat, 320
Schmuck, 298
Schneider, 157, 416, 417
Schnell, 30
schnr **Bartol**, 132
schnr **Dodge**, 72, 383
schnr **Dorchester**, 440
schnr **Eagle**, 485
schnr **Fair**, 386
schnr **Flirt**, 269, 487
schnr **Florilla**, 33
schnr **H M Johnson**, 461
schnr **Industry**, 33
schnr **John Anderson**, 68
schnr **John Roberts**, 437
schnr **Mary**, 117
schnr **Mary Frances**, 3
schnr **Mary Jane**, 224
schnr **Meridian**, 130
schnr **On-ka-bye**, 342
schnr **Oraloo**, 284
schnr **Reeside**, 49
schnr **Ruth**, 11
schnr **Salada**, 49
schnr **Saml 1st**, 387
schnr **Sarah Lavinia**, 204

schnr **Sea Gull**, 7
schnr **Spitfire**, 221, 226, 315
schnr **Two Brothers**, 33
schnr **Victory**, 84
schnr **Water Witch**, 255
schnrs **Frank & Victory**, 277
Scholfield, 56, 210, 410
Schoolcraft, 224
Schreiber, 370
Schroder, 312
Schucking, 379
Schussler, 463
Schuyler, 190, 232, 366, 488, 505
Schwartstraber, 54
Schwartz, 157, 408, 416
Schwartzenburg, 351
Schwartztrawber, 45, 82, 108, 156
Scoggin, 112
Scot, 347
Scott, 24, 41, 45, 59, 79, 84, 86, 89, 110, 113, 152, 177, 196, 208, 210, 225, 236, 240, 249, 289, 291, 292, 294, 300, 310, 342, 343, 344, 347, 355, 361, 366, 374, 392, 398, 408, 412, 429, 444, 445, 449, 454, 479, 490, 493
Scovel, 496
Scoville, 327, 473
Scrivener, 14, 316, 483
Scrivner, 192
Scroggins, 256, 392
Scudder, 46, 192, 331
Seabrook, 168
Seamans, 122
Searight, 281, 347
Searle, 291
Sears, 62, 98, 175, 443, 474
Seaton, 92, 216, 347, 455
Seaver, 493
Seawell, 422
Second Addition to Culver's Chance, 435
Seddon, 310, 341, 508
Seely, 46, 221, 429

Segar, 454
Segur, 507
Seibert, 200
Seiler, 281, 429
Seitz, 481, 483
Selby, 328
Selden, 147, 236, 363, 389
Sellers, 45, 195
Sellman, 171, 441
Semimes, 408
Seminoles, 85
Semmes, 26, 62, 122, 153, 179, 227, 236, 296, 298, 347, 374, 375, 377, 417, 435, 463, 470, 480, 489, 493
Sengstack, 416
Sentmanat, 255
Sergeant, 100, 493
Serrin, 248
Serro, 170, 303
Servant, 316
Sessford, 126, 177, 248, 281, 456
Sevier, 136, 144, 353
Sevin, 290
Sewall, 1, 12, 75, 110, 138, 142, 149, 177, 180, 273, 294, 319, 333, 366, 371, 485
Sewell, 101, 310, 311, 468
Sexsmith, 159, 218, 236
Seymour, 136, 160, 254, 366, 454
Shad, 9, 389
Shadd, 416
Shaeffer, 462
Shafer, 475, 482
Shaffer, 488
Shallenberger, 347
Shanks, 387, 392, 398, 454
Shannon, 291
Shap, 429
Sharetts, 339
Sharkey, 298
Sharp, 144, 220, 249, 382
Sharpe, 210, 247
Sharpless, 327

Sharrett, 490
Shaw, 2, 3, 44, 50, 52, 55, 89, 121, 126, 187, 287, 290, 304, 342, 377, 380, 458, 473, 504
Shawk, 392, 408
Sheahan, 255, 389, 478
Sheckell, 416, 417
Sheckels, 245
Shed, 47
Sheels, 327, 366
Sheets, 310, 347, 392, 408, 429
Sheirburn, 65, 447
Shekell, 367
Shelby, 194, 353
Shelly, 179
Shelton, 284
Shepard, 196
Shepherd, 137, 161, 213, 225, 227, 228, 235, 266, 334, 445, 453
Sherbaus, 157
Sherburne, 310
Sheriff, 241, 360, 374, 394
Sherman, 2, 5, 168, 258, 287, 311, 366, 384, 473
Sherry, 17
Sherwood, 487
Shiek, 454
Shield, 473
Shields, 80, 153, 291, 362, 385, 392, 454, 477, 484
Shiles, 462
Shinn, 36, 214
ship **Arabella**, 184
ship **Ariadne**, 17
ship **Beard**, 334
ship **Boston**, 340
ship **Carysfort**, 63
ship **Clarissa Andrews**, 318
ship **Columbia**, 188
ship **Columbus**, 147, 193, 358
ship **Congress**, 158
ship **Coromando**, 66
ship **Elizabeth**, 80

ship **Elizawetta**, 183
ship **Erbus**, 218
ship **Erie**, 59, 120
ship **General Pike**, 383
ship **Great Western**, 426
ship **Hibernia**, 335
ship **Hoogly**, 290
ship **Hornet**, 121
ship **Inez**, 351
ship **Jamestown**, 238, 385
ship **John Adams**, 410
ship **Maria Theresa**, 234
ship **Mississippi**, 311
ship of the line **Royal George**, 181
ship **Patrick Henry**, 107
ship **Paul Jones**, 43
ship **Peacock**, 486
ship **Pennsylvania**, 149, 396, 494
ship **Portsmouth**, 25
ship **Potomac**, 342
ship **Powhatan**, 112
ship **Preble**, 121, 385
ship **Princeton**, 69, 261
ship **Ranger**, 353
ship **Saratoga**, 121
ship **St Louis**, 43, 191
ship **St Martins**, 80
ship **Ten Brothers**, 290
ship **Terror**, 218
ship **Vandalia**, 151, 152, 330
ship **Vincennes**, 163
ship **Woodside**, 505
ship **Yorkshire**, 269
ship **Zurich**, 395
Shippen, 347
ships **Thos B Wales** & **Tyrian**, 431
Shiras, 68
Shiraz, 41
Shirley, 70, 259, 260, 450
Shirtliff, 408
Shock, 303
Shoemaker, 222, 392, 455
Shofer, 1

Shonnard, 478
Shorter, 189, 327, 347
Shott, 408
Shreeve, 463
Shreve, 108, 156, 166, 352, 371, 455, 462, 463, 485
Shriver, 191
Shroeder, 57
Shryock, 392
Shubrick, 147, 185, 188, 233
Shufeldt, 259, 260
Shugart, 176
Shuster, 381
Shutter, 195
Sibbet, 141
Sibley, 25, 313, 369, 431, 454, 509
Sibrey, 392
Sickels, 429
Sickles, 195
Siebel, 366
Siecle, 347
Siffkin, 290
Sikin, 296
Silcox, 310
Silliman, 219, 232
Silver Spring, 418
Simeon, 415
Simes, 290
Simmes, 174, 281, 310, 327, 392
Simmons, 7, 8, 40, 52, 82, 83, 88, 92, 106, 310, 327, 366, 429
Simms, 29, 72, 100, 137, 152, 159, 218, 236, 248, 259, 260, 261, 281, 327, 347, 366, 379, 392, 416, 417, 454, 473, 482
Simons, 40, 90, 136, 259, 260, 424
Simonton, 281, 485
Simpers, 20
Simpkins, 43
Simpson, 7, 8, 45, 60, 82, 100, 232, 236, 321, 347, 358, 372, 378, 379, 498
Sims, 16, 163, 493
Simson, 25

Sinclair, 11, 200, 342, 366, 454, 473
Singleton, 210
Singley, 56
Sinnott, 281
Sinon, 356
Sioussa, 219
Sip, 392
Sipple, 323
Sirati, 298
Sisler, 327
Sisson, 122
Sizer, 35, 347
Skaggs, 350
Skerrett, 175
Skidmore, 49
Skinner, 38, 77, 87, 89, 113, 118, 121, 164, 172, 178, 238, 286, 361, 381, 387
Skipwith, 178
Skirving, 56, 451, 462, 463
Slack, 19
Slacum, 157, 162, 204, 408, 473
Slade, 138, 339
Slagg, 45, 62, 82, 107, 156
Slamm, 371, 454
Slater, 76, 219, 298
Slaymaker, 349
Sleater, 90
Sleeper, 95
Slicer, 158, 171, 310, 468
Slidell, 408
Slifer, 372
Sloan, 366
Sloat, 185
Slocum, 34, 82, 97
Slocumb, 411
sloop of war **Preble**, 6, 208
sloop of war **Saratoga**, 147
sloop of war **St Mary's**, 90, 147, 149
sloop of war **Vandalia**, 149
sloop of war **Vincennes**, 147
sloop of war **Yorktown**, 6
sloop-of-war **Boston**, 304
sloop-of-war **John Adams**, 238

Sluper, 347
Slye, 310, 408, 479
Small, 281, 417
Smalley, 27
small-pox, 419
Smallpox, 452
Smallwood, 20, 36, 143, 168, 171, 176, 255, 295, 347, 366, 392, 399, 441, 451
Smallwoon, 374
Smead, 445
Smedes, 162, 464
Smeed, 342
Smetts, 293
Smith, 2, 3, 4, 5, 10, 17, 21, 22, 32, 39, 42, 44, 49, 51, 55, 60, 63, 64, 65, 73, 75, 76, 83, 84, 85, 87, 88, 89, 92, 100, 103, 105, 109, 110, 113, 120, 121, 122, 126, 128, 133, 136, 137, 140, 146, 151, 157, 168, 169, 172, 173, 174, 175, 176, 185, 186, 196, 202, 203, 215, 216, 218, 220, 221, 224, 227, 232, 233, 237, 246, 252, 254, 257, 259, 263, 264, 271, 272, 273, 276, 280, 281, 286, 289, 290, 291, 292, 296, 303, 305, 306, 310, 311, 312, 313, 321, 323, 324, 327, 331, 336, 344, 347, 352, 359, 366, 369, 374, 384, 386, 392, 393, 398, 399, 404, 408, 411, 416, 422, 423, 429, 432, 433, 435, 440, 441, 442, 448, 449, 450, 454, 455, 463, 467, 473, 474, 475, 476, 480, 482, 484, 487, 493, 503
Smithea, 367
Smithson, 37
Smithwood, 85
Smoot, 47, 113, 148, 173, 189, 213, 223, 261, 340, 366, 392, 399, 416, 425, 467, 470, 493
Smoots, 443
Smull, 83, 427
Smyles, 54
Sneed, 462

Sneeder, 15
Snell, 276, 349
Snelling, 272
Snethen, 122, 225, 323
Sneyders, 388
Snider, 240
Snively, 358, 382
Snodgrass, 29, 429, 457
Snow, 56, 69, 189, 190, 197, 315
Snowden, 167, 296, 377
Snowden's Manor Enlarged, 435
Snyder, 310, 398, 451
Sojourner, 298
Soley, 435, 445, 446
Sollers, 26
Somerby, 30
Somerville, 28, 93, 96, 174, 259, 260, 302, 362, 376, 429, 442
Sommers, 144, 281, 403, 429
Sopher, 347
Soran, 171
Sothoron, 456
Souder, 396
Soule, 96, 473
Southall, 149
Southard, 75, 233
Southern, 392
Southgate, 388
Southwick, 424
Southworth, 383
Sower, 351
Spackman, 193
Spaight, 258
Spain, 47
Spalding, 2, 14, 16, 57, 96, 160, 170, 199, 296, 298, 456, 473
Spangler, 30
Spaniard, 199
Sparey, 314
Sparks, 52, 70, 188
Spatz, 56
Spaulding, 310, 366
Speake, 374

Spear, 284, 285
Spears, 63, 327
Speckman, 408
Speed, 474
Speedwell Forges, 165
Speekes, 493
Speer, 281
Speiden, 424
Speir, 327
Speisser, 170, 423
Spellman, 314, 493
Spence, 376
Spencer, 55, 94, 107, 139, 141, 193, 235, 276, 290, 303, 310, 353, 354, 366, 408, 429, 493
Sperling, 392
Sperry, 97
Spicer, 259, 260, 381, 451
Spigwill, 310
Spofford, 230
Spotts, 466
Spradley, 429
Sprague, 70, 157, 221, 360, 488
Spregle, 122
Sprigg, 303, 327, 469, 501
Spring, 460
Spring Garden, 227
Springs, 310
Sprole, 10, 203, 231, 332, 333, 360, 449, 451, 502
Spurrier, 173
Spurvier, 442
Squier, 377
Squire, 139
Squires, 360, 400
St Clair, 94, 119, 143, 221, 317, 392, 446, 483
St Elme, 245
St John, 32
St Paul's Cathedral, 215
St Peter, 351
St Phillip's & Jacob, 403
St Vrain, 87, 89, 486

Stabler, 261
Stafford, 361
Stagg, 291
Stallings, 463, 495, 504
Stambaugh, 199
Stamp, 220
Stanford, 392
Stanhope, 410
Staniford, 290, 446
Stanley, 490
Stanly, 310
Stansbury, 110, 392, 408
Stanton, 243, 408, 429, 474, 477
Stanwood, 56
Staples, 461
Stapleton, 112
Stappar, 319
Stark, 429, 450, 493
Starke, 143
Starkey, 392
Starr, 92, 399
State of Indiana, 222
Statz, 84
Staunton, 392
steamboat **Bourbon**, 274
steamboat **Buckeye**, 1
steamboat **Buffalo**, 427
steamboat **Capitol**, 9
steamboat **Columbia**, 94
steamboat **Columbus**, 437
steamboat **De Soto**, 1
steamboat **Empire**, 41
steamboat **George Washington**, 7
steamboat **Josephine**, 150
steamboat **Lady Madison**, 438
steamboat **Madison**, 449
steamboat **Marquette**, 281
steamboat **Narragasset**, 151
steamboat **New Philadelphia**, 375
steamboat **Pathfinder**, 60
steamboat **Pike**, 118
steamboat **Plymouth**, 438
steamboat **Rainbow**, 151

steamboat **Red Rover**, 115
steamboat **Sultana**, 501
steamboat **Swallow**, 139, 141
steamboats **Saratoga, North America, & Erie**, 370
steamer **Alabama**, 343
steamer **Belle Poule**, 274
steamer **Bertrand**, 182
steamer **Big Hatshee**, 314
steamer **Cambria**, 237
steamer **Cherokee**, 100, 156
steamer **Columbia**, 222
steamer **Confidence**, 439
steamer **Dayton**, 384, 412, 414
steamer **Engineer**, 149
steamer **Express**, 139
steamer **Georgia**, 367
steamer **Great Western**, 316
steamer **Hibernia**, 183, 185
steamer **Kent**, 332
steamer **London**, 332
steamer **Marquette**, 274
steamer **Massachusetts**, 388
steamer **Montezuma**, 473
steamer **NewYork**, 454
steamer **Omega**, 78
steamer **Paul Jones**, 216
steamer **Powhatan**, 47
steamer **Princeton**, 285
steamer **Rochester**, 139
steamer **Union**, 39
steamer **United States**, 389
steamer **Victoria & Albert**, 397
steamer **Water Witch**, 149
steamship **Alabama**, 312
steamship **Great Western**, 360
steamship **Missouri**, 155
steamship **New York**, 194
steamship **Princeton**, 285
Steel, 315
Steele, 138, 313, 320, 323, 324, 349, 360, 366, 379, 463
Steenrod, 362

Steever, 40, 41
Steffens, 293
Steiger, 417
Stein, 45
Steinberger, 303
Steiner, 392
Stelle, 280, 408, 437, 454
Stephen, 134
Stephens, 61, 347, 416
Stephenson, 61, 367, 399, 416, 466
Sterne, 135
Sterrett, 398
Stetson, 285, 347, 392
Stettinius, 15, 60, 114, 132, 140, 141
Steuart, 25, 129
Steuben, 143
Stevens, 26, 183, 259, 260, 313, 450, 473, 498
Stevenson, 53, 55, 147, 179, 461
Steward, 6, 366
Stewart, 35, 50, 53, 65, 67, 77, 85, 98, 99, 113, 135, 136, 137, 140, 156, 163, 171, 198, 199, 215, 217, 237, 271, 273, 281, 284, 310, 322, 327, 332, 342, 347, 355, 366, 392, 408, 417, 429, 454, 473, 479, 493, 508
Stickney, 161
Stiff, 74
Stiles, 24, 110, 259, 260
Stilwell, 170
Stimpson, 276
Stinger, 153, 473
Stinson, 96, 366
Stirling, 11, 21, 143, 291
Stirman, 203
Stitcher, 392
Stith, 87, 500
Stockton, 4, 10, 17, 30, 46, 56, 69, 77, 107, 261, 285, 334, 342, 343, 424, 432, 473, 502
Stoddard, 395
Stoddert, 174
Stokes, 56, 107

Stokvis, 281
Stone, 1, 2, 21, 24, 26, 104, 138, 184, 187, 191, 192, 198, 207, 229, 264, 272, 274, 291, 310, 327, 376, 408, 441, 454, 473, 478, 488
Stoneall, 408
Stoner, 408
Stonestreet, 216, 497
Stoney, 310
Storer, 27, 121, 281, 327
store-ship **Erie**, 275
storeship **Lexington**, 188, 205, 422
Storkwell, 362
Storms, 46
Storor, 310
Story, 262, 362, 434
Stotlemeyer, 358
Stott, 181, 215, 258, 295, 416, 417, 437, 458, 475
Stoub, 392
Stout, 222, 333, 473
Stoutenburgh, 292
Stover, 247
Stovin, 204, 305
Stow, 281, 401, 450
Stowbriski, 454
Stowell, 380
Strader, 347
Strahan, 480
Stratton, 168, 177, 210
Straub, 281
Stribling, 393, 494
Strickland, 197, 238
Strider, 493
Stringer, 84, 401
Stringfellow, 99, 257, 347, 355, 358, 399
Stringham, 247
Strobecker, 64
Strohm, 409
Stroman, 303
Strong, 147, 292, 327, 389, 404, 462
Strother, 213, 392
Stroud, 322

Strunk, 504
Struver, 292
Stryker, 8
Stuart, 61, 122, 144, 147, 153, 259, 260, 298, 465, 488
Stubb, 203
Stubbs, 318
Stull, 179, 418
Sturgess, 310, 448
Stuteley, 366
Stutely, 392
Suarez, 429
Suddards, 399
Suit, 400
Sullivan, 4, 255, 283, 291, 320, 347, 366, 415
Sultzer, 171
Sumby, 255
Summerance, 88
Summeraner, 11, 33, 45
Summers, 182, 278, 321, 454, 498
Sumpter, 144, 353
Sumter, 8, 59, 74
Suter, 118, 263, 489
Sutherland, 180, 190, 208, 287, 408
Sutton, 429, 454
Suydam, 113, 263, 293, 458
Swaine, 395
Swan, 64, 113, 126
Swann, 149, 181, 223, 255, 404, 441, 469, 475, 493
Swartwout, 381, 507
Swartz, 475
Swartze, 366
Swasey, 45
Swatzhawber, 1
Swayne, 408
Swearer, 366
Sweeney, 157, 200, 252
Sweeny, 153, 193, 417, 480
Sweeting, 416, 456
Swett, 99, 450
Swinborne, 292

Swink, 117
Swisher, 423
Switzer, 251
Swope, 61
Sydnor, 224
Sykes, 312
Sylvester, 199, 276, 408
Symington, 310
Symms, 347, 429

T

Tabb, 29
Tabbs, 225
Tabler, 151
Taggard, 292
Taggert, 303, 464
Tailor, 254
Tait, 34, 408, 410
Taite, 281
Talbert, 14, 112, 387
Talbot, 104, 121, 318, 395
Talbott, 291
Talcott, 96
Talking Telegraph, 134
Tallmadge, 75, 253, 265, 356, 454
Talmadge, 325, 392
Talor, 327
Talty, 283, 416
Tamariz, 125
Taney, 477
Tannehill, 404, 442
Tannell, 493
Tanner, 105, 201
Tansil, 392
Tarbell, 425
Tarlton, 105, 353
Tarning, 379
Tarr, 94
Tarring, 17, 31, 167, 185, 188, 202, 221, 283, 396, 398, 417, 438, 480, 507
Tasistro, 281, 473
Tasker, 485
Tastit, 459

Tate, 79, 281
Tattnall, 281
Tayloe, 60, 83, 84
Taylor, 13, 22, 26, 48, 56, 63, 78, 87, 98, 106, 122, 125, 126, 135, 149, 151, 161, 187, 189, 190, 195, 200, 238, 244, 252, 270, 278, 281, 284, 314, 327, 332, 347, 369, 388, 392, 395, 397, 399, 421, 430, 450, 460, 468, 473, 475, 488, 493, 495
Tayman's Land, 387
Tazewell, 102, 455
Teachen, 188
Teachum, 413
Teall, 171, 300
Teas, 11
Teats, 419
Tee, 493
Telnore, 350
Templeman, 447
Templeton, 401
Ten Eyck, 46, 234, 311, 424
Tennant, 508
Tennesley, 255
Tenney, 277, 430
Teprell, 414
Terore, 430
Terrett, 131, 146, 179, 271, 273, 493
Terrinet, 408
Territt, 310
Tete, 297
Thanksgiving, 465
Tharp, 433
Thatcher, 94
Thaxter, 306
Theaker, 130
Theband, 292
Thellerterger, 327
Thibadeaux, 408
Thiel, 393
Thigpen, 98, 156
Thistle, 44
Thockmorton, 66

Thom, 473
Thomas, 12, 34, 40, 41, 60, 61, 82, 92, 95, 99, 105, 111, 118, 180, 187, 230, 251, 302, 311, 327, 347, 351, 361, 366, 384, 392, 403, 408, 454, 455, 473, 478, 482, 493, 506, 509
Thomkins, 430
Thompson, 10, 13, 20, 39, 45, 67, 75, 77, 79, 80, 82, 86, 89, 97, 99, 101, 105, 114, 121, 122, 143, 151, 152, 155, 168, 185, 190, 223, 233, 264, 281, 298, 303, 304, 310, 316, 327, 330, 331, 347, 358, 369, 379, 384, 392, 399, 403, 408, 409, 424, 429, 432, 454, 455, 464, 467, 473, 493, 498
Thomson, 96, 236, 255, 291, 437, 503
Thorburn, 311
Thorn, 102, 125, 127, 408, 454, 508
Thornbury, 493
Thorne, 395
Thornley, 2
Thornly, 235, 478, 498
Thornton, 20, 28, 33, 45, 59, 82, 264, 268, 298, 311, 313, 376, 430, 473
Thornwell, 257
Thorny Point, 302
Thorp, 142, 325
Thriff, 366
Thrift, 429, 493
Throckmorton, 28, 60, 89, 216, 281
Throop, 381
Thruston, 143, 234, 245, 265, 340, 347, 354, 369, 397, 461
Thumb, 473
Thumblert, 327
Thumblet, 327, 347
Thumlert, 294, 416, 479
Thurler, 310
Thurman, 500
Thyson, 417
Tiber Creek, 198
Tiber Mill, 126, 318, 393
Tickle, 175

Ticknor, 147
Tiernan, 460
Tilden, 171
Tileson, 230
Tiley, 191
Tilghman, 42, 342, 347, 378, 424, 429, 441
Tillard, 20
Tiller, 311
Tilley, 38, 306, 392
Tillinghast, 3
Tilton, 43, 169, 376, 392
Timberlake, 408
Timmerman, 292
Timms, 71
Tinslar, 450
Tinsley, 47
Tippett, 366
Tirrell, 425, 431, 507
Tisdale, 385
Titcomb, 241
Titus, 96, 314
Tobacco, 170
Tobey, 177
Toca, 125, 151
Tochman, 475, 479
Tod, 24, 147, 310, 500
Todd, 4, 14, 60, 117, 154, 170, 236, 366, 379, 380, 426, 456, 464, 480
Todhunter, 257
Tolson, 255, 347, 430
Tombert, 285
Tombs, 395
Tomlinson, 64, 104
Tompkins, 46, 176, 396, 473
Tonge, 3, 227
Topliff, 419
Toppin, 473
Torbert, 210
Torbut, 78, 357
Torre, 366
Torrence, 62
Torrey, 141

Torry, 477
Totten, 296
Tousard, 374
towboat **Persian**, 431
towboat **Pilot**, 112
Towers, 215, 493
Towle, 170, 380, 399, 436, 450
Towles, 359, 374, 463
Townley, 328, 338, 392, 408
Towns, 34
Townsend, 32, 33, 123, 200, 256, 287, 293, 327, 367, 454
Townsley, 130
Towson, 208
Tozer, 392
Tracey, 215
Tracy, 473
Tranah, 311
Trapani, 26
Traphagen, 293
Travers, 286, 366, 371, 416, 418, 474, 475
Traverse, 104
Travis, 361
Treat, 32
Tree, 222, 335, 403
Tree Hill, 186
Trepagnier, 83
Tribe, 392
Trice, 404
Trinity Church, 306
Triplett, 402, 409
Trist, 336
Tristler, 299
Troost, 459
Trott, 62, 243, 450
Troubat, 288
Trouman, 366
Troxell, 243
Troy, 274
True, 168, 366, 408, 429, 473
Trueman, 172, 442
Truemen, 172

Truman, 444
Trumbull, 265, 327
Truscott, 167, 366, 430
Trusmels, 251
Truston, 466
Truuill, 315
Truxton, 493
Tryson, 374
Tschieffly, 473
Tucker, 13, 21, 23, 33, 81, 103, 187, 188, 207, 281, 304, 314, 316, 347, 356, 358, 362, 368, 374, 379, 408, 417, 437, 454, 456, 460, 473, 493, 498, 499, 507
Tuckerman, 13
Tudor, 137
Tuffey, 454
Tufiakin, 129
Tufts, 298
Tuion, 292
Tuley, 251
Tuleyries, 251
Tull, 177
Tully, 429
Tumbler, 366
Tump, 302, 505
Tunsill, 393
Tupper, 74
Turgeon, 297
Turley, 425
Turner, 49, 67, 113, 120, 216, 220, 243, 249, 275, 281, 314, 320, 333, 366, 392, 408, 454, 500
Turpin, 211, 274, 454, 468, 473
Turrills, 424
Turton, 214
Tuston, 10, 80, 116, 125, 203, 259, 287, 486, 502
Tutt, 123
Tuttle, 484
Tuzer, 327
Tweedy, 381
Twiggs, 313, 321

Twogood, 251
Twyford, 401
Twyman, 34
Tyler, 7, 42, 67, 75, 78, 88, 91, 92, 110, 114, 149, 151, 202, 246, 250, 311, 347, 367, 374, 402, 416, 454, 489
Tyndale, 500
Tyner, 252
Tyson, 52, 108, 152, 156, 236
Tyson's Mills, 386

U

Ufford, 197
Ulshoeffer, 381
Umphries, 493
Underhill, 324, 499
Underwood, 332, 408, 430
Union Tavern, 196
Upperman, 236, 493
Upsala, 125
Upshur, 233, 494
Upton, 311
Urquhart, 439
Utermoehle, 462, 463
Utermohle, 417
Utermuhle, 417
Utica, 464
Uttermoehle, 482
Uttermuhle, 135

V

Vaas, 456
Vail, 129
Valentine, 87, 139, 311, 392
Valentine's Grove, 14
Vallentine, 454
Valley Farm, 482
Van Alstine, 168
Van Antwerp, 225
Van Arsdale, 290
Van Buren, 46, 75, 196, 324, 328, 369, 381, 477
Van Cleve, 57

Van Couvre, 452
Van Dewater, 366
Van Dieman's Land, 348, 361
Van Dusen, 180
Van Groning, 363
Van Horne, 312
Van Horseigh, 37, 40, 386, 484
Van Ness, 21, 33, 36, 84, 86, 126, 140, 161, 231, 288, 404, 437, 473, 483
Van Nest, 325
Van Ney, 408
Van Pelt, 239
Van Rensselaer, 243, 505
Van Resiwck, 23
Van Reswick, 197, 216, 379, 481, 498
Van Sicklen, 269
Van Steenburgh, 360
Van Tyne, 266
Van Valkenburgh, 484
Van Winkle, 290
Van Zandt, 168, 239
Vance, 20, 33, 45, 62, 88, 311, 315, 408, 500
Vancoble, 187, 338
Vandegrift, 311
Vanderford, 468
Vandergrift, 281
Vanderhoost, 408
Vandewater, 464
Vandyck, 61
Vanhorn, 408
Vanhorseigh, 170
Vann, 164
Vanzandt, 215
Varden, 80, 108, 456
Varnum, 281
Vass, 211
Vatican, 150
Vattemare, 69, 72
Vaughan, 80, 126
Vaux, 250
Veazy, 171
Venable, 213, 433, 498

Venner, 493
Verden, 80
Verdie, 57
Verdin, 473
Verhaegan, 325
Vermillion, 403
Vermilye, 325
Vernet, 388
Vernon, 76, 116, 360
vessel **Asia**, 66
vessel **Cadoz**, 107, 155
vessel **Hunter**, 64
vessel **John Mason**, 139
vessel **Manchester**, 221
vessel **Ruby**, 115
vessel **Sancala**, 220
vessel **Truxton**, 221
vessels of war **Levant & Cyane**, 113
Vhrel, 84
Viall, 290
Vickery, 386
Vienne, 388
Viers, 473
Villagrand, 311, 350
Villard, 160
Villaumez, 242
Villiers, 70
Vincens, 292
Vincent, 154
Vinson, 251
Vinton, 132, 222
Visser, 378
Vivan, 181
Vivans, 83, 84, 228, 233
Von Groening, 290
Von Schmidt, 33, 45, 53, 59, 74, 79, 82
Von Steenbergh, 379, 463
Vondelehr, 327
Voorhees, 100, 158, 199, 217, 220, 247, 266, 478
Vose, 297, 445, 446
Voss, 99, 402
Vought, 183

Vowell, 201, 412
Vredenburgh, 291

W

Wachter, 458
Waddell, 92
Wade, 22, 24, 167, 209, 297, 313, 327, 392, 454
Wadsworth, 60, 347, 466
Waggaman, 80
Waggoner, 33
Wagner, 188, 281, 388, 431
Wagoner, 493
Wailes, 62
Wainwright, 147, 404, 450
Wait, 121, 147
Waite, 148, 215, 273
Wake, 217, 221
Wakefield, 278
Walback, 408, 454
Walch, 327
Waldo, 141, 215, 275
Waldroff, 102
Waldron, 23, 34, 311, 384
Walker, 15, 29, 31, 36, 45, 47, 51, 63, 71, 72, 82, 97, 101, 108, 139, 141, 147, 158, 166, 170, 172, 181, 186, 197, 215, 233, 252, 281, 282, 287, 294, 311, 327, 329, 347, 366, 374, 375, 380, 392, 408, 430, 439, 450, 454, 458, 463, 473, 486, 493, 497, 503
Wall, 116, 147, 215, 256, 292, 311, 313, 327
Wallace, 16, 94, 281, 301, 430, 464, 467, 500
Wallach, 65, 78, 129, 288, 303, 334, 339, 390
Waller, 163, 281, 374, 417, 460
Wallingford, 195
Wallington, 366
Wallis, 299, 311, 315, 408, 454, 493
Waln, 327
Walsh, 4, 120, 147, 392, 408, 419, 481

Walston, 24, 193
Walter, 82, 327, 374
Walters, 311, 392, 430
Walton, 197
Walworth, 74, 124
Wander, 408
Wankowiez, 501
Ward, 4, 14, 31, 45, 76, 88, 167, 190, 203, 207, 218, 222, 224, 237, 263, 267, 272, 291, 300, 311, 327, 340, 348, 350, 392, 408, 417, 430, 451, 454, 467, 493, 495, 509
Wardell, 333
Warden, 436
Warder, 111
Ware, 42, 329, 499
Warfield, 173, 285, 444
Waring, 138, 214, 250, 324, 334, 339, 340, 387, 399, 424
Warman, 378
Warner, 50, 142, 281, 291, 402, 450, 454, 456, 473
Warren, 33, 45, 88, 281, 285, 292, 366, 392, 408, 430, 464
Warrington, 41, 92, 228, 311, 366, 424
Warters, 454
Washington, 7, 11, 14, 15, 19, 21, 31, 45, 60, 61, 66, 70, 72, 75, 78, 119, 134, 143, 144, 164, 178, 198, 199, 201, 256, 258, 280, 281, 311, 324, 337, 338, 356, 368, 392, 412, 417, 430, 435, 454, 473
Wason, 362
Wast, 347
Waterhouse, 408
Waterman, 15, 401
Waters, 137, 173, 225, 248, 300, 311, 322, 327, 347, 386, 392, 410, 417, 430, 435, 437, 442, 454, 456, 473, 493
Watkins, 114, 160, 201, 385, 442
Watrons, 454

Watson, 39, 45, 47, 48, 81, 88, 121, 199, 269, 311, 322, 366, 406, 408, 418, 430, 454, 473, 485, 493
Watt, 186
Watterson, 430
Watterston, 87, 102, 399, 440
Watts, 180, 284
Waugh, 29, 73, 75, 436
Way, 76, 210
Waydell, 291
Wayne, 143, 327, 347, 477
Weasner, 366, 493
Weatherbee, 116
Weatherspoon, 327
Weaver, 347, 408, 430, 469
Webb, 28, 38, 94, 180, 238, 256, 259, 260, 281, 327, 376, 437
Webber, 162, 493, 505
Weber, 449, 470
Webster, 31, 75, 112, 183, 211, 353, 392, 455, 473
Weed, 16, 162
Weeden, 322
Weedon, 447
Weeks, 38, 325, 347
Weightman, 2, 72, 100, 235, 347, 376, 401
Weinhagen, 72
Weir, 291
Weisse, 2
Welch, 171, 272, 281, 311, 454
Weld, 272
Weller, 122
Wellford, 464
Wellman, 64, 188
Wellner, 347
Wells, 31, 33, 56, 103, 201, 228, 246, 276, 285, 342, 366, 423, 424, 455, 466
Welmer, 176
Welsh, 57, 180, 355, 493
Wentling, 23, 45, 77, 88
Wentworth, 144
Wenwood, 488

Werner, 417
Wescott, 63, 64, 493
Wesson, 311
West, 37, 61, 105, 117, 121, 136, 147, 169, 223, 281, 340, 412, 416, 430, 496, 510
West Grove, 316
Westcott, 267, 430, 479
Westendorff, 79
Westerfield, 38, 135
Westervelt, 291
Weston, 6, 99, 109, 385
Westwood, 134
Wethby, 430
Wethered, 382
Wetmore, 101, 113, 381
Wetton, 249
Wever, 34, 376, 409
whaleship **Audley Clarke**, 286
Whalley, 184
Whallon, 240
Whalon, 311
Wharton, 245, 247, 281, 311, 313, 366
Whatley, 176
Whealer, 430
Wheat, 206, 265, 389
Wheatland, 154
Wheatly, 417
Wheaton, 83, 194
Wheeler, 60, 144, 240, 258, 281, 301, 338, 395, 417, 473, 493, 505
Wheelock, 423
Wheelwright, 247, 336
Whetcroft, 383
Whipple, 151, 241, 340, 369
Whistler, 430, 445
Whiston, 88
Whitaker, 389, 414
Whitall, 271, 411
White, 45, 49, 69, 71, 75, 82, 95, 96, 107, 120, 130, 137, 145, 156, 165, 180, 183, 185, 193, 213, 223, 240, 257, 258, 281, 298, 311, 321, 323, 347, 355, 362, 375, 381, 384, 386, 392, 399, 401, 408, 417, 454, 462, 473, 478, 493, 495
White Hall, 285
White Haven, 403
Whitehill, 81
Whitehorn, 92
Whitelock, 4
Whitfield, 470
Whiting, 77, 98, 147, 153, 179, 208, 271, 289, 301, 412
Whitlock, 78, 366, 430
Whitman, 13, 228
Whitmore, 355, 430, 463
Whitney, 32, 87, 192, 211, 218, 222, 245, 422, 454, 473, 499
Whitson, 45, 54, 361
Whitten, 2, 7, 8, 33, 60, 82
Whitting, 342
Whittle, 342, 424, 454
Whittlesey, 117, 313, 325, 379, 445, 454, 473, 476
Whittock, 454
Whitton, 13
Whitwell, 29, 332
Wick, 264, 493
Wickenshop, 347
Wickham, 331
Wickhan, 361
Wickliffe, 168, 194
Wicks, 97, 499
Widdicombe, 209, 242, 459
Wiel, 366
Wiggin, 473, 493
Wight, 366
Wignants, 205
Wilbor, 255
Wilbur, 58, 123, 180, 292
Wilcocks, 484
Wilcockson, 81
Wilcox, 119, 121, 221, 264, 281, 298, 405, 419
Wilcoxson, 259, 260

Wilde, 4, 15, 449
Wilder, 24
Wildman, 495
Wiley, 311, 366
Wilford, 366
Wilhelm, 454
Wilke, 356
Wilkes, 163, 371
Wilkin, 80
Wilkins, 92, 165, 281, 408
Wilkinson, 175, 230, 311, 327, 497
Wilkison, 209
Will, 347
Willard, 254, 311, 352
Willet, 482
Williams, 15, 22, 29, 33, 45, 49, 60, 61, 63, 68, 71, 81, 98, 99, 100, 103, 118, 122, 126, 133, 139, 142, 144, 156, 168, 171, 173, 210, 220, 221, 225, 237, 242, 244, 254, 281, 285, 292, 302, 311, 327, 329, 343, 347, 353, 354, 366, 378, 386, 392, 398, 408, 422, 430, 432, 435, 441, 442, 444, 454, 463, 469, 473, 475, 483, 484, 489, 493, 499
Williamson, 39, 82, 101, 185, 258, 366, 395, 450, 493
Willingham, 25
Willins, 45
Willis, 75, 193, 203, 220, 268, 450, 496
Willner, 338
Willoughby, 366
Willow Brook, 105
Willow Brooke, 119
Wills, 401, 482
Wilmarth, 94
Wilmer, 42, 133, 178, 349, 490
Wilmot, 33, 55, 77, 172, 175
Wilmott, 56
Wilson, 10, 12, 13, 29, 37, 56, 58, 63, 74, 85, 91, 95, 122, 137, 142, 152, 162, 178, 186, 210, 215, 223, 241, 249, 257, 258, 264, 281, 296, 311, 327, 335, 337, 347, 358, 361, 366, 374, 375, 383, 389, 401, 408, 414, 416, 430, 433, 454, 460, 475, 493, 495, 500
Wilson's Delight, 257
Wiltberger, 134, 168, 248
Wimberly, 509
Wimer, 238
Wimpsatt, 473
Wimsatt, 49, 50, 191, 248, 416, 467
Winans, 6, 102
Wincard, 311
Winchell, 366
Winchester, 173, 442, 443
Winder, 120, 173, 393, 441, 493
Windsor, 22
Wines, 360
Wing, 31, 206
Wingard, 311
Wingerd, 222, 507
Winn, 292, 330, 454
Winne, 347, 500
Winser, 311
Winship, 313
Winslow, 147, 244
Winston, 22, 28, 349, 353, 395, 473
Winter, 171
Winters, 251, 402, 430
Winterson, 210
Winthrop, 184
Wirt, 11, 133, 313
Wischering, 431
Wise, 24, 63, 64, 75, 84, 87, 202, 208, 223, 283, 317, 342, 347, 366, 392, 423, 430, 432
Withers, 375
Wolf, 92, 281, 311, 392, 473
Womack, 24
Wood, 38, 44, 73, 101, 139, 141, 183, 236, 248, 271, 272, 311, 322, 327, 366, 369, 387, 399, 403, 431, 444, 463, 473
Wood Park, 183

Woodall, 267, 281
Woodard, 94
Woodbridge, 17, 448
Woodbury, 75, 78, 268, 367, 381, 477, 509
Woodcock, 366, 493
Woodford, 143, 301
Woodhall, 281
Woodley, 38, 133, 313, 478
Woodrock, 430
Woodruff, 265, 408
Woods, 278, 282, 367, 454
Woodside, 260, 493
Woodson, 201
Woodville, 167
Woodward, 19, 63, 110, 133, 170, 171, 269, 296, 306, 358, 375, 379, 454, 469, 479
Woodworth, 7, 49, 56, 72, 74, 82, 107, 187, 311, 466
Wool, 435
Woolfolk, 457
Woolford, 172, 173, 441
Woolley, 17
Woomer, 327
Wooton, 12
Workman, 178
Wormley, 7, 36
Wormly, 374
Worrall, 281
Worrel, 420
Worrell, 384
Worseley, 347
Worth, 266
Worthen, 484
Worthington, 122, 170, 277, 387, 395, 459, 474, 480, 482, 503
Wratcliff, 311
Wren, 347
Wright, 16, 24, 30, 33, 35, 45, 55, 71, 75, 82, 107, 118, 137, 151, 160, 162, 167, 173, 183, 195, 225, 243, 248, 264, 294, 311, 314, 327, 342, 347, 352, 355, 360, 374, 379, 381, 382, 387, 392, 408, 411, 418, 430, 439, 443, 456, 463, 473
Wrightman, 195
Wrigley, 473
Wrixon, 347, 408, 454, 493
Wroe, 73, 463, 475
Wyatt, 185, 284, 299
Wyche, 130
Wylie, 93
Wyman, 28, 147, 193, 268, 503
Wynne, 327

X

Xaveria, 311

Y

Yardy, 327
Yarnall, 108, 147
Yates, 408
Yates' Hope, 405
Yearsley, 102
Yearwood, 362
Yeates, 166
Yeatman, 311, 347
Yell, 194, 281, 297
Yetman, 209
Yohn, 405
Yong, 493
York, 35, 117, 499
Yost, 408, 438
Young, 4, 9, 10, 12, 28, 65, 111, 114, 147, 166, 167, 187, 207, 215, 219, 246, 281, 282, 297, 311, 327, 330, 333, 347, 366, 373, 375, 376, 381, 383, 388, 392, 398, 408, 415, 416, 430, 433, 454, 455, 473, 478, 493
Younger, 493

Z

Zabriskie, 78, 493
Zachmann, 460

Zackman, 416
Zantzinger, 3, 22, 74, 89, 110
Zeilin, 424
Zeller, 295, 303

Zimmerman, 95, 292, 327, 408
Zolkowski, 501
Zurbano, 15

www.ingramcontent.com/pod-product-compliance
Lightning Source LLC
Chambersburg PA
CBHW071712300426
44115CB00010B/1390